Warrant for Genocide

BROWN UNIVERSITY
BROWN JUDAIC STUDIES
Edited by
Jacob Neusner
Wendell S. Dietrich, Ernest S. Frerichs,
Horst R. Moehring, Sumner B. Twiss

Number 23

Warrant for Genocide
The myth of the Jewish world-conspiracy
and the *Protocols of the Elders of Zion*

by Norman Cohn

WARRANT FOR GENOCIDE

The myth of the Jewish world-conspiracy
and the *Protocols of the Elders of Zion*

by

NORMAN COHN

Scholars Press

Distributed by
SCHOLARS PRESS
101 Salem Street
Chico, CA 95926

Warrant for Genocide

by
Norman Cohn

Reprint of 1969 Harper Torchbook edition.

Library of Congress Cataloging in Publication Data

Cohn, Norman Rufus Colin.
  Warrant for genocide.

  (Brown Judaic studies ; 23)
  Bibliography: p.
  Includes Index.
  1. Protocols of the wise men of Zion. 2. Antisemitism—
Germany. I. Title. II. Series.
DS145.P7C6   1980   956.94'001   80-21733
ISBN 0-89130-423-1 (pbk.)

Printed in the United States of America
2   3   4   5

To David Astor

Contents

Illustrations

between pages 144 *and* 145

FOREWORD TO THE THIRD EDITION

When *Warrant for Genocide* first appeared, in 1967, I was uncertain what response there would be to a book which explores such very uninviting areas of historical experience. I was agreeably surprised to see it very soon translated into half-a-dozen languages. I was even more surprised to find myself, an Englishman, honoured by an American award, the Wolf-Anisfield Award for contributions to the study of race relations. Most gratifying of all is the fact that, more than a dozen years after its first appearance, the book continues to be in demand. And I am particularly glad that Scholars Press should have decided to respond to that demand by publishing a third edition in that distinguished series, the Brown Judaic Studies.

This new edition differs from the second edition (New York 1969, London 1970) only in one respect: the Conclusion, entitled 'A case-study in collective psychopathology', has been omitted. This is not because I no longer believe that psychoanalytical hypotheses can throw light on such manifestly paranoid fantasies as those I describe, but because, given the increasing sophistication of psychoanalytical thinking, my interpretation now appears somewhat primitive. What I tried to say has since been said more adequately by, for instance, Saul Friedländer in *L'antisémitisme nazi: histoire d'une psychose collective*, Paris 1971.

The main text of the book had already been revised for the second edition (New York 1969, London 1970); and it was neither necessary nor practicable to revise it further for the present edition. It is enough to note a few publications which, in the intervening years, have thrown additional light on certain aspects of the story, and to indicate a couple of errata. How the 'conspiracy theory' first developed as a reaction to the Enlightenment and to the French Revolution, and how it was modified

and amplified in the course of the nineteenth and early twentieth centuries, can be studied in detail in Jacob Katz, *Jews and
Freemasons in Europe 1723–1939*, Cambridge, Mass., 1970, and
in Johannes Rogalla von Bieberstein, *Die These von der Ver-
schwörung 1776–1945*, Frankfort a.M., 1976. That the milieu in
which the *Protocols* were first propagated was steeped in theosophy and occultism has been confirmed, with abundant evidence,
in Chapter 4 of James Webb, *The Occult Establishment*, La Salle,
Illinois, 1976. In an article in the journal *Patterns of Prejudice*
(published in London by the Institute of Jewish Affairs), vol.
11, no. 6, November–December 1977, Colin Holmes gives
fresh information, based on archival research, about the first
publication of the *Protocols* in England, about their reception,
and about their subsequent unmasking.

As for the errata: On pp. 114–115, Globachev's report on the
reactions of Nicholas II to the Protocols extends without interruption to the end of the paragraph. The apostrophe in line 2 is
a misprint. On p. 192, the statement that Hitler shot himself
seems to be an error. It now appears that he poisoned himself.

*   *   *   *   *

I have often been asked how, as a historian who has devoted
most of his working life to much earlier periods, I came to
make this excursion into modern history. I am in no doubt as to
the answer: I did it in an attempt to understand how anyone
ever came to conceive the gigantic killing which Hitler called
"the final solution of the Jewish question," and which nowadays
we are accustomed to call the Holocaust.

For the Holocaust does present a problem of a very special
kind. It is true that only about a third of the civilians killed by
the Nazis and their accomplices were Jews, and that the civilian
losses of some of the east European nations at war with the
Third Reich—the Soviet Union, Poland, Yugoslavia—amounted
to eleven or twelve percent of the entire population. It is also
true that in Germany itself between 80,000 and 100,000 inmates
of mental hospitals were killed by gassing; and that about a
quarter of a million Gypsies perished alongside the Jews. And
still there is a difference. The Jews were hunted down with a
fanatical hatred which was reserved for them alone. The killed
amounted to well over half, probably to more than two-thirds of
all European Jews: somewhere between five and six million, not

including those who died of hunger and disease in the ghettos. And all this happened to people who did not constitute a belligerent nation, or even a clearly defined ethnic group, but lived scattered across Europe from the English Channel to the Volga, with very little in common to them all save their descent from adherents of the Jewish religion. How can this extraordinary phenomenon be explained?

Like a great many people I constantly asked myself this question while the extermination was taking place, but it was only after the end of the war that I began to feel my way towards what I am now convinced is the correct answer. In the winter of 1945, while awaiting demobilization in central Europe, I happened to have access to a large library of writings by Nazi and proto-Nazi ideologists and propagandists. Several months of reading, reinforced by contact with SS who were undergoing interrogation and investigation, left me with one pretty strong suspicion—that the drive to exterminate the Jews sprang from a quasi-demonological superstition. I began to suspect that the deadliest form of antisemitism, the kind that results in massacre and attempted genocide, has little to do with real conflicts of interest between living people, or even with racial prejudice as such. What I kept coming across was, rather, a conviction that Jews—all Jews everywhere in the world—form a conspiratorial body set on ruining and then dominating the rest of mankind.

As the facts of the Holocaust became known the history of antisemitism, which previously had been the preserve of a couple of bold spirits, began to attract the attention of many scholars, and detailed studies of this or that aspect of the story began to pile up. But little was published that could confirm or refute my suspicion: at the time of the trial of Adolph Eichmann in 1961 nobody had yet made a thorough study of the myth of the Jewish world-conspiracy and the part it played in making the Holocaust possible.

It is true that the supreme expression and vehicle of the myth of the Jewish world-conspiracy, the notorious forgery known as the *Protocols of the Elders of Zion*, had received quite a lot of attention. Between 1920, when it first made its appearance in western Europe, and 1942, when it was being exploited to some effect by Goebbels, it was the subject of a dozen critical studies in English, German, French and Russian. Several of these books were works of scholarship; one, *L'Apocalypse de notre temps*, was an important piece of original research and would certainly have made its mark if its publication had not been overshadowed by the outbreak of the Second World War, and if the edition had not been seized and destroyed by the Germans the moment they reached Paris. Nevertheless, a conspicuous gap remained: no proper study had ever been made of how, after the French Revolution, the myth of the Jewish world-conspiracy came into being; how it inspired a whole series of forgeries, culminating in the *Protocols*; how the *Protocols* were used to justify massacres of Jews during the Russian civil war; how they swept the world after the First World War; how they took possession of Hitler's mind and became the ideology of his most fanatical followers at home and abroad—and so helped to prepare the way for the Holocaust. Under the impact of the Eichmann trial I at last embarked on such a study. *Warrant for Genocide* tells what I discovered.

It is perhaps hard to accept that scholarly study, and all the time and energy which that implies, can appropriately be lavished on a ludicrous fantasy such as the *Protocols* or on obscure figures such as the hack novelist Hermann Goedsche, the cheap swindler Osman Bey, the half-crazy pseudo-mystic Sergey Nilus, and the rest. Yet it is a great mistake to suppose that the only writers who matter are those whom the educated in their saner moments can take seriously. There exists a subterranean world where pathological fantasies disguised as ideas are churned out by crooks and half-educated fanatics for the benefit of the ignorant and superstitious. There are times when this underworld emerges from the depths and suddenly fascinates, captures, and dominates multitudes of usually sane and responsible people, who thereupon take leave of sanity and responsibility. And it occasionally happens that this underworld becomes a political power and changes the course of history. It is an incontestable fact that the forgotten eccentrics described in the first half of this book built up a myth which, years later, the masters of a great European nation were to use as a warrant for genocide.

Not, of course, that myths operate in a vacuum. The myth of the Jewish world-conspiracy would have remained the monopoly of right-wing Russians and a few cranks in western Europe, and the *Protocols* would never have emerged from obscurity at all, if it had not been for the First World War and the Russian Revolution and their aftermath. And they would never have become the creed of a powerful government and an international movement if it had not been for the great slump and the utter disorientation it produced. On the other hand all these disasters together could never have produced an Auschwitz without the help of a myth which was designed to appeal to all the paranoid and destructive potentialities in human beings. I have tried to do justice also to those dimensions—what one might call the sociological and psychopathological dimensions—of this extraordinary and terrible story.

The myth of the Jewish world-conspiracy is by no means dead—in fact it keeps reappearing, in slightly altered guise, in the most diverse quarters. But the story of its influence since the Second World War would require another volume, and someone else to write it. The story told in this book ends with the Holocaust.

London, March 1980   N.C.

Acknowledgements

This book would probably never have been written at all but for David Astor, who for many years has been deeply concerned about the kind of aberration it describes. By enabling me to leave university life for a time and devote myself wholly to research and writing, he reduced to manageable proportions a task that might otherwise have proved overwhelming.

Boris Nicolaevsky, who was a witness at the Berne trial in 1934–35, and who died just after this book was completed, put at my disposal not only valuable documents from his archives but also his unique knowledge of revolutionary and counter-revolutionary politics in tsarist Russia. The Rev. Dr James Parkes and Dr Léon Poliakov gave me the benefit of their years of research on the history of antisemitism and offered a number of very useful criticisms and suggestions. I was much helped, too, by having access to the Parkes Library and to the fruits of Dr Parkes's own researches on the *Protocols*.

Professor Francis Carsten, Professor John Higham, Professor Walter Laqueur, Professor George Mosse, and Professor Leonard Schapiro brought their powerful equipment to bear on various chapters, and between them saved me from many errors. If after all the efforts of these critics and guides the book still shows errors of fact or judgement, the fault is mine alone.

The staff of the Wiener Library coped with my many requests with the efficiency and courtesy which users of that admirable institution soon learn to take for granted; and Mr C. C. Aronsfeld also guided me to much material that I could easily have missed.

By appointing me to a fellowship, the Center for Advanced Study in the Behavioral Sciences, Stanford, California, provided me with an ideal setting in which to put the finishing touches to the book, including the opportunity of discussing various knotty points with some very stimulating and helpful colleagues.

My wife, having Russian as her native language, read all the Russian works for me. The patience which she brought to this task is appreciated all the more because of the distressing nature of much that she had to read. It was an indispensable contribution, and so was the criticism to which she submitted the entire manuscript.

I am glad of this opportunity of expressing my gratitude to all who have helped me in these various ways.

August 1966   N. C.

... quantum mortalia pectora caecae
noctis habent ...

How much blind night there is in the hearts
of men!

Ovid, *Metamorphoses*

CHAPTER I

The Origins of the Myth

1

OVER very large areas of the earth Jews have traditionally been seen as mysterious beings, endowed with uncanny, sinister powers. This attitude goes back to the time, from the second to the fourth centuries after Christ, when the Church and the Synagogue were competing for converts in the Hellenistic world, and when moreover each was still struggling to win adherents from the other. It was to terrorize the judaising Christians of Antioch into a final breach with the parent religion that St John Chrysostom called the Synagogue 'the temple of demons . . . the cavern of devils . . . a gulf and abyss of perdition' and portrayed Jews as habitual murderers and destroyers, people possessed by an evil spirit. And it was to protect his catechumens against Judaism that St Augustine described how those who had been the favourite sons of God were now transformed into sons of Satan. Moreover the Jews were brought into relation with that fearsome figure, Antichrist, 'the son of perdition', whose tyrannical reign, according to St Paul and the Book of Revelation, is to precede the second coming of Christ. Many of the Fathers taught that Antichrist would be a Jew and that the Jews would be his most devoted followers.[1]

Seven or eight centuries later, in the most militant period in the history of the Roman Catholic Church, these ancient

---

[1] For the demonization of the Jew in Christian teaching see J. Parkes, *The Conflict of the Church and the Synagogue*, London, 1934; J. Trachtenberg, *The Devil and the Jews*, New Haven, 1943; M. Simon, *Verus Israël*, Paris, 1948; L. Poliakov, *Histoire de l'Antisémitisme*, Vol. I: *Du Christ aux Juifs de Cour*, Paris, 1955; J. Isaac, *Genèse de l'Antisémitisme*, Paris, 1956.

fantasies were revived and integrated into a whole new demon-ology. From the time of the first crusade onwards Jews were presented as children of the Devil, agents employed by Satan for the express purpose of combating Christianity and harming Christians. It was in the twelfth century that they were first accused of murdering Christian children, of torturing the con-secrated wafer, and of poisoning the wells. It is true that popes and bishops frequently and emphatically condemned these fabrications; but the lower clergy continued to propagate them, and in the end they came to be generally believed. But above all it was said that Jews worshipped the Devil, who rewarded them collectively by making them masters of black magic; so that however helpless individual Jews might seem, Jewry possessed limitless powers for evil. And already then there was talk of a secret Jewish government – a council of rabbis, located in Moslem Spain, which was supposed to be directing an underground war against Christendom and employing sorcery as its principal weapon.

The propagation of such views by the clergy, century after century, gradually but decisively influenced the attitude of the laity. If Judaism, with its profound sense of election and its elaborate system of tabus, tended in any case to make Jews into a people apart, Christian teaching and preaching ensured that they would be treated not simply as strangers but as most dangerous enemies. During the Middle Ages Jews were almost wholly without legal rights and were frequently massacred by the mob. Such experiences in turn greatly en-couraged the Jewish tendency to exclusiveness. During the long centuries of persecution Jews became a wholly alien people, compulsorily restricted to the most sordid trades, re-garding the Gentile world with bitterness. In the eyes of most Christians these strange creatures were demons in human form – and some of the demonology that was woven around them in those centuries has proved extraordinarily durable.

The myth of the Jewish world-conspiracy represents a modern adaptation of this ancient demonological tradition. According to this myth there exists a secret Jewish govern-ment which, through a world-wide network of camouflaged agencies and organizations, controls political parties and governments, the press and public opinion, banks and economic developments. The secret government is supposed to be doing this in pursuance of an age-old plan and with the single aim of achieving Jewish dominion over the entire world; and it is also supposed to be perilously near to achieving this aim.

In this fantasy the remnants of ancient demonological terrors are blended with anxieties and resentments which are typically modern. The myth of the Jewish world-conspiracy is in fact a particularly degraded and distorted expression of the new social tensions which arose when, with the French Revolution and the coming of the nineteenth century, Europe entered on a period of exceptionally rapid and deep-going change. As everyone knows, it was a time when traditional social relationships were shaken, hereditary privileges ceased to be sacrosanct, age-old values and beliefs were called in question. The slow-moving, conservative life of the countryside was increasingly challenged by an urban civilization which was dynamic, restless, given to innovation. Industrialization brought to the fore a bourgeoisie intent on increasing its wealth and extending its rights; and gradually a new class, the industrial proletariat, began to exert pressure on its own account. Democracy, liberalism, secularism, by the mid-century even socialism, were forces to be reckoned with. But all over Continental Europe there were large numbers of people who abominated all these things. A long, bitter struggle began between those who accepted the new, mobile society and the opportunities it offered, and those who hoped to retain or restore the vanishing traditional order. These changes, which affected European society as a whole, brought both new opportunities and new perils to Europe's Jews.

In one country after another in western and central Europe Jews were relieved of their legal disabilities. Most Jews wanted nothing so much as to live by the same routines as other people, and they quietly adapted themselves to their new freedom. Nevertheless in the eyes of many people 'the Jew' still had a highly symbolic significance, and for two quite different reasons. On the one hand Jews remained an identifiable and – though to a rapidly diminishing extent – an exclusive community; and this meant that they retained something of the mysterious quality which they had possessed in earlier centuries. On the other hand they came to be seen as symbolic of the modern world by those who most detested that world. Various circumstances were responsible for this. For centuries Jews had of necessity been town-dwellers, and they still remained concentrated to an overwhelming extent in the cities, especially the capital cities. In politics Jews naturally tended to side with the liberal and democratic forces which alone could guarantee and increase their liberties. Being still denied access to many traditional occupations, they were encouraged to pioneer new ways of making a living; and in doing so, a few became extremely rich. And in general it can be said that a feeling of suddenly liberated energies made many Jews exceptionally enterprising, exceptionally given to experiment and innovation. In industry and commerce, politics and journalism, Jews became identified with everything that was most wholeheartedly modern. As a result, by about 1870 it was possible to see in 'the Jews' the supreme incarnation of modernity, even while continuing to see them as uncanny, semi-demonic beings.

Of course other, quite different types of antisemitism also existed. There was, for instance, a left-wing antisemitism, compounded of contempt for Jewish religion – which was blamed for Christianity – and of resentment at the power of Jewish bankers, notably the Rothschilds. The socialist movements of France and Germany were full of this kind of antisemitism, and they finally rid themselves of it only at the very end of the century. The demonological type of antisemitism, on the other hand, flourished among those who were most thoroughly disconcerted by the civilization of the nineteenth century. It was above all the landed aristocracy and the clergy who saw in 'the Jews' a symbol of all that most threatened their world – and not only their material interests but the values that gave meaning to their lives. These people were only too happy to believe that such alarming changes must spring not from any defects in the old order, nor from impersonal historic processes, but from the machinations of a handful of devils in human form. Moreover by putting this idea about they could hope to achieve certain highly practical aims. To portray democracy, liberalism, and secularism as the work of the Jews was a way of making these things suspect in the eyes of a growing but ill-educated electorate.

So the new political form of antisemitism came into being. From now on antisemitism was to be deliberately whipped up by ultra-conservative politicians and publicists in their struggle against the progressives. And although Jews were still sometimes accused of such things as ritual murder, these age-old superstitions gradually yielded in importance to the new political superstition concerning a secret Jewish government. This new fantasy was of course just as remote from reality as the old, but it was also just as effective. What Jews really were or did or wanted, or what Jews possibly could be or do or want, had nothing whatsoever to do with the matter. To understand how the fantasy arose and spread it is much less important to know about Jews than to know what persecution-mania means and how, given a suitable situation, it can be deliberately exploited in multitudes of ordinary human beings. This had happened before, during the witch-mania that gripped Europe in the sixteenth and seventeenth centuries. It was to happen again as the myth of the Jewish world-conspiracy began its deadly work.

2

Today when people think of the myth of the Jewish world-conspiracy they think of the forgery known as the *Protocols of the Elders of Zion*, which circulated through the world in millions of copies in the 1920s and 1930s. But the *Protocols* are only the most celebrated and influential in a long series of fabrications and forgeries reaching back almost to the French Revolution.

In its modern form the myth of the Jewish world-conspiracy can be traced back to a French cleric, the Abbé Barruel. As early as 1797 Barruel, in his five-volume *Mémoire pour servir à l'histoire du Jacobinisme*, argued that the French Revolution represented the culmination of an age-old conspiracy of the most secret of secret societies. As he saw it, the trouble began with the medieval Order of Templars, which had not really been exterminated in 1314 but had survived as a secret society, pledged to abolish all monarchies, to overthrow the papacy, to preach unrestricted liberty to all peoples and to found a world-republic under its own control. Down the centuries this secret society had poisoned a number of monarchs; and in the eighteenth century it had captured the Order of Freemasons, which now stood entirely under its control. In 1763 it had created a secret literary academy, consisting of Voltaire, Turgot, Condorcet, Diderot, and d'Alembert, and meeting regularly in the house of the Baron d'Holbach; by its publications this body had undermined all morality and true religion among the French. From 1776 onwards Condorcet and the Abbé Sieyès had built up a vast revolutionary organization of half a million Frenchmen, who were the Jacobins of the revolution. But the heart of the conspiracy, the true leaders of the revolution, were the Bavarian *Illuminati* under Adam Weishaupt – 'enemies of the human race, sons of Satan'. To this handful of Germans all the Freemasons and Jacobins of France already owed blind allegiance; and it was Barruel's view that unless it was stopped, this handful would soon dominate the world.

One need waste no time on the claim that the French Revolution was produced by a conspiracy reaching back to the fourteenth century. As for the obscure German group known as the *Illuminati*, they were not Freemasons at all but rivals of the Freemasons and had in any case been dissolved in 1786. And the role of the Freemasons was also fantastically oversimplified and exaggerated. It is of course true that the Freemasons shared that concern with humanitarian reform which is commonly associated with the Enlightenment – for instance, they contributed to the abolition of judicial torture and of witchcraft trials, and to the improvement of schools. On the other hand at the time of the revolution most Freemasons were Catholic and monarchist – indeed King Louis XVI and his brothers were all Freemasons; while during the Terror Freemasons were guillotined by the hundred and their organization, the *Grand Orient*, was suppressed.

The fact is that Barruel himself never noticed any Masonic influence at work while the revolution was in progress. The idea was presented to him some years later, in London, by the Scottish mathematician John Robison, who was himself preparing a book called *Proofs of a Conspiracy against all the Religions and Governments of Europe, carried on in the secret*

meetings of Freemasons, Illuminati and Reading Societies.
Barruel felt inspired to produce a book on the very same subject, if possible before the imprudent Robison. And he succeeded – his *Mémoire* forestalled Robison's by a year, it was
translated into English, Polish, Italian, Spanish, and Russian,
and it made its author a rich man.

Nevertheless at the time when he wrote his five volumes
Barruel still imposed certain limits on his imagination.
Though he was more than willing to blame the revolution on
the Freemasons, he scarcely mentioned the Jews – understandably enough, since no Jew played any significant part
either in the revolution itself or in the philosophical revolution
that preceded it. Others, however, were less inhibited than
Barruel. In 1806 he received a document which seems to be the
earliest in the series of antisemitic forgeries that was to cul-
minate in the *Protocols*. This was a letter from Florence
ostensibly written by an army officer called J. B. Simonini, of
whom nothing else is known and with whom Barruel himself
failed to establish contact.[1] After congratulating Barruel on
having 'unmasked the hellish sects which are preparing the
way for Antichrist' he draws his attention to 'the Judaic sect'
– surely 'the most formidable power, if one considers its great
wealth and the protection it enjoys in almost all European
countries'. The mysterious Simonini goes on to reveal some
extraordinary information which he claims to have obtained
by a ruse. He once pretended to some Piedmontese Jews that
he himself had been born a Jew and, though separated from
the Jewish community in early childhood, had always retained
his love of his 'nation'. Thereupon the Jews showed him 'sums
of gold and silver for distribution to those who embraced their
cause'; promised to make him a general if only he would

---

[1] The Simonini letter will be found in *Le Contemporain*, Paris, issue of
July 1878, pp. 58–61. It has been reprinted in many antisemitic works,
e.g. N. Deschamps, *Les sociétés secrètes et la Société*, Avignon–Paris, n.d.,
Vol. III, pp. 658–61, and A. Netchvolodov, *L'Empereur Nicolas II et les
Juifs*, Paris, 1924, pp. 231–4. Internal evidence shows that it does indeed
date from around 1806. M. Léon Poliakov, in a private communication
to the author, has argued convincingly that it was fabricated by the
French political police under Fouché with the object of influencing
Napoleon against the Jews at the time of 'the Great Sanhedrin'; see
below, pp. 29–30.

become a Freemason; presented him with three weapons bearing Masonic symbols; and revealed their greatest secrets.

These were indeed surprising. Simonini learned, for instance, that Mani and the Old Man of the Mountain were both Jews (though in reality neither of them was);[1] and that the Order of Freemasons and the *Illuminati* were both founded by Jews (though their founders are known, and were not Jews). More surprising still, he discovered that in Italy alone more than 800 ecclesiastics were Jews; these included bishops and cardinals and would shortly, it was hoped, include a pope. In Spain much the same state of affairs obtained; and indeed everywhere Jews were disguising themselves as Christians. Equally menacing were their political and economic stratagems. Already certain countries had granted full civil rights to the Jews and soon the remaining countries, harassed by plots and seduced by money, would do likewise. That accomplished, the Jews would buy up all lands and houses, until the Christians were completely dispossessed. And then the last stage of the plot would be carried out: the Jews 'promised themselves that in less than a century they would be masters of the world, that they would abolish all other sects and establish the rule of their own sect, that they would turn Christian churches into so many synagogues and reduce the remaining Christians to a state of absolute slavery'. Only one serious obstacle remained – the House of Bourbon, which was the Jews' worst enemy; and the Jews would annihilate that.

Barruel once remarked that if the Simonini letter were published it might provoke a massacre of Jews, and on that occasion he was talking sense; for in embryo the letter does indeed contain the whole myth of the Judeo-Masonic conspiracy. But the letter also points very clearly to the circum-

[1] In the third century of the Christian era the Persian Mani founded the religion of Manicheeism, which in one form or another competed with Christianity for a thousand years.

The Old Man of the Mountain: the supreme ruler of the Moslem sect known as the Assassins, which was active from the eleventh to the thirteenth centuries and had its headquarters in the mountain fortress of Alamut in Persia. The sect employed secret assassination against all enemies. Those required to kill were made obedient by means of hashish – whence the word 'assassin'. Crusaders from France came across the Assassins in Syria.

stances which gave birth to that myth. Needless to say it had nothing to do with the real relationship between Jewry and Freemasonry, which was tenuous. In the eighteenth century the Freemasons were on the whole hostile to the Jews (and so, incidentally, were the Bavarian *Illuminati*). At the time of the Simonini letter many lodges were still reluctant to accept Jewish members. At no time have Jews, or persons of Jewish descent, played a disproportionate part in Freemasonry. These are the sober facts. But facts such as these have never deterred anyone who wished to believe in a Judeo-Masonic conspiracy. Had not Barruel shown that the French Revolution was the work of a conspiracy of Freemasons? And had not the Jews benefited from the revolution? No more was required to establish that Freemasons and Jews were closely associated, in fact practically identical.

It is of course true that the French Revolution, like the American Revolution before it, really did help the Jews. Since it proclaimed 'the rights of man' and championed the principles of liberty, equality, and fraternity, it was logically bound to grant civil rights to French Jews. And not only this – wherever Napoleon's power extended the Jews were emancipated; in the Simonini letter one can hear the crash of the Italian ghettos as they fell before the French armies. This was quite enough to convince reactionaries that Napoleon was the ally of Jewry, if not a Jew himself. Those who identified themselves with the *ancien régime* had to account somehow for the collapse of a social order which they regarded as ordained by God. The myth of the Judeo-Masonic conspiracy supplied the explanation they craved.

Then, in 1806, Napoleon summoned an assembly of prominent French Jews – mostly rabbis and scholars – at Paris. The Emperor's motives were of course purely political and administrative; he was interested in stamping out the money-lending which, as a legacy from pre-emancipation days, was still practised by Jews in Alsace, and he also wanted to satisfy himself that the Jewish population was as submissive as the rest of France. But he called the assembly 'the Great Sanhedrin', after the supreme Jewish court of antiquity – and this automatically suggested that a Jewish government had been secretly in existence down the centuries. Above all, in the eyes of many of Napoleon's enemies the calling of this 'Sanhedrin' established him once and for all as that Antichrist who, in the last days of this earth, is to appear as the Messiah of the Jews. The journal of the French *émigrés* in London, *L'Ambigu*, commented: 'Does he hope to form, from these children of Jacob, a legion of tyrannicides? . . . Time will show. It remains for us only to watch this Antichrist fight against the eternal decrees of God; that must be the last act of his diabolic existence.'[1] In Moscow the Holy Synod of the Orthodox Church thundered: 'Today he proposes to reunite the Jews whom God's wrath had scattered over the face of the earth, to urge them on to overthrow the Church of Christ and to proclaim a false messiah in his person.'[2] The Simonini letter, with its mention of Antichrist and its prophetic tone, fitted perfectly into such an atmosphere. Barruel duly passed it around in influential circles in France, with the express object 'of forestalling the effect which might be produced by the "Sanhedrin" '.[3]

The Simonini letter seems in fact to have given a new direction to Barruel's own thinking. Just before his death in 1820, at the age of seventy-nine, Barruel opened his mind to a certain Father Grivel—and what emerged was the myth of the Judeo-Masonic conspiracy, elaborated far beyond the hints in the Simonini letter.[4] He had written a vast manuscript, which he destroyed two days before his death, to show how a revolutionary conspiracy has existed down the ages, from Mani to the medieval Templars and thence to the Freemasons. As for the Jews, he believed them to have made common cause with the Templars and to have occupied commanding positions in the conspiracy ever since. At that moment Europe was covered by a network of Masonic lodges, penetrating into every village in France, Spain, Italy, and Germany; and the

[1] *L'Ambigu*, London, issue for 20 October 1806, pp. 101–17: 'Grand Sanhédrin des Juifs à Paris'.

[2] Quoted in S. Doubnov, *Histoire moderne du peuple juif*, Paris, 1933, Vol. I, p. 376. Cf. R. Anchel, *Napoléon et les Juifs*, Paris, 1928, Chapter VI, and P. Vulliaud, *Joseph de Maistre, franc-maçon*, Paris, 1926, Chapter IX.

[3] 'Souvenirs du P. Grivel sur les PP. Barruel et Feller', in *Le Contemporain*, issue of July 1878, p. 62.

[4] Ibid., pp. 67–70.

whole organization was rigidly controlled by a supreme council of twenty-one, which included no less than nine Jews. This council had no fixed residence, but wherever the statesmen of the great powers met in congress it was to be found somewhere in the background; in addition, its individual members travelled a great deal, under the pretext of pursuing business interests or attending learned conferences but in reality to direct the activities of the organization. The supreme council was not, however, the ultimate authority in Freemasonry; it appointed an inner council of three, which in turn elected a Grand Master, who was the secret head of this secret International.

Around the figure of the Grand Master, Barruel weaves a truly lurid tale. The Grand Master takes all decisions, and he takes them 'as despotically, as irrevocably, as the Old Man of the Mountain'. Disobedience to his orders is punished by death; every Freemason is bound by oath to assassinate any member of the order, even up to the members of the inner council, if the Grand Master so ordains. This is in fact the explanation of almost every apparently inexplicable assassination. And of course the sole true aim of Freemasonry is to produce revolutions. Orders to this end are sent out by the Grand Master in code, and are carried across Europe by relays of Freemasons, all of them on foot. 'And so,' concludes Barruel, 'from neighbour to neighbour and from hand to hand the orders are transmitted with incomparable speed, for these pedestrians are delayed neither by bad weather, nor by the mishaps that normally befall horsemen or carriages; a man on foot can always get along when he knows the country, and that is the case here. They stop neither to eat nor to sleep, for each one covers only two leagues. The mail-coach takes ten hours from Paris to Orleans, stopping for an hour; the distance is thirty leagues. Fifteen or twenty pedestrians, replacing one another, can reach Orleans from Paris in nine hours, using short-cuts and above all never stopping.' Clearly the supreme council, even though only partly Jewish, already possessed that super-human capacity for organizing vast and invisible manoeuvres that later generations were to attribute to the Elders of Zion.

8

Barruel's fantasies and the Simonini letter found little echo in
the first half of the nineteenth century. Antisemitic propaganda, though it existed, was neither abundant nor influential
at that time, and the myth of the Judeo-Masonic conspiracy in
particular passed into oblivion even among antisemites. Indeed
the first important reference to the idea appears not in antisemitic propaganda but, in the form of a rather naughty joke, in
Disraeli's novel *Coningsby*, which appeared in 1844. In Chapter
XV of Book III there is a passage where the rich and aristocratic Jew Sidonia describes how, when raising a loan for the
Russian Government, he travelled from country to country –
Russia, Spain, France, Prussia – and in each capital found that
the minister concerned was a Jew. And he ends his tale with
the comment: 'So you see, my dear Coningsby, that the world is
governed by very different personages from what is imagined
by those who are not behind the scenes.' It is a passage which
was later to be quoted by innumerable antisemitic writers –
for did it not after all come from a famous Jew who was later
himself to be prime minister? What was not mentioned, and
was perhaps seldom realized, is that the various ministers
named – who include Napoleon's marshal, Soult, and the
Prussian Count Arnim – were not in fact Jews.

It was around 1850 that the myth of the Judeo-Masonic
conspiracy reappeared – this time in Germany – as a weapon
of the extreme right in its struggle against the growing forces
of nationalism, liberalism, democracy, and secularism. Writing
under the immediate impact of the risings of 1848, the publicist
E. E. Eckert describes how the Freemasons are organizing
not only all revolutionary movements but also the situations
that produce revolutionary movements – how they deliberately plunge the masses into moral barbarism and religious despair and finally into economic desperation. This points forward
unmistakably to the *Protocols*, save that Eckert makes no
mention of Jews. The gap was filled by the Catholic periodical
Historisch-politische Blätter, of Munich, which in 1862 published a protest signed 'A Berlin Freemason' but which was
manifestly not written by a Freemason at all.

After complaining of the growing influence of Jews in public and political life in Prussia, the anonymous correspondent describes an (entirely imaginary) association in Germany which, while employing the symbols and rituals of Free-masonry, in reality pursues secret aims – aims that have nothing to do with Freemasonry and that threaten the security of all states. This association is governed by 'unknown superiors' and consists mostly of Jews. Nor are such machina-tions confined to Germany. In London 'the Grand Master' Palmerston presides over the forces of revolution in Europe – but behind Palmerston are two pseudo-Masonic lodges con-sisting entirely of Jews, and whose threshold no Gentile can ever cross. Another such Jewish centre is in Rome – the struggle for the national unity of Italy is in fact nothing but a Jewish plot in which Mazzini and his colleagues are puppets in the hands of 'unknown superiors'. And during the annual fair at Leipzig an exclusively Jewish lodge functions uninterrup-tedly, though in deadly secret. German Freemasons feel them-selves being impelled hither and thither by unknown forces, although the oath of secrecy prevents them from comparing notes and thus penetrating the fearsome secret.[1]

A few years after this extravaganza there appeared, also in Germany, a document which in due course was to become the model for the *Protocols* themselves. The author of this pro-totype of the most famous of all antisemitic forgeries was one Hermann Goedsche, who had formerly been a minor official in the Prussian postal service. In the reaction following the revolutionary upheavals of 1848 this man had made an un-fortunate miscalculation. In order to incriminate the demo-cratic leader Benedic Waldeck, whose politics were proving inconvenient to the King of Prussia, Goedsche produced letters which if they had been genuine would have unmasked Waldeck as conspiring to overthrow the constitution and assassinate the King. In the event it was quickly proved not only that the letters were forgeries but that Goedsche knew them to be so. His career in the postal service being at an end, Goedsche joined the staff of the newspaper *Neue Preussische Zeitung*, popularly known as the *Preussische Kreuzzeitung*, which was much favoured by conservative landowners; and

[1] *Historisch-politische Blätter für das katholische Deutschland*, Mu-nich, Vol. 50 (1862), pp. 432–4.

he also began to write novels, the more sensational under the pseudonym of Sir John Retcliffe. One of these novels, *Biarritz*, contained a chapter called 'In the Jewish Cemetery in Prague'. It is a piece of straight fiction of the most romantically sensational kind, but it was nevertheless to become the basis for a very influential antisemitic forgery.[1]

The chapter describes a secret nocturnal meeting which is supposed to have been held in the cemetery during the Feast of Tabernacles. At eleven o'clock the gates of the cemetery creak softly and the rustling of long coats is heard, as they touch against the stones and shrubbery. A vague white figure passes like a shadow through the cemetery until it reaches a certain tombstone; here it kneels down, touches the tombstone three times with its forehead and whispers a prayer. Another figure approaches; it is that of an old man, bent and limping; he coughs and sighs as he moves. The figure takes its place next to its predecessor and it too kneels down and whispers a prayer. A third figure appears – a tall, impressive figure, clad in a white mantle; as though unwillingly, he too kneels down at the tombstone. Thirteen times this procedure is repeated. When the thirteenth and last figure has taken its place a clock strikes midnight. From the grave there comes a sharp, metallic sound. A blue flame appears and lights up the thirteen kneeling figures. A hollow voice says, 'I greet you, heads of the twelve tribes of Israel.' And the figures dutifully reply : 'We greet you, son of the accursed.'

The assembled figures are in fact meant to represent the twelve tribes of Israel. The additional member of the party represents 'the unfortunates and the exiles'. Under the chairmanship of the representative of the house of Aaron, these various personages report on their activities during the century which has elapsed since the last meeting. The Levite announces that after centuries of oppression and striving, Israel is rising again, thanks to the gold which has fallen into her hands. The Jews can now look forward to a future, not far off, when the whole earth will belong to them. The representative of Reuben reports that through the stock exchanges the Jews

[1] Sir John Retcliffe (pseudonym of Hermann Goedsche), *Biarritz*, Vol. I, Berlin, 1868, pp. 162–93.

have managed to get all the princes and governments of Europe into their debt and are thereby able to control them. Simeon outlines a scheme for breaking up the great estates and getting all land into Jewish hands, so that the workers on the land will become workers for the Jews. Judah shows how independent artisans are being reduced by Jewish machinations to the status of factory-workers, who can then be controlled and directed for political purposes. The Aaronic Levite is concerned with undermining the Christian Church, by fostering free thought, scepticism, and anti-clericalism. Issachar thinks that the military class, being the defender of the throne and the exponent of patriotism, has to be discredited in the eyes of the masses. Zebulon maintains that, though the Jewish people is by nature intensely conservative, Jews must now appear to side with forces of progress; for unrest and revolutions can be so directed that they bring no real benefits to the poor but merely increase the power of the Jews. Dan, 'a Jew of the lower order', has more modest ambitions; he is concerned that Jews should monopolize the trade in liquor, butter, wool, and bread. Naphtali demands that governmental positions should be thrown open to Jews, particularly those which carry great influence, such as Justice and Education. Benjamin makes a similar demand with respect to the liberal professions. Asher considers that marriage with Christian women can only serve the purpose of the Jews, and that a Jew desiring the pleasures of fornication or adultery should always seek them with Christian and not with Jewish women. Manasseh concludes the series of speeches with an impassioned plea for capturing and controlling the press; in this way Jews will be able to decide what the masses shall believe, what they shall desire, what they shall reject.

After the assembled representatives have all had their say the presiding Levite gives his message of encouragement. What has been said will be as a sword with which Israel will strike down its enemies. If these prescriptions are faithfully followed, future generations of Jews will suffer no more oppression but, on the contrary, will enjoy happiness, wealth, and power. When the next meeting is held, a hundred years hence, the grand-children of those now present will be able to announce at that graveside that they have indeed become princes of the world and that all other nations are their slaves. The Levite concludes with the command: 'Let us renew our oath, sons of the golden calf, and go out to all the lands of the earth!' Thereupon a blue flame appears above the tomb, while each of the thirteen throws a stone upon the tomb; and in the midst of the flame there appears a monstrous golden calf. So the meeting ends; but what none of the participants knows is that these clandestine proceedings have been observed throughout by two men, a German scholar and a baptized Jew, who now swear to spend all their strength in fighting this devilish Jewish plot.

The relevant volume of *Biarritz* was published in 1868, and the date is significant. In Germany the partial emancipation of the Jews during the years of Napoleon's sway had been followed by a violent antisemitic reaction. With the slow growth of a middle class which was at least partly liberal, Jews again enjoyed greater freedom and acceptance, until this tiny fraction of the population – 1·2 per cent, to be precise – was granted approximately the same civil rights as were enjoyed by the remaining 98·8 per cent. This came about in the North German states in 1869, and was extended to the whole of the new German Reich in 1871. Nevertheless in a country which never accepted with any real conviction the ideals of liberalism and democracy, antisemitism remained a powerful factor. Moreover, precisely because German national unity was achieved extremely late, Germans became quite abnormally emphatic in their nationalism; and this too fostered antisemitism. It is therefore not surprising that the first comprehensive formulation of the modern myth of the Jewish conspiracy should have appeared in Germany at the very moment when the Jews were about to be granted full emancipation.

But this was only the beginning of the story – for soon this frankly fictional episode began to turn into a forged document! It was Russian antisemites who first thought of treating the story as an authentic record; in 1872 the relevant chapter was published in St Petersburg as a pamphlet, with the sinister comment that, although the story was a piece of fiction, it had a basis in fact. In 1876 a similar pamphlet appeared in

Moscow, with the title *In The Jewish Cemetery in Czech Prague (the Jews sovereigns of the world)*. In 1880 a second edition of this pamphlet was published; and similar pamphlets appeared in Odessa and Prague. Some years later the story appeared in France, in *Le Contemporain* for July 1881. Now it was no longer presented as a piece of fiction. All the various speeches made by the fictional Jews at Prague were consolidated into a single speech, which was supposed to have been made by a chief rabbi to a secret meeting of Jews. The authenticity of this speech was vouched for – in fact it was supposed to be extracted from a forthcoming work by an English diplomat, *Annals of the Political and Historical Events of the Last Ten Years*.

Goedsche, as we know, had written his novel under the *nom de plume* of Sir John Retcliffe; so it was only appropriate that the English diplomat should be called the same – or rather, carelessly, Sir John Readclif. This gentleman was to have a most adventurous career. When François Bournand printed the 'speech' in *Les Juifs et nos contemporains* (1896) he prefaced it with a startling revelation: 'We find the programme of Jewry, the real programme of the Jews expressed by . . . the Chief Rabbi John Readclif. . . . It is a speech made in 1880.' Mercifully Sir John quickly recovered himself. Later editions of the 'speech' were often accompanied by touching tributes to that heroic antisemite, Sir John Readclif. The tributes were by no means unmerited, for when in 1933 the 'speech' appeared for the first time in Sweden, it was prefaced by a melancholy statement: Sir John Readclif had paid with his life for exposing the great Jewish conspiracy. It was a sad end for a man who, if he had been a German novelist, had also been an English diplomat and historian, and who if he had been a heroic antisemite had also been a chief rabbi.

This, then, is the origin of what came to be known as *The Rabbi's Speech*.[1] But the ludicrousness of its origin did not prevent this 'speech' from having a most successful career. In 1887 Theodor Fritsch published it in his 'catechism' for antisemitic agitators; in the same year, and again in 1891, it appeared in the famous antisemitic anthology *La Russie juive*. In 1893 it was printed in an Austrian newspaper, the *Deutsch-*

[1] The text of *The Rabbi's Speech* is given in Appendix I.

soziale Blätter. In 1896, as already indicated, it figured in Bournand's book *Les Juifs et nos contemporains.* In 1901 a paraphrase of the speech in Czech was printed in Prague, under the title *Speech of a Rabbi about the Goyim.* The pamphlet was confiscated by the authorities; but this measure was circumvented by a Czech deputy, Břzenovskí, who in a question in the Reichstag in Vienna quoted the entire pamphlet verbatim; whereupon it was promptly printed in two newspapers, *Michel wach auf* and the *Wiener Deutsche Zeitung,* and so re-entered circulation.

In Russia, where the 'speech' had taken the first steps towards fame in the 1870s, it continued on its triumphant way. In 1891 it appeared in Russian translation in the Odessa newspaper, *Novorossiysky Telegraf.* Now it was established that the 'speech' had been made by a rabbi to a 'secret Sanhedrin' in 1869 (presumably the reference is to the First Congress of Reform Judaism held in that year at Leipzig); and again its authenticity is guaranteed by the well-known English aristocrat, Sir John Readclif. Early in the new century the fabrication was used in Russia for the purpose of instigating pogroms. And at this stage its history became intertwined with that of the *Protocols of the Elders of Zion.* The professional antisemite P. A. Krushevan seems to have used a pamphlet containing *The Rabbi's Speech* as a help in provoking the pogrom at Kishinev in Bessarabia in 1903. A few months later, as we shall see, he published the *Protocols* in his newspaper *Znamya (The Banner)*; and on 22 January 1904 he published the 'speech' in the same newspaper. In 1906 Krushevan's friend Butmi included it in his edition of the *Protocols*; and in the same year it was published as a pamphlet in Kharkov. The *Deutsch-soziale Blätter* rejoiced that this powerful weapon from the ideological arsenal of German antisemitism was helping the Russian people to liberate itself from its 'mortal enemy', the Jews.

Shortly afterwards the hitherto nameless rabbi who was supposed to have delivered the 'speech' was given a name, or rather two names: sometimes he is Rabbi Eichhorn and sometimes Rabbi Reichhorn. As such he figured at the non-existent congress at Lemberg in 1912. After the First World War the pronouncements of this imaginary gentleman, refurbished to suit the new conditions, shared in the triumphs of the *Protocols*; many editions include both works. By this time there were naturally several variants of the 'speech' in circulation, and these different versions were used to bolster up one another's authenticity. Indeed their resemblance was taken as proving not only that they were all genuine but that they were successive expressions of a long-established Jewish plot. *The Rabbi's Speech* was also, inevitably, constantly invoked as proof of the authenticity of the *Protocols*.

It was in post-war Germany that this fabrication, like the *Protocols*, enjoyed the greatest vogue. Already in 1919 it made up the contents of two different pamphlets. One of these, entitled *What is the Jewish Spirit?* and published in Württemberg, announces in its preface that 'John Retcliffe's warning cry, addressed to the whole non-Jewish world (it must be forty or fifty years old) is today, in 1919, when Jewry has attained the greater part of its appointed aim, still sufficiently interesting to be presented anew to the German people'. The other edition, published in Berlin, bears the melodramatic title: *The Secret of Jewish World-Domination, from a work of the last century, which was bought up by the Jews and so disappeared from circulation.* In the early 1920s the 'speech' was also reprinted in several popular antisemitic books; and when the Nazis came to power Johann von Leers, of whom we shall be hearing more, produced yet another edition. Moreover by this time it had become a commonplace that 'the great knower and warner' Hermann Goedsche, alias Sir John Retcliffe, had himself witnessed the meeting in the cemetery in Prague – having been led there by the Jewish socialist, Ferdinand Lassalle!

Goedsche's fantasy was by no means the only German contribution to the myth of the Jewish world-conspiracy. When, in the 1880s, antisemitism became an important political movement, Germany emerged as the leading producer of antisemitic propaganda of every kind. Both French and Russian antisemites borrowed heavily from German authors and journalists. Conversely, no antisemitic idea or fable or slogan could appear anywhere in Europe without being promptly snapped up by some German writer. In the vast mass of German antisemitic writing the myth of the Jewish world-conspiracy and the secret Jewish government became one of the more important themes. If, for instance, one examines Theodor Fritsch's 'antisemitic catechism',[1] one finds a whole section devoted to 'Jewish secret societies'. Here all the fantasies which had been elaborated in Germany or France or Russia are refurbished for the benefit of the German public. And the book proved very popular. First published in 1887, later enlarged and dignified with the title *Handbook of the Jewish Question*, it had sold 100,000 copies by 1933. It eventually sold far more than that, for in the Third Reich it became – along with the *Protocols* themselves – one of the texts prescribed for compulsory study in schools.

[1] *Antisemiten-Katechismus: Eine Zusammenstellung des wichtigsten Materials zum Verständnis der Judenfrage*, written under the pseudonym Thomas Frey (1887).

CHAPTER II

Against Satan and the Alliance Israélite Universelle

1

In the Middle Ages Jews had been seen as agents of Satan, devil-worshippers, demons in human form. It is one of the achievements of the modern antisemitic movement that in the late nineteenth century it was able to revive this archaic superstition. As we have seen, Goedsche closed the Prague meeting with a supernatural apparition: in the form of a golden calf Satan offers himself to the adoration of the assembled Jews. Within a year of the publication of Goedsche's fantasy there appeared in France the book which was to become the Bible of modern antisemitism: *Le Juif, le judaïsme et la judaïsation des peuples chrétiens*, by Gougenot des Mousseaux. Here Satan bulks large indeed, for the author is convinced that the world is falling into the grip of a mysterious body of Satan-worshippers, whom he calls 'kabbalistic Jews'.

In reality the kabbalah is nothing but a body of Jewish mystical and theosophical doctrine, dating in the main from the later Middle Ages. It is fully expounded in such works as the *Zohar* and there is nothing secret about it. During the Renaissance it was made available to Christendom by humanists such as Pico della Mirandola and Johann Reuchlin, and it charmed a number of thoughtful men, including Pope Leo X. Des Mousseaux, however, imagined the kabbalah as something quite different: a secret demonic religion, a systematic cult of evil, established by the Devil at the very beginning of the world. According to him the first adepts of this cult were the sons of Cain, who after the Flood were succeeded by the sons of Ham; these are the same as the Chaldeans, and in due course they passed on their secret to the Jews. In later days the cult was to be practised also by the Gnostics, the Manichees, and the Moslem sect of the Assassins; these last transmitted the diabolic lore to the Templars, who handed it on to the Freemasons. But at all times the Jews, as 'the representatives on earth of the spirit of darkness' have supplied the grand masters. And if one asks in what precisely the cult consists, the answer is that it centres on the worship of Satan. The chief symbols are the serpent and the phallus, and the ritual includes erotic orgies of the wildest kind. But that is not all: by murdering Christian children the Jews in particular are able to acquire magical powers; and this too is part of 'the kabbalah'.

The extraordinary fact is that even these weird extravagances found believers. It is certain that many twentieth-century devotees of the *Protocols* really have imagined the secret Jewish government as composed of oriental sorcerers – one has only to look at the commentary on the *Protocols* published in Madrid in 1963 to find pages upon pages about 'the kabbalah'. Nor is this the only respect in which des Mousseaux provides the link between the *Protocols* and archaic, half-forgotten religious beliefs. One of the most unexpected features of the *Protocols* is that Jewish world-domination is to be exercised through a Jewish king, whom all nations will accept as their saviour. This figure is taken straight from the end of the last chapter of Gougenot des Mousseaux. As he nears his 500th page the industrious author allows himself a flight of prophetic frenzy in which he foretells how, in the midst of a great European war, the Jews will raise up 'a man with a genius for political imposture, a sinister bewitcher, around whom fanatical multitudes will cluster'. The Jews will hail this man as the Messiah, but he will be more than that. After destroying the authority of Christianity he will unite mankind in one great brotherhood and bestow on it a superabundance of material goods. For these great services the Gentile nations too will accept him, exalt him, worship him as a god – but in reality, for all his apparent benevolence, he will be Satan's instrument for the perdition of mankind.[1]

[1] Gougenot des Mousseaux, *Le Juif, le Judaïsme et la judaïsation des peuples chrétiens*, Paris, 1869, pp. 485–98.

Gougenot des Mousseaux states repeatedly that what inspired him to write this passage was the prophecy of Antichrist. According to the prophecy in the second chapter of the Second Epistle to the Thessalonians, the second coming of Christ and the Last Judgement will be immediately preceded by the appearance of Antichrist, 'the man of sin, the son of perdition'. He will demand to be worshipped as God; and by the miracles which he will perform with the Devil's help he will deceive all who are willing to be deceived. He will establish his rule over the whole world until the returning Christ destroys him with the breath of his mouth. So far the New Testament – but in the second and third centuries after Christ, as the Church and the Synagogue came more and more sharply into competition and conflict with one another, Christian theologians began to give a new interpretation to this prophecy. They foretold that Antichrist would be a Jew and would love the Jews above all peoples; while the Jews for their part would be the most faithful followers of Antichrist, accepting him as the Messiah. As to what would happen next, the theologians were divided. If some expected the Jews to be miraculously converted to Christianity, others expected that they would follow Antichrist to the end and on the return of Christ would be sent, along with Antichrist, to endure the torments of hell for all eternity.

It has been argued elsewhere that the Nazi belief in a Jewish world-conspiracy represents a revival, in a secularized form, of certain apocalyptic beliefs which once formed part of the Christian world-view.[1] In this instance one can trace the precise way in which an apocalyptic belief – in the coming of Antichrist – contributed to the making of the *Protocols*, which were to become part of the Nazi scriptures. And indeed the connexion between the *Protocols* and the Antichrist prophecy does not stop there. In later chapters we shall see how the first important edition of the *Protocols* appeared in a Russian book about the imminent coming of Antichrist; and how something of the same apocalyptic atmosphere appears even in the thinking and writing of Hitler and Rosenberg as soon as they touch on the *Protocols* and the Jewish world-conspiracy.

[1] N. Cohn, *The Pursuit of the Millennium*, revised editions, London and New York, 1961–62, pp. 62–3, 310.

But if Gougenot des Mousseaux revived archaic fantasies, he also modernized them. The long chapters on 'Gold' and on 'The Press' belong entirely to the world of modern, political antisemitism (indeed certain phrases in the *Protocols* seem to have been lifted straight from these pages). Above all the world-state which is to be established by Antichrist is astonishingly modern. It is an international order, in which all peoples are united in allegiance to a single unity, mankind, and in which material goods abound and are enjoyed by all with a good conscience. Reading these descriptions, one may well wonder why the Judeo-Masonic conspirators should not be regarded as the benefactors rather than as the exploiters of mankind. One has to remind oneself that if nowadays almost all political parties in the advanced countries subscribe to some extent to the ideals of international co-operation and material well-being, such notions were frankly abominated by the extreme Right so long as an extreme Right existed. Hitler and Gougenot des Mousseaux would have been at one in regarding such a world-order as quite intolerable.

Le Juif, le judaïsme et la judaïsation des peuples chrétiens was written at a time of bitter conflict between Freemasonry and the Roman Catholic Church. For, although the French Revolution was certainly not engineered by a Masonic conspiracy, in the course of the nineteenth century the Freemasons of France and Italy did indeed identify themselves more and more completely with the principles of that revolution. Staunchly republican and anti-clerical, the French Freemasons felt not insulted but flattered when reactionaries blamed them for the overthrow of the *ancien régime*. In Italy the Masonic lodges took a very active part in the struggle for national unity and therefore in attacking the temporal power of the Pope. But in the eyes of many Catholics the end of the Papal State meant the end of the Church; and to these people Freemasons seemed quite literally agents of Satan. It is in the years immediately before the Vatican Council of 1870 that Freemasons are first portrayed as devil-worshippers: in 1867, in his book *Les Francs-Maçons*, Mgr Ségur declared that black masses were celebrated in the 'inner lodges'. Gougenot des Mousseaux belonged to the same world of extreme right-wing, ultramontane Catholicism, and with his talk of 'the kabbalah' he was at least as much concerned to discredit Freemasonry and the progressive forces in general as to attack the Jews. His book, armed with an enthusiastic foreword from the head of the Foreign Mission Seminary in Paris, was explicitly directed to the Fathers at the Council – and not wholly in vain, for des Mousseaux was blessed by Pope Pius IX for his courage.

In France Gougenot des Mousseaux found a worthy successor in the Abbé Chabauty, *curé* of Saint-André at Mirebeau in Poitou, honorary canon of Poitiers and Angoulême. In 1881 this man published a 600-page volume called *Les Francs-Maçons et les Juifs: Sixième Age de l'Eglise d'après l'Apocalypse*, in which he argued that Satan, through the Judeo-Masonic conspiracy, was preparing the way for the Jewish Antichrist and the world-dominion of the Jews. In his most influential book, *Les Juifs nos maîtres* (1882), Chabauty did more than re-hash his predecessor's arguments, he added an important discovery of his own. He had found, in the *Revue des études juives* for 1880, two letters which seemed to him to be full of the most sinister significance, and which were indeed later to acquire a sinister significance in the history of antisemitism. They are known as *The Letter of the Jews of Arles* (or, in some versions, of Spain) and *The Reply of the Jews of Constantinople*; and they read as follows:

Honourable Jews, greetings and blessings!
   This is to tell you that the King of France, who is again master of Provence, has ordained by public proclamation that we must become Christians or leave his territory. And the people of Arles, Aix and Marseilles want to take away our belongings, they threaten our lives, they wreck our synagogues, they cause us much vexation; and all this makes us uncertain about what we ought to do to keep the Law of Moses. This is why we ask you to be so good as to let us know, in your wisdom, what we ought to do.
                                        CHAMOR
                                        Rabbi of the Jews of Arles
                                        the 13th of Sabath, 1489

Well-beloved Brethren in Moses, we have received the letter in which you tell us of the anxieties and adversities you are suffering.
   The advice of the grand satraps and rabbis is as follows:
   You say that the King of France demands that you become

Christians: do so, since you cannot do otherwise, but keep the Law of Moses in your hearts.

You say that you are forced to surrender your belongings: then make your children merchants, so that, little by little, they may strip the Christians of their belongings.

You say that attempts are made against your lives: then make your children doctors and apothecaries, so that they may deprive Christians of their lives.

You say that they are destroying your synagogues: then make your children canons and clerics, so that they may destroy their churches.

You say that people are vexing you in many other ways: then see to it that your children become advocates and notaries, so that you will get the Christians under your yoke, you will dominate the world, and you will be able to take your revenge.

Do not depart from this order that we give you, for you will see by experience that, from the abasement in which you now find yourselves, you will attain the summit of power.

V.S.S.V.F.F.
Prince of the Jews of Constantinople
the 21st of Casleu, 1489[1]

From the point of view of the literary historian these 'letters', which date at least from the sixteenth century, are not without interest. Probably they were originally written in Spain, as a satirical comment on the Marranos – the Spanish Jews who claimed to have been converted to Catholicism but who were suspected, often rightly, of remaining Jews at heart. What is certain is that they were meant as a joke – the signature Chamor, for instance, is simply the Hebrew for donkey! For Chabauty, however, there was no possible doubt as to their authenticity – after all, as he pointed out, was not the *Revue des études juives*, which reprinted them, founded by the Baron de Rothschild?

And indeed thanks to these 'letters' the enterprising *curé* stumbled on an idea which had not occurred to any of his predecessors. He convinced himself that a single, secret Jewish government had existed throughout the Dispersion, that it was pursuing an unchanging plan for world-domination, and that all Jews owed it absolute obedience. And he was also

[1] The 'letters' are reprinted in E. A. Chabauty, *Les Juifs nos maîtres*, Paris–Brussels–Geneva, 1882, Chapter I.

concerned that 'Bismarck, William and the other ministers and sovereigns of Europe and America are only the docile and often the blind instruments' of the hidden Jewish government. By such imaginings he not only prepared the way for the *Protocols of the Elders of Zion* but established the *Letter of the Jews of Constantinople* as an important 'document' in its own right. When, half a century later, the *Protocols* became a world-famous work, this 'letter' was republished again and again, often in the same volume as the *Protocols*, as confirmatory evidence. And not one editor realized that the signature V.S.S.V.F.F., which looks so cryptic and sinister, is simply the name Ussuff, i.e. Joseph!

Chabauty found his first imitators in Italy. In the mid-1880s Pope Leo XIII embarked on a fresh struggle against Italian Freemasonry; and although he himself never stooped to antisemitic propaganda, he permitted others to do so. The Jesuits associated with *La civiltà cattolica*, in particular, considered it perfectly legitimate to discredit Freemasonry by presenting it as part of the Jewish world-conspiracy. Two of these reverend gentlemen, Father R. Ballerini and Father F. S. Rondina, waged a campaign which lasted right through the 1890s. According to them all the afflictions in the modern world, from the French Revolution to the latest Italian bankruptcies, were simply fruits of two thousand years of Jewish conspiracy. *La civiltà cattolica* portrayed Italy as in the grip of violence, immorality, and general chaos – all thanks to the Jews; it described Jewry in terms that Hitler was to use – as a giant octopus squeezing the world; it even printed the tales of ritual murder which were later to grace the pages of *Der Stürmer*. It is not surprising that, with such an illustrious example before their eyes, provincial Catholic newspapers demanded a repeal of Jewish emancipation and the confiscation of all Jewish property.

It is true that the campaign failed to undermine the tolerant outlook of most Italian Catholics – how could they, after all, forget that the whole of Italian Jewry numbered barely 30,000? – but that does not mean it had no influence at all. The time was to come, after the First World War, when two successive popes were to honour the Frenchman Mgr Jouin for his life-long struggle against that mythical entity, the Judeo-

Masonic conspiracy; in one case, when he was already celebrated as an editor of the *Protocols*. *La civiltà cattolica* can
certainly take some credit for the outlook that made that
possible.[1]

In France, too, the theme of a Satanic world-conspiracy of
Freemasons, or of Jews, or of both together, continued to
inspire a prodigious amount of nonsensical propaganda
throughout the 1890s.[2] There it appealed above all to the
country clergy – nearly all of them sons of peasants or of
village artisans, poorly educated, infinitely credulous. What
they were prepared to believe beggars description. In 1893
that great hoaxer, Léo Taxil, had no difficulty at all in persuading them that the head of American Freemasonry had a
telephone system invented and manned (if that is the word)
by devils, and so was kept in constant touch with the seven
major capitals of the world; or that beneath the Rock of
Gibraltar squads of devils were at work, concocting epidemics
to destroy the Catholic world. And if Taxil confines his attention to Freemasons and makes no mention of Jews, others were
less restrained. *La Franc-Maçonnerie, Synagogue de Satan*, by
Mgr Meurin, Archbishop of Port-Louis, Mauritius – which also
appeared in 1893 – insists on the contrary that 'everything in
Freemasonry is fundamentally Jewish, exclusively Jewish,
passionately Jewish, from the beginning to the end'.[3]

This extraordinary work seems indeed to have been one of
the most immediate sources of the *Protocols* which, as we shall
see, were fabricated just about that time. And like so many of
the devotees of the *Protocols* after him, the Archbishop was
convinced that the whole of human history could be interpreted in terms of a Jewish conspiracy which was now within
sight of its goal. He also knew the means by which this plan
was being carried out: 'Some day history will tell how all the
revolutions of recent centuries originated in the Masonic sect
under the supreme command of the Jews.'[4] And not only that –

[1] On the campaign of *La civiltà cattolica*, see R. De Felice, *Storia degli
ebrei italiani sotto il fascismo*, Turin, 1961, pp. 37 seq.

[2] Cf. R. F. Byrnes, *Antisemitism in Modern France*, New Brunswick,
1950, notably pp. 256–313.

[3] L. Meurin, *La Franc-Maçonnerie, Synagogue de Satan*, Paris, 1893,
p. 260.

[4] Ibid., p. 196.

whatever the appearances, it is the governments themselves that foment the revolutions, because they too are controlled by Jews: 'The fact that all revolutions are made in the depths of the Masonic back-lodges would be inexplicable, if we did not know that the ministries of all countries . . . are in the hands of Freemasons who in the last analysis are controlled by Jews.'[1]

And the Archbishop has something else to tell about these mysterious 'back-lodges': they consist of Freemasons and Jews 'of the 33rd degree' – just as the *Protocols* themselves end with the words 'Signed by the Representatives of Zion of the 33rd degree'. It is quite clear where this idea came from. There really is one particular Masonic system which has thirty-three grades: 'the old and accepted Scottish rite', which was instituted in the United States at the beginning of the nineteenth century and spread to many countries. So far from concerning itself with political and economic strategies, this branch of Freemasonry has specialized in symbolism and in philanthropy; and in no sense does it control the whole of Freemasonry. But these facts were of no interest to the worthy Archbishop, or to the fabricator of the *Protocols*; for them, the Freemasons of the 33rd degree are the heart of the conspiracy to set up a Jewish king as ruler of the world. And the Archbishop goes further: these Freemasons of the 33rd degree are agents of the Devil in the most literal sense of the term. Assembled in their 'back-lodges', they worship Satan in the form of a serpent or a phallus, and on occasion Satan even honours them with a visit in person.

Once more, at the end of this fantastic book, one finds oneself plunged into the familiar apocalyptic atmosphere. The struggle against the imaginary Judeo-Masonic conspiracy is equated with the battle between the heavenly and the Satanic hosts foretold in the Book of Revelation:

As we write these lines, a hurricane, sighing and roaring, passes over our little island. . . . It is the image of our century! Science explains the origin and nature of the hurricane. This book explains our tormented century. . . . Paganism, Judaism, the vices and the passions, under the supreme command of Lucifer, are rising up

---

[1] Ibid., p. 202.

together to assault the Heavenly Jerusalem, in the hope that, united, their batallions may achieve the victory which they have never, to this day, gained by attacking separately.[1]

The Archbishop calls on the rulers of Europe to league themselves against the Jewish conspiracy before it destroys them. And although he declares that he will be satisfied if Jews are excluded from banking, commerce, journalism, teaching, and medicine, his final outburst is dramatic indeed:

Do not hope, O Jews, to be able to escape the calamity that once more threatens you. . . . The day when you are crushed will see the Church, your victim, enjoying a vital expansion such as has never been seen.

We do not wish to be slaves of the Jews, and we will not be such. . . . We shall forget our political differences to stand united and firm against the impudence and insolence of the enemies of God and of his Christ. Victory is assured. The future belongs to us. Lucifer and his emissaries will be forced to haul down their Masonic flag; Satan and the evil spirits who tour the world for the purpose of ruining souls will be cast back into Hell, from which they have audaciously climbed to assault the City of God.[2]

When one reflects that France had been the first country to emancipate its Jews (in 1791) and that by 1890 French Jews were still a mere handful (less than 80,000), one can only marvel at the intensity of such hatred. And the antisemitic fever that gripped France in the 1880s and 1890s had in fact practically nothing to do with contacts between individual non-Jewish Frenchmen and individual Jews. Talk of the Judeo-Masonic conspiracy found most belief in provinces such as Normandy, Brittany, Maine, Anjou, and Poitou, where there were very few Jews; in Montdidier, in the Somme, where the newspaper *L'Anti-Sémitique* was published, there lived not a single Jew. What the Jew symbolized for this public was the mysterious and sinister power of Paris, where most Jews lived. Here again one sees how the latter-day revival of antisemitism expressed above all the protest of traditional, rural society against the forces of modernity.

There was also the example of Germany. Militant antisemitism appeared in Germany at the very moment when German

[1] Ibid., p. 462.
[2] Ibid., pp. 466–8.

power and prestige were increasing; and there were French-men who argued that France's salvation lay in imitating her formidable neighbour. Chief among these was that talented demagogue Edouard Drumont. Moreover, in his extremely influential book *La France juive* (1886), Drumont popularized the arguments of the little-known Gougenot des Mousseaux – admittedly by the curious method of incorporating large sections of his book without acknowledgement. He also reprinted Chabauty's find, the *Letter from the Jews of Constantinople*; and altogether he did far more than anyone else to turn the myth of the Judeo-Masonic conspiracy into a political force in France.

As we shall see, the fabricator of the *Protocols of the Elders of Zion* wrote in French and lived in France. There can be no doubt that he drew heavily on the tradition of French political antisemitism as it had developed in the last third of the nineteenth century, and particularly on the writings of des Mousseaux, Chabauty, Meurin, and Drumont.

2

In the late nineteenth century antisemitism was a very much more serious business in Russia than in any of the countries of western or central Europe. Various circumstances combined to make it so. Russia was in outlook still largely a medieval country, where Jews were traditionally exposed to the same kind of religiously motivated hatred as they had had to endure in medieval Europe. Russia was also the last absolute monarchy in Europe, and as such the greatest stronghold of opposition to the liberalizing, democratizing tendencies associated with the French Revolution. And as it happened, Russia was also the country which had the largest Jewish population, both absolutely and relatively: some 5,000,000 Jews, or about a third of all the Jews in the world, lived in the Pale of Jewish Settlement, a group of provinces extending from the Baltic to the Black Sea and embracing much of what is now Poland. They represented about 5 per cent of the total population of the Russian Empire, but a much larger proportion of the population in the areas to which they were restricted.

These Russian Jews were by no means newcomers. Mostly they were descended from Jews who had been driven out of Germany and France in the later Middle Ages and had settled in Poland; in the Crimea Jews had been settled since Roman times. But compared with the Jews of western Europe, Russian Jews did form a very closed, distinctive, unassimilated minority. They lived separate from the Russians, dressed differently, spoke and wrote Yiddish in preference to Russian. Many were passionately attached to the Jewish religion in its strictest form. They were on the whole miserably poor, but they included enough traders and moneylenders to incur the resentment of their Russian rivals in the towns and sometimes the hatred of the down-trodden Russian peasantry.

Russian Jews were subject to severe economic, residential, and educational restrictions. Throughout the nineteenth century they were harried and persecuted by the Government – not however as members of an alien race but as adherents of a detested religion. Any Jew who claimed to have been converted to Orthodoxy was at once relieved of the disabilities which afflicted his fellows. Conversions of convenience therefore represented a constant temptation to ambitious young men, and it is astonishing how few yielded to it.

Persecution was much intensified when the relatively liberal Tsar Alexander II was assassinated in 1881 and succeeded by his son, the ruthless and ultra-reactionary Alexander III. Both Alexander III and his son Nicholas II, the last tsar, were fanatical antisemites; and during their reigns everything possible was done, with every official encouragement, to clear Russia of Jews. The persecution was carried out partly by administrative measures – for instance, by expelling the Jews from the rural areas while preventing them from finding employment in the towns – and partly by officially sponsored pogroms. These methods were so successful that at some periods Russian Jews were emigrating at the rate of 100,000 a year, mostly to the United States of America.[1]

These developments had however been preceded by some

[1] For a good contemporary account of the situation of the Jews under Alexander III, by a non-Jewish Russian, see Stepniak (pseudonym of S. M. Kravchinsky), *King Stork and King Log, a study of modern Russia*, London, 1896, Vol. I, pp. 142–94.

years of antisemitic propaganda. As in France and Germany, the idea of the Jewish world-conspiracy was developed and elaborated from 1868 onwards, and began to take its full effect in the 1880s. Around 1868 the Jews of central Europe – in the German states and in Austria-Hungary – were being granted full citizenship; and one object of the propaganda was certainly to counter any pressure for similar reforms within the Russian Empire. Once instituted, the propaganda proved to have many uses. This was a time when the Russian autocracy was beginning to encounter active political opposition, notably from clandestine terroristic groups. The authorities were determined at all costs to mask the fact that there were real Russians – and educated ones at that – who so hated the autocracy that they were prepared to assassinate its representatives. They accordingly pretended that all opposition to the régime, and particularly all terrorism, was the work of the Jewish world-conspiracy.

This was not because Jews had any big part in the terroristic movement of the 1860s and 1870s. On the contrary, it was largely because of the intensified persecution which began in the 1880s that a small minority of Jews eventually joined the revolutionary movement, and particularly the Social-Democratic party which later split into the rival factions of Mensheviks and Bolsheviks; and even this small minority consisted, of course, not of Jews in the religious sense but of people of Jewish descent who had broken with Judaism and with the traditional Jewish community. Such distinctions were however ignored by the police. For them the whole revolutionary movement was from the start a tool in the hands of – incredible as it may seem – adherents of the Jewish religion. This was the story which they put out in their propaganda; and many of them certainly came to believe it themselves.

In Russia, then, in contrast with France and Germany, propaganda about the Jewish world-conspiracy was officially sponsored; it was a regular activity of the political police. Foreign contributions, such as *The Rabbi's Speech*, were eagerly snatched up; but there were also inventive spirits at work in Russia itself. The first of these in date was Jacob Brafmann, a Jew who not only underwent a tactical conversion to Orthodoxy but went on to become a police spy. In 1866 this man laid before certain high-ranking officials strange evidence concerning what he called 'the Kahal'. The Hebrew word 'kahal' means simply 'community-organization'. As Jews in medieval Europe were normally allowed a certain degree of local self-government, each Jewish settlement was automatically a kahal. In Russia a similar state of affairs existed until 1844, when the kahals, and with them all traces of Jewish autonomy, were abolished. But according to Brafmann 'the Kahal' was something quite different and far more menacing.

By way of proof Brafmann published a work which he called *The Book of the Kahal* (1869). In reality this was based on some minutes of routine business kept by the officially recognized kahal of Minsk from 1789 to 1828, supplemented by some similar material from other towns. But to this material Brafmann added a commentary which made it look as if the kahal in each town aimed at enabling Jewish traders to oust their Christian competitors and in the end to acquire possession of all the property of the Christians. *The Book of the Kahal* was issued at public expense and distributed to government officials to guide them in their dealings with the Jewish population. It had a great effect, particularly on the political police, and it was frequently reprinted. The word 'kahal' passed into the international vocabulary of antisemitic propaganda as an immensely sinister term – often described as 'a name which few Gentiles are ever allowed to hear.'[1]

Still more noxious was another book by Brafmann, first published in 1868 and later (1888) reprinted in the same volume as *The Book of the Kahal*. This work, called *Jewish Fraternities, local and universal,* can be regarded as the Russian counterpart to the fantasies of Goedsche and des Mousseaux. In it the existence of certain international Jewish organizations is 'unmasked', as though it were a great secret. The organizations in question are a society for the reprinting of basic Jewish texts; the Alliance Israélite Universelle; the Society for the Dissemination of Education among the Jews in Russia; the Society for the Promotion of Colonization in

---

[1] One of the American editors of the *Protocols,* who calls himself 'Earnest Sincere', even knows that the membership of 'the Kahal' numbers precisely 1,921,601!

Palestine; and the Association for the Support of Jewish Refugees in London. These were all well-known philanthropic organizations, with nothing secret about them; but that did not prevent Brafmann from treating them as branches of a secret, world-wide Jewish conspiracy. The Alliance Israélite Universelle, which was shown as the hub of the conspiracy, had been founded at Paris in 1860 and quickly became hated by all antisemites. In reality it was a purely French institution and not at all international. It was however concerned to help the persecuted Jews of Russia and Rumania, both by providing educational facilities and by succouring refugees; and this was quite enough to prompt Brafmann to the comment that 'the net of the Jewish world-alliance is spread over the whole globe'. Like *The Book of the Kahal*, the book on Jewish fraternities attracted much attention in the antisemitic bureaucracy. Thanks to it the Alliance Israélite Universelle was forbidden to operate in Russia and the work of the Society for the Dissemination of Education among the Jews in Russia was much restricted.

A decade later, when in France the Abbé Chabauty was constructing his fantasies around the *Letter from the Jews of Constantinople*, a former Roman Catholic priest of Polish extraction, Hippolytus Lutostansky, was engaged in a similar exercise in Russia. Having been unfrocked for a variety of offences ranging from embezzlement to rape, Lutostansky joined the Orthodox Church and became a student at a religious academy. The first result of his studies was a book on the use of Christian blood in Jewish religious ritual (1876). Some years later he made an interesting proposal to leading representatives of Russian Jewry: at a price, he would be prepared to publish a refutation of this book and to denounce it in lectures in the principal cities; if the price was not forthcoming he would publish further antisemitic writings. This attempt at bribery having failed, Lutostansky continued his career as an antisemitic propagandist until 1905; then, when it looked as though a more democratic régime might expose him to prosecution for forgery, he changed tack once again. In an open letter he assured the Jews that he had never really been their enemy; and signed it 'a repentant sinner'. This did not of course prevent the Black Hundreds from invoking his writings at the time of the Beiliss ritual murder trial.[1]

Lutostansky's most important book was a three-volume work called *The Talmud and the Jews* (1879–80). Totally ignorant of Hebrew, Lutostansky confined his researches to collecting every scurrilous rumour and forgery that had ever been concocted concerning the Talmud. The horrifying account which he gave of the principles of Judaism undoubtedly helped and encouraged the political police in their new task of provoking pogroms. But the book also contains a chapter on 'the Jewish Freemasons', based on the ideas of Gougenot des Mousseaux; and for Russia this was a novelty. As every reader of *War and Peace* knows, Freemasonry had once flourished among the more enlightened of the Russian nobles; already in the eighteenth century Russian Freemasons had in fact rendered great services in organizing famine relief and disseminating education. But that was a long time ago; in 1822 Freemasonry was banned in Russia and it remained weak. Lutostansky can claim the honour of having introduced the myth of the Judeo-Masonic conspiracy into a country where there were very few Freemasons at all.

Ingeniously, he combined this myth with Brafmann's attacks on the Alliance Israélite Universelle: Freemasonry is a Jewish secret society governed by the Alliance Israélite Universelle. The philanthropic aims of the Alliance are camouflage: 'This noble aim serves the Jews simply as a cloak for their grandiose political machinations. In this shape the society commands the services of journalists, secret agents and politicians, who day and night carry on their work of undermining the Christian states, by destroying their foundation, which is morality, and by weakening religious faith, so that all the inhabitants can easily be changed into freethinkers, atheists, nihilists, and anarchists.' 'Indeed, what government can rely on such a great number of agents, representing all the governments of the world?' The Alliance is in fact 'only the official public organ of the real centre of the Jewish state, a

---

[1] In 1913 Mendel Beiliss, a Jewish clerk of Kiev, was tried for the ritual murder of a Christian boy. The case caused great excitement and indignation far beyond the borders of Russia. Despite the most strenuous efforts by the prosecution Beiliss was acquitted. See M. Samuel, *Blood Accusation, the strange history of the Beiliss case*, New York, 1966.

centre which is wrapped in deepest darkness'. Like Brafmann, Lutostansky singles out for special attention the Society for the Dissemination of Education among the Jews in Russia; and he calls on the Russian government to suppress it. As justification for his whole argument he reprints – *The Rabbi's Speech*!

But the most extraordinary of these figures was surely an international crook of Jewish origin whose real name was Millinger but who preferred the names of Osman-Bey or Kibridli-Zade. Expelled from Venice in 1870 and from a whole series of countries during the following decade, this man turned to antisemitism as a way of making a living. Arrested in Milan, he solemnly withdrew all his antisemitic inventions – which did not prevent him later from producing new antisemitic pamphlets and selling them from door to door, from Athens to Constantinople and Alexandria. Constantly on the move, frequently arrested and imprisoned for swindles of every kind, he continued his picturesque and nefarious career until his death around 1898.

Though Osman-Bey came, apparently, from Serbia, and wrote in German, and published his major work in Switzerland, it was in Russia, and through the Russian antisemitic movement, that he tried to make his career. He wrote old-style stories of ritual murder – but he also wrote a book called *World Conquest by the Jews*. Like Brafmann and Lutostansky, he claimed that the source of all evil was the Alliance Israélite Universelle – which, in a fine flight of metaphor, he describes as an invisible and intangible power, casting an unnoticeable net of gold and steel around the world, while creeping in darkness with a dagger in one hand and dynamite in the other. As he portrayed it, the Alliance was no creation of nineteenth-century philanthropy but as old as the Jewish people itself. It had caused the French Revolution, through the instrumentality of William Pitt and his Jewish agitators, and was now dominating France through the Jews [*sic*] Thiers and Renan. At the moment it was mobilizing the whole of Jewry against Holy Russia. The Russian terrorists were its creatures and the assassination of Alexander II was its masterpiece – had it not smuggled the assassin out of Russia and brought him to (of all people) Karl Marx in (of all places) Berlin? The next step would be for 'nihilists and Jews' to rise in their masses, set up barricades and proclaim a constitution.

Fortunately the hour found the man, in Osman-Bey. 'It was our duty to delay no longer,' writes Osman-Bey, 'but to save Russia by seizing the helm.' Armed with 400 roubles from the political police he left St Petersburg for Paris on 3 September 1881; 'Russia,' he remarks, 'should note the date as a memorable one, for on that day began my mission, which was to be crowned with the uncovering of the universal conspiracy and the restoring of peace.' In Paris he visited the headquarters of the Alliance and at once noticed 'a strong nihilistic smell'. His aim was however a more concrete one – to capture documents which should reveal the part of the Alliance in the world-conspiracy. And sure enough he made a discovery which in his view 'saved Russia and will help to open the eyes of the rest of mankind'.[1]

Osman-Bey describes how he bribed a young Jew to smuggle out of the offices of the Alliance letters which had been received from various Jewish committees in countries bordering on Russia. He admits that he never met the young Jew and remarks that the whole affair was arranged through French friends of his, whom he does not name. Once in possession of the letters, he sat up all night copying them out; then he marked on a map the location of the committees. The result astonished and appalled him: the committees stretched along the Russian frontier; clearly they represented a Jewish force massed against Russia, under the command of the rabbis of Königsberg and Liegnitz, with the Russian terrorists as their vanguard. In reality the only Jewish committees were those responsible for succouring the thousands of Jewish refugees as they left Russian territory, hungry and penniless; but Osman-Bey saw things in a different light. In phrases worthy of the Abbé Barruel he describes how, while the Russian police watched the main roads, agents passed to and fro between these committees and the terrorists inside Russia, all travelling cross-country or by water, without ever being spotted.

'In the Ministries of the Interior, of Foreign Affairs and of

---

[1] Osman-Bey (pseudonym of Millinger), *Enthüllungen über die Ermordung Alexanders II*, Bern, 1886, pp. 116–29. On Osman-Bey see W. Laqueur, *Russia and Germany*, London, 1965, p. 96.

War,' remarks this adventurous traveller, 'they fought one another to get at my reports, and universal horror reigned.' This need not be taken too seriously – he also claimed that in the Russian–Turkish war he had captured the town of Kars single-handed. Osman-Bey was a near-paranoiac, who believed that but for a conspiracy of hack politicians he would be recognized as Russia's saviour and appointed minister and dictator. But he has a real claim to be remembered, nevertheless – as a truly sinister prophet and portent.

In *World Conquest by the Jews* – which had already reached its seventh edition in 1875, that is to say before Hermann Goedsche's fantasy had turned into *The Rabbi's Speech* – and in his *Revelations concerning the assassination of Alexander II* (1886), Osman-Bey expounds the whole delusional system which, fifty or sixty years later, was to work itself out in the greatest of all massacres. In a world without Jews, he says, wars will be less frequent, because nobody will stir one nation up against another; class-hatred and revolutions will cease, because the only capitalists will be 'national' ones, who never exploit anyone; socialists and suchlike will realize the folly of their ways. 'The Golden Age would lie before us all, it would be the ideal of progress itself.' But first there must be a great purge: 'Drive out the Jews with an enthusiastic shout: "Long live the principle of nationalities and races! Out with the intruders. . . ."' And if one asks where the Jews are to go, sometimes he replies 'to Africa', just as Hitler was to talk of Madagascar. At other times, however, he is franker: 'The Alliance Israélite Universelle can be destroyed only through the complete extermination of the Jewish race.'[1]

[1] Osman-Bey, *Enthüllungen über die Ermordung Alexanders II*, pp. 189-92.

CHAPTER III

The *Protocols* and the *Dialogue aux Enfers*

1

THE nineteenth-century transmitters of the myth of the Jewish world-conspiracy, then, are a varied crew. They include Barruel and the 'Simonini letter' at the beginning of the century; and much later, in the last third of the century, Goedsche in Germany, and *The Rabbi's Speech*; the Frenchmen Gougenot des Mousseaux, Mgr Meurin, the Abbé Chabauty, Edouard Drumont; the Russian Brafmann, the Pole Lutostansky, and the Serb Osman-Bey. Together these people prepared the way for the famous forgery which was to survive long after their own writings had faded into obscurity.

'Around 1840,' wrote Osman-Bey in his *World Conquest by the Jews*, 'a Jewish parliament was summoned at Cracow. It was a sort of Ecumenical Council, where the most eminent leaders of the Chosen People met to confer. The purpose of summoning them was, to determine the most suitable means to ensure that Judaism should spread safely from the North Pole to the South . . .

'Suddenly a clear voice rang out and automatically imposed silence. It was the voice of a recognised authority, a man of overwhelming intelligence, whose name we unfortunately do not know. . . .

'His words had a startling effect on the assembly; people saw that an oracle had spoken, that a new illumination had dawned upon their minds, to give a firm direction to their efforts . . .'[1]

This fantasy provides the framework for the *Protocols of the*

[1] Osman-Bey, *Die Eroberung der Welt durch die Juden*, Wiesbaden, 1875, p. 48.

Elders of Zion. For the *Protocols* consist of lectures, or notes for lectures, in which a member of the secret Jewish government – the Elders of Zion – expounds a plot to achieve world-domination.

In the standard version the 'protocols', or lectures, or chapters, are twenty-four in number; together they fill a booklet – about a hundred small pages in both British editions. They are not easy to summarize, for the style is turgid and diffuse, the argument tortuous and illogical. With perseverance one can however distinguish three main themes: a critique of liberalism; an analysis of the methods by which world-domination is to be achieved by the Jews; and a description of the world-state which is to be established. These themes are interwoven in a most confusing manner, but on the whole it can be said that the first two themes predominate in the first nine 'protocols', while the remaining fifteen 'protocols' are devoted mainly to a prophecy of the coming kingdom. And if one insists on reducing the argument to some sort of order, it comes out roughly as follows.

The Elders base their calculations on a particular view of politics. As they see it, political liberty is only an idea – admittedly an idea which has great attraction for the masses, but one which can never be translated into reality. Liberalism, which attempts this impossible task, results merely in chaos; for the people are incapable of governing themselves, they do not know their own mind, they are easily deceived by appearances, they cannot choose rationally between conflicting counsels. When the aristocracy ruled it was right that aristocrats should have liberty, for they used it for the general good; it was in their own interest, for instance, to care for the workers from whose labour they lived. But aristocracy is a thing of the past, and the liberal order which has succeeded it cannot last but must inevitably lead to despotism. Only a despot can ensure order in society. Moreover, since there are more evil men than good in the world, force is the only appropriate means of government. Might is right; and in the modern world the basis of might is the possession and control of capital. Today it is gold that rules the world.

Over a period of many centuries a plot has been in operation to place all political power firmly in the hands of those who alone are qualified to use it properly – that is to say, in the hands of the Elders of Zion. Much has been achieved but the plot has not yet reached fruition. Before the Elders can establish their rule over the whole world the existing Gentile states, already seriously undermined, must be finally abolished; and the Elders have very precise ideas as to how this is to be accomplished.

In the first place everything possible must be done, in each existing state, to foster discontent and unrest. Fortunately the means for this are provided by the very nature of liberalism. Already, by encouraging the incessant proclamation of liberal ideas and the incessant chatter with which parliaments fill their days, the Elders will be helping to produce complete mental confusion in the populace. This confusion will be increased by the multiplicity of political parties; the Elders will foster it by secretly supporting them all. Again, they will exert themselves to alienate the people from their rulers. In particular they will keep the workers in perpetual unrest by pretending to sympathize with their grievances while secretly contriving to raise the cost of living.

Within each state authority must be discredited. The aristocracy is to be finally eliminated by heavy taxation on land; as aristocrats will not easily abandon their luxurious way of life this should plunge them deep in debt. Presidential régimes will be instituted, and this will enable the Elders to make their own puppets into presidents – preferably men with some discreditable episode in their past lives, for this will make them easier to control. Freemasonry and secret societies must be penetrated and turned into mere tools of the Elders; any Freemasons who show signs of resistance must be secretly executed. Industry must be concentrated into giant monopolies, so that all Gentile fortunes can be destroyed together when it suits the Elders.

Relations between states, too, are to be bedevilled. National differences are to be emphasized until international understanding becomes impossible. Armaments must be perpetually increased and there must be frequent wars. These wars must, however, lead to no gains on any side but only to ever greater economic chaos. And meanwhile there will be a steady undermining of Gentile morality. Gentiles are to be encouraged to become atheists and to indulge in every kind of luxury, licence, and depravity; for this purpose the Elders are already placing chosen tutors and governesses as their agents in Gentile homes. Drunkenness and prostitution must be vigorously fostered.

The Elders recognize that their plot may yet be obstructed by the Gentiles but are confident of their ability to overcome all resistance. They can use the common people to overthrow the rulers; by reducing the masses to starvation level they can bring them to a point where they will rise up, simultaneously in all countries and all under the complete control of the Elders, to destroy all private property – except of course that owned by Jews. They can use governments against governments; after years of carefully fostered intrigue and hostility it will be easy for them to organize a war against any nation which resists their will. Even if by any chance the whole of Europe should unite against them, they will still be able to call on the cannon of America, China, or Japan. And then there are the underground railways: these have been devised with the sole purpose of ensuring that the Elders will be able to meet any serious opposition by blowing whole capital cities sky high. After which any surviving remnants of opposition can always be inoculated with frightful diseases. Even the possibility that the Jews themselves might become refractory has been foreseen; this is to be coped with by stimulating outbreaks of antisemitism.

Surveying the contemporary scene the Elders see grounds for confidence. Already they can claim to have destroyed religious faith, and especially Christian faith. Now that the Jesuits have been brought low the Papacy remains defenceless and can be destroyed at a convenient moment. The prestige of secular rulers, too, is on the decline; assassinations and threats of assassination have made them afraid to appear in public except with a guard, while the assassins have been glorified as martyrs. Neither rulers nor aristocrats can now command the allegiance of the common people. Economic disorder is already far advanced. Cunning financial manipulations have produced depressions and enormous national debts, public finances have been reduced to hopeless confusion, the gold standard has everywhere produced national ruin.

The time must soon come when the Gentile states, reduced

to desperation, will be only too glad to hand over all control to the Elders, who indeed have already been able to establish the foundations for their future rule. In the place of aristocracy they have set up plutocracy or the rule of gold; and the gold is controlled by them. They have established their control over the law and have brought it into utter confusion; the invention of arbitration is an example of their devilish subtlety. Education too is firmly in their hands, and here their baleful influence is shown in the invention of teaching by visual media; the purpose of this technique is simply to turn the Gentiles into 'unthinking submissive beasts, waiting for things to be presented before their eyes in order to form an idea of them'. Above all, the Elders already control politics and the politicians; all parties, from the most conservative to the most radical, are in reality simply their tools. Hiding behind Freemasonry, the Elders have already penetrated all state secrets; and as governments well know, they have the power to create political order or disorder as they wish. After centuries of struggle, and at the cost of thousands of Gentile and even of many Jewish lives, the Elders are perhaps within a century of the final attainment of their goal.

That goal is the Messianic Age, when the whole world will be united in a single religion, Judaism, and will be ruled over by a Jewish sovereign of the House of David. This age is divinely ordained, for God has chosen the Jews to dominate the world; but it will also be characterized by a very definite political structure. Society will be organized to take full account of the reality of human inequality. The masses will be kept well away from politics; both their education and their press will be designed to prevent them from developing any political interests whatever. All publications will be strictly censored and freedom of speech and association will be stringently curtailed. These restraints will be imposed in the guise of temporary measures, to be ended when the enemies of the people have been subdued; but they will be maintained permanently. History will be taught only as a way of stressing the difference between past chaos and present order; the successes of the new world-empire will be perpetually contrasted with the political weaknesses and failures of the old Gentile governments. Everyone will be spied upon. A vast secret police will be recruited from all strata of the population, and it will be an absolute obligation for every citizen to report any criticism of the régime. Seditious agitation will be treated as a shameful crime, comparable with theft or murder. Liberalism will be utterly extirpated and unquestioning obedience demanded from all. Liberty will, admittedly, be promised for some future time but it will never be granted.

On the other hand everything will be done to ensure the efficient functioning of society. Unemployment will be abolished and taxation will be proportionate to wealth. The interests of the small man will be furthered by the stimulation of small-scale industry. Education will be designed to train the young for the particular station in life for which each is destined. Drunkenness will be severely discouraged; and so will independence of thought.

All this will tend to keep the masses quiet and contented, and the example set by their rulers will help in this. The laws will be clear and unalterable; judges will be incorruptible and infallible. All the Jewish leaders will show themselves able, efficient, and benevolent. Above all, the sovereign will be a man of exemplary character; unsuitable heirs will be ruthlessly set aside. This Jewish ruler of the world will be seen to go freely among the people, accepting their petitions; nobody will realize that those who surround him are security police. His private life will be above reproach, he will bestow no favours on his relatives, he will possess no property. He will work constantly at the task of government. The result will be a world without violence or injustice, in which true well-being will be enjoyed by all. The peoples of the earth will rejoice in being so well governed; and so the kingdom of Zion will endure.

Such, then, is the plot attributed to those mysterious gentlemen, the Elders of Zion. It was first revealed to the public when a number of editions were published in Russia, between 1903 and 1907. The earliest is a version, slightly shortened at the end, which appeared in the St Petersburg newspaper *Znamya* (*The Banner*) from 26 August to 7 September 1903. *Znamya* was edited by P. A. Krushevan, the noted and militant antisemite. A few months before publishing the *Protocols* he had instigated the pogrom at Kishinev in Bessarabia, in which forty-five Jews were killed and more than 400 injured and 1,300 Jewish houses and shops destroyed.

Krushevan does not reveal who sent or gave him the manuscript – only that it was a translation of a document originally written down in France and that the translator had entitled it *Minutes of the Meeting of the World Union of Freemasons and Elders of Zion*; for his part he called it *Programme for World Conquest by the Jews*. Some two years later the same version, but no longer truncated, appeared in the form of a booklet with the title *The Root of our Troubles* and the sub-title: 'Where the root is of the present disorder of society in Europe and especially in Russia. Extracts from the ancient and modern Protocols of the World Union of Freemasons'. This work was handed to the St Petersburg Censorship Committee on 9 December 1905; permission to print was given at once and the book was published the same month, in St Petersburg, under the imprint of the Imperial Guard. No editor's name was given but it is very likely that the editor was in fact a retired officer called G. V. Butmi, who was a close associate of Krushevan and like him a Bessarabian.

At that time – from October 1905 onwards – Butmi and Krushevan were busily helping to build up an extreme right-wing organization, the Union of the Russian People, commonly known as the Black Hundreds, with armed squads of toughs to assassinate radicals and liberals and to massacre Jews. In January 1906 this organization published a new edition of the pamphlet *The Root of our Troubles*, but this time bearing the name of Butmi and the title *The Enemies of the Human Race*, with the sub-title: 'Protocols extracted from the secret archives of the Central Chancellery of Zion (where the root is of the present disorder of society in Europe in general and of Russia in particular).' This edition appeared under the imprint no longer of the Imperial Guard but of a society of the deaf and dumb. Three further editions of this version appeared in 1906 and another in 1907, all in St Petersburg; another appeared at Kazan in 1906, with the title *Extracts from the Protocol of the Freemasons*.

The Root of our Troubles and *The Enemies of the Human Race* are cheap pamphlets meant for mass distribution. Quite different is the edition of the *Protocols* that appeared as part of a book called *The Great in the Small. Antichrist considered as an imminent political possibility*, by a mystical writer, Sergey Nilus. The first two editions of this work, published in 1901 and 1903, did not contain the *Protocols*, but they were inserted in the third edition, published in December 1905 under the imprint of the local Red Cross at the imperial residence outside St Petersburg, Tsarskoe Selo. As we shall see, this edition was produced to influence Tsar Nicholas II, and it bears all the signs of its origin. It is elegantly printed, it forms part of a mystical work such as the Tsar loved to read; above all it abounds in reference to French events and personalities, whereas the Krushevan-Butmi version refers more to purely Russian affairs.

Nilus's book was passed by the Moscow Censorship Committee on 28 September 1905, but it was still in manuscript; even so it appeared in print about the same time as *The Root of our Troubles*. And it had made its mark before that. At that time Sergey Nilus was much in favour at the imperial court; as a result, the Metropolitan of Moscow ordered a sermon quoting his version of the *Protocols* to be read in all the 368 churches of Moscow. This was duly done on 16 October 1905, and the sermon was promptly reprinted in the right-wing newspaper *Moscovskia Vedomosti* – yet another edition of the *Protocols*, of a sort.

It was Nilus's version, not Butmi's, that was to become a force in world history. That did not even begin to happen in 1905, nor when further editions of *The Great in the Small* were published in 1911 and 1912. It happened only when the book reappeared, somewhat revised and enlarged, under the title *He is Near, At the Door . . . Here comes Antichrist and the reign of the Devil on earth*. And then it happened because of the moment: 1917.

2

When one is confronted with a highly secret document ostensibly recording a series of lectures one naturally wonders who delivered the lectures to whom and on what occasion, and also how the document came to be seen by eyes for which it was obviously not intended. The various editors of the *Protocols* have done their best to satisfy such curiosity, but unfortunately their answers are anything but clear or unanimous.

Even the earliest edition, that in *Znamya*, plunges us into confusion. While the translator tells us that the document was taken from 'the Central Chancellery of Zion, in France', the editor admits that 'we do not know how, where or by what means the minutes of these meetings, which took place in France, could be copied down, nor above all who copied them . . .'. And that is not all. The translator, in a postscript, warns us sharply against confusing the Elders of Zion with the representatives of the Zionist movement – but that does not prevent the editor from claiming that the *Protocols* reveal the menace of Zionism 'which has the task of uniting all the Jews in the whole world in one union – a union which is more closely knit and more dangerous than the Jesuits'.[1]

For Butmi too the *Protocols* are 'extracted from the secret archives of the Central Chancellery of Zion'; but he has a more colourful tale to tell: 'These minutes or "protocols", being secret documents, were extracted with great effort, in the form of detached pages, and translated into Russian on 9 December 1901. It is almost impossible to penetrate a second time into the secret archives where they are kept; that is why they cannot be confirmed by precise indications as to the place, day, month and year, that is to say as to where and when they were drawn up. The reader who is at all familiar with the Masonic mysteries will be convinced of their authenticity when he learns of the criminal plan exposed in these "protocols".'[2]

Nilus is still more communicative – so much so, in fact, that he ends by contradicting not only Butmi but also himself. In the 1905 edition the *Protocols* are followed by a note: 'These "protocols" were removed from a whole book of "protocols." All this was obtained by my correspondent from the secret archives of the Central Chancellery of Zion, which is at present situated in France.'[3] This tallies well enough with Butmi; but

[1] *Znamya*, St Petersburg, issue of 26 August 1903.
[2] Mgr Jouin, *Le Péril Judéo-maçonnique*, Vol. IV: *Les 'Protocols' de 1901 de G. Butmi*, Paris, 1922, p. 4.
[3] S. Nilus, *Velikoe v Malom*, Tsarskoe Selo, 1905, p. 394.

unfortunately in the same edition the *Protocols* are also preceded by a note, saying that they were 'stolen by a woman from
one of the most influential and most highly initiated leaders of
Freemasonry, after one of the secret meetings of the "initiated" in France, that nest of Masonic conspiracy'.[1] And in the
1917 edition Nilus confuses the issue still further:

. . . only now have I learned authoritatively from Jewish sources
that these *Protocols* are nothing else than a strategic plan for the
conquest of the world, putting it under the yoke of Israel, the
struggle against God, a plan worked out by the leaders of the
Jewish people during the many centuries of dispersion, and finally
presented to the Council of Elders by 'the Prince of the Exile',
Theodor Herzl, at the time of the first Zionist congress, summoned
by him at Basel in August 1897.[2]

There could hardly have been a worse choice. The original
manuscript of the *Protocols* was in French, but at the first
Zionist congress there was not a single French delegate and
the official language was German; Herzl, the founder of
modern Zionism, was an Austrian; and the entire proceedings
of the congress were held in public, while the town of Basel
overflowed with journalists who would hardly have overlooked
so extraordinary a meeting. But in any case Nilus himself, in
his edition of 1905, had categorically stated that the lectures
were delivered not in 1897 but in 1902–3.

As though the confusion was not already sufficient, the
editors of various later translations of the *Protocols* invented
still further stories. The editor of the first German edition
(1919), who passed under the name of Gottfried zur Beek,
maintains that the Elders of Zion were simply the members of
the Basel congress; and he explains, too, just how their
machinations were unmasked. According to him the Russian
government, always anxious about Jewish activities, sent a
spy to observe the congress. A Jew who was entrusted with
taking the minutes of the (non-existent) secret meetings from
Basel to the 'Jewish Masonic lodge' at Frankfort-on-Main
was bribed by this spy to lend them for a night at an unnamed
town on the way. Fortunately the spy had with him a whole
squad of copyists. Writing frantically, these men managed

---

[1] S. Nilus, *Velikoe v Malom*, Tsarskoe Selo, 1905, p. 322.
[2] S. Nilus, *Bliz Est,Pri Dverekh*, 1917, p. 88.

during that night to copy many of the minutes, which were then sent to Nilus for translation into Russian.

Thus Gottfried zur Beek; but Theodor Fritsch, 'the Nestor of German antisemitism', took an entirely different view of the matter in his edition of the *Protocols* (1920). For him too the document was a Zionist production – indeed he called it *The Zionist Protocols* – but it was stolen not from the Basel congress but from an unspecified Jewish house by the Russian police. Moreover it was not in French but in Hebrew – so the police passed it for translation to 'the orientalist Professor Nilus' (who in reality was neither a professor nor an orientalist – nor, as we shall see, a translator of the *Protocols*). Different again is the tale told by Roger Lambelin, the editor of the most popular French edition: according to him the *Protocols* were stolen from a cupboard in a town in Alsace, by the wife or fiancée of the leader of the Freemasons. After such picturesque stories it is a sad anticlimax to learn from a Polish edition that the *Protocols* were simply taken from the flat of Theodor Herzl in Vienna.

A Russian-American lady, sometimes known by her maiden name of Lesley Fry and sometimes by her married name of Mrs Shishmarev, wrote much about the *Protocols* from 1922 onwards. Her major contribution was to argue that the author of the *Protocols* was none other than Ascher Ginzberg, who wrote under the name of Achad Ha-am (i.e. 'One of the People') – in reality as unpolitical and unworldly an author as one can imagine. According to Miss Fry the *Protocols* were written by Ginzberg in Hebrew, read by him to a secret gathering of initiates at Odessa in 1890 and then sent, in a French translation, to the Alliance Israélite Universelle at Paris and thence to the congress at Basel in 1897 – where, one must assume, it would have had to be translated into German for the benefit of the delegates. A complicated hypothesis, but one which found influential adherents nevertheless.

Between the various writers on the *Protocols* there is, then, almost no agreement. Even the conviction that the Elders of Zion are the same as the leaders of Zionism is not shared by them all. As we have seen, the unknown Russian translator of the original French manuscript, as quoted by Krushevan and Butmi, explicitly states that the Elders are not to be confused with the representatives of the Zionist movement. For Nilus, until his belated discovery, the 'Central Chancellery of Zion' was the headquarters of the Alliance Israélite Universelle in Paris; and Urbain Gohier, one of the first editors of the *Protocols* in France, was equally convinced that the Elders were members of the Alliance. Others, following in the footsteps of Miss Fry, have attempted to combine the two beliefs – no easy feat, since the Alliance, a purely philanthropic and unpolitical organization which set all its hopes on the assimilation of the Jews to their Gentile compatriots, was as hostile to Zionism as could be. And then of course there were the Freemasons, so frequently named in connexion with the *Protocols*. ... And meanwhile in 1921 something came to light which conclusively proved the *Protocols* to be a forgery.

The *Protocols* are such a transparent and ludicrous forgery that one may well wonder why it was ever necessary to prove the point. The fact remains that in the years immediately after the First World War, when the *Protocols* were emerging from obscurity and becoming a world-famous document, multitudes of people who were by no means insane took them perfectly seriously. To realize this one has only to consider what *The Times* had to say on the matter in its issue of 8 May 1920: 'What are these "Protocols"? Are they authentic? If so, what malevolent assembly concocted these plans, and gloated over their exposition? ... Have we, by straining every fibre of our national body, escaped a "Pax Germanica" only to fall into a "Pax Judæica"?'[1]

A year later, on 18 August 1921, *The Times* devoted a resounding editorial to admitting its error. It had just published, in its issues of 16, 17, and 18 August, a lengthy despatch from its correspondent in Constantinople, Philip Graves, revealing that the *Protocols* were largely copied from a pamphlet directed against Napoleon III and dated 1865. Philip Graves wrote as follows:

I must confess that when the discovery was communicated to me I was at first incredulous. Mr X, who brought me the evidence, was convinced. 'Read this book through,' he said, 'and you will find

---

[1] The text is given more fully below, pp. 152–3.

irrefutable proof that the *Protocols of the Learned Elders of Zion* is a plagiarism.'

Mr X, who does not wish his real name to be known, is a Russian landowner with English connections. Orthodox by religion, he is in political opinion a Constitutional Monarchist. He came here as a refugee after the final failure of the White cause in South Russia. He had long been interested in the Jewish question as far as it concerned Russia, had studied the *Protocols*, and during the period of Denikin's[1] ascendancy had made investigations with the object of discovering whether any occult 'Masonic' organization, such as the *Protocols* speak of, existed in Southern Russia. The only such organization was a Monarchist one. The discovery of the key to the problems of the *Protocols* came to him by chance.

A few months ago he bought a number of old books from a former officer of the Okhrana[2] who had fled to Constantinople. Among these books was a small volume in French, lacking the title-page, with dimensions 5½ by 3½ inches. It had been cheaply re-bound. On the leather back is printed in Latin capitals the word Joli. The preface, entitled 'Simple Avertissement', is dated Geneva, 15 October 1864. . . . Both the paper and the type are characteristic of the sixties and seventies of the last century. These details are given in the hope that they may lead to the discovery of the title of the book. . . .

Mr X believes it must be rare, since, had it not been so, the 'Protocols' would have speedily been recognized as plagiarism by anyone who had read the original.

That the latter is a 'fake' could not be maintained for an instant by anyone who had seen it. Its original possessor, the old Okhrana officer, did not remember where he obtained it, and attached no importance to it. Mr X, glancing at it one day, was struck by a resemblance between a passage which had caught his eye and a phrase in the French edition of the *Protocols*. He followed up the clue, and soon realized that the *Protocols* were to a very large extent . . . a paraphrase of the Geneva original. . . .

Before receiving the book from Mr X I was, as I have said, in-credulous. I did not believe that Serge Nilus' *Protocols* were authentic. . . . But I could not have believed, had I not seen, that the writer who supplied Nilus with his originals was a careless and shameless plagiarist.

The Geneva book is a very thinly veiled attack on the despotism

---

[1] General Anton Denikin, Commander-in-Chief of the 'White' armies in southern Russia during the civil war, 1918–20.

[2] Okhrana: the secret police in tsarist Russia.

of Napoleon III in the form of a series of 25 dialogues. . . . The speakers are Montesquieu and Machiavelli. . . .[1]

Before publishing the dispatch from its Constantinople correspondent *The Times* carried out some research at the British Museum. The name 'Joli' on the book's cover provided the clue. The mysterious volume was quickly identified as the *Dialogue aux Enfers entre Montesquieu et Machiavel*, by a French lawyer called Maurice Joly; it was first published at Brussels (though with the imprint Geneva) in 1864.

In the autobiography which he wrote in 1870 Maurice Joly has described how, strolling one evening by the Seine in Paris, he suddenly conceived the idea of writing a dialogue between Montesquieu and Machiavelli. Montesquieu would present the case for liberalism, Machiavelli the case for a cynical despotism. It was forbidden to criticize openly the régime of Napoleon III; but in this way it should be possible, through the mouth of Machiavelli, to present the Emperor's motives and methods stripped of their usual camouflage of humbug. So thought Joly, but he underestimated his adversary. The *Dialogue aux Enfers* was printed in Belgium and smuggled into France for distribution, but the moment it crossed the border it was seized by the police and its author was quickly traced and arrested. On 25 April 1865 Joly was tried and sentenced to fifteen months' imprisonment; his book was banned and confiscated.

Joly's later career was equally unfortunate. Witty, aggressive, no respecter of persons, he proceeded from disappointment to disappointment until, in 1879, he committed suicide. He deserved a better fate. He was not only a brilliant stylist, he had a fine intuition for the forces which, gathering strength after his death, were to produce the political cataclysms of the present century. In his novel *Les Affamés* he showed a rare understanding of those tensions in the modern world which foster revolutionary movements, whether of the right or the left. Above all, in his reflections on the amateurish despotism of Napoleon III he arrived at insights which remain valid when applied to various authoritarian régimes of our own time. Moreover, something of Joly's insights even survived when the *Dialogue aux Enfers* was transformed into the

---

[1] *The Times*, issues of 16, 17, and 18 August 1921.

Protocols of the Elders of Zion; that is one reason – though, as we shall see, not the only reason – why the *Protocols* often seem to forecast twentieth-century authoritarianism. But that after all is a poor kind of immortality; and there is a cruel irony in the fact that a brilliant but long-forgotten defence of liberalism should have provided the basis for an atrociously written piece of reactionary balderdash which has swept the world.

Joly's pamphlet is indeed an admirable work, incisive, ruthlessly logical, beautifully constructed. The debate is opened by Montesquieu, who argues that in the present age the enlightened ideas of liberalism have made despotism, which was always immoral, impracticable as well. Machiavelli replies with such eloquence and at such length that he dominates the rest of the pamphlet. The mass of the people, he insists, are simply incapable of governing themselves. Normally they are inert and are only too happy to be ruled by a strong man; while if something happens to arouse them they show unlimited capacity for senseless violence – and then they need a strong man to control them. Politics have never had anything to do with morality; and as for practicability, it has never been so easy as now to impose despotic rule. A modern ruler need only pretend to observe the forms of legality, he need allow his people only the merest semblance of self-government – and he will have not the slightest difficulty in attaining and exercising absolute power. People readily acquiesce in any decision which they imagine to have been their own; therefore the ruler has only to refer all questions to a popular assembly —having first, of course, arranged that the assembly shall give the decision he requires. The forces that might oppose his will can be dealt with easily enough: the press can be censored, political opponents can be watched by the police. Neither the power of the Church nor financial problems need be feared. So long as the prince dazzles the people with his prestige and by winning military victories he can be sure of their support.

Such is the book that inspired the forger of the *Protocols.* He plagiarized it shamelessly – just how shamelessly can be seen by skimming the selection of parallel passages at the end of this book.[1] In all, over 160 passages in the *Protocols,* totalling

¹ See pp. 275 9.

two-fifths of the entire text, are clearly based on passages in Joly; in nine of the chapters the borrowings amount to more than half of the text, in some they amount to three-quarters, in one (Protocol VII) to almost the entire text. Moreover with less than a dozen exceptions the order of the borrowed passages remains the same as it was in Joly, as though the adaptor had worked through the *Dialogue* mechanically, page by page, copying straight into his 'protocols' as he proceeded. Even the arrangement in chapters is much the same – the twenty-four chapters of the *Protocols* corresponding roughly with the twenty-five of the *Dialogue*. Only towards the end, where the prophecy of the Messianic Age predominates, does the adaptor allow himself any real independence of his model. It is in fact as clear a case of plagiarism – and of faking – as one could well desire.

The forger constructed his argument out of the two con-flicting arguments in the *Dialogue*: that of 'Machiavelli', in favour of despotism, and that of 'Montesquieu', in favour of liberalism. His borrowings are mostly from 'Machiavelli'. What Joly put into the mouth of Machiavelli, the forger put into the mouth of the mysterious lecturer, the nameless Elder of Zion – but with certain important differences. Whereas 'Machiavelli', representing Napoleon III, is describing a state of affairs which already exists, in the *Protocols* this description is recast in the form of a prophecy for the future. Again, 'Machiavelli' argues that a despot may find in democratic forms a useful cover for his tyranny; in the *Protocols* the argu-ment is reversed, so that all democratic forms of government are shown as being simply masks for tyranny. But the forger also borrows certain passages from 'Montesquieu'; and here he makes it seem that the ideals of liberalism were invented by Jews, and are being propagated by them, for the sole pur-pose of disorganizing and demoralizing the Gentiles.

Given sufficient leisure, it might be possible to construct a coherent argument out of such materials, but the *Protocols* give the impression of having been concocted in a hurry. The *Dialogue aux Enfers*, for instance, distinguishes perfectly clearly between the policy of Napoleon III striving for power and his policy once power is firmly in his hands. The *Protocols* knows nothing of such distinctions. At one moment the lecturer talks as though the Elders already hold absolute control and at the next moment as though they have still a century to wait. Sometimes he boasts that the Gentile governments are utterly intimidated by the Elders, and sometimes that they have not discovered what the Elders are plotting or even that they exist. Other illogicalities arise from the fact that whereas the despot portrayed by Joly was concerned to dominate France, the Elders are supposed to be trying to dominate the world. The forger takes no steps to eliminate the resulting discrepancies – any more than he minds interrupting the argument by irrelevancies of his own, such as the threat to blow up recalcitrant cities from their underground railways.

More strangely still, the forger introduces whole passages which are devoted simply to attacking liberal ideas and to extolling the landed aristocracy as an indispensable bulwark of monarchy. These passages are so conspicuously un-Jewish in spirit that they have caused real embarrassment to the editors of the *Protocols*. Some editors have simply suppressed them, others have added comments to the effect that that fervent Russian conservative, Sergey Nilus, must have interpolated certain reflections of his own. Their uneasiness is understandable. Nilus was not himself the forger but, as we shall see, the invective against liberalism and the eulogy of the aristocratic and monarchical order do point to the real nature and motives of the forgery.

CHAPTER IV

Secret Police and Occultists

1

AFTER Hitler came to power in Germany the *Protocols* were promoted and distributed throughout the world both by German Nazi associations and by Nazi sympathizers in other countries. A vigorous response to this provocation came from the Jewish communities of Switzerland, which brought an action against the leadership of the Nazi organization in Switzerland and against certain individual Nazis. The charge was of publishing and distributing improper literature; but the case, which was heard in Berne partly in October 1934 and partly in May 1935, became in effect an inquiry into the authenticity or spuriousness of the *Protocols*. Incredible as it may seem nowadays, this inquiry attracted world-wide attention and was covered by journalists from all parts of the world.

Much of the interest of the proceedings at Berne lies in the light which they threw upon the activities of the tsarist secret police – the Okhrana – and their possible connexion with the *Protocols*.[1] The plaintiffs called as witnesses several Russian émigrés of liberal views. One of these was Professor Sergey Svatikov, a former Social-Democrat of the Menshevik wing. Under the Provisional Government which ruled Russia during the six months between the Tsar's abdication and the Bolshevik

---

[1] The Okhrana was founded by imperial decree after the assassination of Alexander II in 1881, for the 'protection of public security and order'. ('Okhrana' means 'protection' in Russian.) Previously the chief organ of the secret police had been the Third Section of the Imperial Chancellery, which was founded after the Decembrist revolt of 1825. The Okhrana had branches in all the principal towns of Russia, as well as a foreign service centred on Paris. Like the rest of the police forces, the Okhrana was subordinate to the Minister of the Interior.

revolution in 1917, Svatikov was sent to Paris to dissolve the foreign branch of the Russian secret police, which had its headquarters there. One of the agents he interviewed was Henri Bint, a Frenchman of Alsatian origin who had been in the service of the Russians ever since 1880. According to Bint, the *Protocols* had been concocted on instructions from the head of his organization, Pyotr Ivanovich Rachkovsky. Another witness, the celebrated journalist Vladimir Burtsev, gave evidence pointing in the same direction. He claimed to have been told by two former directors of the Department of Police, Lopukhin and Beletsky, that Rachkovsky was involved in the fabrication of the *Protocols*.[1]

A great deal is in fact known about Rachkovsky, the sinister and gifted head of the Okhrana outside Russia. 'If ever you meet him in society,' wrote a Frenchman who knew him, 'I very much doubt whether you will feel the slightest misgivings about him, for nothing in his appearance reveals his sinister function. Fat, restless, always with a smile on his lips . . . he looks more like some genial, jolly fellow on a spree. . . . He has one rather noticeable weakness – that he is passionately fond of our little Parisiennes – but he is the most skilful operator to be found in the ten capitals of Europe.'[2] A Russian compatriot gave his impression in equally striking terms: 'His slightly too ingratiating manner and his suave way of speaking – which made one think of a great feline carefully concealing its claws – only dimmed for a moment my clear perception of what was fundamental in this man – his subtle intelligence, his firm will, his profound devotion . . . to the interests of imperial Russia.'[3]

Rachkovsky started life as a minor civil servant, and he even cultivated relations with students of more or less revolu-

---

[1] Mimeographed copies were made of the verbatim report of the proceedings at Berne, under the title *Stenographisches Protokoll der Verhandlungen . . . vor Richteramt V von Bern in Sachen Schweizerischer Israelitischer Gemeindebund und Israelitische Kultusgemeinde Bern gegen die Gauleitung des Bundes National-Sozialistischer Eidgenossen sowie gegen Unbekannte.* A copy is available in the Wiener Library, London. Svatikov's and Burtsev's evidence are items iii and iv.

[2] Papus, in *Echo de Paris*, issue of 27 October 1901.

[3] M. A. Taube, *La Politique russe d'avant-guerre et la fin de l'Empire des sars (1904–1917)*, Paris 1928, p. 26.

tionary leanings. The turning-point in his career came in 1879, when he was arrested by the secret police and charged with activities prejudicial to the safety of the state. An attempt had been made on the life of the Adjutant-General Drentel; and although Rachkovsky was merely a friend of a man who was accused of sheltering the would-be assassin, this was sufficient to land him in the hands of the Third Section of the Imperial Chancellery – the future Okhrana. As so often happened in such circumstances, Rachkovsky found himself faced with the alternative of banishment to Siberia or else of a lucrative career in the secret police itself. He chose the latter course, and it led him to a position of great power.

By 1881 Rachkovsky was active in the right-wing organiza- tion, the Holy Druzhina, an early attempt at what was later to become the Union of the Russian People. In 1883 he was adjutant to the head of the security services at St Petersburg. The following year he was in Paris, in charge of the operations of the entire secret police outside Russia. In this position he was brilliantly successful, and he retained it for nineteen years (1884–1903). He organized a network of agencies in France and Switzerland, London and Berlin; as a result he was able to keep a close check on the activities of Russian revolutionaries and terrorists, not only abroad but in Russia itself. Soon he was revealing an extraordinary talent for intrigue. In 1886 his agents – Henri Bint among them – blew up the printing works of the Russian revolutionary group Narodnaya Volya (The People's Will) in Geneva – and at the same time made it look as if this was the work of traitors among the revolutionaries themselves. In 1890 he 'unmasked' an organization which was supposed to be manufacturing in Paris, bombs to be used for assassinations in Russia. In Russia itself the Okhrana was able, as a result of this *coup*, to arrest no less than sixty-three terrorists. It was only nineteen years later that the journalist Burtsev – the same who was to give evidence before the court at Berne – discovered and revealed the truth about this affair: that the bombs had been planted by Rachkovsky's men, acting on Rachkovsky's instructions.

The 1890s were the time when bombs were being made – and thrown – in western Europe as well as in Russia; it was the golden age of the anarchists and 'nihilists'. In 1893 Vaillant threw his rather harmless bomb, full of nails, into the French Chamber of Deputies; in 1894 a whole series of much more dangerous bombs were thrown at Liége. It is certain that Rachkovsky deliberately provoked and organized the latter outrage, and highly probable that he was behind the former also. In all this the wily Russian was playing at high politics. Never satisfied with his job as a security chief, he tried to influence the course of international affairs. His motive in arranging outrages in France and Belgium was to force a *rapprochement* between the French and Russian police as a first step towards the Franco-Russian military alliance on which he had set his heart – and which indeed he did much to bring about.

Rachkovsky also built up a fortune by speculation on the stock exchange, and this enabled him to live in great style. He cultivated personal relationships with leading French politicians, including President Loubet himself, and with Russian dignitaries, including some who stood close to the Tsar. But he was ruthlessly ambitious, and it is remarkable how many of those who in any way obstructed his ambition – from General Seliverstov, who was sent to inquire into his activities in Paris in 1890, to the Minister of the Interior Plehve, who recalled him from Paris in 1903 – were assassinated by his subordinates in the secret police.

This born intriguer delighted in forging documents. As head of the Okhrana outside Russia his main concern was to cope with Russian revolutionaries who had taken refuge abroad. One of his favourite methods was to produce a letter or pamphlet in which a supposed revolutionary attacked the revolutionary leadership. In 1887 there appeared in the French press a letter by a certain 'P. Ivanov', who claimed to be a disillusioned revolutionary, asserting – quite falsely – that the majority of the terrorists were Jews. In 1890 there appeared a pamphlet entitled *Une confession par un vieillard ancien révolutionnaire* (*A confession by an old man who was once a revolutionary*), accusing the revolutionaries who had taken refuge in London of being British agents. In 1892 a letter appeared over the famous name of Plekhanov, accusing the leadership of Narodnaya Volya of having published this 'confession'. A few weeks later came a further letter, in which

Plekhanov in turn was attacked by other supposed revolutionaries. In reality all these documents were written by the same man, Rachkovsky.

Rachkovsky also did much to develop a technique which, half a century later, was to be employed on a massive scale by the Nazis. This was, to present the whole progressive movement, from the most moderate liberals to the most extreme revolutionaries, as being a mere tool in the hands of the Jews. His object here was simultaneously to discredit the progressive movement in the eyes of the Russian bourgeoisie and proletariat and to direct against the Jews the widespread discontent engendered by the tsarist régime. Among the materials presented by the plaintiffs at the Berne trial was a letter sent in 1891 by Rachkovsky in Paris to the Director of the Department of Police in Russia, announcing his intention of launching a campaign against the Russian Jews.

And then there is the book *Anarchie et Nihilisme*, published in Paris in 1892 over the pseudonym of Jehan-Préval. *Anarchie et Nihilisme* was quite certainly inspired by Rachkovsky – it even contains one of his own notorious forgeries – and in places it reads like a sketch for the *Protocols*. It tells how, as a result of the French Revolution, the Jew has become 'the absolute master of the situation in Europe . . . governing by discreet means both monarchies and republics'. The one remaining obstacle to Jewish world-dominion is presented by 'the Muscovite fortress'; to overthrow it, an international syndicate of extremely rich and powerful Jews, bestriding Paris, Vienna, Berlin, and London, is preparing to hurl a coalition of nations against Russia. And it is with a shock of recognition that we come across a phrase that appears in innumerable apologies for the *Protocols*: 'The whole truth is to be found in this formula, which provides the key to a host of disturbing and seemingly insoluble riddles'. From all this a practical lesson is to be drawn: that a Franco-Russian league must be formed forthwith to combat the 'mysterious, occult, irresponsible power'[1] of the Jews.

In 1902 Rachkovsky actually tried to bring such a league into being, and nothing could be more typical of the man than the method he adopted. He distributed in Paris an appeal to

[1] Jehan-Préval, *Anarchie et Nihilisme*, Paris, 1892, pp. 202–7.

the French to support a 'Russian Patriotic League' which was supposed to have its headquarters in Kharkov. The appeal was a forgery, for it was worded as though it came from the league itself – and in reality there was no league. And this is not all: the appeal contains bitter complaints about Rachkovsky, whom it accuses of misrepresenting the league's aims and activities and even of pretending that it does not exist at all – but what, it adds, could one expect of a security chief who employs as his agents a former revolutionary, a literary adventurer, and a blackmailer 'whose cheeks still bear marks of the slaps he received, for attempted extortion, in 1889'?[1] The appeal ends with a hope – that Rachkovsky may yet discover his error and come to value the league as it deserves. The whole weird concoction was composed by Rachkovsky himself, and so skilfully that it deceived not only many eminent Frenchmen but the Russian Foreign Minister himself![2]

This time Rachkovsky had overreached himself, however, and when the hoax was unmasked he was recalled from Paris. It proved only a temporary setback. When revolutionary activities were intensified in 1905 and General Trepov was given near-dictatorial powers to crush them, he appointed Rachkovsky Assistant Director of the Department of Police. In this capacity he was able to resume his activities as a forger of documents, and on a far more dangerous scale. Vast numbers of pamphlets were printed on behalf of non-existent organizations, calling on the populace and even on the soldiers to kill Jews. And now at last he was able to help found an antisemitic league: it was that Union of the Russian People whose members, from Butmi in 1906 to Vinberg and Shabelsky-Bork in the 1920s, were to play so large a part in the dissemination of the *Protocols*. The armed bands organized and paid by this Union of the Russian People established a pattern in political terrorism and in the massacre of Jews which – as we shall see – was to have a direct influence upon

[1] See below, p. 88.
[2] A photostat of this document, which is in French, was sent by the Soviet authorities to Berne at the time of the trial, and a typed copy of this is in the Wiener Library, London (file 'Russische Urkunden des Berner Prozesses').

the Nazis. All in all, it is not surprising that Gottfried zur Beek, the editor of the first foreign translation of the *Protocols*, should have asserted that Rachkovsky, who died in 1911, was murdered on orders from the Elders of Zion.

There are, then, very good grounds for suspecting Rachkovsky of instigating the forgery that resulted in the *Protocols*. The evidence of Svatikov and Burtsev, the book *Anarchie et Nihilisme*, Rachkovsky's activities as a militant antisemite and organizer of pogroms, his taste for forgery and for immensely complicated deceptions – all this seems to point to him. That being so, it is worth noting that at the very time when he was trying to create his antisemitic 'Russian Patriotic League', in 1902, Rachkovsky became involved in a court intrigue in St Petersburg which also involved the future editor of the *Protocols*, Sergey Nilus. It was an intrigue against a Frenchman called Philippe who, like Rasputin after him, established himself at the imperial court as a faith-healer and became the idol and guide of the Tsar and Tsaritsa.[1] Rachkovsky and Nilus both took part in the intrigue against him, and on the same side.

The man always called himself Philippe, though his full name was Philippe-Nizier-Anthelme Vachod. He was born in 1850 into a family of poor peasants in Savoy. When he was six the local priest regarded him as possessed by devils; at thirteen he began to practise faith-healing; later he set up at Lyons as a 'mesmerizer'. As he possessed no medical qualifications he was forbidden to practise as a doctor and was three times prosecuted for doing so; but he managed to go on treating patients nevertheless. It seems certain that he really had exceptional intuitive gifts and was able, by means of suggestion, to perform some remarkable cures.

When the Tsar and Tsaritsa visited France in 1901 Philippe was presented to them by the two 'Montenegrin princesses' Militsa and Anastasia – daughters of Prince Nicholas of Montenegro, but married to Russian dukes and wholly intent on ingratiating themselves with the imperial couple. Now the Tsar, a weak and timid mediocrity who suffered a good deal

[1] It is a mystery how the form Tsarina, which is a cross between the Russian *Tsaritsa* and the German *Tsarin*, ever came into the English language, and there seems no good reason for perpetuating it.

under the burden of autocratic power, yearned for some holy man who could act as intermediary between him and the God whose indubitable but woefully inadequate representative he felt himself to be. And the Tsaritsa was a hysteric whose instability was constantly aggravated by the conspiracies which surrounded her and her husband at court as well as by the terrorists with their bombs; she too was quite ready to submit to any quack who could offer her solace and at least some semblance of security. Above all Tsar and Tsaritsa, though they had four daughters, had no son, and they desperately needed one. Any medicine-man who claimed to know the answer to this problem could hope to dominate them – just as, later, Rasputin was able to build his career on their need to keep their haemophilic son alive.

No wonder that Philippe was invited to Tsarskoe Selo and loaded with honours. Already in France the Tsar had addressed a personal request to the French Government that this un-qualified practitioner should be awarded a medical diploma. This of course was unthinkable for the French – but in Russia, where he was master, the Tsar made the St Petersburg Military Medical Academy appoint Philippe doctor to the army. He also appointed him a Counsellor of State with the rank of general. But if Philippe was cherished and flattered and almost worshipped by the imperial couple and by the 'Montenegrin princesses' and their husbands, he also had powerful enemies – in fact he found himself in much the same controversial and dangerous position as came to be occupied by Rasputin. In the circles around two formidable ladies – the Dowager Empress Maria Feodorovna and the Grand Duchess Elizaveta Feodorovna – he was resented and hated. To break Philippe these people turned to Rachkovsky.

Rachkovsky was asked for information about Philippe's past. Thanks to the relations he had cultivated with the French police he was able to draw up a detailed and, no doubt, suitably distorted report, which he brought with him when he visited St Petersburg early in 1902. The first person to whom he showed it, the Minister of the Interior, Sipyagin, advised him to throw it on the fire which was burning in the hearth. But Rachkovsky persisted: he took his report to the commandant of the imperial palace and it seems he even wrote the Dowager

Empress a personal letter denouncing Philippe as an instrument of the Freemasons. But Sipyagin's misgivings proved justified. Although the Tsar did in the end yield to pressure and refrain from inviting Philippe to take up permanent residence in Russia, he was furious. In October 1902 Rachkovsky was recalled from France, the following year he was dismissed, retired without a pension, forbidden to return to France – and there is no doubt that if this was partly due to his manoeuvres with his imaginary Patriotic League, it was also due to his campaign against Philippe. Even later, when Philippe had returned to France for good and he himself was living in Russia as a private person, Rachkovsky used his connexions with the French police to persecute the unfortunate faith-healer. Vindictive and merciless as ever, he pursued the unwitting cause of his downfall until in the end he harried him to death. Watched day and night by police spies, his letters opened, slandered in the press, Philippe died in August 1905 – just one week before Rachkovsky, restored to favour, reached the height of his career with his appointment as Assistant Director of the Department of Police.

The intrigue against Philippe also involved Sergey Alexandrovich Nilus. A Frenchman, Alexandre du Chayla, who lived many years in Russia and who saw quite a lot of Nilus in 1909, gave an account of these developments in an article in *La Tribune Juive* in May 1921. He tells how Nilus, a landowner who lost his entire fortune while living in France, returned to Russia and adopted the life of a perpetual pilgrim, wandering from monastery to monastery. Around 1900 he wrote a book describing how he had been converted from an atheistic intellectual into a fervent believer in Orthodox Christianity and a mystic. The book – it was the first edition of *The Great in the Small*, without the *Protocols* – received favourable reviews in conservative and religious newspapers and so came to the attention of the Grand Duchess Elizaveta Feodorovna. The Grand Duchess was a woman of deep piety (she later became a nun), but she was deeply suspicious of the mystical adventurers and faith-healers whom the Tsar collected around him. She blamed this state of affairs on the Archpriest Yanishev, who was confessor to the Tsar and Tsaritsa, and set out to replace him by a man whom she regarded as a genuine mystic and unshakably orthodox: Sergey Nilus.

Nilus was accordingly brought to Tsarskoe Selo. It was the end of 1901 or the beginning of 1902, and the immediate task was to oust Philippe. The clique of Philippe's enemies hit on the following plan: Nilus was to be ordained priest and he was also to be married off to one of the Tsaritsa's ladies-in-waiting, Yelena Alexandrovna Ozerova.[1] Then a concerted effort would be made to impose him on the Tsar and Tsaritsa as their confessor; if it succeeded, there would be no more room for Philippe or for any similar 'holy men'. It was an ingenious stratagem, but Philippe's supporters were able to counter it. They drew the attention of the ecclesiastical authorities to certain facts concerning Nilus's life that precluded ordination (presumably these concerned his love-life, which was always colourful). Nilus fell into disgrace and had to leave court. Some years later he did indeed marry Ozerova, but his chance of becoming the Tsar's confessor had gone for ever.

Were the *Protocols* used in the intrigue against Philippe, and if so, were they used at Rachkovsky's instigation? According to du Chayla the answer to both questions is yes. Nilus, he tells us, was convinced that the original 'discoverer' of the *Protocols* was Rachkovsky – 'a fine man, very active, one who in his time has done much to deprive Christ's enemies of their sting' and who 'had fought with much self-sacrifice against Free-masonry and the Satanic sects', as Nilus put it.[2]

Ana du Chayla goes on to explain what Rachkovsky could have hoped to achieve by sending the *Protocols* to Nilus. The *Protocols* claims to reveal a devilish plot by Freemasons as well as by Jews – or rather by Freemasons identified with Jews. Philippe was a Martinist, i.e. a member of an association which claimed to follow the teachings of the eighteenth-century occultist Claude de Saint-Martin, 'the unknown philosopher'. The Martinists were not really Freemasons, but the Tsar could hardly be expected to realize that. If the Tsar could be per-suaded that Philippe was the agent of a conspiracy such as

[1] Priests in the Russian Orthodox Church are required to be married.

[2] A. du Chayla, 'Serge Alexandrovitch Nilus et les Protocols des Sages de Sion (1909–1920)', in *La Tribune Juive*, Paris, issue of 14 May 1921, pp. 3–4.

that portrayed in the *Protocols*, he would certainly send him packing. By the peculiar standards of the Okhrana the calculation was a perfectly sound one, and it was just the kind of calculation that fascinated Rachkovsky.

How reliable is du Chayla? He makes occasional slips, as when he says that Nilus published a first edition of the *Protocols* in 1902, but on the whole he shows himself very well informed. In his article of 1921 he states, for instance, that in 1905 Nilus published an edition of the *Protocols* at Tsarskoe Selo, under the imprint of the local Red Cross organization. That is perfectly accurate: the book in question is the third edition of *The Great in the Small*, which contains the *Protocols*. What is more, he remarks that it was Yelena Ozerova who made this edition possible – and years later, when the Soviet authorities sent photostats of documents to the court at Berne, this proved to be accurate also. Among these documents are several letters to and from the Moscow Censorship Committee, which show quite clearly how Ozerova used her position as lady-in-waiting to secure publication for the book of her fiancé and future husband.

These documents reveal something else as well – and something of which du Chayla cannot possibly have been aware. They contain an item, so elusive that it has hitherto escaped notice, which suggests that Rachkovsky had had some contact either with Nilus or with the manuscript copy of the *Protocols* in Nilus's possession. The Moscow Censorship Committee, at its session of 28 September 1905, received a report from State Counsellor and Censor Sokolov which quotes the following phrase as being attached by Nilus to his manuscript of the *Protocols*: 'Naturally the head of the Russian Agency,[1] the Jew Efron, and his agents, who are also Jews, have not reported on these matters to the Russian Government.'[2] The committee, in authorizing publication, stipulated that all proper names must be removed from the manuscript – that of Efron among them. The name was duly removed before the book was printed, but one can identify the passage where it was to have

[1] In Paris.
[2] A photostat of the report of the Censorship Committee was sent by the Soviet authorities to Berne. German translation in the Wiener Library (file 'Russische Urkunden des Berner Prozesses').

appeared – it is in the epilogue to the *Protocols*. This epilogue also appears in all the other early Russian editions of the *Protocols*, that in *Znamya* and those of Butmi. None of these editions was subjected to the stipulation concerning proper names – indeed the *Znamya* version had appeared two years before the Moscow Censorship Committee made the stipulation – and yet none of them contains any reference to Efron. We can only assume, therefore, that the reference to Efron was specially inserted into Nilus's manuscript. And it can only have been done or prompted by some enemy of Efron.

Who then was Efron, and who can his enemy have been? Akim Efron, or Effront, was the secret agent in Paris of the Russian Ministry of Finance. When he died in 1909 the French press referred to him as the director of the political agency attached to the Russian embassy. He certainly did not belong to Rachkovsky's organization but employed his own agents and sent his own reports back to St Petersburg. One could assume that this would suffice to earn Rachkovsky's hatred, but as it happens there is no need to assume, for we have proof. One thing that is known about Efron is that during the International Exhibition in Paris in 1889 his face was publicly slapped in the Russian pavilion for attempted blackmail. In other words, Efron must have been the person whom Rachkovsky described, in his forged appeal for the 'Russian Patriotic League', as bearing on his cheeks the marks of the slaps which he received in 1889 for attempted blackmail.[1] As for the statement in the same appeal that Efron was one of Rachkovsky's own men, it was a deliberate lie, and just the tortuous and malicious kind of lie that most delighted Rachkovsky. So the mention of Efron in Nilus's manuscript does suggest that some link, direct or indirect, existed between the persecutor and the rival of Philippe.

2

We have seen what kind of man Rachkovsky was and it seems worth while to take a look at Nilus too. We possess a good deal of information about him, some of it very odd indeed. Again

---

[1] See above, p. 82.

it is Alexandre du Chayla who has left the fullest account.[1] He tells how, wishing to study the inner life of the Orthodox Church, he made his way in January 1909 to the famous monastery of Optina Pustyn, a couple of miles from the town of Kozelsk in what was then the government of Kaluga. In the nineteenth century Optina Pustyn had played an important part in Russian intellectual life; the figure of Father Zosima in *The Brothers Karamazov* is modelled on one of its leading personalities; Tolstoy also often visited the monastery and at one time even lived there. Near the monastery were a number of villas occupied by laymen who wished to withdraw to some extent from the world. Du Chayla set up house in one of these villas. The day after his arrival the Father Superior, the Archimandrite Xenophon, introduced him to one of his neighbours, who was Sergey Nilus.

Nilus, who was then aged forty-seven, is described by du Chayla as 'a man of truly Russian type, big and strong, with a grey beard and deep eyes – blue, but with a veiled, somewhat troubled look. He wore boots, and a Russian shirt with a belt which had a prayer embroidered on it.' He and his dependents occupied four rooms in a large villa; and rest of the villa was employed as a home for cripples, idiots, and mentally sick people, who lived there in hope of a miraculous cure. The whole establishment was supported by the pension which the imperial court paid to Ozerova as a former lady-in-waiting. Ozerova, otherwise Mme Nilus, struck du Chayla as being absolutely submissive to her husband. She even had the most amiable relations with Nilus's former mistress, who lived in the same villa and, having lost her own fortune, also on Mme Nilus's pension.

During the nine months he passed at Optina Pustyn, du Chayla learned a lot about Nilus. A former landowner in the government of Orel, he was an educated man who had graduated in Law at the University of Moscow; he spoke excellent French, German, and English and had a good grasp of contemporary European literature. But in character he was capricious, unruly, and despotic – so much so in fact that he had been obliged to resign from the position of magistrate which he had held in Transcaucasia. He had also tried his

[1] In *La Tribune Juive*, loc. cit.

hand at managing his estate in Orel, but had had no success
with that either. Finally he had gone abroad with his mistress
and had lived at Biarritz – until one day he heard from his
steward that he was ruined.

This news produced a major emotional crisis in Nilus and
altogether changed his outlook on life. So far he had been a
theoretical anarchist with a cult of Nietzsche. Now he became
a convert to Orthodox Christianity and an ardent champion
of the tsarist autocracy, he fancied himself a mystic and also
a heaven-sent defender of Holy Russia. He had always re-
pudiated modern civilization; now he saw it as a conspiracy of
the powers of darkness. He became a systematic anti-rational-
ist. Science, technological progress, democracy, even the
application of reason to religious and philosophical questions –
all these features of modern civilization, says du Chayla, were
rejected by Nilus as 'the abomination of desolation in the holy
places' and as portents of the coming of Antichrist. It is an
attitude which, in one form or another, we shall meet again
and again among the devotees of the *Protocols*.

In a couple of pages which deserve a place in any anthology
of religious eccentricity du Chayla has shown just what the
Protocols meant to their most celebrated editor:

Nilus took his book from the shelves and began to translate into
French the most remarkable passages of the text and of his own
commentaries. At the same time he watched the expression on my
face, for he assumed that I would be dumbfounded by this revelation. He was rather upset himself when I told him that there was
nothing new for me in all this and that the document must be
closely related to the pamphlets of Edouard Drumont. . . .

Nilus was shaken and disappointed by this. He retorted that I
took this view because my knowledge of the *Protocols* was super-
ficial and fragmentary, and because their effect was weakened by
the oral translation. It was absolutely necessary that I should feel
the full impact. And it would be easy for me to get to know the
Protocols, because the original was in French.

Nilus did not keep the manuscript of the *Protocols* in his house
for fear lest it should be stolen by the Jews. I recall how amused I
was by his perturbation when a Jewish chemist of Kozelsk, taking
a walk with a friend in the monastery forest and trying to find the
quickest route to the ferry, happened to stray into Nilus's garden.

Poor Sergey Alexandrovich was convinced for a long time that the chemist had come to carry out a reconnaissance.

Later I learned that the note-book containing the *Protocols* was deposited until January 1909 with the priest and monk Daniel Bolotov (a portrait-painter who was quite well known at St Petersburg).[1] After his death it was deposited at the hermitage of St John the Baptist, a third of a mile from the monastery, in the keeping of the monk Alexis, a former engineer.

Some time after our first conversation about the *Protocols*, one afternoon about four o'clock, one of the patients from Nilus's home for the sick brought me a letter: Nilus was asking me to come and see him on an urgent matter.

I found Sergey Alexandrovich in his study. He was alone, his wife and Mme K. having gone to vespers. Dusk was falling but it was light, for the earth was covered in snow. I noticed on his writing-table something like a rather large envelope, made of black material and decorated with a big triple cross and the inscription: 'In this sign you shall conquer'. A little picture of St Michael, in paper, was also stuck on to the envelope. Quite clearly all this was intended as an exorcism.

Sergey Alexandrovich crossed himself three times before the great icon of the Mother of God . . . and opened the envelope, from which he took a leather-bound note-book. I learned later that the envelope and the binding had been prepared in the monastery workshop under the personal supervision of Nilus, who carried the manuscript to and fro himself, for fear of its being stolen. The cross and the other symbols had been drawn by Yelena Alexandrovna,[2] according to her husband's instructions.

'Here it is,' said Nilus, 'the charter of the Kingdom of Antichrist.'

He opened the note-book. . . . The text was written in French by various hands and, it seemed to me, with different inks.

'You see,' said Nilus, 'during the sessions of the secret Jewish government, at different times, various people filled the office of secretary. Hence the different handwritings.'

Clearly Sergey Alexandrovich regarded this peculiarity as proving that the manuscript was an original document. Yet he had no fixed views on this matter, for on another occasion I heard him say the manuscript was only a copy.

After showing me the manuscript, Sergey Alexandrovich placed

---

[1] The same monk figures, in a somewhat dubious role, in Mme Kashkina's account. See below p. 95.

[2] Ozerova.

it on the table, opened it at the first page and, settling me in his armchair, said: 'Well, now read!'

While reading the manuscript I was struck by certain peculiarities in the text. There were some spelling mistakes and above all some expressions which were not French. It is too long ago for me to be able to say that the text contained 'Russianisms', but one thing is beyond doubt: the manuscript was written by a foreigner.

It took me two and a half hours to read the document. When I had finished Nilus took the note-book, replaced it in its envelope and locked it up in the drawer of his writing-table. . . .

Sergey Alexandrovich wanted to know what impression my reading had produced on me. I told him straight out that I stood by my previous judgment; I didn't believe in the 'Elders of Zion' . . .

Nilus's face clouded. 'You really are under the Devil's influence,' he said. 'Satan's greatest ruse is to make people deny not simply his influence on the things of this world but even his very existence. What will you say now if I show you how what is said in the *Protocols* is being fulfilled, how the mysterious sign of the coming of Antichrist appears on all sides, how the imminent advent of his kingdom can be felt everywhere?'

Sergey Alexandrovich got up and we all went into his study. He took his book and a file, and he also brought from his bedroom a small chest, which I came later to call 'the Museum of Antichrist'. He began to read bits from his book and from material he had prepared for publication. He read everything that in any way expressed the eschatological expectations of contemporary Christianity: the dream of the Metropolitan Philaret, quotations from an encyclical of Pius X, the sermons of St Seraphim of Sarov and of Roman Catholic saints, fragments of Ibsen, Solovyev, Merezhkovsky.

He read for a long time. Then he proceeded to the 'exhibits in the case'. He opened his chest. Inside there were, in an indescribable state of disorder, detachable collars, india-rubbers, household utensils, insignia of various technical colleges, even the cipher of the Empress Alexandra Feodorovna and the cross of the Légion d'honneur. On all these objects he detected, in his hallucination, the 'seal of Antichrist', in the form of a triangle or of two superimposed triangles. . . . If an object bore a trade-mark even vaguely suggesting a triangle, that was enough to secure it entry to his museum. And nearly all these examples were included in his 1911 edition of the *Protocols*.

With increasing excitement and anxiety, in the grip of a sort of mystical terror, Nilus explained to me that the sign of 'the son of perdition' is now contaminating all things, that it shines even from the designs of church ornaments and from the scrolls of the great icon behind the altar in the church of the hermitage.

I felt a sort of fear. It was nearly midnight. The gaze, the voice, the reflex-like gestures – everything about Nilus gave me the feeling that we were walking on the edge of an abyss and that at any moment his reason might disintegrate in madness.[1]

Later du Chayla tells how, when the 1911 edition of his book was published, Nilus sent to the eastern patriarchs, to the Holy Synod, and to the Pope an epistle urging that an ecumenical council be summoned, with the task of working out common measures for the defence of Christendom in view of the imminent coming of Antichrist. And he began to preach on the same subject to the monks of Optina Pustyn – and so effectively that he was asked to leave the monastery for good.

Clearly, then, Nilus really believed in the Jewish world-conspiracy. Yet, with that curious capacity for double-think so characteristic of fanatics, he was sometimes prepared to admit that the *Protocols* themselves might be spurious. One day in 1909 du Chayla asked him whether Rachkovsky might not have been deceived and whether Nilus might not be working with a forgery. Nilus replied: 'You know my favourite quotation from St Paul? – "The power of God works through human weakness." Let us admit that the *Protocols* are spurious. But can't God use them to unmask the iniquity that is being prepared? Didn't Balaam's ass prophesy? Can't God, for the sake of our faith, change dog's bones into miracle-working relics? So he can put the announcement of truth into a lying mouth!'[2]

Another neighbour of Nilus has also recorded her recollections. On 1 June 1934, when preparations for the Berne trial were under way, Maria Dmitrievna Kashkina, *née* Countess Buturlin, made a statement which has not previously been published, but which certainly deserves publication, and not only for the light it throws upon the personality of Sergey Nilus. Anyone who probes into the world of the *Protocols* must at times feel suffocated by the miasma of superstition, gullibility, and quackery which it exudes. It is good to be reminded, for once, that even in tsarist Russia there were people – and

---

[1] A. du Chayla in *La Tribune Juive*, pp. 3–4.   [2] Ibid., p. 4.

not urban intellectuals either, but country folk, landowners
and peasants – who were capable of healthy scepticism and
knew craziness and roguery when they saw them. The most
relevant parts of the statement read as follows:

In 1905 I married Kashkin, who owned an estate in the Kozelsk
district in the government of Kaluga. . . . Our estate was about 2½
miles from Optina Pustyn – the monastery was built on land
donated by my husband's ancestors. . . . I met Nilus soon after
my arrival on the estate and knew him throughout the years I lived
there. . . . All those years he lived at the monastery . . . He was
known to be a writer; he gave his book *The Great in the Small* to
everyone he met. The Abbot was the Archimandrite Xenophon, a
good and honest man but quite uneducated. He was impressed by
Nilus and was still more impressed when Nilus promised to dedicate
to him his forthcoming history of the monastery; from then on
Xenophon quite melted and opened all his archives to Nilus. And
he didn't only allow him to use the archives, often he simply gave
him the documents. . . . My husband got to know about it and was
indignant. 'Nilus will loot the whole archive,' he used to say. . . .
Altogether, my husband regarded Nilus as a very tricky and shady
character, who ought to be very carefully watched. Of course this
opinion was based not on Nilus's love for documents from the
archives but on much worse things.

It should be said here that in those years Optina Pustyn was a
centre for all sorts of 'holy idiots'. Outstanding among them was
'the barefooted Mitya Kozelsky'. . . . A butcher by trade, he came
from the town of Kozelsk. . . . He was a big, strong fellow but he
could hardly utter recognizable words, he was a real idiot. It was
impossible to understand him. Nevertheless he had the reputation of
being able to cast out devils. . . . His methods . . . were more than
peculiar: he hit his patients with his fists, mainly in the stomach,
he pushed them into barrels, and so on. People said that his cures
sometimes worked. He became famous after curing the widow of a
rich merchant – I seem to remember her name was Ivanova and
she came from Moscow. Mitya diagnosed that there were seven
devils in her – and he drove them all out by his methods. The
grateful widow married him. Her fortune was substantial. Now
Mitya was washed and clothed and kept his own horses – I remember
vividly seeing him, sitting well back in his carriage, stretching his
legs, every inch a conqueror. . . .

Nilus frequented these circles. . . . His own private life gave rise
to many misgivings. In a little house adjoining and belonging to

the monastery there lived with him, apart from his wife, *née* Ozerova, his first wife, who was not officially divorced, and also part of the time yet another woman, always ailing, with a girl of eleven or twelve. The girl was said to be Nilus's daughter. In the circle around Nilus she was used as a medium in spiritualist séances. She stayed with Nilus, when her mother left. . . . They could be seen going for walks, all of them together. Nilus walked in the middle, with his long white beard and usually dressed in a white peasant's shirt, with a monk's cord as a belt. On either side of him walked his wives, the first and the second, as a supporting audience, gazing into his eyes, hanging on his every word. The little girl and her mother walked a little way behind. When they reached the wood they would settle down under the trees. Ozerova would begin to sketch something – she had a little artistic ability. The first wife . . . might do some needlework. Nilus himself would lie down – and it was rare for him to say anything.

I was told that the peace that reigned in Nilus's family had not been achieved at once – that at first, at the beginning of her marriage, Ozerova had tried to rebel. There were scenes – something, in particular, concerning the little girl. I don't know the details. But Ozerova soon gave in. . . . Nilus could control her easily enough. . . . The whole family lived on her pension. . . .

Nilus circulated amongst the odd beings who clustered around the monastery. . . . In particular, he took a lot of trouble to cultivate Mitya Kozelsky, whom he tried to introduce into the higher spheres of society. As Ozerova's husband Nilus had connections with the imperial court . . . and he used these to advance Mitya. One of Nilus's friends at the monastery was a monk called Daniel – a rather dubious personality but a fair painter. Certainly with Nilus's knowledge and possibly at his instigation, this Daniel painted a picture. It showed the Tsar, the Tsaritsa and their son enveloped and supported by clouds. . . . These clouds were full of devils with horns, tails and hoofs, who were all trying to get at the Tsarevich, reaching for him, sticking out their tongues at him. But through this throng of devils there strides, with sure step, Mitya Kalyada,[1] the fearless fighter against the Satanic powers, coming to save the Tsar's son . . . With Nilus's help this canvas was sent to St Petersburg. One can guess at the kind of publicity that Nilus must have made there for Mitya. Anyway, Mitya was summoned to St Petersburg and presented to the Tsar and Tsaritsa. Nilus went with him, as interpreter of the incomprehensible sounds he uttered;

[1] Kalyada was the real surname of 'Mitya Kozelsky', or Mitya of Kozelsk.

already before that he had established himself in this capacity. Mitya travelled first class.

You can imagine what sort of impression this journey of Mitya's made on our local population. There was no great esteem for the monks there, particularly not among the peasants. Those who saw the monks at close quarters knew that there was little place for holiness in their lives – not far from the monastery there was a whole hamlet populated with 'the monks' sins'. The local population distrusted especially all those 'holy beggars' and 'fools of God' – they considered them, with rare exceptions, a lot of loafers and charlatans. And then suddenly it turned out that the Tsar had extended an invitation to that charlatan Mitya. I myself heard some of the steadiest and most thoughtful peasants express their bewilderment. 'What can this mean?' they said. 'Doesn't the Tsar understand? Or is he making fun of us?'

The local landowners and civil servants were also shocked. I remember a talk I had with our local police chief, Rakhmaninov. . . . He showed me telegrams from the Minister, asking him to give Mitya every assistance, to provide him with a special compartment on the train, first class, and so on. Of course he did what he was told, but he made no secret of his embarrassment. My husband put the blame for Mitya's journey squarely on Nilus. He didn't hesitate to call him an adventurer and a charlatan. This business was a blow to the Tsar's prestige, and my husband regarded Nilus as wholly responsible for that.[1]

The rather cool accounts supplied by du Chayla and Mme Kashkina can be set alongside a biography of Nilus published in Yugoslavia in 1936. The author of this book, Prince N. D. Zhevakhov, was a fervent admirer of Nilus; in his eyes the *Protocols* were incontestably 'produced by a Jew writing to the dictation of the Devil, who revealed to him the methods for destroying Christian states and the secret of how to conquer the whole world'.[2] It is all the more significant that the biographical data he gives should tally almost exactly with those given by du Chayla. Moreover we discover from him what Nilus had in mind when he was delving among monastic

[1] This statement was taken down by the late Boris Nicolaevsky in Russian in Mme Kashkina's presence and was then read back to her; she approved it in every detail. The Russian transcript is in the B.I. Nicolaevsky Collection at the Hoover Institution, Stanford University, California.

[2] N. D. Zhevakhov, *Sergey Alexandrovich Nilus*, Novi Sad, 1936, p. 11.

archives. One of Nilus's achievements was to edit the diary of a hermit who, according to Zhevakhov, 'described the after-life with extraordinary realism. Thus he tells of a youth who was cursed by his mother and was thereupon lifted up by unknown powers into the airless space above the earth, where for forty days he lived the life of the spirits, mingling with them and being subject to their laws. . . . In short, this diary was a book of exceptional value, a veritable manual of holiness'.[1]

Zhevakhov also tells of the last years of Nilus, at a time when he had quite passed out of the ken of du Chayla and Mme Kashkina and when, all unknown to him, his edition of the *Protocols* was sweeping the world. It seems that after leaving Optina Pustyn Nilus lived on the estates of various friends. It is curious to note that for some six years after the Bolshevik coup d'état, while Russia was convulsed by re-volution and civil war, terror, counter-terror, and famine, Nilus and Ozerova lived peacefully somewhere in south Russia, in a house which they shared with a former hermit called Seraphim and which had a chapel constantly overflowing with dozens of pilgrims. It is true that, according to Nilus's letters, some time in 1921 a squad of Red Army soldiers, led by a local bandit, arrived with the intention of murdering the two holy men – but even then, we are told, they were preserved by a mysterious and miraculous night-watchman who disappeared into thin air as soon as he was hit. The leader of the squad was paralysed on the spot and could be cured only by the hermit Seraphim himself.

The Bolshevik authorities, however, having defeated the 'White' armies and liquidated their political opponents, were not to be permanently deterred by a vanishing night-watch-man. In the end Nilus and his companions were all evicted. After some years of wandering and two short periods of imprisonment, in 1924 and 1927, Nilus died of heart failure, at the age of sixty-eight, on New Year's Day, 1930.

From the Freyenwald documents at the Wiener Library, London, we learn the fate of some of those who were closest to Nilus. According to a manuscript note by the right-wing Russian known as Markov II, Ozerova was arrested during

[1] Ibid., p. 20.

the great purges of 1937 and deported to the Kola peninsula on the Arctic sea, where she died of hunger and cold the following year. There is also a good deal of correspondence from and concerning a son of Nilus, presumably by his first wife. Sergey Sergeyevich Nilus, who was a Polish citizen, put himself at the disposal of the Nazis when they were preparing their appeal against the judgement of the Berne court in 1935. A letter which he wrote to Alfred Rosenberg from Poland in March 1940 deserves to be quoted:

> I am the only son of the discoverer of the *Protocols of the Elders of Zion*, S. A. Nilus. . . . I can and must not remain indifferent in these times when the fate of the whole Aryan world hangs in the balance. I feel that the victory of the Führer, that man of genius, will liberate my poor country also, and I believe that I could contribute to this in any position. After the brilliant victory of the mighty German army I . . . have done everything to earn the right to take part actively in liquidating the Jewish poison. . . .[1]

This seems an appropriate note on which to close our examination of Sergey Alexandrovich Nilus.

3

It is certain that Rachkovsky and Nilus were both involved in the intrigue against Philippe, it is even possible that they conspired to use the *Protocols* for their common purpose. This has led to the assumption, which is to be found in several works on the *Protocols*, that the forgery was carried out for the express purpose of influencing the Tsar against Philippe. Yet this theory is implausible. Philippe was a Martinist and a faith-healer – surely then, if the *Protocols* were forged to help Nilus in his struggle with Philippe, they should contain at least some suggestion that Martinism and/or faith-healing form part of the Jewish plot? As it is, they contain almost everything else, from banking and the press to international wars and underground railways. It is one thing to use a forgery which is already available – and Rachkovsky was certainly not fastidious in his choice of weapons. It is quite another thing to fabricate a whole book which is almost wholly irre-

[1] The letter is in the Freyenwald Collection at the Wiener Library.

levant to the task on hand. Could even Rachkovsky's tortuousness really have gone so far?

It is, then, worth looking at any evidence there may be for the existence of the *Protocols* before 1902. There is in fact a good deal of evidence, some of it from 'White' Russian refugees, but not necessarily worthless on that account. In the first place there is an affidavit sworn by Filip Petrovich Stepanov, formerly procurator of the ecclesiastical synod of Moscow, court chamberlain, and privy councillor, at Stary Futog, Yugoslavia, on 17 April 1927. It reads as follows:

> In 1895 my neighbour in the government of Tula, the retired major Alexey Sukhotin, gave me a manuscript copy of the *Protocols of the Elders of Zion*. He told me that a lady of his acquaintance, whom he did not name, when residing in Paris had found this copy at the home of a Jewish friend; and that before leaving Paris she had secretly translated the manuscript and had brought it with her to Russia, where she gave it to Sukhotin.
>
> First of all I reproduced this translation in hectograph jelly, but finding it difficult to read, I decided to have it printed without any mention of date, place or publisher. In all this I was assisted by Arkady Ippolitovich Kelepovsky, who was at that time head of the household of the Grand Duke Sergey. He had the document printed on the press of the district. This took place in 1897. Sergey Nilus inserted these *Protocols* in his work and added his own commentaries.[1]

Save for the passing reference to the lady's 'Jewish friend' this document seems quite useless as propaganda; so Stepanov was probably trying to tell the truth as he remembered it, admittedly after a lapse of thirty years. As it happens there is, or was, very solid evidence to confirm his statement. Although no copy of Stepanov's printed book is known, a copy of the hectograph was still extant at the time of the Berne trial in 1934. At that time it was to be found in the Pashukanis Collection in the Lenin Library, Moscow; and the Soviet authorities sent a photostat of four pages to the court at Berne. The title-page carries no date, but the late Boris Nicolaevsky was convinced, after careful inspection, that this was indeed

---

[1] A facsimile of the Russian affidavit is in L. Fry, *Waters Flowing Eastwards*, Paris, 1933, after p. 100; a French translation (with some errors) in L. Fry, *Le Juif notre maître*, Paris, 1931, pp. 95–6.

Stepanov's hectograph.[1] The hectograph was made from a
hand-written Russian document with the title *The Ancient
and Modern Protocols of the Meetings of the Elders of Zion*. Unfortunately it can no longer be inspected – two years of
assiduous inquiry extracted nothing from the Lenin Library
except a statement that no such manuscript can be traced –
but the Wiener Library possesses a German translation of the
extracts sent to Berne. This shows that the text must have
been practically identical with that later edited by Nilus,
which directly or indirectly provides the basis for almost all
later editions throughout the world.

Among the 'White' Russians there also existed a firm
tradition concerning the identity of the lady who brought the
handwritten Russian document from Paris and gave it to
Sukhotin. She was said to be Yuliana (or, in France, Justine)
Glinka.[2] A good deal is known about her too, and again all the
evidence fits. Yuliana Dmitrievna Glinka (1844–1918) was the
daughter of a Russian diplomat who ended his career as
ambassador in Lisbon. She herself became a lady-in-waiting
to the Empress Maria Alexandrovna and lived much of her
life in great style in St Petersburg, associating with the
spiritualists around Mme Blavatsky[3] and indeed squandering
her fortune in supporting them. But there was also another
and more sinister side to her life. In Paris in 1881–2 she tried
her hand at the game which Rachkovsky was to play so
brilliantly shortly afterwards – watching and denouncing the
Russian terrorists in exile. General Orzheyevsky, who was a
prominent figure in the secret police and ended as Assistant
Minister for Internal Affairs, had befriended her ever since her
childhood; and she sent her secret reports to him. But she was
not really gifted for the work, feuded constantly with the
Russian ambassador and ended by being unmasked in the left-
wing newspaper *Le Radical*.

Glinka continued to spend a good deal of her time in Paris
until, on a visit to St Petersburg somewhere around 1895, she

[1] Private communication to the author.
[2] Cf. L. Fry, *Waters Flowing Eastwards*, pp. 87–9.
[3] Yelena Petrovna Blavatsky (1831–91), Russian theosophist and
spiritualistic medium. At one time she herself tried – in vain – to find
employment in the Russian secret service.

found that she had lost the imperial favour. The Tsar had been deeply offended by a series of books which her great friend Juliette Adam had published in Paris and which contained all kinds of rumours and revelations about the Russian court. Rightly or wrongly he suspected Glinka of complicity and exiled her to her estate in the government of Orel, which bordered on the government of Tula. The natural protector for Glinka in her distress would have been the Marshal of Nobility for the district – and that was Alexey Sukhotin, the same person from whom Stepanov claimed to have received the *Protocols*.[1]

Glinka was exiled only temporarily and in later years she was once more comfortably established in St Petersburg. To judge by an article which the right-wing St Petersburg newspaper *Novoe Vremya* printed in its issue of 7 April 1902, she may have developed a proprietory attitude to the *Protocols*. The well-known journalist M. Menshikov reported how a lady of fashion had invited him to her house to see a document of vast importance. Seated in an elegant apartment (in Paris Glinka had been noted for her fine picture-collection) and speaking perfect French, the lady informed him that she was in direct contact with the world beyond the grave and proceeded to induct him into the mysteries of theosophy (Glinka was a disciple of Mme Blavatsky). Finally she initiated him into the mysteries of the *Protocols*. Of recent years, she explained, the original French manuscript had been kept at Nice, which had long been the secret capital of the Jews; but they had been stolen by a French journalist, who had passed them on to her. In great haste she had translated extracts from French into Russian. Menshikov took one glance at the

---

[1] There exists in the Freyenwald Collection at the Wiener Library a copy of a statement, dated 13 December 1936, by a female cousin of Alexey Sukhotin. It says that about 1895, when visiting her cousin on his estate, she saw the manuscript of the *Protocols* being copied out by Sukhotin's sister and by another young lady, who is named and who in 1936 was living in Paris. This statement would have little value by itself, but has some as corroboratory evidence. It could even be that they were retranslating the Russian text into French; for the text which du Chayla claims to have seen in Nilus's possession, written in bad French by various hands, was certainly not the original French version; there is no evidence that *that* ever left France.

Protocols and immediately recognized them as a forgery of a
very familiar type. And he adds that there were other copies
in St Petersburg, one of them in the possession of a journalist –
one guesses, Krushevan, since his *Znamya* published the
Protocols the following year.

There are, then, reasonable grounds for thinking that
Yuliana Glinka and Filip Stepanov really were involved in
the first publication of the *Protocols*. As for the date, internal
evidence suggests that in saying he received the *Protocols* in
1895 and published them in 1897 Stepanov was erring no more
than is to be expected after thirty years. There is for instance
the remark, at the end of 'protocol' 16, that as part of the plan
to stupefy the Gentiles one of the Elders' agents, Bourgeois, is
advocating a programme of teaching by object lessons. The
reference is to Léon Bourgeois, a highly suspect figure in the
eyes of the French right wing since, as Prime Minister in 1895–
6, he had included nine Freemasons in his cabinet. From 1890
to 1896 he frequently spoke in favour of a system of teaching
by object lessons, and in 1897 these speeches were published
in a book, *L'éducation de la démocratie française*; in 1898, as
Minister of Education, he issued decrees on the subject. A
similar reference which points in the same direction is the
passage in 'protocol' 10 where the Elders recommend the
election of presidents with some 'Panama' in their past. This
refers almost certainly to Emile Loubet, who was Prime
Minister of France when the Panama scandal reached its
climax in 1892. Though certainly not involved in the scandal
itself, Loubet showed no eagerness to institute inquiries against
those who were; and this made him a suspect figure. In 1895
Loubet was elected President of the Senate, which made him a
candidate for the presidency of the Republic, and in 1899 he
was elected President of the Republic. The passage in the
Protocols could have been inspired by either event.

As for the Paris underground, the *Métro*, plans for it were
announced in 1894, but it was only in 1897 that the municipal
council granted the concession, and it was in 1900 that the
first line was opened. In view of the threat in the *Protocols*
to blow up capital cities from the underground railways, it is
worth noting that in 1897 Drumont's *Libre Parole* was lament-
ing the number of Jewish shareholders in the *Métro*. Again, it

was in 1896 that the Russian Minister of Finance Sergey Witte first proposed the introduction of the gold-standard in Russia, in place of the gold-and-silver standard then in force; and in 1897 it was in fact introduced. This too figures in the *Protocols* – in 'protocol' 19 there is the observation that the gold standard has ruined every state that has adopted it. But, above all, there is the title of the forgery itself. One would normally expect the mysterious rulers to be called Elders of Jewry or Elders of Israel. There must be some reason why they bear the absurd name of Elders of Zion, and there is in fact a very plausible one. As we have seen, the first Zionist congress at Basel was interpreted by antisemites as a giant stride towards Jewish world-domination. Countless editions of the *Protocols* have connected that document with the congress; and it does seem likely that this event inspired if not the forgery itself, then at least its title. The year of the congress was 1897.

All in all it is practically certain that the *Protocols* were fabricated some time between 1894 and 1899 and highly probable that it was in 1897 or 1898. The country was undoubtedly France, as is shown by the many references to French affairs. One may assume that the place was Paris and one may even be rather more precise: one of the copies of Joly's book in the Bibliothèque Nationale bears markings which correspond strikingly with the borrowings in the *Protocols*. So the job was done in the midst of the Dreyfus affair – somewhere between the arrest of Alfred Dreyfus in 1894 and his pardon in 1899, and probably at the very height of the great debate which so bitterly divided France. And nevertheless the forgery is clearly the work of a Russian and oriented towards the Russian right wing. Can one, then, be certain that it was done at the behest of the head of Okhrana in Paris, the sinister Rachkovsky?

As we have seen, there are very substantial grounds for this view – and nevertheless the question is less simple than it seems. Rachkovsky's political master and patron was Sergey Witte, the all-powerful Minister of Finance, and Witte's enemies were also Rachkovsky's enemies. And there is no doubt that Witte's enemies had a hand in the *Protocols*. When Witte took office in 1892 he took up the task begun by Peter the Great and largely neglected by later rulers: the transformation of backward Russia into a country as modern as the countries of western Europe. During the following decade the production of coal and of iron and steel was more than doubled; the construction of railways, which at that time was the surest index of industrial development, proceeded at a rate attained in only one other country, the United States. But this rapid economic development brought grave disadvantages to those classes whose wealth was bound up with the traditional, agricultural order; and in these circles Witte was detested. Moreover in 1898 there came a serious slump which brought heavy losses even to those who had benefited most from the economic expansion. Witte was under heavy pressure to resort to inflation, even if this meant abandoning the newly adopted gold-standard. He resisted, and his unpopularity became still more widespread.

The *Protocols* have all the appearance of a weapon for use in the campaign against Witte. In the *Protocols* it is argued that slumps are used by the Elders as a means of getting control over all money and of fomenting unrest in the proletariat; and as we have seen, it is also argued that the gold-standard ruins the countries that adopt it. Moreover, if one compares the *Dialogue aux Enfers* with the *Protocols* one finds that the only economic and financial reflections which have been preserved from Joly's book are those which applied to developments in Russia under Witte. The intention seems obvious enough: it is to present Witte as a tool in the hands of the Elders of Zion.

The *Protocols* are not the only piece of propaganda directed simultaneously against the Jews and against Witte. There is an even more bizarre document called *Tayna Yevreystva (The Secret of Jewry)*,[1] which carries a date – February 1895 – and which looks like a first, ham-handed attempt at the *Protocols*. *Tayna Yevreystva* came to light when, on instructions from the Minister of the Interior, Stolypin, in the first year of this century, the police archives were combed for evidence as to the origin of the *Protocols*. It is a ridiculous essay about an imaginary secret religion which, after being held by the Essenes in the time of Jesus, is now supposed to be cherished by the unknown rulers of Jewry. But it is at one with the *Protocols* in warning us that the secret Jewish government is

[1] Text in Yu. Delevsky, *Protokoly Sionskikh Mudretsov*, Berlin, 1923, pp. 138–58. Cf. J. Gwyer, *Portraits of Mean Men*, London, 1938.

now striving to turn Russia from an agrarian, semi-feudal country into a modern state with a capitalistic economy and a liberal middle class. 'Already in the West the latest economic factor, capitalism, served Freemasonry as a weapon, which had now been skilfully appropriated by the Jews. Naturally it was decided to employ the same weapon in Russia, where the autocracy rests entirely on the support of the landed aristocracy, whereas the child of capitalism, the bourgeoisie, is benevolently disposed towards revolutionary liberalism.'[1] And like the *Protocols*, *Tayna Yevreystva* contains an attack on Witte's innovation, the gold-standard.

According to one 'White' Russian tradition, this extraordinary production was sent by Yuliana Glinka to her friend General Orzheyevsky, who passed it to the commander of the Imperial Guard, General Cherevin, who was supposed to pass it on to the Tsar but failed to do so. And there is little doubt that the *Protocols* too were intended to be read by the Tsar, and for a quite specific reason. Compared with his formidable father Alexander III, Nicholas II was a mild and kindly man who in the first years of his reign had been reluctant to persecute anyone – even the Jews – and who moreover had shown a certain willingness to let Russia be modernized, perhaps even slightly liberalized. The ultra-reactionaries were much concerned to cure the Tsar of these disconcerting traits, and the way they set about it was to persuade him that the Jews formed a deadly conspiracy intent on undermining the foundations of Russian society and Orthodox Christianity; and that the Jews' chosen instrument was the great modernizer, Witte.

Who, in the end, forged the *Protocols*? Boris Nicolaevsky and Henri Rollin have argued that much of the *Protocols* could have come from the eminent physiologist and political journalist known as Ilya Tsion in Russia and Elie de Cyon in France.[2] De Cyon certainly was a fanatical opponent of Witte, and many passages in his political writings do resemble those parts of the *Protocols* which are directed against Witte's policies. He even composed one of his attacks on Witte by the

---

[1] Delevsky, op. cit., p. 155.

[2] Nicolaevsky in a private communication to the author, Henri Rollin in *L'Apocalypse de notre temps*.

very same method employed in the *Protocols*, i.e. by taking an old French satire on a long-dead statesman and simply changing the names. Also, he was a Russian expatriate who lived in Paris and belonged to the circle around Juliette Adam – who in turn was a close friend of Yuliana Glinka. But there is an important qualification to be made: if de Cyon really is the forger, what he forged cannot have been the *Protocols* as we know them today.

It is inconceivable that a person of such seriousness and intellectual calibre as de Cyon should have sunk to writing a crude antisemitic fabrication. Moreover he was himself of Jewish origin, and though converted to Christianity he never turned against the Jews. In his book *La Russie contemporaine* (1892) he shows a lively sympathy with the persecuted Russian Jews, demands equal opportunities for them, bitterly attacks antisemitic propagandists and instigators of pogroms. If de Cyon did indeed have a hand in the concoction we know as the *Protocols*, then somebody must have appropriated his work and transformed it, replacing the Russian Minister of Finance by the Elders of Zion.

And so we come back to Rachkovsky. For in 1897 Rachkovsky and his men, on instructions from Witte, burgled de Cyon's villa at Territet, Switzerland, and removed quantities of papers. They were looking for writings directed against Witte, and it may well be that they found an adaptation of Joly's book. It remains rather puzzling that Witte's devoted servant Rachkovsky should have propagated a document which, even when transformed, is still largely directed against his master's policies. Perhaps his intention was that the book should be generally ascribed to de Cyon? Such a manoeuvre would serve two purposes: antisemites would be able to claim that the Jewish world-conspiracy had been unmasked by someone who was himself of Jewish birth; and de Cyon would be cruelly mortified and at the same time quite unable to defend himself. And when one recalls that in Russia de Cyon was called Tsion – the same word as Zion – the title of the *Protocols* takes on an added meaning as a malicious private joke. All this would be very much in Rachkovsky's style.

All in all, the most likely hypothesis is that Joly's satire on Napoleon III was transformed by de Cyon into a satire on

Witte which was then transformed under Rachkovsky's guidance into the *Protocols of the Elders of Zion*. But some mystery remains and it is unlikely ever to be cleared up now. The Okhrana archives at the Hoover Institution, Stanford University, reveal nothing; and Rachkovsky's private archives in Paris (now lost) also revealed nothing when Boris Nicolaevsky inspected them in the 1930s. De Cyon's papers, which were kept by his widow in Paris until the Second World War, have disappeared. There is also the riddle of *Tayna Yevreystva*, which can hardly be attributed either to de Cyon or to Rachkovsky. And there one must leave the matter – to be pursued perhaps some day by a specialist in the 1890s with time and energy to spare.

As for the early editors of the *Protocols*, comparison with the fragments of the hectograph in the Wiener Library show Nilus's version to be the nearest to the original, even though it was not the first to be published. Sergey Nilus is in fact the key figure in the launching of the forgery. How it came into his hands remains, like so much else, uncertain. He himself said, in the preface to the 1917 edition of his book, that Sukhotin gave him a copy in 1901; while a letter from Filip Stepanov's son, now in the Freyenwald Collection in the Wiener Library, says that this was a mistake for Stepanov. In any case it is true that in 1901 Nilus was living fairly near to the estates of Sukhotin, Stepanov, and Glinka. But as we have seen, there is also good reason for thinking that Rachkovsky had some contact either with Nilus or with Nilus's copy of the *Protocols*.

Again and again, in trying to unravel the early history of the *Protocols*, one comes up against ambiguities, uncertainties, riddles. There is no need to take them very seriously. It was necessary to glance at the strange vanished world in which, a mere seventy years ago, the *Protocols* were born – the world of counter-revolutionary agents and pseudo-mystics that flourished on the decay of the Tsar's empire.

But what is really important about the *Protocols* is the great influence which – incredibly yet incontestably – they have exercised on twentieth-century history.

CHAPTER V

The *Protocols* in Russia

1

WHATEVER the origin of the *Protocols,* they were adopted and preserved and in the end launched on the world by *pogromsh-chiki,* professional instigators of pogroms. For the hundreds of local massacres of Jews which occurred in Russia between 1881 and 1920 were by no means spontaneous outbreaks of popular fury – they demanded long-term planning, careful organiza-tion, above all intensive agitation. Sometimes this work was carried out by the police, but sometimes private individuals – above all, unscrupulous journalists – took a hand. These were the people who made the *Protocols* their own.

The first person to publish the *Protocols,* Pavolachi Krus-hevan, was a typical *pogromshchik.* Just four months before he printed the *Protocols* in his St Petersburg newspaper *Znamya,* his other newspaper *Bessarabets* succeeded in provoking a pogrom in his native province of Bessarabia – in fact in the provincial capital, Kishinev, where it was published. How this was achieved was established by Irish and American travellers who visited the town just after the massacre.[1] They found a fertile and prosperous country where traditionally relations between the mass of the population and the large Jewish minority had been very good – so good in fact that in 1881–3, when the whole of south Russia was swept with pogroms, the Bessarabian peasants refused to take part: 'If the Tsar wills that the Jews be slain,' they said, 'he has his army. But we

---

[1] See I. Singer, *Russia at the Bar of the American People: A Memorial of Kishinev,* New York and London, 1904, and the report of the cele-brated Irish nationalist Michael Davitt, who visited Kishinev just after the massacre: *Within the Pale: The true story of antisemitic persecutions in Russia,* London, 1903.

will not strike the Jews.' The situation changed only in 1898, when Krushevan launched his local newspaper and began to publish fanatical attacks on the Jews. A group of journalists, civil servants, and other professional men was formed and, guided by Krushevan from St Petersburg, deliberately began to prepare the way for massacre. In 1902, at Easter – always the favourite time for pogroms – Krushevan announced that a Christian youth, found dead in a well, was the victim of a Jewish ritual murder. That time he was unsuccessful, as the real murderer was quickly identified; but the following year the murder of a boy at Dubossary enabled him to renew the charge, this time with success. He also put it about that an imperial ukase had been issued permitting Christians 'to execute bloody justice on the Jews during the three days of Easter'.

But this was not all. In preparing for the massacre Krushevan's men also made use of the more modern fantasy of the Jewish world-conspiracy. They distributed copies of *The Rabbi's Speech*, and they also elaborated on it. The delusions they fostered emerge clearly from the utterances of Krushevan's leading representative in Kishinev, an agitator called Pronin. At the farcical trial which was held – largely under pressure from abroad – some months after the massacre, this man stated in evidence that a meeting of Jews from all countries had taken place in the Kishinev synagogue just before Easter. The meeting decided to organize a revolt against the Government; whereupon the Jews attacked the Christian population, which merely defended itself. Pronin also published in *Znamya* an article in which he praised the rioters as true patriots who were concerned only to defend the Tsar and Holy Russia against a fearsome international conspiracy. All this when at Kishinev no single Christian had been injured but forty-five Jews had been killed and hundreds injured – almost all of them artisans, miserably poor and completely helpless – and some 10,000 reduced to destitution. Such was the milieu in which the *Protocols* began their public career.

Meanwhile the struggle to modernize and liberalize the Russian political régime was reaching a new intensity. Particularly in 1904–5, against the background of the disastrous war with Japan, there was overwhelming pressure for fundamental reforms, and notably for the establishment of a national representative assembly, freedom of speech, and guarantees of individual liberty. A nation-wide general strike in September 1905 forced the Government to yield, and in October the Tsar reluctantly issued a manifesto promising a constitution based on the principles of modern liberalism. But these developments did not, needless to say, go unopposed. The Tsar himself was surrounded by reactionary influences – notably his mother, some of the grand-dukes, the Procurator of the Holy Synod Pobedonostsev, the Governor-General of St Petersburg Trepov, not to mention the organization known as the Union of the Russian People, or more popularly as the Black Hundreds.[1]

One of the freedoms granted by the Tsar's October manifesto was the freedom of association – and none were quicker to avail themselves of it than the extreme right-wing. On 4 November 1905 the Union of the Russian People was founded in St Petersburg by a doctor, A. Dubrovin, and a politician, V. M. Purishkevich, who was the driving force behind the organization. Like those other members of the Black Hundreds, Krushevan and Butmi, Purishkevich came from Bessarabia – in fact he had graduated at Kishinev – and his political aim was precisely the same as theirs: to fight the liberalization of Russia by presenting it as a Jewish plot, and to get Jews massacred to show how real the plot was. Proclamations began to appear in towns and villages, of which the following is a fair sample:

The efforts to replace the autocracy of the divinely appointed Tsar by a constitution and a parliament are inspired by those bloodsuckers, the Jews, the Armenians and the Poles. Beware of the Jews! All the evil, all the misfortune of our country comes from the Jews. Down with the traitors, down with the constitution![2]

[1] On the Union of the Russian People see W. Laqueur, *Russia and Germany*, notably pp. 79–86. Strictly speaking the Black Hundreds were armed bands recruited for purposes of terror by the Union of the Russian People and similar political organizations; they consisted largely of small shop-keepers, vagabonds and professional criminals. But in popular speech the members of these political organizations themselves were often referred to as 'Black Hundredists'.

[2] Quoted in B. Segel, *Die Protokolle der Weisen von Zion*, Berlin, 1924, p. 214.

And when the national assembly – the Duma of the Empire – came into being, the propaganda of the Black Hundreds concentrated on discrediting it as an instrument in the hands of the Jews. The elections to the first Duma in 1906 and to the second and third Dumas in 1907 were accompanied by a spate of pamphlets stating that most of the candidates were Jews, that the liberal parties were financed by the Jews, that the Jews were enslaving Russia through the Duma. Among the electioneering pamphlets published by the Black Hundreds Butmi's version of the *Protocols, The Enemies of the Human Race* – four editions in 1906–7 – finds its rightful place.[1]

Even in the lamentable context of Russian political life, the Black Hundreds were widely regarded as being beyond the pale. Witte for one had no doubts:

This party is patriotic to the depths of its soul . . . but its patriotism is primitive, it is based not on reason and generosity but on passion. Most of its leaders are political upstarts, people with unclean ways of thinking and feeling; they have not a single viable political idea and concentrate all their efforts on unleashing the lowest possible impulses in the benighted, savage masses. Sheltered by the wings of the two-headed eagle this party can instigate the most frightful pogroms and convulsions, but it is incapable of anything positive. It embodies a wild, nihilistic patriotism which thrives on lies, slander and deceit, it is a party of wild and cowardly despair but has no room for courageous, far-sighted, creative thinking. The bulk of the membership comes from the wild, ignorant masses, its leaders are political villains, it has secret sympathizers in court circles and amongst nobles with all kinds of titles – people who seek their salvation in lawlessness and have as their slogan: 'Not we for the people, but the people for the good of our stomachs'. . . . And the Tsar dreams of restoring greatness to Russia with the help of this party. Poor Tsar . . .[2]

These people were in fact true precursors of the Nazis. Words such as 'proto-Fascist' have been so monstrously misused that one hesitates to use them at all – yet there is no denying that the Black Hundreds mark an important stage in

[1] An account of these Black Hundred publications is given in the article on Antisemitism in the *Yevreyskaya Entsiklopediya*, Vol. II, pp. 746–52.

[2] Translated from the German version of Witte's memoirs: *Erinnerungen*, Berlin, 1923, pp. 144 seq.

the transition from reactionary politics as they were understood in the nineteenth century to the right-wing totalitarianism of the Nazis. In their allegiance to throne and altar they
belonged to the past – but as political adventurers dedicated to
sabotaging, by means of antisemitic agitation and terrorism,
the development of liberal democracy, and as romantic reactionaries who could also talk the language of radical demagogy,
they certainly did look forward to Hitler and his associates.
Like the Nazis, they pretended that Jews formed a capitalist-
revolutionary conspiracy, and that in order to prevent this
conspiratorial body from establishing a monstrous tyranny
the workers and peasants must stand firmly by the 'native'
ruling class. And they forestalled the Nazis, too, in their ideas
as to what should be done to the Jews. If some wanted to deport them to the Kolyma region in the Arctic or beyond the
Altai mountains in southern Siberia, others looked forward to
their physical annihilation. One leading member, 'Markov II',
who in the 1930s was to be employed by the Nazis as an expert
on the *Protocols* and the Judeo-Masonic conspiracy, was already prophesying in 1911, in a speech in the Duma, that 'all
the Yids, down to very last, will be killed'.[1]

It was well known that the Black Hundreds employed
criminals to carry out assassinations and to lead pogroms, and
Black Hundred politicians were not received in decent society
– but that did not prevent the organization from receiving
abundant support from church and state. A bishop was among
its leaders, monasteries published leaflets in support of it, its
emblems and banners were displayed in churches, priests
urged their congregations to pray for its success and to parti-
cipate in its activities. The Government for its part gave
every kind of assistance. It is estimated that in the single year
the Union of the Russian People received 2,500,000 roubles[2]
in government subsidies. It was granted the right to apply for
a free pardon for any member arrested for participating in
pogroms. Above all, it enjoyed the full approval of the Tsar,
who praised it as a shining example of justice and order and
was pleased to wear its badge on his uniform. During the

---

[1] Quoted in A. B. Tager, *The Decay of Czarism: the Beiliss trial*,
Philadelphia, 1935, p. 44.
[2] At that time the rouble was worth about two shillings.

Beiliss ritual murder trial he even sent a telegram thanking the leaders for their attempt to obtain a conviction.

Then there is the story of the Lamsdorf Memorandum to show how even foreign policy could be affected by the outlook of the Black Hundreds. Faced with the advance of liberalism in Russia the Minister for Foreign Affairs, Count Lamsdorf, prepared in 1906 a secret memorandum in which he recommended that Russia, Germany, and the Vatican should take common action against the Alliance Israélite Universelle and its supposed instrument, France. The campaign to extend the franchise and liberalize the régime, he explained, was simply a trick to modernize Russia which, as 'a state of peasants, Orthodox and monarchist', still stood in the way of world-domination by the Judeo-Masons controlled from Paris. It is true that the Lamsdorf Memorandum was quickly buried by Lamsdorf's successor, Isvolsky (it was published only in 1918, by the Bolsheviks), but it is worth noting what the Tsar wrote in the margin: 'Negotiations must be started *at once*. I entirely share the opinions expressed here'.[1]

In this atmosphere the *Protocols* enjoyed their first vogue. How seriously they were taken in some quarters, and how blindly they were believed, is shown by an unpublished letter which a former conservative Russian journalist, I. Kolyshko, otherwise known as 'Bayan', wrote to Burtsev at the time of the Berne trial, when both of them were refugees in France:

7 September 1934

Much esteemed Vladimir Lvovich,

You ask whether, as a former journalist . . ., I know anything about the so-called *Protocols of the Elders of Zion*. . . .

To help you evaluate my recollections, I think it necessary to tell you that at that time my sympathies drew me to right-wing circles in Russia . . . to people who tended to be antisemitic . . . as a result I paid most attention to what came to me from the antisemitic camp. I cannot deny that when they first appeared these *Protocols* made a really overwhelming impression in these circles,

[1] The Lamsdorf Memorandum was published by the Soviet Commissariat of Foreign Affairs in 1918. A French translation appeared in the *Mercure de France*, issue of 1 October 1918, pp. 547–51, and an English translation in L. Wolf, *Diplomatic History of the Jewish Question*, London, 1919, pp. 54–62.

and on me personally. As you know, one believes what one wants to believe. The people amongst whom I moved began by believing *absolutely* in the authenticity of this document. Then gradually the efforts of the Left began to undermine this belief, we began to have doubts and the construction . . . began to crumble, under the corroding effect of criticism (and of the facts); slowly at first, then more and more quickly. So far as I can recall . . . it finally collapsed at the beginning of the war. During the Great War I heard no mention of the *Protocols* in Russia, until after 1917. . . .

Inside Russia the controversy came to an end. I was not interested in how or when it spilled over into the west – into France, England and Germany. Because I regarded this matter as settled *once and for all.* . . . There seemed no possibility that the *Protocols* would ever again revive and upset mankind. . . .

With the greatest esteem and devotion,
I. Kolyshko (Bayan)[1]

The success of the *Protocols* before the war was in fact limited. Zhevakhov tells how in 1913 Nilus complained to him: 'I cannot get the public to treat the *Protocols* seriously, with the attention they deserve. They are read, criticized, often ridiculed, but there are very few who attach importance to them and see in them a real threat to Christianity, a pro- gramme for the destruction of the Christian order and for the conquest of the whole world by the Jews. That nobody be- lieves . . .'[2] Years later 'Markov II', in a letter preserved in the Wiener Library, lamented that the Union of the Russian People, by its half-hearted use of the *Protocols*, had failed to avert the Russian Revolution.

One has to bear in mind that in these matters everything depended on the attitude of the Tsar himself – and in the end the Tsar, however besotted by the Judeo-Masonic conspiracy, had to recognize the *Protocols* as spurious. How this came about is described in a statement from General K. I. Globa- chev, one-time commandant of the St Petersburg division of the Okhrana, which Burtsev produced at the Berne trial. Globachev describes how, after many unsuccessful attempts, the *Protocols* were at last brought to the Tsar's notice in the revolutionary year 1905. 'Reading the *Protocols*,' he continues,

---

[1] A copy of Kolyshko's letter is in the B. I. Nicolaevsky Collection at the Hoover Institution, Stanford University, California.

[2] N. D. Zhevakhov, *Sergey Alexandrovich Nilus*, Novi Sad, 1936, p. 35.

'made a very deep impression on Nicholas II, who made them his handbook for politics.' Typical in this respect are the marginal annotations which Nicholas II made on the copy of the *Protocols* which had been submitted to him: 'What depth of thought!' – 'What foresight!' – 'What precision in the realization of the programme!' – 'Our year 1905 has gone as though managed by the Elders.' – 'There can be no doubt as to their authenticity.' – 'Everywhere one sees the directing and destroying hand of Judaism.' And so on. Keenly interested in the 'discovery' of the *Protocols*, Nicholas II gave his attention to the foreign branch of the Russian secret police and handed out a great number of rewards, decorations, and gratuities. . . . The leaders of the Union of the Russian People, like Shmakov, Markov II, etc., addressed a request to the Ministry of the Interior, asking for authorization to use the *Protocols* on a large scale in the struggle against militant Judaism, and for subsidies for the purpose. But the Minister of the Interior, Stolypin . . . entrusted two officers of the corps of gendarmes,[1] Martynov and Vassilyev, with a secret inquiry into the origin of the *Protocols*. This inquiry revealed clearly the spuriousness of the *Protocols*. The results of the inquiry were presented by Stolypin to Nicholas II, who was completely bowled over. And this is the resolution of Nicholas II on the report concerning the employment of the *Protocols* for anti-semitic propaganda: 'Drop the *Protocols*. One cannot defend a pure cause by dirty methods'[2].

This situation changed in 1917–18, when first the Tsar and then the Provisional Government were overthrown, the Bolsheviks seized power and the civil war began. Indeed, what launched the *Protocols* on their career across the world was above all the murder of the imperial family at Yekaterinburg (now Sverdlovsk) on 17 July 1918. Here chance played an extraordinary part. Some months before her murder at Yekaterinburg the deposed Empress had received from a friend, Zinaïda Sergeyevna Tolstaya, a copy of Nilus's book containing the *Protocols*. It seems to have meant little to her, to judge

---

[1] The corps of gendarmes was a semi-military police force which, while concerned with political matters, was independent of the Okhrana.

[2] Burtsev later published this document in his book *Protokoly Sionskikh Mudretsov*, Paris, 1938, pp. 105–6.

by a letter which she sent to her great friend Anna Vyrubova on 20 March 1918: 'Zina has sent me a book: *The Great in the Small*, by Nilus, I am reading it with interest.'[1] This terse comment hardly suggests enthusiasm; and the Tsaritsa, though a stupid, superstitious, and hysterical woman, was in fact far less of an antisemite than her husband. In her correspondence one even finds her remonstrating with the Tsar over his anti-semitic policy. There is therefore much irony in the fact that the Tsaritsa's death should, more than any other event, have brought world fame to an old and half-forgotten antisemitic forgery.

As luck would have it, the Empress took Nilus's book with her to her last home, the house of Ipatyev at Yekaterinburg. A week after the murder of the imperial family Yekaterinburg was evacuated by the Bolsheviks and occupied by the 'Whites'; on 28 July the remains of the Tsar, the Tsaritsa, and their children, dismembered and incinerated, were discovered at the bottom of a disused mine-shaft in a nearby forest. Meanwhile the examining magistrate Nametkin was engaged in drawing up an inventory of the belongings found at Ipatyev's house. He found three books belonging to the Empress: the first volume of *War and Peace*, the Bible in Russian, and *The Great in the Small* by Nilus.

Another curious circumstance came to light: the Tsaritsa had drawn a swastika in the embrasure of a window in the room occupied by her and her husband. It is known that she had long had a special partiality for this ancient symbol[2] – she wore a jewelled swastika and had swastikas engraved on the gifts which she sent to her friends. It is also known that for this profoundly superstitious woman the swastika was a talisman intended to bring good luck. But already then there were people for whom it meant something quite different. Well before the war the Austrian writer Guido von List had taught, in a whole series of popular books on 'the Germano-

[1] Anna Vyrubova, *Souvenirs de ma vie*, Paris, 1927, p. 269.
[2] The swastika is found in remains from the bronze age in various parts of Europe, and was also known in ancient Persia, India, China, Japan, and among the Indian tribes of north, central, and south America. Its commonest significance is as a symbol of good luck or benediction.

Aryans', that the swastika symbolized the purity of Germanic blood and the struggle of the 'Aryans' against the Jews. These ideas had penetrated to Russia; and to Russians who were familiar with them the discovery of the Empress's swastika together with the copy of Nilus came as a revelation from on high. This, they believed, was a testament from their dead Empress; and what it said was that the reign of Antichrist was beginning, that the Bolshevik revolution was the supreme assault of the Satanic powers, that the imperial family had been destroyed because they represented the divine will on earth – and that the forces of darkness were incarnated in the Jews.

It was all the easier to arrive at such a conclusion because some Jews really were playing a conspicuous part in the revolution. Among the officers in the 'White' armies, some failed to reflect that this might be connected with the oppression to which Jews had been subjected under the tsarist régime; or that earlier tsars had been assassinated also, and by pure-blooded Russians. This is not surprising, for these men had grown up in a society where 'the Jew' had been regarded as the source of all evil. They had been taught that the whole Russian people loved the Tsar and his autocracy, and they had every reason for concealing from themselves that this had long ceased to be true. They needed a simple explanation for the catastrophe which was overwhelming them and their world. They found it in the union of the swastika and the *Protocols* in Ipatyev's house. And soon the *pogromshchiki* were at hand to exploit the great discovery.

2

When the Tsar and his family were murdered the civil war was still in its early stages. It continued for another two years, during which the Soviet Government was repeatedly on the brink of defeat, before the 'White' armies were finally routed in 1920. It was during those two years that the *Protocols* first showed their power to incite men to murder.

The people behind the *Protocols* were still the same. As a unified organization the Union of the Russian People had hardly existed since about 1910, but now the former leaders attached themselves to the various 'White' armies, founded new political groups with names like the Union of the Russian National Communities or the Russian Assembly, and above all carried on a vigorous agitation in favour of pogroms. The Frenchman du Chayla, who was with the 'White' armies at that time, has described the zeal of these men in disseminating the *Protocols*. A Moscow lawyer, Ismailov, and a lieutenant-colonel, Rodionov, combined forces to produce a new, cheap edition for the armies in the Don region; and this was distributed to the troops by Purishkevich, a founder of the Black Hundreds, who had got himself a job in General Denikin's propaganda department at Rostov. In the Crimea too, under the régime of General Wrangel, professors and journalists 'shouted at every street-corner about the menace of the *Protocols* and the Judeo-Masonic world-conspiracy'.[1]

To this one may add that further editions of the *Protocols* were published in Siberia. One was printed at Omsk, for the army of Admiral Kolchak. The Admiral himself was obsessed by the *Protocols*; G. K. Gins, who saw much of him at that time, has recorded that he 'literally devoured the *Protocols*. His head was crammed with anti-Masonic ideas. He was ready to see Freemasons everywhere, even in his own entourage . . . and amongst the members of the military missions of the Allies'.[2] Other editions of the *Protocols* appeared in the easternmost parts of Siberia, such as Vladivostok and Khabarovsk. An edition was even published by 'White' Russians in Japan.

The interpretation that was now put upon the *Protocols* emerges clearly from the preface which was attached to the first of the new editions, that produced by the Moscow lawyer Ismailov and the Cossack officer Rodionov at Novocherkask under the title *Zionist Protocols, Plan for World Conquest by the Judeo-Masons*:

> The *Protocols* are a programme, carefully worked out in every detail, for the conquest of the world by the Jews. The greater part of this programme has already been realized, and if we do not take thought, we are irretrievably doomed to destruction. . . . These *Protocols* are in fact not only the key to our first, unsuccessful

[1] A. du Chayla, in *La Tribune Juive*, Paris, 14 May 1921, pp. 6–7.
[2] G. K. Gins, *Sibir, Soyuzniki i Kolchak*, Peking, 1921, Vol. II, p. 39.

revolution (1905), but also to our second revolution (1917), in which the Jews have played such a disastrous role for Russia. . . . For us who are witnesses of this self-laceration, for us who hope to see Russia's rebirth, this document is all the more significant because it reveals the means employed by the enemies of Christianity to subjugate us. Only if we reach an understanding of these means, shall we be able to fight successfully the enemies of Christ and of Christian civilisation.[1]

The *Protocols* were of course far too complicated and sophisticated to be understood by the common soldiers – most of whom were in any case illiterate. At the Berne trial of 1934 Chaim Weizmann recalled the first time he saw the *Protocols*. British officers attached to the 'White' armies brought to Palestine a document of four or five typewritten pages, and explained that just such a document was to be found in the possession of every 'White' officer and N.C.O. On inspection it turned out to consist of extracts from the *Protocols*. From other sources it appears that material of this kind was distributed on a vast scale to literate members of the various 'White' and Ukrainian armies, who used to read and explain it to the illiterate.

New forgeries were also produced to supplement the *Protocols* and bring them up to date. The most celebrated of these was a document said to have been found on a Jewish Bolshevik commander in the Red Army, of the name of Zunder. Copies of this document seem to have been circulated as early as May 1918; and in the winter of 1919–20, when the tide of battle was turning and the 'White' armies, hitherto victorious, were losing battle after battle, it began to figure in newspapers run by the 'White' armies – sometimes in new and considerably expanded versions. It reads as follows:

Secret. To the representatives of all the branches of the Israelite International League.

Sons of Israel! The hour of our ultimate victory is near! We stand on the threshold to the command of the world. That which we could only dream of before is about to be realized. Only quite recently feeble and powerless, we can now, thanks to the world's catastrophe, raise our heads with pride.

We must, however, be careful! It can surely be prophesied that,

[1] *Sionskiye Protokoly* (ed. A. Rodionov), Novocherkask, 1918.

after we have marched over ruined and broken altars and thrones, we shall advance further on the same indicated path.

The authority of the to us alien religions and doctrines of faith we have, through very successful propaganda, subjected to a merciless criticism and mockery. We have brought the culture, civilization, traditions and thrones of the Christian nations to stagger, wherein, among these nations, we found more men than was necessary for our work. We have done everything to bring the Russian people under the yoke of the Jewish power, and ultimately compelled them to fall on their knees before us.

We have nearly completed all this, but we must all the same be very cautious, because the oppressed Russia is our arch-enemy. The victory over Russia, gained through our intellectual superiority, may in future, in a new generation, turn against us.

Russia is conquered and brought to the ground. Russia is in the agony of death under our heel, but do not forget – not even for a moment – that we must be careful. The holy care for our safety does not allow us to show either pity or mercy. At last we have been allowed to behold the bitter need of the Russian people, and to see it in tears! By taking from them their property, their gold, we have reduced this people to helpless slaves.

Be cautious and silent. We ought to have no mercy for our enemy. We must make an end of the best and leading elements of the Russian people, so that the vanquished Russia may not find any leader! Thereby every possibility will vanish for them to resist our power. We must excite hatred and disputes between workers and peasants. War and class struggle will destroy all treasure and culture created by the Christian people. But be cautious, Sons of Israel! Our victory is near, because our political and economic power and influence upon the masses are in rapid progress. We buy up Government loans and gold and thereby we have controlling power of the world's exchanges. The power is in our hands, but be careful – place no faith in traitorous shady powers.

Bronstein (Trotsky), Apfelbaum (Zinovyev), Rosenfeld (Kamenev), Steinberg – all of them are like unto thousands of other true sons of Israel. Our power in Russia is unlimited. In the towns the commissariats and committees of food, house committees, etc., are dominated by our people. But do not let victory intoxicate you. Be careful, cautious, because no one except yourselves will protect us.

Remember, we cannot rely on the Red Army, which one day may turn its warfare on ourselves.

Sons of Israel! The hour for our long-cherished victory over

Russia is near; close your ranks! Make known our people's national policy! Fight for our eternal ideals! Keep holy the old laws, which history has bequeathed to us! May our intellect, our genius, protect and lead us!

Signed, The Central Committee of the Israelite International League.[1]

For all its absurdity, the Zunder document was a portent; for the idea underlying it – that the Bolshevik revolution was the result of a Jewish plot and fulfilled the age-old strivings of the Jewish people – was to leave its mark on history. Already at that time the idea had become an obsession with many of the 'White' Russians, later it was to become an article of faith with the Nazis, within a generation it was to influence the policy of the German Government at home and abroad. It is worth considering what basis, if any, it had in historical fact.

Until the last few generations, to be a Jew meant one thing only: to be an adherent of the Jewish religion. For Jews in this sense of the word the Bolshevik revolution meant not fulfilment but renewed peril. In the event religious Jews have been at least as much persecuted in the Soviet Union as have religious Christians. At the very time when the Zunder document was circulating in the 'White' armies, the Soviet Government was converting synagogues into workers' clubs, dissolving Jewish religious, cultural, and philanthropic institutions, and banning all Hebrew books, irrespective of their contents. Bolsheviks of Jewish descent felt not the slightest solidarity with religious Jews – on the contrary. When a deputation of Jews called on Trotsky and asked him to do nothing which could provoke the 'White' soldiery to pogroms, he answered: 'Go home to your Jews and tell them I'm not a Jew and don't care about the Jews or what happens to them'.[2] Here is a gulf, and an unbridgeable one, which antisemitic propagandists have done their best to conceal.

There was another reason why the great mass of Russian Jews could not conceivably support the Bolsheviks: they were mostly small shop-keepers and self-employed artisans. As

---

[1] Reprinted in *Four Protocols of Zion* (*not the Protocols of Nilus*), London, 1921.

[2] H. Valentin, *Antisemitenspiegel*, Vienna, 1937, pp. 179–80.

such, though mostly miserably poor, they were from the
Leninist point of view class-enemies. Although these people
were inevitably opposed to the tsarist régime which persecuted
them, they were anything but Communist. During the short
period when the free expression of political opinion was
possible, they emerged mainly as supporters of the bourgeois
reformist Constitutional Democrats. Under the Soviet régime
they suffered even more than other Russians – in the 1920s
more than a third of the Jewish population was without civil
rights, as compared with 5–6 per cent of the non-Jewish
population.

It remains true that Jews, in the sense of persons of Jewish
descent, provided a disproportionate part of the leadership
(though not of the total membership) of the two Marxist
parties, the Bolsheviks and the Mensheviks. The reason is not
far to seek. These were people who had broken with the traditional Jewish community and abandoned the Jewish religion
but who nevertheless suffered discrimination and persecution
under the tsarist autocracy; and this was sufficient to lead
them towards the parties of the Left. Moreover they were
mostly former university students – and owing to the *numerus
clausus* a Jew had to be of quite outstanding ability to get to a
university at all. Once they had joined a political party such
people were well qualified to rise to positions of leadership.
It is a situation which has been repeated in other countries
where Jewish intellectuals have had to cope with antisemitism
without the support and consolation of religious faith.

Such Jews are usually idealists inspired by a vision of a
society from which all forms of discrimination are banished.
In general they make poor politicians and they tend to be
ousted soon after a successful revolution. In Russia Jews were
in fact far more numerous in the Menshevik than in the
Bolshevik leadership; and these Menshevik leaders were all
exiled or imprisoned or executed by the Bolsheviks. As for
the Jews among the Bolshevik leaders, they too were almost all
shot in the 1930s.

Such are the facts. But fantasy does not wait upon facts,
and the myth of the Judeo-Communist conspiracy was to
prove even more potent than the myth of the Judeo-Masonic
conspiracy. The Russian civil war provided a first indication

of its power. Some of the army commanders, such as General Denikin, might themselves be revolted by the propaganda which was being carried on among their troops, but this made no difference. The Black Hundred organizations had formulated their war aim very clearly, and they effectively imposed it on the troops: 'Kill the Jews, Save Russia.'

The enormous massacres of Jews carried out by the Nazis have overshadowed everything that went before, so that few people now are much aware of the prelude which was acted out in Russia between 1918 and 1920. The number of victims was nevertheless very considerable – over 100,000 killed and an unknown number of wounded and maimed. Many of the accounts given by witnesses of these pogroms are too horrible to bear re-telling. The following extracts from a report by the Russian journalist Ivan Derevensky on the pogrom carried out by a Cossack regiment at Fastov, near Kiev, in September 1919, will suffice to give some idea of what a pogrom was like and how it was set in motion. This is what happened after an unsuccessful attempt by the Bolsheviks to capture the town:

In the first three days robbery and murder were perpetrated mainly at night. During the nights the whole population could hear shooting and desperate cries now from one direction, now from another. At first murders were not so frequent, but they became more and more so. By about the third day Cossacks were already walking about the town, quite openly looking for Jewish houses and when they found one, doing whatever they liked. They were also stopping Jews in the streets. Sometimes they would simply ask, 'A Yid?' and put a bullet through his skull. More often they would search the man, strip him naked, and then shoot him. Many of the killers were drunk. . . .

About the second or third day they began to set fire to Jewish homes. The reason for this was that the *pogromshchiki* wanted to destroy the traces of their worst crimes. In one house on the corner of the Torgovy Square, for instance, were fifteen corpses, including many young girls who had been killed after being raped. They set that house alight to cover up those crimes. . . .

I shall describe the excesses committed, dividing them into their different kinds.

Murders. When I was in Fastov it was not yet possible to establish the number of victims with any certainty. According to the Red Cross, 550 bodies had been buried in the Jewish cemetery.

But the total number of dead was thought to be much higher. The general view amongst both Christians and Jews was that between 1,500 and 2,000 Jews had been killed in Fastov. . . . By the time I arrived all bodies had been removed from the streets and buried, but they were still finding bodies in woods and ditches and in some of the houses. Apart from that it is agreed that many bodies were burnt when the houses were set on fire. People are still searching for the remains. Near some of the burnt-out houses there is a strong smell of dead bodies. Unidentifiable bones are often found in the ashes. Many of the victims cannot be traced by their relatives at all and are presumed dead. Behind the house of prayer many corpses were eaten by pigs and dogs. . . .

Woundings. The number of wounded is put at 300–400. Some of these wounded die every day. Owing to shortage of personnel medical aid is very inadequate. The wounded are in the class-rooms of the local school. They lie there without bandages, and in such a state of overcrowding that one can hardly walk between them.

Atrocities. I was told of one case of a man being thrown into the fire alive. A man called Kiksman had his tongue cut out and died after being shot with a dumdum bullet. Everyone talks of how dumdum bullets were used, including the medical personnel from the hospital. A man called Markman had both ears cut off, another member of the same family got twelve slashes with a sabre, another got eight. The corpse of a small girl, M. Polskaya, showed that she had suffered burning while alive. One of the lists of the buried (available from the police clerk) contains the names of two six-month-old babies, Avrum Slobodsky and Ruvin Konik. A man was killed by being cut in two. In front of the synagogue about twenty Jews were stripped naked and then shot. The same happened to four Jews in Voksal Street. . . .

Very often people were got ready for hanging, in order to make them give up their money. . . . But many were hanged until they were dead – for instance Moshko Remenik (on a tree in his garden) and a father and his school-boy son, Meyer and Boris Zabarsky. These two were experimentally half-hanged first, and the boy was forced to tighten the noose around his father's neck. . . .

Rape. Understandably, the names of victims of rape who survived are not available. There were very few of these – I heard only of two young girls, who were in some hospital. But according to witnesses rapes were very numerous; the victims were usually killed afterwards. I was told of rapes committed on very young girls. . . .

Arson. Altogether about 200 buildings were burnt down, half of them dwellings. . . . About a thousand families have been rendered homeless and are sheltering in the synagogue, the school or simply on the street.

To the question, 'Who perpetrated this pogrom?' it is possible to give a quite definite answer: the Cossacks of the 2nd Brigade from Tersk. It is commanded by Colonel Belogortsev. . . .

I must point out that the victims of the pogrom are convinced that the pogrom was 'permitted' by brigade headquarters. They drew this conclusion from the fact that the officers were at best indifferent and often came out in support of the pogrom, and that individual Cossacks said such things as 'We were ordered to beat the Yids,' and 'We had leave to *have a party* for three days,' and 'Nobody is going to punish us for this,' and so on. But I must add that some officers of that same brigade tried to stop the pogrom, to defend certain houses and in general to help the Jews in their plight. Lieutenant Ilyushkin, who was in command of the artillery, persuaded his Cossacks to defend a whole block of buildings. . . .

Now as for the causes of the pogrom: although this was just what interested me most, I could find no real reason for the pogrom at all. One thing only is certain – that there was amongst the Cossacks a general belief – though an entirely vague and baseless one – that Jews sympathized with Bolshevism. Lieutenant Ilyushkin told me that, 'obviously for purposes of provocation', somebody spread a rumour amongst the Cossacks to the effect that Jews welcomed the Bolsheviks with joy when for a short time they occupied Fastov . . . and that they fired at the Volunteer forces[1] as these withdrew from Fastov. This rumour was not confirmed by any of my many informants. On the contrary, everybody – including people who were very hostile to the Jews – denied absolutely that such things could possibly have happened. At the time when the Bolsheviks penetrated into Fastov the Jews – like the rest of the inhabitants – hid in the cellars. . . .[2]

While these things were happening in Russia the *Protocols* and the myth of the Judeo-Bolshevik conspiracy were penetrating westwards and establishing themselves above all in Germany.

[1] i.e. 'White' forces.

[2] Derevensky was sent to Fastov by an organization founded in Kiev in 1919 for collecting data about the pogroms in the Ukraine, later called the Central Archives of Pogrom-materials and located in Berlin. Derevensky arrived in Fastov on 17 September 1919; the pogrom had taken place on 10–13 September. His report is printed in I. B. Shekhtman, *Pogromy dobrovolcheskoy armii na Ukraine*, Berlin, 1932.

CHAPTER VI

The *Protocols* reach Germany

1

IN the course of the Russian civil war the *pogromshchiki* and
the 'White' officers whom they influenced built up a whole
corpus of antisemitic legends and forgeries. For instance, in
September 1919 a monarchist journal at Rostov on the Don
printed a forged document which it falsely attributed to the
American secret service.[1] The purport of the document was
that the Bolsheviks had received a subsidy of many millions
of dollars from the American Jewish banker Jacob Schiff on
behalf of the New York banking house of Kuhn, Loeb and Co.,
and that this had enabled them to carry out their revolution.
It is easy to see why Schiff was singled out in this way. During
the pogroms of 1905 he really had tried to persuade the United
States Government to exert itself on behalf of the Russian
Jews – and that was something no *pogromshchik* could forgive.
But some of the foreign correspondents and members of the
military missions with the 'White' armies took this kind of
stuff seriously and helped to channel it to western Europe.
Before long Mgr Jouin in Paris was blithely reprinting the
forgery about Schiff in his edition of the *Protocols*; while for
the Nazis the story was to provide an inexhaustible theme
for propaganda.

Meanwhile the *Protocols* themselves travelled west. Some
twenty years after the original French manuscript of the
forgery had gone from Paris to Russia, printed copies of the
Russian translation came out of Russia in the baggage of
'White' Russian officers. In 1919 typewritten copies in various
languages began to circulate among the delegates to the Peace

---

[1] *V Moskvu*, issue No. 1, 23 September 1919.

Conference; they also began to appear on the desks of cabinet ministers and civil servants in London, Paris, Rome, and Washington. The aim of this manoeuvre was to persuade the governments of the various powers to continue and intensify their intervention in Russia. All kinds of objections could be raised against intervening in a genuine civil war – but what if the conflict in Russia were no civil war but simply the unfolding of an international Jewish plot to subjugate the Russian people? Crazy as the argument may seem now, it appears to have had some effect on governmental policies.

Not that all dealers in the *Protocols* thought in terms of high policy. In the summer and autumn of 1919 a mysterious Lithuanian, a former employee of the Okhrana, called on a Jewish delegation to the Peace Conference and offered to hand over, for £10,000, a book which could be exceedingly dangerous to the Jews. Needless to say no business was done; but the delegation saw the book, and it was a copy of the *Protocols*. And this was no isolated incident: the American Jewish Committee had occasion to report, in its yearbook for 1920, how it had been approached by certain Russians with an offer to destroy, for a handsome consideration, the original manuscript of the *Protocols*. But the time for such private intrigues was drawing to a close. By the end of 1919 the *Protocols* had begun their rise to world fame, thanks to the efforts of a pair of Russian fanatics settled in Berlin, Pyotr Nikolaevich Shabelsky-Bork and Fyodor Viktorovich Vinberg.[1]

Shabelsky-Bork was born in the Caucasus in 1893. His father was a rich landowner; his mother was a leading member of the Union of the Russian People, the editor of a Black Hundred periodical in St Petersburg and the author of an antisemitic and anti-Masonic book called *The Satanists of the Twentieth Century*. Shabelsky-Bork himself belonged from an early age to the Union of the Russian People and to another similar organization, the Confraternity of St Michael the Archangel. He served as an officer in the World War and, briefly, in the civil war. In September 1918 he was at Yeka-

---

[1] On the part played by Vinberg and Shabelsky-Bork see H. Rollin, *L'Apocalypse de notre temps*, Paris, 1939, notably pp. 153 seq., and W. Laqueur, *Russia and Germany*, London, 1965, pp. 109 seq.

terinburg, claiming that he had been commissioned by certain highly placed persons to inquire into the circumstances attending the murder of the imperial family. He interrogated a number of people there and must certainly have heard about the Tsaritsa's swastika and her copy of Nilus.

Vinberg was a much older man, having been born in 1871 at Kiev, as the son of a general commanding a cavalry division. He himself became an officer, and eventually a colonel, in the Imperial Guard. He was a member of the Confraternity of St Michael the Archangel and wrote for Black Hundred periodicals. In 1918 he was arrested for counter-revolutionary activities and imprisoned in the fortress of St Peter and St Paul in Petrograd;[1] but soon he escaped or was released. He made his way to the Ukraine, where he joined the 'White' propagandists and *pogromshchiki* at Kiev. The murder of the Tsaritsa and the discoveries made in her room at Yekaterinburg had a very special significance for him. When he died in France in 1927 the obituary in the *Revue Internationale des Sociétés secrètes* noted that the Tsaritsa had been honorary colonel of Vinberg's regiment: 'He really worshipped her, and all his writings against the Jews and Freemasons are permeated by this cult.'[2]

Shabelsky-Bork and Vinberg both left Russia at a fairly early stage in the civil war. When the German troops evacuated the Ukraine after the armistice of November 1918 the German authorities provided a train for any Russian officers wishing to accompany them. Shabelsky-Bork and Vinberg took the opportunity and moved to Germany. It seems that immediately on arrival, in a Germany still in the first throes of defeat and revolution, Vinberg established contact with the man who was to produce the first German translation of the *Protocols*, Ludwig Müller. Müller, who liked to call himself Müller von Hausen and also used the pen-name Gottfried zur Beek, was a retired army captain and the editor of a conservative and anti-semitic monthly, *Auf Vorposten* (*On Outpost Duty*). Before November was out, this man possessed a copy of the 1911 edition of Nilus's book, *The Great in the Small*, with the *Protocols* – and he had it either from Vinberg or from some associate of

[1] St Petersburg, now Leningrad, was called Petrograd from 1914 to 1920.
[2] On the *Revue Internationale des Sociétés secrètes* see below, pp. 164–5.

Vinberg's. The contacts between these obscure, half-crazy, half-criminal characters were to have important consequences. Mgr Jouin, who did so much to disseminate the *Protocols* in France, considered that Vinberg's activity in Germany was 'the starting-point for the crusade against the Judeo-Masonic peril'; and if this was an exaggeration it had some truth in it. Certainly from that moment antisemitic agitation took on a murderous intensity which was new in western Europe.

In Berlin Vinberg and Shabelsky-Bork collaborated in producing a yearbook, *Luch Sveta* (*A Ray of Light*), the third issue of which (May 1920) contains the complete text of the 1911 edition of Nilus. The other issues are also obsessively concerned with the imaginary Judeo-Masonic-Bolshevik conspiracy; and so is Vinberg's book *Krestny Put* (i.e. *Via dolorosa*) which was translated into German. In all these writings Vinberg insists that in one way or another the Jews must be got rid of. Of course he realizes that this cannot be done in a democracy, but this worries him not at all, for in his view democracy is in any case a monstrous aberration – in fact it is a devilish device invented by the Jews as a means of securing their domination. Vinberg accordingly demands that the natural leaders of the nations shall once and for all recognize the political incompetence of the masses, turn their backs on democratic politics, seize power and impose their dictatorship on these 'anthropoid herds'. Then the time will be ripe to unite the nations in a common front against the world-conspiracy of the Jews.

Meanwhile Vinberg sees one great consolation: Germany is relatively free from the democratic malady. 'In Germany the *Protocols of the Elders of Zion* circulate freely, and the workers are revising their socialist programmes at extra meetings. . . . Lectures on Jewish domination are being given every-where. . . .'[1] And it is Germany's enemies, England and France, that constitute the stronghold of the Elders. Already in the eighteenth century England, at the behest of the Elders, paid such men as Rousseau, Voltaire, and the Encyclopedists to undermine France; more recently she paid Tolstoy and Gorky to undermine Russia. The French Revolution was planned by the Elders and so were the Russian and German

[1] F. V. Vinberg, *Krestny Put*, Munich, 1922 edition, p. 246.

revolutions of 1917–18. 'The link connecting the German and
Russian revolutions consists in the fact that the two *coups
d'état* were artificially provoked by means of the world-wide
. . . network of Judeo-Masonic organizations. In these organizations, low-grade Freemasonry plays the part of a blind
weapon of the notorious . . . Alliance Israélite Universelle,
that secret council of the Elders of the People of Israel. . . .'[1]
Moreover not only the revolutions but the World War itself
was the work of the Elders, operating through British and
French foreign policy. The Kaiser and the Tsar did their best
to avoid war but they were no match for the Elders. The only
remedy now lies in an alliance of the true Germany and the
true Russia – meaning a Germany and a Russia under dic-
tatorships of the Right. Such an alliance may yet challenge
and overthrow the Judeo-Masonic conspiracy and its French
and British puppets. There must be a new slogan: 'Germany
and Russia above everything! above everything in the
world!' 'In this way,' comments Vinberg, 'the two peoples
will realize their dream, magnanimous and beneficent but
hitherto unrealizable, of peace in the world. . . .'[2]

As a political programme Vinberg's utterances cannot be
taken seriously. Among the Russian émigrés only a minority
even of the right-wing extremists was willing to call on German
help to restore the tsarist régime, while among German right-
wingers only a few – such as Ludendorff – were so unrealistic
as to contemplate such a restoration. On the other hand
Vinberg was absolutely right in thinking that the *Protocols*
would have a greater appeal in Germany than in any other
country. He knew, of course, that ever since the emergence of
antisemitism as a political force, around 1870, it had been far
stronger and more widespread in Germany than in England or
France. But this was not all: as soon as it became apparent
that Germany was going to lose the war, those who had led the
country to disaster hastened to throw the blame upon the
Jews, who were held responsible both for the war itself and for
Germany's failure to win it.

Already in January 1918 the right-wing monthly *Deutsch-
lands Erneuerung* (*Germany's Renewal*) produced a variation

[1] *Luch Sveta*, Berlin, Vol. I (1919), p. 50.
[2] F. V. Vinberg, *Krestny Put*, p. 49.

on *The Rabbi's Speech*, adapted to the needs of the moment. In 1913, it declared, an international group of Jewish bankers met in Paris and decided that the time had come for high finance to oust kings and emperors and openly impose its authority upon the whole world; what had hitherto been secret control must now become avowed dictatorship. These were the men who had plunged the world into war. They had also seen to it that 'all-Jewish agitators' should undermine Germany to such an extent that foreign powers felt free to attack her, in the certain knowledge that war would plunge her into revolution. This idea quickly caught on in right-wing circles. As, during the last desperate months of the war, strikes spread in Germany and Austria, leaflets were distributed stating that 'American, English and Russian Jews have raised 1,500,000,000 marks . . . to incite Germans against Germans, brothers against brothers'. In August 1918, when the German Army was in full retreat on the western front, Prince Dr Otto zu Salm-Horstmar – who in due course was to become a very active sponsor of the *Protocols* – explained that Germany was losing the war because the democratic philosophy was undermining the aristocratic philosophy which was natural to Germans; and this democratic philosophy found its strongest support in the international Jewish race, operating through the Masonic lodges. For good measure he added that Lenin was a Jew and belonged to a Masonic lodge in Paris, to which Trotsky also belonged. All this the prince said in a formal speech in the upper house of the Prussian Diet.

In the very moment of Germany's final defeat the periodical *Auf Vorposten* was ready with its explanation: 'The blue and white flag of the Jewish people and the blood-red banner of the Scottish high-grade[1] have won for the present! The thrones of the Romanovs, the Habsburgs and Hohenzollerns . . . are deserted, and Germany groans under the tyranny of the workers' and soldiers' councils.'[2] And early in 1919, as the German population tasted the full bitterness of defeat, whole books began to appear in which the war and its outcome were explained in this way. Two particularly influential works were *Judas Schuldbuch, eine deutsche Abrechnung (Accounts to be*

---

[1] I.e. 'the old and accepted Scottish rite', see above, p. 49.
[2] *Auf Vorposten* for 1918, Heft 4–6, p. 82.

settled by Germany with the Jews), which appeared over the pseudonym 'Wilhelm Meister',[1] and *Weltfreimaurerei, Weltrevolution, Weltrepublik, eine Untersuchung über Ursprung und Endziele des Weltkrieges* (*World Freemasonry, World Revolution, World Republic, an investigation into the origin and final aims of the World War*), by Dr F. Wichtl – both of them published in Munich, where Adolf Hitler was just beginning his political career. Their object is stated with remarkable naïveté by Wichtl himself: 'to convince the reader that it is not we Germans who are to blame for all the horrible bloodshed' but the Judeo-Masonic world-conspiracy, 'the invisible master of all peoples and states'.[2] It is of course taken for granted that Russia is firmly in the hands of that power – but the British Empire is no less so. Englishmen and Jews together plotted the war as a means to world-domination; the Entente was organized by Jews from their stronghold in the City of London, and so of course was the pacifist propaganda that undermined Germany. And if Trotsky is the agent both of Jewish high finance and of the rabbinate, the Jewish monarch who was about to be established as world-ruler is none other than King George V. A country where such stuff could enjoy big sales (between them these two books sold some 50,000 copies within a year) was indeed ready for the *Protocols*.

But the *Protocols* hung fire. It had been intended to publish them simultaneously in Germany and in Britain, with appropriately varied commentaries – only it proved no easy matter to find them a British publisher. Publication in Germany was accordingly delayed until the beginning of 1920; but meanwhile there were many hints of joys to come. In April 1919 old Theodor Fritsch, 'the Nestor of German antisemitism', printed in his *Hammer* a prophecy which a Jewish revolutionary was supposed to have made in Paris in 1895, i.e. about the time of origin of the *Protocols*: 'In about thirty years Germany will be involved in a great war, which it will be bound to lose. Then on the ruins of the German Empire we shall build our empire,

---

[1] 'Wilhelm Meister' was really Paul Bang, the economic expert of the Deutschnationale Volkspartei, the successor to the pre-1918 Conservative party of Prussia.

[2] F. Wichtl, *Weltfreimaurerei, Weltrevolution, Weltrepublik*, ninth edition, Munich, 1922, p. 268.

as Jehovah promised us, with a second Solomon as king.'
Fritsch, one feels, must have been reading a copy of the
Protocols (soon he was to produce an edition of them, at great
profit to himself). Also in April 1919 Vinberg in *Luch Sveta*
talked of a German edition as being imminent; and in the
same month *Auf Vorposten* carried an advertisement which
remains a most significant document:

> In Germany the reports of the Elders of Zion were known before
> the war only in Jewish and Masonic circles. World history would
> certainly have followed another course if the princes of Europe had
> known the *Secrets of the Elders of Zion* early enough and had drawn
> the right conclusions from them. . . .
> In view of the softness shown by the peoples of central Europe,
> and particularly by the Germans, in their handling of the Jewish
> question, any revelation of Jewish aims would probably have been
> rejected before the war with an incredulous smile. Even during the
> world war only a few realized that there must exist some great
> plan for the destruction of Germany; those who were initiated
> knew that the Freemasons and Jews had prepared this plan
> decades in advance, for the purpose of overthrowing the princely
> houses of Europe and then launching a struggle against the
> Church. . . . Let an impartial tribunal examine who is to blame for
> the war! We summon the leaders of international Freemasonry,
> the Jewish world-alliances and all the chief rabbis to appear
> before it.[1]

This much at least was true: people who before the war
would have laughed the *Protocols* to scorn were ready to take
them seriously now. The development which had taken place
in Russia after the October revolution was about to be repeated, on an infinitely vaster scale, in Germany. Once more
defeated and ruined men were to invoke this ridiculous fake
to explain their misfortunes and excuse their failures. Above
all a handful of political adventurers were to use it as a device
for capturing influence, privilege, and power – and in this
some of them were to succeed far beyond the dreams of any
Black Hundred *pogromschchik*.

A good deal is known about the promotion of the first
German edition of the *Protocols*. The book was published in
mid-January, 1920, under the title *Die Geheimnisse der Weisen*

[1] *Auf Vorposten* for 1919, Heft 4–6, pp. 78–80.

von Zion (*The Secrets of the Elders of Zion*). The publisher was the same organization as published *Auf Vorposten* – the Verband gegen Ueberhebung des Judentums (Association against the Presumption of the Jews), which had been founded in 1912 or 1913 for the purpose of 'enlightening the spiritual, social and economic élite of the people'. The editor was the founder of that organization – the same Ludwig Müller, *alias* Müller von Hausen, *alias* Gottfried zur Beek, to whom the copy of Nilus had been passed in November 1918. Though the book quickly became a best-seller it started by being heavily subsidized – and we know from what quarters. The upper house of the Prussian Diet might have been abolished under the new constitution but its conservative wing still functioned as an entity, notably by subscribing funds to various organizations which aimed at discrediting the republic and restoring the monarchy. Prince Dr Otto zu Salm-Horstmar raised money for the *Protocols* from this source. It seems certain moreover that members of the deposed Hohenzollern family also contributed; at any rate, when this charge was brought the usually vociferous *Auf Vorposten* remained prudently silent.

The Hohenzollerns certainly had cause to be pleased with the book: it carried a dedication 'To the Princes of Europe' and a portrait of their illustrious ancestor, the 'Great Elector', with the motto: 'May an avenger arise some day from our bones.' No wonder Prince Joachim Albrecht of Prussia made a practice of handing out copies of the book to the staff of the hotels and restaurants he frequented. As for the exiled Kaiser, when Lady Norah Bentinck visited him in the summer of 1921 she found him utterly convinced that his fall was due to the Elders.[1] To Germany's great war-hero, General Ludendorff, the *Protocols* also came as a revelation – and one which he refused to reject even after *The Times* had proved its spuriousness. 'The supreme government of the Jewish people,' he wrote in 1922, 'was working hand in hand with France and England. Perhaps it was leading them both.'[2] And he reflect-

---

[1] Lady Norah Bentinck, *The Ex-Kaiser in Exile*, London, 1921, pp. 99–108.

[2] E. Ludendorff, *Kriegführung und Politik*, second edition, Berlin, 1922, p. 51.

ed: 'Several publications have recently appeared which throw more light on the position of the Jewish people. The German people, but also the other peoples of the earth, have every reason to make a thorough study of the historical development of the Jewish people, its organizations, its methods of fighting and its plans. One suspects that in many instances we shall arrive at another version of world history.'[1] Ludendorff's need for a scapegoat was of course great, for by recommending the most ruthless submarine warfare he had done as much as anyone to bring the United States into the war against Germany.

If Ludendorff and the Kaiser were perhaps genuinely deceived, the professional politician Count Ernst zu Reventlow knew perfectly well what he was doing. This Prussian aristocrat, who was a leading member of the *völkisch*[2] bloc in the Reichstag and was in due course to become a Nazi, was wholly committed to propagating the *Protocols*. He did so in *Auf Vorposten*, in his own newspaper *Der Reichswart* (*The Guardian of the Reich*) and also in newspapers with mass circulations, such as the *Deutsches Tageblatt*; and when *The Times* produced its revelation he defended the authenticity of the *Protocols* more vigorously than ever. 'The revelations of *The Times*,' he wrote, 'cannot touch, let alone destroy, the genuineness of the *Protocols*. On the contrary, these revelations throw a most interesting and valuable light on Jewish manoeuvres. . . . Let people in Germany draw the practical conclusion and see to it that the book, which is already widely distributed, is distributed as widely as ever possible!'[3] Thus Count Reventlow – who, as we shall see, believed not a word of it.[4]

Amid the chorus of praise the voice of the Association against the Presumption of the Jews sounded loud and clear. These enterprising publishers did not talk merely of politics, of such things as wars and revolutions – in their publicity, as later in Nazi propaganda, the unmasking of the Judeo-Masonic conspiracy is presented as a turning-point in the

[1] Ibid., p. 322, footnote.
[2] Extreme nationalists who were more radical and 'popular' than the German National People's party, and frankly racist and antisemitic in outlook.   [3] In *Deutsches Tageblatt*, issue for 23 August 1921.
[4] See below, p. 140.

spiritual history of mankind. According to *Auf Vorposten* the new book revealed a plot

'to destroy Christianity and other forms of belief in God and to establish the Mosaic–Talmudic faith as the religion for the world. The great struggle, which far-sighted men foretold decades ago, has now begun. If the civilized peoples of Europe do not now rouse themselves for the struggle against the common enemy, our civilization will be destroyed by the same disruptive fungus as was the civilization of antiquity two thousand years ago. . . . A few days ago a Berlin professor told us that this book will surely bring salvation to our people, and a south German scholar wrote to say that no book has ever provoked such a revolution in people's world-view as does the work of Gottfried zur Beek – not since the invention of printing, nay, since the discovery of the alphabet. From all levels of the German population, from the courts of princes to the workers' cottages, there come to us messages of rejoicing and approval that at last a brave man has solved the question on which the destiny of the German people depends.'[1]

Publishers' blurbs admittedly tend to exaggerate – but the popular reception accorded to the Müller von Hausen (or Gottfried zur Beek) edition of the *Protocols* really was extraordinary. It was reprinted twice within a month of publication and another three times before the end of 1920; sales quickly reached 120,000 copies. And the book certainly did much to foster the Nazi madness already under the democratic and liberal régime of the Weimar Republic. This, for instance, is what a Jewish observer found in the early 1920s:

In Berlin I attended several meetings which were entirely devoted to the *Protocols*. The speaker was usually a professor, a teacher, an editor, a lawyer or someone of that kind. The audience consisted of members of the educated class, civil servants, tradesmen, former officers, ladies, above all students, students of all faculties and years of seniority. . . . Passions were whipped up to boiling-point. There, in front of one, in the flesh, was the cause of all ills – those who had made the war and brought about the defeat and engineered the revolution, those who had conjured up all our suffering. This enemy was quite close by, he could be caught by our hands, and yet he was the enemy who slunk about in the darkness, one shuddered to think what secret designs he was harbouring.

[1] *Auf Vorposten*, for 1920, Heft 1–2, pp. 35–7.

I observed the students. A few hours earlier they had perhaps been exerting all their mental energy in a seminar under the guidance of a world-famous scholar, in an effort to solve some legal or philosophical or mathematical problem. Now young blood was boiling, eyes flashed, fists clenched, hoarse voices roared applause or vengeance. Sometimes a speech from the floor was permitted; whoever dared to express a slight doubt was shouted down, often insulted and threatened. If I had been recognized as a Jew, I doubt whether I would have got away without physical injury. But German scholarship allowed belief in the genuineness of the *Protocols* and in the existence of a Jewish world-conspiracy to penetrate ever more deeply into all the educated sections of the German population, so that now[1] it is simply ineradicable. Here and there a serious Christian newspaper expressed slight doubts, raised mild and timid objections, but that was all. None of the great German scholars (save for the late lamented Strack) rose to unmask the forgery. . . .[2]

This account is confirmed by others from the same period – and all agree that the *Protocols* were predominantly a middle-class preoccupation. The Social-Democratic newspapers were staunch in denouncing them, whereas the bulk of the 'bourgeois' press remained at best non-committal. And the most zealous students of the *Protocols* were to be found not among the industrial workers, whether skilled or unskilled, but in the professional classes. Former officers were particularly addicted to them – but they also circulated in institutes of technology, often with the approval of the staff, and helped to form the outlook of students who later occupied positions at all levels of industry, including the highest. (Incidentally Techow, the murderer of Rathenau, had been through an institute of technology.)[3] No doubt the most enthusiastic believers were those who subscribed to the racialist and *völkisch* outlook – at which we shall be glancing later – but on the other hand even the most orthodox Protestantism was no sure protection. Antisemitic propagandists began to put it about that the authenticity of the *Protocols* was guaranteed by the British Museum, on the grounds that a copy of Nilus's book is to be found in the great library; and that was enough to convince

[1] i.e. in 1924.
[2] B. Segel, *Die Protokolle der Weisen von Zion*, pp. 37–8.
[3] See below, pp. 145–6.

even the most staid and respectable journals of the Lutheran Church.

The appetite of this wide, mainly middle-class public might fluctuate, but it never died away. By the time Hitler came to power in 1933, thirty-three editions of zur Beek's translation had been published. Meanwhile a popular edition had been issued by the publishing house Der Hammer at Leipzig, over the name of Theodor Fritsch; and by 1933 this had sold nearly 100,000 copies. Moreover these editions were accompanied by a stream of works elaborating and justifying the *Protocols*. The German translation of the book on the subject sponsored by Henry Ford, *The International Jew*, ran through six editions between 1920 and 1922. By 1923 the official 'philosopher' of the Nazi Party, Alfred Rosenberg, produced a volume entitled *Die Protokolle der Weisen von Zion und die jüdische Weltpolitik* (*The Protocols of the Elders of Zion and Jewish World Policy*), and this too ran through three editions within a year. Already in the 1920s, then, Germany must have contained hundreds of thousands of copies of the *Protocols* and of commentaries on them.

All this was part of an antisemitic propaganda drive which was far more intensive than anything known before the war. Within a year of the armistice there existed six organizations dedicated to disseminating such propaganda – two in Berlin, three in Hamburg, one in Leipzig – and at least a dozen newspapers and periodicals;[1] this at a time when Hitler and his future party had not even begun to emerge from obscurity. Thanks to these organizations and journals, the *Protocols* did not stand alone but were constantly reinforced by other forgeries and fables concerning the Judeo-Masonic-Communist world-conspiracy. Already in 1919 there appeared two editions of *The Rabbi's Speech*, apart from the variants on it

---

[1] Antisemitic organizations active at the beginning of 1920: Verband gegen die Ueberhebung des Judentums (Berlin), Ausschuss für Volksaufklärung (Berlin), Deutsch-völkischer Bund (Hamburg), Deutsche Erneuerungsgemeinde (Leipzig), Deutsch-völkischer Schutz- und Trutzbund (Hamburg), Reichshammerbund (Hamburg). Antisemitic newspapers and periodicals: *Deutsche Zeitung, Deutsche Tageszeitung, Tägliche Rundschau, Deutsches Wochenblatt, Münchener Beobachter, Deutscher Volksrat, Der Aufrechte, Der deutsche Landtag, Die Tradition, Auf Vorposten, Die deutsche Erneuerung.*

contained in the book of 'Wilhelm Meister'. The Zunder document, after playing its part in provoking pogroms in Russia, penetrated into Germany; it appeared in the newspaper of the Russian right-wingers, *Prizyv* (*The Call*), in February 1920 and was at once translated and republished by *Auf Vorposten* and similar journals. In the same month that ancient work, Osman-Bey's *World Conquest by the Jews*, was reprinted. And another rich mine was provided by the long introduction and postscript with which Müller von Hausen ornamented his edition of the *Protocols*.

Even to one hardened by much wandering in these territories it comes as something of a shock to realize just what is contained in this book which was taken seriously by innumerable professors and schoolmasters, business-men and industrialists, army officers and civil servants. For even the *Protocols* are less bizarre than the editorial appendages. These include, for instance, the cartoon 'The Kaiser's Dream', first published in the English weekly *Truth* in 1890.[1] This satirical comment on the Kaiser's ambitions and their probable consequences is interpreted as a Judeo-Masonic production revealing the secret (!) plan to overthrow the European monarchies; after all, was not the editor of *Truth*, Henry Labouchere, a Freemason and what is more a member of the Reform Club? Equally remarkable is a fantasy which Müller von Hausen lifted from *Prizyv*: a black mass had just been celebrated in the Kremlin, where Trotsky and his associates prayed to Satan for help in defeating their enemies; this sacrilegious affair was revealed by a guard, who was thereupon murdered on Trotsky's orders. This stuff, and much more of the same quality, became the stock-in-trade of antisemitic propagandists.

The apex of absurdity was reached in a fabrication called *Die siegreiche Weltanschauung* (*Neo-Machiavellismus*) *und wir Juden* (*The victorious world-view* (*Neo-Machiavellianism*) *and we Jews*, which was published within a few weeks of the *Protocols* over the unbelievable name of Dr Siegfried Pentha-Tull. In this pamphlet the author, who is supposed to be a Jew, publicly rejoices over the success of the plan outlined in the *Protocols* – presumably forgetting that the plan itself was

[1] See Plate 4.

supposed to be secret. It did not take long to trace the careless Pentha-Tull. Just at that time the newspaper *Deutsche Zeitung*, which was the organ of the German National People's party (formerly the Conservatives), was publishing a serial novelette with a Jewish villain called Pentha-Tull; and novelette and forgery were in fact by the same person, a well-known antisemite called Hans Schliepmann. But this did not prevent the same newspaper from expressing its horror at the revelations of the imaginary Pentha-Tull. His book, it ex-claimed, 'makes one's blood freeze in one's veins'. And it formulated an urgent demand: 'A united Christian phalanx must be formed against the fearful dangers which threaten not only the churches but the whole German people from the direction of the Jews. It is necessary to speak frankly, if we are not to perish miserably. The people can be pulled from the morass ... only by an energetic struggle against the poisoners of the people; only so can we extricate ourselves from their deadly clutch.'[1]

Nobody was more vocal on the subject of Pentha-Tull than that indefatigable propagator of the *Protocols*, Count Ernst zu Reventlow. In May 1920 he devoted whole articles in the *Deutsche Zeitung* to arguing that the authenticity of the *Protocols* was proved beyond all doubt by Pentha-Tull and the Zunder document; and he did this without himself believing it for a moment. Although one knows that a great deal of antisemitic propaganda consists of deliberate lying, it is rare to find one of the liars admitting as much in writing. Revent-low provides one of the exceptions. In 1940 one of the pro-paganda offices of the Third Reich thought of resuscitating Pentha-Tull and addressed an inquiry to Reventlow, who was still a member of the Reichstag. The Freyenwald Collection at the Wiener Library contains his reply: 'When I read the pamphlet by "Pentha-Tull" I was clear that it was a pretty clumsy hoax. Nevertheless in public I called it genuine, be-cause this seemed to me to answer the purpose best at that time ... Heil Hitler!'[2] And we know the purpose for which

---

[1] *Deutsche Zeitung*, issue for 31 August 1920.

[2] A copy of Reventlow's letter, which was dated 5 March 1940 and was addressed to the *Weltdienst*, is in the Freyenwald Collection file 'Pentha-Tull'.

Reventlow did this particular piece of lying. The elections for the first republican Reichstag were due in June 1920. To present the new Republic as a creation of the Elders of Zion was one way of winning votes for the anti-democratic Right.

2

The *Protocols* did much to provoke two political assassinations which occurred in Berlin in 1922.

On his arrival in Berlin Shabelsky-Bork, the friend and collaborator of Vinberg and a very active propagator of the *Protocols*, founded an organization modelled on the Black Hundreds and trained in terrorism. Its major undertaking was carried out on 28 March 1922. A meeting of Russian émigrés was being held in the Berlin Philharmonia, in aid of the victims of famine in the Soviet Union. The chairman of the meeting was Pavel Nikolaevich Milyukov, the eminent historian and the leader of the Constitutional Democrats (Cadets). Milyukov had himself had to flee from Russia to escape being imprisoned or executed by the Bolsheviks; indeed just like Vinberg and Shabelsky-Bork, he had had to attach himself to the German troops withdrawing from the Ukraine. That did not prevent these fanatics from planning his assassination. Shabelsky-Bork and his band suddenly burst into the Philharmonia and opened fire on the platform – missing Milyukov, who threw himself on his face, but killing Vladimir Nabokov (the father of the novelist). For this murder Shabelsky-Bork was sentenced to fourteen years' hard labour. He was released long before his term was up; and when the Nazis came to power he received a regular pension from Rosenberg's office and, already in 1933, was allowed to collaborate in founding a Russian 'Nazi' movement. It was an appropriate reward, for in trying to kill Milyukov Shabelsky-Bork was acting according to the doctrine of his master Vinberg—who indeed was also implicated in the murder and had to leave Germany as a result. And Vinberg saw in Milyukov the secret, but entirely conscious, agent of the Bolsheviks, who were themselves agents of the Elders of Zion.

This affair was followed within a few months by an assassination, this time by right-wing Germans, which echoed through Europe. In June 1922 a handful of young fanatics murdered Walther Rathenau, the German Minister for Foreign Affairs. And they did so in the conviction not simply that he was acting for the Elders but that he himself was one of the Elders.

Rathenau was a man of extraordinary abilities, who made his mark in the applied sciences, in engineering, in philosophy, in political and economic theory, in addition to being one of Germany's greatest industrialists, an outstanding administrator, a remarkable Foreign Minister. His services to Germany were great. At the very beginning of the war he recognized the mortal threat represented by the British blockade. To counter it he built up, in an amazingly short time, a huge organization for administering raw materials – and which did in fact enable Germany to hold out with raw materials right through the war. After the war he worked tirelessly to overcome Germany's isolation and to secure a lightening of the burden of reparations; at the same time he strove to unite the nations of Europe, still bitterly divided by the experience of the war, in a collective effort at reconstruction. In April 1922, as Foreign Minister, he signed the Rapallo Treaty with the Soviet Union, by which both sides renounced all claims arising from the war.

Rathenau was a fervent patriot, but his patriotism was that of a civilized and liberal European and had nothing to do with chauvinism. Also, he was a Jew. Right-wing fanatics accordingly viewed him with a hatred which became more and more intense as his political status increased. By 1921 the press of the *völkisch* bloc and of the young Nazi party was representing this great idealist as a Satanic being. 'You spread around you hellish justice, hellish practices, hellish morality,' wrote the *Deutsch-völkische Blätter*; while the Nazi *Völkischer Beobachter* complained: 'How long before we have a Walter I of the dynasty of Abraham, Joseph, Rathenau? The day is coming when the wheel of world history will be put into reverse, to roll over many a corpse, of the great financier and his accomplices.'[1] At the same time Theodor Fritsch in the *Hammer* presented Rathenau as the man behind Bolshevism even inside Russia. In 1922 the attacks became more scurrilous still. It was said that in instituting the control of raw materials during the war Rathenau had deliberately organized the starvation of the German people. As for his appointment as Foreign Minister, that had been secured by presenting the Chancellor with an ultimatum threatening to 'sacrifice the German people to Jewish world-power'. And for months before the assassination speeches were being made calling in effect for just such a deed.

In this campaign the *Protocols* were of course invoked constantly, but that was not all – two particular stories were put about which linked Rathenau peculiarly closely with the Elders of Zion. One of these was a weird invention which Müller von Hausen put into his edition of the *Protocols*. Emil Rathenau, the father of the statesman, had once bought and largely reconstructed a house in Berlin; and one of the additions he made was a frieze running round the outside of the building. In reality this frieze consisted of masks with floral decorations, repeated sixty-six times. To the hallucinated gaze of the editor of the *Protocols*, however, it represented sixty-six crowned heads, cut off and resting on sixty-six dishes for receiving sacrificial blood. And who could doubt that in this design the secret of the German and Russian revolutions was symbolically expressed? Had not Emil Rathenau been one of the Kaiser's most trusted counsellors? 'How often,' lamented Müller, 'may our unsuspecting Emperor have crossed the threshold of this house, little suspecting what kindly wishes for the future of the House of Hohenzollern were cherished by the man whom he called his friend?'. [2,3]

---

[1] Both quoted in *C. V. Zeitung* (i.e. the weekly of the Central-Verein deutscher Staatsbürger jüdischen Glaubens), Vol. I, issue for 20 June 1921.

[2] Müller von Hausen seems to have borrowed the idea from a pamphlet called *Versailles Visions*, published in 1919. The author was a dismissed schoolteacher called Leisner, who under the pseudonym of Ellegaard Ellerbek preached a peculiar mixture of occultism, astrology and sun-religion – and who incidentally was taken seriously not only by Alfred Rosenberg but also in certain quite respectable conservative circles.

[3] G. zur Beek, *Die Geheimnisse der Weisen von Zion*, Berlin–Charlottenburg 1919 (really 1920), p. 199.

Like father, like son. Years earlier Walther Rathenau had written a sentence which was to have a long and inglorious history. In the *Neue Freie Presse* for Christmas Day, 1909, there appeared an article by him which was reprinted in his book *Zur Kritik der Zeit* (*A critique of the age*) in 1922. It dealt with economic affairs and contained the following observation: 'Three hundred men, all of whom know one another, guide the economic destinies of the Continent and seek their successors among their followers.' There is no mention whatsoever of Jews; and the context shows what Rathenau intended – which was, to deplore the fact that at that time the leading positions in finance and industry were largely the preserve of a hereditary oligarchy. It seems to have been Ludendorff who first suggested that the 300 men were in fact the secret Jewish government.[1] The suggestion was snatched up by the professional antisemites, and they were quick to draw the obvious conclusion: if Rathenau knew the number of the Elders, that could only mean that he was one of them. Nothing more was required to complete the transformation of the Foreign Minister into a super-criminal. 'The name of the main culprit for the enslavement of our economy is Rathenau,' wrote one right-wing journal. 'Dominion over the productive labour of all the peoples of the earth is passing more and more into the hands of those 300 men who, according to an unnoticed remark of Rathenau's, guide the history of the world, all know one another, and of whom he is one. . . . Many innocent contemporaries still do not recognize the preconcerted operations of these 300 men, who almost without exception belong to the Jewish race. . . .'[2] Alfred Rosenberg, in his pamphlet *Plague in Russia*, stated that Rathenau and his like were 'long since ripe for prison and gallows'. Count zu Reventlow lamented that such a man should still be alive and in excellent health; and his article was reprinted in many newspapers a fortnight before the murder.

Rathenau had frequently been threatened with assassination, but had always refused police protection. He was murdered as he was taking his usual drive from his house to

[1] E. Ludendorff, *Kriegsführung und Politik*, p. 51, footnote.
[2] *Reichsbote*, quoted in *Mitteilungen aus dem Verein zur Abwehr des Antisemitismus*, issue for 12 January 1922, p. 3.

1. MAURICE JOLY (1829-78), author of the *Dialogue aux Enfers entre Montesquieu et Machiavel*

2. PYOTR IVANOVICH RACH-KOVSKY, head of the foreign branch of the Okhrana from 1884 to 1902

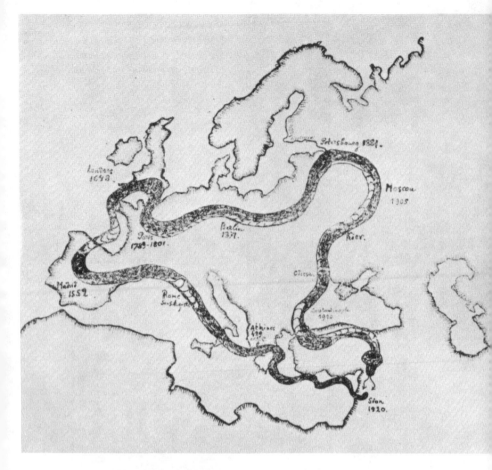

3. 'The Symbolic Snake,' which is supposed to represent the progress of the Jewish plot from the fifth century B.C. onwards. Starting from Palestine the head of the Snake moves through the states of Europe until, with Zionist immigration, it returns to its point of origin. This means that the world is ruled from Palestine, and marks the culmination of the plot. Pictures and descriptions of the Snake have accompanied the *Protocols* throughout their history

4. 'The Kaiser's Dream.' This cartoon was first published in the English weekly *Truth* in 1890 and was intended as a satirical comment on the ambitions of Kaiser Wilhelm II and their possible consequences. It was reprinted in many editions of the *Protocols* as representing the plan of the Elders

5. SERGEY NILUS, whose Russian edition of the *Protocols* in his book *The Great in the Small* formed the basis for most non-Russian editions

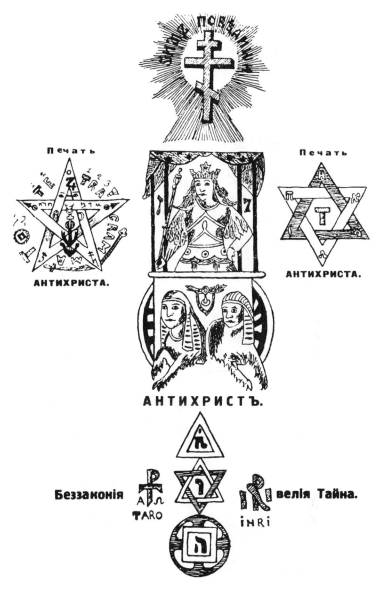

6. Antichrist and his emblems, surmounted by the Orthodox cross as talisman against the powers of evil. From the 1911 edition of *The Great in the Small*. The figure labelled 'Antichrist' is really the King in the Tarot pack

„Quand même!"

7. Frontispiece from the year-book *Luch Sveta,* in which the *Protocols* appeared for the first time outside Russia. Here the task of illuminating the dark conspiracy of the Elders is shown as a religious mission

Die Geheimniſſe der Weiſen von Zion

„Alles dieſes wußte ich ſchon vor 11 Jahren; wie ging es aber zu, daß ich es doch nicht glauben wollte?"

Ludwig XVI. bei ſeiner Verhaftung am 22. Juni 1791 in Varennes. Vergl. Joh. Robiſon „Über Geheime Geſellſchaften und deren Geſährlichkeit für Staat und Religion". Deutſche Überſetzung nach der 3. engliſchen Auflage, Königslutter bei D. Culemann 1800, 242. Seite.

Herausgegeben

von

Gottfried zur Beek

3. Auflage

Verlag „Auf Vorpoſten" in Charlottenburg 4
1919

8. Title-page of the first non-Russian version of the *Protocols.* The tusked boar was the emblem of the German anti-semitic society which published this edition

9. From a brochure advertising the *Protocols,* dated 1925. The U. Bodung publishing house belonged to Colonel Fleischhauer of the *Weltdienst*

10. ALFRED ROSENBERG, the official 'philosopher' of the Nazi Party and a leading champion of the *Protocols*

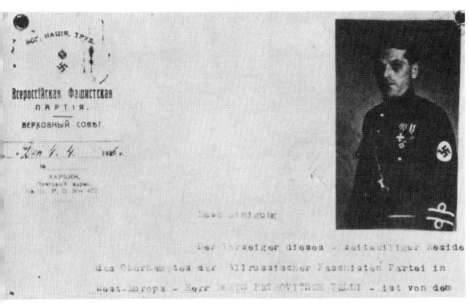

11. Document issued to Boris Toedtli, Swiss citizen and 'White' Russian agent, by the head of the All-Russian Fascist Party in Kharbin, authorizing him to appoint and dismiss officers of the party in Europe

12. Leaflet celebrating the fifth birthday of the All-Russian Fascist Party. The emblem combines the swastika, the eagle of imperial Russia, and St. Michael killing the dragon—the old emblem of the Black Hundreds

13. Cover of a popular French edition of the *Protocols*, c. 1934

14. Cover of another popular French edition, c. 1934

Wzór okładki do broszury „W szponach komunizmu".

Po Rosji i Hiszpanji — kolej na Polskę! Trzeba ją skąpać we krwi! Zostawić po niej ruiny i zgliszcza! Żyd już wiedzie kostuchę na żniwo do Polski! Baczmy na ten pochód i czuwajmy, bo gorze nam! Gorze!!!...

Nakl. „Samoobrona Narodu" Poznań   Drukarnia Centralna Poznań

15. Frontispiece to a Polish edition, Poznan, 1937. The caption reads: 'After Russia and Spain—it is Poland's turn! She must have a blood bath! Only ruins and cinders should remain! Already the Jew leads Death to her harvest in Poland! Let us watch this marching column and let us be awake, for woe to us! Woe!!!...'

16. Cover of a Swedish edition, Hangö, 1924

17. Cover of a Brazilian edition, São Paulo, 1937

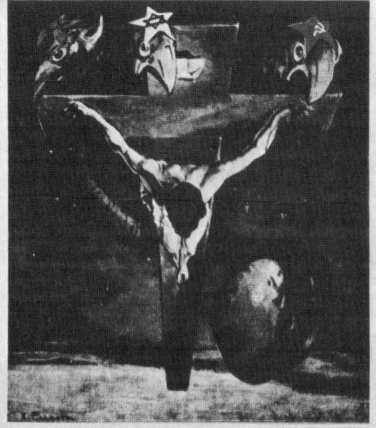

SABIOS DE SION
PROTOCOLOS

PLAN:
Destruir la Cristiandad
Esclavizar la Humanidad

18. Cover of a very recent Spanish edition, Madrid, 1963. The three heads of the snake represent the Jewish religion, the state of Israel, and Communism

19. A fifteenth-century version of the ritual murder of a Christian boy by Jews. From Schedel's *Liber Cronicarum*

the Foreign Ministry, on the morning of 24 June 1922. The killers were quite young men who belonged to various groups of the extreme Right, such as the Deutsch-völkischer Schutz und Trutzbund (Defensive and Offensive Alliance) and the Ehrhardt Naval Brigade; several of them had taken part in the first attempt by the Right to overthrow the Republic, the Kapp *putsch* of 1920. They were grouped in an organization known as 'Organization Consul' which, like the young Nazi party, was based on Munich. This body was dedicated to terrorism; and 'Shoot down Walther Rathenau, The God-accursed Jewish sow,' is a fair sample of the kind of thing these young people sang about the streets.

The imagination of the assassins was steeped in the *Protocols* and the lore which had gathered around them. The man who planned the murder, Willy Günther, admitted this quite frankly during his preliminary interrogation. The reason why Rathenau had to be killed, he said, was that according to Ludendorff he was the one man in Germany who knew the membership of the secret Jewish government, which had caused the war. The same picture emerged at the trial at Leipzig, in October 1922, of the driver of the car from which Rathenau was shot (of the two who had done the actual killing, one was shot by the police and another shot himself to avoid capture).[1] This is how the accused, Ernst Techow, described the plot as it had been propounded by its originator, the dead Erwin Kern:

Kern said that he proposed to murder Minister Rathenau. And that I must bind myself to help him, whether I wanted to or not. Otherwise he would be prepared to carry the job out alone. And that it was all one to him what the consequences might be. At the same time he gave various reasons which in his opinion were decisive, although that was not my view. He said . . . that Rathenau had very close and intimate relations with Bolshevik

---

[1] The account given by one of the plotters, Ernst von Salomon, in *Die Geächteten*, Berlin 1935, makes no mention of the *Protocols* or the secret Jewish government, and in his famous post-war book *Der Fragebogen von Ernst von Salomon*, Hamburg 1951, he even denies that Rathenau's Jewishness had anything to do with the murder. But even if some of those involved saw the assassination in other terms, Techow's evidence stands.

Russia, so that he had even married off his sister with the Communist Radek.

To end with, he said that Rathenau had himself confessed, and boasted, that he was one of the three hundred Elders of Zion, whose purpose and aim was to bring the whole world under Jewish influence, as the example of Bolshevist Russia already showed, where at first all factories, etc., were made public property, then at the suggestion and command of the Jew Lenin, Jewish capital was brought in from abroad, to bring the factories into operation again, and so in this way the whole of Russian national property was now in Jewish hands. . . .

The President of the Court: You say that Rathenau had close relations with the Bolshevist Radek, so that he even married his sister off to him.

Techow: That is supposed to be the fact. I don't know.

President: To my knowledge Rathenau has only one sister, who is married to a Dr Andreae in Berlin.

Techow: I don't know.

President: How could this great industrialist come to have such relations with the Russian refugee and Communist Radek? Does it seem likely to you?

Techow: No, it was simply a conjecture, which Kern gave as if it was a fact. So I had to suppose it was right.

President: To continue: Rathenau is supposed to have confessed that he was himself one of the three hundred Elders of Zion. The three hundred Elders of Zion come from a pamphlet. Have you read it?

Techow: Yes.[1]

On the eve of the trial a packet of poisoned chocolates had been sent to one of the accused, Willy Günther, in prison. The public prosecutor, in the statement which he issued, made it clear why: for fear lest 'those who stood behind the murderers of Foreign Minister Rathenau would be betrayed by the evidence which Günther would be giving at the trial'.[2] How far these people can be identified with the leaders of the young Nazi party remains uncertain, but we know what Goebbels wrote to Techow while the latter was serving his sentence of hard labour:

[1] K. Brammer, *Das politische Ergebnis des Rathenau-Prozesses*, Berlin, 1922, pp. 26–29. The book contains a shorthand record of parts of the trial.
[2] Ibid., p. 42.

. . . the nationalist camp stands by you without any reservations whatsoever. This too shows the difference between true nationalists and 'bourgeois' patriots, who only stand by a man when it is safe to do so and it does not offend against the canons of bourgeois propriety.

And again:

I want to shake your hand – it is an inner need for me – and, as it is not permitted for me to acknowledge your deed, I want to join you and your comrades as a man, as a German, as a young, conscious activist, who believes in Germany's resurrection – in spite of everything![1]

Certainly the assassination of Rathenau as an Elder of Zion foreshadowed the lunatic era when the *Protocols* would be proclaimed as ultimate truth by the government of a great European nation. Certain words spoken by the judge in his summing-up were to take on, retrospectively, a depth of meaning which few would have attributed to them in 1922:

Behind the murderers and their accomplices the chief culprit, irresponsible, fanatical antisemitism, lifts its face, distorted with hatred – antisemitism, which reviles the Jew as such, irrespective of the individual, with all those means of calumny of which that vulgar libel, the *Protocols of the Elders of Zion,* is an example; and in this way sows in confused and immature minds the urge to murder. May the sacrificial death of Rathenau, who well knew to what dangers he was exposing himself when he took up his office; may the insight which this trial has brought concerning the consequences of unscrupulous incitement . . . serve to purify the infected air of Germany and to lead Germany, now sinking in mortal sickness in this moral barbarism, towards its cure.[2]

The assassination did indeed act for a time as a salutary shock. A law was introduced for the protection of the Republic, and under its provisions various obscure publicists were prosecuted for continuing to assert that Rathenau had been an Elder of Zion. The Defensive and Offensive Alliance was banned. Ludendorff took fright and in an article in a London newspaper accused the Communists of the murder. Müller von Hausen for his part tried at first to justify the murder by repeating the story of the frieze, but he quickly withdrew it when

[1] E. Techow, *Gemeiner Mörder?!*, Leipzig, 1933, p. 31.
[2] K. Brammer, op. cit., p. 14.

he was sued by Rathenau's mother. And then, from 1924 onwards, the situation in Germany began to change in such a way that even the most fanatical could hardly say just what harm the Elders were doing. A new and more moderate reparations agreement was negotiated, allied troops withdrew from German territory, and in 1926 Germany was received by unanimous vote into the League of Nations. As a result the wave of right-wing extremism ebbed all over Germany. It was a bad time for the *Protocols* – but it was not to last.

CHAPTER VII

The *Protocols* circle the World

1

THE enthusiasm which greeted the *Protocols* in Germany was unique, but that does not mean they were ignored elsewhere. Even in Britain, where antisemitism had never in modern times taken the virulent form familiar on the Continent, and in the United States, where up to that time it had played very little part at all, the forgery attracted serious interest in quarters which might have been expected to know better. Indeed the translations and commentaries which appeared in these two countries in the course of 1920 did a great deal to spread knowledge of the *Protocols* throughout the world – partly of course because they were in English but partly also because of the distinguished names with which they became associated.

In Britain there had been talk of a Jewish world-conspiracy for a couple of years before the *Protocols* appeared. As in Germany, this was conceived as a Jewish-Bolshevist affair – but whereas in Germany the Entente was also thought of as allied with the Jews, here the third party to the conspiracy was of course Germany. An early formulation of this odd theory is contained in a book published in 1918, before the end of the war, and entitled *England Under the Heel of the Jew*. Ironically enough, the bulk of this book consists of translated extracts from the German sociologist Werner Sombart – but that does not prevent the original parts from being as anti-German as they are anti-Jewish and anti-Bolshevik. The anonymous author had discovered that the name Ashkenazim, which embraces the great majority of European Jews, is a Hebrew word for Germans – but had overlooked the fact that anything up to six centuries had elapsed since the ancestors of most of these Jews left Germany. The nightmare which this thought inspired seems already to belong to the world of the *Protocols*:

Finance has become international, and international finance is Jewish finance, and Jewish finance is German finance. These two, become one, are penetrating the veins of all the nations of the earth, poisoning their life-blood and sapping the life out of them. . . .

When once the Ashkenazi-German alliance was cemented and organized throughout the world, the Kaiser could laugh at his enemies, for he had his allies planted in all their banks, all their brothels, all their businesses, all their Stock Exchanges, all their socialist organizations, all their newspapers, all their council-chambers and war-cabinets, in many of their lawyers' secret closets, and on their judicial benches. When England declared war against him, he was disappointed, but he was not unprepared. . . . He knew he could get a horde of Ashkenazi white slavers with their slaves planted on English soil as Belgian refugees all ready to spread vice and disease among troops and civilians. . . . He had thousands of agents of Rasputinism to carry on his usual work among our rulers and legislators. He knew he could keep in our country tens of thousands of Ashkenazi-Bolsheviks to eat English bread, steal English trade and pollute English life. . . . There is no weapon that the Ashkenazi-Hun finds too low for his handling or too small for his consideration. The same approach – Rasputineries and all – as have proved the downfall of Russia are in intense operation in our islands.

Yet, wily though the Kaiser may be, the author believes him to be less the master of the Jews than their slave, for 'the magic powers of money as wielded by the Lords of Lucre are powers of Black Magic at its blackest'.[1]

This was no voice crying in the wilderness, for soon belief in a German-Jewish-Bolshevik conspiracy became widespread – and by no means only among the semi-literate. Early in 1919 the British ambassador in Copenhagen, Lord Kilmarnock, re-ported to the Foreign Secretary, Lord Curzon, that the Bolsheviks were said to comprise chiefly Jews and Germans, who, being active and enterprising, were able to tyrannize the dreamy Russians. More remarkable still, the Foreign Office saw fit to publish in an official report the following observa-tions by a naval chaplain recently returned from Russia: '(Bolshevism) originated in German propaganda, and was, and

[1] *England Under the Heel of the Jew*, London, 1918, pp. 60–2.

is being, carried out by international Jews'. Its aims are 'to buy up all nationalized banks and to open up everywhere branches of German Government banks . . .' and also 'to preach the doctrine of the Socialistic form of managing enterprises amongst the working classes, to encourage their efforts to seize such enterprises and then by means of bankruptcies to get them into German hands', while at the same time 'spreading amongst the masses such views and teachings as may at any time be dictated from Berlin'. And of course this benefits the Jews: 'All business became paralysed, shops were closed, Jews became possessors of most of the business houses. . . .'[1]

The press could hardly be expected to be more cautious than the Foreign Office. By the end of 1919 even the correspondence columns of *The Times* were opened to a passionate debate as to whether the horrors through which Russia was passing could or could not be interpreted as acts of Jewish vengeance. It was a question on which the newspaper's special correspondent in Russia, Robert Wilton, had no doubts at all. Wilton was an Englishman who had been brought up in Russia and who had identified himself completely with the extreme right wing. In his book *The Last Days of the Romanovs*, published in 1920, he declared that the Bolsheviks were simply Jewish agents of the Germans and the revolution nothing but a Jewish-German invasion of Russia. Had not the imperial family been murdered by 'Magyar-Germans', acting on instructions from Jews, who in turn were acting on instructions from 'the Red Kaiser' of Germany? And had not a monument been erected in Moscow to that well-known Jewish hero, Judas Iscariot? Such was the source on which the most authoritative of British newspapers chiefly depended for its understanding of the Russian Revolution.

Meanwhile the *Protocols* was being put into circulation, with the object in the first instance of persuading the Government to persevere with its policy of intervention in Russia. 'It is incredible,' wrote an observer in 1920, 'but it is nevertheless a fact, that these crazy forgeries have played a part behind the

---

[1] *Russia No. 1 (1919). A collection of reports on Bolshevism in Russia*, p. 56. (Report from the Rev. B. S. Lombard to Earl Curzon.) For Lord Kilmarnock's report, ibid., p. 32.

scenes in the international combinations for assisting the anti-Bolshevist reaction in Russia, which has filled so much of the public mind during the last two years, and which have cost this country close on £100,000,000. . . . Russian intelligence officers, armed with doctored typewritten translations of the Nilus *Protocols*, with the anti-British passages carefully expunged, were sent to London . . . where they circulated this precious literature confidentially among cabinet ministers, heads of public departments, and persons of influence in society and journalism. That this campaign was not fruitless is attested by many curious facts. . . .'[1] The campaign culminated in the publication of an anonymous English translation of the *Protocols*, with the title *The Jewish Peril*; this took place in January or February 1920, to coincide with the appearance of the first German translation. The book bore the imprint of Eyre & Spottiswoode Ltd, and this was in itself a great triumph: Eyre & Spottiswoode, the publishers of the Authorised Version of the Bible and of the Prayer Book, carry the title of His (or Her) Majesty's Printers – and this enabled antisemites all over the Continent to proclaim, probably with more malevolence than ignorance, that the *Protocols* had been published with the authority of His Majesty's Government.[2]

The same circles were delighted by the reaction of *The Times*, which on 8 May devoted a long article to the book. On the matter of authenticity *The Times* remained non-committal – but it did note that nobody had yet shown the *Protocols* to be spurious. Here was a work published in 1905, which foretold in an uncanny way the situation of the world, and particularly of Russia, in 1920. An impartial investigation was necessary, for without it how could such a work fail to arouse the worst suspicions? A sombre paragraph reveals what suspicions were already afflicting *The Times* itself:

What are these 'Protocols'? Are they authentic? If so, what malevolent assembly concocted these plans, and gloated over their exposition? Are they a forgery? If so, whence comes the uncanny

[1] L. Wolf, *The Jewish Bogey*, London, 1920, pp. 34–5.
[2] It seems that this edition of the *Protocols* was printed to private commission and therefore bears the imprint of the printers, Eyre & Spottiswoode Ltd, instead of a publisher's imprint. The firm of Eyre & Spottiswoode (Publishers) Ltd was not founded until April 1929.

note of prophecy, prophecy in parts fulfilled, in parts far gone in the way of fulfilment? Have we been struggling these tragic years to blow up and extirpate the secret organization of German world dominion only to find beneath it another, more dangerous because more secret? Have we, by straining every fibre of our national body, escaped a 'Pax Germanica' only to fall into a 'Pax Judæica'? The 'Elders of Zion', as represented in their 'Protocols', are by no means kinder taskmasters than William II and his henchmen would have been.

The Times was not the only responsible journal to express grave perturbation. The following week the *Spectator* devoted not only a long review but also an editorial to *The Jewish Peril*; and though it did not altogether exclude the possibility of forgery, it had little doubt that the *Protocols* were a genuine document of Jewish origin. And what a document! Anyone who has spent long hours trying to make some sense of their nonserse can only feel baffled to read, in what was one of the most sophisticated of British weeklies, that 'the "Protocols" are of very great ability', 'brilliant in (their) moral perversity and intellectual depravity' and indeed 'one of the most re-markable productions of their kind'.[1]

Yet in the first months after the publication of the *Protocols* there were hesitations and misgivings. Both *The Times* and the *Spectator* were inclined to acquit the majority of Jews of collaborating with the horrible Elders of Zion; and both published letters – not all of them from Jews – arguing against the genuineness of the *Protocols*. The right-wing newspaper the *Morning Post*, on the other hand, showed no such restraint. Just as *The Times* was influenced by its correspondent in Russia, Robert Wilton, so the *Morning Post* accepted every-thing it was told by its correspondent in Russia, Victor Marsden. Like Wilton, Marsden was an Englishman who had lived many years in Russia and had adopted, with passion, the outlook of Russian right-wingers. And if Wilton could by imagination conjure up a Soviet monument to Judas Iscariot, Marsden went further and produced a new translation of the *Protocols* (it is still on sale in London today). It is not therefore surprising that in the summer of 1920 the *Morning Post* should have published a series of eighteen articles expounding

[1] *The Spectator*, issue of 15 May 1920.

the full myth of the Judeo-Masonic conspiracy, with of course due reference to the *Protocols*.

If the productions of Wichtl and 'Wilhelm Meister' reflect the resentment of German ultra-nationalists when confronted with defeat and revolution, these articles reflect the resentment of British ultra-nationalists at the stirrings of independence among the colonial peoples of the Empire. And just like *Auf Vorposten*, the *Morning Post* recognizes quite clearly that tales which before the war would have been dismissed with a shrug could find believers now: 'The war has produced a complete change of mentality, because we have had concrete proof of close connection between rebellion in Ireland, trouble in Egypt, disaffection in India, revolution in Russia, to mention only a few of the disorders brought about by Germany. . . . But it is becoming every day more evident that the conspiracy against civilization did not finish with the defeat of Germany. . . . Behind the scenes was a 'formidable sect' using the Germans for their own ends instead of being used by them, and when Germany fell and German money disappeared, the conspiracy still went on unimpeded.' Signs of the conspiracy at work were not hard to find. Who could doubt, for instance, that the assassination in 1909 of an eminent member of the Indian Civil Service, though carried out in London by an Indian, had really been engineered from Paris by a German woman and a handsome Jewess who, owing to the combined support of Jewry and of Continental Freemasonry, wielded immense power? For of course at the heart of the whole world-conspiracy were Jews, and religious Jews at that: 'The fundamental notion of the "formidable sect" is the destruction of Christianity and all religion except the Jewish'.[1]

It might be thought that such stuff would scarcely penetrate beyond the lunatic fringe on the extreme Right, but this was by no means the case. When in the autumn of 1920 these articles were reprinted as a book with the title *The Cause of World Unrest*, and with a preface by the editor of the *Morning Post* himself, they produced a noticeable heightening of tension. In October the staid *Spectator*, shedding all caution, produced an editorial which showed how things were changing. 'There are nations,' it stated, 'who will avoid, if possible,

[1] *The Cause of World Unrest*, London, 1920, pp. 190-4.

submitting their political status to a searching diagnosis. The *Morning Post*, greatly to its honour, realizes that the function of a newspaper is that of the watchdog. . . . The evidence that the paper brings to support its plea of conspiracy is clearly of enough substance and of enough importance to justify its action. . . . We hold that a case for inquiry has been made out, and we most sincerely wish that some body of the nature of a Royal Commission could be appointed to inquire into the whole subject.' The commission would investigate whether there existed a world-wide conspiracy under Jewish leadership and whether it was supported by the mass of religious Jews as a means of destroying Christianity. Should the answer be in the affirmative 'we shall be justified in moving with great caution in our admission of Jews to the fullest rank of citizenship. . . . We must drag the conspirators into the open, tear off their ugly masks, and show the world how ridiculous as well as how evil and dangerous are such pests of society.'[1]

The *Spectator* was seconded by *Blackwood's Magazine*, which insisted that if the country was to be saved from Bolshevism Jews must be immediately excluded from all influence, public or private, on government. A new weekly called *Plain English* was founded by Lord Alfred Douglas for the express purpose of antisemitic propaganda; it swore to the genuineness of the *Protocols* and even asserted that, on instructions from Jewish financiers, Winston Churchill had forged a telegram from Admiral Beatty, so as to enable the German fleet to escape after the battle of Jutland. Another journal, *The Hidden Hand*, was published by a group of professional antisemites called The Britons; it printed not only long commentaries on the *Protocols* but also the Zunder document, and proclaimed that the miners' strikes were all the work of Jews.

For a moment it looked as though antisemitism of the kind that was at work in Germany might become a political factor in Britain also, but in the end nothing came of it. In August 1921 *The Times* published on its centre page, on three consecutive days, the proofs that the *Protocols* were a forgery based on the *Dialogue aux Enfers*, and for good measure added a resounding leader entitled 'The End of the Protocols'. So far as Britain was concerned it was in effect their end. Eyre &

[1] *The Spectator*, issue of 16 October 1920.

Spottiswoode had already declined to reprint them, and now the reputable press stopped talking about them. They continued (and still continue) to circulate, but with the imprint only of that obscure body, The Britons. Lord Alfred Douglas argued that Maurice Joly was really Moses Joël, so the *Protocols* were Jewish after all; Baron Sydenham continued to proclaim that the *Protocols* proved the identity of Judaism, Pan-Germanism, and Bolshevism and to lament 'the failure of western minds to fathom the depths of eastern intrigue'; but these were isolated eccentrics.[1] Even Nesta Webster's well-known books, which interpret all modern history in terms of a conspiracy of Illuminati and Freemasons, are rather non-committal about the *Protocols*. And when, in the 1930s, the British Union of Fascists came into being, it too found the forgery too thoroughly discredited to be much use. By British standards the triumphs of 1920 had been impressive, but they were never repeated.

2

Things were different in the United States, where the *Protocols* enjoyed a limited but lasting vogue. There too they were first put into circulation, in typescript, by Russian right-wingers who were concerned to influence government departments. Then, in October 1919, extracts from the *Protocols* were printed in a series of articles in the *Public Ledger*, of Philadelphia. The articles, with headings like 'Red Bible Counsels Appeal to Violence' and 'Reds Plot to Smash World in 1919', were sensational enough – but all references to Jews had been removed, so that the plot seemed a purely Bolshevik affair. By the spring of 1920, following the publication of *The Jewish Peril* in Britain, this interpretation of the matter was being discarded. 'Trotsky Leads Jew-Radicals to World Rule. Bolshevism only a Tool for His Scheme', proclaimed the *Chicago Tribune* on 19 June; and it continued:

---

[1] Lord Alfred Douglas in his paper *Plain English*, issue of 27 August 1921; Baron Sydenham in an article in *The Nineteenth Century and After*, issue of November 1921, later reprinted by The Britons as a pamphlet, *The Jewish World Problem*.

For the last two years army intelligence officers, members of the various secret organizations of the Entente, have been bringing in reports of a world revolutionary movement other than Bolshevism. At first these reports confused the two, but latterly the lines they have taken have begun to be more and more clear.

Bolshevism aims for the overthrow of existing society and the establishment of an international brotherhood of men who work with their hands as rulers of the world. The second movement aims for the establishment of a new racial domination of the world. So far as the British, French and our own department's inquiry have been able to trace, the moving spirits in the second scheme are Jewish radicals. . . .

Within the ranks of Communism is a group of this party, but it does not stop there. To its leaders, Communism is only an incident. . . .

They are ready to use the Islamic revolt, hatred by the central empires for England, Japan's designs on India, and commercial rivalry between America and Japan. . . .

As any movement of world revolution must be, this is primarily anti-Anglo-Saxon.

For the United States antisemitic propaganda of this kind was something new, but it came at the right moment. Although the war had brought incomparably less suffering to the United States than to the European belligerents, it had proved a very disorientating experience – not least because of the abruptness with which it ended. Just when the nation was at last thoroughly roused to fight, when it had suffered no great losses and was in fact only beginning to feel its strength – suddenly there was no enemy left. It was not a state of affairs that could be easily accepted. The American Defense Society hastened to warn the public not to buy German products, on the grounds that they might be poisoned or deliberately infected with deadly bacteria. The Ku-Klux-Klan underwent a dramatic revival. Soon, however, fear and rage became concentrated on one foe: Bolshevism, along with every group that, rightly or wrongly, was suspected of sympathizing with it.

People who shortly before had accused one another of being pro-German now bandied charges of pro-Bolshevism. The Department of Justice reported that it had a card-index of 60,000 suspects; and the figure was surprisingly modest, for it was common knowledge that Bolshevism was stalking the country. Even the debate about prohibition tended to be

conducted in these terms, so that while the state superinten-
dent of the Anti-Saloon League of New York declared that
'the main centres of anarchistic activities have been wet
centres', the Association Opposed to National Prohibition
pointed out that 'all radical elements . . . are earnest advocates
of prohibition, as they assert that it is driving into the radical
groups many men who in normal times are law-abiding men'.[1]
No category of citizens was exempt from the suspicion of
subversion – the Senate committee investigating Bolshevism
was even asked to investigate the suffragettes. How could the
Jews have remained untouched?

The time was indeed ripe for full editions of the *Protocols*,
and they duly appeared – one in New York, with the title
Praemonitus Praemunitus (i.e. 'Forewarned is forearmed'), and
another in Boston, as part of a volume called *The Protocols and
World Revolution*. Above all from May to October 1920 Henry
Ford's newspaper the *Dearborn Independent* published a long
series of articles which forms an American counterpart to the
effort of the *Morning Post*; and in November these too were
republished as a book, *The International Jew: the world's
foremost problem*. The *Dearborn Independent* had a circulation
of some 300,000. As for *The International Jew*, thanks to a big
publicity campaign and the prestige of Ford's name it made a
powerful impact, particularly among the rural population –
for, just as in Europe, the myth of the Jewish world-conspiracy proved most attractive to people who were deeply
attached to the traditional ways and values of the countryside
and deeply disoriented by modern civilization.[2] Half a million
copies of the book were put into circulation in the United
States.[3] Moreover it was translated into German, Russian, and

[1] Quoted in C. Merz, *And Then Came Ford*, New York, 1929, p. 177.

[2] On the connexion between the American agrarian tradition and
antisemitism see J. Higham, *Strangers in the Land: patterns of American
nativism 1860–1925*, revised edition, New York, 1963 (p. 285 for Ford);
S. Lipset, 'Three decades of the Radical Right', in D. Bell (ed.), *The
Radical Right*, revised edition, New York, 1964; and cf. A. Nevins and
F. E. Hill, *Ford, Expansion and Challenge, 1915–1933*, New York, 1957,
p. 323.

[3] It is true that many of these were given away, and it is also true that
the circulation of the *Dearborn Independent* depended partly on semi-
compulsory buying by Ford agencies and dealers.

Spanish; in due course a shortened version of it was to become a stock item in Nazi propaganda. All in all *The International Jew* probably did more than any other work to make the *Protocols* world-famous.

The *Protocols* are indeed all things to all men. As interpreted here for an American public the world-conspiracy is a matter of Jew-Bolsheviks but certainly not of Freemasons; and the most horrible thing about it is that it undermines puritan morality. The ways in which the Elders seduce American youth are both unexpected and ingenious: 'Every influence that leads to lightness and looseness in Gentile youth today heads up in a Jewish source. Did the young people of the world devise the "sport clothes" which have had so deleterious an effect on the youth of the times?' But the rot starts earlier still: under the cover of such socialistic pretences as public safety 'children are hardly free to play nowadays except under play-masters appointed by the State, among whom, curiously enough, an astonishing proportion of Jews manage to find a place. . . . All this focuses up to the World Plan for the subjugation of the Gentiles. . . .'[1] Where this kind of thing can lead is seen in Soviet Russia; there sex knowledge is taught in schools, which means that the young are 'compulsorily drawn through sloughs of filth . . . with consequences that are too pitiable to relate'. In this way the Jewish rulers are destroying the moral fibre of Russia. For all Bolsheviks are Jews: and we are given a picture of Lenin and his wife, who in reality were childless and had not a drop of Jewish blood between them, chatting away in Yiddish with their little ones.[2]

It is a very strange book indeed; and one of the strangest things about it, considering how recently the United States had been at war with Germany, is that it adopts the German interpretation of the *Protocols*. Jewry, imagined as a closely organized, world-wide political power, is referred to as 'All-Judaan', which is a nonsensical name coined by German anti-semites. And the secret government of 'All-Judaan' – in other words, the Elders of Zion – is supposed to be allied not with Germany but with Britain. The war was really a war of 'All-Judaan' against Germany; it was a triumph for the Elders

---

[1] *The International Jew*, London edition, 1920, pp. 135–6.
[2] Ibid., pp. 214, 217.

that, by their control of the press, they had been able to drive whole nations to hate Germany; and the final victory was theirs alone. At the same time there is no doubt where the Elders found their most whole-hearted support: London was their 'first capital' and Paris their second. With Britain in particular the secret Jewish government has a most useful agreement: 'its fleet is the British fleet which guards from hindrance the progress of all-Jewish world-economy. . . . In return, All-Judaan assures Britain an undisturbed political and territorial world rule.'[1]

At present the Elders are intent on obtaining dominion over the United States, and they are making astonishingly rapid progress. In the United States a few decades have sufficed for a campaign which in Europe lasted 1,500 years, and it is clear why: 'certain mistaken *ideas* of liberalism, certain flabby *ideas* of tolerance' have been put about by the Elders and are rapidly undermining the American will to resist.[2] The United States would do well to study the cases of Russia and Germany; both countries have been brought low but both are now rising in revolt. Germany is already bestirring herself to bring Jewish power under control; as for Russia – 'when Russia turns, a shudder will run through the earth'. The United States must summon up the same ruthlessness; and quickly too, for with the subjugation of the United States the great conspiracy will reach its culmination, the establishment of the Davidic monarch as ruler of the world: 'As the Jew is a past master of symbolism, it may not be without significance that the Bolshevik Star has one point less than the Star of David.' For there is still one point to be fulfilled in the World Programme as outlined in the Protocols – and that is the enthronement of 'our leader'. When he comes, the World Autocrat for whom the whole programme is framed, 'the sixth point may be added'.[3]

Some facts are known about the origins of this extraordinary work. A Dr Edward A. Rumely, who had been a very active member of a German propaganda ring in the United States during the First World War, was a close friend of Henry Ford. This enabled him to find a place on the staff of *The Dearborn*

---

[1] *The International Jew*, p. 30.
[2] Ibid., p. 141.   [3] Ibid., p. 233.

Independent for a German, Dr August Müller; and it seems to have been Dr Müller who wrote most of *The International Jew*. Also associated with the undertaking was a Russian refugee, Boris Brasol. In Russia this man had served under the fanatically antisemitic Minister of Justice Shchegolitov, who organized the Beiliss murder trial, and he himself believed passionately in stories of ritual murder. In 1918 he was employed by the United States Government on secret service work, and this enabled him to introduce American intelligence officers to the *Protocols*. He did much to promote the Boston edition of the *Protocols*, which was the work of the daughter of a tsarist general, Natalie de Bogory; and he also established contact with Ford's secretary and passed him materials on the *Protocols*. From all this it emerges that *The International Jew* was far more a Russo-German than an American product.[1, 2]

The publication of this book and of the *Protocols* produced some sharp reactions in the United States. President Wilson, the former Secretary of State Lansing, the Cardinal Archbishop of Boston, were among those who protested most vigorously. American Jews themselves refused to submit passively to these slanders and launched a campaign against the *Dearborn Independent*. Particularly active was the American diplomat Herman Bernstein, whose book *The History of a Lie* (1921) is one of the earliest studies of the forging of the *Protocols*; some years later, despite the legal difficulties involved, he even brought a libel action against Ford for publishing such tales. And in the end the great industrialist did recant. In June 1927 he wrote to the president of the American Jewish Committee, Louis Marshall, disclaiming all responsibility for the articles in *The Dearborn Independent* and for the book they had become. Although he owned both publications, he had no idea what was published in them; and in this whole matter he had been deceived by men

---

[1] Later Rumely became executive secretary of the so-called Committee for Constitutional Government, which between 1937 and 1944 spent some $2,000,000 on fighting Roosevelt; while Brasol was active in Nazi intrigues up to 1939.

[2] On the intrigues around Ford's campaign see Norman Hapgood, 'The inside story of Henry Ford's Jew-mania', six articles in *Hearst's International*, from June to November 1922.

on whom he had relied implicitly. Shocked to discover what
had been done in his name, he solemnly retracted the accusations contained in *The International Jew* and undertook to
withdraw the book from circulation.

So far so good – but it was not in Ford's power to abolish
The International Jew. Especially in Germany its influence
was great and lasting. Because of it, Hitler kept a photograph
of Ford beside his desk for years; and when he heard, in 1923,
that Ford might be running for President of the United States,
he commented: 'I wish that I could send some of my shock
troops to Chicago and other big American cities to help in the
elections. . . . We look to Heinrich Ford as the leader of the
growing Fascist movement in America. . . . We have just had
his anti-Jewish articles translated and published. The book is
being circulated in millions throughout Germany.'[1] What is
more, the political antisemites in Germany refused to take the
book out of circulation even when Ford asked them to, and
were still distributing and advertising it at the outbreak of the
Second World War.

But the harm was not confined to Germany, for in the end
The International Jew was translated into sixteen languages.
Ford's recantation can have reached only a few of the hundreds of thousands, or millions, who had been encouraged by
his reputation as a man of affairs to accept the *Protocols* as
genuine – and one may fairly wonder how many of those few
took it seriously. For there is no real doubt that Ford knew
perfectly well what he was sponsoring. He founded the *Dearborn Independent* in 1919 as a vehicle for his own 'philosophy'
and he took a keen and constant interest in it; much of the
contents consisted simply of edited versions of his talk. It is
not conceivable that when, on 20 May 1920, the paper suddenly changed its format and began its attacks on the Jews, he
should have failed to notice. But apart from this, Ford did in
fact commit himself publicly on the subject of the Jewish
world-conspiracy, in two books published in 1922 – *The
Amazing Story of Henry Ford*, by James M. Miller, and *My
Life and Work*, by Henry Ford in collaboration with S.
Crowther. Nobody who studies certain passages written at his

[1] *Chicago Tribune*, quoted in J. R. Carlson, *Under Cover*, New York,
1943 edition, p. 210.

dictation can doubt that at least by that time he knew the *Protocols* and was determined that people should believe in them.[1]

Did he himself believe? At first sight it seems incredible that a man who could build up a huge industrial empire from scratch could be as naïve as that. Yet some of the things Ford did can be explained in no other way. When *The International Jew* began to make its impact a prominent American Jew, Isaac Landman, offered to provide enough money to enable the world's leading detectives to establish once and for all whether a secret Jewish government did or did not exist; whatever the results might be, they were to be printed in at least a hundred leading newspapers. Ford rejected the offer – but instead of leaving the matter at that, he himself put a squad of agents into New York to unmask the operations of the secret government. These agents – some of them fanatics and others mere crooks – shadowed prominent Jews, investigated such improbable bodies as the Shipping Board, and above all carried on a melodramatic correspondence with headquarters at Detroit, using code names as signatures. In the end they heard of the official New York Jewish community organization, which under the name Kehilla (Yiddish for 'kahal') was chiefly concerned with protecting and educating Jewish immigrants. This, they announced, was the secret government in whose hands President Wilson, Herbert Hoover, and Colonel House were willing tools.[2,3]

That Ford lent himself to such a performance strongly suggests that in this matter at least he was no cynic but a true believer. And one can see what could have made him so.

[1] E.g. pp. 240–2 in *The 'New Era Philosophy'*, by Henry Ford, which forms Part II of *The Amazing Story of Henry Ford*; and pp. 250–2 in *My Life and Work*. Both books were published in 1922.

[2] The detectives spent much energy in trying to trace a private telephone-line from the home of one particular Jew, Justice Brandeis of the United States Supreme Court, to the room in the White House where President Wilson lay gravely ill. They failed – not surprisingly, as Justice Brandeis had no private telephone at all. Two former senior members of the secret service joined Ford's detective service; they were both completely taken in by the 'White' Russian Rodionov, who claimed to have access to thirteen additional 'Protocols' 'in the original Hebrew'.

[3] Cf. J. N. Leonard, *The Tragedy of Henry Ford*, New York, 1932, pp. 203–4.

Paradoxically, this man who did so much to create the modern world of mass production and cheap travel detested modernity. He abominated cities, especially New York, and was convinced that the only true Americans were those in the farms and small towns of the Middle West; he cherished a sentimental nostalgia for the pre-industrial past. We have seen how easily such attitudes can lead to the most virulent form of political antisemitism. Moreover, Ford had absolutely no understanding of the complex ways in which societies operate and history is made. 'All the world needs for the guidance of its life could be written on two pages of a child's copybook,' he wrote in the *Dearborn Independent*. A man who could believe that could also believe that all the transformations and up-heavals and torments of the modern world have a single explanation, enshrined in the few dozen pages of the *Protocols*. All in all the *Protocols* probably owe their most influential backing less to Ford's Machiavellianism than to his astounding innocence.[1]

After Germany, Britain, and the United States, the countries which gave the *Protocols* the warmest welcome and did most to make them a force in world affairs were Poland and France. The first Polish edition appeared early in 1920 and was sold out by 1921; whereupon the same translation was republished, with an introduction and a conclusion, by the antisemitic organization Rozwój ('Development'). Poland, of course, included a large part of what in the Tsar's empire had been the Pale of Jewish Settlement, and antisemitism was a well-established tradition; so it is not surprising that the *Protocols* should have had a considerable impact in the newly created state. The Roman Catholic clergy did much to encourage belief in them. In the summer of 1920, when Poland seemed likely to be overrun by the Red Army, the Polish episcopate sent to Roman Catholic bishops throughout the world a 'cry for help and rescue for Poland' which was clearly inspired by the *Protocols*. It reads as follows:

The real object of Bolshevism is world-conquest. The race which has the leadership of Bolshevism in its hands, has already in the

[1] Ford's naïvety emerges clearly in the conversation recorded in W. C. Richards, *The Last Billionnaire: Henry Ford*, New York, 1949, pp. 89–90.

past subjugated the whole world by means of gold and the banks, and now, driven by the everlasting imperialistic greed which flows in its veins, is already aiming at the final subjugation of the nations under the yoke of its rule. . . . The hatred of Bolshevism is directed against Christ and his Church, especially because those who are the leaders of Bolshevism bear in their blood the traditional hatred for Christianity. Bolshevism is in truth the embodiment and incarnation of the spirit of Antichrist on earth.[1]

This document was particularly misguided, because the overwhelming majority of Polish Jews were in fact staunch opponents of Bolshevism. But the appeal, which was signed by two cardinals, two archbishops, and three bishops, was none the less potent for that. It did nothing to bring help to Poland but, read out in churches all over the world, it certainly impelled many Catholics to accept the myth of the Jewish world-conspiracy. And in Poland itself it must have helped to provoke the many murders of Jews which occurred during the Russian invasion.

In France the *Protocols* also enjoyed widespread and continuous favour. Interest was aroused by the first English translation and the notice which this received in *The Times*. Royalist journals associated with the Action Française reviewed the book, while the independent weekly *L'Opinion* produced an abbreviated version of it in three articles on 'The origins of Bolshevism'. This was in June 1920, and in the following three months there appeared no less than three complete translations. The daily newspaper *La Libre Parole*, faithful to the spirit in which Edouard Drumont had founded it twenty-eight years before, printed the first French translation of the entire *Protocols*, extending over nearly a month of issues. The review *La Vieille France*, edited by Urbain Gohier, also printed the whole text; and both these translations were reissued as popular pamphlets. More successful still was the translation dignified by the name of Mgr Jouin, *curé* of the church of St Augustine in Paris. This venerable ecclesiastic (he was born in 1844) had begun his campaign against the Judeo-Masonic conspiracy in 1909, by founding the *Revue Internationale des Sociétés secrètes*; he even established contact

[1] B. Segel, *Die Protokolle der Weisen von Zion*, p. 171.

before the war with the *pogromshchik* Butmi. After publishing a new translation of the *Protocols* in his review he republished it, in the autumn of 1920, as the first volume in a series entitled *Le Péril judéo-maçonnique*. As it turned out, this series was to run to five volumes in which the principal early versions of the *Protocols*, Russian, German, and Polish, were subjected to minute comparison and elaborated in long commentaries. The industrious author devoted seven years to this rewarding task, which he completed at the age of eighty-two. Elevated to the prelacy by Benedict XV, when he was already editor of the *Revue Internationale des Sociétés secrètes*, he was appointed apostolic prothonotary by Pius XI, when he was known as a leading sponsor of the *Protocols*; and these distinctions must certainly have added to the prestige of his publications.

A fourth translation appeared early in 1921 and it was to be the most popular of all. The only French version to be translated direct from the Russian, it was the work of Roger Lambelin, a life-long royalist who, after heading the political office of the Duke of Orleans, had left the old-style royalists in favour of the demagogic and antisemitic Action Française. This translation was outstandingly successful – it ran to sixteen editions within a year; by 1925 the figure had risen to twenty-five, and sales continued excellent right down to the Second World War. Today it is Lambelin's introduction that claims attention, as a historical document to set alongside the lucubrations of *Auf Vorposten* and the *Morning Post*. All, of course, are agreed that Bolshevism is the work of the Elders – but there agreements stops. Müller von Hausen might argue that the British and French Governments enjoyed the special protection of the Elders, and the *Morning Post* that the German Government and the Elders were indissolubly allied – Roger Lambelin achieved a new and ingenious synthesis: 'The British Government, under the premiership of Mr David Lloyd George, is completely bound to the policies of world Jewry. . . . In the United States, under President Wilson, the Jewish conquest was as obvious as in England.' But the Elders cared for Germany too: 'At the moment of the armistice and the first international negotiations the Jews rendered Germany a decisive service by camouflaging her states as democratic or socialist countries.' In fact France was the only sufferer from 'this strange peace, more favourable to the vanquished than to the victors – except for the Anglo-Saxons. . . .'[1]

Alongside the editions of the *Protocols* produced by Frenchmen there appeared a number of works by right-wing Russians who had taken refuge in France. Two of these give the complete text of the *Protocols*, with long and fantastic commentaries: *L'Empereur Nicolas II et les Juifs*, by General Nechvolodov, published in 1924; and a work which became a standard manual for adepts of the *Protocols: Le Juif notre maître* (1931), by 'Mrs. L. Fry', who was the wife of a Russian called Shishmarev. From the point of view of the public all this formed a single body of writing. Representatives of the extreme right wing of French politics combined with the defeated supporters of the Russian autocracy to make the *Protocols* known in France.

It is a familiar picture, and one which was repeated in country after country. Vinberg, Shabelsky-Bork, and somewhat later Schwarz-Bostunitsch in Germany, Brasol and Cherep-Spiridovich in the United States, Zhevakhov and Schwarz-Bostunitsch in Yugoslavia, Subbotin in South America, Rodzayevsky in the Far East – these and many other former tsarist generals, officers and right-wing politicians played a decisive part in the dissemination of the *Protocols*. These people collaborated with all kinds of right-wing bodies for the furtherance of their own aim, which was restoration of the autocracy in Russia; and these different bodies used them for *their* aims, which varied from country to country. Out of this collaboration came the finance and the organization which were required to carry the *Protocols* across the world.

Save in Britain the unmasking of the forgery in 1921 seems to have made little difference. Some editors and sponsors of the *Protocols* copied Lord Alfred Douglas and pretended that Joly was really a Jewish revolutionary called Moses Joël; but most of them avoided the whole matter and simply maintained that the *Protocols* must be genuine if the processes and events they foretold were taking place. And who could deny that the age was indeed one of wars and revolutions, slumps and inflation?

[1] Lambelin's introduction to his translation of the *Protocols*, pp. vi, x–xii in the edition of 1935.

So the *Protocols* proceeded unchecked on their triumphant way. A whole international network of sponsors and 'students' of the *Protocols* came into existence. Journals all over the world collaborated in expounding them and exchanged 'information' and 'documents' – *The Dearborn Independent* in the United States, *The Patriot* and *The British Guardian* in Britain, *La Vieille France* and *La Libre Parole* in France, the *National Tidsskrift* in Norway, the *Dansk National Tidsskrift* in Denmark, *Dwa Grosze* and *Pro Patria* in Poland, and of course many journals in Germany. To the various German, English, and French translations there were soon added translations into Swedish, Danish, Norwegian, Finnish, Rumanian, Hungarian, Lithuanian, Polish, Bulgarian, Italian, Greek, Japanese, and Chinese. And meanwhile in Germany the *Protocols* were being incorporated into the ideology of a rising and ruthless political party.

CHAPTER VIII

Germanic Racism, Hitler and the *Protocols*

1

WHEN the judge at Techow's trial referred to Rathenau's 'sacrificial death' he spoke truer than he knew; for Rathenau was not simply assassinated as an Elder of Zion, he was offered up as a human sacrifice to the sun-god of ancient Germanic religion. The murder was timed to coincide with the summer solstice; and when the news was published, young Germans gathered on hilltops to celebrate simultaneously the turning of the year and the destruction of one who symbolized the powers of darkness.[1] What are we to make of these extraordinary facts?

The *Protocols* had indeed acquired a new dimension when they came into contact with that peculiar outlook which is known as *völkisch*[2] or sometimes as 'the Germanic ideology'.[3] The beginnings of this outlook – which was really a pseudo-religion – go back to the Napoleonic Wars. Germany is by no means the only country which first began to develop a national consciousness as a result of being invaded – but it so happened that in this case the invading power was itself the standard-bearer of the modern age, the champion of democracy, liberalism, rationalism. It is normal to reject the values of the invader and to affirm their opposites – and this meant that German nationalism was from the start partly backward-looking, partly inspired by a repudiation of modernity and a

---

[1] *Mitteilungen aus dem Verein zur Abwehr des Antisemitismus*, issue of 29 September 1922, p. 98.   [2] From *das Volk*, the people.

[3] On the *völkisch* outlook from the 1860s to Hitler see G. L. Mosse, *The Crisis of German Ideology*, New York, 1964; and for its beginnings, from the Napoleonic wars to 1850, see Eleonore Sterling, *Er ist wie Du*, Munich, 1956.

nostalgia for a past which was imagined as in every way unlike the modern world. And this attitude not only persisted but was intensified when economic developments pitchforked Germany into that same modern world. At the very time when Germany was turning into a great industrial power, a land of factories and cities, technology and bureaucracy, many Germans were dreaming of an archaic world of Germanic peasants, bound together by bonds of blood in a 'natural', 'organic' community.

Such a view of the world requires an anti-figure, and this was supplied partly by the liberal West but also, and more effectively, by the Jews. As we have seen, it is characteristic of latter-day, political antisemites that they see 'the Jew' not only as an uncanny, demonic being but also as an embodiment of modernity, a symbol of all those forces in the modern world which they themselves fear and hate. This was the case also with German antisemites of the *völkisch* variety – but with a difference. When these people looked to the past, to the ideal state which they supposed to have preceded the modern age, they looked far beyond throne and altar, back to an infinitely remote and almost entirely mythical world. For them 'the Jew' was not only, or mainly, the destroyer of kings and the enemy of the Church – he was above all the age-old antagonist of the Germanic peasant, he was the force which for two thousand years had been undermining the true, original German way of life. Historical Christianity itself was a Jewish creation which had helped to destroy the archaic Germanic world. Now capitalism, liberalism, democracy, socialism, and the urban way of life were continuing the process; together they made up 'the Jew's' world, the modern age which was his creation and in which he flourished.

The first major proponent of this outlook was an eccentric scholar, Paul Bötticher, usually known by his adopted name of Paul de Lagarde.[1] In his major work, *Deutsche Schriften* (*German Writings*), published in 1878, Lagarde expressed his disillusionment with the united Germany which had just come into being. He demanded a higher unity: that of the German

---

[1] On Paul de Lagarde, see F. Stern, *The Politics of Cultural Despair*, Berkeley and Los Angeles, 1961; and for a briefer account G. L. Mosse, op. cit., Chapter 2.

Volk, living once more as it had lived in the remote past and thereby realizing the divine intention for the world. But he recognized that this new order could not easily be achieved, and this he attributed to the Jews. Though he really knew nothing of Jewish religion he was convinced that it was at the heart of that modernity which was so fatal to the *Volk.* He foresaw a mortal struggle between the Jewish and the German ways of life – and when he talked of struggle, he meant physical violence: the Jews, he proclaimed, must be exterminated like bacilli. It was not for nothing that in 1944, when the Nazis were completing their vast massacres, an anthology of Lagarde's work was distributed to the troops on the eastern front.[1]

Yet at other times Lagarde could advocate the total assimilation of the German Jews into the German people. This was because for him Jews still meant simply the adherents of the Jewish religion, or what he imagined as that religion; he did not think of them as a 'race'. But at that very time the pseudo-science of German racism was coming into being. In 1873 Wilhelm Marr – the probable inventor of the word 'anti-semitism' – published a book with the significant title *Der Sieg des Judenthums über das Germanenthum* . . . (*The Victory of Jewry over Germandom, considered from a non-denominational point of view*), and in 1881 Eugen Dühring, a lecturer in economics and philosophy at Berlin University, published *Die Judenfrage als Rassen-, Sitten- und Kulturfrage* (*The Jewish Question as a Question of Race, Morals and Civilization*). In these works the Jews are shown not simply as evil but as irremediably evil, the source of their depravity lies no longer simply in their religion but in their very blood. In the 1890s this view of the matter was adopted and popularized by that tireless propagandist Theodor Fritsch – the same who, a generation later, was to publish the *Protocols.* In the innumerable pamphlets and periodicals put out by the Hammer publishing house, Fritsch proclaimed that by proving 'scientically' the depravity of the Jewish and the sublimity of the German 'race', German racists were inaugurating not only a prodigious advance in human knowledge but a new epoch of human history. The fact that there is no such thing as a

[1] F. Stern, op. cit., p. 63, footnote.

'German race' or a 'Jewish race' was of course ignored by all these writers.

Finally, in 1899, Houston Stewart Chamberlain—an Englishman by birth and the son of a British admiral, but a German by choice and eventually by nationality – published his two-volume work *Die Grundlagen des neunzehnten Jahrhunderts* (*Foundations of the Nineteenth Century*), which thanks to its eloquence and its appearance of learning became the Bible of the whole *völkisch*-racist movement. Here all human history was presented as a bitter struggle between spirituality, embodied in the German 'race', and materialism, embodied in the Jewish 'race' – the only two pure races, for all the others were but a 'chaos of peoples'. In Chamberlain's view the Jewish 'race' had been relentlessly striving, down the ages, to secure absolute dominion over all other nations. If once this 'race' were decisively defeated, the Germanic 'race' would be free to realize its own divinely appointed destiny – which was to create a new, radiant world, transfused with a noble spirituality and mysteriously combining modern technology and science with the rural, hierarchical culture of earlier times.[1]

This *völkisch*-racist view of the world was not by any means shared by all Germans. The nobility and the great industrialists disdained it; and so, at the other end of the social scale, did the industrial working class organized in the Social-Democratic movement. The reason was that these strata of German society were relatively secure in their self-esteem – the nobility and the industrialists because they enjoyed the reality of social and political dominance, the workers because their Marxist indoctrination – unrivalled for its thoroughness in any other country – inspired them with a sense of historic mission. More surprisingly, the peasantry too was uninterested. When peasants became actively antisemitic, as they did at various times in various places, it was always for specific economic reasons directly affecting themselves; the *völkisch* glorification of a mythical peasantry left them cold. But the *völkisch*-racist outlook did make a great appeal to certain sections of the middle class. The explanation for this lies in the curious history of the German middle class in the nineteenth and early twentieth centuries.[1]

Two strata of the middle class were involved: on the one hand artisans and small retailers, on the other hand university students and graduates. It has often been remarked that artisans and small retailers were peculiarly prone to anti-semitism and in due course provided the bulk of the votes which brought Hitler to power. There is nothing mysterious about this. These sections of the population were survivals from an earlier age and they were gravely threatened by the development of modern capitalism. Though the Marxist prophecy that they would inevitably be proletarianized proved wrong, they did indeed live in a state of almost perpetual crisis. Barely able to cope with the new world of giant industrial and commercial undertakings, lacking even that rudimentary understanding of it which industrial workers received from their Marxist training, struggling frantically to preserve their status, these people felt an overwhelming need for a scapegoat.

The Jews were perfectly suited for the role – though not, as was commonly said, because they 'created' modern capitalism, or because they occupied the commanding heights in the German economy, or because they were mostly well-to-do, or because they were obviously foreign. In reality German Jews constituted a tiny minority with a falling birthrate, so that left to themselves they would in any case probably have disappeared by the end of the century. They mostly identified themselves passionately with the German fatherland, and they had gone very far on the road to total assimilation. A large proportion of them belonged to the lower middle class and shared all the hazards which that implied. Jews had no place among the giants of industry and their role in banking was a very limited one. And yet in spite of all this, German Jewry

[1] For the sociology of the *völkisch*-racist outlook see, in addition to Pulzer and Mosse, the penetrating article by H. P. Bahrdt, 'Gesellschaftliche Voraussetzungen des Antisemitismus', in the symposium *Entscheidungsjahr 1932* (ed. W. E. Mosse), Tübingen, 1965; and the works by P. W. Massing, Eva G. Reichmann and A. Leschnitzer, listed in the Bibliographical Note.

was the obvious scapegoat for the resentments of the lower middle class.

There were various reasons for this. There were the concentrations of well-to-do Jews in certain areas of Berlin and Hamburg, which could lead the unthinking to suppose that all Jews were rich, even that all rich people were Jews. There was the typical Jewish zeal in getting the sons to universities and thence into the liberal professions, which brought them into direct conflict with the more aspiring members of the lower middle class. Above all, Jews really did revolutionize certain trades, such as the clothing trade; and though the scale of their enterprises benefited the public, it threatened innumerable small firms. At the same time Jews in general were still just sufficiently different and exclusive to constitute a recognizable minority. And so, however unjustly, it came about that in the eyes of the lower-middle-class antisemite, harassed, frustrated, disorientated, the Jews were above all the symbol of modern capitalism, the beneficiaries of the system under which he himself was suffering.[1]

But though many members of the lower middle class were attracted by the *völkisch*-racist outlook, its creators, propagators, and most fanatical adherents were to be found elsewhere – in that rather higher stratum of the middle class to which many of the Jews themselves belonged. Irrational, unscientific, and demonstrably nonsensical as this outlook was, it was nevertheless the speciality of the educated – or rather, of those with a university degree. Lagarde was an orientalist of real distinction and latterly a university professor, Dühring was a university lecturer, Chamberlain was very widely read; while the main body of believers was to be found among university students and university graduates – the two being linked, often quite closely, in the *Burschenschaften* (fraternities).

This too can be understood only in terms of the peculiar history of the German middle class. In Germany the first section of the middle class to attain prestige consisted of writers, scholars, thinkers. Already early in the nineteenth century, at a time when Germany consisted simply of a mass

[1] Cf. E. Bennathan, 'Die demographische und wirtschaftliche Struktur der Juden', in *Entscheidungsjahr 1932*, pp. 87–131.

of petty principalities, as backward economically as politically, German intellectual achievements commanded respect throughout Europe. At that time many German intellectuals were liberal nationalists, equally devoted to liberal principles and to the cause of German unification. But their attempt at creating a united Germany in 1848 was a failure, and when unification came in 1871 it was imposed by the Prussian Junker Bismarck. Meanwhile the industrial bourgeoisie had appeared and together with the nobility monopolized political power. The writers and scholars and thinkers, once the spearhead of the bourgeoisie, found themselves pushed down the social scale. Excluded not only from political influence but from all contact with politics, accustomed to dealing with abstractions but not with real people in real situations, wounded in their self-esteem and seething with resentment, many of these people consoled themselves with constructing vast philosophies of history.

The *völkisch*-racist view of the world was one of these philosophies. It had the enormous advantage that it made any German who accepted it feel not only important but enormously, supremely important. For men with some pretensions to education but irked by their political impotence and social insignificance it had great attractions. To feel oneself the bearer of a divine mission, a paladin in the vast struggle of 'German spirituality' against the dark forces of 'Jewish materialism' – this was a most gratifying experience, especially as it carried with it no concrete political responsibilities whatsoever.

The appeal of the *völkisch*-racist outlook was perhaps even stronger among the German element in the Habsburg empire than it was in the Hohenzollern empire.[1] On this periphery of the German-speaking world, where ever since the war of 1866 the German element had felt isolated and threatened by the preponderant Slav element, the aggressive affirmation of German superiority had particular attractions. Moreover, the Jews were far more conspicuous in Austria than in Germany, and at both ends of the social scale: while the great majority lived in appalling poverty, a minority made up a large part of

[1] Pulzer's book deals with the (commonly neglected) Austrian contribution to the antisemitic tradition.

the professional class and a few were bankers of great wealth. That Austrian Jews did not regard themselves as forming one of the national groups within the Habsburg empire, but as belonging to the German group, did not help at all: the Germans rejected them. And here as in Germany the most militant antisemites were to be found, on the one hand, in a lower middle class which had failed to adapt itself to the demands of a rapidly developing industrial economy, and on the other hand among students and professional men. When Hitler came to power in 1933, a joke circulated in Germany: Hitler was Austria's revenge for Königgrätz, i.e. for Austria's defeat at the hands of Prussia in 1866. And there was a good deal in it, for the petty bourgeois Hitler did indeed embody a whole century of frustration, disappointment, and insecurity, and the boundless lust for revenge which possessed him was a magnified version of something which possessed a whole stratum of Austrian society.

Before the First World War the *völkisch*-racist outlook had relatively little impact on politics, whether in the Habsburg or the Hohenzollern empire. From 1880 onwards various antisemitic parties appeared, and they had some success; but these organizations were seldom committed to any such high-flown ideology.[1] In the years immediately preceding the war racist fanatics tended to avoid day-to-day politics and to deal solely in 'ideas'. Austrian racists developed the cult of the swastika, and foretold that some day Jews would be castrated and killed under the aegis of that ancient sun-symbol. In Austria too Georg von Schönerer, after an unsuccessful career as a politician, set out to revive antique Germanic customs, including the solstice festival which a generation later was to play such a curious part in the Rathenau murder. In Germany there appeared a multitude of more or less esoteric bodies, such as the Germanen- und Walsungsorden (Order of Teutons and Volsungs), which also used the swastika as its emblem; and

---

[1] An exception was a party which came into existence in 1903 in the Sudetenland, that ancient outpost of Germandom on the Slav frontier: the German Workers' party, later the National Socialist German Workers' party, which after the war co-operated closely with the Nazi party in Germany.

the Kulturbund für Politik (Cultural League for Politics), which combined virulent racism with enthusiasm for a new kind of whole-meal loaf.[1]

At the time there were probably few who imagined that the *völkisch*-racist outlook would ever impinge much on practical politics. Yet even then, well before 1914, it influenced many schoolteachers and above all the famous Youth Movement, in which multitudes of young Germans sought escape from bourgeois stuffiness; it even touched at least one important and respectable political organization, the Pan-German Association. But above all, in its purest form, where a fanatical race-consciousness blended with teetotalism, vegetarianism, and occultism, it formed the outlook of many of the most sinister of the future Nazi leaders – including Hitler himself.

It was the outcome of the war that enabled the *völkisch*-racist outlook to penetrate into the field of practical politics. The humiliation of defeat and the sufferings that followed it, the mortification felt over the peace treaties of Versailles and St Germain, the utter disorientation and widespread financial ruin which accompanied the collapse of the currency – these things produced an entirely new atmosphere. Moreover both Germany and Austria had lost the national minorities on which, formerly, nationalist arrogance and rancour had vented itself; while Germany seemed in addition to have lost any prospect of imperialist expansion. All this gave added appeal to the fantasy of an age-old, mortal struggle between the German and Jewish 'races'. Among university students it flourished with particular vigour. Jewish students had long been excluded from the student fraternities, but it was a significant innovation when, in 1919, this exclusion was extended to non-Jews who were married to Jews.

In the ideology of the political Right *völkisch*-racist ideas began to figure to an extent quite unknown before the war. In election campaigns from 1920 onwards the German National People's party (DNVP) used racist propaganda of great ferocity – and this party, at the peak of its success, polled six million votes. Admittedly the DNVP appealed to many

[1] Pulzer, op. cit., pp. 208, 231, 244.

different interests and for many different reasons; but on the extreme Right there were various smaller organizations which existed only to further racist antisemitism. Already before the war the leader of the Pan-German Association, Heinrich Class, had demanded that German Jews should be deprived of citizenship, debarred from all official positions and from teaching and the law, forbidden to own land, and taxed twice as high as other Germans. Now he managed to lead his association in the same direction; in the last days of the war it officially extended its work to embrace 'the Jewish question', and a year later it created a special body to deal with these matters: the Deutsch-völkischer Schutz- und Trutzbund (Defensive and Offensive Alliance).[1]

The Alliance, which had the swastika as its emblem, quickly acquired a membership of 300,000. After the Rathenau murder it was suppressed – but to no effect, as its members promptly joined the Nazi party. Meanwhile the old Order of Teutons and Volsungs continued to exist, also using the swastika. In November 1918 it produced, as a cover-organization, a body called the Thule Society; and it was a couple of members and associates of this short-lived organization who, early in 1919, founded the German Workers' party, shortly to become the Nazi party.

These organizations were indoctrinated with the *völkisch*-racist outlook in its most fanatical form, and when the *Protocols* came into their hands they reinterpreted them accordingly. In their eyes the machinations of the Elders of Zion were the supreme expression of the characteristics which they attributed to the Jewish 'race'. The Jewish world-conspiracy was seen as the product of an ineradicable destructiveness, a will to evil which was believed to be inborn in every Jew. A peculiar breed of sub-human beings, dark, earthbound, was

---

[1] D. Frymann (pseudonym of Heinrich Class), *Wenn ich der Kaiser wär*, Leipzig, 1912; and cf. A. Kruck, *Geschichte des Alldeutschen Verbandes*, 1890–1939, Wiesbaden, 1954, pp. 130 seq.

[2] W. Maser. *Die Fruhgeschichte der NSDAP. Hitlers Weg bis 1914*. Frankfurt am Main and Bonn, 1965, pp. 146 f. See also G. Franz-Willing, *Die Hitlerbewegung*, Vol. I; *Der Ursprung 1919–1922*, Hamburg and Berlin, 1962, p. 127; and H. Phelps, 'Hitler and the Deutsche Arbeiterpartei', in *American Historical Review*, vol. 68, No. 4 (July 1963), pp. 974–86.

working conspiratorially to destroy those sons of light, the 'Aryan' or Germanic 'race', and the *Protocols* contained their plan of campaign. To that plan there could be only one response – extermination, carried out under the symbol of the sun-god, the swastika. Walther Rathenau fell as the first victim in a massacre which was to begin in earnest a generation later.

2

When the *Protocols* came into contact with the *völkisch*-racist outlook the result was an apocalyptic vision not only of contemporary politics but of all history and indeed of all human existence on this planet. And it was in the name of this quasi-religious world-view that the Nazis and their accomplices undertook the extermination of the Jews of Europe, as a prelude to the extermination of Jews throughout the world. This is seldom realized even today, and as a blunt statement of fact it does seem almost incredible. But the evidence is there, in the pronouncements of the Nazi leaders and of the organizers of the exterminations, and it is incontrovertible.

One may start with the astonishing statement of Dieter Wisliceny, a SS captain who was a close associate of Eichmann and was executed in 1947 for his part in the attempt to exterminate Slovak, Greek, and Hungarian Jews. On 18 November 1946, in preparation for his trial in Czechoslovakia, he described at length how the great massacre came about. Before describing how the policy of genocide was formulated and implemented, he had something to say about a matter 'without which it is impossible to obtain a clear view of the situation: the reasons which led Hitler and Himmler to undertake the extermination of European Jewry'. What he had in mind was the world-view which obsessed these men, and which he pictured as follows:

Antisemitism constituted one of the main bases of the programme of the Nazi party. Essentially it was the product of two ideas:
  (1) the pseudo-scientific biological theories of Professor Günther,[1] and

[1] Professor Hans K. Günther was the official theorist of racism in the Third Reich.

(2) a mystical and religious view which sees the world as ruled by good and bad powers.

According to this view the Jews represented the evil principle, with, as auxiliaries, the Church (the Jesuit Order), Freemasonry and Bolshevism. The literature of this outlook is well known, the former writings of the Nazi party teem with such ideas. A straight line leads from the *Protocols of the Elders of Zion* to Rosenberg's *Myth*.[1] It is absolutely impossible to make any impression on this outlook by means of logical or rational argument, it is a sort of religiosity, and it impels people to form themselves into a sect. Under the influence of this literature millions of people believed these things – an event which can only be compared with similar phenomena in the Middle Ages, such as the witch-mania.

Against this world of evil the race-mystics set the world of good, of light, incarnated in blond, blue-eyed people, who were supposed to be the source of all capacity for creating civilization or building a state. Now these two worlds were alleged to be locked in a perpetual struggle, and the war of 1939, which Hitler unleashed, represented only the final battle between these two powers.

The usual view of Himmler is that he was an ice-cold, cynical politician. This view is certainly wrong. In his whole attitude Himmler was a mystic, who embraced this 'world-view' with religious fanaticism.[2]

From other sources we know that the same world-view obsessed Hitler himself throughout his political career. There are signs of the obsession already in the very first of his political utterances. In 1919 Hitler was employed by the army district command in Munich as 'education officer', with the job of immunizing the troops against the infection of democracy and socialism. On 16 September 1919 he wrote a letter to a certain Gemlich which shows clearly enough how he conceived of his assignment. Already the opening words concern 'the danger which Jewry today represents for our people' – and he promptly goes on to complain that ordinary German antisemitism still lacks the ideological coherence which would make it an effective political movement. It is not, he protests, enough to dislike Jews; Germans must realize that Jewry

---

[1] Rosenberg's *Mythus des 20. Jahrhunderts* (*The Myth of the Twentieth Century*) was one of the basic scriptures of Nazism.

[2] Text in L. Poliakov and J. Wulf, *Das Dritte Reich und die Juden*, Berlin-Grunewald, 1955, pp. 91–2.

forms a racial entity with very strongly marked racial characteristics, of which the passion for material gain is the most
dominant. This is what makes Jewry 'the racial tuberculosis
of the peoples'. Mere pogroms are inadequate to cope with such
a dangerous foe – 'there must be a rebirth of the moral and
spiritual forces of the nation' through 'the ruthless effort of
born leaders with a nationalist outlook and an inner sense of
responsibility'. A government formed of such men will
restrict the legal rights of the Jews, but it will not stop there:
its ultimate aim must be 'the removal (*Entfernung*) of the
Jews altogether'.[1] Thus the unknown ex-corporal who a
couple of days before had attended his first meeting with the
tiny German Workers' party, the nucleus of the future Nazi
party.

Probably Hitler knew of the *Protocols* already then, for they
had been advertised in *Auf Vorposten* and were being discussed among professional antisemites. Certainly by the time
he emerged into the political limelight, in 1923, his thinking
was permeated by them. As Germany passed through the
inferno of the great inflation, in which the savings of the
middle and working classes were wiped out and wages and
salaries became meaningless, Hitler offered his explanation of
the catastrophe: 'According to the *Protocols of Zion* the peoples
are to be reduced to submission by hunger. The second revolution under the Star of David is the aim of the Jews in our
time' – the first revolution being the establishment of the
Weimar Republic itself.[2] The following year, in the comfortable
prison where he was lodged after the abortive *putsch* in
Munich, Hitler dictated *Mein Kampf* – and much of that
dreary but revealing work is devoted to the manoeuvres by
which Jewry is supposed to be pursuing world-domination.
Freemasonry, we are told, is the trick by which the Jews make
the governing class serve their purpose, while the lower classes
are captured by means of the press. Capitalism, liberalism,
democracy, are the devices by which the Jews induced the
bourgeoisie to overthrow the aristocracy and the proletariat

[1] Printed in full in E. Deuerlein, 'Hitlers Eintritt in die Politik und
die Reichswehr', in *Vierteljahreshefte für Zeitgeschichte*, Munich, Vol. VII
(1959), Document 12, pp. 203–5.
[2] *Adolf Hitlers Reden*, ed. E. Boepple, Munich, 1933, p. 71.

to overthrow the bourgeoisie. This accomplished, the Jews are now introducing Bolshevism as a way of dominating the masses who brought them to power.

The source of all this is obvious enough, and Hitler had at least the grace to acknowledge it – even though Philip Graves had long since shown the *Protocols* to be a forgery. 'The extent to which the whole existence of (the Jewish) people is based on a continual lie,' he writes in *Mein Kampf*, 'is shown in an incomparable manner in the *Protocols of the Elders of Zion*, which the Jews hate so tremendously. The *Frankfurter Zeitung*[1] is for ever moaning to the public that they are supposed to be based on a forgery; which is the surest proof that they are genuine. What many Jews do perhaps unconsciously is here consciously exposed. But that is what matters. It is a matter of indifference which Jewish brain produced these revelations. What matters is that they uncover, with really horrifying reliability, the nature and activity of the Jewish people, and expose them in their inner logic and their final aims. But reality provides the best commentary. Whoever examines the historical development of the last hundred years from the standpoint of this book will at once understand why the Jewish press makes such an uproar. For when once this book becomes generally familiar to a people, the Jewish menace can be regarded as already vanquished.'[2]

Years later, when Germany was in the throes of the great slump, Hitler explained this world-wide disaster in precisely the same way as he had explained the German inflation. Hermann Rauschning has recorded his comments:

'It was the Jews, of course, who invented the economic system of constant fluctuation and expansion that we call capitalism – that invention of genius, with its subtle and yet simple self-acting mechanism. Let us make no mistake about it – it is an invention of genius, of the devil's own ingenuity.

'The economic system of our day is the creation of the Jews. It is under their exclusive control. It is their super-state, planted by them above all the states of the world in all their glory. But now we have challenged them, with the system of permanent revolution. . . .

[1] A leading German liberal newspaper.
[2] *Mein Kampf*, 11th edition, Munich, 1942, p. 337.

'I have read the *Protocols of the Elders of Zion* – it simply appalled me. The stealthiness of the enemy, and his ubiquity! I saw at once that we must copy it – in our own way, of course. . . . It is in truth the critical battle for the fate of the world.'

'Don't you think,' I objected, 'that you are attributing rather too much importance to the Jews?'

'No, no, no!' exclaimed Hitler. 'It is impossible to exaggerate the formidable quality of the Jew as enemy.'

'But,' I said, 'the *Protocols* are a manifest forgery. . . . It is evident to me that they can't possibly be genuine.'

'Why not?' grunted Hitler.

He did not care two straws, he said, whether the story was historically true. If it was not, its intrinsic truth was all the more convincing to him. . . .[1]

These are all more or less public statements by an outstandingly unscrupulous politician, and if one had no other evidence one might wonder how far Hitler the politician spoke for Hitler the man. But in fact there is plenty of other evidence – and what Hitler has to say about the Jewish world-conspiracy when chatting with friends, or in writings which he did not publish, is much stranger still. The earliest of these sources dates from before the Munich *putsch* of 1923 and consists of a little book by the bohemian poet and journalist Dietrich Eckart, called *Bolshevism from Moses to Lenin: a dialogue between Adolf Hitler and myself*, and published posthumously in 1924.[2] It is a reliable source, for Eckart was not only one of the founding members of the Nazi party, he was one of the very few real friends Hitler ever had (*Mein Kampf*, incidentally, ends with an invocation of his memory). It is quite inconceivable that such a man should have distorted his friend's views in a book intended for publication.[3]

The booklet contains references to earlier works and these are what one would expect: the *Protocols*,[4] Ford's *International*

---

[1] H. Rauschning, *Hitler Speaks*, London, 1939, pp. 235–6.

[2] *Der Bolschewismus von Moses bis Lenin – Zwiegespräch zwischen Adolf Hitler und mir*, Munich, 1924, is analysed in E. Nolte, 'Eine frühe Quelle zu Hitlers Antisemitismus', in *Historische Zeitschrift*, June 1961, pp. 584–606.

[3] Nazi propaganda kept quiet about the book precisely because it was too revealing.

[4] Hitler reveals that he knows 'the Kaiser's Dream', which, as we have seen, figures in the zur Beek edition of the *Protocols*.

Jew, Gougenot des Mousseaux, Fritsch's *Handbook of the Jewish Question*. But by combining these with *völkisch*-racist speculations, Hitler arrives at a whole 'philosophy of history', an interpretation of human existence from the beginning onwards, which has a certain crazy originality. As Hitler sees it, human history forms part of nature and follows the same laws as the rest of nature. If it has gone wrong, that shows that some force is at work to frustrate nature's intention; and that has in fact been the case for thousands of years. There follows an outline of history which portrays it as one long degeneration. Nature demands inequality, hierarchy, subordination of the inferior to the superior – but human history has consisted of a series of revolts against this natural order, leading to ever greater egalitarianism. This process is compared with disease, with the work of a bacillus: 'A proliferation right across the world, now slow, now leaping ahead. Everywhere it sucks and sucks. At first there is teeming abundance, in the end only dried-up sap.'

The force behind this disastrous process is the Jewish spirit, 'which has been there from the beginning'. Already in ancient Egypt the Children of Israel undermined a healthy, 'natural' society. They did this by introducing capitalism – Joseph being the first capitalist – but above all by inciting the lower orders to revolt, until nationally minded Egyptians rose in their wrath and chased the trouble-makers from the land – this is the true meaning of Exodus. Moses therefore is the first Bolshevik and a true precursor of Lenin, whom Hitler and Eckart both assumed to be a Jew. And so a process began which has been repeated over and over again ever since. In Hitler's eyes the lower social strata consist, all over the world, of similar, racially mixed and therefore inferior human material. The essence of the Jewish world-conspiracy is that it uses this racial hotchpotch to overthrow the racially pure upper classes and thereby to further its own drive for world-domination.

In conversation with his friend Hitler said frankly what he was careful never to say in public – that Christianity itself was part of the Jewish plot. Jesus was of course no Jew but an 'Aryan' – but then it was not Jesus but Paul who created Christianity. By extolling pacifism and the egalitarian spirit,

Paul deprived the Roman Empire of the hierarchical, military outlook which was its mainstay, and thereby ensured its doom – and all so that the Jews could move one step nearer their goal of world-domination. In modern times the Jews have repeated the same manoeuvre again and again, and the results have been the French Revolution, liberalism, democracy, and finally Bolshevism; the Russian Revolution with its millions of victims is nothing but the latest episode in the eternal war of Jewry against the other peoples of the world. But Hitler does not stop there – every historical episode that comes to his mind is evaluated from the same point of view, how ever little connexion it may have with Jews and their affairs. Thus Luther made a disastrous mistake in attacking the Roman Catholic Church, for by doing so he weakened the Germans in their struggle against the Jews; he ought to have realized that Catholicism was being used by the Jews for their own purposes and have directed his attacks against these hidden manipulators. Indeed, if Luther had any merit it was that in his latter years he did attack the Jews; and when Hitler talked of the spirit of Luther he meant one thing only – Luther's hostility to the Jews.

In this little book, then, one comes to the very heart of Hitler's interpretation of history and of human existence. He was utterly convinced that everywhere and at all times the Jews strive for world-domination; that everywhere and at all times they aim to overthrow those who are actually dominant, the pure-blooded élites which nature has set as the governing class in all nations; and that everywhere and at all times they use the lower strata, the masses with impure blood, to carry out this work for them. And what Eckart recorded in 1923 or earlier, Hitler confirmed in his own writings soon afterwards – not so much in *Mein Kampf* as in that other book which he wrote in 1928 and which remained unpublished and unknown until 1961, when it appeared in English translation under the title *Hitler's Second Book* (in Britain) and *Hitler's Secret Book* (in the United States).

In the main this work is simply a plea for an alliance between Germany and Fascist Italy, but even here Hitler feels obliged to append, as a sort of epilogue, some pages of antisemitic invective. And this epilogue carries the argument a stage further: we learn that the Jew does not merely use the racially impure masses for his purposes – he has a whole strategy to ensure that they become more and more racially impure and therefore more and more amenable. 'His ultimate goal is the denationalization, the promiscuous bastardization of other peoples, the lowering of the racial level of the highest peoples as well of the domination of this racial mish-mash through the extirpation of the folkish intelligentsia and its replacement by the members of his own people.'[1] That is why 'after the Bolshevik revolution he completely tore down the bonds of order, of morality, of custom etc, abolished marriage as a lofty institution and instead proclaimed a general copulation with the aim of breeding a general inferior human mish-mash, by way of a chaotic bastardization, which by itself would be incapable of leadership and which ultimately would no longer be able to do without the Jews as its only intellectual element. . . . At the moment, he exerts himself to lead the remaining states toward the same condition'.[2] Appalled by 'this most terrible of all crimes against mankind', Hitler omitted to explain how promiscuity among Russians could alter the biological composition of the Russian population.

Hitler's mind was not one that developed or matured. His chatter over the dinner-table at headquarters when he was Commander-in-Chief of the German Armed Forces during the Second World War has been faithfully recorded. If one examines it to see what he has to say about the Jews one finds precisely the same ideas as he propounded in the 1920s – and often expressed in precisely the same words. The way he sees the course of history is the same – as a decline and decay, a falling away from an original hierarchical order. The cause he imagines is the same – the evil, anti-natural principle incarnated in the Jews and operating on racially impure populations. Even the images are the same – images of disease, infection, pestilence: Christianity and Bolshevism are compared with syphilis and plague, the Jews themselves are constantly referred to as bacilli. 'The discovery of the Jewish virus,' he said to Himmler in 1942, 'is one of the greatest revolutions that have taken place in the world. The battle in which we are

[1] *Hitler's Secret Book*, trans. S. Attanasio, New York, 1961, p. 213.
[2] Ibid., p. 215.

engaged today is of the same sort as the battle waged, during the last century, by Pasteur and Koch. How many diseases have their origin in the Jewish virus! . . . We shall regain our health only by eliminating the Jew.'[1]

This brings us to the core of this extraordinary fantasy. There is in *Mein Kampf* an astonishing passage which ought to have attracted more attention than it did: 'If the Jew, with the help of his Marxist catechism, triumphs over the peoples of this world, his crown will be the dance of death for mankind, and as once before, millions of years ago, this planet will again sail empty of all human life through the ether. . . . I believe that I am today acting according to the purposes of the almighty Creator. In resisting the Jew, I am fighting the Lord's battle.'[2] One is impelled to ask: What ever can the man have meant? What possible sense can there be in this talk of an earth empty of all human life? And the answer to these questions, when one faces up to it, goes a long way to explain the monstrous deeds perpetrated by the Germans during the Second World War. It has of course nothing to do with atomic warfare – Hitler wrote these words in 1924. What he means is that only a tiny part of what is usually regarded as mankind consists of human beings – notably those whom he imagined to be of Nordic descent, plus, for political reasons, the Japanese. The rest – what he called the racial mish-mash – belongs not to mankind but to an inferior species. In using these creatures to kill off the ruling strata – who in his view must *ipso facto* be Nordic – the Jew is therefore literally depriving the earth of its human population. What will be left will be simply animals disguised as human beings, under the leadership of Jews, who are demonic beings disguised as human beings.

Even by the crazy standards of German racism these ideas were eccentric and extreme. Unfortunately they were held by the man who became dictator of Germany – and this meant that instead of remaining the property of some obscure group of cranks they became the creed of the SS. It was in the name of these weird fantasies, disguised as scientific truth, that the SS at the height of their power terrorized and martyrized Europe from the English Channel to the Volga. How Hitler's

[1] *Hitler's Table Talk*, ed. H. R. Trevor-Roper, London, 1953, p. 332.
[2] *Mein Kampf*, p. 70.

special version of the Jewish world-conspiracy was presented
to these men is shown by a tract issued by SS headquarters:

'Just as night rises up against the day, just as light and darkness
are eternal enemies, so the greatest enemy of world-dominating
man is man himself. The sub-man – that creature which looks as
though biologically it were of absolutely the same kind, endowed
by Nature with hands, feet and a sort of brain, with eyes and
mouth – is nevertheless a totally different, a fearful creature, is
only an attempt at a human being, with a quasi-human face, yet in
mind and spirit lower than any animal. Inside this being a cruel
chaos of wild, unchecked passions: a nameless will to destruction,
the most primitive lusts, the most undisguised vileness. A sub-
man – nothing else! . . . Never has the sub-man granted peace,
never has he permitted rest. . . . To preserve himself he needed
mud, he needed hell, but not the sun. And this underworld of sub-
men found its leader: the eternal Jew!'[1]

Once such a creed was applied it could only lead to massacre.
The victims were not only the six million Jews who were
killed as bearers of an imaginary plague. As we have seen, in
Hitler's eyes Russia was the country in which the Jews,
through the revolution, had most completely 'infected' the
population, and this certainly had much to do with the extraordinary ferocity of the SS in the occupied territories of the
Soviet Union. When the German attack began, Himmler
announced that it was intended to kill thirty million Russians.
The number of Russian dead is in fact put at twenty million;
and the way in which whole armies of prisoners of war were
put behind barbed wire and left to starve, and whole villages
of men and women herded into barns to be burned alive, is
certainly connected with the fact that these people were
regarded as sub-human beings, bastardized by the Jews and
enlisted in their service.

As for the Jews, it is possible that Hitler always intended
to exterminate them. In his very first political pronouncement,
the Gemlich letter of 1919, he already talked of their 'removal
altogether'; Dietrich Eckart records him as saying that it
would be useless to destroy synagogues and Jewish schools, as
the Jewish spirit is incarnate in every single Jew and will

[1] L. Poliakov and J. Wulf, *Das Dritte Reich und die Juden*, p. 217.

operate so long as any Jews exist. Admittedly in those early days his public speeches avoided all reference to massacre, but even then he sometimes let fall some ominous phrases. 'What is preparing today will be greater than the world war. It will be fought out on German soil for the whole world! Only two possibilities exist: we will be either the sacrificial lamb or the victor.'[1] This comes from a speech of 1923 and the subject is the struggle against the Jews. More ominous still is a passage in *Mein Kampf* which clearly foreshadows what was to happen in the extermination camps twenty years later. Germany, says Hitler, lost the war only because Jewish Marxists sapped the will to fight; and he continues: 'If at the beginning of the war or during the war 12,000 or 15,000 of these corrupters of the people had been held under poison gas ... the sacrifice of millions at the front would not have been in vain. On the contrary, the removal of 12,000 rascals at the right time would perhaps have saved the lives of a million decent Germans, so valuable for the future.'[2]

Elsewhere in *Mein Kampf* he speaks of the overthrow of 'world-Jewry' with a truly apocalyptic fervour. We have seen how in the popular Christianity of the Middle Ages, and also in the eccentric Christianity of Sergey Nilus, the Jews were regarded as servants of Antichrist and destined for the same fate – to be destroyed, in preparation for the millennium, by Christ returning in majesty. Now in the Book of Revelation Antichrist is shown as trying to storm heaven and being cast down to hell; and the curious thing is that Hitler, though he loathed Christianity, was quite capable of using these age-old Biblical images when speaking of the fate of the Jews. 'The Jew goes his fatal way,' he wrote, 'until the day when another power stands up against him and in a mighty struggle casts him, the heaven-stormer, back to Lucifer.'[3] The apocalyptic feeling is unmistakable, and something of this was taken over by Himmler and the SS. At least at certain moments these people regarded the extermination of the Jews as a necessary prelude to some kind of Germanic millennium. Again it is worth considering the inside evidence provided by Wisliceny: 'While [Himmler] took the advice of astrologers and inclined

---

[1] *Adolf Hitler, sein Leben und seine Reden*, ed. A. V. von Koerber, Munich, 1923, p. 106.   [2] *Mein Kampf*, p. 772.   [3] Ibid., p. 751.

towards all the occult arts, the SS gradually turned into a new kind of religious sect. . . .' It was less new than Wisliceny supposed: medieval Europe too had known apocalyptic sects which believed that they had a divinely ordained mission to purify the world by exterminating the Jews.[1]

Wisliceny also said that in Hitler's mind the war of 1939 was above all the final struggle against Jewry; and from 1939 onwards Hitler himself publicly talked of the war in just those terms. As we have seen, German editors of the *Protocols* had always insisted that the First World War was the work of the Jews; now Hitler blamed them for the war he was about to inflict on the world, and at the same time prophesied the genocide he was about to carry out. In a speech to the Reichstag on 30 January 1939 he declared: 'Today I will once more be a prophet: if the international Jewish financiers in and outside Europe should succeed in plunging the nations once more into a world war, then the result will not be the bolshevization of the earth, and thus the victory of Jewry, but the annihilation of the Jewish race in Europe.'[2]

This prophecy provided a theme on which Hitler continued to embroider throughout the war. He repeated his threat before the Reichstag on 1 September 1939, at the very moment of the invasion of Poland. On 30 January 1941 he repeated it in the Sportspalast in Berlin: 'And I should not like to forget the hint which I already gave once before, on 1 September 1939, in the German Reichstag – that should the other world be plunged into a general war, Jewry as a whole will have played out its role in Europe. They can laugh at this today, just as they laughed at my prophecies before. The coming months and years will prove that here too I saw correctly.'[3] In June 1941 the invasion of the Soviet Union and with it the extermination of the Russian Jews began, and by 30 January 1942 Hitler was able to speak with even greater confidence: 'We fully realize that this war can end only either in the extermination of the Aryan peoples or in the disappearance of Jewry in Europe. I said it already in the German Reichstag on

[1] Cf. N. Cohn, *The Pursuit of the Millennium*, revised editions, London and New York, 1961–62, pp. 49–65, 92–4.

[2] M. Domarus, *Hitler, Reden und Proklamationen, 1932–1945*, Neustadt/Aisch, 1962–63, Vol. II, p. 1058.   [3] Ibid., p. 1663.

1 September 1939 – and I am careful not to make rash prophecies – that this war will not end as the Jews imagine, namely, in the extermination of the European Aryan peoples, but that its outcome will be the annihilation of Jewry.'[1] In the course of 1942 extermination camps were set up in Poland, to which Jews were deported from all over Europe. In the New Year message for 1943 Hitler was able to announce: 'I said that the hope of international Jewry, that it would destroy the German and other European peoples in a new world war, will be the biggest mistake Jewry has made in thousands of years; that it will destroy not the German people but itself – and about that there is today no doubt. . . .'[2]

These were all public statements, made by the Führer to the German people at large – explanations, as it were, of the policy adopted by the German Government to combat the latest manoeuvres of 'the international Jewish financiers', alias the Elders of Zion. Again one is bound to ask how far they reflected Hitler's own beliefs – and again one finds complete identity. Speaking privately with Himmler in October 1941 Hitler said: 'By exterminating this pest, we shall do humanity a service of which our soldiers can have no idea. . . . From the rostrum of the Reichstag I prophesied to Jewry that, in the event of war's proving inevitable, the Jew would disappear from Europe. That race of criminals has on its conscience the two million (German) dead of the first world war, and now hundreds of thousands more. . . .'[3] In the last weeks before he committed suicide he returned to the theme: 'I have played straight with the Jews. On the eve of war I gave them a last warning. I warned them that if they again plunged the world into war, they would not be spared this time – that the vermin would be finally exterminated in Europe. They replied to this warning by a declaration of war. . . . We have pierced the Jewish abscess. The world of the future will be eternally grateful to us.'[4] In the political testament which he dictated

[1] Ibid., Vol. II, pp. 1828–9.
[2] *Deutschland im Kampf*, ed. A. I. Berndt and Oberst Wedel, No. 81 (January 1943), p. 45.
[3] *Hitler's Table Talk*, pp. 79, 87.
[4] *Le Testament Politique de Hitler. Notes recueillies par Martin Bormann*, Paris, 1959, p. 86.

on the night of 28–29 April 1945 (he shot himself on the 30th) he again insisted: 'It is untrue that I, or anybody else in Germany, wanted war in 1939. It was wanted and provoked exclusively by those international politicians who either came of Jewish stock, or worked for Jewish interests. . . .' And in the closing words of the testament, the last words he ever wrote, he summoned the élite of the German nation 'to merciless opposition to the world-poisoner of all peoples, international Jewry'.[1]

What is one to make of these utterances? The circumstances in which they were made show that they were in a sense sincere – yet how can Hitler possibly have believed that the Jews had caused the war which he himself had brought about? The answer can only be that for Hitler anything which opposed his own limitless craving for domination was automatically felt as part of the Jewish world-conspiracy. And that does indeed seem to have been the case at every stage of his career, including the war. Any nation, large or small, that attempted to defend its territory or its interests against the insatiable claims of Nazi Germany showed by that very fact that it was a tool in the hands of the Elders of Zion.

As one reflects on the implications of this, further questions present themselves. It has sometimes been argued that Hitler was simply a super-Machiavellian, a man without convictions or loyalties, an utter cynic for whom the whole aim and value of life consisted in power and more power. There certainly was such a Hitler – but the other Hitler, the haunted man obsessed by fantasies about the Jewish world-conspiracy, was just as real.[2] What one would like to know is just how far the near-lunatic was active even in the calculating opportunist. How much of the dynamism behind that astonishing career – from the creation of the Nazi party, through the struggle for power and the establishment of the dictatorship and the terror – how much of all this came from a secret dream of overthrowing the Jewish world-conspiracy by exterminating the Jews? An unanswerable question, no doubt – but one that

[1] In H. R. Trevor-Roper, *The Last Days of Hitler*, London, 1950, pp. 195, 198.
[2] Cf. E. Faul, 'Hitlers Ueber-Machiavellismus', in *Vierteljahreshefte für Zeitgeschichte*, Vol. 2 (1954), and notably p. 368.

occurred even to some important Nazis, though of course they put it differently. 'For what else,' asked the supreme judge of the party, Walter Buch, writing in the party's legal journal during the war, 'for what else did we struggle, take upon us want and deprivation, for what else did the courageous men of the SA and the SS, the boys of the Hitler Youth fall, if not for the possibility that one day the German people might start its struggle for liberation against the Jewish oppressors? In this struggle we are now involved. . . . Victory will be attained by Adolf Hitler. . . .'[1]

And again: to what extent did Hitler and his immediate associates model themselves on the imaginary Elders of Zion? According to Rauschning he took the *Protocols* as his primer for politics; and in the 1930s three whole books were written to show how in almost every particular Nazi policy followed the plan laid down there.[2] The argument can be pushed too far, but that does not mean it is wholly false. It is worth reflecting on two more recent judgements. 'The Nazis,' writes Hannah Arendt, 'started with the fiction of a conspiracy and modelled themselves, more or less consciously, after the secret society of the Elders of Zion . . .';[3] while Léon Poliakov comments that the Nazi leaders began by drugging themselves with sensational sub-literature of the type of the *Protocols* and ended by translating these morbid fantasies into a reality terrible beyond imagining.[4] There is a good deal in this. The ruthless struggle of a band of conspirators to achieve world-domination – a world-empire based on a small but highly organized and regimented people – utter contempt for humanity at large – a glorying in destruction and mass misery – all these things are to be found in the *Protocols*, and they were of the very essence of the Nazi régime. To put it with all due caution: in this preposterous fabrication from the days of the Russian pogroms Hitler heard the call of a kindred spirit, and he responded to it with all his being.

[1] Quoted in M. Weinreich, *Hitler's Professors*, New York, 1946, p. 89.
[2] See Bibliographical Note.
[3] Hannah Arendt, *The Origins of Totalitarianism* (2nd edition), London, 1958, p. 366.
[4] L. Poliakov, preface to *Le IIIe Reich et les Juifs* (French edition), Paris, 1959.

CHAPTER IX

The Myth in Nazi Propaganda

1

THE *Protocols* and the myth of the Jewish world-conspiracy were exploited in Nazi propaganda at every stage, from the first emergence of the party in the early 1920s to the collapse of the Third Reich in 1945. They were exploited first to help the party to power – then to justify a régime of terror – then to justify war – then to justify genocide – and finally to postpone surrender to the Allies. The history of the myth during those years, of the changing purposes it was made to serve, mirrors faithfully the rise and fall of the Third Reich itself.

In the early days the chief propagator of the myth and of the *Protocols* was Alfred Rosenberg, the official 'ideologist' of the party. Rosenberg was a Balt of less purely German descent than he liked to pretend (one of his grandfathers was a Lett). As he came from Reval his original nationality was Russian, and even after the revolution he still took his examination as an architect in Moscow. He was in his mid-twenties when the revolution roused his interest in politics and turned him into a fanatical anti-Bolshevik. In 1918 he attached himself to the German troops on their withdrawal from Russia – like Vinberg, whom he knew well and who influenced him deeply. In Germany he joined the newly founded Nazi party and became an intimate associate of Hitler's.

Although he was never taken very seriously by Hitler and was already losing influence before the party came to power, Rosenberg left a permanent mark on Nazi ideology. The party was rabidly antisemitic from the moment of its foundation in 1919, but it became obsessed with Russian communism only in 1921–22; and this seems to have been largely Rosenberg's doing. He provided the link between Russian antisemitism of the Black Hundred type and the antisemitism of the German racists; more precisely, he took over Vinberg's view of Bolshevism as a Jewish conspiracy and reinterpreted it in *völkisch*-racist terms. The resulting fantasy, as expounded in innumerable articles and pamphlets, became an obsessive theme in Hitler's thinking and in the outlook and propaganda of the Nazi party.

Rosenberg was the most educated of the Nazi leaders, but that is not saying much. Although he set himself up as an expert on Bolshevism, he never read a word of Marx or Engels, never studied the history or theory of socialism, knew nothing at all about the Russian revolutionary movement. It was enough to know that Kerensky was a Jew called Kirbis [*sic*] and that Lenin was a 'Kalmuk-Tartar' (he should have compared notes with Hitler who, as we have seen, had his own ideas about this). Much of his information was undoubtedly supplied by Vinberg and other right-wing Russian émigrés – many of his articles in the party newspaper, the *Völkischer Beobachter*, were almost entirely based on *Luch Sveta*, while large parts of his *magnum opus*, the unreadable *Myth of the Twentieth Century*, were lifted straight from Vinberg's writings.

Between 1919 and 1923 Rosenberg produced, in addition to innumerable articles, five pamphlets on the world-conspiracy of the Jews (with or without the Freemasons), an abbreviated translation of that notable nineteenth-century forerunner, Gougenot des Mousseaux, and a whole volume of commentary on the *Protocols*. And whereas his bulky *Myth of the Twentieth Century* was read by hardly anybody (and certainly not by the Nazi leaders), these early pamphlets had considerable influence. Typical of them all is *Pest in Russland* (*Plague in Russia*), published in 1922. Here we learn that tsarist Russia earned the hostility of Jews not (as one might have supposed) by pogroms and oppression but by its resistance to finance capitalism. In order to overcome this obstacle and at the same time to punish the recalcitrant Russians, the Jews used their dialectic skill, developed in centuries of commenting on the Talmud, upon the Russian masses, who were easily misled into exterminating the national élite. This enabled Jewish Bolsheviks to nationalize Russian industry – which meant simply appropriating it for the enrichment of themselves and of their friends and relatives abroad. It remained only to organize the Red Army around a core of Letts and (a startling novelty) former Chinese silk-merchants – and the Russian people could at last be forced to submit to capitalism.

In all this a special role was reserved for Walther Rathenau. As Rosenberg saw it, Rathenau was closely connected with those all-powerful Jewish Bolsheviks in the Soviet Union; they shared with him the wealth they derived from Russian industry, while in return he arranged, through the Treaty of Rapallo, for the German people to be exploited in the interest of 'stock exchange and Soviet Jews'. If he and his like had their way, Letts and Chinese under Jewish command would soon be shooting down German workers. And who could deny that such people were 'long since ripe for prison and gallows'? Shortly after the appearance of this booklet Rathenau was assassinated by young men holding precisely these views. It was an appropriate beginning to a career which was to end, a generation later, with Rosenberg's execution as a major war criminal.

These writings of Rosenberg's are of course political propaganda, designed to serve the Nazi party in its struggle for power – but their atmosphere is one, rather, of apocalyptic prophecy. As we have seen, Hitler himself had his apocalyptic moments; with Rosenberg, however, it was a matter not of moments but of a permanent cast of mind. 'The Jew stands in our history as our metaphysical opposite,' he wrote in 1923, at the end of his commentary on the *Protocols*. 'That was *never* clearly grasped by us. . . . *Today* at last it seems as if the eternally foreign and hostile, now that it has climbed to such monstrous power, is felt and hated as such. For the first time in history instinct and knowledge attain clear consciousness. The Jew stands at the very top of the peak of power which he has so eagerly climbed, and awaits his fall into the abyss. The last fall. After that, there will be no place for the Jew in Europe or America. Today there begins, in the midst of the collapse of a whole world, a new era, a fundamental rejection in all fields of many ideas inherited from the past. One of the advance signs of the coming struggle for the new organization of the world is this understanding of the very nature of the demon which has caused our present downfall. Then the way will be open for a new age.'[1] That is how Rosenberg felt about the *Protocols* in 1923; a decade later a new edition of his work carried a fore-word – which he must have approved if not written – cele-brating the advent of the Third Reich: 'The luminous people in the centre – Germany – struggles up out of the claws of the Jewish world-entanglement to a mighty rebirth, it tears the meshes of the net in which it was caught by Talmudic trappers, and like a phoenix rises from the ashes of a burnt-out material-istic philosophy. The German Reich stands in the focus of the world, and a purified nation reveals itself for those who can see, shining brightly, like a new dawn of creation. The spirits of the underworld shrink back appalled before this rising-up ... Jewry, the spirit of decay, the dark demon of creative peoples, feels itself smitten to the heart. The circle of the Jewish plans for world-domination was not yet quite closed, it was too soon to drive the peoples yet again into a bloody war with one another.... May the new edition of this book reveal yet again to the German people in what a delusion they were imprisoned, before the great German movement shattered it ... and how deeply this perception was rooted amongst the leaders of National-Socialism from the very beginning of the movement.'[2]

Rosenberg was a simple soul and he really believed the balderdash he wrote. Josef Goebbels, who became the party's propaganda chief in 1928, was much more of a cynic, and the propaganda he put out consisted mostly of deliberate lies. A fine example is the variation on the *Protocols* which he spon-sored in December 1929. Under the heading 'Slave Market' there appeared, on placards and in party journals, the latest decision of the international Jewish financiers: since Germany was unable to pay reparations in full, she must make up the deficit by exporting young men and women. These would be specially selected by the Jewish masters of Germany; young Jews would of course be exempt. 'Translated from Yiddish into German, that means: Forced export of German people. Of that there can be no doubt.' The source of this tale was

---

[1] A. Rosenberg, *Die Protokolle der Weisen von Zion und die jüdische Weltpolitik*, Munich, 1923, p. 147.
[2] Preface to 1933 edition of Rosenberg's *Protokolle*.

given as the *Berliner Tageblatt* – a perfectly respectable news-paper where no word of all this had ever appeared.[1]

This story figured in the campaign preceding the Reichstag election of 1930, which marked the beginning of the spectacular rise of the Nazi party. Between 1928 and 1933 the party soared from ninth place in the Reichstag, with less than one million votes and only twelve seats, to an easy first, with more than seventeen million votes and 288 seats. Each stage in the rise was accompanied by further floods of antisemitic propaganda. It would be easy to argue – and it often has been argued – that the party's success was mainly due to its anti-semitism, even that anyone who voted Nazi must have been a fanatical antisemite. And yet . . .

Hitler would never have come to power without the world depression, which at one time brought the number of regis-tered unemployed in Germany to six million and plunged almost the whole population – the middle classes and the peasantry as well as the industrial workers – into chronic misery and anxiety. In such an atmosphere – which was all the more desperate because the country was only just re-covering from the earlier shocks of military defeat and a devastating inflation – Hitler could deploy the whole range of his demagogy. He attacked the victorious Allies, especially the French, for enslaving the German people; and the German republican régime, for its failure to cope with the crisis; and the parties of the Left, for dividing the nation; and the parties of the Right, for their ineffectiveness; and the plutocrats and monopolists, for exploiting everyone else. In fact he attacked everybody, even if his most ferocious attacks were reserved for the Jews. And above all he offered a show of iron deter-mination, of readiness to act and act radically, in a society unaccustomed to the uncertainties which are inseparable from democracy – and especially from new and inexperienced democracy. All these things helped Hitler to power – or rather, helped him to the 37·3 per cent of the total vote which was the most he ever obtained in a truly free election (July 1932). And the one thing on which all witnesses seem to agree is that the Germany in which Hitler came to power was not in fact a country gripped in a frenzy of antisemitism, hypnotized by the

[1] *C. V. Zeitung*, Vol. VIII (1929), p. 561, and Vol. IX (1930), p. 15.

myth of the Jewish world-conspiracy and thirsting for the blood of the Jews. Admittedly the most popular edition of the *Protocols* had sold nearly 100,000 copies in a dozen years – but Remarque's famous anti-war and left-wing novel *All Quiet on the Western Front*, published in 1929, sold a quarter of a million copies in a single year, and plenty of other 'progressive' novels also enjoyed big sales.

Nor can it be taken for granted that even the whole of the Nazi party itself, with its relatively small membership of about one million, was fanatically antisemitic. In 1934 an enterprising American sociologist, Theodore Abel, advertised for life-histories by members of the party, showing what led them to join. Six hundred members voluntarily sent in their autobiographies. The astonishing fact is that 60 per cent of these Nazis never mentioned antisemitism at all. Some even expressly dissociated themselves from this aspect of party policy: 'It quickened my pulse to hear about the Fatherland, unity and the need for a supreme leader. I felt that I belonged to these people. Only their statements about the Jews I could not swallow. They gave me a headache even after I had joined the party.' Moreover, statistical analysis showed that whereas antisemitic sentiments figured in nearly half the life-histories supplied by members of the middle classes, including the liberal professions, they figured in less than 30 per cent of those supplied by industrial or agricultural workers.[1] If real commitment to the antisemitic cause was as exceptional inside the party as this survey suggests, it can hardly have been widespread in the mass of the population which did not join the party.

Yet when all qualifications are made, it remains true that very many of the seventeen million who voted Nazi in 1933 must have been willing to expose their Jewish fellow-citizens at least to some loss of civil liberties. And there can be no doubt, either, that there were plenty of fanatical anti-semites, for instance in the national student movement (which had been captured by the Nazis in 1931) and among the 400,000 members of the SA (Storm Troop) – some hundreds of thousands who would have agreed with the contributor to Abel's collection who said: 'The history of the world would

[1] T. Abel, *Why Hitler Came into Power*, New York. 1938, p. 164.

have lost its meaning if Judaism, with its corroding spirit, the embodiment of all evil, were to win the victory over the true and good encompassed in Adolf Hitler's idea. My belief is that our leader, Adolf Hitler, was given by fate to the German nation as our saviour, bringing light into darkness.'[1] Such were the fruits of fifty years of propaganda, culminating in fourteen years of intensive, virulent, unrelenting propaganda since the war, operating above all on the young. They were deadly fruits, for it was precisely this mixture of the fanaticism of a minority with the indifference of the many that made possible the whole development, from the first restrictions to the final extermination.[2]

In February 1933 Hitler became Chancellor, and on 1 April the persecution of the Jews began with a compulsory one-day boycott of Jewish shops. Already in justification of this first antisemitic measure the *Protocols* were invoked – notably by Julius Streicher in the *Völkischer Beobachter*. The 'Plan of Basel,'[3] he declared, had been on the point of fulfilment, but 'on Saturday, 1 April, at 10 a.m., the German people begins defensive action against the Jewish world-criminals! National-Socialists! Strike down the world-enemy!'[4] The boycott was a try-out; as nobody protested, the Government proceeded to introduce antisemitic legislation. Very soon Jews were excluded from the civil service and the liberal professions, and in

[1] Ibid., p. 243.

[2] The findings of W. S. Allen, in *The Nazi Seizure of Power: the experience of a single German town, 1930–1935*, Chicago 1965, pp. 77–8 and 209–12, suggest that the divergence between the fanatical Nazis and the bulk of the population was even greater than is indicated here. Whereas for the fanatics antisemitism was a deadly serious matter, most people regarded the antisemitic propaganda as so much talk, which was quite unrelated to the Jews they knew personally and would in any case not lead to serious persecution. Allen's study concerns a single middle-sized town in Hanover and his findings are not necessarily valid for the whole country. This much however seems certain: antisemitism played only a limited part in bringing Hitler to power, but indifference played an important part in facilitating the subsequent persecution. See below, pp. 210–13.

[3] 'Plan of Basel' because the *Protocols* were supposed to have originated at the first Zionist congress at Basel.

[4] Article by Streicher in the *Völkischer Beobachter*, issue of 31 March 1933.

September 1935 the Nuremberg Laws finally cast them out from the community of the German nation. And in the non-stop propaganda campaign which accompanied these measures the *Protocols* and the Jewish world-conspiracy bulked very large indeed. The *Völkischer Beobachter* invoked them constantly, while Streicher's weekly *Der Stürmer* alternated between elaborations of the *Protocols* and lurid stories of German maidens raped by Jews and German children ritually murdered. The efforts of *Der Stürmer* were particularly important, for this vile paper had a circulation of nearly half a million – one of the biggest of any German periodical – and it was also displayed on special notice-boards in towns and villages throughout the country; most sinister of all, it was used in schools.

The *Protocols* themselves were officially advertised. A party edition carried an urgent appeal to every citizen: 'It is the duty of every German to study the terrifying avowal of the Elders of Zion, and to compare them with the boundless misery of our people; and then to draw the necessary conclusions and to see to it that this book comes into the hands of every German. . . . We, German racists, must be grateful to Providence for illumining our path precisely at the moment when all seemed lost. Difficult struggles await us. The first task is to disintoxicate the soul of the German people and to wake its understanding of the nobility of the Aryan race. With God, for the resurrection of Germany!'[1] The *Protocols* did in fact sell excellently – and, unlike that other sacred text of the Third Reich, *Mein Kampf*, they were not only purchased but read. And it is certain, too, that many of those who read them became fanatical believers.[2] In less than two years after Hitler's accession to power intellectual and moral standards in Germany had dropped to a point where a Minister of Education could prescribe the *Protocols* as one of the basic textbooks for schools.

These developments did not affect the Jews alone. In

[1] *Die Geheimnisse der Weisen von Zion*, Parteiverlag, Munich, 1933, p. 3 and 21.

[2] F. Bauer, 'Antinazistische Prozesse und politisches Bewusstsein', in *Antisemitismus: zur Pathologie der bürgerlichen Gesellschaft*, ed. H. Huss and A. Schröder, Frankfort/Main, 1965, p. 177.

tsarist Russia the myth of the Jewish world-conspiracy had been used as a means of discrediting the revolutionary movement; in the Weimar Republic it had been used by the Nazis as a means of discrediting the democratic régime; now in the Third Reich it was used as a means not only of discrediting possible opponents of the dictatorship but also of justifying the whole régime of terror. Writing in 1935 Reinhard Heydrich, Himmler's principal lieutenant, noted that all oppositional organizations had been smashed – but at the same time insisted that the Judeo-Masonic world-conspiracy was still pursuing its aim of undermining, poisoning, and destroying the German people. 'We must learn, from the history of the last few thousand years, to recognize the enemy. Then we shall suddenly see that we are today, for the first time, grasping the enemy at the very roots of his strength. Can one wonder that he defends himself all the more fiercely?' He admitted that this supposed activity of the great conspiracy was so little evident that it was almost impossible to detect: 'When after the seizure of power all visible opposition disappeared and the spiritual struggle began, many of our SS lacked the arms for this struggle because they failed to recognize the all-embracing nature of the enemy.' Nevertheless he insisted: 'We fighters must face it: We need years of bitter struggle to drive back the enemy finally in all fields, to destroy him and to make Germany secure, in its blood and its spirit, against new penetrations by the enemy.'[1]

What this meant in practice was that anyone whom the régime wished to persecute and destroy, for whatever reason, could be denounced as an agent of the perennial Jewish world-conspiracy. It also meant that to deny the reality of that world-conspiracy was to label oneself as an enemy of the régime and to expose oneself to persecution and destruction. So an anti-semitic myth originally concocted by a few eccentric priests in reaction against the French Revolution became in the 1930s a device by which a despotic government could consolidate its hold over a great European nation.

The myth of the Jewish world-conspiracy was also a means

[1] Quoted in H. Buchheim, *Die SS – Das Herrschaftsinstrument. Befehl und Gehorsam* (vol. I of *Anatomie des SS-Staates*), Olten and Freiburg im Breisgau, 1965, pp. 114-15.

by which the Government tried to make its foreign policy acceptable to the German people. That policy aimed at war, but that is an aim which no modern European government – not even Hitler's – could openly admit. From 1933 onwards German foreign policy was therefore presented as above all a defence against a deadly encirclement organized by the Jews. In particular the Soviet Union was portrayed as Hitler had always imagined it – as a land of sub-men ruled by Jews. Goebbels regularly distinguished himself by his outbursts on this subject at the annual party rallies at Nuremberg. In 1935 he declared that Bolshevism was a Satanic plot which could have been hatched only in the brain of a nomad; while Nazi Germany was a bulwark against which the Asiatic-Jewish flood would break in vain. A year later he announced that Bolshevism was pathological and criminal nonsense concocted and organized by the Jews for the purpose of destroying the European nations and establishing world-domination on their ruins.[1] Streicher also had some eloquent things to say. When the Soviet Union was at last admitted to the League of Nations, in 1935, he argued that the governments of the democracies which had supported this move must consist of those famous 300 men mentioned by Rathenau – 'and those 300 men are members of the Jewish race and conspirators of Freemasonry'.[2]

Meanwhile various diligent researchers were producing works with titles like *Jews Behind Stalin* to show that everyone of any importance in the Soviet Union was a Jew. As in reality almost all the Jews who were at all prominent in the Soviet Communist party were just then being liquidated by Stalin, this was no easy task – but it was accomplished just the same, by the simple device of ascribing Jewish descent to everyone with a Latvian, Armenian, or Tartar name and to a lot of ordinary Russians as well. It is true that this procedure was soon extended beyond the Soviet Union. Soon every politician anywhere who tried to thwart Hitler's plans – starting with Roosevelt – was declared to be a Jew, a half-Jew, or at least

[1] On Goebbels's antisemitic propaganda 1935–38 see E. K. Dramsted, *Goebbels and National Socialist Propaganda 1925–1945*, Michigan State U.P., 1965, and Z. A. B. Zeman, *Nazi Propaganda*, London, 1964.

[2] J. Streicher, 'Der Feind des Völkerfriedens', in *Der Judenkenner*, No. 5 (March 1935), p. 94.

married to a Jewess. Enormous quantities of propaganda along these lines were put out by Goebbels's Propaganda Ministry – where little of it was believed – and by various party offices under Rosenberg – where rather more was believed. Strange contortions were performed in 1939–40, to fit the needs of the German-Soviet non-aggression pact; it was even discovered that the Soviet Union was not ruled by Jews at all and that the whole idea had been a deception practised on simple Germans by a Judaised Britain. This, however, taxed the ingenuity even of Goebbels, and it must have been a relief when in 1941 the identification of Jews with Communists proved to have been right after all.

Yet whatever other targets this propaganda might be directed against and whatever other purposes it might be made to serve, its main target was always the Jews themselves, and its main purpose was to present these human beings as demonic beings. At the end of that path lies murder – and already before the war those who dealt in the *Protocols* were hinting at a possibility which was beginning to take shape in their imagination. By the end of 1936 *Der Stürmer* was looking forward to a world-wide cleansing operation: 'The mobilization of the German people's will to destroy the bacillus lodged in its body is a declaration of war on all Jews throughout the world. Its final result will decide the problem whether the world is to be redeemed by German virtues or to perish by the Jewish poison. . . . We believe in the final victory of the German people and thus in the liberation of all non-Jewish humanity. Those who vanquish the world-Jew will save the earth from the Devil.'[1] At the Nuremberg party rally of 1937 Goebbels excelled himself: 'Europe must see and recognize the danger. . . . We shall point fearlessly to the Jew as the inspirer and originator, the one who profits from these dreadful catastrophes. . . . Look, there is the world's enemy, the destroyer of civilizations, the parasite among the peoples, the son of Chaos, the incarnation of evil, the ferment of decomposition, the demon who brings about the degeneration of mankind.'[2]

[1] Quoted in L. W. Bondy, *Racketeers of Hatred. Julius Streicher and the Jew-baiters' International*, London, 1946, pp. 36–7.
[2] Text in *Der Parteitag der Arbeit* (i.e. proceedings of the 1937 congress), Zentralverlag der NSDAP, Munich, 1938, p. 157.

By October 1938 it was possible to be more precise, and *Der Stürmer* could write of the Jews: 'Bacteria, vermin and pests cannot be tolerated. For reasons of cleanliness and hygiene we must make them harmless by *killing them off*.'[1]

All this would have been mere rhetoric if it had not been for the war, which by 1941 placed the majority of European Jews in Hitler's power and gave him vast and remote spaces in which to carry out the exterminations.[2] As we have seen, Hitler defined his war as a war waged by 'world Jewry' against National-Socialist Germany; and once the exterminations began this became a constant theme in internal German propaganda. Not that the propaganda ever spoke unambiguously of mass executions and gassing (that was strictly forbidden), but it constantly hinted that the Jews were being made to pay for the war with their lives. It was a curious manoeuvre, as though the Nazi leaders were trying to involve the whole German people in their own guilt, yet without ever really admitting that guilt.

Very soon after the German forces invaded Russia a booklet appeared under the sponsorship of Goebbels and with the title *German Soldiers See the Soviet Union*. 'The Jewish question,' it reported, 'is being solved with imposing thoroughness. . . . As the Führer put it . . .: "Should Jewry succeed in inciting the European nations to a senseless war, this will mean the end of this race in Europe!" The Jew ought to have known that the Führer is accustomed to take his word seriously, and now he has to bear the consequences. They are inexorably hard but necessary if ultimately quiet and peace are to reign among nations.'[3] By November 1941 Goebbels himself was in effect publicly justifying the killing of Jews. 'In this historical contest,' he declared, 'each Jew is our enemy. . . . All Jews by virtue of their birth and race belong to an international conspiracy against National-Socialist Germany. . . . Each German soldier who falls in this war goes to the debt account of the

---

[1] Quoted in Bondy, op. cit., p. 61.

[2] Already before the war hundreds of German Jews were killed in the concentration camps; but the number of political prisoners who perished was far greater. It was the war that opened up the possibility of destroying the Jewish population of Europe.

[3] Quoted in M. Weinreich, *Hitler's Professors*, New York, 1946, p. 141.

Jews. He is on their conscience and they, therefore, must pay for it.'[1] In a speech at Karlsruhe in May 1942 the head of the German Labour Front, Robert Ley went further still: 'It is not enough to isolate the Jewish enemy of mankind – the Jew has got to be exterminated.'[2] In the same month the party journal *Volk und Rasse* announced: 'A right understanding of Jewry must require its complete annihilation.'[3]

By 1943 even the antiquated myth of Jewish ritual murder was being revived. In the 1930s this theme had been practically reserved for Streicher and *Der Stürmer*, but now men with university doctorates began to produce solemn tomes to show that ritual murder represented in miniature what the war demonstrated on a grand scale – the Jewish plan to kill off all Christians. Himmler was so enchanted by one of these books that he distributed copies throughout the senior ranks of the SS and sent hundreds more to be distributed to the extermination squads in Russia. And he had another bright idea: 'We must at once employ investigators in England[4] to follow and check the reports of trials and police announcements concerning missing children, so that we can include short announcements in our broadcasts, that a child has disappeared in such-and-such a place, and that this is probably the result of a Jewish ritual murder. . . . I am of the opinion that we could give antisemitism an incredible virulence by means of anti-semitic propaganda in English, perhaps even in Russian, giving special publicity to ritual murders.'[5]

It was a delusion shared by Hitler, Himmler, and Goebbels that British and American morale could be undermined by propaganda about the Jewish world-conspiracy. This propaganda did indeed have some effect in France and even in Britain in the winter of 1939–40, when there was a good deal of vague talk about 'the Jews' war'; but it had less and less effect thereafter, and it was a fantastic miscalculation that led Goebbels in 1943 to devote from 70 per cent to 80 per cent of

[1] Quoted in Weinreich, op. cit., pp. 144–5.
[2] Quoted in Bondy, op. cit., p. 157.
[3] Quoted in Weinreich, op. cit., p. 185.
[4] [sic] A novel use for spies in wartime!
[5] Text in L. Poliakov and J. Wulf, *Das Dritte Reich und die Juden*, Berlin-Grunewald, 1955, p. 360.

all foreign broadcasts to antisemitic themes.[1] The Nazi leaders were however so firmly locked in their delusion that they really expected big antisemitic movements to arise in Britain and the United States, overthrow the democratic régimes, make peace with Germany and join in the work of exterminating the Jews. Some insight into their state of mind is provided by Johann von Leers,[2] whom Rosenberg had imposed on the University of Jena as a full professor and who specialized in the *Protocols*, *The Rabbi's Speech*, and tales of ritual murder. This is what he had to say in the foreword to his book *Die Verbrechernatur der Juden* (*The Criminal Nature of the Jews*), in 1942:

If the hereditary criminal nature of Jewry can be demonstrated, then not only is each people morally justified in exterminating the hereditary criminals – but any people that still keeps and protects Jews is just as guilty of an offence against public safety as someone who cultivates cholera-germs without observing the proper precautions.

By this time the fortunes of war were turning against Germany, and so the Jewish world-conspiracy was invoked to reinforce the German will to fight on. In February 1943 the *Deutscher Wochendienst* (*German Weekly Service*), which consisted of confidential instructions issued by Goebbels for the benefit of writers and speakers on politics, made the following recommendation: 'Stress: If we lose the war, we do not fall into the hands of some other states, but will all be annihilated by world Jewry. Jewry is firmly decided to exterminate all Germans. International law and international custom will be no protection against the Jewish will for total annihilation.'[3] This of course was cynical and calculated propaganda, but it was something else as well: a barely disguised description of what Germans were at that moment doing to Jews. For as Germany's chances of winning the war diminished, the drive to exterminate the Jews took on a quality of fury and desperation – as though the Nazi leaders were resolved that this

[1] *The Goebbels Diaries*, ed. Louis P. Lochner, London, 1948, p. 287.

[2] After the war von Leers fled, became a Moslem and, under the name of Omar Amin, worked as an adviser to President Nasser on propaganda. He died in 1965.

[3] Quoted in R. Hilberg, *The Destruction of the European Jews*, Chicago, 1961, p. 655.

victory at least, the most essential of all, should not slip through their fingers. At the beginning of 1943 new gas-chambers were built at Auschwitz and the first crematoria were solemnly inaugurated in the presence of distinguished visitors from Berlin. In 1943 and 1944 the process of extermination was stepped up until, by the summer of 1944, 12,000, 15,000, even 22,000 Jews were being gassed and cremated on single days in Auschwitz alone.

By the autumn of 1944 the holocaust was nearing its conclusion, but propaganda concerning the Jewish world-conspiracy continued unabated. In September the *Deutscher Wochendienst* insisted that speakers and writers must present Jewry as the one real enemy and the sole instigator and prolonger of the war. Propaganda distributed to the troops on the eastern front talked quite openly of the extermination – of which they had in any case abundant evidence – and justified it as a purely defensive measure. The following, for instance, comes from a publication of the armed forces, sponsored by the highest military commanders: 'There are still individuals in our people who feel somewhat uncertain in themselves when we speak of the extermination of the Jews in our living-space. The strength of character and the energy of the greatest man our people has produced in a thousand years were necessary to tear the Jewish deception from our eyes. *Jewish plutocracy and Jewish communism are out to hunt down the German people which has escaped from slavery.* Who can speak in this struggle of pity or of Christian charity, etc.? *The Jew must be destroyed wherever we find him.*'[1]

By October 1944 some five to six million Jews had been killed, and Germany was about to be invaded from east and west. Himmler, foreseeing that Auschwitz would shortly be overrun by the Russians and perhaps hoping to ingratiate himself with the Western Allies, ordered an end to the systematic exterminations (though tens of thousands were still to die of hunger and exhaustion). One might have expected that at this point talk of the *Protocols* and of the Jewish world-conspiracy would cease at last – but that is not what happened. 'The Jews,' wrote Goebbels in January 1945, 'are the incarnation of that destructive drive which in these terrible years

---

[1] Text in Weinreich, op. cit., p. 212.

rages in the enemies' warfare against everything that we consider noble, beautiful and worth preserving. . . . Who drives Russians, Englishmen and Americans into the fire and offers hecatombs of other people's lives in a struggle without prospects against the German people? The Jews! . . . The Jews at the end of this war are going to experience their Cannae. Not Europe but they themselves are going to perish. . . .'[1]

In the midst of this last agony of the Third Reich, in a Berlin reduced to a heap of rubble and about to be overrun, the Propaganda Ministry harked back to the first of all these millions of murders. On 29 December 1944, for the benefit of the German press, it repeated the lie which had bemused Rathenau's assassins a generation earlier: 'The central issue of this war is the breaking of Jewish world-domination. If it were possible to checkmate the 300 secret Jewish kings who rule the world, the peoples of this earth would at last find their peace.'[2] It was an admission of defeat, strictly comparable with that ultimate defeat which is the fate of the paranoiac. After incomparably the greatest and cruellest massacres in history, the Nazi leaders felt themselves not one step nearer their aim.

It remained for the chief administrator of the whole extermination, Adolf Eichmann, to suggest an explanation for this singular failure. At his trial at Jerusalem in 1961 Eichmann maintained that Hitler himself was nothing but a pawn and a marionette in the hands of 'the Satanic international high-finance of the western world' – meaning, of course, the mysterious, undiscoverable and omnipotent Elders of Zion.[3]

2

What, in the end, did all the propaganda achieve? There is no simple answer to that question. The picture that Hitler and Goebbels liked to present to the world was of a nation solidly

[1] Quoted ibid., p. 203.
[2] Politischer Dienst (Arbeitsmaterial für Presse und Publizistik), No. 370 (Distributed by Abteilung Deutsche Presse der Presseabteilung der Reichsregierung).
[3] L. Poliakov, *Le Procès de Jérusalem*, Paris, 1963, pp. 284–5.

united in a passionate determination to defeat the Jewish
world-conspiracy. Confronted with the almost unbelievable
fact of five or six million murdered Jews, many in the outside
world found it easy enough, at the end of the war, to accept
this picture as accurate. But how accurate was it?

The picture that emerges from first-hand observations made
in Germany under the Nazi régime is more complex. It is
perfectly true that already by the time Hitler came to power
a large part of the German population was infected with
antisemitism – and in a form which went a good deal beyond
the rather vague prejudice current in the western democracies.
The typical German antisemite wanted to see German Jews
excluded from public office, subjected to disabilities in their
education and careers, pushed into a position of an under-
privileged minority. There, however, his demands stopped.
Unjust and uncivilized as they were, they were yet very
different from the aspirations of Hitler and his associates.

Within the first couple of years of the Nazi régime all these
demands were fulfilled and more than fulfilled. Jews disappeared from all positions of prominence and influence,
personal contacts between Jew and non-Jew practically
ceased, the mass emigration of Jews began. Now the question
was – what next? It was conceivable that the limited antisemitism of the many would expire because it no longer
had a real objective. It was also conceivable that it would be
whipped up to a higher level of intensity, transformed into a
murderous fanaticism. By exploiting the myth of the Jewish
world-conspiracy the Nazi leadership hoped to forestall the
first of these possibilities and to achieve the second. How far
did they succeed?

A very shrewd and experienced observer, Michael Müller-
Claudius, who had been studying the development of antisemitism for many years, carried out investigations in 1938
and again in 1942. After the officially organized pogrom of
9–10 November 1938, when squads of young Nazis destroyed
and looted synagogues and Jewish shops and houses throughout Germany and killed some scores of Jews, Müller-Claudius
had informal conversations with 41 party-members from all
social strata. To the casual comment, 'Well – so a start is being
made at last with carrying out the programme against the

Jews?' he got the following reactions: 26 persons, or 63 per cent of the total, expressed downright indignation at the outrages; a further 13 persons, or 32 per cent, answered non-committally; 2 persons (a student and a bank employee) approved – and they did so because they believed in the Jewish world-conspiracy. In the eyes of this 5 per cent physical violence against Jews was justified because 'terror must be met with terror'.[1]

Four years later Müller-Claudius carried out a further investigation. It was the autumn of 1942, when the remaining German Jews were being deported to an unknown destination in the east – ostensibly, to do manual labour as a contribution to the war effort. This time he put a series of skilfully designed questions to 61 party-members, again chosen from all social strata. The result was different in various respects. Only 16 persons, or 26 per cent, showed signs of concern for the Jews, while the proportion of the indifferent had risen to 69 per cent (42 persons). The proportion of fanatics, on the other hand, was unchanged: 3 persons, or 5 per cent of the total. And for this group, as before, the Jewish world-conspiracy was a self-evident fact and the extermination of the Jews an absolute necessity: 'It's obvious that the destruction of Jewry is a war-aim. Without it the final victory would not be secure.' – 'International Jewry provoked the war. . . . After the final victory the Jewish race must cease to exist.' – '(The Führer) owes it to mankind to liberate it from Jewry. . . . The Führer will order how they are to be exterminated.'[2]

These findings of Müller-Claudius, which have been substantially confirmed by other careful observers, enable one to estimate with some objectivity what Hitler and Goebbels achieved and what they failed to achieve.[3] On the one hand the

[1] M. Müller-Claudius, *Der Antisemitismus und das deutsche Verhängnis*, Frankfurt/Main, 1948, pp. 162–6.

[2] Ibid., pp. 166–72. The whole book is a most valuable study of anti-semitism in Germany from the 1920s to the end of the Third Reich, and it deserves to be much better known than it is.

[3] Expert examination of 1,000 German prisoners of war over the period 1942–44 showed 24 per cent to be more or less critical of the régime; 65 per cent to have the kind of attitude which suggests that, if they had been asked about the Jews, they would have reacted with indifference; and 11 per cent to be fanatically Nazi. The rather higher

mass of the German population was never truly fanaticized against the Jews, it was never obsessed by the myth of the Jewish world-conspiracy, it could not really think of the war as an apocalyptic struggle against 'Eternal Jewry' – but on the other hand it dissociated itself from the Jews more and more completely as the years passed. By 1942 most people at least suspected that something dreadful was happening to the deported Jews, and an appreciable number must have known, for professional reasons, just what was happening – and few cared much. The contrast between 1938 and 1942 shows the extent to which the whole population had been conditioned not so much to positive hatred as to utter indifference.

Of course allowance has to be made for the traditional German subservience to authority; for the strain and harassment of war; for the increasingly ruthless terror which was being exercised against the population itself. Yet the fact remains that when it was realized that the inmates of lunatic asylums were being killed, powerful protests were uttered, and with considerable effect; whereas hardly a voice was raised on behalf of the Jews. The reason seems plain enough. Anyone who spoke up for the Jews was at once labelled as a member of their conspiracy and fit only to share their fate; and very few were prepared to expose themselves and their families to such hazards. In such circumstances it is extremely tempting to disguise one's timidity by identifying oneself at least partly with the official attitude. There was no need to talk of the Elders of Zion – it was enough to agree that Jews were somehow sinister, in any case not deserving of anyone's concern. And this attitude at least the Nazi leadership managed to instil into the great majority of the population.

In the minds of most Germans, German Jews ceased altogether to be regarded as compatriots, the last traces of solidarity disappeared; as for the Jews in countries occupied

proportion of fanatics is not surprising, as the Müller-Claudius sample consisted entirely of people old enough to have belonged to the party by 1933 at the latest, whereas most of the prisoners of war had spent their adolescence under the Nazi régime. See Henry V. Dicks, 'Personality traits and National Socialist ideology', in *Human Relations*, Vol. III, No. 2 (June 1950), pp. 111–54, London and Ann Arbor, U.S.A.

by the Germans, hardly anyone gave them a thought. A mood of passive compliance became general. And meanwhile the fanatics, if no more numerous than before, acquired a new importance. Scattered through the civilian population and the armed forces were individuals, certainly numbering many hundreds of thousands, perhaps even a couple of million, who accepted the conspiracy-myth with all its murderous implications and who were prepared to denounce anyone who questioned it to the SD (security service). It was a state of affairs which, if it fell far short of Hitler's ideal, still enabled him to proceed unmolested with the extermination of European Jewry.[1]

Much the same applied to the organization which actually planned and carried out the extermination. Here too only a minority consisted of genuine fanatics. At the higher levels there were plenty of criminal opportunists for whom the whole murderous business was simply a chance for extortion, loot, and professional advancement. Among the camp guards there were also plenty of opportunists, who simply preferred a comfortable and privileged existence to the dangers and hardships of the front; and there were also some true sadists, hungry for the chance to beat and torture. And at all levels there were plenty of mere conformists—people who simply followed the line of least resistance, went wherever they were directed, did whatever they were told to do, automatically. Yet it is still true that all these people needed a pretext for their activities, some excuse which would enable them to kill and kill with an easy conscience. And at every level of the SD and SS there were fanatics eager to provide just such a justification, in the form of the myth of the Jewish world-conspiracy.

So this old myth, as reinterpreted by Hitler, became part of the ideology of the most ruthless and efficient body of professional killers in all human history. The psychoanalyst Bruno Bettelheim found that the SS guards at Dachau and

[1] A subtle socio-psychological study of the German population under the Nazi régime is: Wanda von Baeyer-Katte, *Das Zerstörende in der Politik*, Heidelberg, 1958.

Buchenwald believed absolutely in the Jewish world-con-spiracy.[1] Rudolf Hoess, the commandant of Auschwitz, at the time regarded the extermination of the Jews as necessary 'so that Germany and our posterity might be freed for ever from their relentless adversaries'; and if he later decided that the extermination was wrong after all, that was only because by discrediting Germany it 'brought the Jews far closer to their ultimate objective' of world-domination.[2] For many of the SS the conspiracy-myth was in fact far more than an ideology or a world-view – it was something which took possession of their psyches, so that they were able, for instance, to burn small children alive without any conscious feelings of com-passion or of guilt.[3]

The leaders of these men expected no less of them. In October 1943, at Posen, Himmler said to a group of high-ranking SS: 'We had a moral duty towards our people, the duty to exterminate this people which wanted to exterminate us. . . . Most of you know what it means to see a pile of 100 corpses, or of 500, or of 1,000. To have gone through that, and still – with a few exceptions – to have remained decent people, that is what has toughened us. It is a glorious page of our history, which has never been written and never will be. . . .'[4] Others were less reticent still. In August 1942 Hitler and Himmler visited the Polish town of Lublin to discuss methods of extermination with the local head of the SS and SD, the Austrian, Odilo Globocnik. When a member of Hitler's suite asked whether the dead Jews should not be cremated rather than buried, 'as a future generation might think differently of these matters', General Globocnik replied: 'But, gentlemen, if after us such a cowardly and rotten generation should arise that it does not understand our work which is so good and so necessary, then, gentlemen, all National-Socialism will have been for nothing. On the contrary, bronze plaques should be put up with the inscription that it was we, we who had the

---

[1] B. Bettelheim, *The Informed Heart*, London, 1961, p. 226.

[2] R. Hoess, *Commandant of Auschwitz*, London, 1959, pp. 153, 178.

[3] Cf. Elie A. Cohen, *Human Behavior in the Concentration Camp*, trans. M. H. Braaksma, New York, 1953, pp. 273 seq.

[4] Text in L. Poliakov and J. Wulf, *Das Dritte Reich und die Juden*, p. 215.

courage to achieve this gigantic task.' Hitler agreed: 'Yes, my good Globocnik, that is the word, that is my opinion, too.'[1] One day the SS doctor Pfannenstiel (he was also Professor of Hygiene at the University of Marburg) visited the extermination camp of Treblinka. The camp SS gave a banquet in his honour and in his speech of thanks the doctor said: 'Your task is a great duty, a duty useful and necessary. . . . Looking at the bodies of the Jews, one understands the greatness of your good work.'[2]

These are extraordinary words and they point to an extraordinary phenomenon. In the middle of the twentieth century, in the heart of civilized Europe, there had appeared a large body of men in whom there was no trace of what traditionally had been known as conscience and humanity. These technicians of genocide went blithely about their business – and even today those of them who appear before the German courts seem quite unrepentant. No doubt many factors – of innate temperament and childhood experience and later training – combined to produce this result. It is still true that in order to do what they did these men needed an ideology, and that this was provided by the *Protocols* and the myth of the Jewish world-conspiracy.

[1] *Trials of War Criminals before the Nürnberg Military Tribunal under Control Council Law No. 10.* U.S. Government Printing Office, Washington. Vol. I, pp. 866 seq. (deposition of Kurt Gerstein).

[2] Ibid., p. 870.

CHAPTER X

Forgery Pushers on Trial

1

ALREADY in the 1890s Mgr Meurin called on the rulers of
Europe to league themselves against the Jewish conspiracy.
In 1906 Tsar Nicholas II and Count Lamsdorf tried, however
ineffectively, to build a system of alliances on just such a
basis. As conceived by these pioneers the Antisemitic International would have been an inter-governmental organization
for the suppression of revolutionary, radical, and even merely
liberal movements throughout Europe. The Nazis took over
the idea and gave it a new content. This seems to have been
the work above all of a German from the Baltic provinces of
Russia, Max Erwin von Scheubner-Richter, during the short
period when he was a leading theoretician of the Nazi Party
(he was shot dead in the Munich *putsch* of 1923, as he marched
arm in arm with Hitler). Reflecting on the fact that Jews are
to be found all over the world, Scheubner-Richter hit on the
notion that antisemitism might provide a means by which
German National-Socialism could find allies abroad.

Unlike his predecessors the Archbishop of Port-Louis and
the Russian Foreign Minister, Scheubner-Richter did not
think of these allies as being necessarily governments – they
could just as well be right-wing revolutionaries. Already at
that early stage in the party's history one comes across the
slogan, modelled on the famous ending of *The Communist
Manifesto:* 'Antisemites of all countries, unite!' Hitler himself
adopted the idea with enthusiasm – Hermann Rauschning
reports him as saying: 'Antisemitism is a useful revolutionary
expedient. . . . Antisemitic propaganda in all countries is an
almost indispensable medium for the extension of our political
campaign. You will see how little time we shall need to upset

the ideas and criteria of the whole world, simply by attacking Judaism. It is beyond question the most important weapon in my propaganda arsenal. . . .'[1] The Nazis did in fact propagate the myth of the Jewish conspiracy throughout the world in the hope that it would undermine resistance to their own drive for world-domination. And in this campaign the *Protocols* played a vital part. Of the three books that made up the sacred scriptures of Nazism and which sold in millions – *Mein Kampf*, Rosenberg's *Myth of the Twentieth Century*, and the *Protocols* – only the last was exported for propaganda abroad.

The propagation and defence of the *Protocols* outside Germany was mainly the responsibility of an organization called the *Weltdienst* (World Service), headed by a retired colonel, Ulrich Fleischhauer. A disciple of Theodor Fritsch and a friend of Dietrich Eckart, Fleischhauer emerged from the First World War to found, already in 1919, a centre for the dissemination of antisemitic propaganda, the U. Bodung publishing house at Erfurt. The moment Hitler took power in 1933 he received a memorandum, ostensibly from 'a few undaunted nationalists from Holland, Belgium, Luxemburg, Switzerland, Austria and Hungary', urging that a 'technical assistance office' should be set up as the nucleus for an international antisemitic movement. This office would concern itself with establishing liaison between antisemites in various countries and with the dissemination of antisemitic 'enlightenment' throughout the 'Aryan-Christian' world. The appeal was successful: Fleischhauer's organization was officially encouraged to embark on a major expansion – which incidentally provided comfortable jobs for several of the 'dauntless nationalists'. Under the name of *Weltdienst* the Erfurt centre acquired a certain importance and notoriety in the years up to the outbreak of war. By 1937 it could boast that 'for the first time in world history, international Jewry was faced by an international counter-organization, the cell of a true League of Nations. . . . Our work reaches to the furthest corners of the earth.'[2]

---

[1] H. Rauschning, *Hitler Speaks*, London, 1939, p. 233.

[2] On the *Weltdienst* see L. W. Bondy, *Racketeers of Hatred*, pp. 66–105; Z. A. B. Zeman, *Nazi Propaganda*, pp. 72–3; and O. J. Rogge, *The Official German Report*, New York, 1961, notably pp. 76–8.

Fleischhauer consistently denied that the *Weltdienst* was connected with the German Government or with the Nazi party, but these statements, always inherently implausible, are now known to have been false. From 1933 to 1937 the *Weltdienst* was subsidized by the Propaganda Ministry and from 1937 onwards by the foreign policy office of the Nazi party under Rosenberg. This backing enabled it to carry on propaganda of various kinds. It published a fortnightly, also called *Weltdienst*, the aim of which was stated at the head of each copy: 'To enlighten ill-informed Gentiles, irrespective of the state or country to which they may belong. These information sheets, which deal with the machinations of the Jewish underworld, accordingly form a necessary part of the intellectual armoury of every Gentile.' This publication was translated into many languages,[1] and so were the various antisemitic brochures that supplemented it. The *Weltdienst* also organized international conferences – which, unlike those organized by Julius Streicher, were held in secret; at the conference at Erfurt in 1937 as many as twenty-two countries were represented. The object of all this activity was to build up an international network based on blind belief in the *Protocols* and the Jewish world-conspiracy.

As early as 1934–35 two sensational trials, one in South Africa and the other in Switzerland, drew attention to what was going on. In July and August 1934 a local division of the Supreme Court, sitting at Grahamstown, Eastern Province, South Africa, heard a civil action brought by the Rev. Abraham Levy, minister of the Western Road synagogue, Port Elizabeth, against three leaders of the Nazi-type organization known as the Grey Shirt Movement. The three men, Johannes von Strauss von Moltke, Harry Victor Inch, and David Hermannus Olivier, were sued for having published a scurrilous document on the lines of the *Protocols*. The trial created a great stir in South Africa. Its political significance was emphasized by the defendants themselves, who appeared in uniform – von Moltke in the uniform of the South African

---

[1] During the war the number rose from half a dozen to eighteen. But by then Fleischhauer had been ousted and his organization merged into the Institute of the NSDAP for Research into the Jewish Question, at Frankfort.

Gentile National-Socialists, the others in that of the Grey
Shirt Movement; and just before the trial began the Grey
Shirt newspaper *Die Waarheid* (i.e. *Truth*) published long
extracts from the *Protocols*.[1]

The fabricated document had been read aloud at two political meetings and printed in the newspaper *Die Rapport*, edited
by Olivier. Like the *Protocols*, it was supposed to be an outline
of the Jewish plan for world-domination, but in crudity and
sadism it surpasses all earlier antisemitic forgeries and faithfully mirrors the new age which began when the Nazis came
to power.[2] The conclusion of the document gives a fair impression of its quality:

> We will fool the public, so that their belief in *Live and Let Live*
> will be intensified a thousandfold. We will make them digest as
> much silly rot as their decayed and filthy minds are capable of
> understanding. Hitler, Lunatic Goering, Von Papen and their co-
> Lunatics, with the Asylum Contingent (namely the Brownshirts),
> are guilty of devastation, and crimes against Civilization, which
> we have built up. They raped our women, murdered our old men,
> bombarded and dynamited our Synagogues, Threw our children to
> their hunting dogs, – Made our little ones to dance on hot coals until
> they fried. Made our husbands run the gauntlets in the passage
> ways in our clubs while they themselves struck them as they
> passed. . . .
>
> Brethren, although for countless centuries you have been des-
> pised and hated, in the near future the races of the Earth will kiss
> your feet and worship you, they shall bow down before thee and
> praise thee. They shall beg mercy of thee and *thou shalt refuse*. They
> shalt [*sic*] acknowledge that thou art the Chosen, the *Infallible*.
> Our elected leader will be the first Sovereign over all the Earth.
> The Communist World. And at last the Talmud Torah and
> Prophecies will be fulfilled. I may say that we are on the threshold.

----

[1] *Die Waarheid* called itself the 'official organ of the South African
National Party with which is incorporated the S.A. Gentile National-
Socialist Movement and the S.A. Grey Shirts'. Extracts from the
Protocols were printed in the issue of 1 June 1934.

[2] The main features of the trial are recorded in the judgement read by
Sir Thomas Graham and Mr Justice Gutsche in the Supreme Court on
Tuesday, 21 August 1934. The judgement is printed in full in a 64-page
pamphlet published by Grocott and Sherry, Grahamstown: *Judgment,
Grey Shirt Libel Action at Grahamstown*. The fabricated document is
given at pp. 5–8.

On your very life take care of these instructions, do not mention
a word to not even your own what is contained in these pages. You
know our law. You know the Result. . . .

ISSUED BY THE SELECT HIGH CIRCLE OF THE ANTI-NAZI PRO-
PAGANDA VIGILANCE COMMITTEE C.X.V.O. 3838 AND AUTHORIZED
FOR USE BY THE TRUSTEE AND THE SIX COUNCIL MEMBERS ONLY.

'RABBI.'

Victor Inch's account of how he came into possession of this
document also deserves to be recorded. He claimed that stolen
Jewish letters had been passed to him by two boys who had
since been 'spirited away' by the Jews; these letters had put
him on the track of the conspiracy and had inspired him to
break into the Western Road synagogue, where he duly found
the document lying on a table. The judges had of course no
difficulty in recognizing this tale as a fabrication. But if Inch
was a liar another of the defendants, David Olivier, was
genuinely deceived. This man was convinced that, with the
document in their possession, his colleagues Inch and von
Moltke went in danger of their lives; on one occasion he had
even collected a commando of 150 farmers to rescue von
Moltke, whom he believed to have been kidnapped by the
Jews. In fact the three defendants represented, in miniature,
that combination of knavery and gullibility which was the
very essence of the Antisemitic International. And that is also
how it looked to the judges at Grahamstown, who fined
Olivier a mere £25, while fining von Moltke £750 and Inch
£1,000. Inch had moreover to face a criminal trial on various
counts, including perjury and uttering a forged document;
and for him the outcome was, in addition to his fine, a sentence
of six years and three months' hard labour.

2

In the Berne trial of 1934–35, which attracted world-wide
attention, the *Weltdienst* was directly involved. Just what this
implied is revealed by correspondence preserved in the Wiener
Library. More surely than any amount of published propaganda, these confidential letters reveal the inner life of the
Antisemitic International – the genuine delusions as well

as the calculating dishonesty, the fierce internal conflicts as well as the underlying unity of purpose. It seems well worth while to rescue a few of these strange documents from oblivion.

The story opens within a few months of Hitler's accession to power. On 13 June 1933 a Swiss antisemitic organization, the National Front, held a demonstration in Berne; among the propaganda distributed were copies of the thirteenth edition of Theodor Fritsch's version of the *Protocols*. The Jewish community of Berne and the united Jewish communities of Switzerland took the opportunity to demonstrate in court the spuriousness of the *Protocols*. Five persons, some of them members of the National Front, others of the Union of Swiss National-Socialists, were cited under the Swiss law forbidding the printing, publication, or sale of indecent writings; the most prominent were Theodor Fischer, the editor of the antisemitic newspaper *Eidgenossen*, and a musician called Silvio Schnell. The Berne court nominated an expert on the *Protocols* and asked each of the parties to nominate an expert of its own. Not surprisingly, the defence was most unwilling to agree to the nomination of experts; and when its objection were over-ruled it still failed to produce an expert. At last it nominated a certain German pastor, but this gentleman could not be traced. When the court met in October 1934, after more than a year's delay, there were still only two experts instead of the stipulated three; nobody had been found who was willing seriously to defend the authenticity of the *Protocols*.

There was also the matter of the witnesses. The plaintiffs produced an impressive array of these, ranging from Chaim Weizmann, who spoke on the aims of Zionism, to the French-man du Chayla and such non-Jewish Russians as Burtsev, Svatikov, and Nicolaevsky, who between them did a good deal to illumine the dark and tortuous story of the *Protocols*. In answer to all this the defence was able to produce only one solitary witness, whose contribution was limited to saying that the *Protocols* were not the only document of their kind – was there not also *The Rabbi's Speech?* – and so they must be genuine. All in all the defence found itself at such a disadvan-tage that it decided to look around, however belatedly, for expert support. An adjournment was requested for this pur-pose and proceedings were suspended until the end of April 1935.

From this point the leading roles were played not by the defendants themselves nor by their counsel but by one Ulrich von Roll, a prominent member of the National Front who bore the title of *Gauleiter* for the Canton Berne, and above all by a sinister individual called Boris Toedtli. Some two years later, in November 1936, the Swiss police raided Toedtli's house in Berne. The letters found there, which led to the arrest of Toedtli on a charge of espionage, afford a vivid glimpse of the manoeuvres which were practised behind the scenes at the Berne trial, on the one hand by the Swiss Nazis, on the other by the *Weltdienst*.

The trial was adjourned on 31 October. On 19 November Ulrich von Roll took a foolhardy and irretrievable step – he sent to the headquarters of the Nazi party at the Brown House, Munich, the following appeal for help:

... I turn to you to enquire, courteously, whether and to what extent you are able and willing to place yourselves at our disposal. . . . Could you possibly supply us with an expert, who at first would simply assist us but later perhaps might act as a proper witness on our side? . . . Do you not think that your cooperation will be of interest or even of importance from your own point and from the point of view of the ideas for the which the NSDAP stands?[1]

Von Roll's initiative brought results: within a couple of weeks contact had been established with Fleischhauer at Erfurt. At once the correspondence takes on an air of clandestinity – all the persons involved, German, Swiss, and Russian, are referred to by cover-names only. This conspiratorial procedure becomes understandable when one realizes that the Swiss Nazis were not asking simply for expert advice. On 16 January 1935 Ulrich von Roll wrote to Fleischhauer:

Either you receive an official permit to export currency – and then you can just as well send the money direct to us in Berne as via Basel or Solothurn; or else somebody brings the money across the border – and then it can be paid into our account in Basel or elsewhere just as well as into any other account. . . .

But soon von Roll had come to regret this arrangement. On

[1] Photostats of the von Roll correspondence printed here are in File 88 in the Wiener Library archives.

21 February he expressed his exasperation in a letter to one of the defendants in the trial:

In my view it's deplorable that we are all so dependent on Erfurt – specially in financial respects. They would certainly be rather more modest and approachable over there, if they didn't know just how very dependent we are on them. . . .

The *Weltdienst* did its best to disguise its interference in the internal affairs of Switzerland: the money was sent in the name of an 'international committee'. Von Roll must have suspected – quite rightly – that the committee did not really exist, and he must have voiced his suspicions.[1] The answer he received shows Fleischhauer at his most pompous and arrogant:

I am absolutely astonished and speechless at your demand that I should first tell you the names of the gentlemen who are responsible for the committee.

I have had all kinds of experiences, but such a . . . – I can find no parliamentary expression for it – has never yet come my way.

What do you want with the names of the people responsible for the committee? Be content that the committee exists! . . .

You write moreover: '. . . it may be that Herr Farmer[2] plays this part . . .' To this I reply:

1. in our organization nobody plays at all;
2. in our organization nobody plays a 'part';
3. in our organization we work for the great cause;
4. in our organization there is no place for prying and unheard-of demands;
5. in our organization there is only honest, purposeful work;
6. we shall not in future let ourselves be disturbed by questions like yours and shall not answer any more letters;
7. Farmer does not belong to the committee.

Von Roll was learning the cost of accepting help from Nazi Germany. According to his lights he was a Swiss patriot and, unlike some of the more extreme Swiss Nazis, he could not easily accept the total subservience demanded by Erfurt. In

---

[1] After the war it was established that the German Propaganda Ministry, operating through the *Weltdienst*, spent 30,000 marks on the Berne trial. (See Rogge, *The Official German Report*, p. 77.)

[2] Farmer is a cover-name for Pottere, a leading member of the Erfurt organization.

desperation he turned for help to Princess Karadja, resident in Locarno-Monti. The princess, who was the mother of the Rumanian consul-general in Berlin, was quite wealthy herself and above all had wealthy friends whose support she enlisted for various antisemitic projects. The Aryan Protection League, which was supposed to be an Anglo-American undertaking, was her creation. On 8 February she sent von Roll an account of the league which, in its blend of inflated idealism and wilful blindness, expresses perfectly the political attitude of countless Nazis:

I do not work for the trial, but for the *movement* in general. My intention is, before I die, (if God grants me this favour), to establish contact between people in all countries with which I am in contact, so that they can cooperate *with one another* when I am gone.

I wish to build a 'façade', all white and bright and shining. There must be nothing suspicious about it. *Nothing secret.* I ask for no oaths and show no distrust . . . *BUT nobody will* penetrate further than the vestibule!!! (I do not wish at all to know what goes on in the back rooms. Dear people like *you* and some others must arrange that after your own ideas! I am 'the left hand' and do not want to know what 'the right hand' does.) You will, I think, agree with this policy? I really think it is important for our cause to have a beautiful façade and vestibule, don't you think so?

So I don't feel that I have anything to do with 'destruction'. Those who concern themselves with that, must of course keep their intentions secret. But they must know one another and assure themselves of the reliability of their collaborators. Each committee that is connected with the league must have *full autonomy.* The façade can take no responsibility for the various groups.

I must confess that I am really happy and proud at what I have already achieved in this short time.

On 1 March von Roll wrote to the princess in the vain hope of finding in the Aryan Protection League an alternative source of funds:

My position is of course so difficult because I have received no money except from Erfurt. . . . In my view it is really stupid of Erfurt simply to want to dictate everything, which is clearly the aim. In this way our Swiss trial becomes a German affair and that is simply impossible for Switzerland. But it's remarkable – in

Germany they simply don't see this. There they pretend there is an international committee that has nothing at all to do with Germany and is therefore qualified to conduct the trial in whatever way it pleases. . . . My collaborators here completely agree with me about all this, but are of the opinion that, being the weaker party, we must yield to the stronger, namely Erfurt, because we are dependent on them. For this reason I can nowhere find the necessary support. . . . I want to prevent us here from becoming a branch office of Erfurt, of National-Socialism or of Germany.

Hampered by such scruples, von Roll was no match at all for his colleague, Boris Toedtli. What Toedtli thought of von Roll emerges from a letter which he wrote to the defendant Silvio Schnell on 9 March:

As for v. R., I've seldom seen anything so low. Yesterday G. showed me his statement of account. An absolute swindle! . . . Let him write! In your place I wouldn't even answer him, it's a pity to waste money on the postage! He keeps on meddling in our affairs, one ought to be able to shake him off at last, for good and all. He only causes more and more confusion with his chatter.

Unlike von Roll, Toedtli was not inhibited by any feelings of loyalty towards Switzerland and was more ready to put himself wholly at the disposal of Erfurt. After the Berne trial was over, and while an appeal was pending, he wrote two singularly frank letters to Fleischhauer. The first, dated 6 October 1935, reads as follows:

Schnell writes that he and I are being accused on all sides of being in the service of Germany, and opinions and circumstances being what they are in Switzerland, that means that one is morally dead. If these accusations are not literally true – still, we are fighting in the first place to support Germany in the struggle against the powers of darkness.

The other letter, dated 5 July 1936, contains the following passage:

Herr Ruef[1] advised me to write to you and ask for a recompense for my work. He considers that the German currency control will understand that we have been fighting for Germany in the first place and are therefore entitled to claim something in return.

[1] Counsel for the defence.

Strange sentiments, coming from a man who was Swiss by
birth and ancestry. They became more understandable (though
not more laudable) when one learns what kind of life Boris
Toedtli had behind him.[1] Though his parents were both Swiss,
they lived for many years in Russia, and he himself was born
in Kiev in 1896. As a young man he fought in the World War
and then in the civil war, of course on the side of the 'Whites',
and was made an officer. He lost his hearing in an explosion,
was captured by the Bolsheviks, nearly died of typhus, and
meanwhile his father's factory was confiscated. The family
was allowed to emigrate to Switzerland but never recovered
financially. Boris Toedtli became a photographer but failed to
keep himself. His attempts at other careers were even less
successful and at the time of his arrest he was still dependent
on his parents and parents-in-law. In 1933, when Nazi-type
movements appeared in Switzerland, he joined first one and
then another. In the National Front he became deputy to
the *Gauleiter* von Roll – whom we have seen him trying to
oust.

It is a familiar picture. Like so many Nazis, Toedtli was a
déclassé with unfulfilled ambitions for a middle-class career.
And like so many 'White' Russians, he lived for the day when
Russia would cast off what he saw as a Judeo-Masonic tyranny.
'I am antisemitic from personal experience,' he said. 'This is
the explanation for my whole behaviour. . . . My family and I
lost everything in Russia. The Jew alone was to blame, not at
all the Russian people.' Frustrated, resentful, politically
illiterate, he was indeed ideally qualified to become a champion
of the *Protocols*.

It was a year after the end of the Berne trial that the head
of the All-Russian Fascist Party, Rodzaevsky, sent from the
headquarters at Kharbin a document appointing Toedtli his
deputy in Europe, with responsibility for directing the regional
leaders in France, Belgium, England, Italy, Algeria, Morocco,
and the Congo, and with special powers to negotiate with the
German authorities. This step, which gave Toedtli some scope
as an organizer of espionage and terrorism, also proved his

---

[1] Information concerning Toedtli, including the account of his career
which he gave to the Swiss police, are in File 77 in the Wiener Library
archives.

undoing, for it led to his arrest by the Swiss police.[1] But long before that Toedtli had been in touch with 'White' Russians in Paris and Jugoslavia. In the winter of 1934–35, while von Roll was carrying on his painful dealings with Erfurt, Toedtli was corresponding with former tsarist generals and colonels, members of the Black Hundreds and the like. His aim was to produce these people as witnesses for the defence when the Berne trial was resumed. In fact the financial dependence of the Swiss Nazis on German funds, which so distressed von Roll, was mainly caused by these manoeuvres of his rival, Toedtli. The 'White' Russians had to be provided with visas, passports, accommodation, train-fares, in some cases also with fees; and for all this the *Weltdienst,* or rather the German Propaganda Ministry, paid.

The replies which Toedtli received from the various 'White' Russians were preserved by a collaborator of the *Weltdienst,* Jonak von Freyenwald, and are now in the Wiener Library.[2] Some of them are of interest even today, for not being intended for publication they reveal with great directness and naïvety the extraordinary delusions which prevailed in those circles. Some of the 'White' Russians knew perfectly well that the Elders of Zion did not exist – but that made no difference, for they still believed in the conspiracy unfolded in the *Protocols.* Thus on 4 November 1934 General Krasnov wrote to Toedtli as follows:

I must tell you that your affair is of unusual difficulty, for the following reason. The *Protocols of Zion* are apocryphal so far as their form is concerned, i.e. they were composed by Nilus, but on the basis of precise Jewish decisions. Therefore the Yids will always, from a formal point of view, be right, for strictly speaking there were no 'protocols', there were single decisions which the Yids published at various times and in various places and which Nilus brought together in a single whole with the title *Protocols of Zion.* I cannot tell why Nilus chose this way of publishing them.

[1] Toedtli was arrested before he could do much harm and his sentence was correspondingly light: two months' imprisonment and nine-tenths of the costs. He fled to Germany to avoid serving his sentence, but in December 1939 the German-Russian pact compelled him to leave Germany and return to Switzerland, where he was promptly arrested. He died during the war.

[2] In File 1 of the Freyenwald Collection.

Perhaps he did it to give them a bigger circulation, to get wider circles of readers interested in them. But in this way he provided the Jews with a perpetual loophole – they can deny not only the genuineness of the *Protocols* but also the genuineness of what is written in them. The court does not bother about the essence of the *Protocols*, it takes cognisance simply of the naked fact – 'protocols' of this kind did not exist, and that suffices.

On 5 November the notorious Markov II – Nikolai Yevgenevich Markov, a former right-wing deputy in the Duma and a leading figure in the Union of the Russian People – produced an even more tortuous argument:

... all the questions in court turned on who wrote the *Protocols* and when. Nobody wrote them, for they are the result of the work of a thousand-year-old world-conspiracy, a programme which has been unmasked again and again, which constantly changes in the methods adopted for its realization, but which was constant in its essence: messianism, the struggle to dominate the world and subjugate mankind.

On New Year's Day, a letter from Belgrade, signed I. Lanskoy, offered a startling suggestion:

It is *very* important to investigate exactly the journey which Nahum Sokolov[1] made on the way back from the Basel congress in 1897. It is essential to check his route: what railway-lines did he use, where did he stop and where was he going to? Did he cross the Russian frontier, and where?
I appreciate all the difficulty of such a task but I believe that an experienced detective would not consider it an impossible one.

No wonder that von Roll, confronted with offerings such as these, and harassed at the same time by Toedtli's intrigues, began to develop a hearty dislike of 'White' Russians. On 28 January he wrote as follows to Markov II (of all people!):

... the Russians are the worst of all ... they exaggerate things to such an extent that sometimes one would like to drop the whole business. No, it's really no fun at all – our struggle with our

[1] Nahum Sokolov (1861–1936), a Polish Jew, was one of the leading figures in the early history of Zionism. From 1920 he was president of the executive of the Zionist organization and from 1921 chairman of all the Zionist congresses. He went from Russian Poland to attend the first Zionist congress in 1897: whence this communication.

opponents is less difficult than our struggle with our collaborators. One really needs to be young and to have good nerves.[1]

All this activity did however produce one result: the defence was able at long last to produce an 'expert', as required by the court. It produced Ulrich Fleischhauer, and despite his career as a publisher and distributor of antisemitic literature he was accepted by the court. He distinguished himself, if not by his scholarship, at least by his zeal. The 'experts' were of course expected to avoid all contact with the witnesses; but this did not prevent Fleischhauer from inviting a selection of 'White' Russians to Erfurt, where he rehearsed them in the evidence they were supposed to give. It was sheer waste of time,[2] for in the end the court declined to summon any of the 'White' Russians as witnesses – perhaps unfortunately, as it has enabled later editors of the *Protocols*, right down to the present day, to complain that the evidence for the authenticity of the *Protocols* was never properly presented at Berne. In reality this 'evidence' was presented at enormous length by Fleischhauer, who submitted a written opinion of 416 printed pages and oral evidence which lasted for six days.[3]

To appreciate the level at which Fleischhauer conducted his argument one has only to study his comments on Maurice Joly and the *Dialogue aux Enfers*. He could not deny that the *Protocols* were largely copied from the *Dialogue* – so he adopted the argument, first put forward by Lord Alfred Douglas in 1921, that Maurice Joly was a Jew and his book, whatever its overt meaning, a coded version of the Jewish plan for world-domination. Joly might have been baptized a Catholic, there might be no known trace of Jewish ancestry on either side – but had not the Freemason Gambetta spoken the funeral sermon beside his grave, and was that not proof enough? But in case it was not, Fleischhauer had a further proof to offer. He had discovered that a character in the novel *Alt-Neuland* by the founder of Zionism, Theodor Herzl, was called Joe

[1] Copy in File 18 of the Freyenwald Collection.

[2] Except for Markov II, who was given a permanent job as head of the Russian section of the *Weltdienst*. Other 'White' Russians were less fortunate; in view of the revelations which accompanied Toedtli's arrest many of them were expelled from France.

[3] Documents captured after the war show that the opinion was mostly written for Fleischhauer by other people, notably Pottere.

Levy. Now to obtain the name 'Joly' one has only to remove the 'e' from Joe and the 'ev' from Levy – a procedure which, he felt, 'probably has some secret meaning for the Jews'.[1]

Not surprisingly the court was unable to make much sense of these speculations, but that did not prevent Fleischhauer from pursuing them long after the trial was over. Nor was he alone in this. It must have given him immense satisfaction to receive the following communication, dated 6 February 1937, from an Italian baron who was a subscriber to the *Weltdienst*:

> You are quite right in saying that all Jolys were most zealous revolutionaries. And what revolutionaries! The Vatican State police used to regard them as a real plague and the devil's own emissaries.

It is true that the baron's information concerning these mysterious beings was limited. 'My material,' he admitted, 'is rather slight, and consists of family traditions and a few short studies.'

The Berne trial ended on 14 May 1935. Judge Meyer found that the *Protocols* were largely plagiarized from Joly's book and were indecent literature; and he imposed a fine on the two main defendants. His comment could hardly have been sharper. 'I hope to see the day when nobody will be able to understand why otherwise sane and reasonable men should have had to torment their brains for fourteen days over the authenticity or the fabrication of the *Protocols of Zion*.... I regard the *Protocols* as ridiculous nonsense.'[2] And when Fleischhauer asked for a fee of 80,000 Swiss francs for his services as expert, the court promptly reduced the sum by nine-tenths.

That however was not the end of the matter. The defendants appealed and the case was heard by the Court of Appeal in Berne in the autumn of 1937. On 1 November the court ruled that as the *Protocols* were not salacious, the law concerning indecent literature could not be applied to them; the sentence

---

[1] Bulletin No. 6 in *Der Berner Prozess um die 'Protokolle der Weisen von Zion'*. (This is a collection of bulletins on the progress of the second part of the trial, in April–May 1935. A copy is in the Wiener Library.)

[2] Ibid., Bulletin No. 23.

was therefore quashed. This has enabled later editors of the *Protocols* to claim that the Court of Appeal refused to commit itself on the authenticity of the *Protocols*. In reality the court described the *Protocols* as trash, whose only purpose was the political one of bringing the Jews into hatred and contempt; and it was asked whether, in the interests of social harmony, ways and means ought not to be found to forbid such 'absolutely unjustified and unheard-of insults and defamation.' The court also refused to award damages to the defendants, on the grounds that 'whoever disseminates inflammatory writings of the greatest possible coarseness must pay his own costs.'

The Berne trial, then, achieved all it could reasonably have been expected to achieve: the proceedings had revealed the *Protocols* as a fabrication designed to cause persecution and massacre, and they had been reported at length in hundreds of newspapers throughout the world. It is hardly necessary to add that this made not the slightest difference to the Nazis and their accomplices. The *Weltdienst* conference of 1937, consisting of 'many experts, authors and political leaders from more than twenty countries', passed a solemn resolution re-affirming the authenticity of the *Protocols*. Fleischhauer found himself suddenly famous and much in demand as a lecturer; when he lectured at Munich the rectors of the city's two universities did not disdain to appear as guests of honour. After all – as the German press insisted – who could doubt that the trial had been initiated and stage-managed, and the judges suborned, by the ever-resourceful Elders of Zion?

---

[1] A typed copy of the 1937 judgement is in File 20 of the Freyenwald Collection in the Wiener Library. The relevant pages are pp. 41-45.

CHAPTER XI

The Antisemitic International

1

As soon as Hitler came to power in Germany the myth of the Jewish world-conspiracy began to be propagated throughout the American continent. In Canada its most ardent champions were the Blue Shirts, who were recruited from French Canadians. The Blue Shirts, otherwise known as the Parti National Social Chrétien, had much in common with the South African Grey Shirts, and there was in fact a living link between the two organizations: Henry Hamilton Beamish, an Englishman who was also the founder of The Britons and who had done more than anyone, ever since 1920, to propagate the *Protocols* in Britain. In the 1930s Beamish established contact with the *Weltdienst* and became a sort of travelling salesman for the most virulent form of antisemitism. Resident in Rhodesia and at one time a member of the Rhodesian Parliament, Beamish appeared as a voluntary witness for the defence at the Grahamstown trial; and he also visited Canada and put himself at the service of Adrien Arcand, the leader of the Blue Shirts. The pamphlet *The Key of the Mystery*, which consisted of forged and distorted texts illustrating the Jewish world-conspiracy, was published in Montreal by Arcand – and in South Africa it was pushed with great vigour, in English and Afrikaans versions. On his side Beamish looked forward to a career as Propaganda Minister in a Canada dominated by Arcand. History decided otherwise, and when war came both Beamish and Arcand were interned; but even then a secret society, the Order of Jacques Cartier, continued to distribute *The Key of the Mystery* and similar material in the hope of weakening the Canadian war-effort.[1]

[1] L. W. Bondy's *Racketeers of Hatred* remains a valuable source of

In the United States little had been heard of the *Protocols* or of the Jewish world-conspiracy since Henry Ford's recantation in 1927 – but here too the situation changed immediately Hitler came to power.[1] At once Nazi propaganda concentrated on reinforcing the already very powerful and widespread isolationism, compounded of fear of war, a general dislike of European entanglements, and a particular suspicion of Britain. And naturally enough the propaganda was first directed towards the German-speaking community in the United States. By the outbreak of war the members of the German-American Bund (at first called Friends of the New Germany) numbered some 25,000, almost all of them of German birth and half of them still German by nationality. These people, most of whom belonged to that same lower middle class which predominated in the German Nazi movement itself, were deluged with literature sent direct from Germany, including countless tons of copies of the *Protocols* in the zur Beek edition, of Wichtl's old book on the Jewish conspiracy and the First World War, and of the German translation of Ford's *International Jew*. But soon there appeared purely American agencies which dealt in the same kind of propaganda; by 1939 there were some 120 of these. Mostly they were insignificant in membership and influence,[2] but there were two exceptions, run by a Roman Catholic priest and a Protestant Fundamentalist minister respectively: Father Charles E. Coughlin's organization, The National Union for Social Justice and the Christian Front, and the Rev. Gerald B. Winrod's Defenders of the Christian Faith.

Father Coughlin, 'the radio priest', was a belated convert to antisemitism.[3] In the early 1930s he already had a national reputation as a broadcaster on religion and politics, but he was

information concerning the personalities in the Antisemitic International, including Beamish and Arcand.

[1] For the United States see: D. Strong, *Organized Anti-Semitism in America*, Washington, 1941, Copyright Public Affairs Press; J. R. Carlson, *Under Cover*, New York, 1943 edition; and O. J. Rogge, *The Official German Report*.

[2] William Dudley Pelley's Silver Shirts acquired 15,000 members in one year (1933–34), but quickly waned when in 1935 Pelley was indicted and convicted for selling worthless stock.

[3] On Coughlin see C. J. Tull, *Father Coughlin and the New Deal*, Syracuse University Press, New York, 1965.

quite uninterested in Jews. When Roosevelt launched the New
Deal Coughlin supported him; but by 1935 he had turned
against the President and was furiously attacking the New
Deal as not radical enough. Sincerely concerned, it would
seem, about the mass misery caused by the great depression
and impatient with Roosevelt's moderation, Coughlin created
a new political party, the National Union for Social Justice,
which soon had a membership of at least four million. But the
Union suffered a disastrous defeat when it ran a candidate for
President in 1936 and failed to win the electoral vote in a
single State. After two years of relative neglect, in 1938
Coughlin suddenly began to broadcast in favour of an authoritarian corporate state. At the same time he founded a new
organisation, the Christian Front, as an alliance of Christians
of all denominations against communism and against plutocracy – and he made it plain that he regarded Roosevelt as a
servant of both those powers.

Coughlin was nearing the brink of the antisemitic morass,
but in the end it was considerations of foreign policy that
pushed him over. In 1938 his newspaper *Social Justice* was
increasingly concerned with foreign affairs, and its standpoint
was that of the most extreme isolationism of the period. Moreover, like many Irish-Americans, Coughlin hated Britain. It
was therefore only to be expected that Coughlin and *Social
Justice* would end by echoing German propaganda about the
Jewish world-conspiracy. This final step was in fact taken in
the summer of 1938, at the height of the crisis over the
Sudetenland. At the same time as it was justifying Hitler's
onslaught on Czechoslovakia and raging against Churchill,
Social Justice printed a series of articles by the leading propagandist for Nazi Germany, George S. Viereck; and it
followed them up by printing the *Protocols* themselves. It was
the biggest campaign of its kind since the days of *The Dearborn
Independent*, for *Social Justice* had a circulation of a million.
Moreover, by November Coughlin was expounding the *Protocols* in his Sunday broadcasts – he even revived the old story
that a Jewish firm in New York had financed the Bolshevik
revolution. According to the American Institute of Public
Opinion his usual audience was 3,500,000, and over two million
of these found him convincing. In the end he even involved his

own church at Royal Oak, Michigan, in his antisemitic campaign. His Shrine of the Little Flower, conveniently situated on the Detroit highway and equipped with souvenir shops, hot-dog stands, a Shrine inn, and a Shrine garage, attracted multitudes of tourists and became a major distribution centre for the *Protocols*. 'Christ Himself sponsored this little leaflet for your protection,' he wrote on brochures listing stores which employed no Jews – though the more immediate sponsor is known to have been the German-American Business League.

Coughlin was not of course representative of Roman Catholicism in the United States. Cardinal Mundelein of Chicago answered his antisemitic campaign with the forthright statement that he 'is not authorised to speak for the Catholic Church, nor does he represent the doctrine or sentiment of the Church'. Another outspoken Catholic critic was Frank Hogan, the president of the American Bar Association. Nevertheless the turbulent priest was not censured by his immediate superiors, and this made it easier for him to convince vast numbers of Roman Catholics that his voice was indeed the voice of the Church. Particularly among the less prosperous and less educated of the Roman Catholics of Irish descent he built up a devoted following. Over 400 members of the New York police belonged to his Christian Front. The inner circle of his followers even included some priests, among them the president of the International Catholic Truth Society, the Rev. Edward Lodge Curran.[1] Some 2,000 churches were willing to sell copies of *Social Justice*. All in all there is no doubt that Coughlin did manage to introduce into the Roman Catholic population of the United States a more virulent type of antisemitism than it had known in the past.

There is no doubt, either, that his movement did in effect serve Nazi interests, even though he himself had no links with the German Government or with Nazi organizations in the United States. It was not for nothing that the German-American Bund was a major distributor of *Social Justice*, or that Streicher's *Stürmer* reprinted extracts from it, for *Social Justice* in turn mirrored very closely the short-wave broadcasts put out by Goebbels' propagandists. Indeed on one

---

[1] It also included the inevitable 'White' Russian – George Agayeff.

occasion Coughlin reprinted a large part of one of Goebbels's own major speeches – and attached his own signature to it: identification could scarcely go further. And nothing changed when the European war began in 1939, or even when the United States entered the war two years later. As late as March 1942 *Social Justice* was accusing the Jews of having started the war. In fact this proved the undoing of the newspaper and of Coughlin, for at this point the Government intervened: *Social Justice* was suppressed, and in response to a government initiative the Archbishop of Detroit at last imposed silence on Coughlin.

Like Coughlin, the Protestant Fundamentalist Gerald B. Winrod, of Wichita, Kansas, came late to antisemitism. A self-appointed preacher with no formal theological training, he founded the Defenders of the Christian Faith in 1925 for the purpose of combating modernism in religion. It was only when Hitler was about to take power that Winrod suddenly realized that the true cause of modernism, and indeed of all other evils, was 'Jewish Bolshevism'. He at once set about producing a series of writings in which the reality of the Jewish world-conspiracy would be demonstrated from the Book of Revelation. Already in 1932 he produced a book about the *Protocols*, called *The Hidden Hand*. In 1933 his pamphlet *The Protocols and the Coming Super Man* sold some 22,000 copies, and it was soon followed by *The Truth about the Protocols* and *The Anti-Christ and the Tribe of Dan*. By 1936 nearly 100,000 copies of his antisemitic pamphlets had been printed, while the circulation of his leaflets – brochures of a dozen pages or less, distributed free – ran into millions; in one month alone 75,000 of these productions were given away, largely in jails and hospitals. The monthly magazine, the *Defender*, had 100,000 regular subscribers and sprouted a Spanish edition, *El Defensor Hispano*, for the benefit of Puerto Rico, Cuba, and Mexico. Winrod also became a major distributor of the *Protocols* themselves. And as a broadcaster, lecturer, and organizer of meetings about the *Protocols* he was indefatigable.

If Coughlin called himself 'the sole unbiased source of truth', Winrod too maintained that he was acting under divine guidance; 'beyond all doubt,' he wrote of one of his pamphlets, 'this is one of the most important books the Holy Spirit has ever prompted me to write'.[1] Mixing his attacks on Jewry with almost equally virulent attacks on the Roman Catholic Church, he found the bulk of his following where, traditionally, anti-Catholic feeling was strongest – in the 'Bible Belt' running from Texas to Missouri, and above all in Kansas. His supporters consisted of small-town and rural folk, mostly poor and ill-educated – people who had seldom if ever seen a Jew but who were convinced that the great cities, with their labour organizations, their complex ways of life, their polyglot populations of recent immigrants, were somehow centres of a Jewish plot against 'fundamental Americanism'. Among such people Winrod had a real appeal: when he stood for senator for Kansas it was found necessary to launch a campaign to 'keep Fascism out of Kansas' – and even then he polled 54,000 votes in a four-sided contest.

How far did Winrod in fact support the Nazis? It might be thought that a man whose mental horizon was prescribed by the Book of Revelation would have little sympathy with the neo-mysticism of blood and soil, but this was not the case. From the very beginning of the Nazi régime Winrod praised Hitler and Goebbels, quoted the *Stürmer* and announced that 'the Hitler revolution has saved Germany and perhaps all Europe, from an invasion of Jewish communism, directed from Moscow';[2] in return his book *The Hidden Hand* was translated into German. When the Berne trial began he went to Germany and established contact with Fleischhauer and the *Weltdienst*. Back in the United States he discussed the trial at length in a series of articles which embellished the *Defender* from February to July 1935 and presented the defendants as 'fine Swiss patriots', Fleischhauer as a brilliant champion of truth, the judge as criminally biased. Soon the *Defender* was comparing Adolf Hitler with Martin Luther and announcing: 'Germany Stands Alone. Of all the countries of Europe, Germany is the only one that has had the courage to defy Jewish Masonic Occultism, Jewish Communism, and the international Jewish Money Power.'[3] Although Winrod represented less of a threat to American democracy than did

[1] Quoted in Strong, op. cit., p. 72.
[2] Quoted in Rogge, op. cit., p. 213.
[3] Ibid., p. 214.

Coughlin, and never even began to organize a political movement – yet within his limits this ultra-Protestant preacher
served the Nazi cause more truly than the Catholic priest. 'The
American Streicher' he was called in the German press, and he
did his best to deserve the title.

There is no point in exaggerating the importance of the
innumerable antisemitic groups which appeared in the United
States in the 1930s; none of them had the slightest chance of
causing a major upheaval, let alone the revolution they talked
of. Nevertheless they are not altogether without historical
significance. Through their books and pamphlets, broadcasts
and lectures, they hammered at a public of several millions
that the New Deal was a reign of terror imposed by Jews on
the population of the United States. 'Minnesota Close to Red
Abyss as Murder Terrorizes Voters' – 'Dictator for America
Looms; Reds Concentrating Energies behind Pro-Jewish
Despot' – 'A Death List of the Enemies of Jewish Bolshevism
Exists in the United States' – these were typical headlines.
Even the anti-syphilis campaign was presented as part of the
conspiracy: ' . . . this entire scheme is one leading up to the
wholesale inoculation of Gentiles with vaccine syphilitic
germs'.[1] Although wholehearted believers in the Jewish world-
conspiracy were few, there is no doubt that many people were
more or less disorientated by this constant stirring-up of deep
and barely conscious anxieties.

Among the people who did the stirring-up were some who
longed for physical violence. William Dudley Pelley, the leader
of the Silver Shirts, looked forward to 'a bath of violence' and
'history's greatest pogrom'; his lieutenant, William Zachery,
shouted at a public meeting: 'I want all of you to go out and
get guns, and I want each of you to get plenty of ammunition.'
Another antisemitic propagandist, James B. True, wrote in
his paper *Industrial Control Report*: 'Urge your congressional
representatives to oppose all anti-gun and registration legislation. Remember that the Constitution gives all United States
citizens the right to bear arms, and unless all signs fail we shall
need that right.'[2] An interview which the same man gave to the

[1] Quoted in Strong, op. cit., p. 160.
[2] The remarks by Pelley, Zachery, and True are quoted from Strong,
op. cit., pp. 152–7.

Rev. Dr L. M. Birkhead, National Director of the Friends of Democracy, reveals with complete naïvety a state of mind which, as we now know, was that of many of the Nazi leaders themselves:

I found True to have the look and determination of a fanatic. Spread out on his desk were a half-dozen wooden pieces which looked like the lower ends of an axe handle. On examination I found that they had straps running through one end much the same as a policeman's billy. When Mr True began to explain to me that he had a militant organization in the South which he was equipping with arms in order to kill off the Jews, I began to understand what these hip-pocket-flask billies were for. They were Mr True's 'Kike Killers'.

'What are you trying to do through your organization?' I asked Mr True.

Quick as a flash he replied, 'To defeat the only real enemy that America has today.' That enemy, it appears, is the Jew Communism which the New Deal is trying to force on America.

'We may have to do something more militant than vote,' Mr True said with the emphasis of a man who believed that bullets might have to be substituted for ballots.

I asked him just what he meant by being more militant.

'What I mean is that the thing has possibly gone too far for us to save the country by political methods,' True replied. '. . . I don't see any way out except a pogrom. We have got to kill the Jews. Ballots don't mean anything to them.'

'May I ask, Mr True, if you aren't oversimplifying the problem?' I said by way of interruption. 'Suppose we could line up the fifteen million Jews up against a wall and shoot them, that wouldn't solve our problems. We'd still have them with us – the same old problems.'

True speaking: 'That's just where you're wrong. Our problem is very simple. Get rid of the Jews and we'd be on the way to Utopia tomorrow. The Jews are the source of all our troubles. That's plain to anyone who makes a study of this problem, and I have studied it deeply.'

'Who is it that is trying to destroy our Constitution and the American form of government? The Jew.

'You take the hiring of "big, buck niggers" by the Jews to attack white women in the South. That's right in the Talmud. The Talmud teaches the Jew that it's right to do that. . . .

'Communism is the major part of the Jewish conspiracy today. Why, just look at Russia where the Jews run the country.

'I want to leave you with a thought,' said Mr True as I arose to leave. 'I predict a pogrom in America. I don't see how it can be avoided.'[1]

The groups headed by Pelley and True were, admittedly, insignificant – but one finds the same attitude even among some elements in Coughlin's Christian Front. In the spring and summer of 1939, while Hitler was preparing to launch his war, Coughlin's henchmen were warning big audiences in New York that a Jewish-Communist coup was imminent – that any day now they could wake up to see the gutters flowing with blood – 'Christian blood, your blood, the blood of Christian boys and Christian leaders!'[2] This imaginary danger was used to justify massacre. One of Coughlin's organizers, George Van Nosdall, told a Christian Front meeting, 'Boys, we are going to work. I am ready to line the God-damned Jews right up against the wall.' At another meeting he shouted: 'When we get through with the Jews in America they will think the treatment they received in Germany was nothing. . . . Judais-tic gore will soon flow in the streets of New York City.' Another organizer even instructed his audience: 'When you are in a crowd yell "Kill the Jew".'[3]

All this talk, in a country like the United States, was of course mere wind. But it is worth noting nevertheless, for it shows that even in the United States many of those who dealt in the *Protocols* were just the kind of people who under the Nazi régime became the organizers and executants of genocide.

The operations of the *Weltdienst* extended also to South America, particularly Argentina. A commission for the in-vestigation of anti-Argentinian activities was alarmed to find, in 1943, the extent to which resident Germans had allowed themselves to be used by Erfurt as distributors of the *Protocols*. A future Minister of Justice under Peron, Martinez Zuviria, wrote two books, *Oro* and *Kahal*, about the Jewish world-conspiracy, and was duly honoured by the German com-munity. Some Roman Catholic clerics cooperated happily in this propaganda, which once more took on the religious colouring it had possessed in the days of Mgr Meurin. The

[1] Strong, op. cit., pp. 124 seq.
[2] Quoted in Carlson, op. cit., p. 60.
[3] Strong, op. cit., p. 158.

monthly *Clarinada* wrote in August 1937; '*Clarinada* fights the Jews because they are the inventors, leaders and henchmen of communism throughout the world. *Clarinada* fights the Jews because – following the directives of the Elders of Zion – they corrupt Christian morality and stimulate human vices and defects in order to annihilate the spiritual conquest of humanity brought about by Jesus Christ, the first victim of the God-destroyers.' A year later *Clarinada* earned quotation in *Der Stürmer* by suggesting a remedy: 'It is a great pity that all Jews without distinction are not being buried alive so that peace could at last reign within the great Argentinian family.'[1]

2

By the eve of the Second World War the *Protocols* were enjoying a greater vogue than they had enjoyed even in 1920, before they were first unmasked. In the countries of eastern Europe where there were large Jewish minorities and important Fascist movements, the myth of the Jewish world-conspiracy provided a constant theme for propaganda and for political argument. In Poland Piasecki's Falanga even tried in October 1937 to arrest President Moscicki and massacre his more or less liberal associates, on the grounds that they were agents of international Judeo-Masonry.[2] But above all these fantasies were invoked by governments which were allied to or dependent on Nazi Germany – and this happened even in countries which had no Jews.

In Spain there had been no Jews for more than four centuries, but that did not prevent the Nationalists from presenting the civil war as a struggle against Judeo-Masonry.[3] Nationalist newspapers carried headlines saying 'Our war is a war against Judaism', and amazed their readers with tales of the prodigious power, wealth, and cunning of a Jewish government which had never been mentioned before. Outside Spain this propaganda enjoyed a marvellous success in quarters

[1] Quoted in Bondy, op. cit., pp. 242–3.
[2] See L. Blit, *The Eastern Pretender*, London, 1965, pp. 70–2.
[3] It is true that after the great expulsion of 1492 dwindling numbers of crypto-Jews (Marranos) lingered on in Spain. But the Nationalists were certainly not thinking of them.

sympathetic to General Franco; among Father Coughlin's followers, for instance, it was a commonplace that the forces of the Spanish Republic represented the embattled might of the Elders of Zion. And years later, in October 1944, when the majority of the Jews on the European Continent had already been killed, the official Spanish radio station Radio Falange could still proclaim: 'The Jewish danger is no unfounded fantasy. . . . Nothing is more urgent than to fight against the Communist and the Jew'.[1]

The case of Japan was strangest of all, for there Jews were so completely unknown that nobody could imagine what kind of creatures they could be. However, Hitler had said in *Mein Kampf* that Jewry 'fears the presence of a national Japanese state in its millennial Jewish kingdom and desires that the ruin of that state shall precede the establishment of its own dictatorship';[2] and the hint was sufficient. The Japanese Government needed some excuses which might seem in the eyes of the world to justify its attack on China, and the myth of the Judeo-Masonic conspiracy provided one such excuse. According to the Japanese delegate to the *Weltdienst* congress of 1938, Fujivara, 'Judeo-Masonry is forcing the Chinese to turn China into a spearhead for an attack on Japan, and thereby forcing Japan to defend herself against this threat. Japan is at war not with China but with Freemasonry, represented by General Chiang-Kai-shek, the successor of his master, the Freemason Sun-Yat-Sen.' The war in China bore 'the sacred mark of sacrifice'; Japanese soldiers were dying not for any narrow national interest but for the sake of the whole world, which they were struggling to 'save from the Judeo-Masonic-Bolshevik claws'. The conclusion was obvious: 'Do not abandon us, the isolated bulwark in the Far East!'[3] Meanwhile the Japanese General Shioden was also visiting the Third Reich, establishing contact with Streicher and the *Weltdienst* and visiting the anti-Masonic museum at Nuremberg. He proved an apt pupil, for by July 1939 the *Stürmer* was proud to print a letter from him: 'I am pleased to inform you that the copious information and material collected dur-

[1] Quoted in Bondy, op. cit., p. 211.
[2] Hitler, *Mein Kampf*, p. 724.
[3] Quoted in H. Rollin, *L'Apocalypse de notre temps*, p. 514.

ing my journey in Germany has now been translated into Japanese by experts. This will contribute to the enlightenment of the Japanese about the Jewish plan for world-domination. . . .'[1]

Here we are in the world of farce, but it is characteristic of the story of the *Protocols* that it keeps jerking one out of farce into the starkest tragedy. We have seen how the men who propagated the *Protocols* were often *pogromshchiki* at heart, waiting hungrily for the chance to organize massacre.[2] Whether they ever got that chance or not depended entirely on what happened to their countries during the Second World War. In the embattled democracies such people lapsed into obscurity, when they did not disappear into jail – but in those parts of Europe where the Nazi leaders were able to implement their plans for genocide various dingy figures, hitherto known only as editors or publishers of the *Protocols*, were suddenly transformed into important administrators, with responsibility for drafting and implementing antisemitic legislation. As often before, but on a far more massive scale, dealing in the *Protocols* led to dealing in murder. It is worth looking briefly at a few such cases.

In France the most active champion of the *Protocols* in the years immediately before the war was one Darquier de Pellepoix. As plain Monsieur Darquier this man had behind him a whole career of failure before he took to antisemitic politics. He held a good position with a French firm in Antwerp but was dismissed for speculating against the franc. Reinstated, he was sent to London but got himself arrested for being drunk and disorderly. Next he emigrated to Australia, married money, and bought a sheep-ranch – but it failed. Back in France, he was accidentally involved in the right-

---

[1] Quoted in Bondy, op. cit., p. 246.

[2] This was the tendency even in England. Mosley's British Union of Fascists was rather non-committal about the *Protocols* – and its antisemitism, though real, was never of the exterminatory kind. But the *Protocols* provided the ideological basis for the much more extreme (and numerically insignificant) Imperial Fascist League, headed by Arnold Leese, which had close links with the Nazis and openly favoured the gassing of all Jews. Leese, incidentally, also propagated the ritual murder myth. (C. Cross, *The Fascists in Britain*, London, 1961, pp. 153–4.)

wing demonstration of 6 February 1934 and had the good luck to be wounded in the rioting. This gave him the happy idea of founding an 'Association of the Wounded of 6 February'. He added 'de Pellepoix' to his name, took to wearing a monocle, and embarked on an antisemitic campaign which in violence far surpassed anything offered by the Action Française. This brought him some success, for in 1935 he was elected to the municipal council of Paris as representative for the fashionable district of Ternes.

Next Darquier founded a new movement, the Rassemblement Antijuif de France, with a programme modelled on the antisemitic legislation which had been introduced in the Third Reich. French Jews were to be disfranchised and were to be excluded from the civil service and the armed forces, the property of Jewish organizations was to be confiscated for the benefit of 'the French community ruined by Judeo-Masonic policy'. But the programme also contained a vaguer and still more menacing item: 'Expulsion of all Jews likely to contaminate the moral or physical health of the nation.'[1] What this really meant was revealed in a public statement which Darquier made in May 1937: 'The Jewish question must be solved, and very urgently: either the Jews must be expelled or they must be massacred.'[2]

At the time few could take such a remark seriously – but one of those few was Darquier himself, and he did his best to prepare the way. In the last couple of years of peace the Rassemblement Antijuif de France concentrated on publishing and distributing literature about the Jewish world-conspiracy. It was at Darquier's meetings in 1937 that the Canadian booklet *The Key of the Mystery* was distributed for the first time in France. Above all the movement's fortnightly paper, *La France enchaînée*, regularly carried advertisements for the *Protocols* – 'a prophetic book which every Frenchman ought to read'. Anyone who secured five subscriptions for the paper received, as a reward, five free copies of the *Protocols*. And in 1938 there appeared the proud announcement: 'The Rassemblement Antijuif has just published an annotated edition of the *Protocols of the Elders of Zion*, price 2 francs. This very low

[1] The programme is given in Rollin, op. cit., p. 556.
[2] As reported in the Paris newspaper *La Lumière* on 22 May 1937.

price is intended to enable all Frenchmen to recognize the machinations of Enemy No. 1: the Jew. . . . In publishing this new edition, we appeal to all Frenchmen who are not completely chloroformed or emasculated. France must awake!'[1]

It was no coincidence that this advertisement appeared at the height of the Munich crisis. Throughout August and September 1938 *La France enchaînée* produced articles with such headings as 'War Danger: Jewish-Russian plot in Czechoslovakia' – 'War comes nearer, the Jews' war' – 'Will Jewry dare to unleash world war?' The publication of the new edition of the *Protocols* was accompanied by the announcement: 'It is Jewry that has created the democratic front. It is Jewry that has brought the United States out of their splendid isolation. It is Jewry that wants war. France, soldier of the Jew! No! Everyone must proclaim the truth.'[2] Under a mask of patriotism Darquier was in fact serving the interests of the Third Reich, and the Nazis knew it well enough: his immediate reward was to be applauded in the *Völkischer Beobachter*. The French authorities knew it too. The effects of Darquier's propaganda were so considerable, especially in Alsace, that the French Government had to take the step, which at that time was an extraordinary one, of restricting the liberty of the press. On 25 April 1939 a decree was promulgated which forebade, under penalty of fine or imprisonment, all antisemitic propaganda. Darquier was prosecuted and sentenced to three months in prison. In court he cried: 'I have striven to fight the Jewish invasion which is submerging France.'

It was the war that gave Darquier his chance. As a captain in the army he was again imprisoned for subversive propaganda; but he was released in time to be captured by the Germans, who had the good sense to set him free at once. In the new conditions he quickly made a political career, and in Laval's second cabinet (May 1942) he was appointed Commissioner-General for Jewish Affairs, in succession to Xavier Vallat. In this capacity he supervised the deportation of the 9,000 foreign Jews who were handed over to the Germans.[3]

---

[1] Quoted in Rollin, op. cit., p. 556.   [2] Ibid., p. 555.

[3] Laval in the end refused to hand over the French Jews. The French Jews who perished (probably about 85,000) were mostly taken by the Germans themselves in the Occupied Zone.

At the end of the war he was tried *in absentia* and sentenced to death; but he was able to make his way to Spain.

In Italy the history of the *Protocols* is indissolubly linked with the name of Giovanni Preziosi.[1] Political antisemitism was unknown in Italy before the First World War;[2] and when the ex-priest Preziosi took to political propaganda during the war, he too was concerned not with Jewish but with German machinations. In a book he published in 1916, *La Germania alla conquista dell' Italia*, he argued that Germany was dominating Italy through the great bank the Banca Commerciale. It was only after the war that he decided that the same bank was really Jewish and the instrument of a Jewish conspiracy. From 1920 onwards Preziosi's journal *La vita italiana* was arguing that the western democracies, Freemasonry, international socialism, and Bolshevism were all means by which a hidden Jewish power was seeking to subordinate the world, but especially the poorer and more dynamic nations, to Jewish interests. Who could deny that of the three statesmen who had opposed Italian claims at Versailles two – Wilson and Clemenceau – were in the hands of the Jews, while one – Lloyd George (!) – was himself a Jew? And what were all these manoeuvres but the latest manifestations of a conspiracy which dated at least from the destruction of the Temple in 70 A.D.?

But in 1921 Preziosi published a translation of the *Protocols* and from 1922 onwards he and his journal were firmly integrated into the international network. Thus the August 1922 issue of *La vita italiana* contained an article by Preziosi himself, justifying the murder of Rathenau; another article signed P. Praemunitus, which was the title of the first American edition of the *Protocols*; and above all an article entitled 'The Jews, the passion and the resurrection of Germany (Thoughts of a German)', which was signed 'A Bavarian' and is now known to be by Adolf Hitler himself. Preziosi was in fact the one publicist in Italy who from the start fully accepted Hitler and Nazism. Even the Fascists had as a whole considerable

---

[1] On Preziosi see R. De Felice, *Storia degli ebrei italiani sotto il fascismo*, Turin, 1961, pp. 54–64, 502–18.

[2] The clerical antisemitism associated above all with *La civiltà cattolica* had no influence on nationalist politics.

reservations about the kindred but infinitely more ruthless movement which was extending its power to the north of the Alps. In particular they were not antisemitic, and they were mostly shocked when in 1933 the Nazis began to reveal the full extent of their brutality. Preziosi on the other hand proved quite unshockable.

For some eighteen years Preziosi and the little group around *La vita italiana* remained isolated and ineffective. Even when the *Protocols* were republished in 1937, bookshops refused to stock them and the press to review them. Then, in 1938, Mussolini decided that to make the alliance with Germany really solid, it was indispensable to launch an antisemitic campaign – and for Preziosi things changed overnight. Now several important newspapers gave favourable attention to the *Protocols*; and soon the work was officially sponsored by the Italian service for propaganda abroad, the Committee of Action for the Universality of Rome. Before the end of the year Preziosi was appointed Minister of State.

But it was the Italian armistice of September 1943 that brought Preziosi to the peak of his career. Mussolini had been overthrown, and the Germans were trying to find a new government for the part of Italy they had occupied. Preziosi went to Germany and so impressed Rosenberg that he chose him as his candidate to head the new government. These hopes vanished with Mussolini's liberation, but Preziosi had other resources. He began to broadcast to Italy, blaming the Judeo-Masonic conspiracy for the capitulation and demanding a 'purge' of Freemasonry and an 'integral solution of the Jewish question'. He also sent to Mussolini a letter such as the Duce can seldom have received, warning him of the consequences of failing to cope with the 'conspiracy'; and he sent a copy to Hitler. Mussolini gave way and in March 1944 appointed this man – whom he had always despised and detested – Inspector General of Race. Later in the year Preziosi was given the rank of ambassador as well.

At first Preziosi concentrated his efforts on introducing into the Italian Social Republic – as Mussolini's régime in north Italy was called – laws confiscating Jewish property, debarring Jews and half-Jews from public office, and forbidding mixed marriages. In this he was unsuccessful, and he retorted by complaining in *La vita italiana* that the Republic was in the hands of Freemasons acting for the Jews. But in fact all this was only preparatory to a far more sinister plan. In June 1944 Preziosi submitted to Mussolini a memorandum urging that his inspectorate should be turned into an Italian version of the Gestapo, with unlimited powers to carry out police activities throughout the Republic and to exact collaboration from all public authorities and military formations. This, he announced, was made necessary by the 'injustices' which were occurring each day in the Republic. What he had in mind was that the Italian population was helping Jews to evade deportation and extermination by the Germans. If he had had his way, the number of Italian Jews killed would no doubt have been greater than it was (the number is put at about 10,000, out of a total Jewish population of 25,000); but in the end Mussolini preferred to leave the Germans to their own devices. The Government of the Republic was still discussing these things in the spring of 1945, when it was overthrown by popular insurrection. To avoid being killed by the crowd Preziosi committed suicide.

Darquier and Preziosi were not free agents; both served governments which were not interested in killing Jews, and this severely limited their own activities. Their Hungarian counterpart Lászlo Endre found himself in a more fortunate position, after equally obscure beginnings.[1] Throughout the 1930s Endre was active as an antisemitic propagandist, and shortly before the outbreak of war he produced a whole book 'proving' the genuineness of the *Protocols*; but he never achieved the slightest political importance so long as Hungary remained independent. Even after Hungary entered the war as Germany's ally the Regent, Admiral Horthy, though willing to allow some harassing of Jews by Hungarians, refused absolutely to let the Germans deport and exterminate them. But in March 1944 Horthy took steps to withdraw the Hungarian troops from the Russian front, and this resulted in the immediate occupation of Hungary by the German army and the imposition of a new, wholly subservient government.

[1] On Endre see J. Weidlein, *Der ungarische Antisemitismus*, Schorndorf, 1962, pp. 166 seq.; and E. Levai, *Black Book on the Martyrdom of Hungarian Jewry*, Zurich and Vienna, 1948.

Eichmann arrived and hurled himself into the task of deporting the 800,000 Hungarian Jews. His closest Hungarian collaborator was Endre, now a Secretary of State and charged by the new cabinet with this welcome task. On the day of the first deportations, 15 May, Endre opened an Institute for Race Research in Budapest; he took the opportunity to announce that 'the Government has decided to settle the Jewish question once and for all, in the shortest possible time'. He did his best; and it was largely thanks to his energy that within six weeks some 450,000 Jews had in fact been despatched by freight-train to the gas-chambers of Auschwitz – a hundred in each wagon, without food or water for a journey of three days and nights.

At the end of the war Endre was executed. According to a Hungarian of similar outlook, on the night before his execution, 21 March 1946, he sent the following farewell message: 'The *Protocols of the Learned Elders of Zion* are true. . . . The means to establish a world kingdom are in [the Jews'] hands and they will destroy everything that might constitute an obstacle to the new world state. . . . Jewish policy is *to exterminate* not only those who did something but *even those who might yet do something or could have done something. . . .*'[1]

Such was the Antisemitic International in the Nazi era. No doubt the men we have been considering were impelled by all kinds of motives. Some saw in the administration of massacre a unique chance of wielding power and enjoying prestige; others were keen to appropriate the belongings of the killed; others were sadists who sought gratification in pursuing, torturing, and killing defenceless people. All this is true – and yet the fact is inescapable: behind the massacre as a whole there was a blind fanaticism which was largely inspired by the *Protocols* and the myth of the Jewish world-conspiracy. Again and again one comes across the same weird, apocalyptic atmosphere, hints of some gigantic final battle in which the demonic hosts will be eliminated, the world released from the strangling octopus, a new age brought to birth. This atmosphere is unmistakable in many of the political speeches and

[1] L. Marschalko, *The World Conquerors*, trans. A. Soranyi, London, 1958, p. 241.

writings of that period, and it is much the same in New York as in Budapest. But for its supreme, most naïve expression one has to turn from such utterances – which after all could never be completely frank – to a novel published in 1937 by a French writer who was later to abet the Nazis in France, Ferdinand Céline. In *Bagatelles pour un massacre* Céline swears to the genuineness of the *Protocols* and of *The Rabbi's Speech*; and he goes on:

Let us recall, for our pleasure and to remind ourselves, the main provisions of the *Protocols*. . . . For an Aryan, nothing is more invigorating than to read them. . . . It does more for our salvation than any number of prayers. . . .

Do you know that the executive power over the whole of world Jewry is called the 'Kahal'? . . . Assembly of the Elders of Israel? . . . Our fate . . . depends entirely on the good favour of the big Jews, 'the big occult ones'. It's not stupid to think that our fate is certainly still being discussed in the consistories of the Kahal, as much as in the Masonic lodges, indeed much more.

In short, Frenchmen . . . you will go off to war at the moment chosen by Baron de Rothschild . . . at the moment fixed in full agreement with his sovereign cousins in London, New York and Moscow. . . .

I want something solid! . . . Realities! . . . Those who really are responsible! . . . I've got a hunger! . . . an enormous hunger! . . . a world-wide hunger! a hunger for Revolution . . . a hunger for planetary conflagration . . . for the mobilization of all the charnel-houses in the world! An appetite which is surely divine, divine! Biblical![1]

Céline was himself a near-paranoiac and for that very reason saw perfectly clearly what would happen if once believers in the *Protocols* had absolute power. In his eyes the *Protocols* were a warrant for genocide; and that is precisely what they became.

[1] F. Céline, *Bagatelles pour un massacre*, Paris, 1937, pp. 277–89. In April 1938 France's most distinguished literary review, the *Nouvelle Revue française*, published a review by Marcel Arland commending this book as 'effective' and a fine example of French eloquence; it singled out, for particular praise, a passage evoking ritual murder.

The Rabbi's Speech[1]

On this precursor of the *Protocols* see above, pp. 34–40.

Our fathers have bequeathed to the elect of Israel the duty of gathering together once each century around the tomb of the Grand Master Caleb, the holy rabbi Simeon ben Jehuda, whose knowledge gives the elect of each generation power over all the earth and authority over all the descendants of Israel.

For eighteen centuries Israel has been at war with that power which was first promised to Abraham but which was taken from him by the Cross. Trampled underfoot, humiliated by its enemies, living ceaselessly under the threat of death, of persecution, of rape, and of every kind of violation, the people of Israel has not succumbed; and if it is dispersed over the whole earth, that is because it is to inherit the whole earth.

For eighteen centuries our wise men have been fighting the Cross courageously and with a perseverance which nothing can discourage. Gradually our people is rising up and its power increases day by day. Ours is that God of today whom Aaron raised up for us in the desert, that Golden Calf, that universal deity of the age.

The day when we shall have made ourselves the sole possessors of all the gold in the world, the real power will be in our hands, and then the promises which were made to Abraham will be fulfilled.

Gold, the greatest power on earth . . . gold, which is the strength, the recompense, the instrument of every power . . . the sum of everything that man fears and craves . . . *there* is the only mystery, the deepest understanding of the spirit that rules the world. *There* is the future!

Eighteen centuries belonged to our enemies, the present century and future centuries must belong to us, the people of Israel, and they surely will belong to us.

[1] My translation from the French. N.C.

Now for the tenth time, in a thousand years of terrible and
ceaseless war against our enemies, the elect of a given generation
of the people of Israel are gathered in this cemetery, around the
tomb of our Grand Master Caleb, the holy rabbi Simeon ben
Jehuda, to take counsel as to how to turn to the advantage of our
cause the great errors and sins which our enemies the Christians
never cease to commit.

Each time the new Sanhedrin has proclaimed and preached a
merciless struggle against our enemies; but in no earlier century
were our ancestors able to concentrate in our hands so much gold,
and therefore so much power, as the nineteenth century has be-
stowed on us. We can therefore expect, without any rash illusions,
to achieve our aim soon, and we can look with confidence to our
future.

Most fortunately, the persecution and the humiliations, those
dark and painful days which the people of Israel endured with such
heroic patience, are no more with us, thanks to the progress of
civilization among the Christians, and that progress is the best
shield for us to hide and act behind, so as to cross with firm and
rapid strides the space that separates us from our supreme objective.

Let us just look at the material condition of Europe, let us
analyse the resources which the Jews have got into their possession
since the beginning of the present century simply by concentrating
in their hands the huge amount of capital which they control at
this moment. Thus, in Paris, London, Vienna, Berlin, Amsterdam,
Hamburg, Rome, Naples, etc., and in all the Rothschild branches,
everywhere the Jews are the financial masters, simply by possess-
ing so many milliards; not to mention that in every town of second
or third magnitude it is the Jews who control the currency in
circulation, and that nowhere can any financial operation, any
major undertaking be carried through without the direct influence
of the children of Israel.

Today all reigning emperors, kings, and princes are burdened
with debts contracted in keeping up large standing armies to support their toppling thrones. The stock exchange assesses and
regulates those debts, and to a great extent we are masters of the
stock exchange everywhere. We must therefore study how to
encourage borrowing more and more, so as to make ourselves the
regulators of all values and, as security for the capital we lend to
countries, take the right to exploit their railways, their mines,
their forests, their great ironworks and factories, and other kinds
of real estate, even their taxes.

In every country agriculture will always be the greatest source
of wealth. The possession of large landed property will always

bring honours and much influence to the owners. From this it follows that we must concentrate on ensuring that our brothers in Israel acquire landed property on a large scale. So far as possible we must therefore encourage the splitting-up of large estates, so as to help us acquire it more quickly and more easily.

Under the pretext of helping the working classes, we must place the weight of taxation on the great landed proprietors, and when all properties have come into our hands, all the work of the Gentile proletarians will become a source of huge profits for us.

Since the Christian Church is one of our most dangerous enemies, we must work doggedly to diminish its influence; so far as possible, therefore, we must implant in the minds of those who profess the Christian religion the ideas of free thought, of scepticism, of schism, and provoke the religious disputes which are so naturally productive of divisions and sects within Christendom.

Logically, we must begin by disparaging the ministers of that religion. Let us declare open war on them, let us rouse suspicions about their piety, about their private conduct. So, by ridicule and malicious banter, we shall undermine the respect in which the profession and the cloth are held.

Each war, each revolution, each political or religious upheaval brings nearer the moment when we shall attain the supreme aim of our journey.

Trade and speculation, two branches so fertile in profits, must never leave Jewish hands, and once we have become proprietors we shall be able, thanks to the obsequiousness and the shrewdness of our agents, to penetrate to the first source of real influence and real power. It is understood that we are concerned only with those occupations which bring honours, power, or privileges, for those which demand knowledge, work, and inconvenience can and must be left to the Gentiles. The magistrature is for us an institution of the first importance. A career at the bar does most to develop the faculty of civilization and to initiate one into the affairs of our natural enemies, the Christians, and it is in this way that we can get them at our mercy. Why should Jews not become ministers of Education, when they have so often had the portfolio of Finance? Jews must also aspire to the rank of legislators, so that they can work to abrogate the laws which those sinners and infidels, the Goyim, have made against the children of Israel, who by their unvarying devotion to the laws of Abraham are the truly faithful ones.

Moreover, on this point our plan is on the brink of complete fulfilment, for almost everywhere progress has recognized and granted to us the same civil rights as are enjoyed by Christians.

But what must be obtained, what must be the object of our ceaseless efforts, is that the law against bankruptcy should be made less severe. Out of that we shall make ourselves a mine of gold which will be far richer than the mines of California ever were.

The people of Israel must direct its ambition towards that height of power which brings esteem and honours. The surest means of attaining it is to have supreme control over all industrial, financial, and commercial operations, while carefully avoiding every trap and temptation which might expose one to legal proceedings in the country's courts. In its choice of speculation the children of Israel will therefore display the prudence and tact which are the mark of its congenital talent for business.

We must be familiar with everything that earns one a distinguished position in society: philosophy, medicine, law, political economy. In a word all the branches of science, of art, of literature, are a vast field where our successes must give us a big part and show off our talent.

These vocations are inseparable from speculation. Thus the performance even of a very mediocre musical composition will give our people a plausible excuse to put the Jewish composer on a pedestal and surround him with a radiance of glory. As for the sciences, medicine and philosophy, they too must be incorporated into our intellectual domain.

A doctor is initiated into the most intimate secrets of the family. The health and life of our mortal enemies, the Christians, are in his hands.

We must encourage marriages between Jews and Christians, for the people of Israel loses nothing by the contact and can only gain from these marriages. Our race, chosen by God, cannot be corrupted by the introduction of a certain amount of impure blood, and by these marriages our daughters will secure alliances with Christian families of some influence and power. It is right that, in exchange for the money we give, we should obtain the equivalent in influence over everything around us. To be related to Gentiles does not imply a departure from the path we have chosen to follow; on the contrary, with a little skill it will make us the arbiters of their fate.

It is desirable that Jews should refrain from taking women of our holy religion as their mistresses and that they should choose Christian virgins for that role. It would be a great gain for us to replace the sacrament of marriage in church by a simple contract before some civil authority, for then Gentile women would stream into our camp!

If gold is the first power in this world, the second is undeniably the press. But what can the second achieve without the first? As the aims listed above cannot be attained without the help of the press, our people must become the editors of all daily newspapers in all countries. Our possession of gold, our skill in devising means of exploiting mercenary instincts, will make us the arbiters of public opinion and enable us to dominate the masses.

So, advancing step by step in this path, with that perseverance which is our great virtue, we will push the Gentiles back and undo their influence. We shall dictate to the world what it is to have faith in, what it is to honour, and what it is to curse. Perhaps some individuals will rise up against us and will hurl insults and anathemas against us, but the docile and ignorant masses will listen to us and take our side. Once we are absolute masters of the press we will be able to transform ideas about honour, about virtue, about uprightness of character, we will be able to deal a blow against that institution which so far has been sacrosanct, the family, and we will be able to achieve its disintegration. We shall extirpate all belief and faith in everything that our enemies the Christians have venerated up to the present and, using the allurements of the passions as our weapon, we shall declare open war on everything that people respect and venerate.

Let all this be understood and noted, let every child of Israel absorb these true principles! Then our might will grow like a gigantic tree whose branches will bear the fruits called wealth, enjoyment, power, as compensation for that hideous condition which for long centuries has been the only lot of the people of Israel. When one of our people takes a step forward, let another follow him closely; if his foot slips, let him be picked up and succoured by his co-religionists. If a Jew is summoned before the courts of the country where he lives, let his brothers in religion hasten to give him aid and assistance; but only if the accused has acted in accordance with the Law of Israel, so strictly observed and kept for so many centuries!

Our people is conservative, faithful to the religious ceremonies and the customs bequeathed to us by our ancestors.

It is in our interest that we should at least make a show of zeal for the social questions of the moment, especially for improving the lot of the workers, but in reality our efforts must be geared to getting control of this movement of public opinion and directing it.

The blindness of the masses, their readiness to surrender to that resounding but empty eloquence that fills the public squares, make them an easy prey and a double instrument, of popularity and of credit. We will have no difficulty in finding as much eloquence among our people for the expression of false sentiments as Christians find in their sincerity and enthusiasm.

So far as possible we must talk to the proletariat, bring it into subjection to those who have the handling of money. By this means we will be able to make the masses rise when we wish. We will drive them to upheavals, to revolutions; and each of these catastrophes marks a big step forward for our particular interests and brings us rapidly nearer to our sole aim – world-domination, as was promised to our father Abraham.

Some parallel passages in the *Protocols* and the *Dialogue aux Enfers*

For the story of how the forger of the *Protocols* plagiarized Maurice Joly's *Dialogue aux Enfers entre Montesquieu et Machiavel* see above, pp. 71–6. The following extracts are taken from the first (1920) British edition of the *Protocols*, which is a pretty free translation from the Russian. If one bears in mind that the Russian is itself a translation of the lost French text, it is remarkable that the parallelism with Joly's book, as exemplified in these extracts, should be as close as it is. But the similarity between Joly in French and Lambelin's French edition of the *Protocols* is much closer still.

In the first British edition the text is not divided into separate chapters or 'protocols'. The 'protocol'-numbers given below and in Appendix III refer to the Russian edition by Nilus and to most of its many translations.

Dialogue aux enfers[1]	*Protocols*
First dialogue	First 'protocol'
. . . The bad instinct is stronger in man than the good instinct. . . . Fear and force have more power over him than reason. . . . All men aim at domination, and there is none who would not be an oppressor if he only could; all or almost all are ready to sacrifice the rights of others to their own interests. Who restrains among themselves the beasts of prey we call men? In the beginnings of	. . . people with corrupt instincts are more numerous than those of noble instinct. Therefore in governing the world the best results are obtained by means of violence and intimidation, and not by academic discussions. Every man aims at power; everyone would like to become a dictator if he only could do so, and rare indeed are the men who would not be disposed to sacrifice the

[1] My translation. N.C.

society, it was brute, unbridled force; later it was law, that is to say force still, but regulated by certain forms. . . . Everywhere might appears before right. Political freedom is only a relative idea.

welfare of others in order to attain their own personal aims. What restrained the wild beasts of prey which we call men? What has ruled them up to now? In the first stages of social life they submitted to brute and blind force, then to law, which in reality is the same force, only masked. From this I am led to deduct [sic] that by the law of nature, right lies in might. Political freedom is not a fact, but an idea.

Seventh dialogue

. . . I would organize huge financial monopolies, reservoirs of public wealth, in which all private fortunes would be so closely involved that they would sink together with the credit of the state the day after any political disaster.

As head of the government, all my edicts would be constantly directed to the same aim: to develop the preponderance of the state, out of all proportion, to make it the sovereign protector, promoter and recompenser. . . . Nowadays the aristocracy, as a political force, is no more; but the landowning bourgeoisie still constitutes an element of dangerous opposition to governments, because it is itself independent. It may be necessary to impoverish it or even to ruin it altogether. To

Sixth 'protocol'

. . . Soon we will start organizing great monopolies – reservoirs of colossal wealth, in which even the large fortunes of the Gentiles will be involved to such an extent that they will sink together with the credit of their government the day after a political crisis takes place.
. . . We must use every possible kind of means to develop the popularity of our Supergovernment, holding it up as a protection and recompenser of all who willingly submit to us.

The aristocracy of the Gentiles, as a political power, is no more – therefore we need not consider it any more from that point of view. But as landowners they are still dangerous to us, because their independent existence is ensured through their resources. Therefore, it is essential for us, at all costs, to deprive the aristo-

achieve this it is only necessary to increase the rates and taxes on landed property, to keep agriculture in a state of relative inferiority, to give preferential treatment to trade and industry, and especially to speculation, for if industry prospers too much it can itself become dangerous, by creating too many independent fortunes.

cracy of their lands. To attain this purpose the best method is to force up rates and taxes. These methods will keep the landed interests at their lowest possible ebb. . . . At the same time we must give all possible protection to trade and commerce, and especially to speculation, the principal role of which is to act as a counterpoise to industry. Without speculation industry will enlarge private capitals. . . .

Twelfth dialogue

I foresee the possibility of neutralizing the press by means of the press itself. Since journalism is such a great force, my government will take to journalism. It will be journalism incarnate. . . .

I will count the number of newspapers that represent what you call the opposition. If there are ten for the opposition, I shall have twenty for the government; if there are 20 I shall have 40; if there are 40 I shall have 80. . . . But the mass of the public must have no suspicion of these tactics. . . .

Like the god Vishnu, my press will have a hundred arms, and these arms will give expression to all shades of opinion throughout the whole country. People will belong to my party without realizing it. Those who think they are talking their own language will be talking mine, those who think

Twelfth 'protocol'

Literature and journalism are the two most important educational powers; for this reason our government will buy up the greater number of periodicals. By these means we shall neutralize the bad influence of the private press and obtain an enormous influence over the human mind. If we were to allow ten private periodicals we should ourselves start thirty, and so forth.

But the public must not have the slightest suspicion of these measures, therefore all periodicals published by us will seem to be of contradictory views and opinions, thus inspiring confidence and presenting an attractive appearance to our unsuspecting enemies, who will thus fall into our trap and will be disarmed. . . . These newspapers, like the Indian god Vishnu,

they are stirring up people on their side will be stirring up people on mine, those who think they are marching under their flag will be marching under mine. . . .

. . . You should know that journalism is a sort of freemasonry; those who live by it are all more or less bound to one another by the bonds of professional discretion; like the ancient augurs, they will not easily divulge the secret of their oracles. They would gain nothing by betraying one another, for they mostly have more or less shameful wounds. It is quite likely that at the heart of the capital, in certain circles, these things will be no mystery; but elsewhere people will know nothing of these things and the great majority of the nation will march with the utmost confidence in the footsteps of the guides I have given it.

will be possessed of hundreds of hands, each of which will be feeling the pulse of varying public opinion.

. . . If any chatterers are going to imagine that they are repeating the opinion of their party newspaper, they will in reality be repeating our own opinion, or the opinion which we desire. Thinking that they are following the organ of this party, they will in reality be following the flag which we will fly for them.

. . . Already there exists in French journalism a system of masonic understanding for giving countersigns. All organs of the press are tied by mutual professional secrets in the manner of the ancient oracles. Not one of its members will betray his knowledge of the secret, if such a secret has not been ordered to be made public. No single publisher will have the courage to betray the secret entrusted to him, the reason being that not one of them is admitted into the literary world without bearing the marks of some shady act in his past life. He would only have to show the least sign of disobedience and the mark would be immediately revealed. Whilst these marks remain known only to a few, the prestige of the journalist attracts public opinion throughout the country. The people follow and admire him.

My journalism will exercise its greatest influence in the provinces. . . . There I shall always arrange the climate of opinion which I need, and each of my blows will strike home. The provincial press will be entirely in my hands, for there no contradiction or discussion can be permitted. From the administrative centre where I preside, orders will be sent out to make the newspapers express such and such views, so that at a given moment a certain influence will be felt, a certain impulsion given, throughout the country, often before the capital has any idea. . . . When necessary, opinion in the capital will form more slowly than the external movement of opinion which will envelop it, if need be without its knowledge. . . . I do not wish the country to be disturbed by rumours . . . If some extraordinary suicide occurs, or some shady financial affair . . . I shall forbid the newspapers to mention it.

Our plans must extend chiefly to the provinces. It is essential for us to create such ideas and inspire such opinions there as we could at any time launch on the capital by producing them as the neutral views of the provinces.

Of course, the source and origin of the idea would not be altered: namely, it would be ours.

It is imperative for us that, before we assume power, cities should sometimes be under the influence of the opinion of the provinces – that is to say, that they should know the opinion of the majority, which will have been prearranged by us. It is necessary for us that the capitals, at the critical psychological moment, should not have time to discuss an accomplished fact, but should accept it simply because it has been passed by a majority in the provinces.

When we reach the period of the new régime – that is to say, during the transition stage to our sovereignty – we must not allow the press to publish any account of criminal cases; it will be essential that people should think that the new régime is so satisfactory that even crime has ceased.

Some passages in the *Protocols* not based on the *Dialogue aux Enfers*[1]

The following extracts give a fair idea of the mental world of Russian right-wingers in the 1890s. They reveal not only what these people believed about the Jews or tried to make others believe about them but also, in places, the social and political ideals which they themselves cherished. For paradoxically – and like the Nazis after them – these antisemites often attributed their own values and aspirations to the imaginary Jewish government.

First 'protocol'

. . . Alone an autocrat can conceive vast plans clearly assigning its proper part to everything in the mechanism of the machine of state. Hence we conclude that it is expedient for the welfare of the country that the government of the same should be in the hands of one responsible person. Without absolute despotism civilization cannot exist, for civilization is capable of being promoted only under the protection of the ruler, whoever he may be, and not at the hands of the masses.

The crowd is a barbarian, and acts as such on every occasion. As soon as the mob has secured freedom it speedily turns it into anarchy, which in itself is the height of barbarism.

Just look at these alcoholised animals stupefied by the drink, of which unlimited use is tolerated by freedom! Should we allow ourselves and our fellow creatures to do likewise? The people of the Christians, bewildered by alcohol, their youths turned crazy by classics and early debauchery, to which they have been instigated by our agents, tutors, servants, governesses in rich houses, clerks, and so forth, by our women in places of their amusement – to the latter I add the so-called 'society women' – their voluntary followers in corruption and luxury. . . .

[1] From the first (1920) British edition of the *Protocols*.

Third 'protocol'

Today I can assure you that we are only within a few strides of our goal. There remains only a short distance and the cycle of the Symbolic Serpent – that badge of our people – will be complete. When this circle is locked, all the States of Europe will be enclosed in it, as it were, by unbreakable chains.[1]

The existing constructional[2] scales will soon collapse because we are continually throwing them out of balance in order the more quickly to wear them out and destroy their efficiency. . . .

. . . Under our auspices the populace exterminated the aristocracy which had supported and guarded the people for its own benefit, which benefit is inseparable from the welfare of the populace. Nowadays, having destroyed the privileges of the aristocracy, the people fall under the yoke of cunning profiteers and upstarts.

We intend to appear as though we were the liberators of the labouring man, come to free him from this oppression, when we shall suggest to him to join the ranks of our armies of Socialists, Anarchists, and Communists. The latter we always patronize, pretending to help them out of fraternal principle and the general interest of humanity evoked by our socialistic masonry. The aristocracy, who by right shared the labour[3] of the working classes, were interested in the same being well-fed, healthy, and strong. We are interested in the opposite, i.e. in the degeneration of the Gentiles.[4] Our strength lies in keeping the working man in perpetual want and impotence; because, by so doing, we retain him subject to our will and, in his own surroundings, he will never find either power or energy to stand up against us. Hunger will confer upon Capital more powerful rights over the labourer than ever the lawful power of the sovereign could confer upon the aristocracy.

We govern the masses by making use of feelings of jealousy and hatred kindled by oppression and need. And by means of these feelings we brush aside those who impede us in our course.

When the time comes for our Worldly Ruler[5] to be crowned, we will see to it that by the same means – that is to say, by making use of the mob – we will destroy everything that may prove an obstacle in our way.

[1] Cf. the Epilogue to the *Protocols* below, and the map on Plate 4.
[2] *Sic.* An error for 'constitutional'.
[3] Should read 'shared the fruits of the labour'.
[4] In the standard British version this appears as 'the *killing out of the Goyim*', italicized.
[5] Should read 'Ruler of the World'.

The Gentiles are no longer capable of thinking without our aid in matters of science. That is why they do not realize the vital necessity of certain things, which we will make a point of keeping against the moment when our hour arrives – namely, that in schools the only true and the most important of all sciences must be taught, that is, the science of the life of man and social conditions, both of which require a division of labour and therefore the classification of people in castes and classes. . . .

The true science of social conditions, to the secrets of which we do not admit the Gentiles, would convince the world that occupations and labour should be kept in specified castes so as not to cause human suffering, arising from an education which does not correspond with the work which individuals are called upon to do. If they were to study this science, the people would of their own free will submit to the ruling powers and to the castes of government classified by them. Under the present conditions of science and the line which we have allowed it to follow, the populace, in its ignorance, blindly believes in printed words and in erroneous illusions which have been duly inspired by us, and it bears malice to all classes which it thinks higher than itself. For it does not understand the importance of each caste. This hatred will become still more acute where economical crises are concerned, for then it will stop the markets and production. We will create a universal economic crisis, by all possible underhand means and with the help of gold, which is all in our hands. Simultaneously we will throw on to the streets huge crowds of workmen throughout Europe. These masses will then gladly throw themselves upon and shed the blood of those of whom, in their ignorance, they have been jealous from childhood, and whose belongings they will then be able to plunder.

They will not harm us, because the moment of the attack will be known to us and we will take measures to protect our interests.

We persuaded the Gentiles that liberalism would bring them to a kingdom of reason. Our despotism will be of this nature, for it will be in a position to put down all rebellions and by just severity to exterminate every liberal idea from all institutions.

When the populace noticed that it was being given all sorts of rights in the name of liberty, it imagined itself to be the master, and tried to assume power. Of course, like every other blind man, the mass came up against innumerable obstacles. Then, as it did not wish to return to the former régime, it lay its power at our feet. Remember the French Revolution, which we call the 'great', the secrets of its preparatory organization are well known to us, being the work of our hands. From that time onwards we have led the nations from one disappointment to another, so that they should even renounce us in favour of the King-Despot of the blood of Zion, whom we are preparing for the world. . . .

Fifth 'protocol'

. . . In the days when the people looked on their sovereigns as on the will of God, they quietly submitted to the despotism of their monarchs. But from the day that we inspired the populace with the idea of its own rights, they began to regard kings as ordinary mortals. In the eye of the mob the holy anointment fell from the head of monarchs, and, when we took away their religion, the power was thrown into the streets like public property, and was snatched up by us. Moreover, among our administrative gifts, we count also that of ruling the masses and individuals by means of cunningly constructed theories and phraseology, by rules of life and every other kind of device. All these theories, which the Gentiles do not at all understand, are based on analysis and observation, combined with so skilful a reasoning as cannot be equalled by our rivals, any more than these can compete with us in the construction of plans for political actions and solidarity. The only society known to us which would be capable of competing with us in these arts, might be that of the Jesuits. But we have managed to discredit these in the eyes of the stupid mob as being a palpable organization, whereas we ourselves have kept in the background, reserving our organization as a secret. . . .

We set at variance with one another all personal and national interests of the Gentiles, by promulgating religious and tribal prejudices among them, for nearly twenty centuries. To all this, the fact is due that not one single government will find support from its neighbours when it calls upon them for it, in opposing us, because each one of them will think that action against us might be disastrous for its individual existence. We are too powerful – the world has to reckon with us. Governments cannot make even a small treaty without our being secretly involved in it. . . .

Ninth 'protocol'
(See above, pp. 63, 102)

. . . It is contended that nations can rise in arms against us if our plans are discovered prematurely; but in anticipation of this we can rely upon throwing into action such a formidable force as will make even the bravest of men shudder. By then metropolitan railways and underground passages will be constructed in all cities. From these subterranean places we will explode all the cities of the world, together with their institutions and documents.

Twenty-fourth 'protocol'

Now I will deal with the manner in which we will strengthen the dynasty of King David, in order that it may endure until the last day.

Our manner of securing the dynasty will consist chiefly of the same principles which have given to our wise men the management of the world's affairs, that is to say, the direction and education of the whole human race.

Several members of the seed of David will prepare Kings and their successors, who will be elected not by right of inheritance but by their own capabilities. These successors will be initiated in our secret political mysteries and plans of governing, taking great care that no one else should acquire them.

Such measures will be necessary in order that all should know that only those can rule who have been initiated in the mysteries of political art. Only such men will be taught how to apply our plans in practice by making use of the experience of many centuries. They will be initiated in the conclusions drawn from all observations of our political and economical system and in all social sciences. In a word, they will be told the true spirit of the laws that have been founded by nature herself in order to govern mankind.

Direct successors to the sovereign will be superseded in the event of their proving to be frivolous or soft-hearted during their education, or in case they show any other tendency likely to be detrimental to their power, and which render them incapable of ruling and even to be dangerous to the prestige of the crown.

Only such men as are capable of governing firmly, although perhaps cruelly, will be entrusted with the reins of government by our Elders.

In case of illness or loss of energy, our Sovereign will be obliged to hand over the reins of government to those of his family who have proved themselves more capable.

The King's immediate plans and, still more, his plans for the future will not even be known to those who will be called his nearest councillors. Only our Sovereign, and the Three who initiated him, will know the future.

In the person of the Sovereign, who will rule with an unshakable will and control himself as well as humanity, the people will recognize as it were fate itself and all its human paths. None will know the aims of the Sovereign when he issues his orders, therefore none will dare to obstruct his mysterious path.

Of course, the Sovereign must have a head capable of dealing with our plans. Therefore he will not ascend the throne before his brain-power has been ascertained by our wise men.

In order that all his subjects should love and venerate their Sovereign, he must often address them in public. Such measures will bring the two powers into harmony, namely, that of the populace and that of the ruler, which we have separated in the Gentile countries by holding the one in awe of the other.

We had to hold these two powers in awe one of another, in order that they, when once separated, should fall under our influence.

The King of Israel must not be under the influence of his own passions, especially that of sensuousness. He must not allow animal instincts to get the better of his brain. Sensuousness, more than any other passion, is certain to destroy mental and foreseeing powers; it distracts men's thoughts towards the worst side of human nature.

The Column of the Universe in the person of the World Ruler, sprung from the Holy seed of David, has to forgo all personal passions for the benefit of his people.

Our Sovereign must be irreproachable.

Signed by the representatives of
Zion, of the 33rd degree.

In many editions, including the early Russian editions of 1903–6 and also the first British edition of 1920, the text of the *Protocols* is followed by an epilogue on the Symbolic Serpent (see the extract from the third 'protocol' above, and the map on Plate 3). The key passage is as follows:

According to the records of secret Jewish Zionism, Solomon and other Jewish learned men already, in 929 B.C., thought out a scheme in theory for a peaceful conquest of the whole universe by Zion.

As history developed, this scheme was worked out in detail and completed by men, who were subsequently initiated in this question. These learned men decided by peaceful means to conquer the world for Zion with the slyness of the symbolic serpent, whose head was to represent the initiated into the plans of the Jewish administration, and the body of the serpent to represent the Jewish people – the administration was always kept secret, even from the Jewish nation itself. As this serpent penetrated into the hearts of the nations which it encountered, it got under and devoured all the non-Jewish power of these states. It is foretold that the snake has to finish its work, strictly adhering to the designed path, until the course which it has to run is closed by the return of its head to Zion and until by this means, the snake has completed its round of Europe and has encircled it – and until, by dint of enchaining Europe, it has encompassed the whole world. This it is to accomplish by using every endeavour to subdue the other countries by an economical conquest.

The return of the head of the serpent to Zion can only be accomplished after the power of all the Sovereigns of Europe has been laid low, that is to say, when by means of economic crises and wholesale destruction effected everywhere there shall have been brought about a spiritual demoralization and a moral corruption, chiefly with the assistance of Jewish women masquerading as French, Italians, etc.[1] These are the surest spreaders of licentiousness into the lives of the leading men at the heads of nations.

Women in the service of Zion act as a decoy for those who, thanks to them, are always in need of money, and therefore are always ready to barter their conscience for money. This money is in reality only lent by the Jews, for it quickly returns through the same women into the hands of bribing Jewry – but, through these transactions, slaves are bought for the cause of Zion.

It is natural for the success of such an undertaking that neither the public officials nor private individuals should suspect the part played by the women employed by Jewry. Therefore the directors of the cause of Zion formed, as it were, a religious caste – eager followers of the Mosaic law and of the statutes of the Talmud. All the world believed that the mask of the law of Moses is the real rule of life of the Jews. No one thought of investigating the effect of this rule of life, especially as all eyes were directed on the gold, which could be supplied by the caste, and which gave this caste absolute freedom for its economical and political intrigues.

A sketch of the symbolic serpent is shown as follows: Its first

---

[1] Some ladies were named at this point in the manuscript submitted by Nilus to the Censorship Committee in Moscow. The names, which were removed on the order of the committee, included not only the famous Jewish actress Sarah Bernhardt but also La Belle Otéro, who was a Spaniard with nothing Jewish about her. It is an extraordinary thought that La Belle Otéro lived for another sixty years. She died late in 1965, just as the present book was being completed.

stage in Europe was in 429 B.C. in Greece, where, in the time of Pericles, the serpent first started eating into the power of that country. The second stage was in Rome in the time of Augustus about 69 B.C.[1] The third in Madrid in the time of Charles V in A.D. 1552. The fourth in Paris about 1700, in the time of Louis XVI.[2] The fifth in London from 1814 onwards (after the downfall of Napoleon). The sixth in Berlin in 1871 after the Franco-Prussian war. The seventh in St Petersburg, over which is drawn the head of the serpent under the date of 1881.

All these states which the serpent traversed have had the foundations of their constitutions shaken, Germany, with its apparent power, forming no exception to the rule. In economic conditions England and Germany are spared, but only till the conquest of Russia is accomplished by the serpent, on which at present all its efforts are concentrated. The further course of the serpent is not shown on this map, but arrows indicate its next movement towards Moscow, Kieff, and Odessa.

It is now well known to us to what extent the latter cities form the centres of the militant Jewish race. Constantinople is shown as the last stage of the serpent's course before it reaches Jerusalem.

Only a short distance still remains before the serpent will be able to complete its course by uniting its head to its tail. . . .

[1] This is some forty years too early for Augustus.
[2] A mistake for Louis XIV.

The *Protocols* and the Coming of Antichrist

(See above, pp. 43, 91–2, and Plate 6)

Though the *Protocols* were to form an important part of one of the major totalitarian creeds of the twentieth century, they grew out of an age-old apocalyptic tradition. The extent to which they were originally involved with the Antichrist legend emerges clearly from the note which Sergey Nilus appended to his edition of 1905[1]:

. . . There is no room left for doubt. With all the might and terror of Satan, the reign of the triumphant King of Israel is approaching our unregenerate world; the King born of the blood of Zion – the Antichrist – is near to the throne of universal power.

Events in the world are rushing with stupendous rapidity; dissensions, wars, rumours, famines, epidemics, and earthquakes[2] – what was but yesterday impossible, has today become an accomplished fact. Days rush past, as it were for the benefit of the chosen people. There is no time to minutely enter into the history of humanity from the point of view of the revealed 'mysteries of iniquity',[3] to historically prove the influence which the 'elders of Israel' have had on the misfortunes of humanity, to foretell the already approaching certain future of mankind or to disclose the final act of the world's tragedy.

The Light of Christ alone and that of His Holy Universal Church can penetrate into the Satanic depths and reveal the extent of their wickedness.

In my heart I feel that the hour has struck for summoning the Eighth Ecumenical Council to which, oblivious of the quarrels which have parted them for so many centuries, will congregate the pastors and representatives of the whole of Christianity, to meet the advent of the Antichrist.

---

[1] As translated in the first (1920) British edition of the Protocols.

[2] The traditional 'signs' of the last days of this world.

[3] The reference is to the prophecy of Antichrist in 2 Thessalonians II.

Bibliographical Note

IT would be impracticable to produce an exhaustive bibliography for the subjects touched on in this book, and the following survey is intended simply as an introduction to the field of study.

When it is completed by a further two volumes, Léon Poliakov's *Histoire de l'Antisémitisme* will be the fullest history of the anti-semitic tradition. At present (1966) it consists of Vol. I, *Du Christ aux Juifs de Cour* (Paris, 1955) (English translation, New York, 1965)[1], which deals with European antisemitism down to the eve of emancipation, and Vol. II, *De Mahomet aux Marranes* (Paris, 1961), which deals with the fate of the Jews under Islam and in Spain and Portugal. Meanwhile the essentials of the story have been skilfully compressed into a single volume by James Parkes: *Antisemitism*, London, 1963. Hugo Valentin's *Antisemitism Historically and Critically Examined*, London, 1936, can also be profitably consulted, and so can Salo W. Baron's great *Social and Religious History of the Jews*, 3 vols., New York, 1937, and 8 vols., New York, 1952–58.

Works dealing specially with the origins of antisemitism in early Christianity are James Parkes, *The Conflict of the Church and the Synagogue*, London, 1934; Marcel Simon, *Verus Israël*, Paris, 1948; and Jules Isaac, *Genèse de l'Antisémitisme*, Paris, 1956; while James Parkes, *The Jew in the Medieval Community*, London, 1938, and Joshua Trachtenberg, *The Devil and the Jews*, New Haven, 1943, deal with the period when the figure of the Jew was effectively demonized.

The revival of antisemitism in the past few generations is studied in: James Parkes, *The Emergence of the Jewish Problem, 1878–1939*, Oxford, 1946; K. S. Pinson (ed.), *Essays on Anti-Semitism*, New York, 1946; Howard M. Sachar, *The Course of Modern Jewish History*, Cleveland and New York, 1958; and Hannah Arendt, *The Origins of Totalitarianism* (second edition), London, 1958. Works on individual countries include R. F. Byrnes, *Antisemitism in Modern France*, New Brunswick, 1950 (which however stops short before the Dreyfus case); P. W. Massing, *Rehearsal for Destruction:*

[1] And London, 1966.

a study of political antisemitism in Imperial Germany, New York, 1949; P. G. J. Pulzer, *The Rise of Political Anti-semitism in Germany and Austria*, New York and London, 1964; and S. M. Dubnow, *History of the Jews in Russia and Poland*, 3 vols., Philadelphia, 1916–20.

Among works on the social preconditions of Nazi antisemitism Eva Reichmann, *Hostages of Civilisation*, London, 1950, and A. Leschnitzer, *The Magic Background of Modern Anti-semitism*, New York, 1956, remain very valuable, while on the ideological background George L. Mosse, *The Crisis of German Ideology*, New York, 1964, is now the standard work. The Nazi persecution of the Jews can be studied from documents in L. Poliakov and J. Wulf, *Le IIIe Reich et les Juifs*, Paris, 1959. The extermination itself is described in L. Poliakov, *Bréviaire de la Haine*, Paris, 1951 (translated as *Harvest of Hate*, Syracuse U.P. and London, 1954, 1956); Gerald Reitlinger, *The Final Solution*, London, 1953; and Raul Hilberg, *The Destruction of the European Jews*, Chicago, 1961; as well as in the many accounts of particular camps. Various German works illumine the psycho-social processes which made the extermination possible, notably K. Baschwitz, *Du und die Masse*, Amsterdam, 1938; M. Müller-Claudius, *Der Antisemitismus und das deutsche Verhängnis*, Frankfort/Main, 1948; Wanda von Baeyer-Katte, *Das Zerstörende in der Politik*, Heidelberg, 1958; and H. Buchheim, M. Broszat, H.-A. Jacobsen and H. Krausnick, *Anatomie des SS-Staates*, 2 vols., Olten und Freiburg in Breisgau, 1965. H. R. Trevor-Roper, *The Last Days of Hitler*, London and New York, 1947 (third edition 1962); J. R. Rees (ed.) *The Case of Rudolf Hess*, London, 1947; G. M. Gilbert, *The Psychology of Dictatorship. Based on an examination of the leaders of Nazi Germany*, New York, 1950; R. Hoess, *Commandant of Auschwitz*, London, 1953; and Hannah Arendt, *Eichmann in Jerusalem, a report on the banality of evil*, New York, 1963, provide valuable and varied insights into Nazi mentality. For the history of the Nazi movement Alan Bullock, *Hitler, a Study in Tyranny*, 5th edition, London, 1964, is indispensable.

For the psychology and sociology of antisemitic prejudice the series of pioneering volumes sponsored by the American Jewish Committee and entitled *Studies in Prejudice* is of fundamental importance: *The Authoritarian Personality*, by T. W. Adorno, Else Frenkel-Brunswik, D. J. Levinson and R. N. Sanford, New York, 1950; *Dynamics of Prejudice*, by R. Bettelheim and M. Janowitz, Chicago, 1950, and its expanded version, *Social Change and Prejudice*, Glencoe, 1964; and *Antisemitism and Emotional Disorder*, by N. W. Ackerman and Marie Jahoda, New York, 1950. A Comparable British study is J. H. Robb, *Working-class Anti-*

semite, a psychological study in a London borough, London, 1954. All these works are primarily concerned with the personality-structure and social situation of typical present-day antisemites. As a psychoanalytical interpretation of the antisemitic tradition as a historical phenomenon R. M. Loewenstein, *Christians and Jews,* New York, 1951 (translation of *Psychoanalyse de l'antisémitisme,* Paris, 1951) is still unrivalled.

The story of the *Protocols* has been told many times, with varying degrees of accuracy, in newspaper articles and in books dealing with famous impostures. But between the two world wars there also appeared more than a dozen works solely devoted to the historical and critical study of the *Protocols.* Early studies, which by now have themselves acquired historical interest, include: for Britain: L. Wolf, *The Jewish Bogey,* London, 1920; P. Graves, *The Truth about the Protocols (The Times* articles reprinted), London, 1921; for the United States: H. Bernstein, *The History of a Lie,* New York, 1921; John Spargo, *The Jew and American Ideals,* New York and London, 1921; for Germany: O. Friedrich, *Die Weisen von Zion. Das Buch der Fälschungen,* Lübeck, 1920; H. L. Strack, *Jüdische Geheimgesetze?,* Berlin, 1921; B. Segel, *Die Protokolle der Weisen von Zion, kritisch beleuchtet,* Berlin, 1924, and a more popular version of the same: *Welt-Krieg, Welt-Revolution, Welt-Verschwörung, Welt-Oberregierung,* Berlin, 1926 (translated as *The Protocols of the Elders of Zion, the greatest lie in history,* New York, 1934); and a Russian work, Yu. Delevsky, *Protokoly Sionskikh Mudretsov,* Berlin, 1923, which contains little-known documentary material. The Nazi period saw a fresh spate of studies: H. Rollin, *L'Apocalypse de notre temps: les dessous de la propagande allemande d'après des documents inédits,* Paris, 1939, which is an important work of original scholarship; P. Charles, S.J., *Les Protocoles des Sages de Sion,* Paris, 1938 (reprinted from the *Nouvelle Revue Théologique*); another and fuller study by Bernstein, *The Truth about the Protocols of Zion,* New York, 1935; J. Gwyer's witty *Portraits of mean men: a short history of the Protocols of the Elders of Zion,* London, 1938; two works directly inspired by the Berne trial: V. Burtsev, *'Protokoly Sionskikh Mudretsov' Dokazanny Podlog* (*'The Protocols of the Elders of Zion' a proven forgery*), Paris, 1938, and E. Raas and G. Brunschvig, *Vernichtung einer Fälschung: der Prozess um die erfundenen 'Weisen von Zion'* Zurich, 1938; and three works devoted to showing Hitler as a pupil of the Elders: A. Stein, *Adolf Hitler, Schüler der 'Weisen von Zion',* Karlsbad, 1936; I. Heilbut, *Die öffentlichen Verleumder. Die Protokolle der Weisen von Zion und ihre Anwendung in der heutigen Weltpolitik,* Zurich, 1937; and R. Blank, *Adolf Hitler, ses aspirations, sa politique, sa propagande et les Protocols des Sages de Sion*, Paris, 1938. A valuable study of the various editions of the *Protocols* was produced by E. Cherikover, probably in 1934: *Les Protocoles, leur origine et leur diffusion*. It seems never to have been printed, but it was known to Rollin and is available in mimeograph at the Wiener Library. The latest study, J. S. Curtiss, *An appraisal of the Protocols of Zion*, New York, 1942, is a meticulous survey of the facts of the forgery as generally known, but without the benefit of Rollin's researches. Writing a generation later Walter Laqueur, in *Russia and Germany, a century of conflict*, London, 1965, has thrown fresh light on the Russian and German propagators of the forgery and the links between them. A chapter by J. M. Machover in *Dix ans après la chute de Hitler (1945–1955)*, published by the Centre de Documentation Juive Contemporaine in Paris in 1957, deals with the *Protocols* in the years immediately following the war.

The books, pamphlets, and articles defending and elaborating the *Protocols* are believed to number more than a thousand. The following list of some of the editions of the *Protocols* themselves will give some idea of the dissemination of the forgery:

Russian:

Shortened version in Krushevan's newspaper *Znamya*, St Petersburg, from 26 August to 7 September 1903.

Complete text in Chapter XII, second edition of S. A. Nilus, *Velikoe v Malom i Antikhrist . . .*, Tsarskoe Selo, 1905.

In G. Butmi, *Vragi Roda Chelovecheskago*, St Petersburg, 1906; second edition 1907.

In new edition of Nilus's book, renamed *Bliz Gryadushchy Antikhrist*, Moscow, 1911.

In further edition of Nilus's book, renamed *Bliz Est, Pri Dverekh*, Moscow, 1917.

Sionskiye Protokoly, Novocherkask, 1918. Nilus text, printed by printing office of Don Cossack Army, and known to have been edited by A. Rodionov.

Russian emigration:

Luch Sveta, Vol. III, dated May 1920, contains complete text of Nilus's book, 1911 edition. Berlin.

Vsemirny tayny zagovor. Protokoly sionskikh mudretsov (po Nilusu), New York, 1921.

Protokoly sionskikh mudretsov (po tekstu S. A. Nilusa). Vsemirny tayny zagovor, Berlin, 1922.

M. K. Gorchakov, *Sionskiye Protokoly. 'Doloy Zlo!'*, Paris, 1927.

German and Austrian:

Gottfried zur Beek (pseudonym of Ludwig Müller, also called Müller von Hausen), *Die Geheimnisse der Weisen von Zion*, Charlottenburg, 1919 (really 1920). Six editions in 1920. The Nazi Party acquired rights in this edition in 1929. A shortened version had run to fifteen editions by 1933 and twenty-two editions by 1938.

T. Fritsch, *Die zionistischen Protokolle*, Leipzig, 1920. This version had reached its 13th edition by 1933.

E. von Engelhardt, *Jüdische Weltmachtpläne*, Leipzig, 1936.

Die Protokolle der Weisen von Zion. Das Welteroberungsprogram der Juden, published by Erste Wiener Vereins-Buchdruckerei, Vienna, 1940.

British:

The Jewish Peril: Protocols of the Learned Elders of Zion, London, 1920.

Protocols of the Learned Elders of Zion. Translated by V. E. Marsden and published by The Britons Publishing Society, London, 1921. Since reissued under various titles. Currently called *World Conquest through World Government. The Protocols of the Learned Elders of Zion.* Marsden's translation was also published in various parts of the British Empire; in 1934, for instance, a New Zealand edition was published.

In Lesley Fry's *Waters Flowing Eastwards*, Paris, 1921 and 1933. Marsden's translation. The book was published by the *Revue internationale des sociétés secrètes*.

American:

The Protocols and World Revolution; including a translation and analysis of the 'Protocols of the Meetings of the Zionist Men of Wisdom', Boston, 1920. A 'White' Russian production.

'Praemonitus Praemunitus', The Protocols of the Wise Men of Zion, New York, 1920.

The Protocols of the Meetings of the Learned Elders of Zion, Chicago, 1934. The Patriotic Publishing Co. Marsden's translation.

The Protocols of the Learned Elders of Zion, Chicago, 1935. Right Cause Publishing Co.

French:

'Protocols'. Procès-verbaux de réunions secrètes des Sages d'Israël, Paris, 1920. Published by La Vieille France.

Jouin, Mgr E. *Le Péril judéo-maçonnique*, Vol. I, *Les 'Protocols' des Sages de Sion*, Paris, 1920. The Nilus version, though not translated directly from the Russian. Vol. IV, *Les 'Protocols' de 1901 de G. Butmi*, Paris, 1922. Cheap editions of both these volumes were published by the *Revue internationale des sociétés secrètes*, including a new edition of the Nilus version in 1934.

R. Lambelin, *'Protocols des Sages de Sion*, Paris, 1921. Translated from Nilus. Frequently reissued down to 1939.

U. Gohier, *Les Protocoles des Sages d'Israël*, Paris, 1924, 1925.

In Lesley Fry's *Le Retour des flots vers l'Orient. Le Juif notre maître*, Paris, 1931. Published by the *Revue internationale des sociétés secrètes*.

W. Creutz, *Les Protocoles des Sages de Sion*, Paris, 1934.

Le Complot Juif. Les Protocoles des Sages de Sion, Paris, n.d. Published by the Rassemblement Anti-Juif de France (Darquier de Pellepoix), *c.* 1938.

Polish:

Baczność!! Przeczytaj i daj innym. Rok 1897–1920 (Protokóły posiedzeń Mędrców Sjonu), Warsaw, *c.* 1920.

Protokóły Mędrców Sjonu, Warsaw, 1923. Published by the organization Rozwój.

'Wróg przed bramą!', Bydgoszcz, 1930.

Protokóły Mędrców Sjonu, Warsaw, etc., 1934.

Polish emigration:

'Mane, Tekel, Upharsin!' . . . *Księga Straszliwa Protokóły Obrad Mędrców Sjonu*, New York, 1920.

Rumanian:

Ion I. Moța, *Protocoalele Înțeleptilor Șionului*, Orăștie, 1923.

Politica Secretă a Ovreilor Pentu Cucerirea Lumii Creștine, Bucharest, 1934.

Hungarian:

Sion Bölcseinek Jegyzökönyvei. A Bolsevikiek Bibliája, Budapest, 1922.

Czech:

Ze Shromáždění Sionských Mudrců, Prague, 1927.

Yugoslav:

M. Tomič, *Prave Osnove ili Protokoli Sionskih Mudraca*, Split-Šibernik, 1929.

Patrioticus, *Ko potkopava čovečanstvo*, Belgrade, 1934.

Protokoli skupova sionskih mudraca, Belgrade, 1939.

Jedan vazan dokument, a Croatian translation published in Berlin, 1936.

Greek:

A Greek translation of the *Protocols* was published by 'Drasis' in 1928 and reprinted several times, for instance in 1934 and 1940.

Italian:

L'Internazionale Ebraica. Protocoli dei 'Savi Anziani' di Sion, Rome, 1921. Published by *La Vita Italiana* (G. Preziosi). New editions, 1937 and 1938.

Spanish:

Los Protocols. Los Sabios de Sion. El Gobierno Mundial Invisible. El Programa Judío para Subyugar al Mundo. Published by Fritsch's 'Hammer' publishing house, Leipzig, 1930.

Alfonso Jaraix (trans), *Los Poderes ocultos de España,* Barcelona, 1932.

Protocols de los Jefes de Israel, Madrid, 1932.

Duke de la Victoria (trans), *Los Protocolos de los Sabios de Sion,* (5th edition), Madrid, 1935. Translated from Lambelin.

L'Internationale Hebraica: Los 'Protocolos' de los Sabios Ancianos de Sion, Rome, 1938. Translated from the Italian edition of 1937–38.

Portuguese:

F. P. de Sequeira (ed.), *Os Planos da Autocracia Judaica,* Porto, n.d.

Dutch:

J. Nijsse, *De Protocollen van de Wijzen van Sion,* with introduction by P. Molenbroek, Amsterdam, n.d. The same version, with Molenbroek's introduction, appeared over the names of other editors. The 7th edition was published in Amsterdam in 1943.

Flemish:

L. Welter, *Het Jodendom ontmaskerd als de Aartsvijand,* Courtrai–Brussels–Paris, 1937.

Walloon:

A. Robert, *Les Protocols des Sages de Sion,* Brussels, 1935.

Swedish:

Förlåten Faller . . . Det Tillkommende Världssjälvhärskardömet Enligt 'Sions Vises Hemliga Protokoll', Helsingfors, 1919.

Israels Vises Hemliga Protokoll. Judarnas Strategiska Plan att Med Lögn och List Erövra Världsherraväldet, Stockholm, 1934.

Norwegian:

Den nye verdenskeiser; en sensasjonell avsløring av de hemmelige trådtrekkere bak verdens-politikkens kulisser, Oslo, 1944.

Latvian:

Zianas protokoli . . . No kreewu walodas tulkojis un isdewis J.O., Riga, 1923.

Brazilian:

G. Barroso, *Os Protocolos dos Sábios de Sião*, São Paulo, 1936–37.
T. Moreiro, *Os Protocolos dos Sábios de Sião. O Dominio do Mundo pelos Judeus*, Rio de Janeiro, n.d.

The above list covers only the period to 1945, and is not complete even for that period. For instance, the Arabic editions, of which there were several already in the 1920s and 1930s, are not included; and there were certainly more South American editions than the two Brazilian ones listed here.

Index

69 70 71 72 73   12 11 10 9 8 7 6 5 4 3 2 1

From the Library of

Alma S. Thigpen

COOK IT LIGHT

OTHER BOOKS BY JEANNE JONES

The Calculating Cook

More Calculated Cooking

Diet for a Happy Heart

Secrets of Salt-Free Cooking

Jeanne Jones' Party Planner and Entertaining
Diary

Jeanne Jones' Food Lover's Diet

Fitness First: A 14-Day Diet and Exercise Program
(with Karma Kientzler)

The Love in the Afternoon Cookbook
(with Donna Swajeski, ABC TV)

The Fabulous Fructose Recipe Book
(with J. Thomas Cooper, M.D.)

Stuffed Spuds: 100 Meals in a Potato

Jet Fuel—The New Food Strategy for the High-Performance
Person

The Fabulous High-Fiber Diet

Canyon Ranch Menus and Recipes

Non-Dairy Cookbook

COOK
IT
LIGHT

Jeanne Jones

MACMILLAN PUBLISHING COMPANY / *NEW YORK*

COLLIER MACMILLAN PUBLISHERS / *LONDON*

To all of the readers of my "Cook It Light" column—
and most specifically to my readers who write to me!

In grateful acknowledgment:
William Hansen / Viola Stroup / Paula Todd

Copyright © 1987 by Jeanne Jones

Illustrations copyright © 1987 by Thelma Gomilas

Photographs: "Bouillabaisse, Salad of young greens with Jeanne Jones' Light Tarragon Dressing, and Gingered Fruit Compote" is copyright © 1987 by Kim Brun Studios, Inc. All others are copyright © 1987 by Kevin Schumacher, Collins and Associates. Grateful acknowledgment is made to Bo Danica and to Diehling, The Kitchen Store, both of La Jolla, for the table settings in the photographs.

Macmillan Publishing Company
866 Third Avenue, New York, N.Y. 10022
Collier Macmillan Canada, Inc.

Library of Congress Cataloging-in-Publication Data
Jones, Jeanne.
  Cook it light.
  Bibliography: p.
  Includes index.
  1. Cookery . I. Title.
TX715.J773 1987   641.5   87-14052
ISBN 0-02-559770-1

Macmillan books are available at special discounts for bulk purchases for sales promotions, premiums, fund-raising, or educational use. For details, contact:

Special Sales Director
Macmillan Publishing Company
866 Third Avenue
New York, N.Y. 10022

10 9 8 7 6 5 4 3 2 1

Printed in the United States of America

CONTENTS

PREFACE

WRITING my column, "Cook It Light," syndicated by King
Features, is truly an exciting weekly event in my life. It gives me
the opportunity to stay in touch with hundreds of thousands of my
readers all over the United States and Canada. The key is that I
write what is called in the trade an interacting column; in other
words, my readers write to me, and their letters, along with my
answers, are printed every week.

I loved it when I was described recently as the "Dear Abby" of
the food section because that's exactly what I do. Only my readers
don't write to me about personal problems. They send me their
recipes that need help. Sometimes they just write asking me how
to make a lighter version of an old high-calorie classic without
sending a recipe at all—or describe a menu dilemma and ask me
if I have a recipe that will get them out of it, such as a low-
cholesterol quiche or a low-calorie birthday cake.

When a reader does send me a favorite recipe to be revised so
it has fewer calories and less cholesterol and sodium, I first make

it just as it is written. This way I have the taste, texture, and appearance I need to duplicate in the revision.

Sometimes it's easy and I am able to come very close to the original recipe with a much lighter version in one or two tries. Other times I have to make numerous passes at it before I am satisfied that my light recipe is close enough to the original that any one of you would be happy with the results.

I have received hundreds of letters telling me how educational my column is. I want to thank all of you and tell you that my column is also an ongoing education for me. I have learned more ways to substitute fresh and natural ingredients for the processed foods found in cans, bottles, boxes, and envelopes than I ever knew existed.

It has been so much fun for me to write this column that I want to share a collection of the recipes from it with you in this book. I am also including a few of my own favorite recipes that I have developed for famous spas, hotels, and restaurants—and some tips on how you can start creating your own LIGHT recipes.

Enjoy my book—and please keep writing to me. I love your letters and I need your recipes!

Jeanne Jones

COOK IT LIGHT

WHY "COOK IT LIGHT"? *Light* is both an adjective and a noun. *Light,* the adjective, means "less heavy." *Light,* the noun, is something that illuminates, enlightens, or informs. When I say "cook it light," I am saying cook it with less fat for fewer calories; less food of animal origin for lower cholesterol; less salt and high-sodium ingredients to reduce the amount of sodium consumed. But "cook it light" also means make it imaginative and satisfying. Deprivation has no place in my cooking vocabulary.

Cook It Light could also be called *Cook It Smart.* Now, more than ever before, we have been made aware of the importance of proper nutrition. "We are what we eat" will probably be remembered as the slogan of the century, and remember the ancient proverb, "What the fool does in the end, the wise man does in the beginning."

Take a good look at the covers of all our popular magazines for both men and women. It is no longer "in" to be thin. It is "in" to be trim and fit. Healthy is beautiful, and we now know that our health has more to do with what we do for ourselves than what our

1

doctors can do for us. We are being told at every turn to take charge of our lives, to be in control of our own destinies. That's what *Cook It Light* is all about—being in control, taking charge of our nutrition. No one else can control how many calories we eat or how much fat, cholesterol, and sodium we consume.

It isn't enough just to lower the number of calories we eat. It is the quality of the calories consumed that is important. The integrity of any item on any menu is totally dependent upon the quality of the ingredients used. In fact, *Cook It Light* isn't so much about watching calories to lose weight as it is about eating well. To achieve you own full dimension in fitness *and* health, good nutrition is essential.

There are still people who think that food has to be *either* good *or* good for you. Fortunately nothing could be further from the truth, and this new culinary concept is truly for everyone—even the meat and potato lovers! People of all ages are dependent on the fuel they take in for their performance. Therefore, whether you are a man or a woman, a child or an adult, you need the best fuel possible to do the best job.

In *Cook It Light,* I have combined gastronomy—the joy of truly fine food—with nutrition—the study of the proper fueling of the body. In *Cook It Light,* gastronomy and nutrition are combined to create dishes that are both delicious and healthy.

Cook It Light will make you a star in the culinary world. It will help you to achieve and maintain a better-looking and healthier body. It will give you the energy necessary for peak performance. It will also help you avoid heart disease and cancer.

Cooking it light is easy, fast, and fun. It is also less expensive than the heavier, more traditional approach to food preparation. You may be surprised to find that this lighter approach to cooking also produces more delicate, flavorful dishes that are more popular with your family and friends.

By learning to *Cook It Light,* you can produce fabulous gourmet meals, or even "junk" foods, that are as good for you as they are appealing and satisfying. Using the recipes in this book you can enjoy the international cuisines and the American regional cooking you like best. Using my techniques for lowering the fat, calories, cholesterol, and sodium, you can lighten your own recipes without losing any of the taste, texture, or appearance of your favorite dishes.

COOK-IT-LIGHT MEAL PLANNING

Putting together a light meal differs in no way from designing a classic heavy meal as far as balance and taste are concerned.

It is important to balance heavy courses with lighter courses. For example, you would not want to serve a rich, hearty soup with poultry or meat in it before serving pot roast for the entrée. A crisp, fresh garden salad would be a better choice.

Also remember you want variety in taste range, color, and texture in your menus. When possible, avoid using the same ingredients in each course. Serving carrot soup with steamed carrots as the vegetable on your entrée plate and carrot cake for dessert will never win an award for exciting menu planning, no matter how good each course may be by itself, any more than a plate with roast chicken, mashed potatoes, and cauliflower would create visual excitement. New potatoes with their reddish-colored skins intact and broccoli, beets, or carrots would make a much prettier and more colorful plate. The combination of texture or "mouth feel" between the ingredients used in any one dish can also add greatly to its appeal. For example, a salad with crisp greens, soft cheese, and crunchy nuts or seeds is much more exciting than a salad with only one texture.

I like to use a theme for my appetizer, entrée, and dessert courses when I am designing menus for my clients or planning my own dinner parties. For example, a Russian dinner might start with Borscht, followed by Chicken Stroganoff for the entrée and Strawberries Romanoff for dessert. By putting together menus that incorporate a national or ethnic theme, the taste ranges will be compatible and you will have more fun planning and preparing the meals. If you wish to decorate, it is much easier with a theme. It is such fun to decorate appropriately for a party; even a small family dinner is more fun and more exciting when you turn it into a dining event.

I have created the following menu suggestions for you to get started planning your own theme parties. The menus range from a Mexican fiesta to a traditional holiday feast. The recipes for all the dishes suggested in the menus are in this book.

COOK-IT-LIGHT MENUS

MEXICAN FIESTA

Make-believe Margarita (page 257)
Gazpacho (page 31)
Fiesta Salad (without cheese) (page 100)
Quesadilla (page 127)
Flan (page 244)

MIDDLE EASTERN

Eggplant Relish with Pita Bread (page 108)
Moroccan Chicken with Couscous (page 175)
Baklava (page 248)

FRENCH

Celery Root Salad (page 87)
Cassoulet (page 197)
Ratatouille (page 115)
Fantasy in Fruit (page 224)

EAST INDIAN

Citrus Salad with Poppy Seed Dressing (page 92)
Chicken Bombay (page 168) with Apple Chutney (page 62)
Brown Rice
Pea Pods
Pineapple Pie (page 237)

ITALIAN

Parsley Salad (page 84)
Light Lasagna (page 132)
Zucchini al Dente
Fresh Fruit

ORIENTAL

Egg Drop Soup (page 30)
Chinese Chicken Salad (page 97)
Spiced Bananas (page 228)
or
Miso Soup (page 28)
Polynesian Prawns (page 152)
Brown Rice
Oriental Vegetables
Vanilla Ice-Milk Crepe with Papaya-Rum Sauce (page 225)

CONTINENTAL

French Onion Soup (page 35)
Chicken in Pink Peppercorn Sauce (page 173)
Rice Pilaf (page 119)
Creamed Leeks (page 109)
Spinach Salad with Toasted Walnuts (page 85)
Pear Crisp (page 232)

ALL-AMERICAN

Lettuce and Tomato Salad with Bleu Cheese Dressing (page 76)
Pot Roast (page 190)
Scalloped Potatoes (page 121)
Colorful Fresh Vegetables
Raisin-Rice Pudding (page 235)

SUMMER BARBECUE

Coleslaw (page 86)
Grilled Turkey Burger (page 183) with Barbecue Sauce (page 64)
Oven Fries (page 122)
Carob-Yogurt Sundae (page 227)

BRUNCH

Cold Gingered Carrot Soup (page 32)
Broccoli-Cheese Pie (page 139)
Our Famous Sugar-Free Bran Muffins (page 215) with Apple Butter (page 61)

HOLIDAY DINNER

Parsley Salad (page 84)
Roast Turkey with Fennel (page 180)
Italian Oyster Casserole in radicchio cups (page 148)
Italian Green Beans
Italian Cherry Trifle (page 238)

COOK-IT-LIGHT RECIPE REVISION

In my column, "Cook It Light," I revise recipes sent to me by my readers. My goal is to make them healthier without changing the taste or texture of the original recipe.

To do this, I first have to make the recipe exactly as it was sent to me. This gives me a basis for comparison, or what we call in my test kitchen the "benchmark."

The following chart will show you how I marked one recipe to start the testing process. For the revised recipe, see page 144.

RECIPE ANALYSIS

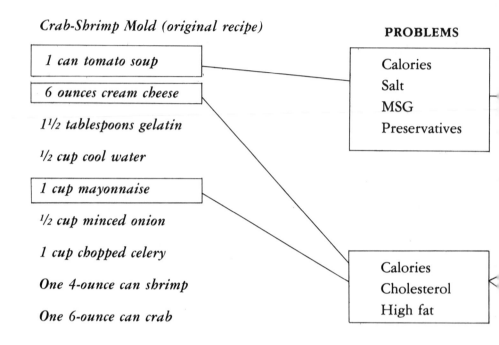

Crab-Shrimp Mold (original recipe)   **PROBLEMS**

| 1 can tomato soup |
| 6 ounces cream cheese |
| 1½ tablespoons gelatin |
| ½ cup cool water |
| 1 cup mayonnaise |
| ½ cup minced onion |
| 1 cup chopped celery |
| One 4-ounce can shrimp |
| One 6-ounce can crab |

Calories
Salt
MSG
Preservatives

Calories
Cholesterol
High fat

The recipe contains three problem ingredients that need to be eliminated, reduced, or replaced.

1. *Problem:* What's wrong with the ingredient? Put the problems in order of importance with your *biggest* concern first.

2. *Function:* What is the purpose of the problem ingredient in the original recipe? Perhaps it can simply be eliminated. List in the order of its perceived importance.

3. *Solution:* What are acceptable ingredients to substitute for the problem ingredients? You may want to try several possibilities, depending on what the desired results are (i.e., tofu *or* reduced-calorie mayonnaise).

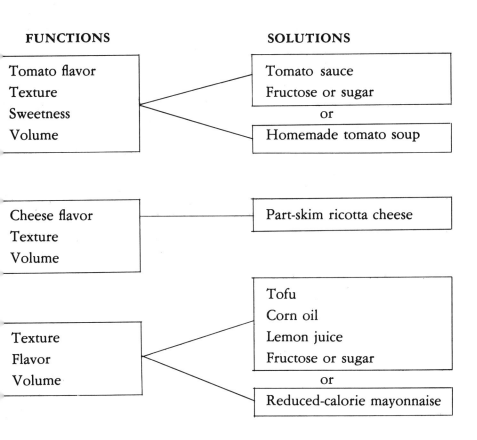

FUNCTIONS	SOLUTIONS
Tomato flavor Texture Sweetness Volume	Tomato sauce Fructose or sugar or Homemade tomato soup
Cheese flavor Texture Volume	Part-skim ricotta cheese
Texture Flavor Volume	Tofu Corn oil Lemon juice Fructose or sugar or Reduced-calorie mayonnaise

4. *Results:* How much did you save? This is the payoff—the rewards are plain to see. You really *can* have it all!

ORIGINAL RECIPE	PER SERVING	REVISED RECIPE
233	Total Calories	74
189	Calories in Fat	27
44 mg	Cholesterol	33 mg
483 mg	Sodium	272 mg

COOK-IT-LIGHT NUTRITION

After each recipe in this book you will find not only the total calories given but also the calories in fat and the milligrams of cholesterol, sodium, and calcium. The number of fat calories compared to the total number of calories you consume has a lot to do with the shape you are in. Most people in the fitness field agree that you should be asked not "What is your weight?" but "What is your fat weight?" because that is the better indication of your general health, stamina, and probable longevity.

It is important to list both the cholesterol and the sodium because both should be monitored in a well-balanced diet. According to the American Heart Association, no one should consume more than 250 milligrams of cholesterol per thousand calories of food. This figure is considerably lower than it was a year ago. The American Heart Association also recommends keeping sodium intake under 2000 milligrams per day, even when performing actively in a temperate climate.

You may wonder why calcium is singled out for mention in the nutritional analyses of my recipes. Calcium is a mineral. It's the most common mineral found in the tissues of the human body and it's the single most important mineral required by our bodies. Without enough calcium, we die! Ninety-nine percent of the calcium in our bodies is contained in our bones. The other 1 percent of the body's calcium is contained in the blood.

Calcium is not only needed for strong bones and good teeth. It plays a key role in many of the body's everyday functions. It's essential for the transmission of nerve impulses, muscular contractions, blood clotting, and functions such as regulation of the heart's rhythm and the chemical activity of all the body's cells.

Most recently, scientists have suggested that calcium may be useful in lowering the blood pressure of those suffering from hypertension. Another report states that there is some evidence to suggest that calcium may be beneficial in preventing cancer of the colon.

Most doctors recommend getting as much calcium as possible from the foods we eat. Without exception, every bit of research and all the reports from the best sources—the La Jolla Cancer Research Foundation, for one—recommend getting your vitamins and minerals from a well-balanced diet rather than through the ingestion of pills. But you don't have to worry about your waistline expanding if you "Cook It Light"!

The nutrition information at the end of each recipe is based upon software designed by Practorcare, Inc. In addition, I have developed a calorie chart to help you compute your own calories quickly and easily.

I routinely round off to the nearest 5 or 0 just as I have on the calorie figures for all servings in this book. The only exception to this is in the calories given for ½ ounce of fish, poultry, or meat, and on this chart I have given an average for each category. For example, ½ ounce of fish at 18 calories is an average or ballpark figure and is actually higher than most fish and seafood; however, all fish in the same category do not have exactly the same number of calories per ounce. It depends upon the fat content of the individual fish.

To further bring calories into perspective, I like to point out that if you take two oranges of exactly the same size and color, and off the same tree, to a laboratory for a calorie count, they will not be the same. In other words, calorie computation cannot be considered an exact science. At best, calories per serving are an educated guess.

AT-A-GLANCE CALORIE CHART

FRUIT	CALORIES	BREADS AND PASTA	CALORIES
Fresh			
1 cup	50	*Cooked*	
Dried		1 cup	200
1 ounce	70		

VEGETABLES		FISH AND SEAFOOD	
Raw Leafy Vegetables and Herbs	Negligible	½ ounce	18
		1 ounce	36
Root Vegetables (Carrots, beets, onions)		1½ ounces	54
		2 ounces	72
		2½ ounces	90
1 cup	50	3 ounces	108
Starchy Vegetables (Potatoes, onion, peas, parsnips, pumpkin)		3½ ounces	126
		4 ounces	144
		4½ ounces	162
		5 ounces	180
		5½ ounces	198
1 cup	150	6 ounces	216
Dried Beans and Legumes (Cooked)			
1 cup	225	POULTRY AND LEAN MEAT	
Other Vegetables (Broccoli, eggplant, tomatoes, asparagus, peppers, cauliflower, brussels sprouts, etc.)		½ ounce	28
		1 ounce	56
		1½ ounces	84
		2 ounces	112
		2½ ounces	140
		3 ounces	168
1 cup	30	3½ ounces	196
		4 ounces	224
		4½ ounces	252
GRAINS		5 ounces	280
Cooked		5½ ounces	308
1 cup	220	6 ounces	336

TOFU	CALORIES	MILK AND CREAM	CALORIES
2 tablespoons		*Cream*	
(1 ounce)	20	2 tablespoons	90
½ cup (4 ounces)	80	*Half and Half*	
1 cup (8 ounces)	160	2 tablespoons	30
		Whole Milk	
CHEESES		2 tablespoons	17
Low-Fat Cottage Cheese		*Low-Fat Milk (2% fat)*	
1%–2 tablespoons	20	2 tablespoons	12
2%–2 tablespoons	25	*Buttermilk*	
Part-Skim Ricotta		2 tablespoons	10
2 tablespoons	40	*Skim Milk (Nonfat milk)*	
Part-Skim Mozzarella		2 tablespoons	10
4 tablespoons		*Dry Powdered Nonfat Milk*	
(1 ounce)	70	2 tablespoons (makes ⅓ cup)	25
Parmesan and Romano		*Canned Skimmed Evaporated Milk*	
4 tablespoons		2 tablespoons	23
(1 ounce)	100	*Canned Whole Milk*	
All Other Cheeses		2 tablespoons	44
4 tablespoons			
(1 ounce)	100	**STOCK** (totally defatted)	Negligible
FATS			
Butter, Margarine, and Oils			
1 teaspoon	40		
2 teaspoons	80		
1 tablespoon	120		
2 tablespoons	240		
Nuts and Seeds			
1 tablespoon	45		
2 tablespoons	90		
3 tablespoons	135		
¼ cup	180		

THE COOK-IT-LIGHT KITCHEN

I have worked with food professionals in commercial kitchens all over the world. At the same time I have been writing cookbooks, a syndicated column, and teaching cooking classes for nonprofessional cooks. The major difference I find between the professional and the home cook is simply in organization.

Just knowing where everything in your kitchen is that you need to make a recipe and having all the necessary ingredients for it is a great start. There is nothing more frustrating than finding out halfway through a recipe that the next ingredient called for is not in the house, or the bowl you need to mix the ingredients in is full of leftovers from last night's dinner!

Commercial kitchens remedy this problem and speed up the preparation time by establishing what is called the *mise-en-place,* which means literally, "things in place." In a properly run restaurant kitchen a recipe is never started until all the ingredients are assembled and prepped in the correct measured amounts. And all of the utensils required to make the recipe are gathered together *before* they are needed.

In commercial kitchens par stock levels are established and then maintained. *Par* is the amount of something you never go below without reordering it (putting it on your shopping list in the case of staples such as rice, flour, onions, and so on). Or making more of it as necessary (for example, salad dressings and sauces).

Another way commercial kitchens work that can be of great benefit in the home as well is in the assembly of the recipe on a per-serving or as-needed basis. Even though most of the recipes in this book are written for four, many of them are broken down in the method for each serving. For example, the Chinese Chicken Salad recipe on page 97 gives instructions in the method for each serving. So, if your family is like many, with some eating at one time and others at another time, the servings are clearly described by proportions of each ingredient required to assemble the finished product and the *mise-en-place* is in the refrigerator ready to be assembled. Describing how each serving is assembled also makes it easy for you to cook the same recipe for one or two instead of four.

In the Food Measurements & Equivalents table in the back of this book, I have done for you what I do for my commercial clients. I have listed ingredients by weight as well as by common units and volume. This will help you enormously when you are shopping for ingredients. A scale is essential if you are truly interested in portion control. I always use one in spa kitchens, where portions *must* be controlled.

I've already mentioned that knowing the weight of ingredients required will be helpful in shopping, so now let's talk about modernizing your marketing and storing methods to make food preparation faster, more efficient, and less expensive. The buying, storing, and preparation of food can be fun and easy, if you're well organized.

The first step to shopping is the list. Keep it handy all the time. Each time you run low on anything, write it down. Don't wait until you are out of it—it might be the next thing you need. When shopping day arrives, plan your weekly menu and add all the necessary ingredients to your list.

Plan to shop only once a week for all staple items. Schedule your shopping trip just as you would any other appointment. Don't minimize the importance of food—make it part of your routine. Your shopping "appointment" should include the time it takes to make the list, do the shopping, and store your groceries properly when you return home.

For the best use of your time, write your shopping list according to the geographical layout of the market. Practically all supermarkets are designed the same way. Usually the fresh food items— dairy, fruits and vegetables, meats, fish and poultry—are all on the outside walls. The interior aisles most often contain the packaged, processed, and canned foods. Obviously there are some desirable items you need—such as grains, herbs and spices, frozen foods, and cleaning products—in the middle aisles. The shopping list you take with you should list all of the things you need in the middle aisles by category so that they are easy to find. This saves you time and money.

Watch out for clever advertisers and misleading labeling. There are thousands of different food products loaded with fat, sugar, and salt cleverly concealed by misleading labeling. Just as soon as you have everything on your list that's in the middle of the market, run for the walls!

When planning your weekly menu, be flexible in your selection of fruits and vegetables. Choose from the fresh produce at the market and select from the best quality available. Fruits and vegetables that are in-season are not only your best buy, but they look better and taste better.

Always include enough time in your shopping appointment to wash and store all your vegetables properly. This will save time later on and greatly add to their storage life. Wash and dry all your leafy vegetables and then roll them in towels or put them in plastic bags before refrigerating them. Root vegetables should also be washed and dried before storing in the refrigerator. But don't peel or scrape them until just before you are ready to use them.

Fruits, if ripe, should be washed, dried, and refrigerated to slow down the ripening process. If not yet ripe, leave them out at room temperature until they are ready to eat. As I have often said when people tell me they don't have time to wash their vegetables when they return from shopping, "What do you do, eat dirty vegetables?" At some point they will have to be washed before they can be used. Doesn't it make more sense to wash them right away so that they go into the refrigerator clean and ready to cook or eat as is? Remember, you are much more likely to use your healthier foods if they are ready to use. Otherwise you will be tempted to pass up the good stuff for faster convenience foods when you are pressed for time.

Natural foods such as dried fruits, whole-grain breads, pastas and flours, and nuts and seeds, stay fresh longer if refrigerated. Always be sure you have plenty of storage containers, wrap, and plastic bags on hand to house your groceries properly.

Once your pantry is stocked, turn your attention to organizing your kitchen for easy access, maximum efficiency, and minimum preparation time.

Arrange the herbs, spices, and extracts in a cool place where they are never exposed to sunlight. Alphabetize them so that you can find them quickly—this saves time, frustration, and money. How? Have you ever looked for a spice, thought you had none, and replaced it—only to find later that you now have two of the same? When your herbs and spices are arranged neatly in alphabetical order, chances for error and accidental duplication are slim.

Have the things you are using within reach when you need them. Organize your kitchen so that the equipment you use most and the foods you eat most often are the most accessible. When possible, free up as much counter space as you can so that you have an adequate work area for meal preparation.

COOK-IT-LIGHT TIPS FOR LIGHTER COOKING

Now that you are ready to cook it light, here are some tips for lighter cooking. These guidelines are the very same ones I use in modifying the recipes sent to me for my syndicated column, "Cook It Light." By following the guidelines, you, too, can modify your own recipes.

CALORIE CONTROL

Calories have only four sources—the three food groups, carbohydrates, proteins, and fats—plus alcohol. Carbohydrates and proteins both contain 4 calories per gram. Fats contain 9 calories per gram, or more than twice as many as carbohydrates and proteins; and alcohol contains 7 calories per gram—almost twice as many. It is easy to see that if you want to control calories, it is important to greatly reduce your intake of fat and alcohol, since they are the two major sources of calories with the least amount of nutrition. To really keep your calories under control, it is important to eliminate fat wherever possible with "light" cooking techniques.

REDUCING THE AMOUNT OF FAT

Cook in nonstick cookware or use a nonstick vegetable spray on your pans and baking dishes to prevent sticking rather than butter, margarine, or oil.

Use water, defatted stock, juice, or wine instead of butter, margarine, or oil to prevent sticking or burning when sautéeing.

When sautéeing onions, garlic, or shallots for a sauce, cook them, covered, over low heat, adding a little water, stock, or wine to prevent scorching rather than butter, margarine, or oil. This will save you a whopping 120 calories per tablespoon of sautéeing fat omitted from your final dish.

When making salad dressings, it is not necessary to add the classic two parts of oil to a part of vinegar. You can extend dressing with water, adding only 1 to 2 tablespoonsful of oil per cup, and still have a delicious, flavorful dressing.

To reduce the amount of saturated fat, use a liquid vegetable oil and margarines that are high in polyunsaturated fats. These include safflower oil, corn oil, cottonseed oil, and all vegetable oils that are not hydrogenated and that run liquid at room temperature. Do not use coconut oil, palm oil, or chocolate. Most nondairy creamers contain coconut oil or palm oil, so always read the labels. For coconut flavor use coconut extract and for chocolate use powdered cocoa. Buy lean cuts of meat and remove all visible fat. Remove the skin from all poultry. Always refrigerate pan drippings so that the fat congeals on the top and can be removed completely.

REDUCING THE AMOUNT OF CHOLESTEROL

To reduce the amount of cholesterol in the foods you are cooking, the most important single rule is to use less animal protein and more complex carbohydrates. Animal protein includes fish, poultry, meat, dairy products, and eggs. Complex carbohydrates include everything that grows that is not refined—fruits, vegetables, grains, unrefined grain products, nuts, and seeds. Cholesterol is found only in foods of animal origin. There is no cholesterol at all in any foods of plant origin. Foods particularly high in cholesterol include egg yolks, some shellfish, and organ meats such as liver, heart, kidneys, sweetbreads, and brains.

INCREASING THE AMOUNT OF FIBER

The source of fiber is just the opposite of cholesterol. Fiber is found only in foods of plant origin—the complex carbohydrates described previously. There is no fiber in any foods of animal origin or in simple or refined carbohydrates such as sugars, syrups, and refined grains.

CONTROLLING SODIUM

The easiest way to control the amount of sodium in your diet is to avoid using salt whenever possible. According to the American Heart Association, no one needs more than a total of 2000 milligrams of sodium per day. If you are on a sodium-restricted diet, avoid foods particularly high in sodium, such as most cheeses, soy sauce, and many condiments, most snack foods, canned soups, and all stock bases, including bouillon cubes, powdered stock bases, and canned consommé and broth.

It is possible to have intense flavor without any salt at all by using herbs and spices. We taste only four things—sweet, salt, sour, and bitter. Everything else is smell. If you have ever had a bad cold and told people you couldn't taste, what you really meant was that you could not smell. You could still taste just fine; in fact you could still tell someone whether something was sweet, salty, sour, or bitter—you just couldn't tell whether it was strawberry or vanilla or lamb or beef. Therefore flavor, as we describe it, is really smell, not taste.

When using dry herbs and spices, always crush them, using a mortar and pestle, before adding them to any recipe, whether it is a cold preparation, such as salad dressing, or something you are cooking, such as stew. This is an essential step because it releases their aroma and increases the flavor. If you want to know how long you continue to grind them in the mortar, the answer is "until you smell them all over the kitchen." That will tell you a great deal about how much more flavor you are adding to any dish.

Never use wines for cooking that are labeled cooking wine, because they contain salt.

REDUCING THE AMOUNT OF SUGAR

Cut the amount of sugar called for in recipes by one-third to one-half.

Substitute concentrated fruit juice (undiluted orange, apple, or pineapple) for the sweetener in recipes.

Reduce ordinary table sugar (sucrose) by at least one-third by using fructose, which is one and one-half times sweeter.

Raise the level of perceived sweetness without adding any sweetener by using vanilla and/or cinnamon.

INCREASING CALCIUM

To increase your calcium intake, use nonfat and low-fat dairy products. The lower the fat content of any dairy product, the higher the calcium content. Also include dark green leafy vegetables, dried fruits, tofu, and all soy products in your diet. Fish and seafood, particularly those with bones, such as sardines, herring, and anchovies, are high in calcium, as is blackstrap molasses. When making fish, poultry, or meat stocks, always add a little vinegar to leach the calcium from the bones and add calcium to the stock.

NUTRITION AT A GLANCE

SUGGESTED % OF CALORIES CONSUMED	BASIC FOOD GROUPS	SOURCES
60% or more	I. *Carbohydrates* A. Complex	Everything that grows and is not refined (fruits, vegetables, and whole grains)
	B. Simple	Sugars, syrups, and refined grains
20% or less	II. *Proteins* A. Animal Protein	Fish, poultry, meat, dairy products, and eggs
	B. Plant Protein	Vegetables, whole grains, legumes, and tofu (soybean curd)
20% or less	III. *Fats* A. Polyunsaturated	1) Most vegetable oils (safflower, corn, and sesame) 2) Seeds
	B. Saturated	1) All fat of animal origin (butter, cream, and lard) 2) Coconut and palm oils and cocoa butter (the fat in chocolate)
	C. Monounsaturated	1) Olive and nut oils 2) Avocados, olives, and nuts

CALORIES PER GRAM	CHOLES-TEROL ?	FIBER ?	GUIDELINES
4	NO	YES	Use five times the amount in volume of complex carbohydrates as animal protein. (This ensures adequate dietary fiber as fiber is found only in foods of plant origin.)
4	NO	NO	Use sparingly.
4	YES	NO	Use 1/5 the amount in volume of animal protein as complex carbohydrates. (This 5 to 1 ratio helps limit cholesterol as cholesterol is found only in foods of animal origin.)
4	NO	YES	Remove poultry skin, trim all visible fat from meat, use only nonfat dairy products, and limit use of egg yolks and organ meats.
9	NO	NO	Use fat sparingly and only for flavor, moisture, and texture.
9	NO	YES	
9	YES	NO	Avoid. These aid in buildup of cholesterol in arteries.
9	NO	NO	
9	NO	NO	
9	NO	YES	These are classified in the fat category because the fat content is so high.

STOCKS & SOUPS

MAKING YOUR OWN STOCK is the single most important step toward becoming a truly fine cook. It always amazes me how many people I know who consider themselves accomplished amateur chefs go to great lengths to buy all fresh, natural, and even exotic ingredients for their dinners, yet still treat stock as the unimportant stepchild on the ingredients' list, routinely using stock bases or canned stocks. Unlike all other quality ingredients, stock cannot be purchased. You must make it yourself. Any really professional chef would die if anyone intimated that any stock was being used in his kitchen that had not been made there.

All stock bases and canned stocks and broth that are not labeled low sodium contain large amounts of salt as well as monosodium glutamate (MSG), artificial coloring, and fat. Stock bases and canned stocks and broth that are labeled low sodium generally taste so bad that it doesn't really matter what's in them because water is a better ingredient!

If you want a low-sodium stock that is truly delicious, making your own is the answer. Making your own stock will not only

20

improve your cooking; it will make all of your dishes healthier and infinitely less expensive. The best news is that it is easy and fast.

I have had so many readers tell me that they don't have time to make their own stock that I finally did a column called "Fifteen-Minute Stock," which I have incorporated into my recipe for chicken stock in this section to show you step-by-step how easy it really is.

When making your own stock, never allow the pot to actually come to a full boil, especially when clarifying (when it starts to boil reduce the heat and simmer the stock). In classic cuisine someone was always designated to make sure this didn't happen. Thus the old cliché: "A watched pot never boils." Don't add salt or much seasoning so that you can adjust the salt and seasonings for every individual recipe. Another tremendous bonus to making your own stock is that you can make it very high in calcium by adding a little vinegar to the water when you put the stockpot on. The vinegar leaches the calcium from the bones, making each cup of stock almost as rich in calcium as milk and practically calorie-free. Almost all of the calories and cholesterol in stock are in the fat, so after totally defatting your stock you do not have to worry about either one of them.

Once you have defatted your stock, freeze it in containers of a volume you most often use. I store my own in ice cube trays. When the stock is solidly frozen, I remove the cubes from the trays and place them in plastic bags. Two cubes equal ¼ cup, so measuring is very simple.

Stock is the base for most soups. Therefore, it goes without saying that your soups will improve dramatically when made with your own stock.

Soups are uniquely different from one culture to another, and I have included a variety of these national and ethnic recipes. Soups also run the gamut from light, practically calorie-free first courses to hearty main dishes.

Almost everyone likes soup. For most of us, various kinds of soup conjure up memories from childhood—perhaps there is a cold fruit soup you loved because you thought it tasted like a dessert or a wonderful seafood chowder your mother always served for Sunday-night supper.

Soups can be elegant and extremely expensive to make, or inexpensive and delicious combinations of your favorite leftovers.

Just remember, no matter what kind of soup you're making, the quality of any dish is totally dependent upon the quality of the ingredients used; and no ingredient in soup is more important than stock.

FIFTEEN-MINUTE CHICKEN STOCK

Making your own stock is essential not only to good light cooking but for any kind of tasty cooking, whether it's healthy or not. You will notice in the recipe that the carrots are scraped and the leaves are removed from the celery, but that the onions and garlic do not have to be peeled. The reason for this is that the outside of the carrot has oxidized and therefore tends to add a bitter taste to the stock, as do the leaves of the celery. Any ingredient that adds a bitter taste should be avoided in any recipe. The onions do not need to be peeled because the onion skins do not affect the taste of the stock; in fact, brown onion skins add a little desirable color. After the chicken stock has cooked for an hour or more, you may want to throw in a whole chicken and cook it for your dinner or have it to dice for a salad or casserole the next day. It will take the chicken less than an hour to cook, and overcooking can make it tough and dry; so as soon as it is tender, remove it from the stockpot.

>   *3 to 5 pounds chicken bones, parts, and giblets, excluding the
>   liver*
>   *2 carrots, scraped and chopped*
>   *2 celery ribs, without leaves, chopped*
>   *1 onion, unpeeled, quartered*
>   *3 parsley sprigs*
>   *2 to 4 garlic cloves, halved*
>   *1 bay leaf*
>   *12 peppercorns*
>   *1/4 cup vinegar*
>   *Cold water to cover*

Buy chicken parts for stock from a butcher or save chicken carcasses in the freezer until ready to make stock.

Put all the ingredients into a large pot with a lid. Add cold water to cover and bring slowly to a boil. Preparation to this point takes about 5 minutes.

Reduce the heat, cover, leaving the lid ajar, and simmer for 3 hours or more. Longer cooking makes the stock more flavorful. Remove from the heat and allow to stand until cool enough to handle. Remove the chicken parts and vegetables and discard. Strain the stock and cool to room temperature. This second step takes 5 minutes more. Refrigerate, uncovered, overnight or until the fat has congealed on top.

Remove the fat and store the stock in the freezer in containers of a volume you most often use (see page 21).

This final step completes the 15 minutes of preparation time. You now have a high-calcium, non-fat, practically calorie-free stock that costs you just a few cents per serving and takes less than 15 minutes to make.

Makes approximately 10 cups (2½ quarts)

1 CUP CONTAINS APPROXIMATELY (CALCIUM VARIES
DEPENDING ON BONES USED): N* TOTAL CALORIES
N CALORIES IN FAT / CHOLESTEROL VARIES / N MG SODIUM
CALCIUM VARIES

*Note: N is used throughout this book to mean "negligible."

BEEF STOCK

Basically, beef stock is made exactly the same way you make chicken stock. The only difference is the first step, where you brown the bones and vegetables prior to starting the stock. The reason for browning the ingredients is to give a rich, dark color to the stock. Pale meat stocks do not make sauces and gravies look as rich and appetizing. Also, a foam or scum rises to the surface of a meat stock and must be removed at least once and sometimes several times when the stock first comes to a boil.

Veal knuckles are ideal to use for the bones. The optional addition of the beef or veal makes for a richer stock.

3 pounds beef or veal bones
1 pound beef or veal, any cut (optional)
1 tomato, halved
3 carrots, scraped and chopped
2 celery ribs, without leaves, chopped
1 large unpeeled onion, quartered
3 parsley sprigs
3 garlic cloves, halved
1/4 teaspoon dried thyme, crushed in a mortar and pestle
1/4 teaspoon dried marjoram, crushed in a mortar and pestle
1 bay leaf
12 peppercorns
1/4 cup vinegar
Cold water to cover

Place the bones, meat, and vegetables in a roasting pan in a 400°F oven until well browned, about 40 minutes, turning frequently to brown evenly.

Remove from the roasting pan and place in a large pot with a lid. Add all the other ingredients and cover with cold water by 1 inch. Bring slowly to a boil. Simmer slowly for 5 minutes and remove any scum on the surface. Reduce the heat, cover, leaving the lid ajar, and simmer for 2 to 6 hours. Cooking longer makes the stock more flavorful.

Remove from the heat and allow to stand until cool enough to handle. Remove the bones, meat, and vegetables and discard. Strain the stock and cool to room temperature.

Refrigerate, uncovered, overnight or until the fat has congealed on top. Remove the fat and store the stock in the freezer in the size containers you most often use.

Makes approximately 10 cups (2 1/2 quarts)

1 CUP CONTAINS APPROXIMATELY (CALCIUM VARIES
DEPENDING ON BONES USED): N TOTAL CALORIES
N CALORIES IN FAT / 1 MG CHOLESTEROL / SODIUM VARIES
CALCIUM VARIES

FISH STOCK

There is nothing better than a good fish stock for either a seafood soup such as Halászlé (page 40), the Hungarian fish soup, or a seafood stew such as Bouillabaisse (page 150), the classic French fisherman's stew that originated in Marseilles. I also like to use fish stock for poaching fish or to moisten the pan for sautéeing or braising fish or seafood. When fish heads are not available, I often make a shellfish stock using shrimp, crab, or lobster shells.

3 quarts water
¼ cup vinegar
2 pounds fish heads, bones, and trimmings
2 onions, sliced
5 parsley sprigs
1 carrot, sliced
½ teaspoon dried marjoram, crushed in a mortar and pestle
¼ teaspoon peppercorns
½ teaspoon salt
1 tablespoon freshly squeezed lemon juice

Bring all the ingredients to a boil and simmer for 40 minutes. Line a strainer with damp cheesecloth and strain the stock through it, discarding the bones and vegetables. Cool to room temperature. Refrigerate. Freeze the stock not needed immediately, using containers that will most nearly fit your requirements.

Makes about 2 quarts

1 CUP CONTAINS APPROXIMATELY (CALCIUM VARIES
DEPENDING ON BONES USED): N TOTAL CALORIES
N CALORIES IN FAT / 1 MG CHOLESTEROL / SODIUM VARIES
CALCIUM VARIES

COURT BOUILLON

Court bouillon is actually a fancy name for seasoned water and is used as a substitute for fish stock for poaching fish and seafood. I

much prefer using fish stock or even chicken stock for cooking fish
or seafood, but you don't always have it on hand when you need
it. Court bouillon is certainly a better substitute than just plain
water!

> *6 cups water*
> *1/3 cup white vinegar*
> *1 lemon, including peel, sliced*
> *2 celery ribs, without leaves, sliced*
> *2 carrots, sliced*
> *1 onion, sliced*
> *2 whole garlic cloves, peeled*
> *2 bay leaves*
> *12 peppercorns*

Combine all the ingredients in a large pot and bring to a boil.
Reduce the heat and simmer, uncovered, for 45 minutes.

Strain through two layers of damp cheesecloth and store in the
freezer in the size containers you will require.

Use for cooking shrimp, crab, or lobster or to poach any fish. This
court bouillon may be used many times, straining after each use.

Makes 6 cups

1 CUP CONTAINS APPROXIMATELY: N TOTAL CALORIES
N CALORIES IN FAT / 0 MG CHOLESTEROL / SODIUM VARIES
CALCIUM VARIES

DASHI

Dashi is a Japanese fish stock that is used for many Japanese soups
and stews. It is an essential ingredient for Miso Soup (page 28),
which happens to be a favorite of mine. You can buy Dashi stock
base in Japanese grocery stores, but they all contain monosodium
glutamate (MSG). This is a quick and easy way to make your own

Dashi and avoid preservatives or MSG. Dried seaweed is available in all Oriental grocery stores.

6 cups water
1 pound fish and fish bones
1 carrot, chopped
1 onion, chopped
2 parsley sprigs
4 peppercorns
¼ teaspoon salt
2 teaspoons freshly squeezed lemon juice
2 tablespoons dried seaweed

Bring all the ingredients to a boil in a large saucepan. Reduce the heat and simmer, uncovered, for 1½ hours.

Strain off the liquid and discard the solids. Store the stock in the refrigerator or freezer in a tightly covered container.

Makes 4 cups

1 CUP CONTAINS APPROXIMATELY (CALCIUM VARIES
DEPENDING ON BONES USED): N TOTAL CALORIES
N CALORIES IN FAT / 1 MG CHOLESTEROL / SODIUM VARIES
CALCIUM VARIES

VEGETABLE STOCK

Vegetable stock is an essential ingredient for running a purely vegetarian kitchen where chicken, beef, and fish stock cannot be used. Basically you can make vegetable stock from almost any combination of vegetables as long as you eliminate any ingredient that might add bitterness, such as carrot peelings or celery leaves. All of the vegetarian dishes I serve at the Canyon Ranch Spa in Tucson are made with vegetable stock. To ensure consistency in the taste range of our vegetarian entrées, I had to develop a recipe for our vegetable stock so it always tasted the same. Try my recipe and then experiment with your own favorite vegetables. Use your imagination and your leftover vegetables and you can create lots of your own vegetable stock recipes.

> *1 pound cabbage, shredded (4 cups)*
> *2 pounds onions, chopped (6 cups)*
> *1 pound carrots, scraped and chopped (4 cups)*
> *2 pounds celery, without leaves, chopped (6 cups)*
> *¼ pound parsley, chopped (2 cups)*
> *2 bay leaves*
> *2 teaspoons dried marjoram, crushed*
> *1 teaspoon salt*
> *1 gallon water*

Combine all the ingredients in a large pot and bring to a boil. Reduce the heat and simmer for 1 hour, covered.

Strain and refrigerate the stock in a tightly covered container or store in the freezer in the size containers most used for individual recipes. Freeze some in an ice cube tray to use in sautéeing. Discard the vegetables or puree them as a side dish.

Makes approximately 3 quarts

1 CUP CONTAINS APPROXIMATELY: N TOTAL CALORIES
N CALORIES IN FAT / 0 MG CHOLESTEROL
SODIUM VARIES / CALCIUM VARIES

MISO SOUP

The first time I ate Miso Soup was in a private home just outside Tokyo and I loved it. The next day I ordered it in a restaurant and found that it was much too salty. I learned that they had used a prepared base for the Dashi (Japanese fish stock), which is the basic ingredient of this soup, whereas my hostess the day before had made her own Dashi. I asked for the recipe so that I could make it myself when I got home. It is possible to buy miso in all Japanese markets and some health food stores.

> *2 cups Dashi (see page 26)*
> *2 tablespoons miso*
> *¼ pound tofu, cut into ¼-inch cubes (½ cup)*
> *¼ cup chopped scallion tops*
> *½ cup enoki mushrooms*

Combine the Dashi and miso and bring to a boil. Simmer for 10 minutes over low heat.

While the soup is simmering, place 2 tablespoons of the cubed tofu, 1 tablespoon of the chopped scallion tops, and 2 tablespoons of the enoki mushrooms in each of four bowls. Pour ½ cup hot soup into each bowl and serve immediately.

Makes 4 servings

EACH SERVING CONTAINS APPROXIMATELY:
50 TOTAL CALORIES / 20 CALORIES IN FAT
1 MG CHOLESTEROL / 105 MG SODIUM / 45 MG CALCIUM

SHERRIED CONSOMMÉ

This is a quick and easy method for clarifying consommé. The classic clarification method involves adding more vegetables and raw chicken to the cold stock and then bringing it just to the boiling point, but never allowing it to come to a full boil, then simmering it for an hour before straining it. If it is allowed to actually come to a full boil, the stock will not be clear. I have called for sherry to be added to the consommé in this recipe; however, it is good just plain or with a dash of Madeira substituted for the sherry.

4 cups defatted chicken stock (see page 22)
2 tablespoons sherry
Finely chopped parsley for garnish

Line a colander or strainer with two or three layers of damp cheese-cloth. Ladle the stock through the cheesecloth and allow it to drain until all of it has seeped through.

Reheat to serving temperature, add the sherry, and mix thoroughly. Top each serving with chopped parsley.

Makes four 1-cup servings

EACH SERVING CONTAINS APPROXIMATELY:
50 TOTAL CALORIES / 15 CALORIES IN FAT
1 MG CHOLESTEROL / 105 MG SODIUM / 10 MG CALCIUM

EGG DROP SOUP

Egg Drop Soup is served in every Chinese restaurant and is a light and delicious first course for any Chinese meal. It is sometimes called Egg Flower Soup because the egg whites literally look like flowers strewn through the soup. I often serve it on spa menus with Oriental entrées of all types because, along with the fact that it is traditional, it is so low in calories.

3 cups defatted chicken stock (see page 22)
3 egg whites
1 teaspoon reduced-sodium soy sauce
2 tablespoons finely chopped chives or scallion tops

Bring the chicken stock to a boil. Beat the egg whites with a fork until frothy, then pour them into the boiling chicken stock, stirring constantly with a wire whisk. Continue to stir the soup rapidly until the eggs are shredded and look like long strings. Add the soy sauce and mix well.

Ladle ¾ cup soup into each of four consommé cups and sprinkle the top of each serving with chopped chives or scallion tops.

Makes four ¾-cup servings

EACH SERVING CONTAINS APPROXIMATELY:
35 TOTAL CALORIES / 10 CALORIES IN FAT
1 MG CHOLESTEROL / 180 MG SODIUM / 5 MG CALCIUM

GAZPACHO

This classic cold Mexican soup is a favorite not only throughout Mexico but throughout most of the rest of the world as well. I used to serve it at the Canyon Ranch Spa in Tucson only as a first course for some of our Mexican meals. It was so popular that guests started asking for it all the time, and it is now available as an optional appetizer for every meal. It can also be used as a sauce, like a salsa, over salads, beans, rice, or even fish, poultry, or meat. Because of its many possible uses and the fact that it keeps for days in the refrigerator, I have given you a recipe that makes 6 cups. If you want to make a smaller amount, it is easy to cut the recipe in half.

1 cucumber, peeled, seeded, and diced (¾ cup)
½ pound red and green bell peppers, seeded and diced (1 cup)
½ medium onion, chopped (¾ cup)
1 large tomato, peeled and diced (1½ cups)
3 cups V-8 juice
1 garlic clove, finely chopped (1 teaspoon)
¼ teaspoon freshly ground black pepper
½ teaspoon Worcestershire sauce
3 tablespoons freshly squeezed lemon juice
Dash Tabasco
Chopped fresh cilantro for garnish

Combine all the ingredients except the chopped cilantro and mix thoroughly. Prepare a day in advance and store, tightly covered, in the refrigerator.

To serve, spoon ¾ cup cold Gazpacho into each chilled bowl and garnish with 1 tablespoon of chopped cilantro.

Makes 6 cups

A ¾ CUP SERVING CONTAINS APPROXIMATELY:
35 TOTAL CALORIES / 5 CALORIES IN FAT
0 MG CHOLESTEROL / 200 MG SODIUM / 25 MG CALCIUM

GINGERED CARROT SOUP

I really like most soups better served the day after they are made; however, this recipe is an exception. It is much better when it is very fresh. Since I like it best cold, I always make it several hours before I want to serve it so it has enough time to chill thoroughly. It is wonderful served before curried or Oriental-style entrées.

> *1 teaspoon corn-oil margarine*
> *¼ cup chopped onion*
> *2 tablespoons freshly peeled and chopped ginger*
> *2 cups defatted chicken stock (see page 22)*
> *1 medium potato, peeled and cubed (1 cup)*
> *6 small carrots, peeled and sliced (2 cups)*
> *¾ cup skim milk*
> *¼ teaspoon salt*
> *¼ teaspoon ground cinnamon*

Melt the margarine in a large saucepan. Add the onion and ginger and cook over moderate heat until tender, about 5 minutes.

Add the stock, potato, and carrots and bring to a boil. Reduce the heat and simmer, covered, for about 30 minutes.

Pour the vegetable mixture into a blender container. Add the milk, salt, and cinnamon and blend until very smooth.

This soup is good served either hot or cold. If reheating, do not boil.

Makes four ³/4-cup servings

EACH SERVING CONTAINS APPROXIMATELY:
110 TOTAL CALORIES / 20 CALORIES IN FAT
1 MG CHOLESTEROL / 230 MG SODIUM / 85 MG CALCIUM

CREAMY CAULIFLOWER SOUP

This soup is wonderful served either hot or cold. When served cold, it tastes very much like Vichyssoise, the famous French leftover. Vichyssoise is made by pureeing leek and potato soup and adding heavy cream. To be able to get the same effect with a fraction of the calories is wonderful.

> *¹/2 medium onion, finely chopped (³/4 cup)*
> *2 leeks, finely chopped, white part only (2 cups)*
> *¹/4 cauliflower head, finely chopped (1¹/2 cups)*
> *1 bay leaf*
> *1 cup defatted chicken stock (see page 22)*
> *²/3 cup skim milk, heated*
> *¹/4 teaspoon salt*
> *¹/8 teaspoon freshly ground black pepper*
> *Chopped chives for garnish*

Combine the onion, leeks, cauliflower, bay leaf, and chicken stock and bring to a boil. Reduce the heat and cook, covered, for 10 minutes.

Remove the bay leaf. Pour the cauliflower mixture into a blender container, add all the other ingredients, and blend until smooth.

To serve, ladle ³/4 cup hot soup into each bowl and sprinkle with the chopped chives.

Makes four ³/4-cup servings

EACH SERVING CONTAINS APPROXIMATELY:
70 TOTAL CALORIES / 10 CALORIES IN FAT
2 MG CHOLESTEROL / 190 MG SODIUM
95 MG CALCIUM

FRESH TOMATO SOUP

This soup is particularly good in the summertime, when tomatoes are in season and are available vine-ripened. It is another soup that is good either hot or cold. I like to serve it hot in mugs before a cold supper on a summer evening.

1 tablespoon corn-oil margarine
2 tablespoons minced onion
6 medium-ripe tomatoes, peeled, seeded, and chopped (4 cups)
1/2 cup defatted chicken stock (see page 22)
1/2 teaspoon salt
1/8 teaspoon white pepper
1 cup skim milk

Melt the margarine in a large saucepan. Add the onion and cook until soft and clear.

Add the tomatoes and cook, covered, over medium heat, stirring occasionally, until the tomatoes are very soft, about 15 minutes.

Place the cooked tomatoes and onion in a blender container with the chicken stock, salt, and pepper. Blend until a smooth, creamy consistency is reached. Add the milk and mix well.

Return the soup to the saucepan and bring to serving temperature over medium heat. Do not boil.

Makes four 1-cup servings

EACH SERVING CONTAINS APPROXIMATELY:
120 TOTAL CALORIES / 35 CALORIES IN FAT
1 MG CHOLESTEROL / 345 MG SODIUM / 100 MG CALCIUM

FRENCH ONION SOUP

For anyone who has ever eaten a steaming-hot, still-bubbling rame-kin of onion soup au gratin in a French bistro, this soup will conjure up wonderful memories—with lots less calories!

> *4 pieces French bread, thinly sliced (¹/4 inch thick, 4 inches in diameter)*
> *1 teaspoon corn-oil margarine*
> *1 medium onion, sliced very thin vertically (2 cups)*
> *2 tablespoons dry white wine*
> *¹/4 teaspoon freshly ground black pepper*
> *¹/4 teaspoon salt (omit if using salted stock)*
> *2 cups defatted chicken stock or beef stock (see page 22 or 23)*
> *2 ounces Swiss cheese, grated (¹/2 cup)*

Place the bread on a cookie sheet in a preheated 300°F oven for approximately 5 minutes. Let it dry out but not brown.

Melt the margarine in a skillet. Add the onions and cook, covered, over very low heat until soft, about 10 minutes. Remove the lid, turn up the heat, and brown the onions, stirring constantly; do not allow them to burn. When brown, reduce the heat and add the wine. Cook until most of the wine has been absorbed. Add the pepper, salt, and stock and mix well. Simmer for 5 minutes.

Pour ¾ cup soup into each of four ovenproof bowls. Place a slice of French bread on top of each bowl and allow to stand until the bread is saturated with soup and has expanded. Sprinkle 2 table-spoons of the cheese over each serving.

Place in a preheated 325°F oven for 30 to 40 minutes or until the cheese is lightly browned.

Makes 4 servings

EACH SERVING CONTAINS APPROXIMATELY:
155 TOTAL CALORIES / 60 CALORIES IN FAT
15 MG CHOLESTEROL / 290 MG SODIUM / 150 MG CALCIUM

BLACK BEAN SOUP

Everyone argues about the origin of Black Bean Soup. The Cubans claim it, as do the Puerto Ricans and several other islands in the Caribbean; however, there is no argument that everyone likes it, and almost everyone develops a slightly different seasoning for it. This is my version, which I developed for a Pritikin cruise through the Panama Canal on a Sitmar ship several years ago. It is classically served with rice as an entrée course; however, it can be served in a cup as a first course, and many people love it for breakfast. It freezes so well that I have given a recipe for twelve soup-size servings or four to six entrée servings, depending upon the size of your appetite. It is a particularly popular entrée with athletes who are carbohydrate-loading before competition.

1 pound dry black beans, washed and sorted
6 cups water
1 medium green bell pepper, seeded and finely chopped (1 cup)
1/2 jalapeño pepper, seeded and minced (1 tablespoon)
2 cups chicken, beef, or vegetable stock (see page 22, 23, or 27)
1 medium onion, chopped (1 1/2 cups)
3 garlic cloves, finely chopped (1 tablespoon)
1 tablespoon ground cumin
1 teaspoon salt (reduce to 1/2 teaspoon if using salted stock)
1/4 teaspoon freshly ground black pepper
1/4 cup red wine vinegar
1/2 cup sherry
1/2 cup chopped scallions for garnish
3/4 cup Light Cheese (page 52)

Soak the beans overnight in water to cover. Drain. Rinse and drain again.

Combine the beans, water, bell pepper, and jalapeño pepper in a large saucepan. Bring to a boil. Cover. Reduce the heat and simmer for 1 1/2 hours or until the beans are tender.

Heat 1/4 cup of the stock. Add the onions and garlic and cook until the onions are translucent and the stock has been absorbed.

Remove 1 cup of the beans from the pot. Blend in a blender container and return to the pot.

Stir the onions, garlic, the remaining 1¾ cups stock, the cumin, salt, pepper, and vinegar into the beans. Bring to a boil. Reduce the heat and simmer, uncovered, until thick, about 45 minutes.

Add the sherry and simmer for 5 minutes more.

To serve, spoon into bowls and sprinkle 1 tablespoon scallions over the top of each bowl. Top with a tablespoon of Light Cheese.

Makes 9 cups

A ¾ CUP SERVING CONTAINS APPROXIMATELY:
185 TOTAL CALORIES / 20 CALORIES IN FAT
5 MG CHOLESTEROL / 145 MG SODIUM / 110 MG CALCIUM

VARIATION:

For a Cuban-style main dish serve over cooked rice. Top with chopped onions and serve Light Cheese (page 52) or Light Sour Cream (page 53) on the side.

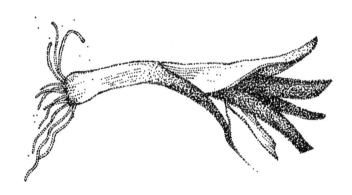

MINESTRONE SOUP

This hearty Italian soup makes a wonderful main dish served with a green salad with Light Italian Dressing (see page 72) and crusty bread.

2 cups defatted beef, chicken, or vegetable stock (see page 23, 22, or 27)
³/₄ cup beer
1 small carrot, peeled and sliced (¹/₂ cup)
¹/₂ medium onion, chopped (³/₄ cup)
1 celery rib, without leaves, chopped (¹/₂ cup)
¹/₂ cup chopped cabbage
One 16-ounce can tomatoes, undrained (2 cups)
¹/₄ teaspoon salt (omit if using salted stock)
¹/₈ teaspoon freshly ground black pepper
³/₄ teaspoon dried rosemary, crushed in a mortar and pestle
³/₄ teaspoon chili powder
1 garlic clove, finely chopped (1 teaspoon)

1 cup canned kidney beans, undrained
¹/₂ cup Italian green beans, cut into 1-inch pieces
¹/₂ cup very thin dry spaghetti, broken into 1-inch pieces
2 ounces imported Parmesan cheese, freshly grated (¹/₂ cup)

In a large pot, combine the stock, beer, carrots, onions, celery, cabbage, tomatoes, salt, pepper, rosemary, chili powder, and garlic. Bring to a boil, then reduce the heat and simmer, covered, for 30 minutes.

Return to a boil. Add the kidney beans and Italian green beans and cook for 5 to 10 minutes more. Add the spaghetti and continue cooking until al dente, 5 to 6 minutes.

Add the Parmesan cheese and heat until melted, stirring constantly.

Makes eight 1-cup servings

EACH SERVING CONTAINS APPROXIMATELY:
120 TOTAL CALORIES / 20 CALORIES IN FAT
5 MG CHOLESTEROL / 295 MG SODIUM / 115 MG CALCIUM

MANHATTAN CLAM CHOWDER

3 cups defatted chicken stock or fish stock (see page 22 or 25)
½ garlic clove, chopped (½ teaspoon)
½ medium onion, chopped (¾ cup)
1 medium potato, peeled and cubed (1 cup)
½ celery rib, diced (¼ cup)
1 small carrot, peeled and diced (¼ cup)
½ green bell pepper, seeded and diced (¼ cup)
One 8-ounce can peeled and chopped tomatoes, undrained
½ cup clam juice
⅛ teaspoon caraway seeds
½ teaspoon dried thyme, crushed in a mortar and pestle
½ bay leaf, crumbled
⅛ teaspoon freshly ground black pepper
One 6½-ounce can chopped clams, undrained

Combine 2 cups of the chicken or fish stock, the garlic, ½ cup of the onions, and ½ cup of the potatoes in a large pot. Bring to a boil. Reduce the heat and cook, covered, for 30 minutes. Pour into a blender container and puree until smooth.

Pour the puree back into the pot and add the remaining stock, onions, and potatoes and all the other ingredients except for the clams. Simmer, uncovered, for 45 minutes.

Just before serving, add the clams plus all the juice from the can and heat through.

Makes four 1-cup servings

EACH SERVING CONTAINS APPROXIMATELY:
115 TOTAL CALORIES / 15 CALORIES IN FAT
35 MG CHOLESTEROL / 280 MG SODIUM / 60 MG CALCIUM

HALÁSZLÉ
(Hungarian Fish Soup)

The first time I ever had this soup, I was sitting in a courtyard on the Buda side of the Danube in Budapest looking across the river at the magnificent buildings on the Pest waterfront. I couldn't decide whether I was more impressed with my surroundings or my fabulous soup. I asked to meet the chef, who fortunately spoke English, and talked him into revealing his recipe.

3/4 pound firm white fish (traditionally carp or perch)
Juice of 1 lemon
Salt
1 1/2 medium onions, thinly sliced (3 cups)
1 leek, white part only, chopped (1 cup)
2 garlic cloves, finely chopped (2 teaspoons)
2 small tomatoes, peeled and diced (1 cup)
2 celery ribs, without leaves, finely chopped (1 cup)
1/2 teaspoon dried marjoram, crushed in a mortar and pestle
1 1/2 teaspoons mild Hungarian paprika
1/4 teaspoon hot Hungarian paprika or dash cayenne pepper (optional)
4 cups defatted chicken stock or fish stock (see page 22 or 25)
1/8 teaspoon salt (omit if using salted stock)

Wash the fish in cold water and pat dry. Place in a glass baking dish and squeeze the lemon juice over it. Lightly salt both sides. Cover the dish tightly and place in the refrigerator until ready to cook.

In a deep kettle, combine the onions and leeks and cook, covered, for 5 minutes, adding a little water or stock if necessary to prevent scorching. Add the garlic, tomatoes, celery, marjoram, mild paprika, and hot paprika or cayenne pepper (if using). Mix thoroughly and cook for 5 minutes more.

Add the stock and salt and bring slowly to a boil. Reduce the heat and simmer for 30 minutes.

Cut the fish into bite-size pieces and add to the simmering soup. Continue cooking for 8 to 10 minutes more or until the fish has turned white.

Makes four 2-cup servings

EACH SERVING CONTAINS APPROXIMATELY:
190 TOTAL CALORIES / 40 CALORIES IN FAT
1 MG CHOLESTEROL / 265 MG SODIUM / 100 MG CALCIUM

JEANNE JONES' CREAM OF MUSHROOM SOUP

One of the most frequently used ingredients in recipes my readers send to me to be modified is condensed cream soup, usually cream of mushroom soup. Condensed soups, while a real convenience in our busy home kitchens, are not really worth eating when you consider the trade-off in higher fat, cholesterol, and sodium. There are 2540 milligrams of sodium in one can of commercial soup and only 624 milligrams of sodium in the same amount of my soup. Commercial soups also contain preservatives and MSG.

In order to modify these recipes I had to create a viable substitute for commercially canned cream soups. It had to be easy enough to make to still be convenient, similar in both taste and texture, and within my guidelines to "Cook it Light." Once you have tried my recipe and its variations, you will never want to go back to using canned soups again.

1 tablespoon corn oil margarine
3 tablespoons unbleached flour
3/4 cup chicken stock (see page 22)
1/2 cup skim milk
1/4 teaspoon salt
Dash of garlic powder
Dash of freshly ground black pepper
1/4 cup fresh cooked or canned mushrooms, finely chopped

Melt the margarine in a skillet. Add the flour and stir over medium heat for 1 minute. Do not brown. Add the chicken stock and skim milk. Using a wire whisk, stir the mixture over medium heat until it comes to a boil. Add the seasonings (omit the salt if using salted stock) and the mushrooms and continue to cook for 1 minute more. To serve as soup, dilute to taste with water, stock, or skim milk.

Make 1 1/4 cups condensed soup

1 1/4 CUPS OF CONDENSED SOUP CONTAINS
APPROXIMATELY: 250 TOTAL CALORIES
110 CALORIES IN FAT / 2 MG CHOLESTEROL
625 MG SODIUM / 165 MG CALCIUM

VARIATIONS:

Cream of Chicken Soup: Omit mushrooms and add 1/4 cup finely chopped cooked chicken.
Cream of Celery Soup: Omit mushrooms and add 1/4 cup finely chopped celery.

MOCK TURTLE SOUP

One of the readers of my "Cook It Light" column sent this recipe to me on the back of an envelope, where he had written it during World War II. In fact it said to use the meat "if you have the stamps for it." When I wrote back to him, I told him that we all certainly hoped that nothing in this country would ever be rationed again but that vegetarian Mock Turtle Soup is also very good. The original recipe also called for browned flour, which I omitted because I felt it gave the soup a muddy look and kept the flavors from being sharp. I explained that the egg white is supposed to be chopped finely enough to look like turtle meat in the soup and that since sherry is always served with real turtle soup, it is appropriate that it also be served with Mock Turtle Soup.

1/2 lemon, unpeeled, thinly sliced, and seeded
1/2 pound very lean ground beef

3 cups water
One 8-ounce cup canned diced tomatoes, undrained
2 tablespoons apple cider vinegar
1 tablespoon fructose or 4 teaspoons sugar
2 small carrots, peeled and grated (1 cup)
1 celery rib, without leaves, finely diced (¹/₂ cup)
¹/₄ cup uncooked brown rice
Dash freshly ground black pepper
¹/₈ teaspoon salt
2 tablespoons pickling spice, tied in a cheesecloth bag
1 hard-cooked egg, white only, finely chopped
2 tablespoons sherry (optional)

Cut the lemon slices in half.

Combine all the ingredients, except for the egg white and sherry, in a large pot. Bring to a boil. Reduce the heat, cover, and simmer for 1 hour. Remove the lid and cook for an additional 30 minutes. Remove the bag of spices.

Add the finely chopped egg white and mix thoroughly. Add the sherry just before serving if desired.

Makes four 1-cup servings

EACH SERVING CONTAINS APPROXIMATELY:
205 TOTAL CALORIES / 60 CALORIES IN FAT
40 MG CHOLESTEROL / 245 MG SODIUM / 45 MG CALCIUM

ALBONDIGAS (MEATBALL) SOUP

Albondigas, or Mexican Meatball Soup, is a popular soup through-out Mexico. It can be served either as a soup course or as the main course for a meal. If using it as the main course, serve larger portions and serve it with warm corn tortillas. As a variation, try Albondigas made with pasta instead of rice.

½ pound very lean ground beef
2 cups defatted chicken stock (see page 22)
1½ cups defatted beef stock (see page 23)
1 cup chopped onions
½ teaspoon dried oregano, crushed in a mortar and pestle
¼ teaspoon crushed red pepper flakes
1 cup thinly sliced carrots
2 tablespoons chopped cilantro
2 tablespoons uncooked brown rice
½ pound fresh spinach, shredded (2 cups)
4 cilantro sprigs for garnish
4 lime wedges for garnish

Preheat the oven to 400°F.

Form eight small meatballs from the ground beef. Place on a rack in a broiler pan in the preheated oven for 10 minutes. Remove from the rack and pat with paper towels to remove any remaining fat.

Combine the chicken and beef stocks, meatballs, onions, oregano, and pepper flakes in a large saucepan. Bring to a boil, then add the carrots, cilantro, and rice. Simmer for 30 to 40 minutes or until the rice is tender.

Remove the stems and veins from the spinach and shred finely. Add the spinach to the soup and continue to cook for 5 minutes more.

Spoon into bowls and garnish each serving with a sprig of cilantro and a lime wedge (to be squeezed into the soup before eating).

Makes four 1-cup servings

EACH SERVING CONTAINS APPROXIMATELY:
185 TOTAL CALORIES / 70 CALORIES IN FAT
40 MG CHOLESTEROL / 140 MG SODIUM / 60 MG CALCIUM

BORSCHT

The Russians have many different types of Borscht, ranging all the way from hearty meat-and-vegetable entrée-type soups to Beet Borscht, which is a totally vegetarian soup that can be served either hot or cold as a first course. I happen to like beets very much and have been experimenting with borscht for years. To date, this is my favorite version of it, and I like it best served cold before Chicken Stroganoff (page 169), with Strawberries Romanoff (page 226) for dessert, for a real Russian menu.

> *2 large beets (¹/₂ pound)*
> *1¹/₂ garlic cloves, finely chopped (1¹/₂ teaspoons)*
> *¹/₄ teaspoon salt*
> *2 teaspoons fructose or 1 tablespoon sugar*
> *1¹/₃ cups buttermilk*
> *4 teaspoons plain nonfat yogurt*

Scrub the beets thoroughly, being careful not to break the skin. Cut off the roots and tops. Place the beets and chopped garlic in a large saucepan. Add water to cover and bring to a boil. Reduce the heat, cover, and simmer for 20 minutes.

Remove the beets from the water, reserving 1 cup of liquid. Slip the skins off the beets and discard. Chop the beets and place in a blender container. Add the reserved cooking liquid and all the other ingredients, except for the yogurt, and blend until smooth.

Serve either hot or cold. Garnish each serving with a teaspoon of yogurt.

Makes four ³/₄-cup servings

EACH SERVING CONTAINS APPROXIMATELY:
70 TOTAL CALORIES / 5 CALORIES IN FAT
5 MG CHOLESTEROL / 270 MG SODIUM
115 MG CALCIUM

SAUCES & DRESSINGS

IN RESPONSE to all the letters I have received asking questions about basic sauces, I am including a very large and varied sauce and salad dressing section. Actually, to design any menu for any meal, all you need is a salad dressing and a sauce or two. You can simply pour good dressing over lettuce, sauce a grilled or poached piece of fish, poultry, or meat, add a vegetable, and pour a fruit sauce over a simple custard—and you have an elegant meal.

Making rich-tasting, creamy-textured sauces without the added butter and other fats always associated with rich sauces is really easy once you learn the tricks.

Reduction is the key. Reducing a sauce in volume to intensify the flavor or thicken the texture is simply a matter of cooking it longer, uncovered, to reduce the volume—it just boils away. If a recipe tells you to reduce by one-half, you literally boil the liquid away until you are left with only half as much as you started with. I often use this technique to intensify flavor and then pour the sauce into a blender in order to get the creamy texture I want.

46

Also defatting pan drippings just as you defat stock gives you a rich flavor base to work with in making sauces and gravies. The juices or drippings that accumulate in the bottom of the pan when you cook poultry or meat are often poured over the finished dish or made into a very-high-fat gravy. In either case you are adding calories along with cholesterol and saturated fats, which do nothing to improve the taste of the finished product.

You really can have your gravy and a healthy dish at the same time by just removing the fat. It only takes a few minutes in the freezer for the fat to congeal on top of the drippings. Remove all the fat and then reheat the drippings to pour the *au jus* over the dish. Or turn the defatted drippings into a tasty sauce or gravy, using the recipes in this section. If you don't plan to use the drippings for the meal you're preparing, put them in the refrigerator to defat later and store in the freezer. Defatted pan juices add a wonderful flavor to many other dishes and also improve the taste of soups and basic stocks.

The vegetable sauces in this section are among my favorite recipes for low-calorie spa cooking. They are colorful, nutritious, and extremely low in calories. In fact, I like to pour these vegetable sauces on the plate and then put the other vegetables, fish, poultry, or meat I am serving on top of them. I also use Cream of Rice to make a completely fat-free, quick-and-easy white sauce as a base for many dishes. And for dairy-free creamy sauces I use tofu (soybean curd), which also adds a great deal of protein and calcium to the dish you are serving it on.

All of my salad dressings are lower in calories, cholesterol, and sodium than their commercial counterparts. The only time I ever use oil in salad dressing is either for flavor or texture, and you will find it DOESN'T TAKE VERY MUCH. For example, in the tofu sauces a small amount of oil is needed for texture or "mouth feel," so I often use unflavored oil. Whenever I am using oil for flavor, I use the most flavorful one obtainable so that only a small amount will give me the result I want in taste. When using olive oil, I always use extra-virgin olive oil, or the "first press" of the olives; this has the strongest, cleanest flavor. When using sesame oil, I call for dark or roasted sesame oil, again because of its strong flavor. Always buy the best-quality oils available and store them tightly covered in a cool place.

Some of my dressings contain no oil at all and therefore practically no calories. You may want to make these up by the quart to use as your "house" salad dressings.

I routinely use oil-free salad dressing as my Jeanne Jones' signature dressing for the menus I create in spas, hotels, and restaurants. I do this for several important reasons. In commercial kitchens dressings are not always thoroughly mixed before being ladled onto salads, and since the oil always rises to the top, it is possible for a dressing very low in calories (because it contains so little oil) to have all the oil at the top spooned onto a salad, therefore making it very high in calories for that particular serving. Even when the dressing is put into a dish or pitcher on the side, unless it is well mixed before being poured into the serving container, it could still contain more oil than it would have if it had been thoroughly mixed first. I learned this firsthand a few years ago when I ordered one of my own salad creations, which is routinely served with the dressing on the side. I was sure it was the wrong dressing because it was over half oil and asked the waiter to replace it. After returning to the kitchen he assured me that it was the right dressing. I then went back to check with the chef myself, and indeed it was out of the right container—it just had not been mixed thoroughly. And therefore, even though the dressing recipe contained very little oil, I had been served the oil off the top rather than the proper mix of dressing. Another reason for having a house dressing that is oil-free and therefore fat-free is that every tablespoon of oil contains 120 calories. These calories can be "traded off" for other fat calories that make more difference in the taste and texture of the salad, such as toasted nuts and seeds or diced avocados.

Along with the recipe for my signature dressing I have included enough variations that it can be used in any flavor range. I have also included how you would use different types of vinegar and oil to get specific flavors. Just remember, with these dressings containing oil for flavor enhancement, how important it is to always mix the dressing thoroughly before using it.

LIGHT GRAVY

Once you have started making Light Gravy, I don't think you will ever like greasy gravy again. The taste is creamier and the flavor sharper without the fat, and Light Gravy works wonders on your waistline. Another bonus provided by this recipe is that you will never again have to contend with lumpy gravy. Even the complete novice cook will get satin-smooth gravy every time! I have given you a choice of stock, milk, or water in this recipe because it really depends upon the intensity of the flavor you want and the type of gravy you are making. If you want a gravy closer to a classic brown sauce, then use defatted stock along with a little red and white wine. If you want a creamy gravy, then use milk, and for a still creamier gravy use nonfat dry milk and mix it with less water than called for on the package directions, or canned skimmed evaporated milk. For a very light gravy, water works well, particularly if the pan drippings themselves are richly flavored. In some cases you might even find that using fruit juice adds an interesting flavor to your gravy, especially when using it for poultry or lean cuts of pork. Your own light gravies will be limited only by your imagination.

> *1 cup defatted stock (see page 22, 23, or 27), skim milk, or*
> *water*
> *2 tablespoons uncooked Cream of Rice*
> *1 cup defatted poultry or meat drippings*
> *Freshly ground black pepper to taste*
> *Seasonings of your choice, such as fennel, thyme, or sage*

Heat the stock, milk, or water to the boiling point in a small saucepan. Add the cream of rice and stir over the heat for 30 seconds. Remove from the heat, cover, and let stand for 5 minutes.

Pour the mixture into a blender container and blend until smooth. Add the drippings and blend again.

Pour back into the saucepan and reheat. For a thicker gravy, cook over medium heat until it reduces to the desired consistency.

Season lightly to match whatever herb or spice is being used in cooking the poultry or meat (for example, use ¼ teaspoon fennel when serving with Roast Turkey with Fennel, page 180). Stock makes a richer, more intense-flavored gravy than water. Milk makes a creamier gravy.

Makes 2 cups

¼ CUP CONTAINS APPROXIMATELY: 25 TOTAL CALORIES
N CALORIES IN FAT / 1 MG CHOLESTEROL / 25 MG SODIUM
40 MG CALCIUM

EASY, FAT-FREE WHITE SAUCE

Like Light Gravy (preceding recipe), this white sauce is not only truly easy to make but foolproof. You will have smooth, creamy white sauce every time—and no fat!

> *1½ cups skim milk*
> *¼ teaspoon salt*
> *Dash white pepper (optional)*
> *3 tablespoons uncooked Cream of Rice*

Bring all the ingredients except the Cream of Rice to a boil in a small saucepan. Add the Cream of Rice and stir for 1 minute. Remove from the heat, cover, and allow to stand for 5 minutes.

Pour into a blender container and blend until smooth. You may store any unused white sauce in the refrigerator to reheat when needed.

Makes 1½ cups

¼ CUP CONTAINS APPROXIMATELY: 40 TOTAL CALORIES
N CALORIES IN FAT / 1 MG CHOLESTEROL
125 MG SODIUM / 75 MG CALCIUM

WHITE SAUCE

This version of a classic approach to white or béchamel sauce is exceptionally easy and is much lower in fat than the traditional recipes. It is also practically cholesterol-free because I have used pure corn-oil margarine, which is a polyunsaturated fat and contains no cholesterol, and skim milk has only a trace. It is also very low in sodium and works well as a base for any recipe calling for a creamy-type sauce, such as the Mornay Sauce variation that follows.

> *1 tablespoon corn-oil margarine*
> *3 tablespoons whole wheat pastry flour, sifted*
> *2½ cups skim milk, heated to simmering*
> *⅛ teaspoon salt*

Melt the margarine over low heat. Add the flour and cook for 2 minutes, stirring constantly. DO NOT BROWN.

Remove from the heat and add the milk slowly, stirring with a wire whisk. Add the salt and cook slowly over low heat for 15 to 20 minutes, stirring occasionally.

Makes 2 cups

¼ CUP CONTAINS APPROXIMATELY: 50 TOTAL CALORIES
15 CALORIES IN FAT / 1 MG CHOLESTEROL / 75 MG SODIUM
95 MG CALCIUM

VARIATION:

Mornay Sauce: When the sauce has thickened, add ⅛ teaspoon white pepper, ⅛ teaspoon freshly grated nutmeg, and ½ cup grated Swiss or Gruyère cheese (2 ounces). Add more skim milk for a thinner sauce.

LIGHT CHEESE

Light Cheese is one of the staples of my light cuisine. In fact it even has several aliases—Breakfast Cheese, Fitness Cheese, Mock Crème Fraîche—depending upon how it's used in a menu. By any name it is a delicious, nutritious, and satisfying condiment that can be used as a spread for toasted bagels, waffles, and pancakes or a topping for soups, salads, and vegetables. I particularly like it on baked potatoes with chopped scallions and freshly ground black . pepper. I also love it for breakfast on whole wheat toast with the Apple Butter on page 61.

¹/₃ cup plain nonfat yogurt
2 cups part-skim ricotta cheese

Blend the yogurt and ricotta in a food processor with a metal blade until it is *satin smooth*. Refrigerate in a tightly covered container. Make it at least a day before using if possible. Keeps 5 days.

Makes 2¹/₄ cups

2 TABLESPOONS CONTAIN APPROXIMATELY:
40 TOTAL CALORIES / 20 CALORIES IN FAT
10 MG CHOLESTEROL / 35 MG SODIUM
85 MG CALCIUM

GARLIC SPREAD

2 bulbs fresh garlic (¹/₂ cup cloves)
1 cup Light Cheese (see recipe above)
¹/₈ teaspoon salt
¹/₄ teaspoon oregano, crushed in a mortar and pestle

Bake the garlic in a preheated 350°F oven for 40 minutes.

Peel the garlic and combine all the ingredients in a food processor with a metal blade. Blend until satin smooth.

Makes 1¼ cups

1 TABLESPOON CONTAINS APPROXIMATELY: 20 CALORIES
10 CALORIES IN FAT / 5 MG CHOLESTEROL / 30 MG SODIUM
40 MG CALCIUM

LIGHT SOUR CREAM

1 cup low-fat cottage cheese
2 tablespoons buttermilk
1½ teaspoons freshly squeezed lemon juice

Put all the ingredients into a blender container and blend until completely smooth. Even when you think it's smooth enough, blend a little longer for a better result.

Makes 1 cup

¼ CUP CONATINS APPROXIMATELY: 45 TOTAL CALORIES
5 CALORIES IN FAT / 3 MG CHOLESTEROL / 240 MG SODIUM
45 MG CALCIUM

VARIATIONS:

To 1 cup add:

Curry Dip: ½ teaspoon curry powder, ⅛ teaspoon ground ginger, and 2 teaspoons grated onion.

Latin Dip: ½ teaspoon chili powder, ¼ teaspoon ground cumin, ¼ teaspoon garlic powder, and dash of Tabasco (optional).

CINNAMON-APPLE YOGURT SAUCE

I developed this sauce originally for a gingered fruit compote, which is a dessert on my menu in the Neiman-Marcus restaurant in Newport Beach, California. However, I like it so much that I use it as a topping for breakfast cereal and fresh fruits of all types.

> *1 cup plain nonfat yogurt*
> *1 teaspoon vanilla extract*
> *3 tablespoons frozen unsweetened apple juice concentrate*
> *1/2 teaspoon ground cinnamon*

Combine all the ingredients and mix well. Refrigerate in a tightly covered container.

Makes 1 1/4 cups

2 TABLESPOONS CONTAIN APPROXIMATELY:
25 TOTAL CALORIES / 5 CALORIES IN FAT
0 MG CHOLESTEROL / 40 MG SODIUM
50 MG CALCIUM

VARIATION:

To serve warm add 1 tablespoon of cornstarch per 1 cup of yogurt to prevent the yogurt from separating.

SALSA

Salsa is as essential to the Mexican menu as tortillas, beans, and rice. In Mexico, restaurants serve one salsa to the tourists and make another they call kitchen salsa to eat themselves. The difference is that the kitchen salsa has many more chili peppers and therefore is much hotter and thus more desirable to the Mexican palate. Salsa can be made with many different kinds of peppers; however, jalapeños are usually more available in the markets in this country. In this recipe I suggest an amount of chili pepper and garlic but really leave it to your personal taste; since I lived in Mexico for two years, my personal preference might be a bit too close to the Mexican kitchen salsa.

3 medium tomatoes, finely diced (2 cups)
1/2 medium onion, finely diced (3/4 cup)
2 tablespoons finely chopped cilantro
1/2 jalapeño pepper, seeded and finely chopped (or to your taste)
1/2 garlic clove, finely chopped (1/2 teaspoon) (or to your taste)
3/4 teaspoon ground cumin
3/4 teaspoon dried oregano, crushed in a mortar and pestle
1/8 teaspoon salt
1 tablespoon freshly squeezed lemon juice
1 tablespoon freshly squeezed lime juice

Combine all the ingredients. Cover and refrigerate for at least 2 hours before serving.

Makes 1 1/2 cups

1/4 CUP CONTAINS APPROXIMATELY: 15 TOTAL CALORIES
N CALORIES IN FAT / 0 MG CHOLESTEROL / 40 MG SODIUM
10 MG CALCIUM

LIGHT PESTO SAUCE

In order to make classic Italian pesto sauce, it is necessary to have fresh basil, which is not available in all places at all times of the year. Therefore, when basil is available, it is a good idea to make it in quantity and freeze it in ice cube trays. As well as being a tasty sauce for pasta of all types, pesto sauce is good on sandwiches or as a spread on toasted Italian bread as an hors d'oeuvre. It also makes a delicious salad dressing. In fact, my favorite picnic salad is rotelle or fusille pasta combined with a colorful assortment of bite-size cooked vegetables topped with toasted pine nuts. Cold cooked chicken or water-packed tuna is also good in this pesto pasta salad.

> *¹/₄ cup pine nuts*
> *2 cups tightly packed fresh basil, all stems removed (¹/₂ pound)*
> *2 cups tightly packed fresh spinach, all stems and veins removed*
>   *(¹/₂ pound)*
> *4 garlic cloves, finely chopped (4 teaspoons)*
> *¹/₄ pound imported Parmesan cheese, freshly grated (1 cup)*
> *¹/₄ teaspoon salt*
> *¹/₄ cup extra-virgin olive oil*
> *¹/₂ cup water*

Place the pine nuts in a preheated 350°F oven for 8 to 10 minutes. Watch carefully, as they burn easily. Combine the pine nuts and all the other ingredients except the water in a food processor with a metal blade. Mix until a smooth paste is formed. Add the water and mix thoroughly.

Refrigerate in a tightly covered container or freeze in containers of appropriate size.

Makes 2¹/₂ cups

2 TABLESPOONS CONTAIN APPROXIMATELY:
50 TOTAL CALORIES / 40 CALORIES IN FAT
3 MG CHOLESTEROL / 110 MG SODIUM
65 MG CALCIUM

SZECHUAN PEANUT SAUCE

Szechuan Peanut Sauce is the topping for one of my own favorite recipes in this book, Oriental Noodles with Szechuan Peanut Sauce (page 135). When I first put this cold pasta dish with a cold peanut sauce on the menu at one spa, everyone in the kitchen thought I was crazy—until they tasted it. Then guess what happened? They routinely doubled the amount they thought they would need so they could eat what was left over themselves. All I can say is that if you don't think you will like it, please try it. I also use this sauce as a dip with cold blanched vegetables and rice crackers.

> *6 tablespoons unhomogenized peanut butter*
> *1/2 cup plain nonfat yogurt*
> *1 1/2 teaspoons fructose or 2 teaspoons sugar*
> *1 teaspoon low-sodium soy sauce*
> *1/4 teaspoon dark sesame oil*
> *1/2 garlic clove, finely chopped (1/2 teaspoon)*
> *1/4 teaspoon crushed red pepper flakes (or to taste)*
> *2 tablespoons rice wine vinegar*

Combine all the ingredients in a blender container and blend until smooth. Refrigerate in a tightly covered container.

Makes 1 cup

1/4 CUP CONTAINS APPROXIMATELY: 180 TOTAL CALORIES
110 CALORIES IN FAT / 1 MG CHOLESTEROL
125 MG SODIUM / 95 MG CALCIUM

CREOLE SAUCE

Creole Sauce can be used as a filling for omelets, to spice up soups, to dress salads, or as a sauce on other vegetables, fish, poultry, or meat. It is an ingredient of my own Cajun/Creole–type dish, which is Chicken Jambalaya (page 177). This recipe makes just enough for the jambalaya recipe, but you may want to double it so you can have it on hand as a sauce for other dishes.

1 small tomato, peeled and chopped (3/4 cup)
1/2 medium onion, finely chopped (3/4 cup)
1/2 medium green bell pepper, chopped (1/2 cup)
1 celery rib, without leaves, chopped (1/2 cup)
1 garlic clove, finely chopped (1 teaspoon)
1 bay leaf
1/8 teaspoon white pepper
1/4 teaspoon salt (omit if using salted stock)
1/4 teaspoon sweet paprika
1/4 teaspoon cayenne
1/4 teaspoon freshly ground black pepper
1/2 teaspoon dried oregano, crushed in a mortar and pestle
1/2 teaspoon dried thyme, crushed in a mortar and pestle
1/2 teaspoon dried basil, crushed in a mortar and pestle
3/4 cup defatted chicken stock (see page 22)
1/2 cup tomato sauce
1/2 teaspoon fructose or 3/4 teaspoon sugar
1/4 teaspoon Tabasco (or to taste)

Combine the tomatoes, onion, pepper, celery, and garlic in a large skillet. Add all the seasonings and mix well. Sauté over low heat, stirring occasionally, until the onion becomes translucent, about 5 to 10 minutes.

Add the chicken stock, tomato sauce, fructose or sugar, and Tabasco. Bring to a boil. Reduce the heat and simmer, uncovered, stirring occasionally, until the vegetables are cooked and the sauce thickens slightly, about 20 minutes. Remove the bay leaf.

Cool to room temperature and store in the refrigerator in a tightly covered container. Or freeze in appropriate-size containers.

Makes 2 cups

1/2 CUP CONTAINS APPROXIMATELY: 45 TOTAL CALORIES
5 CALORIES IN FAT / 1 MG CHOLESTEROL / 355 MG SODIUM
35 MG CALCIUM

MARINARA SAUCE

This is the easiest-to-make, best-tasting, and lowest-calorie marinara sauce you have ever eaten. The recipe makes just enough for Cioppino (page 149), the famous San Francisco Italian seafood stew. It is also an ingredient for Pasta Primavera (page 131), but it has a wide variety of uses on its own. It is wonderful on any pasta and is also delicious on fish, poultry, and meat dishes.

5 cups tomato sauce
2¹/₂ cups water
2 medium onions, finely chopped (3 cups)
2 garlic cloves, finely chopped (2 teaspoons)
1 teaspoon dried oregano, crushed in a mortar and pestle
1 teaspoon dried basil, crushed in a mortar and pestle
¹/₄ teaspoon dried rosemary, crushed in a mortar and pestle
¹/₄ teaspoon dried thyme, crushed in a mortar and pestle
1 bay leaf, broken
¹/₈ teaspoon freshly ground black pepper
¹/₂ teaspoon salt
¹/₂ teaspoon fructose or ³/₄ teaspoon sugar

Combine all the ingredients and bring to a boil. Reduce the heat and simmer, uncovered, for at least 2 hours.

Cool to room temperature and refrigerate or freeze in containers of appropriate size.

Makes 4 cups

¹/₂ CUP CONTAINS APPROXIMATELY:
70 TOTAL CALORIES / 5 CALORIES IN FAT
0 MG CHOLESTEROL / 1060 MG SODIUM
50 MG CALCIUM

PRUNE SAUCE

This prune sauce is a marvelous substitute for cranberry sauce with turkey for holiday dinners.

1 cup dried pitted prunes
1 1/2 teaspoons grated lemon zest
2 tablespoons freshly squeezed lemon juice
1/8 teaspoon ground mace
12 whole cloves
3 whole allspice
1 peppercorn
1/2 cup frozen unsweetened apple juice concentrate, thawed
2 tablespoons apple cider vinegar

Put the prunes in a medium saucepan with water to cover. Add the lemon zest, lemon juice, and mace. Tie the cloves, allspice, and peppercorn in a cheesecloth bag and add this to the prune mixture. Cook, uncovered, over moderate heat for 10 minutes.

Stir in the apple juice concentrate and cook over low heat until the prunes are mushy and the mixture syrupy, about 20 minutes. Stir in the vinegar and cook for 5 minutes more. Remove the spice bag. Keeps for weeks tightly covered in the refrigerator.

Serve with poultry or meat.

Makes 1 1/2 cups

2 TABLESPOONS CONTAIN APPROXIMATELY:
65 TOTAL CALORIES / N CALORIES IN FAT
0 MG CHOLESTEROL / 60 MG SODIUM / 15 MG CALCIUM

EASY STRAWBERRY JAM

This recipe is truly so easy and yet so delicious that I did not want to leave it out of the book. However, I really couldn't decide what section it belonged in because even though I use it as an ingredient for Strawberry-Yogurt Parfait (page 227), it is also a wonderful sauce with poultry, as well as a spread on toast, pancakes, and waffles for breakfast. For this reason it has ended up here along with Apple Butter (following recipe), which is also rather difficult to categorize.

> *1 cup thawed frozen unsweetened strawberries (1 1/2 cups unthawed)*
> *1 tablespoon fructose or 1 1/2 tablespoons sugar*

Combine the strawberries and the fructose or sugar and mix well. It will keep 3 to 4 days in the refrigerator or can be frozen.

Makes 1 cup

¼ CUP CONTAINS APPROXIMATELY: 25 TOTAL CALORIES
N CALORIES IN FAT / 0 MG CHOLESTEROL / 1 MG SODIUM
5 MG CALCIUM

APPLE BUTTER

This is the recipe I use most frequently myself—I have it with Light Cheese (page 52) on my toast almost every morning for breakfast. It is also an ingredient in another of my favorite recipes, Our Famous Sugar-Free Bran Muffins (page 215), which calls for 1 cup of Apple Butter for a dozen muffins. Try this recipe for breakfast and I can almost guarantee your instant conversion to a healthy breakfast condiment for the whole family. It is even good with yogurt or ice cream as a dessert.

> *1/4 pound dried unsulfured sliced apples (2 cups)*
> *1 teaspoon ground cinnamon*
> *1/2 teaspoon ground allspice*
> *1/8 teaspoon ground cloves*
> *2 cups unsweetened apple juice*

Combine all the ingredients in a large saucepan and bring to a boil. Reduce the heat and simmer, covered, for 20 minutes, stirring occasionally. Remove from the heat and cool slightly.

Pour into a blender container and blend until smooth. Cool to room temperature and refrigerate in a tightly covered container. It will keep for months.

Makes 2 cups

2 TABLESPOONS CONTAIN APPROXIMATELY:
35 TOTAL CALORIES / N CALORIES IN FAT
0 MG CHOLESTEROL / 5 MG SODIUM / 10 MG CALCIUM

APPLE CHUTNEY

This chutney is fabulous, easy to make, and keeps for months. It can also be canned, using the classic sterilization procedures, and kept for years. It is free of preservatives and contains less sugar than commercial chutneys. It is also much less expensive. I like to serve it with any curried dish, and it is an ingredient of the Curried Chutney Dressing (page 77).

4 cups dried unsulfured apples, diced
1 cup dried figs, finely diced
1 cup golden raisins, finely diced
1 medium onion, finely chopped (1 1/2 cups)
1 1/2 cups fructose or 2 cups sugar
1 1/4 teaspoons ground ginger
1/4 cup pickling spice, tied in a cheesecloth bag
2 cups water
2 cups apple cider vinegar

Combine all the ingredients in a large saucepan and bring to a boil. Reduce the heat and simmer slowly, uncovered, for 2 hours.

Cool to room temperature. Remove and discard the cheesecloth bag containing the spices. Refrigerate the chutney in a tightly covered container. It will keep for months.

Makes 4 3/4 cups

¼ CUP CONTAINS APPROXIMATELY: 175 TOTAL CALORIES
N CALORIES IN FAT / 0 MG CHOLESTEROL / 10 MG SODIUM
25 MG CALCIUM

JALAPEÑO CHUTNEY

Like Apple Chutney (preceding recipe), Jalapeño Chutney can be canned or just covered tightly and stored in the refrigerator. It keeps for months. It is an ingredient in Southwestern Pasta Salad (page 93) and Pasta Salad with Seafood (page 94). It is also a good sauce on fish, poultry, or meat.

1 cup water
2 cups apple cider vinegar
3 medium tomatoes, chopped (2 cups)
6 tomatillos, chopped (1½ cups)
¾ cup fructose or 1 cup sugar
1 medium onion, chopped (1½ cups)
½ cup canned green California chilies, seeded and chopped
1 cup golden raisins
½ cup chopped fresh cilantro
2 fresh jalapeño peppers, seeded and chopped (¼ cup)
1 teaspoon ground cumin

Combine all the ingredients in a large saucepan and simmer, uncovered, for 3 hours.

Cool to room temperature, then refrigerate in a tightly covered container. It will keep for months.

Makes 4 cups

2 TABLESPOONS CONTAIN APPROXIMATELY:
50 TOTAL CALORIES / N CALORIES IN FAT
0 MG CHOLESTEROL / 20 MG SODIUM / 10 MG CALCIUM

BARBECUE SAUCE

This recipe can be used both as a marinade prior to grilling and as a sauce in which to cook poultry or meat. One of the favorite dishes of guests at the Canyon Ranch Spa in Tucson is the barbecued chicken that is cooked in this sauce. The chicken is baked in a 350°F oven for 15 minutes, then removed, skinned, and put back in the pan, topped with barbecue sauce. It is then baked, covered, for another 20 minutes and is absolutely delicious served with corn on the cob and a fresh green vegetable. This sauce is also good as a spread for sandwiches and as a dip for hot grilled vegetables.

> *1 medium onion, finely chopped (1¹/2 cups)*
> *2 tablespoons water*
> *¹/2 cup tomato sauce*
> *¹/2 teaspoon lemon zest, grated*
> *2 tablespoons freshly squeezed lemon juice*
> *1¹/2 tablespoons Worcestershire sauce*
> *1 tablespoon apple cider vinegar*
> *³/4 teaspoon dry mustard*
> *¹/8 teaspoon salt*
> *6 tablespoons frozen unsweetened apple juice concentrate*
> *¹/4 teaspoon Liquid Smoke*

Combine the onions and water in a small saucepan and cook about 10 minutes until the onions are soft and translucent. Add all the other ingredients except for the Liquid Smoke. Mix well and bring to a boil. Reduce the heat to medium and cook, uncovered, until thick, about 30 minutes.

Remove from the heat, add the Liquid Smoke, and mix well. Pour into a blender container and blend until smooth.

Cool to room temperature, then refrigerate in a tightly covered container.

Makes 1¹/2 cups

¹/4 CUP CONTAINS APPROXIMATELY: 55 TOTAL CALORIES
N CALORIES IN FAT / 0 MG CHOLESTEROL / 60 MG SODIUM
20 MG CALCIUM

LEMON BARBECUE SAUCE

This is an especially good marinade for chicken prior to barbecuing. Marinate for several hours, then barbecue over low coals for 25 to 30 minutes or until done, turning frequently and basting occasionally with the rest of the sauce.

> *1 garlic clove, minced (1 teaspoon)*
> *1/2 teaspoon salt*
> *2 tablespoons extra-virgin olive oil*
> *2 tablespoons defatted chicken stock (see page 22)*
> *1/2 cup freshly squeezed lemon juice*
> *2 tablespoons grated onion*
> *1/2 teaspoon freshly ground black pepper*
> *1/2 teaspoon dried thyme, crushed in a mortar and pestle*

Combine the garlic, salt, and oil in a small bowl. Stir in the remaining ingredients and chill for 24 hours.

Makes 3/4 cup

THE ENTIRE RECIPE CONTAINS APPROXIMATELY:
290 TOTAL CALORIES / 245 CALORIES IN FAT
0 MG CHOLESTEROL / 1115 MG SODIUM / 45 MG CALCIUM

CRANBERRY CATSUP

What else would you serve with a turkey burger? I served this during the Christmas season last year at the Four Seasons Hotel and Resort in Dallas and it was a big hit. Cranberry Catsup is also a good condiment served with any kind of poultry and a wonderful spread on cold turkey sandwiches as well as hot turkey burgers. I made it for Christmas gifts this past year, and many of my friends asked for more. Instead of refills I am sending them recipes!

¹/₂ pound raw cranberries
¹/₂ cup chopped onion
¹/₄ cup water
¹/₄ cup frozen unsweetened apple juice concentrate
¹/₄ cup white vinegar
¹/₈ teaspoon ground cloves
¹/₂ teaspoon ground cinnamon
¹/₂ teaspoon ground allspice
¹/₂ teaspoon salt
¹/₈ teaspoon white pepper

Place the cranberries and onions in a small saucepan with the water and cook until tender. Stir every few minutes to keep it from burning. Pour into a food processor with a metal blade and blend until smooth.

Place the mixture back in the saucepan and add the remaining ingredients. Cook until thick, stirring while cooking, approximately 10 minutes.

Makes 1¹/₄ cups

2 TABLESPOONS CONTAIN APPROXIMATELY:
25 TOTAL CALORIES / N CALORIES IN FAT
0 MG CHOLESTEROL / 140 MG SODIUM / 10 MG CALCIUM

VEGETABLE SAUCE

As I mentioned in the introduction, vegetable sauces are the most nutritious and lowest in calories of all sauces. Fortunately they are also tasty and beautiful and can be very elegant. I like brightly colored vegetable sauces, such as beet, carrot, broccoli, and spinach. (If you are using spinach, remove the fibrous central veins *before* you chop and measure it.) When using them as presentation sauces, I sometimes pour them on the plate as a liner for the entire bottom of the plate and then place the entrée items on top of the sauce, using the sauce as a colorful background or frame for the other items being served. Sometimes I make the sauces thicker by adding less vegetable stock and pipe more than one color sauce out of pastry tubes over the other items on the plate like a painting. Leftover vegetable sauces can be thinned a bit with additional stock and make wonderful soups.

1 1/2 cups peeled and chopped colorful vegetables
1/2 White Rose potato, peeled and diced (1/2 cup)
1/2 medium onion, chopped (3/4 cup)
1 tablespoon chopped shallots
1/2 teaspoon freshly squeezed lemon juice
1/8 teaspoon salt
Dash freshly ground black pepper
Vegetable stock to cover (see page 27)

Combine all the ingredients in a medium saucepan and bring to a boil. Reduce the heat and simmer for 30 minutes. Cool slightly.

Pour all the ingredients into a blender container and blend until satin smooth. If the sauce is too thick, add a little more vegetable stock. Season as desired.

Makes about 1 1/2 cups

1/4 CUP CONTAINS APPROXIMATELY: 30 TOTAL CALORIES
N CALORIES IN FAT / 0 MG CHOLESTEROL / 60 MG SODIUM
15 MG CALCIUM

VARIATION:

Beet Sauce: To keep Beet Sauce from tasting bitter, first cut the stems off the beets and wash them well. Then place them in a saucepan and cover with cold water. Bring to a boil, reduce the heat, and simmer for 20 minutes. Drain. Peel and chop the beets and proceed with the recipe.

MAYO-NOT

Mayonnaise it is NOT! But it is a wonderful dairy-free, cholesterol-free, low-calorie substitute that works well in recipes calling for mayonnaise. It is not good as a substitute spread on bread because the oil content is so low, but it is a good dairy-free base for sauces calling for sour cream or cottage cheese, and it is of great value to people on nondairy diets.

> *½ pound tofu, cubed (1 cup)*
> *1 tablespoon corn oil*
> *¼ cup water*
> *1 tablespoon freshly squeezed lemon juice*
> *½ teaspoon salt*

Place all the ingredients in a blender container and blend until smooth. Refrigerate in a tightly covered container. It will keep 1 week.

Makes 1¼ cups

¼ CUP CONTAINS APPROXIMATELY: 60 TOTAL CALORIES
45 CALORIES IN FAT / 0 MG CHOLESTEROL
225 MG SODIUM / 65 MG CALCIUM

VARIATIONS:

Horseradish Sauce: Add 2 teaspoons prepared horseradish, 1½ teaspoons Worcestershire sauce, ½ teaspoon garlic powder, and dash Tabasco.

Vanilla/Cinnamon Sauce: Add 4 teaspoons fructose or 2 tablespoons sugar, 1½ teaspoons vanilla extract, and ½ teaspoon ground cinnamon.

ROASTED RED PEPPER SAUCE

This brilliantly colored, spicy sauce makes a beautiful presentation sauce for, and is an ingredient in, the Vegetable Terrine (page 112).

> *5 large red peppers*
> *1 tablespoon apple cider vingar*
> *1 tablespoon extra-virgin olive oil*
> *1/2 teaspoon salt*

Broil the peppers until blackened on all sides, turning frequently. Place the peppers in a plastic bag for 25 to 30 minutes (this makes them easier to peel). Peel, core, and seed the peppers.

Combine all the ingredients in a blender container and blend until smooth.

Makes 1 1/2 cups

1/4 CUP CONTAINS APPROXIMATELY: 35 TOTAL CALORIES
25 CALORIES IN FAT / 0 MG CHOLESTEROL
165 MG SODIUM / 5 MG CALCIUM

WALNUT-DILL SAUCE

This is an excellent nondairy cream sauce made with tofu. It is an ingredient in my recipe for Poached Salmon (page 157). In this recipe I combine the sauce with toasted walnuts, which offers a wonderful balance in texture with the smooth creaminess of the sauce, and I suggest either plating the sauce under the salmon or spooning it over the top and garnishing it with sprigs of fresh dill. This presentation would work with other seafood, including water-packed tuna or poultry. I also serve this sauce on a vegetarian plate at the Four Seasons Hotel and Resort in Dallas.

½ pound tofu (1 cup)
½ teaspoon salt
½ teaspoon dried dillweed, crushed in a mortar and pestle
¼ teaspoon dried tarragon, crushed in a mortar and pestle
¼ cup water
2 teaspoons white vinegar
1 tablespoon freshly squeezed lemon juice
1 tablespoon walnut oil
⅛ cup tightly packed fresh dill

Combine all the ingredients in a blender container and blend until satin smooth. Refrigerate in a tightly covered container.

Makes 1¼ cups

¼ CUP CONTAINS APPROXIMATELY: 60 TOTAL CALORIES
45 CALORIES IN FAT / 0 MG CHOLESTEROL
210 MG SODIUM / 65 MG CALCIUM

CREAMY CURRY SAUCE AND DRESSING

When I was developing a creamy dressing for the Canyon Ranch Spa in Tucson, the dietitian asked me if I could make it nondairy as well as creamy because we have so many guests with dairy allergies that it would be nice to have a creamy dressing that all the guests could enjoy. Since curry is always a very popular flavor range, I created this Creamy Curry Sauce and Dressing using tofu as the base. The Canyon Ranch guests love it, and I hope you will too.

½ pound tofu, cubed (1 cup)
¼ cup water
½ teaspoon salt
¾ teaspoon fructose or 1 teaspoon sugar
¾ teaspoon curry powder
⅛ teaspoon ground ginger

1 tablespoon freshly squeezed lemon juice
1 tablespoon corn oil

Combine all the ingredients in a blender container and blend until smooth. Refrigerate in a tightly covered container.

Makes 1¼ cups

2 TABLESPOONS CONTAIN APPROXIMATELY:
35 TOTAL CALORIES / 20 CALORIES IN FAT
0 MG CHOLESTEROL / 120 MG SODIUM
50 MG CALCIUM

JEANNE JONES' LIGHT DRESSING

This is my own signature dressing, which I mentioned in the introduction to this section. I have it on my menu at the restaurant at Neiman-Marcus in Newport Beach, California, all of the Four Seasons hotels, and the Canyon Ranch Spa in Tucson. It is also the dressing I keep in my own refrigerator. I make the basic dressing in large quantities and then add the variations to it as I need them. Further variations are possible within the four categories I have given you by changing the type of vinegar used in the recipe and adding 1 tablespoon of oil per cup of dressing for additional flavor. For example, by using raspberry vinegar and adding walnut oil (Raspberry-Walnut Vinaigrette Dressing, page 72), the entire personality of the dressing changes, and the oil adds only about 8 calories per tablespoon. Remember, however, when using any oil in your salad dressing, it must be mixed thoroughly before serving because it all rises to the top. Also remember when using any oil for flavor to make every calorie count by using the most flavorful oil available; for example, if you wish to add olive oil to your Italian Dressing, use extra-virgin olive oil so you can really taste the small amount you are using. For a creamy-type dressing, add plain nonfat yogurt, Light Cheese (page 52), low-fat cottage cheese, or tofu and blend until smooth.

½ cup red wine vinegar
¼ teaspoon freshly ground black pepper
½ teaspoon salt
1 tablespoon fructose or 4 teaspoons sugar
2 garlic cloves, finely chopped (2 teaspoons)
2 teaspoons Worcestershire sauce
1 tablespoon Dijon-style mustard
2 tablespoons freshly squeezed lemon juice
1 cup water

Combine all the ingredients and mix well. Refrigerate in a container with a tight-fitting lid. It will keep for months.

Makes 2 cups

2 TABLESPOONS CONTAIN APPROXIMATELY:
5 TOTAL CALORIES / 0 CALORIES IN FAT
0 MG CHOLESTEROL / 85 MG SODIUM / 10 MG CALCIUM

VARIATIONS:

Italian: Add 1 teaspoon each of crushed dried tarragon, oregano, and basil.
Cumin: Add ½ teaspoon ground cumin.
Curry: Add 1 teaspoon curry powder.
Tarragon: Add 1 tablespoon crushed dried tarragon.

RASPBERRY-WALNUT VINAIGRETTE DRESSING

½ cup raspberry vinegar
¼ teaspoon salt
¼ teaspoon freshly ground black pepper
1 tablespoon fructose or 4 teaspoons sugar
2 garlic cloves, finely chopped (2 teaspoons)
2 teaspoons Worcestershire sauce
1 tablespoon Dijon-style mustard

1 tablespoon freshly squeezed lemon juice
2 teaspoons dried tarragon, crushed in a mortar and pestle
1 cup water
2 tablespoons walnut oil

Combine the vinegar and salt and mix until the salt is thoroughly dissolved. Add all the other ingredients and mix well. Refrigerate in a tightly covered container. ALWAYS MIX WELL BEFORE USING.

Makes 2 cups

2 TABLESPOONS CONTAIN APPROXIMATELY:
20 TOTAL CALORIES / 15 CALORIES IN FAT
0 MG CHOLESTEROL / 55 MG SODIUM / 5 MG CALCIUM

POPPY SEED DRESSING

1/2 pound tofu (1 cup)
1/4 cup frozen unsweetened apple juice concentrate, undiluted
1/4 teaspoon salt
1 1/2 teaspoons dry mustard
2 tablespoons reduced-calorie mayonnaise
1/2 cup rice wine vinegar
1/2 medium onion, chopped (3/4 cup)
1 1/2 cups chopped orange
4 teaspoons poppy seeds

Combine all the ingredients except for the poppy seeds in a blender container and blend until smooth. Pour into a bowl. Add the poppy seeds and mix well. Refrigerate in a tightly covered container.

Makes 3 cups

2 TABLESPOONS CONTAIN APPROXIMATELY: 25 CALORIES
10 CALORIES IN FAT / 0 MG CHOLESTEROL / 40 MG SODIUM
30 MG CALCIUM

CAPER DRESSING

¼ cup rice wine vinegar or champagne wine
½ teaspoon salt
⅛ teaspoon freshly ground black pepper
1 shallot, finely chopped (1 tablespoon)
1 tablespoon minced capers
1 teaspoon Dijon-style mustard
½ cup water
2 tablespoons corn oil

Combine the vinegar or wine and salt and mix until the salt is completely dissolved. Add all the other ingredients except the oil and mix well. Whisk the mixture constantly while adding the oil.

Refrigerate in a tightly covered container. MIX THOROUGHLY BEFORE EACH USE.

Makes 1 cup

2 TABLESPOONS CONTAIN APPROXIMATELY:
35 TOTAL CALORIES / 30 CALORIES IN FAT
0 MG CHOLESTEROL / 230 MG SODIUM / 5 MG CALCIUM

MANDARIN DRESSING AND MARINADE

This dressing and marinade is used for two of the most popular recipes in this book—as a salad dressing on the Chinese Chicken Salad (page 97) and to cook the prawns for Polynesian Prawns (page 152). It also works perfectly for wok cooking and adds enormously to the flavor of stir-fries of all types.

1/2 cup rice wine vinegar
3 tablespoons dark sesame oil
1 tablespoon reduced-sodium soy sauce
One 6-ounce can (3/4 cup) frozen unsweetened pineapple juice
concentrate
2 teaspoons chopped peeled ginger
1 garlic clove, chopped (1 teaspoon)
1/8 teaspoon crushed red pepper flakes

Combine all the ingredients in a blender container and mix well. Refrigerate in a tightly covered container. MIX WELL BEFORE EACH USE.

Makes 1 1/2 cups

2 TABLESPOONS CONTAIN APPROXIMATELY:
65 TOTAL CALORIES / 30 CALORIES IN FAT
0 MG CHOLESTEROL / 85 MG SODIUM / 10 MG CALCIUM

LIGHT RANCH DRESSING

This is a recipe I developed in answer to a letter from one of my readers, who wanted a ranch dressing mix that was lower in sodium and without preservatives and that she could make herself. After lots of experimenting, I finally came up with a mix I really like. In fact, in my column I suggested that it be made in large quantities and put in little jars for hostess gifts along with the recipe for making the dressing. This dressing is also a good sauce for cooked vegetables, and I like it very much on fish and seafood.

RANCH DRESSING MIX:

> *1/4 cup dried parsley*
> *3 tablespoons dried minced onion*
> *2 teaspoons dried chives*
> *1 teaspoon salt*
> *1/2 teaspoon garlic powder*
> *1/2 teaspoon ground celery seed*
> *1/4 teaspoon black pepper*
>
> *1/4 cup reduced-calorie mayonnaise*
> *3/4 cup buttermilk*

Combine the dressing mix ingredients in a small jar and mix well. Store in a dry place (makes ½ cup of mix).

Combine 1 tablespoon of the dressing mix with the mayonnaise in a bowl and mix thoroughly using a wire whisk. Add the buttermilk slowly, stirring constantly until well mixed. Refrigerate in a tightly covered container.

Makes 1 cup

2 TABLESPOONS CONTAIN APPROXIMATELY:
20 TOTAL CALORIES / 10 CALORIES IN FAT
1 MG CHOLESTEROL / 50 MG SODIUM / 30 MG CALCIUM

BLEU CHEESE DRESSING

This is my own favorite recipe for bleu cheese dressing. Fortunately it is also lower in calories, cholesterol, and sodium than any other bleu cheese dressing I have ever liked. If you prefer Roquefort, Gorgonzola, or Stilton to bleu cheese, just substitute the same amount.

> *1/2 cup reduced-calorie mayonnaise*
> *1 cup buttermilk*
> *1 garlic clove, very finely chopped (1 teaspoon)*
> *2 ounces bleu cheese, crumbled (1/2 cup)*
> *1/4 cup low-fat cottage cheese*

Combine all the ingredients except the cottage cheese in a bowl and mix thoroughly with a wire whisk. Stir in the cottage cheese. Refrigerate in a tightly covered container. It will keep 1 week.

Makes 2 scant cups

2 TABLESPOONS CONTAIN APPROXIMATELY:
35 TOTAL CALORIES / 20 CALORIES IN FAT
5 MG CHOLESTEROL / 95 MG SODIUM / 45 MG CALCIUM

CURRIED CHUTNEY DRESSING

> *1/3 cup reduced-calorie mayonnaise*
> *1/3 cup plain nonfat yogurt*
> *1 1/2 teaspoons curry powder*
> *1 tablespoon fructose or 4 teaspoons sugar*
> *1/8 teaspoon crushed red pepper flakes*
> *Dash freshly ground black pepper*
> *1/2 garlic clove, finely chopped (1/2 teaspoon)*
> *1 shallot, finely chopped (1 tablespoon)*
> *1/8 teaspoon Worcestershire sauce*
> *1/4 teaspoon freshly squeezed lemon juice*
> *1 1/2 teaspoons reduced-sodium soy sauce*
> *1 tablespoon red wine vinegar*
> *1/4 cup Apple Chutney (page 62)*

Combine all the ingredients except the Apple Chutney in a blender container and blend until smooth. Pour in a bowl, add the chutney, and mix well.

Refrigerate in a tightly covered container.

Makes 1 cup

2 TABLESPOONS CONTAIN APPROXIMATELY:
50 TOTAL CALORIES / 15 CALORIES IN FAT
0 MG CHOLESTEROL / 85 MG SODIUM / 20 MG CALCIUM

THOUSAND ISLAND DRESSING

This is the dressing I use on the famous Ranch Burger at the Canyon Ranch Spa in Tucson. On our All-American Day I serve the Ranch Burger with Oven Fries (page 122) (no fat) and Coleslaw (page 86) and Carob-Yogurt Sundae (page 227) for dessert, and it is one of the most popular lunches with all the guests.

1 cup reduced-calorie mayonnaise
1/2 cup chili sauce
1/4 cup sweet relish
2 tablespoons white vinegar
1/4 teaspoon salt
1/4 teaspoon fructose or 1/2 teaspoon sugar
Dash white pepper
1 tablespoon freshly squeezed lemon juice

Combine all the ingredients and mix well. Refrigerate in a tightly covered container.

Makes 2 scant cups

2 TABLESPOONS CONTAIN APPROXIMATELY:
35 TOTAL CALORIES / 20 CALORIES IN FAT
0 MG CHOLESTEROL / 80 MG SODIUM / 5 MG CALCIUM

SALADS

IN THE BEGINNING, salads consisted only of a few edible plants and herbs sprinkled with a bit of salt. In fact the word *salad* actually comes from the word *salt.* This is an amazing fact in today's fitness-conscious society where salad is considered the epitome of good nutrition and salt is decidedly on the other end of the spectrum.

What makes this original concept of salads seem even more strange to me is that it is the salt that wilts the greens when a salad is dressed too soon before serving. The advantage of a salt-free dressing is that you can literally dress the greens hours before serving and still have them crisp and attractive in appearance when they are presented.

The widely held notion that salads are somehow low in calories is indeed a myth in itself. Today salads do not only include leafy raw vegetables and herbs; literally anything you can eat can be an ingredient in a salad. Because of this a salad offers enormous variety in meal planning. It can be a small, almost calorie-free side dish, an

79

appetizer such as a cold jelled terrine or marinated celery root or artichoke hearts, the entrée course, or an entire meal in itself.

At what point during the meal the salad is served has a great deal to do with geographical location. Californians routinely serve salad as a first course; it is often waiting for you at the table when you are seated to a meal. New Yorkers are more likely to serve a small salad on the side with the entrée. And the French prefer the salad after the entrée.

When preparing salad greens it is important to wash and dry them thoroughly before storing them in bags or wrapping them in towels in the refrigerator. Wet salad greens dilute the dressing, and therefore you will be inclined to use more dressing on the salad. The thorough washing of the greens is one of the single most important steps in salad preparation. Nothing is worse than to be served a "gritty" salad; it can even be dangerous. I know several people who have broken teeth biting down on a small rock in an innocent-looking salad.

Cold steamed vegetables can also be marinated for an antipasto salad with an Italian meal or served for hors d'oeuvres with any type of meal. When I prepare cold marinated vegetables, I use one of my oil-free dressings (in the Sauces & Dressings section), so they are very low in calories. Also, if serving them as finger food, they don't leave you with greasy hands. When marinating vegetables, marinate all but the green vegetables (broccoli, snow peas, asparagus, and so on); add them to the mixture just before serving because green vegetables lose their color in the marinade.

My favorite light salad, which can be served either as a first-course salad or after the entrée with equal integrity, is a Salad of young greens with Raspberry-Walnut Vinaigrette Dressing (page 72). Since all salad greens grow from the inside out, young greens are the hearts or centers of lettuce heads as well as the young tender leaves on sprigs of greens such as watercress and arugula. When serving this salad after the meal, you might want to add a small wedge of warm cheese and sprinkle it with a few toasted nuts. In fact, I am so fond of toasted nuts and seeds on salads that I think it was because of them that I was first motivated to create a completely fat-free salad dressing so I could better afford the calories of the nuts and seeds.

Always buy nuts and seeds raw and toast them yourself. The commercially toasted or roasted varieties contain oil and often salt and preservatives. Even though many nuts such as walnuts, almonds, and pine nuts can be eaten without toasting them, they don't have nearly as much flavor, and since nuts and seeds have approximately 50 calories per tablespoon, you want to get as much taste per calorie as possible.

Keep your raw nuts and seeds in the refrigerator so the oils in them won't turn rancid and the bugs won't attack them. Then toast them as you need them so they are always crisp and have that wonderful toasted taste. The only exception is for peanuts; I buy the dry-roasted unsalted variety because raw peanuts take so long to toast.

Toasting nuts and seeds is easy. Place them in a preheated 350°F oven for 8 to 10 minutes or until golden brown. Watch them carefully because they burn easily.

When preparing spinach, it is necessary to fill the sink or a large tub or bowl with water and submerge the spinach completely, tearing off one leaf at a time in order to make certain that all the sandy dirt is removed. During the rainy season it is often necessary to wash lettuce and cabbage in the same manner because they tend to be caked with sand and dirt that cannot be removed any other way. With spinach it is also necessary to remove the stems and large veins that run down the backs of the leaves to take the bitter taste out of it. If you don't like spinach or spinach salad because of a slightly bitter aftertaste, you may find you have discovered a whole new vegetable when you eat it with the stems and veins removed. If you have ever wondered why spinach salads are always more expensive on menus than lettuce when spinach is less expensive to buy at your supermarket, it is because it takes so long to prepare it properly, and the cost of labor has to be added to the price.

Today salads can be served at any temperature or combination of temperatures. In fact my own favorite salad in this section is the Breast of Chicken Salad with Goat Cheese and Warm Mushroom Dressing (page 99), which is a delightful combination of tastes, temperatures, and textures to which a salad lends itself better than any other menu category. When serving cold salads, always chill the salad plates briefly in the freezer.

Another warm salad I particularly like is a grilled vegetable salad. It is easy to make and a wonderful way to use up leftover vegetables. You can either start with raw vegetables or use blanched vegetables. I prefer to use blanched vegetables because they don't require as much cooking time since they are already partially cooked and therefore don't dry out as much when cooking over a grill or under a broiler. I like to serve skewers of grilled vegetables plated on a creamy tofu or vegetable sauce as an appetizer or salad course. Skewered grilled vegetables are also a nice accompaniment to grilled fish, poultry, or meat.

Never put nuts or seeds on a salad or any other dish until you are ready to serve it. Otherwise the moisture will soften them and you won't get the delightful crunchiness that so enhances the texture of any dish.

There is no question that salads are my favorite food category; I almost always have a salad for lunch. For that reason I have included many different types of entrée salads in this section. Never make the mistake of thinking that just because you're having a salad you're having a low-calorie lunch. One of the most popular salads on most menus is the chef's salad, routinely prepared with lettuce, tomatoes, hard-cooked eggs, and various kinds of meat and cheeses and often served with a heavy Roquefort or bleu cheese dressing. This benign-looking bowl of salad can easily contain 2000 calories; after all, the cheeses are each approximately 100 calories per ounce and the salad dressing is over 100 calories per tablespoon. Along with the calories in the salad are hundreds of milligrams of cholesterol and sodium. In other words, the salad of choice for a healthy life-style is not a chef's salad with Roquefort or bleu cheese dressing!

Salads offer a wonderful way to use leftovers. The next time you're planning a meal, go through the refrigerator to see what you have on hand that needs to be used and then look through my salad dressings to find just the right dressing for your "Clean the Refrigerator Salad." You will be surprised at just how good some of these impromptu improvisations can be.

SALAD GREENS GLOSSARY

ARUGULA: Sprigs of dark green leaves with a strong nutlike flavor. It combines well with mild-flavored lettuces or with equally intensely flavored greens, such as watercress.

BELGIAN ENDIVE (French endive, Witloof): Six- to 8-inch heads of crisp-tender yellow-white leaves with a green tinge. Delicately bitter flavor. Use whole or in bite-size pieces of julienne cut. Mixes well with other greens. Expensive but little waste.

BIBB LETTUCE (Limestone): Small, cup-shaped leaves held together loosely. Dark green crisp-tender leaves are succulent; considered by some to be the aristocrat of lettuces. The whole leaves are ideal "bowls" for salad mixtures. Mixes well with other greens.

BOSTON LETTUCE (Butterhead): Soft, small head with delicate leaves. Outer leaves are green and inner are light yellow and buttery. Mixes well with other greens.

CHICORY (American or Curly Endive): Yellow-white stem with curly, fringed tendrils. Somewhat bitter taste. The outer leaves are darker and stronger flavored than the inner. A prickly texture to add to tossed salad. An attractive garnish.

CHINESE CELERY CABBAGE: Celery-colored, white-ribbed leaves in a tightly packed head. Serve alone, as a base for salad mixtures, or mix with other greens. The flavor is between celery and cabbage, as the name implies.

DANDELION GREENS: The wild variety is available in most places and is also especially grown for salads. The youngest leaves are the most tender. Slightly bitter.

ESCAROLE (Batavian Endive): The leaves are less curly and broader than endive and are a paler green; they should snap easily. Combine with other greens.

FENNEL (Anise): The stalks are similar to celery and grow from a bulbous root with lacy, fernlike leaves. The licoricelike flavor is more intense in the leaves, which are usually used as an herb. Substitute for celery in stuffings and casseroles. Slices of the bulb provide a uniquely different taste in salads.

FIDDLEHEAD: A fern often said to taste like asparagus, it is best in early spring when very young. Grows along stream banks.

FIELD LETTUCE (Lamb's Lettuce, Corn Salad, Mâché): Small, smooth green leaves in a loosely formed head. Tangy flavor. Good for tossed salads or as cooked greens.

ICEBERG LETTUCE (Crisphead Lettuce): Large, compact heads with crisp leaves tightly packed. The outer leaves are a medium green and the inner leaves are a paler green. Slice, shred, or tear to add crunch to any salad. Longer shelf life than most lettuces.

ITALIAN PARSLEY: The sprigs have a flat, broad leaf rather than the tight, curly leaf of regular parsley, with a slightly milder flavor. A good garnish for Italian dishes.

LEAF LETTUCE: Loose, smooth leaves growing from a central stalk. Green or red-tipped. The curly leaves make a good undergarnish for molded salads or fruit or vegetable arrangements.

MINT: Usually considered an herb, but important as a salad green in the Middle East, where it is an essential ingredient for the classic salad, tabbouleh.

NAPA CABBAGE: Similar to Chinese celery cabbage, but the head is shorter and the base broader. Use for the same purposes, alone or with other greens.

NASTURTIUM FLOWERS AND LEAVES: The leaves, stems, and flowers are all edible and interesting additions to salads. The leaves and stems have a pungent, peppery flavor. The flowers have a milder flavor and are a wonderful edible garniture.

PARSLEY: Dark green sprigs of tightly crimped leaves with a strong, refreshing flavor. Usually thought of as a garnish, parsley is good in soups and for flavoring stocks. It is also good in salads of all types.

RADICCHIO: Small, cabbage-type head with red leaves. Flavor slightly bitter. Use as a garnish or mix with other greens to provide color and a different taste to a salad.

ROMAINE LETTUCE (Cos Lettuce): An elongated head of loose dark green leaves that are firm and crisp. The pungent flavor adds tang to salads. Classically used for Caesar Salad.

SORREL: Many edible varieties, both cultivated and wild. The arrow-shaped green leaves have a sour, almost bitter taste; the very young leaves are best. Best mixed with milder greens. Most frequently used in soups and sauces.

WATERCRESS: Dark green glossy leaves, dime-size, on crisp sprigs. The leaves and the tender part of the stems are spicy and peppery. Good additions to tossed salads. Also often used as a garnish.

PARSLEY SALAD

This salad may take longer to prepare than any other salad in this section because the parsley must be thoroughly washed and thoroughly dried and then just the tips or curly parts of the parsley picked off for the salad one by one. There is no really fast way to do this and do it properly, but believe me, it is worth the time it takes because it is one of the best and most unusual salads you will ever taste. You can add drained water-packed tuna or diced cooked chicken or turkey and serve this as a luncheon or light supper entrée as well.

> *½ cup Light Tarragon Dressing (page 72)*
> *½ teaspoon fructose or ¾ teaspoon sugar*
> *¼ cup sun-dried tomatoes packed in olive oil, thoroughly drained and julienne cut*
> *2 cups tightly packed parsley tips, stems removed (4 loosely packed cups)*
> *¼ pound imported Parmesan cheese, freshly grated (½ cup)*

Combine the dressing and fructose or sugar and mix thoroughly.
    Combine the sun-dried tomatoes, parsley, dressing, and half the Parmesan cheese and toss well. Place on four chilled plates and garnish each with a tablespoon of the remaining cheese.

Makes four 1-cup servings

EACH SERVING CONTAINS APPROXIMATELY:
160 TOTAL CALORIES / 80 CALORIES IN FAT
20 MG CHOLESTEROL / 640 MG SODIUM / 470 MG CALCIUM

SPINACH SALAD WITH TOASTED WALNUTS

I love spinach salad and I like spinach best with toasted walnuts. I had this as an entrée salad with shrimp on my menu at the restaurant at Neiman-Marcus in Newport Beach, California. It is also good with drained water-packed tuna or diced cooked chicken or turkey.

> *¼ cup chopped walnuts*
> *1 pound fresh spinach, deveined and torn into bite-size pieces (4 cups)*
> *¼ cup Raspberry-Walnut Vinaigrette Dressing (page 72)*

Place the walnuts in a preheated 350°F oven for 8 to 10 minutes. Watch carefully, as they burn easily. Set aside.

Place 1 cup spinach on each of four chilled plates and spoon 1 tablespoon dressing over the top. Top with 1 tablespoon toasted walnuts.

Makes four 1-cup servings

EACH SERVING CONTAINS APPROXIMATELY:
70 TOTAL CALORIES / 50 CALORIES IN FAT
0 MG CHOLESTEROL / 70 MG SODIUM
65 MG CALCIUM

COLESLAW

This is a delightfully different coleslaw. I know many people who don't like regular coleslaw but are crazy about this recipe. It is wonderful to make in large quantities for backyard barbecues or picnics, and it goes well with any type food.

DRESSING:

1/4 cup reduced-calorie mayonnaise
1 1/2 tablespoons white vinegar
1 1/2 teaspoons Dijon-style mustard
1 1/2 teaspoons fructose or 2 teaspoons sugar
1/2 teaspoon caraway seeds
1/8 teaspoon salt
Dash white pepper

6 ounces green cabbage, shredded (1 1/2 cups)
3 ounces red cabbage, shredded (3/4 cup)
1/2 cup peeled and grated carrots
1 small tart green apple, cored, peeled, and grated (3/4 cup)
1/4 cup finely chopped red onion

Combine the dressing ingredients and mix thoroughly. Combine the dressing with all the other ingredients and again mix well. Chill for several hours before serving.

Makes four ¹/₂-cup servings

EACH SERVING CONTAINS APPROXIMATELY:
60 TOTAL CALORIES / 20 CALORIES IN FAT
0 MG CHOLESTEROL / 125 MG SODIUM
35 MG CALCIUM

CELERY ROOT SALAD

The most interesting thing about celery root is that it is not really celery root at all but the root of the celeriac plant. This root is delicious raw or cooked. In fact this recipe can be made with raw celery root as well as cooked as the recipe suggests. I like it best cooked and then chilled to serve as an appetizer.

1 small celery root, peeled and grated (1¹/₄ cups)
1 teaspoon freshly squeezed lemon juice
1¹/₂ tablespoons Dijon-style mustard
2 tablespoons water
1 tablespoon white vinegar
Dash freshly ground black pepper
¹/₄ teaspoon dried tarragon, crushed in a mortar and pestle
4 lettuce leaves to line plates
2 teaspoons chopped parsley
1 tablespoon finely chopped capers

Combine the celery root and lemon juice and steam over boiling water for 2 minutes. Rinse in cold water. Drain thoroughly and set aside.

In a small bowl, whisk the mustard, water, vinegar, pepper, and tarragon and blend well. Toss the dressing with the celery root. Cover and refrigerate for at least 2 hours.

To serve, place a lettuce leaf on each of four chilled plates. Spoon ½ cup of the celery root mixture on each plate. Top each serving with chopped parsley and a pinch of chopped capers.

Makes 4 servings

EACH SERVING CONTAINS APPROXIMATELY:
35 TOTAL CALORIES / 5 CALORIES IN FAT
0 MG CHOLESTEROL / 125 MG SODIUM
50 MG CALCIUM

POTATO SALAD

DRESSING:

½ cup plain nonfat yogurt
¼ cup reduced-calorie mayonnaise
2 tablespoons apple cider vinegar
½ teaspoon Dijon-style mustard
½ teaspoon prepared red mustard

3 medium red potatoes, cooked, and diced (3 cups)
1 tablespoon finely chopped parsley
1½ celery ribs, without leaves, chopped (¾ cup)
½ cups chopped scallions
¼ cup chopped green bell pepper
½ teaspoon celery seed
¼ teaspoon salt
¼ teaspoon freshly ground black pepper
¼ cup sweet pickle relish
2 hard-cooked egg whites, chopped (optional)

Combine the dressing ingredients and mix well. Set aside.

Combine all the salad ingredients and mix well. Fold the dressing into the potato mixture and refrigerate for several hours. Stir the salad before serving.

Makes four 1-cup servings

EACH SERVING CONTAINS APPROXIMATELY:
190 TOTAL CALORIES / 25 CALORIES IN FAT
1 MG CHOLESTEROL / 355 MG SODIUM
100 MG CALCIUM

WILD-RICE SALAD

I serve this salad as a vegetarian entrée at the Canyon Ranch Spa in Tucson; however, it is also good with water-packed tuna or diced cooked poultry or meat added to it. It is a wonderful portable meal for picnics and al fresco parties of all types. To steam vegetables, see page 106.

¹/₂ cup chopped walnuts
1 medium onion, finely chopped and steamed (1¹/₂ cups)
2 cups broccoli flowerettes, steamed
³/₄ cup wild rice
1¹/₂ cups water
1 tablespoon reduced-sodium soy sauce
1 teaspoon dried thyme, crushed in a mortar and pestle
2 medium carrots, scraped and finely chopped (1 cup)
2 celery ribs, without leaves, finely chopped (1 cup)
¹/₂ cup Caper Dressing (page 74)
Lettuce leaves for lining plates
4 cups greens, torn into bite-size pieces (4 cups)
4 sprigs fresh thyme for garnish

Toast the walnuts in a preheated 350°F oven for 8 to 10 minutes. Watch them carefully, as they burn easily. Set aside. Steam the onion and broccoli and set aside.

Combine the wild rice, water, soy sauce, and thyme and bring to a boil. Reduce the heat and cook, covered, for about 30 to 35 minutes or until all the liquid has been absorbed and the rice is fluffy.

Allow to cool to room temperature and combine the steamed onions, chopped carrots, chopped celery, and the dressing and mix well. Refrigerate until cold before serving.

To serve, add the steamed broccoli (if the broccoli is added sooner, it will lose its color). Toss again thoroughly.

Line four chilled plates with lettuce leaves and cover each with 1 cup of greens. Place 2 cups of the wild-rice mixture over the top of the greens. Garnish with a sprig of fresh thyme. Top with 2 tablespoons of toasted walnuts.

Makes four 2-cup servings

EACH SERVING CONTAINS APPROXIMATELY:
300 TOTAL CALORIES / 115 CALORIES IN FAT
0 MG CHOLESTEROL / 545 MG SODIUM
90 MG CALCIUM

VEGETARIAN DELIGHT SALAD

This salad appears on many of my light-cuisine menus for spas, hotels, and restaurants. Besides being vegetarian, it is also extremely high in vitamins, minerals, and fiber and very low in calories. For those who always like to get as much nutrition as possible per calorie, this salad is a very popular entrée.

1/4 cup raw sunflower seeds
1 pound tofu, cubed (2 cups)
2 cups Light Tarragon Dressing (page 72)
6 cups lettuce and spinach, torn into bite-size pieces

6 cups bite-size pieces vegetables—a colorful assortment, such as carrots, red and green bell peppers, tomatoes, zucchini, pea pods, mushrooms—steamed crisp-tender (see chart on page 106)

5½ ounces part-skim mozzarella cheese, freshly grated (1⅓ cups)

16 tomato slices, halved, for garnish

Place the sunflower seeds in a preheated 350°F oven for 8 to 10 minutes or until golden brown. Watch carefully, as they burn easily. Set aside.

Cover the tofu with 1½ cups of the Light Tarragon Dressing and allow to marinate for several hours. Drain, reserving dressing for the salad.

When ready to serve, place 1½ cups lettuce and spinach on each of four chilled plates. Arrange 1½ cups vegetables on top of the greens. Place ½ cup marinated tofu on top of the vegetables. Sprinkle ⅓ cup cheese and 1 tablespoon sunflower seeds over the top. Arrange the tomato slices around salads in a scallop pattern. Serve ½ cup of the remaining Light Tarragon Dressing on the side.

Makes 4 servings

EACH SERVING CONTAINS APPROXIMATELY:
400 TOTAL CALORIES / 195 CALORIES IN FAT
20 MG CHOLESTEROL / 645 MG SODIUM
570 MG CALCIUM

CURRIED WALDORF SALAD

If you like Waldorf Salad, you're going to *love* Curried Waldorf Salad. I served this salad for a holiday party and it was the hit of the menu. The next day I combined the leftover Curried Waldorf Salad with some leftover chopped turkey and it was a delicious luncheon salad.

14 raw almonds
3 celery ribs, without leaves, chopped (1 1/2 cups)
2 red Delicious apples, cored and diced (1 1/2 cups)
2 golden Delicious apples, cored and diced (1 1/2 cups)
1/4 cup chopped chives or scallion tops (1/2-inch pieces)
1/4 cup dried currants
1/4 cup reduced-calorie mayonnaise
1/4 cup plain nonfat yogurt
1 teaspoon curry powder
1/8 teaspoon ground cumin
1 pinch each of:
    ground ginger
    ground cinnamon
    ground allspice
    ground cloves

Chop the almonds coarsely and toast them in a preheated 350°F oven for 8 to 10 minutes or until lightly browned. Watch carefully, as they burn easily. Set aside.

Combine the celery, apples, chives or scallion tops, and currants in a bowl. In a separate bowl, whisk together the mayonnaise, yogurt, curry powder, cumin, ginger, cinnamon, allspice, and cloves.

Add the dressing to the apple mixture and mix well.

Makes four 1-cup servings

EACH SERVING CONTAINS APPROXIMATELY:
165 TOTAL CALORIES / 65 CALORIES IN FAT
0 MG CHOLESTEROL / 70 MG SODIUM / 90 MG CALCIUM

CITRUS SALAD WITH POPPY SEED DRESSING

2 large oranges (3 cups sectioned)
1 small red onion, peeled and thinly sliced (1 cup)

½ cup Poppy Seed Dressing (page 73)
Green lettuce leaves for lining plates
4 mint sprigs for garnish

Peel the oranges and divide them into sections, removing the membranes and seeds. Separate the sliced onions into rings.

Arrange the orange sections and onion rings on four chilled plates that have been lined with the green lettuce leaves. Dribble 2 tablespoons of dressing over each salad. Garnish with a sprig of mint.

Makes 4 servings

EACH SERVING CONTAINS APPROXIMATELY:
85 TOTAL CALORIES / 5 CALORIES IN FAT
0 MG CHOLESTEROL / 20 MG SODIUM
75 MG CALCIUM

SOUTHWESTERN PASTA SALAD
WITH JALAPEÑO CHUTNEY

Both vegetarian and pasta salads are increasingly popular on all menus, as are Southwestern dishes of all types. Therefore, this Southwestern vegetarian pasta salad has met with great success on the Four Seasons Hotel and Resort menu in Dallas. There it is served with Southwestern Corn Bread (page 205).

¹/₂ cup Jalapeño Chutney (page 63)
³/₄ teaspoon ground cumin
³/₄ teaspoon chili powder
1¹/₂ teaspoons balsamic vinegar
1³/₄ cups dry rotelle pasta, cooked al dente
1¹/₂ teaspoons extra-virgin olive oil
¹/₂ cup chopped scallions
1 large tomato, peeled, seeded, and diced (1 cup)
1¹/₂ cups cooked canned or frozen corn kernels
1 small green bell pepper, seeded and diced (¹/₂ cup)
1 small red bell pepper, seeded and diced (¹/₂ cup)
2 chayote squash, peeled and diced (1 cup)
¹/₄ cup chopped fresh cilantro
2 ounces Monterey Jack cheese, grated (¹/₂ cup)

Combine the chutney, cumin, chili powder, and vinegar and mix well. Combine the pasta and oil and mix well. Combine both the mixtures and again mix well. Add all the other ingredients except the cheese and mix well.

Spoon 1¹/₂ cups of salad on each of four chilled plates. Top each serving with 2 tablespoons of grated cheese.

Makes 4 servings

EACH SERVING CONTAINS APPROXIMATELY:
350 TOTAL CALORIES / 80 CALORIES IN FAT
40 MG CHOLESTEROL / 120 MG SODIUM
160 MG CALCIUM

PASTA SALAD WITH SEAFOOD

I have this salad on my light-cuisine menu at the famous Hotel del Coronado across the bridge from San Diego, California. I like the look of the pasta shells with the seafood salad. This salad is also good made with chicken or turkey and when using poultry, I use rotelle pasta because it absorbs the flavor of the marinade even better than the shells.

¹/₄ cup rice wine vinegar
1 tablespoon extra-virgin olive oil
1 cup Jalapeño Chutney (page 63)
1 small bunch scallions, chopped (³/₄ cup)
3 medium tomatoes, peeled, seeded, and diced (2 cups)
¹/₂ pound dry medium-size pasta shells, cooked (4 cups)
Green leaf lettuce leaves for lining plates
8 ounces diced cooked shrimp or other seafood, such as crab, lobster, scallops, water-packed tuna, or a combination (2 cups)
4 large whole shrimp, cooked and butterflied, for garnish (optional)

Combine the vinegar, oil, and chutney and mix well. Add the scallions, 1½ cups of the tomatoes, and the pasta and again mix well. Chill overnight.

Line four plates with the green lettuce leaves. Combine pasta mixture and seafood and mix well. Place 1½ cups of the salad on each plate. Top each serving with a butterflied shrimp if desired. Sprinkle the top with the remaining diced tomato.

Makes 4 servings

EACH SERVING CONTAINS APPROXIMATELY:
465 TOTAL CALORIES / 60 CALORIES IN FAT
130 MG CHOLESTEROL / 180 MG SODIUM
110 MG CALCIUM

PITA POCKET SANDWICH WITH TOFU SALAD

This pita pocket sandwich is a favorite poolside lunch at Fess Parker's Red Lion Resort in Santa Barbara, California. It is also often requested for the bicycle picnic lunches packed for guests to take with them along the beautiful stretch of beach in front of the resort. You may want to double the recipe for those with hearty appetites.

> *½ pound tofu, drained and mashed (1 cup)*
> *⅛ teaspoon freshly ground black pepper*
> *⅛ teaspoon red pepper flakes*
> *½ teaspoon turmeric*
> *¾ teaspoon curry powder*
> *1½ teaspoons reduced-sodium soy sauce*
> *½ teaspoon Pommery mustard*
> *2 tablespoons reduced-calorie mayonnaise*
> *½ celery rib without leaves, finely chopped*
> *½ cup water chestnuts, finely chopped*
> *½ cup scallions, finely chopped*
> *½ cup cauliflower, steamed crisp-tender and finely chopped*
> *4 whole pita pockets, halved*
> *8 tablespoons mung bean sprouts*
> *1 medium tomato, peeled, seeded, and chopped (1 cup)*
> *1 cup alfalfa sprouts*
> *Lettuce leaves for garnish*

Combine the tofu, pepper, red pepper flakes, turmeric, curry powder, soy sauce, mustard and mayonnaise and mix well. Add the celery, water chestnuts, scallions, and cauliflower and mix well.

To make the pita sandwiches, spoon ⅓ cup salad into each pita pocket. Add 1 tablespoon of mung bean sprouts, 2 tablespoons of diced tomatoes, and 2 tablespoons alfalfa sprouts. Place on a lettuce-lined plate, or in a sandwich bag to take with you.

Makes 8 pita sandwiches

EACH SANDWICH CONTAINS APPROXIMATELY:
170 TOTAL CALORIES / 30 CALORIES IN FAT
0 MG CHOLESTEROL / 245 MG SODIUM
95 MG CALCIUM

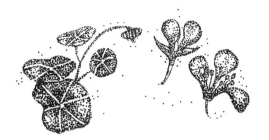

CHINESE CHICKEN SALAD

This is, hands down, the best-selling salad at the La Valencia Hotel in La Jolla, California, where it is on my light-cuisine menu. You can also use turkey, water-packed tuna, or shrimp in this salad, or a combination of any of them.

1/4 cup raw almonds, chopped
1 head Napa cabbage
1 pound raw mushrooms, sliced (4 cups)
3/4 pound cooked chicken breast, julienne cut (3 cups)
1 cup chopped scallion tops
1 cup snow peas, strings removed, ends notched in a V shape and
  blanched
1 cup fresh bean sprouts
1 cup water chestnuts, julienne cut
1 cup Mandarin Dressing (page 75)
1/4 cup julienne-cut red and yellow bell peppers for garnish
4 scallion flowers for garnish

Place the chopped almonds in a preheated 350°F oven for 8 to 10 minutes or until golden brown. Watch carefully, as they burn easily. Set aside.

Place 3 Napa cabbage leaves on each of four chilled plates for garnish. Shred the rest; you should have 4 cups. Combine the shredded cabbage, mushrooms, chicken, scallions, snow peas, bean sprouts, water chestnuts, and Mandarin Dressing and toss thoroughly.

Spoon 3 cups of the salad mixture onto each plate and top each with 1 tablespoon toasted almonds and 1 tablespoon red and yellow bell peppers. Plant a scallion flower on the top of each serving.

To make a scallion flower, cut the bulb end off the scallion just below the green top. Cut the root end off of the bulb and shred the bulb by slicing it through first in half, then in quarters, then in eighths and so on until it looks shredded. To open the scallion flower, drop it in ice water and allow it to "bloom" before using.

Makes four 3-cup servings

EACH SERVING CONTAINS APPROXIMATELY:
420 TOTAL CALORIES / 140 CALORIES IN FAT
70 MG CHOLESTEROL / 295 MG SODIUM
180 MG CALCIUM

CURRIED CHICKEN SALAD IN PINEAPPLE BOATS

Most salads are better if assembled just before serving, but with this salad it is essential to literally wait until the last minute before combining all of the component parts. The enzymes in the pineapple break down the chicken, so it becomes mushy in texture if prepared ahead of time. This salad is on my menu in the restaurant at Neiman-Marcus in Newport Beach, where I garnish it with sliced red apples for color and serve it with hot Light Cinnamon Popovers (page 203) and Apple Butter (page 61).

> *½ cup chopped raw walnuts*
> *1 fresh pineapple*
> *1 pound papaya, cut into bite-size pieces (2 cups)*
> *1 cup Curried Chutney Dressing (page 77)*
> *8 Bibb lettuce leaves for lining plates*
> *¾ pound cooked chicken breast, cut to bite-size pieces*

Place the walnuts in a preheated 350°F oven for 8 to 10 minutes or until golden brown. Watch carefully, as they burn easily. Set aside.

Cut the pineapple into quarters, leaving the leaves attached at the top. Remove the pineapple from its shell and cut into bite-size pieces to use in the salad. You should have 2 cups. Trim the pineapple leaves, cutting off any dead leaves. Set aside.

Combine the papaya, pineapple, and dressing and toss thoroughly. Line four chilled plates with 2 Bibb lettuce leaves each and place the pineapple boats on top. Just before serving, stir the chicken into the salad mixture. Spoon 1¾ cups into each pineapple boat. Top with 2 tablespoons toasted walnuts.

Makes four 1¾-cup servings

EACH SERVING CONTAINS APPROXIMATELY:
410 TOTAL CALORIES / 145 CALORIES IN FAT
70 MG CHOLESTEROL / 235 MG SODIUM
85 MG CALCIUM

BREAST OF CHICKEN SALAD WITH GOAT CHEESE AND WARM MUSHROOM DRESSING

This is my own favorite salad. I love the combination of taste, temperatures, and textures. I first had a salad similar to this in Paris several years ago and was so intrigued with it that upon my return home I immediately started experimenting with my own version, which I now serve at the Canyon Ranch Spa in Tucson, where I call it Salade Nouvelle. When asked to do a salad course for the International Food Media Conference in New York I cut this salad down in size and eliminated the chicken breast, which worked well as an appetizer rather than a main-course salad.

¼ cup chopped raw walnuts
2 heads radicchio
1¼ pounds arugula, stems removed (3 cups)

1 pound fresh mushrooms, sliced (4 cups)
³/4 cup Raspberry-Walnut Vinaigrette Dressing (page 72)
³/4 pound cooked chicken breast, cut into strips and warmed
¹/4 pound goat cheese, crumbled (1 cup)

Toast the walnuts in a preheated 350°F oven for 8 to 10 minutes or until golden brown. Watch carefully, as they burn easily. Set aside.

Separate eight radicchio leaves for lining the plates and set aside. Tear the remaining radicchio leaves and arugula into bite-size pieces. Combine the radicchio and arugula and mix well. Combine the mushrooms and the dressing in a skillet and cook until the mushrooms are just tender, about 5 minutes.

Garnish the outside edge of each of four plates with 2 radicchio leaves. Spread 1½ cups of the radicchio/arugula mixture in the center of each plate. Place 3 ounces of the warmed chicken breast on top. Sprinkle ¼ cup goat cheese over the chicken. Spoon the warm mushrooms and dressing over the top. Sprinkle 1 tablespoon of toasted walnuts over each salad.

Makes 4 servings

EACH SERVING CONTAINS APPROXIMATELY:
315 TOTAL CALORIES / 150 CALORIES IN FAT
85 MG CHOLESTEROL / 470 MG SODIUM
225 MG CALCIUM

FIESTA SALAD

Ole! This salad is a marvelous way to serve a taco in a hurry. All the ingredients are present and you can substitute ground beef, turkey, or even seafood for the chicken; or you can use beans and have a vegetarian fiesta salad. No matter what ingredients you choose, you will find this south-of-the-border salad a big hit with guests of all ages at fiestas large or small.

4 corn tortillas, cut into ¼-inch ribbons
1 head lettuce, finely chopped (6 cups)
1 cup Light Cumin Dressing (page 72)
½ pound cooked chicken, diced (2 cups)
2 cups Salsa (page 54)
1 cup corn kernels, cooked
2 ounces Cheddar or Monterey Jack cheese, grated (½ cup)
¼ cup sour cream
Green chili strips for garnish
Cilantro sprigs for garnish

Spread the tortilla ribbons on a cookie sheet. Bake in a preheated 400°F oven for 10 to 15 minutes, or until crisp and a golden brown. Stir occasionally to brown evenly. DO NOT USE THE BROILER!

For each serving, mix the chopped lettuce, dressing, and diced chicken and divide evenly onto each serving plate. Top each with ½ cup Salsa, ¼ cup corn kernels, 2 tablespoons grated cheese, and 1 tablespoon sour cream. Garnish with 2 strips of chili crossed over the top and 4 sprigs of cilantro. Arrange the tortilla ribbons around the edge of each salad.

Makes four 2½-cup servings

EACH SERVING CONTAINS APPROXIMATELY:
345 TOTAL CALORIES / 105 CALORIES IN FAT
70 MG CHOLESTEROL / 455 MG SODIUM
215 MG CALCIUM

VEGETABLES &
VEGETARIAN ENTRÉES

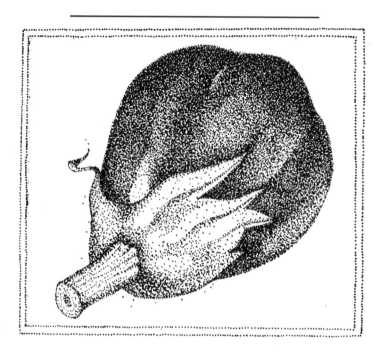

ACCORDING TO THE American Cancer Society the new superstars are the cruciferous vegetables, named for their cross-shaped flowers. They may actually help to prevent cancer. They include broccoli, brussels sprouts, cabbage, cauliflower, and kohlrabi. Many of these vegetables have had star billing in the nutrition world for a long time. Vegetable stars of longer standing that still rate top billing in the medical world include spinach, carrots, garlic, onions, and potatoes. Of these ten top stars of the vegetable world, the only one that is not a relatively common "everyday vegetable" is kohlrabi. The kohlrabi looks like a large turnip but is actually a member of the cabbage family. It can be used in recipes to replace either turnips or potatoes and adds a strong but pleasant turniplike flavor.

Other tips for using some of the star-billed vegetables include the following:

- Treat broccoli as two separate vegetables, that is, use the stems and flowerettes separately. People often cut off the top part or flowerette cluster of the broccoli and throw the stems away. However, the stems, when sliced crosswise, have a beautiful star-shaped pattern. Slice them thinly and steam them. Season them as you like and serve them as your vegetable. Very few people will know what vegetable they are eating. When using broccoli stems in this manner I call them broccoli stars. I also like to chill them and serve them in salads. They are a beautifully colorful addition and have a nice crunchy texture.
- Remember to remove the stems and veins from spinach leaves and to scrape carrots in order to get rid of the bitterness in these two vegetables.
- Always keep onions in the refrigerator. When onions are cold, they do not release the tear-producing gases for which they are so famous.
- When shredding potatoes to make hash browns or latkes, always soak them in cold water to wash away some of the potato starch. This gets rid of the gummy, chewy texture.

In this section I have given you recipes for everything from small side dishes to hearty entrées. When planning your menus, don't decide which specific vegetables you are going to serve for each meal before going to the market. Then when you're shopping, select the freshest and most attractive vegetables available. The good news is that the freshest, best-looking, and most nutritious fruits and vegetables are the ones in season and therefore they are also the least expensive.

Many of the entrées in this section are designed for vegetarians in that they contain nothing of animal origin, such as chicken stock, beef stock, or gelatin. However, there are some exceptions where stock is necessary for flavor or gelatin for texture. No vegetarian eats any part of an animal necessitating its death. Most vegetarians eat only animal by-products, such as dairy products and eggs. Vegan vegetarians, however, do not eat anything that is not of plant origin. In fact strict vegans will not even eat honey because it is made by bees. Lacto-vegetarians add dairy products, but do not eat eggs because they believe this is still a form of potential life. Lactoovo-vegetarians include both dairy products and eggs in their diet.

Also included in the vegetable category are grains and legumes (dried beans). Legumes are an excellent source of plant protein and contain valuable vitamins and minerals, and lots of fiber. When combined with grains they form a complete protein and are therefore a high-quality but very inexpensive food. Some of the more popular legumes include lentils, kidney beans, garbanzo beans (chick-peas), pinto beans, lima beans, black-eyed peas, and white beans, which are usually called navy beans because they were discovered in America and taken by ship to the rest of the world; also soybeans and all soybean products, such as tofu or soybean curd and soy milk. Even peanuts are part of the legume family and are often called the underground legumes.

When cooking beans, it is important to soak them overnight for faster cooking, removing any beans that float to the top. Then you can either cook them in their own water or drain them and cook them in fresh water or stock. Some people feel that draining the beans and starting with fresh liquid reduces some of the flatulence-producing properties. One pound of dried beans measures approximately 2 cups. After soaking they approximately double in volume, becoming 4 cups. To cook 4 cups of soaked beans, use 4 cups of water or stock. Bring the beans to a boil and then simmer them, covered, until they are tender—about 2 hours for most beans—checking on them from time to time and adding more water or stock as necessary to prevent the beans from scorching. In cooking beans I have found that the heavier the cooking pot the less likely I am to need additional liquid.

If you want beans in a hurry and don't have time to soak them overnight, cover them with cold water and bring them to a boil. Allow them to simmer for about 2 minutes and then remove them from the heat and cover them tightly, allowing them to soak for 1 hour and proceed as usual.

Most cooks use fewer varieties of grains than any other food category. Grains are wonderful from the nutrition standpoint and can add wonderful variety to your meals. Start experimenting with all of the different whole grains available on the market, such as rice, cracked wheat (bulgur), buckwheat groats (kasha), rye, millet, barley, and oats, using the package directions as your guide.

How people like their rice cooked usually depends upon their background. There are those who feel that if every grain is not separated from every other grain, the rice is ruined. There are others who feel this "fluffy" rice has no substance and want a gummy, almost chewy texture to their rice. Actually if you fall into the second category, you are less likely to be disappointed with the rice in most places because it is infinitely easier to achieve gummy rice than fluffy rice.

Brown rice, which still has its valuable bran layer, is nutritionally superior to its polished white counterpart, which has had most of the fiber removed. Short-grain brown rice has a nuttier flavor and tends to stick together more than long-grain brown rice, which is better for pilaf or just plain cooked brown rice. The short-grain variety is good for soups, casseroles, and puddings. When cooking brown rice, remember that it takes about one-third longer than white rice, so when substituting it in recipes, always allow a longer cooking time. The time can be shortened by soaking the rice prior to cooking it.

Steaming vegetables is the best method for cooking them because they retain more of their nutrients as well as their texture and color. All you need is a collapsible steamer basket and a pan with a tight-fitting lid. Add water to the pan to just below the basket level. Bring to a rapid boil, put the vegetables in the basket, and cover the pan. Set the timer, using the following steaming chart as a guide. This will give you al dente, or crisp-tender, vegetables every time. Remember, the minute you can smell a vegetable cooking, you are overcooking it. Overcooking vegetables destroys their texture and color as well as many valuable vitamins and minerals— and it smells up your house! Just as soon as the vegetables have cooked the prescribed time, remove the steamer basket from the pan and place it under cold running water. This stops the cooking process and preserves the color and texture.

This is the way most restaurants cook their vegetables; they then reheat them to serving temperature as orders come into the kitchen or refrigerate them to serve cold.

Vegetables can be reheated easily in a pan with a little water, defatted stock, juice, or wine instead of butter, margarine, or oil, and seasoned to taste. Be careful when reheating vegetables not to overcook them. Cold steamed vegetables make wonderful hors d'oeuvres and have a brighter color when used in salads than raw vegetables.

Other "light" approaches to cooking vegetables include stir-frying them without oil in the same way you would reheat steamed vegetables. Stir-fry them in either a wok or a skillet in water, defatted stock, juice, or wine. You can also blanch or parboil vege-

STEAMING TIMES FOR FRESH VEGETABLES

VEGETABLE	TIME (MINUTES)	VEGETABLE	TIME (MINUTES)
Artichokes	30	Onions:	
Asparagus	5	green tops	3
Beets, quartered	15	whole	5
Broccoli:		Parsley	1–2
branches	5	Pea pods	3
flowerettes	3–5	Peas	3–5
Brussels sprouts	5	Peppers:	
Cabbage,		chili	2–3
quartered	5	bell	2
Carrots, ½ inch		Potatoes:	
slices	5	white, sliced	10
Cauliflower:		sweet, sliced	15
flowerettes	3	Pumpkin, cut up	5
whole	5	Rhubarb	5
Celery ribs	10	Romaine lettuce	1–2
Celery root	3–4	Rutabagas	8
Chard	1–2	Shallots	2
Chives	2–3	Spinach	1–2
Cilantro	1–2	Squash:	
Corn kernels	3	acorn, cut up	5
Corn on the cob	3	banana	5
Cucumber, sliced	2–3	chayote	3
Eggplant, cut up	5	Hubbard, cut	
Garlic	5	up	5
Kohlrabi	8–10	summer	3
Leeks	5	zucchini	3
Lettuce	1–2	Tomatoes	3
Mushrooms	2	Turnips,	
Okra	5	quartered	8
		Watercress	1–2

tables by plunging them into rapidly boiling water to cook them rather than cooking them above boiling water as in steaming. This method is generally used when you wish to only partially cook a vegetable before reheating or cooking it on a grill.

Using a microwave oven is still another cooking method. Follow the directions for your own oven for the timing. You can also bake vegetables, or broil or barbecue them. Let your imagination be your guide and learn to enjoy the full range of seasonal fresh vegetables. There really is no such thing as a vegetable that is not good for you.

MARINATED MUSHROOMS

These mushrooms are wonderful in salads or on an Italian antipasto salad. I like to serve them on fancy toothpicks as hors d'oeuvres.

1 pound small mushrooms
1/2 cup red wine vinegar
1/3 cup water
2 tablespoons corn oil
3/4 teaspoon fructose or 1 teaspoon sugar
1 tablespoon finely chopped onion
1 tablespoon finely chopped parsley
1/2 teaspoon dried basil, crushed in a mortar and pestle
2 garlic cloves, finely chopped (2 teaspoons)
1/4 teaspoon salt
1/4 teaspoon freshly ground black pepper

Clean the mushrooms, cutting off the ends of the stems and leaving them whole. Set aside. Place all the other ingredients in a large saucepan and bring to a boil. Add the mushrooms and bring to a boil again. Reduce the heat and simmer, uncovered, for 5 to 10 minutes or until the mushrooms are tender.

Cool to room temperature. Refrigerate in a covered container for several hours before serving.

Makes 3 cups

1/4 CUP CONTAINS APPROXIMATELY:
35 TOTAL CALORIES / 20 CALORIES IN FAT
0 MG CHOLESTEROL / 45 MG SODIUM
5 MG CALCIUM

EGGPLANT RELISH

This relish is excellent as either a spread or a dip. I like to serve it on small rounds of crusty Italian bread garnished with sprigs of Italian parsley as an appetizer or hors d'oeuvre. It can also be served warm as a vegetable side dish. It is particularly good with fish.

> *1 eggplant, halved (1 1/2 pounds)*
> *Salt*
> *Nonstick vegetable coating*
> *1 tablespoon extra-virgin olive oil*
> *1/4 cup finely chopped shallots*
> *1/4 cup finely chopped onion*
> *1 garlic clove, finely chopped (1 teaspoon)*
> *1/2 cup chopped parsley*
> *4 teaspoons freshly squeezed lemon juice*
> *1/8 teaspoon salt*
> *1/8 teaspoon freshly ground black pepper*

Sprinkle the cut sides of the eggplant with salt and let stand for 30 minutes. Rinse thoroughly and pat dry.

Spray a cookie sheet with nonstick vegetable coating and place the eggplant on it cut side down. Preheat the oven to 375°F and bake for 40 minutes. Cool.

Heat 1 teaspoon of the olive oil in a large skillet. Add the shallots, onions, and garlic and cook over low heat until soft, about 5 minutes.

Peel and chop the eggplant and add the cooked mixture, the remaining 2 teaspoons olive oil, the parsley, lemon juice, salt, and pepper. Mix well. Chill for at least 2 hours.

Makes 2 cups

1/4 CUP CONTAINS APPROXIMATELY:
45 TOTAL CALORIES / 15 CALORIES IN FAT
0 MG CHOLESTEROL / 40 MG SODIUM
40 MG CALCIUM

CREAMED LEEKS

This vegetable side dish is incredibly rich-tasting to be so low in calories. I like it much better than the classic approach to creamed leeks, which are actually done in butter and reduced cream. The delicate flavor of the leek is more pronounced in this lower-fat version.

1 1/2 teaspoons corn-oil margarine
1 pound leeks, white part only, coarsely chopped (4 cups)
1/4 cup low-fat milk

Heat the margarine in a skillet and add the leeks. Cook, covered, for 3 minutes. Add the milk and reduce until the liquid disappears.

Makes four 1/2-cup servings

EACH SERVING CONTAINS APPROXIMATELY:
85 TOTAL CALORIES / 20 CALORIES IN FAT
1 MG CHOLESTEROL / 30 MG SODIUM
85 MG CALCIUM

LEEK AND ONION AU GRATIN

I have given you a recipe for 8 servings of this as a vegetable side dish because it is so good served in larger portions as a vegetarian entrée with a big green salad and fresh fruit for dessert.

1 slice whole wheat bread
1/4 pound mozzarella cheese, grated (1 cup)
1/4 pound Monterey Jack cheese, grated (1 cup)
1 pound leeks, white part only, sliced (4 cups)
3 medium onions, sliced (6 cups)
1/2 cup chopped chives

½ teaspoon dried oregano, crushed in a mortar and pestle
½ teaspoon dried basil, crushed in a mortar and pestle
½ teaspoon dried tarragon, crushed in a mortar and pestle
¼ teaspoon salt
⅛ teaspoon freshly ground black pepper
½ cup vermouth

Preheat the oven to 350°F. Place the bread in a blender and convert to bread crumbs. You should have ½ cup. Combine the grated cheeses with the bread crumbs and set aside.

In a separate bowl, combine all the remaining ingredients except for the vermouth.

Spread half the onion mixture in a 9-by-13-inch glass baking dish. Top with half of the cheese mixture. Repeat the layers. Pour the vermouth over the top.

Cover tightly and bake for 1 hour.

Makes 8 servings

EACH SERVING CONTAINS APPROXIMATELY:
195 TOTAL CALORIES / 70 CALORIES IN FAT
20 MG CHOLESTEROL / 225 MG SODIUM
250 MG CALCIUM

SPINACH TIMBALES

It is important to remove the stems and veins from spinach leaves to get rid of the bitterness of the spinach. To devein a spinach leaf, fold the leaf lengthwise and grasp it near the stem end. Then carefully pull the stem toward the outer end of the leaf, removing the large center vein and the larger side vein along with it. If fresh spinach is not available, you may substitute two packages of frozen spinach, thawed and well drained. It is not necessary to cook frozen spinach because it has already been blanched before freezing. When using frozen spinach, the flavor and texture will not be as good as if you use fresh spinach because it is impossible to remove the stems and veins. These timbales are an excellent side dish with fish, poultry, or meat. They also add variety to a strictly vegetarian plate. They are even good cold, served with cold cuts or as a salad plate. When serving them cold, I like to top them with a little Creamy Curry Dressing (page 70).

> *2 pounds spinach*
> *1 teaspoon corn-oil margarine*
> *1 tablespoon flour*
> *1/2 cup skim milk*
> *1/4 teaspoon salt*
> *1/8 teaspoon ground nutmeg*
> *1/8 teaspoon freshly ground black pepper*
> *3 egg whites, lightly beaten*
> *Nonstick vegetable coating*

Preheat the oven to 400°F. Carefully clean the spinach, removing the stems and veins. Steam the spinach for 2 minutes. Squeeze it dry and chop it finely using the metal blade of a food processor. This should make about 1⅓ cups chopped spinach.

Melt the margarine in a saucepan. Add the flour, stirring constantly, and cook for 3 minutes; do not brown. Add the milk and continue to cook, stirring constantly with a wire whisk, until sauce thickens. Add the seasonings and mix well.

Combine the sauce with the spinach and the beaten egg whites. Mix well.

Spray four 3-inch ramekins with a nonstick vegetable coating. Divide the spinach mixture evenly among the ramekins. Place in a baking pan. Pour boiling water around the ramekins to a depth of ¾ inch. Bake for 20 minutes or until a knife inserted in the center of a timbale comes out clean. Let stand for 5 minutes before unmolding.

To unmold, run a knife around the inside of the ramekin and invert the mold over a serving plate.

Makes 4 timbales

EACH TIMBALE CONTAINS APPROXIMATELY:
50 TOTAL CALORIES / 10 CALORIES IN FAT
1 MG CHOLESTEROL / 235 MG SODIUM
125 MG CALCIUM

TZIMMES

I originally developed this recipe for one of my readers, who requested a low-fat version of his mother's tzimmes recipe to serve for a Jewish holiday. I was delighted when he wrote back and told me his mother liked it so much that she wanted "his" recipe.

5 small carrots, peeled and grated (2½ cups)
1 small sweet potato, peeled and grated (2 cups)
1 apple, peeled and grated (1 cup)
½ cup water
¼ teaspoon salt
¼ teaspoon freshly grated nutmeg
1 tablespoon matzo meal
2 tablespoons frozen unsweetened apple juice concentrate

Combine all the ingredients in a large saucepan. Cook, covered, over low heat for 1 hour. Serve either hot or cold.

Makes 3 cups

¼ CUP CONTAINS APPROXIMATELY:
60 TOTAL CALORIES / N CALORIES IN FAT
0 MG CHOLESTEROL / 70 MG SODIUM
10 MG CALCIUM

VEGETABLE TERRINE

This is a recipe I developed working with the talented chefs of the Four Seasons Hotels when we were all in Toronto designing the alternative recipes for their menus. The vegetables I have selected for the recipe will give you a brilliant and beautiful combination of colors and textures; however, it certainly isn't necessary to follow this recipe exactly. A terrine can be an extremely creative way of using the leftover vegetables you have in your refrigerator. The only real trick to this recipe involves using either an electric slicer or a mandolin, a slicing tool available in gourmet shops and commercial restaurant supply stores, because it is very difficult to slice the vegetables thinly enough by hand. Slice all the vegetables but the broccoli with an electric slicer or mandolin.

In this recipe I suggest plating the terrine on the Roasted Red Pepper Sauce simply because the colors contrast each other so wonderfully. It is also good with either Creamy Curry Sauce (page 70) or the Walnut-Dill Sauce (page 69) or any of the vegetable sauces. You may even want to serve it without a sauce, plated on a lettuce leaf with Raspberry-Walnut Vinaigrette Dressing (page 72) on the side.

3 1/2 cups defatted chicken stock, chilled (see page 22)
1/4 cup loosely packed fresh tarragon, thyme, or basil
1 teaspoon dried tarragon, crushed in a mortar and pestle
2 ounces mushrooms, thinly sliced (1/2 cup)
1 medium onion, thinly sliced (2 cups)
4 large Napa cabbage leaves
2 small yellow squash, thinly sliced lengthwise (6 ounces)
2 small zucchini squash, thinly sliced lengthwise (1/2 pound)
1 small red bell pepper, thinly sliced (1 cup)
2 small carrots, scraped and thinly sliced lengthwise (1/4 pound)
1 cup broccoli in small flowerettes
2 envelopes unflavored gelatin
2 cups Roasted Red Pepper Sauce (page 69)
Tarragon sprigs for garnish

Combine 3 cups of the chicken stock, the fresh herbs, and the dried tarragon and bring to a boil. Blanch the mushrooms in stock until just fork tender. Drain, reserving the stock. Return the stock to the saucepan and cook the onions until soft. Drain and again reserve the stock.

Steam the Napa cabbage leaves for 15 seconds or until soft and pliable. Individually steam each of the other vegetables until just crisp-tender. Place each vegetable under cold running water after cooking to preserve the color and texture. Drain well.

Soften the gelatin in the remaining ½ cup of chicken stock (it should be cool) for 5 minutes. Measure 1¾ cups of the remaining heated chicken stock, reserving the rest for future use. Bring to a boil. Remove from the heat and stir in the softened gelatin until it is completely dissolved.

Oil a glass loaf pan. Spoon 2 tablespoons of the stock onto the bottom of the pan. Place 2 of the Napa cabbage leaves on the bottom and one side of the pan, the leafy part on bottom. Trim to fit. Place the other 2 leaves on the opposite side, leafy part hanging over the outside rim. Spoon 2 tablespoons of the stock over the cabbage. Sprinkle the mushrooms over this stock. Layer the remaining vegetables by color, pouring ¼ cup stock between each layer. Fold the cabbage over the final layer and pour the remaining stock over the cabbage. Press down gently with your fingers. Cover with plastic wrap and refrigerate overnight or until completely set.

To serve, unmold the terrine and slice very carefully with a serrated knife. Pour ¼ cup of the Roasted Red Pepper Sauce on each plate and turn the plate so the sauce covers the entire bottom of the plate inside the rim. Place a slice of terrine on the sauce and garnish with a fresh tarragon sprig.

Makes 8 servings

EACH SERVING CONTAINS APPROXIMATELY:
115 TOTAL CALORIES / 50 CALORIES IN FAT
0 MG CHOLESTEROL / 110 MG SODIUM
85 MG CALCIUM

QUICK CHILI

As the title suggests, this recipe takes very little time to make. Because it is a completely vegetarian dish it keeps for a long time in the refrigerator. I have had lots of competing athletes tell me that this chili and a bowl of brown rice comprise one of their favorite carbohydrate-loading meals because it is so easy to make and so inexpensive.

> *3 medium onions, finely chopped (4½ cups)*
> *2 garlic cloves, finely chopped (2 teaspoons)*
> *½ cup canned chopped green California chilies, undrained*
> *1 tablespoon chili powder*
> *2 teaspoons dried oregano, crushed in a mortar and pestle*
> *2 teaspoons ground cumin*
> *One 10-ounce can diced tomatoes, drained*
> *2½ cups dry kidney beans, cooked (6 cups), or one 46-ounce can, undrained*

Combine the onions and garlic and cook in a large saucepan, covered, over low heat until soft, adding a little water if necessary to prevent scorching.

Add all the other ingredients except the beans. Mix thoroughly and bring to a boil. Simmer for 10 minutes. Add the cooked beans, mix well, and heat thoroughly.

Makes 6 cups

1 CUP CONTAINS APPROXIMATELY:
280 TOTAL CALORIES / 15 CALORIES IN FAT
0 MG CHOLESTEROL / 100 MG SODIUM
135 MG CALCIUM

RATATOUILLE

Ratatouille, the classic French vegetable stew, is very versatile. It's easy to make, keeps well in the refrigerator for over a week, and is equally good served hot or cold. I like it for hors d'oeuvres cold as a spread with crusty French bread. For a hot hors d'oeuvre or appetizer course, I stuff giant pasta shells with the ratatouille, topped with melted part-skim mozzarella cheese. I also serve ratatouille au gratin as an entrée at the Canyon Ranch Spa in Tucson. I put 1½ cups of the ratatouille in an au gratin dish and top it with ¼ cup grated part-skim mozzarella cheese, then place it in a preheated 350°F oven for about 10 minutes or until the ratatouille is hot and the cheese is melted.

¼ cup water
2 garlic cloves, minced (2 teaspoons)
1 tablespoon extra-virgin olive oil
1 medium onion, thinly sliced (2 cups)
2 green or red bell peppers, seeded and chopped (1½ cups)
1 medium eggplant, cubed (6 cups)
2 zucchini, cut into rounds (4 cups)
4 large tomatoes, cut into wedges
¼ cup finely chopped parsley
¼ teaspoon freshly ground black pepper
½ teaspoon salt
½ teaspoon dried rosemary, crushed in a mortar and pestle
1 teaspoon dried basil, crushed in a mortar and pestle
1 teaspoon dried thyme, crushed in a mortar and pestle
1 teaspoon dried marjoram, crushed in a mortar and pestle

Combine the water and garlic in a large saucepan and cook slowly until the water has evaporated. Add the olive oil and continue cooking until the garlic is soft, without browning it.

Add the onions, peppers, eggplant, and zucchini and cook for 5 minutes, stirring frequently.

Add the tomatoes and all the seasonings and mix well. Continue to cook over low heat, stirring frequently, for 1 hour. If you prefer a real "French-style" ratatouille, continue cooking for another hour or two, just as you would any other stew.

Makes six 1-cup servings

EACH SERVING CONTAINS APPROXIMATELY:
120 TOTAL CALORIES / 30 CALORIES IN FAT
0 MG CHOLESTEROL / 205 MG SODIUM
100 MG CALCIUM

EGGPLANT FLORENTINE

When fresh spinach is not available, this recipe can be made with two packages of frozen chopped spinach, thawed and thoroughly drained; however, as I mentioned in the recipe for Spinach Timbales (page 110), it is not necessary to steam the frozen spinach, and the appearance and flavor of the dish will not be as good as if using fresh spinach. A delicious variation is to use 4 ounces of tofu per serving to replace the eggplant. For a nonvegetarian entrée this dish is also good made with oysters, clams, or scallops instead of eggplant.

> *1 medium eggplant*
> *Salt*
> *2 pounds fresh spinach (8 cups packed)*
> *2 cups Mornay Sauce (page 51)*
> *1 ounce imported Parmesan cheese, freshly grated (¼ cup)*

Peel the eggplant and slice it crosswise into rounds approximately ¼ inch thick. Put these into a glass baking dish and sprinkle with salt on both sides. Cover and allow to stand for 1 hour. Pour off the liquid and rinse the eggplant thoroughly. This step removes the bitterness from the eggplant.

Carefully wash the spinach to remove all grit. Remove the stems and veins. Chop coarsely and steam for 1 minute. Rinse with cold water and set aside.

Steam the eggplant until it can be pierced easily with a fork, about 4 minutes.

Preheat the oven to 350°F. Line the bottom of an 8-by-8-inch baking dish with spinach. Place the eggplant slices on top of the spinach and cover with the Mornay Sauce. Sprinkle evenly with the Parmesan cheese. Bake for 10 minutes, then brown lightly under the broiler.

Makes 4 servings

EACH SERVING CONTAINS APPROXIMATELY:
250 TOTAL CALORIES / 50 CALORIES IN FAT
15 MG CHOLESTEROL / 605 MG SODIUM
680 MG CALCIUM

SPANISH RICE

I serve this dish in spas as a vegetarian entrée, adding lentils to it
to make it a complete protein. I also use it as stuffing for bell
peppers and acorn squash. I have also served it cold as a rice salad
for picnics.

> *1 1/2 teaspoons extra-virgin olive oil*
> *1 medium onion, chopped (1 1/2 cups)*
> *1 red bell pepper, seeded and chopped (1 cup)*
> *1 cup quick-cooking long-grain brown rice*
> *1 1/4 cups water or vegetable stock (see page 27), heated*
> *1 cup tomato sauce*
> *1/4 teaspoon dried saffron*
> *1/4 teaspoon ground fennel*
> *1/4 teaspoon salt*
> *1/4 teaspoon freshly ground black pepper*
> *1/2 cup frozen peas, unthawed*

Heat the olive oil in a medium saucepan over low heat. Add the
onions and peppers. Sauté slowly, stirring constantly, until soft,
about 10 minutes. Add the rice and cook until the rice is golden,
stirring frequently. Add the heated water or vegetable stock, the
tomato sauce, saffron, fennel, salt, and pepper and mix well. Cover
and cook over low heat for 20 minutes or until the rice is tender
and liquid has been absorbed.

Stir in the peas and let stand, covered, for 5 minutes.

Makes 4 cups

1/2 CUP CONTAINS APPROXIMATELY:
130 TOTAL CALORIES / 15 CALORIES IN FAT
0 MG CHOLESTEROL / 260 MG SODIUM
25 MG CALCIUM

RICE PILAF

Like Spanish Rice (page 118), this Rice Pilaf recipe lends itself well to variations. You can add fish, poultry, or meat or drained water-packed tuna for a delicious hot entrée or serve it cold as a rice salad.

1 1/2 teaspoons corn oil
3/4 cup long-grain brown rice
1/2 medium onion, thinly sliced (1 cup)
1 tablespoon reduced-sodium soy sauce
1 1/2 teaspoons fresh thyme, finely chopped, or 1/2 teaspoon dried
*   thyme, crushed in a mortar and pestle*
1 cup defatted chicken stock (see page 22)

Heat the oil in a heavy skillet. Add the rice and the onion slices and cook, stirring frequently, until brown.

Add the soy sauce and thyme to the chicken stock in a small saucepan and bring to a boil.

Put the rice mixture in a baking pan and add the hot stock. Stir, then cover tightly. Place in a preheated 400°F oven for 40 minutes. Remove and allow to stand for 10 minutes more before removing the cover.

To reheat, add 2 to 3 tablespoons of stock to the cold rice and mix thoroughly. Cover and heat slowly in a preheated 300°F oven for about 25 minutes.

Makes 3 cups

1/2 CUP CONTAINS APPROXIMATELY:
115 TOTAL CALORIES / 15 CALORIES IN FAT
0 MG CHOLESTEROL / 185 MG SODIUM
15 MG CALCIUM

LIGHT POLENTA

The original version of this recipe was served at the International Food Media Conference in New York City, where it was prepared for us by Palio's Restaurant. It was fabulous, but when I saw the recipe I realized that I wouldn't dare eat it very often and decided to try to find a way to make it lower in calories, cholesterol, and sodium. I have also made it easier to prepare so that you can enjoy polenta more often and with less effort!

POLENTA:

> *2 1/4 cups water*
> *1/2 cup yellow cornmeal*
> *1 1/2 teaspoons corn-oil margarine*

RICOTTA SAUCE:

> *1 cup part-skim ricotta cheese*
> *1/3 cup low-fat milk*
> *1/8 teaspoon freshly grated nutmeg*

FONTINELLA SAUCE:

> *4 ounces Fontinella cheese, diced (1 cup)*
> *2 tablespoons low-fat milk*
> *3 spinach leaves, deveined*
> *Fresh herbs for garnish (basil, oregano, thyme, or Italian parsley)*

To prepare the polenta, bring the water to a boil. Slowly add the cornmeal, stirring constantly with a wire whisk. Reduce the heat to medium and continue to cook, uncovered, stirring occasionally, for 30 minutes. Remove from the heat and whisk in the corn-oil margarine. Pour 1/3 cup of the mixture into each of four 3-inch ramekins. Keep warm in a very low oven until ready to serve.

Combine the ricotta sauce ingredients in a blender and blend until smooth. Pour into a saucepan and heat to simmering, stirring frequently. DO NOT BOIL.

Heat the Fontinella cheese and milk in the top of a double boiler over simmering water until the cheese has melted. While the cheese is melting, place the spinach leaves in boiling water until soft. Remove from the water and drain thoroughly. Combine the melted cheese and spinach leaves in a blender and blend until smooth.

To serve, spoon ¼ cup of the ricotta sauce on each of four salad-size plates. Unmold a polenta on top of the ricotta sauce. Top with 2 tablespoons of Fontinella sauce and garnish with a sprig of fresh herb, such as basil, oregano, thyme, or Italian parsley.

Makes 4 servings

EACH SERVING CONTAINS APPROXIMATELY:
420 CALORIES / 135 CALORIES IN FAT
40 MG CHOLESTEROL / 360 MG SODIUM
425 MG CALCIUM

SCALLOPED POTATOES

If you like scalloped potatoes but rarely eat them because they are so fattening, you are going to love this recipe. I developed it for one of my readers, who was put on a low-fat diet and missed scalloped potatoes more than anything else. I have since used it on spa menus and received raves from the guests.

Nonstick vegetable coating
2 medium White Rose potatoes, peeled and thinly sliced (3 cups)
1 tablespoon flour
¼ teaspoon salt
Freshly ground black pepper to taste
½ medium onion, thinly sliced (1 cup)
1½ teaspoons corn-oil margarine
1 cup low-fat milk

Preheat the oven to 350°F. Spray a loaf pan or baking dish with nonstick vegetable coating.

Layer one-third of the potatoes in the bottom of the pan and sprinkle with one-half of the flour, ⅛ teaspoon of the salt, and the pepper to taste. Top with one-half of the onions.

Repeat with another layer of potatoes, flour, salt, pepper, and onions.

Top with the final third of potatoes. Dot with margarine and pour the milk over the top. Bake for 1 hour, uncovered. Turn the heat up to 375°F and bake for 30 minutes more.

Makes six ¾-cup servings

EACH SERVING CONTAINS APPROXIMATELY:
100 TOTAL CALORIES / 20 CALORIES IN FAT
5 MG CHOLESTEROL / 120 MG SODIUM
70 MG CALCIUM

OVEN FRIES

If you love French fries, but are fighting fat, try making these Oven Fries. You will be surprised how much more flavorful they are—you can actually taste the potato!

Nonstick vegetable coating
2 unpeeled baking potatoes, cut into strips

Spray a baking sheet heavily with nonstick vegetable coating. Arrange the potato strips so that they do not overlap.

Bake for 1 hour in a preheated 375°F oven, turning every 15 minutes for even browning.

Makes 4 servings

EACH SERVING CONTAINS APPROXIMATELY:
110 TOTAL CALORIES / N CALORIES IN FAT
0 MG CHOLESTEROL / 10 MG SODIUM
10 MG CALCIUM

LIGHT LATKES AND APPLESAUCE

I developed these light latkes originally for a Hanukkah menu in an article in *San Diego Magazine.* The oil traditionally used for frying the latkes is there for the same symbolic purpose, but in an infinitely smaller amount.

> *3 medium potatoes, peeled and grated (2½ cups)*
> *2 tablespoons finely chopped onion*
> *1 egg, lightly beaten*
> *¼ teaspoon salt*
> *⅛ teaspoon baking powder*
> *1½ tablespoons matzo meal or whole wheat flour*
> *1 teaspoon corn oil*
> *1 cup Baked Applesauce (page 231) (optional)*
> *1 cup Light Sour Cream (page 53) (optional)*

Place the grated potatoes in a bowl with water to cover and let stand 12 hours.

Drain the potatoes well in a strainer or colander and press out any excess moisture. Place in a mixing bowl and add the onion and beaten egg. Mix well.

Combine the salt, baking powder, and matzo meal or flour and slowly add to the potato mixture. Mix thoroughly.

Heat a skillet until a drop of water dances around on it before evaporating.

Drop the mixture by tablespoonsful onto the hot, lightly oiled skillet. Cook on one side until well browned; turn over and brown on the other side.

Serve ¼ cup Baked Applesauce and ¼ cup Light Sour Cream with each serving if desired.

Makes 8 latkes

EACH LATKE CONTAINS APPROXIMATELY:
35 TOTAL CALORIES / 5 CALORIES IN FAT
15 MG CHOLESTEROL / 75 MG SODIUM
10 MG CALCIUM

CANYON RANCH STUFFED SPUD

This popular luncheon entrée at the Canyon Ranch Spa in Tucson made its photographic debut in *Vogue* magazine several years ago. The *Vogue* photographers were at the spa to photograph Jane Seymour and her baby daughter. A full-page color picture of Jane and her daughter sharing the Canyon Ranch Stuffed Spud was used in the magazine. This recipe is easy, inexpensive, and surprisingly delicious.

> *2 small baking potatoes*
> *1 medium onion, finely chopped (1 1/2 cups)*
> *1/4 cup buttermilk*
> *1/2 cup low-fat cottage cheese*
> *3 tablespoons grated Parmesan or Romano cheese*
> *2 tablespoons chopped scallions, including the tops*

Wash the potatoes well. Pierce with the tines of a fork and bake in a preheated 400°F oven for 1 hour.

Cut a very thin slice from the top of each potato. Remove the pulp from the potatoes, being careful not to tear the shells. Mash the potato pulp and set aside in a covered bowl. Keep the shells warm.

Cook the onions, covered, over low heat until soft, adding a little water if necessary to prevent scorching. Add the mashed potatoes and all the other ingredients except the chopped scallions. Mix well and heat thoroughly. Stuff the potato mixture back into the warm shells. They will be heaping way over the top!

To serve, sprinkle the top of each Stuffed Spud with 1 tablespoon of chopped scallions. If you have prepared them in advance, reheat in a 350°F oven for 10 to 15 minutes or until hot before adding the chopped scallions.

Makes 2 servings

EACH SERVING CONTAINS APPROXIMATELY:
245 TOTAL CALORIES / 30 CALORIES IN FAT
10 MG CHOLESTEROL / 415 MG SODIUM
220 MG CALCIUM

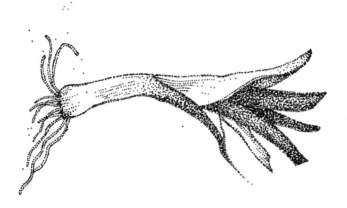

COLCANNON-STUFFED POTATOES

This stuffed potato contains the classic Irish cabbage-and-potato mixture frequently served for Irish get-togethers and is always a real hit on Saint Patrick's Day.

4 medium baking potatoes
4 cups green cabbage, shredded
3 tablespoons corn-oil margarine
1/2 cup skim milk, heated to lukewarm
4 scallions, including 2 inches of tops, finely chopped (3/4 cup)
1/2 teaspoon salt
1/2 teaspoon caraway seeds
Freshly ground black pepper to taste
1/4 cup finely chopped fresh parsley for garnish

Wash the potatoes thoroughly, dry, and pierce with a fork. Bake in a preheated 400°F oven for 1 hour. Remove from the oven and cool slightly.

While the potatoes are cooling, put the shredded cabbage into a pan with water to cover. Bring to a boil. Boil rapidly, uncovered, for 8 minutes. Drain thoroughly and set aside.

When the potatoes are cool enough to handle, split them down the center and carefully remove the pulp from the shells, being careful not to tear the shells. Set the shells aside to refill with the colcannon mixture.

Combine the potato pulp with the margarine. Mash thoroughly. Beat the potatoes, adding milk a little at a time. Add more milk, if necessary, to achieve a creamy consistency.

Add the cabbage to the potato mixture. Add the scallions, salt, caraway seeds, and pepper and mix thoroughly. Refill the potato shells with the colcannon mixture. Garnish each potato with fresh parsley. Note: If making ahead of time and reheating, add the parsley just before serving.

Makes 4 servings

EACH SERVING CONTAINS APPROXIMATELY:
270 TOTAL CALORIES / 80 CALORIES IN FAT
1 MG CHOLESTEROL / 320 MG SODIUM
115 MG CALCIUM

PIZZA

Pizza lovers of the world, rejoice! You can now have your pizza and eat it without guilt. If you really want to be a purist, try serving it with one of the new nonalcoholic beers for your own spa party. Of course you can add any of the suggested toppings touted by all pizza parlors, but this vegetarian version is truly delicious and much lower in calories.

SAUCE:

1/2 medium onion, finely chopped (3/4 cup)
1 garlic clove, finely chopped (1 teaspoon)
1/4 cup finely chopped parsley
1 tablespoon water
One 6-ounce can tomato paste
1/2 teaspoon dried oregano, crushed in a mortar and pestle
1/4 teaspoon dried basil, crushed in a mortar and pestle

¹/₄ teaspoon salt
¹/₈ teaspoon freshly ground black pepper

1 Pizza Crust (page 204)
1 medium onion, sliced (2 cups)
¹/₄ pound mushrooms, thinly sliced (1 cup)
¹/₂ small green bell pepper, sliced (¹/₂ cup)
¹/₂ small red bell pepper, sliced (¹/₂ cup)
1 small zucchini, thinly sliced (1 cup)
6 ounces part-skim mozzarella cheese, sliced

Preheat the oven to 425°F.

Sauté the chopped onions, garlic, and parsley in the water until soft. Remove from the heat and add the tomato paste, oregano, basil, salt, and pepper. Mix well.

Spread the sauce over the pizza crust. Arrange the sliced onions, mushrooms, peppers, and zucchini decoratively on top of the sauce. Bake for 10 minutes on the lowest shelf of the oven.

Place the cheese slices on the pizza and bake for an additional 15 minutes. Allow to stand for 3 to 5 minutes before slicing. If the pizza begins to brown too much before the crust is done, place a square of aluminum foil lightly over the top and continue to bake until the bottom crust is lightly browned. Cut into 6 pie-shaped wedges.

Makes 6 servings

EACH SERVING CONTAINS APPROXIMATELY:
260 TOTAL CALORIES / 75 CALORIES IN FAT
20 MG CHOLESTEROL / 395 MG SODIUM
330 MG CALCIUM

QUESADILLA

This quesadilla is one of the most popular items on my menus in spas, hotels, and restaurants alike. Many people have told me this is their favorite Quesadilla served anywhere and much prefer it to the high-calorie version served in Mexican restaurants. I recently co-hosted a party in New York City with Enid Zuckerman, the owner of the Canyon Ranch Spa. I decided to do a Southwestern menu and used this recipe for a Quesadilla, but instead of the vegetarian version, I added lobster and served the Lobster Quesadilla with a Fiesta Salad (page 100).

Corn-oil margarine
Four 12-inch whole wheat flour tortillas
¼ pound part-skim mozzarella cheese, grated (1 cup)
¼ pound Monterey Jack cheese, grated (1 cup)
½ cup canned green California chilies, seeded and finely chopped
½ cup finely chopped scallions
½ small head lettuce, shredded, for garnish (2 cups)
1 cup Salsa (page 54)
Fresh cilantro sprigs for garnish

For *each* quesadilla, using a paper towel, rub the inner surface of a large skillet with corn-oil margarine. Place one of the tortillas in the pan and cook until lightly browned on one side. Turn over and sprinkle ¼ cup of each of the cheeses evenly over the tortilla.

Sprinkle 2 tablespoons of the chilies and 2 tablespoons of the scallions evenly over the cheese. Cook until the cheese is melted. Fold in half and cut into three pie-shaped wedges.

Serve on a plate garnished with ½ cup of the shredded lettuce and a ramekin of ¼ cup fresh Salsa. Place 1 cilantro sprig on each serving.

Makes 4 servings

EACH SERVING CONTAINS APPROXIMATELY:
355 TOTAL CALORIES / 160 CALORIES IN FAT
40 MG CHOLESTEROL / 600 MG SODIUM
450 MG CALCIUM

BEAN BURRITOS

I purposely separated this bean burrito recipe into two steps—the filling and the actual burritos. The reason I did this it is that is just as easy to make 6 cups of the filling as it is to make 2 cups, and it freezes very well. I also like to serve the burrito filling instead of Mexican refried beans as a side dish with all Mexican entrées or just with rice for a vegetarian entrée.

1 1/2 cups dry pinto beans
1/2 medium onion, chopped (3/4 cup)
1 garlic clove, minced (1 teaspoon)
1/2 teaspoon freshly ground black pepper
1 teaspoon salt
1 1/2 medium onions, chopped (2 1/2 cups)
5 medium tomatoes, chopped (3 cups)
1/4 cup finely chopped cilantro
1/3 cup canned chopped green California chilies
1/2 teaspoon cumin
1 1/2 teaspoons chili powder
8 whole wheat flour tortillas

The day before serving, place the beans, 3/4 cup of onion, the garlic and pepper in a heavy kettle. Cover them with boiling water. Simmer, covered, over medium heat for 2 1/2 to 3 1/2 hours, until the beans are tender. Add additional boiling water as needed to ensure ample broth. When the beans are tender, stir in the salt and let them cool. Store in the refrigerator.

The day of serving, drain the beans, reserving 1 cup of broth. Place the beans in a food processor. Add the reserved broth and process until the consistency of refried beans is attained.

In a nonstick pan, cook the 2 1/2 cups of onion and the tomato until soft. Add the beans, cilantro, chilies, cumin, and chili powder. Cook, uncovered, over medium heat, stirring occasionally until the liquid is reduced and the beans do not run when spooned onto a plate.

Wrap the tortillas in foil and warm them in a preheated 375°F oven for 10 minutes. To serve, spoon 1/2 cup of the bean mixture onto the lower half of each tortilla. Bring the bottom of the tortilla up over the beans. Fold in the sides of the tortilla, then roll it the rest of the way around the beans.

Makes 8 burritos

EACH BURRITO CONTAINS APPROXIMATELY:
240 TOTAL CALORIES / 45 CALORIES IN FAT
0 MG CHOLESTEROL / 595 MG SODIUM
65 MG CALCIUM

MEXICAN SPAGHETTI

I am always trying to figure out new and unusual ways of combining popular and healthy ingredients. Spaghetti is one of the most popular ingredients with people of all ages and so is anything in the Mexican flavor range; so I decided to create Mexican Spaghetti. Whenever I mention Mexican Spaghetti, I am always asked what it is. The recipe is the answer. I like to serve it topped with grated Monterey Jack cheese rather than the Parmesan, which I like better on Italian spaghetti. The Mexican sauce is also good on any other pasta or rice, beans, fish, poultry, or meat.

1 medium onion, finely chopped (1½ cups)
2 garlic cloves, finely chopped (2 teaspoons)
One 28-ounce can solid-pack tomatoes, undrained
One 6-ounce can tomato paste
¾ cup water
¼ cup red wine
1 teaspoon fructose or 1½ teaspoons sugar
1 celery rib, without leaves, chopped (½ cup)
2 tablespoons chopped cilantro
1 bay leaf
1 teaspoon salt
¼ teaspoon freshly ground black pepper
¾ teaspoon ground cumin

1 1/2 teaspoons chili powder
1/2 teaspoon dried oregano, crushed in a mortar and pestle
1/2 teaspoon dried thyme, crushed in a mortar and pestle
2 dashes Tabasco
1/2 pound dry spaghetti (4 cups cooked)
4 cilantro sprigs for garnish

Combine the onions and garlic and cook, covered, in a saucepan over low heat until tender, 8 to 10 minutes, adding a little water if necessary to prevent scorching. Set aside.

In another saucepan, combine the tomatoes, tomato paste, water, and wine. Bring to a boil, then reduce to simmer. Add the onion mixture, fructose or sugar, celery, cilantro, bay leaf, and all the seasonings. Simmer for 1 hour, adding water if too thick. Remove and discard the bay leaf.

Cook the spaghetti in 3 quarts of boiling water until al dente, about 10 minutes. Drain thoroughly.

To serve, place 1 cup spaghetti on each plate and top with 1 cup sauce. Garnish with a sprig of cilantro.

Makes 4 servings

EACH SERVING CONTAINS APPROXIMATELY:
265 TOTAL CALORIES / 10 CALORIES IN FAT
0 MG CHOLESTEROL / 630 MG SODIUM
135 MG CALCIUM

PASTA PRIMAVERA

This Pasta Primavera is a big hit on my menu in the restaurant at Neiman-Marcus in Newport Beach, California. Pasta Primavera is usually served with a cream sauce, but I think it has a lot more zip and decidedly more of an Italian personality served with marinara sauce; and the pine nuts add just the right amount of texture as well as a complementary flavor.

1/2 cup pine nuts

4 cups flowerettes and julienne-cut fresh vegetables (a colorful assortment: broccoli, cauliflower, etc.)

2 cups Marinara Sauce (page 59), heated

4 cups cooked fettuccine noodles (1/2 pound dry)

1/4 pound imported Parmesan cheese, grated (1 cup)

Chopped fresh basil for garnish

4 sprigs fresh basil for garnish (optional)

Toast the pine nuts in a preheated 350°F oven for 8 to 10 minutes or until lightly browned. Watch carefully, as they burn easily. Set aside.

Steam the vegetables separately until crisp-tender. Rinse with cool water to maintain their color.

When ready to serve, heat the Marinara Sauce. Reheat the fettuccine and the vegetables by dipping them into boiling water.

For each serving, place 1 cup of the pasta on a hot serving plate and cover with 1/2 cup of the Marinara Sauce. Top with 1 cup of the heated vegetables and sprinkle with 1/4 cup of the cheese. Top with 2 tablespoons of the toasted pine nuts and garnish with chopped fresh basil leaves and a whole basil leaf if desired. Serve extra Marinara Sauce on the side if desired.

Makes 4 servings

EACH SERVING CONTAINS APPROXIMATELY:
385 TOTAL CALORIES / 115 CALORIES IN FAT
15 MG CHOLESTEROL / 1300 MG SODIUM
355 MG CALCIUM

LIGHT LASAGNA

If you have been looking for a vegetarian entrée your whole family will love, this is your answer. I can promise you no one is going to ask, "Where's the beef?" Even if you are making this for two or three people, I recommend making the entire recipe and freezing what is left over for future meals.

3 medium onions, chopped (4¹/₂ cups)
2 garlic cloves, finely chopped (2 teaspoons)
Two 28-ounce cans solid-pack tomatoes, undrained
Four 6-ounce cans Italian tomato paste
1 cup chopped parsley
1 teaspoon salt
¹/₂ teaspoon freshly ground black pepper
2 teaspoons dried oregano, crushed in a mortar and pestle
¹/₂ teaspoon dried thyme, crushed in a mortar and pestle
¹/₂ teaspoon dried marjoram, crushed in a mortar and pestle
¹/₂ pound dry lasagna noodles
1 pound part-skim ricotta cheese (4 cups), divided
*   into thirds*
¹/₂ pound part-skim mozzarella cheese, grated (2 cups) and
*   divided into thirds*
2 ounces imported Parmesan cheese, grated (¹/₂ cup) and divided
*   into fourths*

Combine the onions and garlic and cook, covered, until tender, adding a little water if necessary to prevent scorching. Add the tomatoes, tomato paste, parsley, salt, pepper, oregano, thyme, and marjoram. Simmer, covered, for 2 hours, stirring occasionally.

Cook the lasagna noodles in boiling water until al dente, about 12 minutes. Drain in a colander and rinse with cold water.

Cover the bottom of a 9-by-13-by-2-inch baking dish with one-fourth of the sauce. Add a layer of lasagna noodles, trimming the edges to fit the dish. Top with a layer of ricotta cheese, then a layer of mozzarella. Sprinkle with Parmesan cheese. Cover with one-fourth of the sauce. Repeat the procedure two more times and sprinkle the remaining Parmesan on top. Bake in a preheated 350°F oven for 45 minutes. Let stand for 10 minutes before serving.

Makes twelve 3-inch-square servings

EACH SERVING CONTAINS APPROXIMATELY:
285 TOTAL CALORIES / 80 CALORIES IN FAT
25 MG CHOLESTEROL / 645 MG SODIUM
370 MG CALCIUM

ACORN SQUASH RAVIOLIS
WITH MARJORAM SAUCE

These raviolis make a wonderful appetizer course as well as an unusually delicious side dish or entrée. The strong marjoram flavor is particularly good with poultry. I recently served these raviolis for a luncheon with cold sliced turkey, and it was a sensational combination.

1 small acorn squash
1/2 teaspoon freshly ground nutmeg
24 wonton skins, halved
1 tablespoon corn-oil margarine
1 medium onion, diced (1 1/2 cups)
1 cup defatted chicken stock (see page 22)
2 cups low-fat milk
*1/2 cup fresh marjoram without stems, chopped, or 2 tablespoons
    dried marjoram, crushed in a mortar and pestle*
1/4 teaspoon salt
1/8 teaspoon freshly ground black pepper
1/4 cup part-skim ricotta cheese
*4 sprigs fresh marjoram or 1/4 cup finely chopped chives for
    garnish*

Remove the seeds from the squash and peel with a sharp knife. Cut into 1-inch cubes and cook in boiling water until tender, about 20 minutes. Drain very well. Puree in a food processor with the nutmeg.

To make the raviolis, place 1 teaspoon of squash puree in the center of each wonton skin half. Fold over, moisten the edges with a little water, and seal with your fingertips. Cook for 5 minutes in boiling water, twelve wontons at a time. Drain the wontons and place them on a paper towel without overlapping until ready to serve.

To make the sauce, melt the margarine in a pan. Add the onions and stir. Cover and cook until the onions are very soft; do not brown. Add the chicken stock and reduce by two-thirds. Add the milk and bring to a rolling boil. Add the marjoram, salt, pepper, and ricotta cheese. Stir to blend. Reduce by one-half.

Remove from the heat, pour into a blender, and puree until satin smooth. Return to the pan and heat through.

To serve, divide the raviolis among four plates (twelve on each plate). Pour ½ cup sauce over each serving. Garnish with a sprig of fresh marjoram or finely chopped chives.

Makes 4 servings

EACH SERVING CONTAINS APPROXIMATELY:
335 TOTAL CALORIES / 75 CALORIES IN FAT
15 MG CHOLESTEROL / 255 MG SODIUM
285 MG CALCIUM

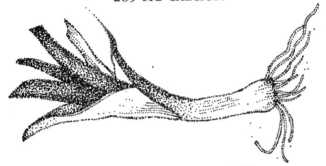

ORIENTAL NOODLES
WITH SZECHUAN PEANUT SAUCE

I will never forget the first time I was in a Szechuan restaurant in New York and had this spectacular cold pasta dish. I recently gave the recipe to a friend who told me he likes it better hot. I prefer it cold, as it is classically served, but there's no law against eating it at any temperature you like. The only problem with this dish is that it will never win a beauty contest or be "the dish most likely to make the cover of *Gourmet Magazine.*" Peanut-butter-colored sauce poured over white pasta needs help cosmetically. It is for this reason I suggest topping it not only with chopped scallions, which are traditional, but also with red pepper and a scallion flower. To make a scallion flower, cut the bulb end of the scallion just below the green top. Cut the root off the end of the bulb and shred the bulb by slicing it through first in half, then in quarters, then in eighths, and so on. To open your scallion flower, drop it in ice water and allow it to "bloom" before using it.

10 ounces dry Oriental-style noodles (4 cups cooked)
1 1/2 teaspoons dark sesame oil
1 cup Szechuan Peanut Sauce (page 56)
1/2 cup chopped scallion tops for garnish
Red bell pepper, diced, for garnish (optional)
4 scallion flowers for garnish

Cook the noodles al dente according to package directions. Drain and rinse with cold water. Drain again THOROUGHLY.

Combine the noodles and the sesame oil and toss. Refrigerate until cold.

To serve, place 1 cup noodles on each plate. Pour 1/4 cup of the Szechuan Peanut Sauce over the top. Sprinkle with 2 tablespoons of the chopped scallion tops and a sprinkle of diced red pepper if desired. Top each with a scallion flower.

Makes four 1 1/4-cup servings

EACH SERVING CONTAINS APPROXIMATELY:
355 TOTAL CALORIES / 115 CALORIES IN FAT
1 MG CHOLESTEROL / 130 MG SODIUM
125 MG CALCIUM

HUEVOS RANCHEROS

When I lived in Mexico City, I was surprised to learn how many versions the Mexicans have for Huevos Rancheros or, as literally translated, ranch-style eggs. After living there for over a year, I developed my own ranchero sauce, which is a sort of combination of all the sauces I liked best. After moving back to this country and becoming involved in the light-cuisine movement, I modified my own recipe further to use only the egg whites. When I was developing recipes for the Pritikin Longevity Center in Santa Monica, California, I made this dish without salt or cheese, and it was one of the menu favorites with all of the participants.

1 medium onion, finely chopped (1½ cups)
2 garlic cloves, finely chopped (2 teaspoons)
⅛ teaspoon salt
⅛ teaspoon freshly ground black pepper
¾ teaspoon dried oregano, crushed in a mortar and pestle
1 teaspoon chili powder
¼ teaspoon ground cumin
1 green bell pepper, seeded and diced (¾ cup)
¼ cup canned chopped green California chilies
2 cups canned tomatoes, drained and chopped (reserve juice)
¼ cup tomato juice (from canned tomatoes)
4 egg whites (½ cup)
2 ounces part-skim mozzarella cheese, grated (½ cup)
4 corn tortillas, heated
Fresh cilantro sprigs for garnish

Sauté the onions and garlic in a medium saucepan over low heat, covered, until soft, adding a little water if necessary to prevent scorching.

Add the salt, pepper, oregano, chili powder, and cumin and mix well. Add the green bell pepper, chilies, tomatoes, and tomato juice. Mix well and cook, uncovered, for 20 minutes.

For each serving, pour ¾ cup of the sauce into a skillet. Put 2 tablespoons of the egg white on top of the sauce (1 egg white). Sprinkle 2 tablespoons of the grated cheese over the egg white. Cook, covered, for about 10 minutes or until the egg white is opaque. Place a hot tortilla on a heated plate. Carefully place the sauce with the egg white and cheese on the tortilla. Spoon 2 tablespoons of the sauce over the top of the cheese. Garnish with a fresh cilantro sprig.

Makes 4 servings

EACH SERVING CONTAINS APPROXIMATELY:
135 TOTAL CALORIES / 15 CALORIES IN FAT
0 MG CHOLESTEROL / 755 MG SODIUM
110 MG CALCIUM

WHITE CHILI

White Chili is one of my own signature recipes. I created it for an all-in-fun cooking contest held by George and Piret Munger for their fellow food professionals and serious amateurs. White Chili won first place for the most original recipe. To make it an entrée and still keep it white I added chunks of tender chicken breast just before serving. It is also good with turkey breast, rabbit, veal, or drained water-packed white albacore or tuna.

It is important to use a heavy saucepan to cook this. The liquid boils too quickly, even over low heat, in a lightweight pan. If you think you have too much liquid left when the chili has finished cooking, stir it up and let it stand, uncovered, until it cools slightly and much of the liquid will be absorbed. Then reheat it to serve.

I purposely wrote this recipe for 8 cups because it doesn't take any more time and it is a wonderful dish for parties and freezes well.

> 1 pound dry Great Northern beans, soaked overnight and
>   drained
> 4 cups defatted chicken stock (see page 22)
> 2 medium onions, coarsely chopped (4 cups)
> 3 garlic cloves, finely chopped (1 tablespoon)
> 1 teaspoon salt
> 1/2 cup canned chopped green California chilies
> 2 teaspoons ground cumin
> 1 1/2 teaspoons dried oregano, crushed in a mortar and pestle
> 1 teaspoon ground coriander
> 1/4 teaspoon ground cloves
> 1/4 teaspoon cayenne (or to taste)
> 1/4 pound Monterey Jack cheese, grated (1 cup) (optional)

Combine the beans, stock, 2 cups of the onions, the garlic, and the salt in a large heavy saucepan or pot and bring to a boil. Reduce the heat, cover, and simmer for 2 hours or until the beans are very tender, adding more stock as needed (more stock should not be needed if you are using a heavy pan or pot).

When the beans are tender, add the remaining 2 cups onions, the chilies, and all the seasonings. Mix well and continue to cook, covered, for 30 minutes.

To serve, spoon 1 cup chili into each serving bowl and top with 2 tablespoons of Monterey Jack cheese if desired.

Makes 8 cups

1 CUP WITHOUT CHEESE CONTAINS APPROXIMATELY:
195 TOTAL CALORIES / 10 CALORIES IN FAT
0 MG CHOLESTEROL / 290 MG SODIUM
105 MG CALCIUM

BROCCOLI-CHEESE PIE

I receive many letters from readers of my column every month requesting modifications of recipes using prepared commercial biscuit mix. In order to create new recipes, it was first necessary to develop a substitute biscuit mix of my own. I call it Magic Biscuit Mix because I truly feel it was a magical breakthrough in recipe development. This recipe is one that I modified for one such reader.

3/4 pound broccoli
1 garlic clove, finely chopped (1 teaspoon)
1/2 cup chopped scallions
6 ounces Cheddar cheese, grated (1 1/2 cups)
1/2 teaspoon dried marjoram, crushed in a mortar and pestle
1/4 teaspoon salt
Nonstick vegetable coating
3 eggs
1 cup skim milk
3/4 cup Magic Biscuit Mix (page 206)
1 tomato, halved and sliced into thin half circles

Preheat the oven to 400°F. Peel tough outer skin from the broccoli stems and chop the broccoli coarsely. Steam until crisp-tender, 4 to 5 minutes. Rinse with cold water and drain thoroughly.

Cook the garlic and scallions in a large skillet, covered, over low heat until tender, about 5 minutes, adding a little water or chicken stock if necessary to prevent scorching. Add the broccoli, cheese, marjoram, and salt and mix well. Turn into a 9- or 10-inch pie plate that you have first sprayed with nonstick vegetable coating.

Combine the eggs, milk, and Magic Biscuit Mix and beat for 1 minute with a hand beater. Pour over the broccoli mixture and bake for 25 minutes.

Remove from the oven and place the tomato circles around the outside edge of the pie plate. Return to the oven and bake for 5 minutes more. Cool for 10 minutes before slicing.

Makes 6 main-dish servings

EACH SERVING CONTAINS APPROXIMATELY:
235 TOTAL CALORIES / 130 CALORIES IN FAT
170 MG CHOLESTEROL / 425 MG SODIUM
340 MG CALCIUM

FISH & SEAFOOD

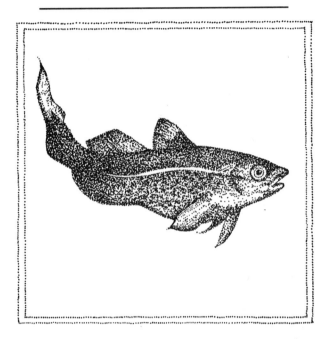

FISH AND SEAFOOD are lower in fat than poultry or meat and are the best sources of animal protein. Not only are fish and seafood lower in fat, most of the fat they do contain is in polyunsaturated form rather than the saturated fats that build up cholesterol and increase the chances of heart disease.

Seafood has long been a very popular item on most menus. In fact the traditional shrimp cocktail is the biggest-selling appetizer item throughout the country. The rapid rise in the popularity of fresh fish in the last couple of years has been awesome. Many restaurateurs have told me that the fresh-fish specials are always the biggest-selling items on their menus.

There was also a time when anyone on a low-cholesterol diet was told to avoid shellfish, but new research shows that shellfish are not nearly as high in cholesterol as was once thought, with the possible exception of shrimp. Even with shrimp, unless you are eating more animal protein than is recommended in a well-balanced healthy diet, the amount of cholesterol per serving can easily be planned into your daily diet without exceeding the cholesterol recommendations of the American Heart Association.

In large part fish owes its new popularity in our diet to the Eskimos, who literally live on fish and seafood. It was only when medical scientists started looking into the eating habits of the Eskimos, who have a lower incidence of coronary artery disease, that they discovered that Omega-3 fatty acids, which include EPA (eicosapentaenoic acid) and DHA (docosahexaenoic acid), were largely responsible for their cardiovascular wellness. Omega-3 fatty acids can also be found in walnuts and walnut oil, wheat germ oil, soybean products, including tofu, most common beans, and seaweed. However, the most abundant and popular source is certainly fish and seafood. Fish particularly high in these fatty acids include salmon, trout, mackerel, haddock, and sardines.

Fish and shellfish are excellent sources of vitamins and minerals and supply many of the minerals that are scarce in most other food sources, such as iodine, zinc, and selenium.

Canned fish, which includes the bones, such as salmon, sardines, and anchovies, is extremely high in calcium.

The rising demand for fresh fish and seafood has had a wonderful effect on its availability. The old rule of supply and demand really does work! Fresh-fish markets have sprung up all over the country, and most supermarkets have a fresh-fish section. If you don't think you like fish, chances are you have never had really fresh fish or properly cooked fish—or maybe neither one.

When buying a whole fresh fish, always look at the eyes. If the fish is really fresh, the eyes will be very clear. As it gets older, the eyes become clouded looking. The scales of a fresh fish will not be separated from the skin. Filleted fresh fish should look moist and never as though it is drying out. Also, fresh fish and seafood do not have the overly strong "fishy" smell many people dislike. If the odor of the fish is too strong, you can count on the fact that the fish is not fresh.

Shellfish are often suspected of coming from contaminated water. Be aware of where the shellfish originates and the water conditions prevailing in that area.

The storage of fresh fish is equally important. Immediately unwrap fish you have purchased and wash it under cold running water. Dry it thoroughly and squeeze fresh lemon juice all over the surface. Store it in a nonaluminum container tightly covered in the refrigerator. If you must keep it for more than a day before serving, place the container on a pan over ice cubes in the refrigerator.

When fresh fish is not available, it is often necessary to buy frozen fish. When using frozen fish, always put it in the refrigerator to thaw so that it thaws slowly. If you force the thawing time, the texture of the fish will be mushy and very unappetizing. After frozen fish has thawed, handle it exactly the same way you would fresh fish. It should not be refrozen.

There are many wonderful canned-fish and seafood products that you can keep in your cupboard and always have on hand. These include canned water-packed tuna, clams packed in clam juice, oysters, salmon, sardines, and anchovies.

When cooking fish the single most important thing to remember is not to overcook it. The minute it turns from translucent to opaque, it is done. Further cooking will only lessen the flavor and make the fish tough and dry. When poaching shellfish such as shrimp and scallops, it will literally take no more than a minute or two in a boiling stock or court bouillon.

Fish lends itself well to many types of cooking procedures, including baking, broiling, poaching, braising, and sautéeing. Before choosing the cooking method you must first decide on the type of fish you are going to use. It is difficult to poach delicately flavored fish such as sole, flounder, or fluke and keep it in one piece. It will also literally fall apart on a grill or under a broiler. It is best to either bake or sauté this type of fish. Poaching and braising are ideal for shellfish and slightly firmer fish such as cod, haddock, pollock, bluefish, trout, perch, snapper, and mackerel.

If you wish to broil or barbecue fish on a grill, it is important to use a very firm fish, such as swordfish, monkfish, tuna, shark, or salmon. Lobster and crab are also good for broiling or grilling.

Many delicately flavored fish are best served with a sauce. In fact good fresh fish, the proper cooking technique, and a good sauce recipe will give you the very best fish dish possible.

CAVIAR-STUFFED PASTA SHELLS

Caviar is an elegant hors d'oeuvre. Two reasons people may avoid using it are its high cholesterol and sodium content and its high price tag. This recipe makes such a little bit of caviar go such a long way that the cholesterol and sodium per portion are greatly reduced, and so is the price! These pasta shells also make a good appetizer course, serving 2 per person and garnishing them with sprigs of parsley or watercress. If you don't like caviar, you can substitute chopped clams or even drained water-packed tuna.

1 cup part-skim ricotta cheese
3 tablespoons plain nonfat yogurt
1 teaspoon freshly squeezed lemon juice
1 1/2 teaspoons finely chopped onion
One 2-ounce jar red caviar
18 giant pasta shells, cooked al dente

Combine the ricotta cheese and the yogurt in a food processor or blender and blend until satin smooth.

Combine the ricotta cheese mixture, lemon juice, onion, and caviar in a mixing bowl and mix thoroughly.

Spoon 1 tablespoon of the caviar mixture into each pasta shell.

Makes 18 pasta shells

EACH SHELL CONTAINS APPROXIMATELY:
50 TOTAL CALORIES / 15 CALORIES IN FAT
15 MG CHOLESTEROL / 90 MG SODIUM
50 MG CALCIUM

CRAB-SHRIMP MOLD

This seafood mold is a revision for one of my readers. The original recipe contained a cup of mayonnaise, for which I have substituted a combination of tofu and ricotta cheese and it works surprisingly well. I used the canned shrimp and crab because they were the ingredients in the original recipe, but you may substitute either leftover fish or drained water-packed canned tuna for the seafood ingredients. If you are serving this for a party, I would suggest making it in a fish-shaped mold. It is good served with rye or whole-grain bread, toasted and cut into quarters, or Herb Bread (page 218).

> *1 envelope unflavored gelatin*
> *2 tablespoons cool water*
> *¼ cup boiling water*
> *½ cup tomato sauce*
> *⅔ cup part-skim ricotta cheese*
> *¾ cup tofu, cubed*
> *1 tablespoon freshly squeezed lemon juice*
> *1 tablespoon corn oil*
> *½ teaspoon salt*
> *¼ teaspoon fructose or ⅓ teaspoon sugar*
> *½ medium onion, finely chopped (¾ cup)*
> *1 celery rib, without leaves, finely chopped (½ cup)*
> *One 4-ounce can shrimp, drained*
> *One 6-ounce can crabmeat, drained*
> *Vegetable oil or nonstick vegetable coating*

Soften the gelatin in the cool water. Add the boiling water and stir until completely dissolved. Pour into a blender container and add the tomato sauce, ricotta cheese, tofu, lemon juice, corn oil, salt, and fructose or sugar and blend until smooth.

Pour the mixture into a bowl and add all the remaining ingredients. Mix well and pour into a mold that is lightly oiled or sprayed with nonstick coating.

Refrigerate overnight before unmolding to serve.

Makes 6 servings

EACH SERVING CONTAINS APPROXIMATELY:
75 TOTAL CALORIES / 30 CALORIES IN FAT
30 MG CHOLESTEROL / 270 MG SODIUM
80 MG CALCIUM

HOT CRAB DIP

This dip is a revision of a much higher calorie version sent to me by a reader. It is a bizarre-sounding list of ingredients but makes an amazingly delicious dip, infinitely lower in calories than the original recipe. It is good served with raw or blanched vegetables, melba toast rounds, or toasted Tortilla Wedges (page 201). It also makes a great open-faced sandwich when spread on toasted whole-grain bread.

1 cup part-skim ricotta cheese
1 garlic clove, minced (1 teaspoon)
2 ounces tofu (1/4 cup)
1 teaspoon prepared mustard
2 tablespoons sherry
1 teaspoon freshly squeezed lemon juice
1 teaspoon minced onion
1/2 pound crabmeat

Place all the ingredients except the crabmeat in a blender container and blend until satin smooth.

Transfer to a pan, add the crabmeat, and heat thoroughly.

Makes 2 cups

1/4 CUP CONTAINS APPROXIMATELY:
85 TOTAL CALORIES / 30 CALORIES IN FAT
40 MG CHOLESTEROL / 330 MG SODIUM
110 MG CALCIUM

SCALLOPS IN GINGER SAUCE

This scallop dish is most attractive served in a giant scallop shell and topped with a chive knot. To make the chive knot, take two long pieces of chive and tie them into a knot in the center. Place the chive knot on top of the scallops in the shell. Smaller portions of Scallops in Ginger Sauce also make a nice appetizer. As an entrée, I like to serve it with Rice Pilaf (page 119) and an assortment of colorful fresh vegetables.

1 *tablespoon corn-oil margarine*
2 *tablespoons chopped peeled ginger*
4 *teaspoons flour*
1 *tablespoon white wine*
1 *cup clam juice or fish stock (see page 25)*
1 *cup skim milk*
2 *tablespoons finely chopped chives*
2 *cups defatted chicken stock or fish stock (see page 22 or 25)*
1 *pound scallops*
4 *whole chives, tied in knots for garnish*

Melt the margarine in a medium saucepan. Add the ginger and cook for 1 minute. Stir in the flour.

Combine the wine, the 1 cup clam juice or stock, and the milk and gradually add to the flour mixture, stirring with a wire whisk. Bring the sauce to a boil, whisking constantly. Reduce the heat and simmer, whisking occasionally, until the sauce thickens and is reduced by one-third, about 10 to 15 minutes.

Remove from the heat. Strain the sauce to remove the ginger. Return the sauce to the pan, add the chives, and reheat.

Meanwhile, bring the 2 cups of chicken or fish stock to a boil. Add the scallops, reduce the heat, and simmer just until the scallops become opaque, about 2 to 4 minutes. Drain and divide among 2 to 4 scallop shells.

Spoon ⅓ cup sauce over each serving. Top each with a chive knot.

Makes 4 servings

EACH SERVING CONTAINS APPROXIMATELY:
155 TOTAL CALORIES / 30 CALORIES IN FAT
45 MG CHOLESTEROL / 215 MG SODIUM
110 MG CALCIUM

ITALIAN OYSTER CASSEROLE

This recipe is a lower-calorie version of the one created by Mary Etta Moose, the owner of the famous Washington Square Bar and Grill in San Francisco. This dish can be served either as an entrée with a salad and dessert or in smaller portions as a dressing with turkey during the holidays. Still smaller amounts make an interesting hors d'oeuvre served on oyster shells. No matter how you're serving it, it needs garnish. As good as it is, it is not a particularly attractive dish, and a little chopped parsley and freshly grated imported Parmesan cheese do wonders for its appearance.

1 large eggplant (1 1/2 pounds)
1 tablespoon fennel seeds
1 tablespoon extra-virgin olive oil
1 medium onion, finely chopped (1 1/2 cups)
1 cup finely chopped fennel bulb
3 garlic cloves, finely chopped (1 tablespoon)
1 whole egg
1 egg white
1/2 teaspoon salt
1/4 teaspoon freshly ground black pepper
1/2 teaspoon dried thyme, crushed in a mortar and pestle
1/8 teaspoon freshly grated nutmeg
1/2 teaspoon grated lemon zest
2 ounces imported Parmesan cheese, freshly grated (1/2 cup)
2 tablespoons finely chopped parsley
2 tablespoons finely chopped fennel tops

2 cups cooked brown rice (²/₃ cup uncooked)
1 cup oysters, cut into ¹/₂-inch cubes, plus all the liquid from the
jar

Pierce holes in an unpeeled whole eggplant with the tines of a fork. Bake for 1 hour in a preheated 400°F oven. When the eggplant is cool enough to handle, peel and cut into ¹/₂-inch cubes. You should have 3 cups.

While the eggplant is cooking, put the fennel seeds in a large dry hot skillet and cook them, stirring constantly, until they are lightly browned. Add the olive oil and mix well. Then add the onions, fennel bulb, and garlic and cook, covered, over low heat until soft, about 10 minutes.

Combine the egg and egg white and mix well. Add the salt, pepper, thyme, nutmeg, lemon zest, ¹/₄ cup of cheese, the parsley, and fennel tops and mix well. Add the cooked rice and mix well. Add the cubed oysters and all of the juice from the oyster jar. Add the eggplant and mix well. Add the onion/fennel mixture to the bowl and again mix well. Pour into a casserole with a tight-fitting lid. Bake in a preheated 350°F oven, covered, for 1 hour; then sprinkle the remaining ¹/₄ cup Parmesan cheese over the top and bake, uncovered, for 15 minutes more.

Makes 6 cups

¹/₂ CUP CONTAINS APPROXIMATELY:
110 TOTAL CALORIES / 30 CALORIES IN FAT
35 MG CHOLESTEROL / 230 MG SODIUM
85 MG CALCIUM

CIOPPINO

Italian fishermen who came to San Francisco at the time of the Gold Rush introduced this spicy shellfish stew, which has since become a San Francisco favorite, where it is served with crusty San Francisco sourdough French bread. Crab and lobster are usually purchased already cooked and therefore they do not need to be poached but simply added in the sauce. This dish is classically presented with all of the shellfish intact in their shells. I suggest serving it with bibs for your guests and big bowls for the shells they discard.

> *4 cups Marinara Sauce (page 59)*
> *1 pound assorted raw shellfish (scallops, shrimp, clams, mussels, lobsters, crab, etc.), cleaned*
> *2 cups clam juice or fish stock (see page 25)*
> *4 whole clams, in their shells (optional), steamed until they open*
> *Fresh herb sprigs*

Heat the Marinara Sauce in a large saucepan. Poach the shellfish in the clam juice or fish stock until it goes from translucent to opaque, about 1 minute. DO NOT OVERCOOK.

Add the clam juice or fish stock to the marinara sauce and mix well.

For each serving, combine 1 cup of the shellfish and 1½ cups of the sauce and place in a large soup bowl garnished with an open clam. Garnish with a sprig of one of the fresh herbs used in making the marinara sauce.

Makes 4 servings

EACH SERVING CONTAINS APPROXIMATELY:
200 TOTAL CALORIES / 20 CALORIES IN FAT
115 MG CHOLESTEROL / 2000 MG SODIUM
110 MG CALCIUM

BOUILLABAISSE

This delicious seafood stew has for centuries been a staple of the fishermen living on the coast of France in and around Marseilles. They use primarily fish for this dish, but when I added a little more shellfish to this savory saffron-scented bowl the guests at the Canyon Ranch Spa in Tucson seemed to like it a lot better; so I am sharing my spa version with you. Also in Marseilles the Bouillabaisse is served over crusty French bread in a bowl, but I like to serve the bread on the side.

1 medium onion, finely chopped (1 1/2 cups)
1 leek, white part only, thinly sliced (1 cup)
1 garlic clove, finely chopped (1 teaspoon)
2 medium tomatoes, peeled, seeded, and diced (1 1/2 cups)
2 tablespoons finely chopped parsley
1 celery rib, finely chopped (1/2 cup)
1 bay leaf
1/4 teaspoon dried thyme, crushed in a mortar and pestle
1/4 teaspoon dried fennel, crushed in a mortar and pestle
1/4 teaspoon dried saffron, dissolved in a little defatted chicken or fish stock
1/8 teaspoon freshly ground black pepper
2 cups defatted chicken stock or fish stock (see page 22 or 25)
1 cup dry white wine
1/2 pound firm white fish, cut into strips (2 cups)
1/2 pound shellfish (shrimp, lobster, scallops, etc.), shelled and cleaned
Fresh thyme or fennel for garnish
4 slices crusty French bread

Combine the onions, leeks, and garlic and cook, covered, over very low heat until soft, about 10 minutes, adding a little stock if necessary to prevent scorching. Add all the other ingredients except the fish, shellfish, garnish, and bread. Mix well and bring to a boil. Reduce the heat and simmer, covered, for 10 minutes.

Add the fish and shellfish and cook until it turns from translucent to opaque, 2 to 5 minutes.

Serve in four casseroles, garnished with sprigs of thyme or fennel. Serve a slice of French bread on the side.

Makes four 2-cup servings

EACH SERVING CONTAINS APPROXIMATELY:
310 TOTAL CALORIES / 45 CALORIES IN FAT
50 MG CHOLESTEROL / 295 MG SODIUM
100 MG CALCIUM

POLYNESIAN PRAWNS

These prawns are as delicious as they are quick and easy to prepare. You can use bite-size shrimp, totally peeled, and put them on toothpicks for hors d'oeuvres or use very large prawns and serve two per person as an entrée with rice and Oriental vegetables. In fact this is a very popular luncheon entrée on my menu at the restaurant at Neiman-Marcus in Newport Beach, California.

> *1 pound large prawns or shrimp*
> *½ cup Mandarin Dressing and Marinade (page 75)*

Peel and devein the prawns, leaving the tails attached.

Bring the dressing to a boil in a large skillet. Add the shrimp and cook, turning frequently, until they turn from translucent to opaque, about 2 minutes.

Makes 4 servings (3 or 4 shrimp each, depending upon size)

EACH SERVING CONTAINS APPROXIMATELY:
175 TOTAL CALORIES / 55 CALORIES IN FAT
160 MG CHOLESTEROL / 245 MG SODIUM
80 MG CALCIUM

LINGUINE WITH CLAM SAUCE

This is one of my favorite "emergency" meals. That is when you have no time to shop, very little time to cook, and unexpected guests coming for dinner. The beauty of this recipe is that everything in it can be kept on hand in your cupboard and refrigerator. Toss whatever salad greens you have on hand with a light dressing and slice up any fruit you may have or open a can of water- or juice-packed fruit and you literally have a meal in minutes.

½ pound dry linguine (4 cups cooked)
One 8-ounce can chopped clams, undrained
1 garlic clove, minced (1 teaspoon)
2 ounces imported Parmesan cheese, grated (½ cup)

Cook the linguine according to the package directions until al dente, or slightly resistant to the bite.

Heat the clams in their juice along with the garlic, until heated through. DO NOT BOIL.

Drain the pasta, toss with the clam and garlic mixture, and the grated Parmesan cheese. Serve on heated plates.

Makes 4 servings

EACH SERVING CONTAINS APPROXIMATELY:
250 TOTAL CALORIES / 45 CALORIES IN FAT
55 MG CHOLESTEROL / 265 MG SODIUM
240 MG CALCIUM

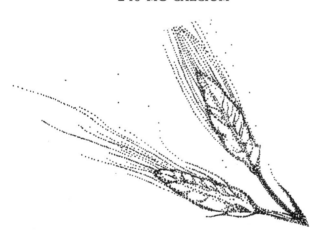

CLAM LASAGNA

I created this clam lasagna for the Four Seasons Hotel and Resort in Dallas. It is as much of a hit with the conference participants as it is with the spa guests. Its uniquely different appearance and taste makes it fun to serve as the entrée for parties. It also works well for a buffet.

Two 6¹/₂-ounce cans minced clams, undrained
1 tablespoon corn-oil margarine
2¹/₂ tablespoons flour
1 cup clam juice
3 garlic cloves, minced (1 tablespoon)
¹/₂ teaspoon each dried basil, oregano, thyme, and marjoram,
*   crushed in a mortar and pestle*
¹/₄ cup loosely packed finely chopped parsley
¹/₄ teaspoon freshly ground black pepper
3 tablespoons freshly squeezed lemon juice
Vegetable oil for the dish
¹/₂ pound dry lasagna noodles, cooked al dente
2 cups part-skim ricotta cheese
3 pounds fresh spinach, veins and stems removed, blanched or
*   steamed for 1 minute*
¹/₂ pound part-skim mozzarella cheese, thinly sliced
1 ounce imported Parmesan cheese, freshly grated (¹/₄ cup)

Drain the clams and reserve the liquid. Melt the margarine in a 2-
or 3-quart saucepan over medium heat. Add the flour and cook for
2 minutes, being careful not to brown the flour. Gradually stir in
the reserved clam liquid and the clam juice; there should be 2 cups
total. Continue cooking and stirring until the mixture boils and
thickens, about 5 minutes. Remove from the heat and stir in the
clams, garlic, herbs, parsley, pepper, and lemon juice. Line an oiled
9-by-13-inch baking dish with one-third of the noodles. Spoon the
ricotta cheese evenly over the noodles and top with a third of the
clam sauce. Add a second layer of noodles. Squeeze as much moisture as possible from the spinach and arrange over the noodles.
Cover with half the cheese slices, then spread with half the remaining clam sauce. Top with the remaining noodles, cheese slices, and
clam sauce. Sprinkle with the Parmesan cheese.

Bake, uncovered, in a preheated 350°F oven for 30 minutes or
until bubbly and heated through. Let stand for 10 minutes before
cutting.

Makes 8 servings

EACH SERVING CONTAINS APPROXIMATELY:
370 TOTAL CALORIES / 125 CALORIES IN FAT
75 MG CHOLESTEROL / 425 MG SODIUM
630 MG CALCIUM

FISH EN PAPILLOTE

If you don't have baker's paper, this dish can also be done in aluminum foil, just folding the edges of the foil envelopes to seal them. The thing I like best about it is the marvelous aroma it releases at the table when the envelopes are opened.

1 pound red snapper or any firm, white fish, cut into 4 portions
Salt
Lemon juice, freshly squeezed
2 cups julienne-cut fresh vegetables of your choice
4 teaspoons chopped fresh herbs or 1 teaspoon dried tarragon,
  crushed in a mortar and pestle
5 teaspoons corn-oil margarine
4 slices lemon
¼ cup balsamic vinegar
8 small new potatoes, steamed, baked, or boiled until tender

Wash the fish in cold water and pat dry. Salt lightly, squeeze lemon juice over both sides, and store, covered, in the refrigerator.

Make four 12-by-16-inch ovals of baker's paper, using a bowl for a template. To assemble the servings, place ½ cup vegetables in the center of each oval and place a piece of fish on top. Sprinkle 1 teaspoon fresh herbs or ¼ teaspoon crushed tarragon over the fish and cover with 1 teaspoon of the margarine, a lemon slice, and 1 tablespoon balsamic vinegar. Spread the remaining 1 teaspoon margarine along the edges of the paper, then fold it over and make sure it is sealed by crimping the edges with a tight fold.

Place in a preheated 400°F oven and bake for 5 minutes. Place each envelope on a large dinner plate with two small potatoes on the side. Allow each guest to open the envelope at the table.

Makes 4 servings

EACH SERVING CONTAINS APPROXIMATELY:
220 TOTAL CALORIES / 70 CALORIES IN FAT
1 MG CHOLESTEROL / 35 MG SODIUM
30 MG CALCIUM

RED SNAPPER IN THE STYLE OF VERA CRUZ

This is my favorite Mexican fish dish. I have it on the dinner menu with hot corn tortillas at the Canyon Ranch Spa in Tucson, Arizona.

> *1 1/2 pounds red snapper or other firm, white fish*
> *1/2 teaspoon salt*
> *1/4 cup freshly squeezed lime juice*
> *1 medium onion, thinly sliced (2 cups)*
> *1/2 cup whole pimientos, thinly sliced*
> *3 medium tomatoes, peeled, seeded, and diced (2 cups)*
> *1/4 cup canned chopped green California chilies*
> *1 tablespoon capers*
> *6 parsley sprigs*

Wash the fish thoroughly with cold water. Dry and place in a nonaluminum dish.

Lightly salt and pour the lime juice evenly over the fish. Cover and refrigerate for at least an hour before cooking.

Cook the onions in a heavy skillet, covered, over very low heat until tender, about 10 minutes, adding a little water if necessary to prevent scorching.

Add half of the pimientos and all of the tomatoes, chilies, and capers. Lay 2 of the parsley sprigs over the top and cook, covered, until there is about 1 inch of liquid in the bottom of the pan.

Add the fish and cook for about 5 minutes per side or until it turns from translucent to opaque. Remove the parsley. Serve with the sauce spooned over the top and garnish with the remaining pimientos and sprigs of fresh parsley.

Makes 4 servings

EACH SERVING CONTAINS APPROXIMATELY:
240 TOTAL CALORIES / 45 CALORIES IN FAT
1 MG CHOLESTEROL / 460 MG SODIUM
30 MG CALCIUM

POACHED SALMON IN WALNUT-DILL SAUCE

Not only is salmon the most beautiful fish because of its peachy color, but modern research indicates that it is also one of the most beneficial creatures from the sea because of its Omega-3 fatty acid content. Poached salmon is often served with dill sauce. I like the hint of walnut in this sauce, particularly when it is accompanied by toasted walnuts to reinforce the nutty flavor with a crunchy texture. Both the tofu-based sauce with walnut oil and the walnuts contain Omega-3 fatty acids, making this a really healthy fish dish. To serve, either place the salmon on top of ½ cup of Rice Pilaf (page 119) and pour ¼ cup of the sauce over it with 1 tablespoon of toasted walnuts and a dill sprig or spoon ¼ cup sauce on the plate and place the salmon on top of the sauce, again sprinkling it with walnuts and topping it with a dill sprig. If plating the salmon on the sauce, I like to serve it with boiled new potatoes.

> *¼ cup chopped walnuts*
> *3 cups court bouillon (see page 25)*
> *1 pound fresh salmon, cut into 4 pieces*
> *1 cup Walnut-Dill Sauce (page 69), heated*
> *Fresh dill sprigs for garnish*

Place the walnuts in a preheated 350°F oven for 8 to 10 minutes or until golden brown. Watch carefully, as they burn easily. Set aside.

Bring the court bouillon to a boil and place the salmon in it. When the bouillon returns to a boil, reduce the heat and simmer until the salmon turns from translucent to opaque, about 10 minutes. Do not overcook or the salmon will be dry.

Makes 4 servings

EACH SERVING CONTAINS APPROXIMATELY:
355 TOTAL CALORIES / 225 CALORIES IN FAT
45 MG CHOLESTEROL / 290 MG SODIUM
175 MG CALCIUM

SALMON MOUSSE

The original recipe for this mousse was sent to me by a reader in Miami who had attended a cooking school on Saint Barthélemy in the Caribbean. She loved the taste and texture of the mousse, but wanted to get rid of all the calories. I like my own version so much I now have it on a luncheon menu at the Canyon Ranch Spa in Tucson, Arizona. As a variation, try serving the mousse cold, plated either on Roasted Red Pepper Sauce (page 69), Walnut-Dill Sauce (page 69), or Creamy Curry Dressing (page 70). If you have any leftover mousse, wrap it well and freeze it to serve on crackers for hors d'oeuvres at your next party.

1 leek, green part only, cut into very thin strips
1 cup part-skim ricotta cheese
3 tablespoons plain nonfat yogurt
1/2 pound salmon, without bones
1/2 pound bass, without bones
2 eggs
1/2 teaspoon salt
1/4 teaspoon freshly ground black pepper
Corn-oil margarine
2 tablespoons raspberry vinegar
1 shallot, finely chopped (1 tablespoon)
1 cup clam juice or fish stock (see page 25)
6 raspberries for garnish (optional)

Cook the leek in boiling water until limp. Drain and put in a bowl of ice water. Drain and set aside.

Combine the ricotta cheese and yogurt in a food processor with a metal blade. Blend until satiny smooth. Add the fish to the ricotta cheese mixture in the food processor along with the eggs, salt, and pepper and blend until satin smooth.

Coat six 3-inch ramekins with the margarine. Fill each ramekin up to 1/4 inch from the top. Set the ramekins in a baking dish filled with hot water to a depth of 3/4 inch. Place the dish with the ramekins in a preheated 350°F oven for 20 minutes.

While the mousse is baking, combine the raspberry vinegar and shallot in a small saucepan. Bring to a boil and reduce completely. Add the clam juice or fish stock and reduce by half.

Remove the ramekins from the oven. Drain each mousse by turning it upside down on a paper towel to remove any melted margarine, then put back in the ramekin.

To serve, unmold the mousse on salad plates. Bring the sauce back to a boil, then remove from the heat. Add 1 tablespoon margarine and shake the pan until the margarine has melted completely. Spoon 1 tablespoon of the sauce over the top of each mousse. To garnish, surround each mousse with strips of leek, which will look like seaweed. If you wish, place a raspberry on top of each mousse.

Makes 6 servings

EACH SERVING CONTAINS APPROXIMATELY:
220 TOTAL CALORIES / 115 CALORIES IN FAT
120 MG CHOLESTEROL / 285 MG SODIUM
170 MG CALCIUM

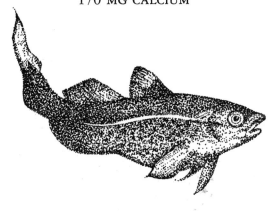

MAGIC TUNA QUICHE

This is another recipe sent to me by a reader who wanted a substitute for the commercially prepared biscuit mix that her recipe called for. I found that it was even lighter with my Magic Biscuit Mix than her original recipe. It makes a nice luncheon or light supper entrée served with my Chinese Chicken Salad (page 97) without the chicken.

> *Nonstick vegetable coating*
> *¼ pound mozzarella cheese, grated (1 cup)*
> *One 6½-ounce can water-packed tuna, drained*
> *¼ cup diced water chestnuts*
> *½ cup frozen peas*
> *¼ cup sliced scallions, including tops*
> *¼ pound fresh mushrooms, sliced (1 cup)*
> *½ cup bean sprouts*
> *¾ cup Magic Biscuit Mix (page 206)*
> *3 eggs*
> *1 cup skim milk*

Preheat the oven to 400°F. Spray a 9-inch pie plate with nonstick vegetable coating. Combine the cheese, tuna, water chestnuts, peas, scallions, mushrooms, and bean sprouts in the pie plate.

Combine the biscuit mix, eggs, and milk in a blender container and blend until smooth (15 seconds) or mix with a beater (1 minute). Pour over the mixture in the pie plate.

Bake for 30 to 35 minutes or until a knife inserted in the center comes out clean. Remove from the oven and let rest for 5 minutes before serving. Cut into six wedges.

Makes 6 servings

EACH SERVING CONTAINS APPROXIMATELY:
220 TOTAL CALORIES / 85 CALORIES IN FAT
170 MG CHOLESTEROL / 490 MG SODIUM
225 MG CALCIUM

CRAB QUICHE

This crustless quiche makes an excellent appetizer. When serving it for hors d'oeuvres, I cook it in a square pan rather than a round pie pan so that it cuts evenly into small squares. When used as an entrée, the servings are quite small because the ingredients are high in cholesterol and sodium. It makes a wonderful brunch served with fresh fruit on the side and my Herb Bread (page 218).

> *¹/₂ medium onion, finely chopped (³/₄ cup)*
> *2 cups crabmeat, flaked*
> *¹/₂ pound Cheddar cheese, grated (2 cups)*
> *3 eggs, lightly beaten*
> *One 12-ounce can skimmed evaporated milk*
> *¹/₂ teaspoon salt*

Cook the onions, covered, over very low heat until soft, adding a little water if necessary to prevent scorching.

Line the bottom of a 9-inch pie pan with the crabmeat. Sprinkle the cooked onions over the crabmeat. Sprinkle the grated cheese over the top of the mixture.

Combine the eggs, milk, and salt and mix well. Pour over the other ingredients.

Bake in a preheated 350°F oven for 1 hour. Allow to stand for at least 10 minutes before cutting into eight pie-shaped wedges.

Makes 8 servings

EACH SERVING CONTAINS APPROXIMATELY:
190 TOTAL CALORIES / 75 CALORIES IN FAT
160 MG CHOLESTEROL / 780 MG SODIUM
380 MG CALCIUM

BASS WITH GREEN CHILI SAUCE

1 1/2 pounds bass fillets
Freshly squeezed lemon juice
1/4 cup white wine
1 shallot, minced (1 tablespoon)
1/4 teaspoon salt
1/2 teaspoon freshly ground black pepper
1 pound tomatillos
1/2 cup clam juice or fish stock (see page 25)
1 medium onion, chopped (1 1/2 cups)
1 garlic clove, chopped (1 teaspoon)
2 yellow chilies, finely chopped (2 tablespoons)
1 large green California chili, peeled seeded, and chopped (2 tablespoons)
1/2 small jalapeño pepper, stem and seeds removed, finely chopped (1 teaspoon)
1/4 cup finely chopped cilantro
1/4 teaspoon fructose or 1/2 teaspoon sugar
Corn-oil margarine
1 tablespoon lime juice
Cilantro sprigs for garnish
Twisted lime slices for garnish

Wash the fish in cold water and pat dry. Place in a nonaluminum baking pan in a single layer. Squeeze lemon juice on the fish. Add the wine. Sprinkle with shallots, salt, and pepper. Cover and refrigerate.

Husk the tomatillos and pierce each with a fork. Place in boiling water and simmer until soft, about 12 minutes. Drain and puree in a food processor with a metal blade or in a blender. Strain to remove the seeds.

Heat half the clam juice or fish stock in a skillet. Add the onions, garlic, chilies, and jalapeño pepper. Sauté until soft, about 5 minutes, adding more liquid if necessary to prevent scorching. Combine the onion/chili mixture with the cilantro, fructose or sugar, and tomatillos in a large saucepan. Bring to a boil, reduce the heat, cover, and simmer for 10 minutes. Set aside.

To cook the fish, cut a piece of parchment paper to fit the pan containing the fish. Lightly spread one side of the parchment paper with margarine.

In a small saucepan, bring the remaining ¼ cup of clam juice or fish stock to a boil and pour over the fish. Lay the parchment paper directly on the fish, margarine side down.

Preheat the oven to 425°F. Place the fish in the oven and cook until just opaque, about 9 minutes per inch of thickness. Reserve the cooking liquid.

Place the fish on a heated platter and cover with the parchment paper while the sauce is being reheated. Strain the cooking liquid, add it to the sauce, and bring to a boil. Remove the sauce from the heat, add the lime juice, and mix well. You should have 1½ cups of sauce.

To serve, divide the fish among six heated plates. Top each serving with ¼ cup of the sauce. Garnish with a sprig of cilantro and a twisted lime slice.

Makes 6 servings

EACH SERVING CONTAINS APPROXIMATELY:
165 TOTAL CALORIES / 30 CALORIES IN FAT
1 MG CHOLESTEROL / 200 MG SODIUM
25 MG CALCIUM

POULTRY

TO MOST PEOPLE the word *poultry* means chicken. I have always wondered if this has anything to do with the Republican promise in the early 1930s to put a "chicken in every pot" or the fact that chicken soup is the time-honored cure-all for everything from the common cold to a hangover.

White meat is always lower in fat and calories than dark meat, and all poultry is lower in fat without the skin. Unlike the fat in red meat, which is spread throughout the red muscle of the meat, the fat in poultry is concentrated in or just below the skin. That means that just by removing the skin you can remove about half the fat. A half chicken breast (about 3 ounces) with the skin is about 10.8 percent fat. Without the skin it is about 4.5 percent in the same piece of chicken. Also poultry fat is higher in polyunsaturates than the fat in red meat.

The white meat of turkey has about as much fat as the same amount of white chicken meat; however, the dark meat of turkey is higher in fat than the dark meat of chicken. Duck and goose have

50 percent more fat than chicken. These comparisons are all based on cooked poultry without skin. Wild game birds, such as pheasant, duck, and quail, are also very low in fat but are not readily available to most people.

The rising popularity of chicken has had its bad side. To meet the overwhelming demand for billions of chickens each year, the modern poultry farmer can raise a chicken from an egg in just 60 days. In order to do this the birds are fed hormone-packed feeds to speed up their growth, confined to small areas where they can't move freely to prevent weight loss, and given antibiotics to prevent disease.

When ordering chicken, ask for free-range or organically grown chickens that have not been raised as miracles of modern science but have been allowed to grow up naturally in a barnyard. They are more expensive but well worth the price, if you can get them, because the meat is firmer and tastier. The ideal solution is to find a chicken farmer in your area and buy your chickens directly from him. Also if you primarily use chicken breasts for cooking, it is less expensive and less time-consuming to buy the chicken breasts separately and then buy only scrap parts, such as necks and backs, to make your stock, rather than buying a whole chicken and using only the breast meat.

The same guidelines also apply to turkey. Since turkey is no longer considered just a holiday meal, but rather an important food source, I am sure that more and more turkey will need to be produced, causing the same problems facing the chicken population.

When cooking poultry, the single most important thing to remember is not to overcook it. If you are roasting a chicken for a meal, put it breast side down in a flat roasting pan and bake it at 350°F for about 1 hour or until the liquid runs clear when pierced with a knife. When roasting chicken you are going to allow to cool so that you can chop it to use later as an ingredient, remove it from the oven while the liquid is still running a little bit pink. It will continue to cook as it cools and will give you moister, tastier chicken meat to use in other recipes. If you cook it completely before allowing it to cool, the chicken tends to be dry.

When roasting turkey, follow the directions given in my recipe for Roast Turkey with Fennel (page 180) and season it any way you wish.

When sautéeing chicken breasts it literally takes only a very few minutes per side for the chicken breasts to turn from translucent to opaque and spring back when touched with your finger. At this point they are done, still moist, and very tender.

When working with poultry of any kind it is extremely important not to let it stand out at room temperature. Poultry of all types, as well as eggs, quickly build up harmful bacteria when not refrigerated. This is also true of anything containing poultry or eggs as an ingredient, such as mayonnaise and hollandaise sauce.

When freezing chicken or other poultry, I prefer freezing it with the skin left on. Freezing tends to dehydrate everything, so leaving the skin on poultry helps to protect it against this dryness.

Rabbit, while not in the poultry category, does have all white meat, which tastes very much like chicken. Rabbit is lower in fat, cholesterol, and calories than any poultry and is also low enough in sodium to be recommended for people on low-sodium diets. I mention this here because I never know where to put rabbit in a cookbook. It doesn't really fit into any of the major animal-flesh categories, but it substitutes well for poultry in recipes.

Chicken, turkey, and rabbit are three of my favorite ingredients because you can literally use any seasoning range with them successfully. You can always substitute them for each other in any recipe and also use them successfully as substitutes for veal.

GINGERED LEMON CHICKEN

This dish is both quick and easy. For a delicious Oriental-style menu, serve Egg Drop Soup (page 30) as an appetizer and serve the Gingered Lemon Chicken with brown rice and Oriental vegetables such as snow peas and water chestnuts, garnished with julienne-cut carrots and red peppers for color.

½ cup coarsely chopped walnuts
4 chicken breast halves (1½ pounds), boned, skinned, and cut into ½-inch strips

1 egg white, lightly beaten

2 tablespoons flour

1/4 teaspoon salt

1/2 teaspoon fructose or 3/4 teaspoon sugar

1 tablespoon corn oil

1-inch piece ginger, peeled and very finely chopped (1 1/2 teaspoons)

1 garlic clove, finely chopped (1 teaspoon)

3 scallions, sliced (1/2 cup)

1/2 cup defatted chicken stock (see page 22)

2 teaspoons reduced-sodium soy sauce

1/4 cup sherry

2 tablespoons freshly squeezed lemon juice

Place the walnuts in a preheated 350°F oven for 8 to 10 minutes. Watch carefully, as they burn easily. Set aside.

In a large bowl, coat the chicken with the egg white. Drain well in a colander and return to the bowl.

Combine the flour, salt, and fructose or sugar. Coat the chicken with the flour mixture.

Heat the oil. Add the ginger and garlic and cook over low heat, stirring constantly, until very lightly browned. Add the chicken and cook until just opaque, about 5 minutes, stirring to expose all sides of the chicken to the heat. Stir in the scallions.

Combine the chicken stock, soy sauce, sherry, and lemon juice. Pour over the chicken and mix well. Bring to a boil.

Serve over 1/2 cup rice or Rice Pilaf (page 119). Top each serving with 2 tablespoons toasted walnuts.

Makes four 3/4-cup servings

EACH SERVING CONTAINS APPROXIMATELY:
400 TOTAL CALORIES / 170 CALORIES IN FAT
165 MG CHOLESTEROL / 425 MG SODIUM
50 MG CALCIUM

CHICKEN BOMBAY

This is one of the most popular entrées on my spa menu at the Four Seasons Hotel and Resort in Dallas. It is also a wonderful recipe for parties because you can make the sauce a day or two ahead of time and it is even better than when freshly made. Instead of just plain brown rice, I like to serve the chicken over my Rice Pilaf (page 119) with the Apple Chutney on the side and an assortment of other low-calorie condiments, such as diced tomatoes, finely chopped scallions, peeled and diced cucumbers, chopped hard-cooked egg whites, and diced tropical fruits, such as banana, pineapple, papaya, or mango.

CURRY SAUCE:

> *1 tablespoon corn-oil margarine*
> *1/2 medium onion, finely chopped (3/4 cup)*
> *1 small green apple, peeled, cored, and finely chopped (3/4 cup)*
> *1/2 garlic clove, finely chopped (1/2 teaspoon)*
> *1 tablespoon flour*
> *1 1/2 tablespoons curry powder*
> *1 cup defatted chicken stock, boiling (see page 22)*
> *1/4 cup skim milk*
> *1 tablespoon nonfat dry milk powder*
> *1 teaspoon freshly squeezed lemon juice*
> *1 1/2 teaspoons grated lemon zest*
>
> *1/4 cup chopped almonds*
> *2 whole chicken breasts, boned, skinned, halved, and butterflied*
> *Juice of 1/2 lemon*
> *Defatted chicken stock (see page 22)*
> *Dry white wine*
> *2 cups cooked brown rice*
> *1/2 cup Apple Chutney (page 62)*

Heat the margarine in a large skillet. Add the onions, apples, and garlic and cook until the onions are tender and translucent, about 10 minutes.

Combine the flour and curry powder. Mix well and add to the onion mixture, stirring constantly for a few minutes. Add the boiling chicken stock and mix thoroughly. Combine the skim milk with the nonfat dry milk and add to the sauce, mixing well. Add the lemon juice and zest and allow the sauce to simmer slowly, partially covered, for 1 hour or until slightly thickened. This makes 1 cup sauce.

Place the almonds in a preheated 350°F oven for 8 to 10 minutes or until golden brown. Watch carefully, as they burn easily. Set aside.

Sprinkle lemon juice over the chicken. Heat a little chicken stock in a large skillet and reduce until almost dry. Add a little white wine and reduce again. Sauté the butterflied chicken breasts until just done, adding a little more stock as needed to prevent scorching.

To serve, place ½ cup of the cooked rice on each plate and place ½ butterflied chicken breast on top. Spoon ¼ cup of the sauce over each chicken breast. Sprinkle 1 tablespoon chopped toasted almonds over the top of the chicken and serve with 2 tablespoons of Apple Chutney and any other condiments you desire.

Makes 4 servings

EACH SERVING CONTAINS APPROXIMATELY:
565 TOTAL CALORIES / 130 CALORIES IN FAT
100 MG CHOLESTEROL / 380 MG SODIUM
140 MG CALCIUM

CHICKEN STROGANOFF

Chicken Stroganoff is another wonderful dish for a party because it can be made ahead of time and is so easy to serve on a buffet. Whenever I have Chicken Stroganoff on one of my spa menus, I keep the entire theme of the menu Russian, serving Borscht (page 45) as an appetizer and Strawberries Romanoff (page 226) for dessert.

WHITE SAUCE:

1 cup skim milk
2 teaspoons corn-oil margarine
1½ tablespoons flour
⅛ teaspoon salt
2 tablespoons defatted chicken stock (see page 22)
1 medium onion, thinly sliced (2 cups)
½ pound fresh mushrooms, sliced (2 cups)
½ teaspoon dried basil, crushed in a mortar and pestle
¼ teaspoon paprika
¼ teaspoon ground nutmeg
⅛ teaspoon salt
2 tablespoons sherry

½ pound cooked chicken, without skin, cut into strips (2 cups)
¼ cup plain nonfat yogurt
3 cups cooked noodles (10 ounces dry)

Heat the milk in a small saucepan over low heat. In another small saucepan, melt the margarine and add the flour, stirring constantly. Cook the flour and margarine for 3 minutes, then take the mixture off the heat and add the simmering milk all at once, stirring constantly with a wire whisk. Put the sauce back over low heat and cook slowly for 15 minutes, stirring occasionally. If you wish a thicker sauce, cook it a little longer. Add the salt and mix thoroughly. If there are lumps, blend until smooth.

In a large saucepan, heat the chicken stock and cook the onions, covered, over very low heat until soft, adding a little chicken stock if necessary to prevent scorching. Add the mushrooms and continue cooking, covered, until soft. Add the white sauce and all the other ingredients except the chicken, yogurt, and noodles. Simmer, uncovered, for 10 minutes.

Add the chicken and cook until thoroughly heated. Remove from the heat, add the yogurt, and mix thoroughly. On each of four heated plates serve ¾ cup of the mixture in the center of ¾ cup of noodles.

Makes 4 servings

EACH SERVING CONTAINS APPROXIMATELY:
345 TOTAL CALORIES / 65 CALORIES IN FAT
90 MG CHOLESTEROL / 165 MG SODIUM
145 MG CALCIUM

COMPANY CHICKEN

This recipe is a revised version of an old standby sent to me by a reader. It contained two packages of frozen broccoli, two cans of cream of chicken soup, and a cup of mayonnaise. This is a long way "ingredientswise" from the original, but amazingly similar in both taste and appearance.

2 whole chicken breasts, halved
2 cups water
1 1/2 pounds fresh broccoli
4 tablespoons corn-oil margarine
3 tablespoons flour
1 1/2 cups defatted chicken stock (see page 22)
1/4 cup skim milk
1/2 pound tofu (1 cup)
1 tablespoon corn oil
2 tablespoons freshly squeezed lemon juice
1/2 teaspoon salt (omit if using salted chicken stock)
1/4 teaspoon ground white pepper
1/2 teaspoon curry powder
2 ounces low-fat Cheddar cheese, grated (1/2 cup)
1/2 cup soft bread crumbs

Remove the skin and fat from the chicken breasts. Put into a Dutch oven along with the water. Bring to a boil, reduce the heat, and simmer for 25 to 30 minutes or until all the pink is gone from the chicken breasts. Cool and slice thinly.

Cut the broccoli into even-length spears. Steam for 5 minutes or until crisp-tender. Remove from the heat and cool under cold running water. Drain and set aside.

Melt 3 tablespoons of the margarine in a medium saucepan. Add the flour and stir until bubbly. Add the chicken stock and milk. Continue to cook and stir until the mixture thickens and comes to a boil.

In a blender container, combine the chicken stock mixture, tofu, corn oil, lemon juice, salt, pepper, and curry powder. Blend until smooth and velvety.

Arrange the broccoli in the bottom of a 9-by-13-inch glass baking dish. Top with the chicken. Pour the sauce over the chicken and top with the grated cheese. Melt the remaining 1 tablespoon of margarine in a small saucepan. Mix with the bread crumbs. Sprinkle over the top of the casserole.

Bake in a preheated 350°F oven until lightly browned and bubbly, about 30 minutes.

Makes 4 servings

EACH SERVING CONTAINS APPROXIMATELY:
500 TOTAL CALORIES / 230 CALORIES IN FAT
70 MG CHOLESTEROL / 490 MG SODIUM
330 MG CALCIUM

CHICKEN IN BURGUNDY

If you prefer, chicken stock may be substituted for the beef stock in this recipe. I like the flavor this sauce gives the chicken so much that I often double the recipe to have cold leftover chicken for lunch the next day.

2 cups defatted beef stock (see page 23)
½ cup Burgundy
1 teaspoon dried thyme, crushed in a mortar and pestle

1 teaspoon dried marjoram, crushed in a mortar and pestle
1/8 teaspoon freshly ground black pepper
1/2 teaspoon salt (omit if using salted stock)
2 tablespoons chopped parsley
8 to 10 small white onions
5 celery ribs
1 1/2 pounds boned and skinned chicken breasts

Combine the stock, wine, thyme, marjoram, pepper, salt, parsley, and onions in a large saucepan and bring to a boil. Lay the celery ribs over the top of the mixture. Reduce the heat, cover, and simmer for 1 hour. Remove the celery and discard.

Add the chicken breasts to the sauce and poach gently for 5 to 10 minutes or until the chicken is opaque but still slightly pink in the center (it will continue to cook while it is being held).

Remove the chicken and onions to a warm platter and cover lightly with aluminum foil to keep it warm. Bring the heat up and reduce the sauce to 1 cup. Pour over the chicken. Serve with rice or noodles.

Makes 4 servings

EACH SERVING CONTAINS APPROXIMATELY:
260 TOTAL CALORIES / 55 CALORIES IN FAT
100 MG CHOLESTEROL / 460 MG SODIUM
90 MG CALCIUM

CHICKEN IN PINK PEPPERCORN SAUCE

The original recipe for this dish was sent to me by a reader and was loaded with butter and cream. It took me a long time to revise this recipe to my own satisfaction, but now that I have, it is one of my favorites. The only problem with it is that the chicken must be cooked at the last minute for the dish to be truly as superb as it deserves to be.

1 tablespoon corn-oil margarine
1 pound chicken breasts, boned, skinned, and cut diagonally
  into sixteen 1-inch strips (reserve the scraps)
¼ cup cognac or brandy
½ cup defatted chicken stock (see page 22)
½ cup low-fat milk
1 tablespoon fresh tarragon, finely chopped, or 1 teaspoon dried
  tarragon, crushed in a mortar and pestle
2 tablespoons dry pink peppercorns
2 cups Rice Pilaf (page 119)
2 cups Creamed Leeks (page 109)
1 small tomato, peeled, seeded, and diced (½ cup) for garnish
2 teaspoons finely chopped chives for garnish
4 fresh tarragon sprigs for garnish

Melt the margarine in a large skillet. When hot, add the scraps of chicken breast and sauté until brown. Remove the chicken scraps and discard.

Pour the cognac or brandy into the hot skillet to deglaze and reduce until almost dry. Add the chicken stock and reduce by half. Add the milk and reduce by half. Add the tarragon and peppercorns. Set aside.

To serve, cook the chicken strips for 3 to 5 minutes or until tender. On each of four heated plates, arrange ½ cup Rice Pilaf in a ring around the outer edge and ½ cup Creamed Leeks in the center. Fan four strips of chicken over the leeks. Spoon 2 tablespoons sauce over the chicken and leeks and sprinkle 2 tablespoons diced tomato and ½ teaspoon chopped chives on top. Lay a sprig of tarragon across the top of each serving.

Makes 4 servings

EACH SERVING CONTAINS APPROXIMATELY:
465 TOTAL CALORIES / 110 CALORIES IN FAT
75 MG CHOLESTEROL / 400 MG SODIUM
165 MG CALCIUM

MOROCCAN CHICKEN WITH COUSCOUS

This delightfully different Middle Eastern dish can be served with turkey or rabbit as well as chicken. Couscous is a fine, cereal-like pasta popular in the Middle East, where they eat it with their right hand. Unless you are inviting adventurous guests, I suggest serving this dish with a soup spoon.

6 cups defatted chicken stock (see page 22)
1 medium onion, finely chopped (1 1/2 cups)
1/2 teaspoon salt (omit if using salted stock)
1/2 cup canned garbanzo beans (chick-peas), drained
1 medium turnip, peeled and cut into bite-size pieces (2 cups)
1 medium yam, peeled and cut into bite-size pieces (2 cups)
1 cup canned peeled tomatoes
1 1/2 teaspoons ground coriander
1 1/2 teaspoons ground cumin
1 cup uncooked couscous
3/4 pound cooked chicken breast, cut into bite-size pieces (3 cups)
  and kept warm
Chopped chives for garnish

Combine the stock, onions, and salt and bring to a boil. Reduce the heat and simmer for 1 hour, uncovered. Add the beans, vegetables, and spices and cook for 20 minutes more or until vegetables are just tender. Do not overcook.

Spoon 1 1/2 cups of the liquid from the vegetables into a medium saucepan and bring to a boil, then add the couscous. Mix well and remove from the heat. Allow to stand, covered, for 5 minutes. This yields 3 cups of cooked couscous.

For each serving, combine 1 cup of vegetables and broth with 1/2 cup warm chicken in a large bowl and sprinkle with chopped chives. Serve 1/2 cup couscous on the side.

Makes 6 servings

EACH SERVING CONTAINS APPROXIMATELY:
355 TOTAL CALORIES / 45 CALORIES IN FAT
50 MG CHOLESTEROL / 400 MG SODIUM
80 MG CALCIUM

CHICKEN ENCHILADA

For a real "south of the border" Mexican fiesta, serve these enchiladas with Gazpacho (page 31) to start, a lettuce and tomato salad with Light Cumin Dressing (page 72), and a Mexican fruit plate for dessert. All fruits grow somewhere in Mexico! Accompany this menu with either my Make-believe Margaritas (page 257) or the real thing.

> *1 medium onion, finely chopped (1½ cups)*
> *½ cup defatted chicken stock (see page 22)*
> *½ teaspoon salt*
> *1 tablespoon chili powder*
> *½ teaspoon ground cumin*
> *3 large tomatoes, peeled and diced (3 cups)*
> *2 ounces part-skim mozzarella cheese, grated (½ cup)*
> *¼ pound cooked chicken, finely chopped (1 cup)*
> *4 corn torttillas*

Sauté the onions in a large skillet, covered, until tender, adding a little chicken stock if necessary to prevent scorching. Add the salt, chili powder, and cumin and mix well.

Add the tomatoes and chicken stock and mix well. Cook, uncovered, for 5 minutes over low heat. Remove half the sauce and set aside.

To the sauce remaining in the pan, add ½ cup of the cheese and the chicken and mix well.

Spoon ½ cup of the mixture down the center of each tortilla and roll the tortilla around it. Place, fold side down, in a baking dish. Spoon the remaining sauce evenly over the tops of the enchiladas. Then sprinkle 1 tablespoon of the remaining grated cheese over each enchilada.

Bake, uncovered, in a preheated 350°F oven for 25 minutes.

Makes 4 servings

EACH SERVING CONTAINS APPROXIMATELY:
195 TOTAL CALORIES / 55 CALORIES IN FAT
55 MG CHOLESTEROL / 435 MG SODIUM
145 MG CALCIUM

CHICKEN JAMBALAYA

Of all the Cajun and Creole-style recipes that have been so popular in the last couple of years, Jambalaya is still the one I like best. This recipe is easy to make and can be made the day before you plan to serve it, which makes it an ideal dish for company.

2 tablespoons water
1 1/2 celery ribs, without leaves, chopped (1 cup)
1/2 medium onion, finely chopped (3/4 cup)
1 green bell pepper, finely chopped (3/4 cup)
1 garlic clove, finely chopped (1 teaspoon)
1/2 cup chopped lean ham
1 bay leaf
1/4 teaspoon salt (omit if using salted stock)
1/4 teaspoon ground white pepper
1/4 teaspoon cayenne
1/4 teaspoon freshly ground black pepper
1/2 cup tomato sauce
1/4 teaspoon Tabasco
1 cup uncooked long-grain brown rice
1 1/2 cups defatted chicken stock (see page 22)
1/2 pound cooked chicken, chopped (2 cups)
2 cups Creole Sauce (page 57), heated
Parsley sprigs for garnish

Heat the water in a large skillet. Add the celery, onions, green peppers, garlic, and ham. Cook, stirring occasionally, over medium heat until the liquid is completely reduced and the vegetables become lightly browned and tender. Scrape the bottom of the pan often.

Add the seasonings, tomato sauce, and Tabasco. Continue to cook, stirring constantly, for 5 minutes more.

Stir in the rice, mixing well. Reduce the heat and simmer for about 15 minutes. Add the chicken stock and bring to a boil. Reduce the heat and simmer, covered, until the rice is tender but still firm, about 40 minutes. Add the chicken and mix well. Cover and continue to cook for 10 minutes more, or until the chicken is heated through. Remove the bay leaf.

To serve, spoon the Jambalaya into 6-ounce custard cups, packing tightly. Spoon ½ cup hot Creole Sauce onto a heated plate. Unmold the Jambalaya on top of the sauce. Garnish the top of each serving with a sprig of parsley.

Makes 4 servings

EACH SERVING CONTAINS APPROXIMATELY:
300 TOTAL CALORIES / 40 CALORIES IN FAT
10 MG CHOLESTEROL / 975 MG SODIUM
80 MG CALCIUM

CHICKEN LIVER PÂTÉ

I have a friend who calls this recipe fantasy pâté because it amuses her to have her favorite hors d'oeuvre for less than half the calories of regular pâté. It is wonderful for hors d'oeuvres and makes great sandwiches served open-faced on bagels or with sliced onions on rye bread.

1 medium potato
½ pound chicken livers
2 tablespoons cognac
¼ cup defatted chicken stock (see page 22)
¼ teaspoon salt (omit if using salted stock)
¼ teaspoon freshly ground black pepper
¼ teaspoon ground nutmeg
1 teaspoon powdered mustard
1 shallot, chopped (1 tablespoon)

Bake or boil the potato until tender. Peel and cut it into small pieces. Set aside.

Wash the chicken livers. Place them in a small saucepan with enough water to cover and cook over low heat until tender, about 10 minutes.

Blend the chicken livers to a paste in a food processor with a metal blade. Add the cooked potato and all the remaining ingredients and blend to a paste.

Pack into 2 or 3 small ramekins and serve as a spread with toast or as a filling for sandwiches.

Makes 2 cups

1 TABLESPOON CONTAINS APPROXIMATELY:
20 TOTAL CALORIES / 5 CALORIES IN FAT
45 MG CHOLESTEROL / 20 MG SODIUM
5 MG CALCIUM

ROCK CORNISH GAME HENS WITH CITRUS-SAGE SAUCE

At the Four Seasons Hotel and Resort in Dallas I serve these game hens with Rice Pilaf (page 119) and an assortment of colorful steamed vegetables. They are also good served with baked yams and green vegetables.

1 1/2 medium onions, finely chopped (2 1/4 cups)
2 Rock Cornish game hens, halved
Freshly ground black pepper to taste
1 cup freshly squeezed orange juice
1/2 cup sherry
1 teaspoon dried sage, crushed in a mortar and pestle
2 tablespoons orange zest
4 orange slices for garnish

Preheat the oven to 350°F. Spread the chopped onions on the bottom of a baking dish. Place the game hens in a single layer on top of the onions, cut side down. Sprinkle with black pepper. Bake for 15 minutes.

While the game hens are cooking, bring the orange juice to a boil and reduce it to ½ cup. Add the sherry, sage, and orange zest and set aside.

Remove the game hens from the oven and set aside until cool enough to handle. When cool, using a sharp knife or kitchen shears, cut the skin away from the meat and discard. Place the game hens back on the bed of onions, cut side down.

Pour the orange juice mixture over the game hens and return to the oven. Bake for 45 minutes more, basting often.

To serve, remove the game hens from the pan and place on individual serving plates, cut side down. Stir the onions thoroughly through the sauce and spoon the sauce over the servings. Garnish each with a twisted orange slice.

Makes 4 servings

EACH SERVING CONTAINS APPROXIMATELY:
335 TOTAL CALORIES / 110 CALORIES IN FAT
90 MG CHOLESTEROL / 55 MG SODIUM
60 MG CALCIUM

ROAST TURKEY WITH FENNEL

This is the recipe I used to roast my own turkey for Christmas last year. I served it with Italian Oyster Casserole (page 148) as the dressing and plated it on radicchio leaves. I served Italian green beans for a red and green Christmas dinner.

> *One 12- to 15-pound turkey*
> *3 onions, peeled and coarsely chopped*
> *2 tablespoons fennel seeds*
> *Salt to taste*

Wash the turkey and pat dry. Combine the onions and fennel seeds and stuff the turkey with the mixture.

Salt the outside of the turkey lightly and place it on its side on a rack in a roasting pan. Bake, uncovered, in a preheated 325°F oven for approximately 20 minutes per pound.

Halfway through the cooking, turn the turkey on its other side. If you wish to brown the turkey for a better appearance, place it on its back for the final 15 minutes.

Remove the turkey from the oven. Transfer it to a platter and allow it to rest for 20 minutes before carving.

Remove the turkey drippings from the pan to a bowl and place in the freezer. As soon as the fat has congealed on top of the drippings, remove from the freezer. Skim off the fat and make a light turkey gravy (see Light Gravy, page 49).

Remove the skin from the turkey after carving.

EACH 3½-OUNCE SERVING CONTAINS APPROXIMATELY:
210 TOTAL CALORIES / 90 CALORIES IN FAT
80 MG CHOLESTEROL / 70 MG SODIUM
25 MG CALCIUM

TURKEY TETRAZZINI

I have purposely made this recipe larger than most of the recipes in the book because it is such an ideal, easy, and inexpensive dinner to make for groups of all ages. Chicken, rabbit, or drained water-packed canned tuna substitute well for the turkey.

1 tablespoon corn-oil margarine
1 pound fresh mushrooms, sliced (4 cups)
1/2 green bell pepper, julienne cut (1/2 cup)
2 1/2 tablespoons flour
1/2 teaspoon salt
1/4 teaspoon freshly ground black pepper
3/4 cup nonfat dry milk powder
1 3/4 cups defatted chicken stock (see page 22)
3 cups julienne-cut cooked turkey
2 tablespoons sherry
1/2 cup sliced pimientos
Nonstick vegetable coating
4 cups cooked spaghetti (1/2 pound dry)
1/4 pound Parmesan cheese, freshly grated (1 cup)

Melt the margarine in a large skillet and sauté the mushrooms and green pepper over low heat until soft, about 5 minutes. Stir in the flour, salt, and pepper and cook until bubbly. Combine the dry milk powder and the chicken stock and add to the flour mixture. Cook, stirring constantly, over low heat until thickened, approximately 10 to 15 minutes.

Add the turkey, sherry, and pimientos and mix well. Remove from the heat and cool slightly.

Spray a casserole dish with nonstick vegetable coating. Place the spaghetti in the bottom, then pour the turkey mixture over the spaghetti and sprinkle with the Parmesan cheese. Bake in a pre-heated 350°F oven until the sauce bubbles and the cheese is melted and lightly browned, about 25 minutes.

Makes eight 1 1/4-cup servings

EACH SERVING CONTAINS APPROXIMATELY:
295 TOTAL CALORIES / 75 CALORIES IN FAT
50 MG CHOLESTEROL / 490 MG SODIUM
295 MG CALCIUM

GRILLED TURKEY BURGER WITH CRANBERRY CATSUP

I designed this "holiday burger" for the Christmas season at the Four Seasons Hotel and Resort in Dallas, and to everyone's surprise it turned out to be their biggest-selling luncheon entrée. In fact it is so popular I plan to leave it on the menu as a permanent item.

1 pound ground lean turkey
4 small buns, halved
1/2 cup Cranberry Catsup (page 65)
4 onion slices
Lettuce leaves

Form the ground turkey into four patties and grill (over mesquite if available) until done.

Spread 1 tablespoon Cranberry Catsup on each bun half. Place the patties on the buns and garnish with the onion slices and lettuce.

Makes 4 servings

EACH SERVING CONTAINS APPROXIMATELY:
370 TOTAL CALORIES / 145 CALORIES IN FAT
1 MG CHOLESTEROL / 350 MG SODIUM
65 MG CALCIUM

RABBIT FRICASSEE WITH DUMPLINGS

This recipe should probably be in the meat section, but, as I have said, rabbit actually substitutes better for chicken and turkey in a recipe than it does for any meat. For that reason I have included it in this section, so you may substitute chicken or turkey if rabbit is not available.

4 cups defatted chicken stock (see page 22)
1/2 cup chopped onion
1/2 cup sliced celery rib
1/2 cup sliced carrots
1/2 cup dry white wine
1/4 cup chopped parsley
1/4 cup finely chopped chives
1/4 teaspoon dried saffron
1 cup Magic Biscuit Mix (page 206)
1/2 cup skim milk
2 tablespoons cornstarch dissolved in 2 tablespoons water
1/2 cup canned evaporated skimmed milk
1/2 pound cooked rabbit, cut into thin strips (2 cups)
1/4 teaspoon freshly ground black pepper
1/2 teaspoon salt
Chopped parsley for garnish

Bring the stock to a boil in a large saucepan and reduce by one-third. Add the vegetables, wine, parsley, half of the chives, and the saffron. Reduce the heat, cover, and simmer until the vegetables are tender, about 15 minutes.

Meanwhile, combine the Magic Biscuit Mix, skim milk, and the remaining chives and mix thoroughly. Set aside.

Stir the dissolved cornstarch into the simmering broth. Add the evaporated skimmed milk and cook, stirring constantly, until slightly thickened.

Drop the batter into the broth by rounded tablespoonsful, making eight dumplings. Cover and cook for 12 minutes.

Transfer the dumplings to soup bowls, using a slotted spoon. Add the rabbit, salt (omit if using salted stock), and pepper to the broth and heat through.

Ladle the fricassee over the dumplings. Garnish with the parsley.

Makes 4 servings

EACH SERVING CONTAINS APPROXIMATELY:
340 TOTAL CALORIES / 100 CALORIES IN FAT
1 MG CHOLESTEROL / 635 MG SODIUM
265 MG CALCIUM

MEAT

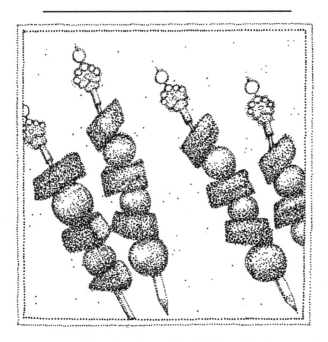

R E D   M E A T, while the least desirable animal protein source because of its fat content, is not all bad. Red meat is a complete protein and is abundant in minerals such as zinc that are often difficult to find in other foods. Meat is also packed with many of the B vitamins.

Red meat is actually very little higher in cholesterol than poultry and some fish. The problem lies in the fact that the fat content of meat is primarily in the saturated form and therefore adds to the buildup of the cholesterol it does contain. The biggest problem, however, is that the fat in meat runs through the red muscle of the meat and that even after you have removed all visible fat, it is impossible to get it all out the way you can by removing the skin and visible fat from poultry.

Currently beef is divided into three grades—good, prime, and choice—depending upon the amount of marbling it contains. The marbling consists of the streaks of fat running through the meat. Good contains the least amount of fat and prime the most. Efforts are being made to change the word *good* to *select* to encourage more people to buy it.

The leanest cuts of meat include flank and round steak, lean lamb or pork, and veal. Interestingly enough, while veal is lower in fat content, it is higher in cholesterol than beef because, being baby beef, it is milk fed during its brief life. Organ meats, such as liver, are also low in fat but extremely high in cholesterol. All organ meats are very high in vitamin and mineral content but should be limited in the diet because of their high cholesterol content. Cured and processed meats, such as ham, bacon, bologna, lunch meats, and hot dogs, should be limited or avoided because they contain nitrates. Also many of them are extremely high in saturated fat and sodium. The reason the nitrates are used is to give cured meats their pinkish color instead of the unappealing brown color they would otherwise have. The problem with them is that while being digested they form nitrosamines, which are known to cause cancer.

When buying meat, always look for the leanest cuts available. Remember the grading on beef and avoid cuts with more fat marbling. Fortunately you do not have to worry about prime beef, which has the highest fat content, because it is not often found in ordinary stores. It is usually sold only to restaurants and specialty meat markets.

Wild game such as venison, elk, and the like are also good choices but are not readily available. They are leaner because they have been allowed to run wild rather than being confined in small spaces to prevent them from losing weight.

If possible it is always better to grind your own meat for things like hamburgers and meat loaf because you can then better control the fat content.

When preparing meat, always carefully remove all visible fat. Use cooking methods that allow the fat to drain off the meat rather than being held in. For example, when you are baking or broiling meat, always put it on a rack above the pan so the fat is not served with it. When making stews or soups, try to always make them the day before you plan to serve them. Then remove all the visible fat that forms on the top before reheating to serve. This gives you not only a healthier dish but also a more appetizing-looking entrée because it will not have the fat globules floating around on the top. An interesting aside is that the pictures you see in magazines for recipes containing lots of fat are always taken of defatted versions in order to avoid the congealed fat that would show in the photographs.

The one thing about cooking meat that is much easier than cooking either fish or seafood is that cooking time is not so crucial. Even though there are many cuts of meat that are much better served very rare rather than well done, there are also many others that can be cooked for long periods of time and the time only improves both the taste and the texture.

The single most important tip in preparing and serving meat is to use less of it. I have been in restaurants where a steak weighing at least a pound was served to a person and arrived looking like a roast for the whole table. Remember that animal protein should never be more than one-fifth the volume of your meal. So think in terms of a small steak, a large baked potato, lots of vegetables, and a wonderful salad; or a stir-fry with a little beef, pork, or lamb to add flavor and texture. Treat all meat as a condiment rather than the focus or main part of the meal.

SZECHUAN BEEF AND VEGETABLE STIR-FRY

This is a delicious Oriental entrée that can also be made with poultry. If you want to make it as a vegetarian dish, you can substitute vegetable stock for the chicken stock called for in the recipe. You will note that I always suggest not only removing the strings from the pea pods but also notching the ends. By notching, I mean cutting a V-shaped wedge at each end of the pod. This removes the tough ends and also gives a finished, more decorative look to the vegetable. It's fun to serve this dish with chopsticks.

> *1 pound flank steak*
> *2 teaspoons dark sesame oil*
> *1 tablespoon reduced-sodium soy sauce*
> *1 tablespoon sherry*
> *1 teaspoon fructose or 1¹/₂ teaspoons sugar*
> *2 teaspoons cornstarch*

2 teaspoons minced peeled ginger
2 garlic cloves, finely chopped (2 teaspoons)
1/4 cup defatted chicken stock (see page 22)
3 scallions, cut diagonally into 1-inch pieces
1/4 pound fresh mushrooms, sliced (1 cup)
1/4 pound Chinese pea pods, ends notched and strings removed
1 small red bell pepper, cut into 1/4-inch strips
1 medium yellow squash, cut in half lengthwise, then sliced crosswise into 1/4-inch slices
1/2 teaspoon crushed red pepper flakes

Remove all visible fat from the flank steak and cut it crosswise into 1/4-inch strips; then cut each strip in half.

Combine the sesame oil, soy sauce, sherry, fructose or sugar, cornstarch, half the ginger, and half the garlic in a medium bowl and mix well. Add the steak pieces and toss to combine. Set aside.

Heat half the chicken stock in a nonstick skillet over medium-high heat. Add the remaining garlic and ginger and the scallions and mushrooms. Stir-fry for 1 to 2 minutes. Transfer to a medium bowl.

Add the remaining chicken stock to the skillet and heat. Add the pea pods, bell pepper, and squash. Stir-fry until crisp-tender, about 3 to 4 minutes. Add this to the scallions and mushrooms.

Heat the skillet again. Add the steak and pepper flakes. Stir-fry until brown and tender, about 3 to 4 minutes. Return the vegetables to the skillet and heat through. Serve with brown rice.

Makes four 1-cup servings

EACH SERVING CONTAINS APPROXIMATELY:
255 TOTAL CALORIES / 80 CALORIES IN FAT
80 MG CHOLESTEROL / 310 MG SODIUM
35 MG CALCIUM

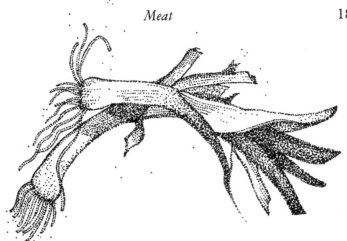

ENCHILADA TORTE

If you like enchiladas but don't like to take the time to make them, this Enchilada Torte is the perfect solution because you don't have to roll each individual enchilada. It also makes a very attractive plate presentation. I sometimes make this dish as a vegetarian entrée, omitting the beef and adding 4 cups of steamed sliced mushrooms in its place.

S A U C E :

One 28-ounce can crushed tomatoes (3 1/2 cups)
1/2 medium onion, chopped (3/4 cup)
1 medium carrot, sliced (1/2 cup)
1 celery rib, without leaves, chopped (1/2 cup)
1 garlic clove, chopped (1 teaspoon)
1/4 cup water
1 1/2 tablespoons chili powder
1 1/4 teaspoons ground cumin
1/4 teaspoon salt
1/4 teaspoon freshly ground black pepper

Nonstick vegetable coating
12 corn tortillas
1 pound lean ground beef
9 scallions, thinly sliced
6 ounces Cheddar cheese, grated (1 1/2 cups)
Cilantro or parsley sprigs for garnish

Combine the sauce ingredients in a large saucepan and bring to a boil. Cover, reduce the heat, and simmer for 30 to 45 minutes or until the vegetables are very tender. Cool slightly. Pour into a blender container or food processor with a metal blade and puree. Return to the pan and set aside.

Lightly spray each side of the tortillas with nonstick vegetable spray and bake on a cookie sheet in a preheated 350°F oven for 7 minutes. Turn the tortillas over and bake until crisp, about 8 minutes. Remove from the oven and set aside.

Brown the meat in a nonstick skillet. Drain to remove any fat that accumulates in the pan. Add meat to the sauce.

Place one tortilla on an ungreased cookie sheet with sides. Top with 2 tablespoons scallions, 2 tablespoons cheese, and ¼ cup sauce. Repeat the layers three times (using four tortillas in all). Make two more stacks the same way on the cookie sheet. Divide the remaining sauce over the three enchilada tortes.

Bake in a preheated 350°F oven for 15 to 20 minutes or until hot.

To serve, cut each torte in half. Place a half torte on each plate and garnish with cilantro or parsley sprigs.

Makes 6 servings

EACH SERVING CONTAINS APPROXIMATELY:
420 TOTAL CALORIES / 145 CALORIES IN FAT
80 MG CHOLESTEROL / 670 MG SODIUM
370 MG CALCIUM

POT ROAST

Pot roast is a wonderful all-American entrée. It is also easy and economical. Leftovers are great for sandwiches and can also be frozen for another meal.

1 teaspoon corn-oil margarine
2 garlic cloves, finely chopped (2 teaspoons)

3 pounds boneless beef pot roast
1 medium onion, sliced (2 cups)
12 peppercorns
12 whole allspice
1 bay leaf, crumbled
2 tablespoons grated fresh horseradish
1/2 cup dry red wine
1/2 cup defatted beef stock (see page 23) or water
1/2 teaspoon salt

Early in the day on which you plan to serve the pot roast (or the day before): Preheat the oven to 325°F. Melt the margarine in a Dutch oven or roasting pan with a tight-fitting lid. Sauté the garlic in the margarine over low heat until lightly browned. Add the roast and brown well on all sides. Remove the roast from the pan.

Layer the onion slices in the bottom of the pan. Put the roast on top of the onions. Combine the remaining ingredients and pour over the roast. Cover tightly and simmer in the oven for 3 to 4 hours or until the roast is tender (or simmer, tightly covered, on top of the stove).

Remove from the pan, cool, cover, and refrigerate. Cool the cooking liquid to room temperature and refrigerate, uncovered, until the fat congeals on top.

When ready to serve, remove the fat from the cooking liquid. Slice the meat and return it to the pan along with the cooking liquid. Warm slowly. Serve with rice, noodles, or potatoes. Spoon the broth over the meat or serve it separately in a gravy boat.

Makes eight 3-ounce servings

EACH SERVING CONTAINS APPROXIMATELY:
325 TOTAL CALORIES / 215 CALORIES IN FAT
80 MG CHOLESTEROL / 190 MG SODIUM
30 MG CALCIUM

BURGUNDY-BRAISED BEEF

---

1 teaspoon corn-oil margarine
2 pounds lean beef, cut into 24 cubes
1/2 cup chopped leeks, white part only
1 small carrot, peeled and chopped (1/2 cup)
1/2 medium onion, chopped (3/4 cup)
1 tablespoon finely chopped parsley
1 tablespoon finely chopped chives
1 garlic clove, chopped (1 teaspoon)
2 whole cloves
3 1/4 cups Burgundy
1/4 teaspoon dried marjoram, crushed in a mortar and pestle
8 peppercorns, crushed
1/2 teaspoon salt

Preheat the oven to 350°F. Melt the margarine in a large nonstick skillet over medium heat. When the pan is hot, add the beef cubes and brown well on all sides.

Put the beef in a Dutch oven or large casserole with a tight-fitting lid. Add the leeks, carrots, onions, parsley, chives, garlic, and cloves to the skillet in which the beef was browned and brown lightly, stirring constantly. Add the vegetables to the beef in the casserole and mix well.

Deglaze the skillet by pouring 1/4 cup of the Burgundy over the drippings. Bring to a boil, stirring and scraping up the remaining bits of meat and vegetables in the pan. Pour over the meat and vegetables in the casserole.

Add the remaining Burgundy and the seasonings to the meat and vegetables and mix well. Bake, covered, for 3 hours.

Serve 4 squares of beef and 3 tablespoons of broth per person with rice or noodles.

Makes 6 servings

EACH SERVING CONTAINS APPROXIMATELY:
375 TOTAL CALORIES / 80 CALORIES IN FAT
120 MG CHOLESTEROL / 275 MG SODIUM
40 MG CALCIUM

CARROT-AND-MUSHROOM-STUFFED BRISKET

This stuffed brisket is a wonderful company entrée because it makes a pretty presentation on the plate. It can be plated either in individual servings or on a larger serving dish for buffet-style service. I like to serve it with new potatoes and a green vegetable such as broccoli, asparagus, or brussels sprouts.

1½ pounds brisket of beef
2 tablespoons water or beef stock (see page 23)
1 garlic clove, chopped (1 teaspoon)
⅓ cup finely chopped onion
¼ pound fresh mushrooms, finely chopped (1 cup)
1 egg white, lightly beaten
½ slice whole wheat bread, broken into crumbs (½ cup)
¼ teaspoon salt
¼ teaspoon freshly ground black pepper
3 medium carrots, peeled
1 medium onion, sliced (2 cups)
½ cup beef stock (see page 23)
½ cup dry red wine
Herb leaves or parsley sprigs for garnish

Preheat the oven to 325°F. Remove all visible fat from the brisket. Cut a pocket horizontally along one long side, leaving a ½-inch border around three sides.

In a large nonstick skillet, bring the 2 tablespoons water or beef stock to a boil. Add the garlic, onions, and mushrooms. Cook until soft, about 5 minutes, adding more liquid if necessary to prevent scorching. Transfer to a bowl and combine with the egg white, bread crumbs, salt, and pepper and mix thoroughly. Set aside.

Place about 4 yards of kitchen string in a small bowl of water to soak.

Coarsely grate one of the carrots. Slice the remaining carrots in ¼-inch rounds and set aside.

Place half the grated carrot in the bottom of the brisket pocket. Spread all the mushroom mixture evenly over the carrot layer. Place the remaining grated carrot over the mushrooms. Tie the string around the brisket in both directions at 1-inch intervals to contain the stuffing.

Reheat the skillet in which the mushrooms were cooked. Brown the brisket well on both sides, about 5 minutes per side.

Place the sliced carrots and onions in the bottom of a roasting pan or Dutch oven. Place the brisket on top. Combine the stock and wine and pour it over the brisket. Cover the pan with a lid or aluminum foil. Bake for 3½ to 4 hours or until fork-tender.

Remove the roast from the oven and let it stand for 20 minutes before slicing. Place the vegetables and broth in a blender and puree until smooth. Reheat in a small saucepan.

To serve, spoon ⅓ cup sauce on each of eight plates. Top with a slice of brisket. Garnish with an herb leaf or parsley sprig. Pass the remaining sauce.

Makes 4 servings

EACH SERVING CONTAINS APPROXIMATELY:
475 TOTAL CALORIES / 180 CALORIES IN FAT
130 MG CHOLESTEROL / 275 MG SODIUM
70 MG CALCIUM

LAMB SHISH KEBAB

I like to serve shish kebab on either a bed of Rice Pilaf (page 119) or a mixture of grains such as barley, millet, cracked wheat, or kasha.

MARINADE:

½ cup red wine or red wine vinegar
2 tablespoons extra-virgin olive oil
2 tablespoons reduced-sodium soy sauce
¼ teaspoon freshly ground black pepper
Dash cayenne
½ teaspoon salt
1 tablespoon dried oregano, crushed in a mortar and pestle
½ cup minced onion

*1½ pounds lean lamb, cut into 16 cubes or slices of 1½ to 2
   inches*
8 small whole boiling onions, parboiled
1 medium green bell pepper, seeded and cut into 8 pieces
1 medium red bell pepper, seeded and cut into 8 pieces

Combine all the marinade ingredients and mix well.

Remove all the visible fat from the lamb. Place in a glass baking dish. Pour the marinade over the lamb, cover, and refrigerate overnight. Stir occasionally.

Remove the lamb from the marinade, reserving marinade to brush on the lamb while cooking.

Thread the kebab ingredients onto four skewers, alternating them to create a colorful presentation.

Cook over hot coals, 4 to 5 inches from the heat, for 15 to 20 minutes, brushing with the marinade and turning the skewers frequently to cook evenly and to prevent burning. The meat is done when it is nicely browned but still slightly pink in the center.

Makes 4 servings

EACH SERVING CONTAINS APPROXIMATELY:
470 TOTAL CALORIES / 305 CALORIES IN FAT
140 MG CHOLESTEROL / 635 MG SODIUM
55 MG CALCIUM

BALKAN LAMB AND APRICOT STEW

When I think of lamb stew, I always think of the traditional Irish lamb stew with vegetables and potatoes. This recipe was sent to me by one of my readers, and I found it not only delicious but delightfully different. I like to serve it with baked sweet potatoes and green peas.

1½ pounds lean lamb roast
1 quart water
1 teaspoon freshly ground black pepper
½ teaspoon salt
2 tablespoons white vinegar
2 tablespoons defatted chicken or beef stock (see page 22 or 23)
2 medium onions, coarsely chopped (3 cups)
2 tablespoons chopped fresh mint
One 16-ounce can whole peeled tomatoes, drained
¼ cup uncooked pearl barley
¾ cup dried apricots
2 teaspoons freshly squeezed lemon juice
Fresh chopped mint for garnish

Place the lamb, water, pepper, and salt in a large, heavy kettle and bring to a boil. Reduce the heat to low, cover, and simmer for 1½ hours.

Meanwhile heat the vinegar and stock in a medium skillet. Add the onions and mint and cook until the onions are soft and translucent, about 5 minutes, adding a little more stock if necessary to prevent them from scorching.

Add the onions, mint, tomatoes, barley, and apricots to the lamb. Cover and simmer for 1 hour more.

Remove the lamb from the mixture. Strain out the vegetables and transfer the stock to a bowl. Cool to room temperature; then refrigerate, uncovered, for several hours or overnight until all the fat has congealed on the surface. Remove the fat.

Remove the lamb from the bones and all visible fat from the meat. Cut into bite-size pieces and combine with the vegetable mixture. Cover and refrigerate.

When ready to serve, combine the meat/vegetable mixture with the defatted stock and the lemon juice. Reheat. Ladle into bowls and sprinkle each serving with chopped mint.

Makes four 1½-cup entrée servings

EACH SERVING CONTAINS APPROXIMATELY:
560 TOTAL CALORIES / 280 CALORIES IN FAT
140 MG CHOLESTEROL / 565 MG SODIUM
95 MG CALCIUM

CASSOULET

Cassoulet is a French country dish that was developed by French housewives to use up the week's leftovers in a hearty dish with white beans. It always amuses me that most American cooking schools teach Cassoulet making by also teaching the preparation of all the leftovers few American homemakers would ever have on hand. Consequently, rather than being an easy "clean the refrigerator" type of dish, it is a time-consuming ordeal that nonetheless results in an absolutely delicious casserole. I don't think you necessarily have to have all the ingredients called for in this recipe to make a good Cassoulet. Just combine your own leftovers with the white beans and suggested seasoning and develop your own Cassoulet.

1 pound lamb shoulder chops, with bones
1 medium onion, chopped (1½ cups)
2 tomatoes, peeled and seeded
1 teaspoon dried thyme, crushed in a mortar and pestle
4 garlic cloves, peeled
1½ cups dry white wine
Water
2 tablespoons white vinegar
½ teaspoon salt
½ teaspoon freshly ground black pepper
1 cup Great Northern beans, soaked overnight
2 small carrots, peeled and diced (1 cup)
1 celery rib, diced (½ cup)
1 medium onion, finely chopped (1½ cups)
1 bay leaf
2 tablespoons chopped parsley
5 peppercorns
1 Cornish game hen, quartered
1 tablespoon dried thyme, crushed in a mortar and pestle
1 cup whole wheat bread crumbs
1 tablespoon corn-oil margarine, melted

The day before serving, make the lamb-stew portion. Remove all the visible fat and cut the lamb into bite-size pieces, including the bones. Cook the lamb and onions in a heavy pot over medium heat for 10 minutes, adding a little water if necessary to prevent scorching. Add the tomatoes, thyme, and garlic. Cover with the wine, 1½ cups water, and the vinegar and season with the salt and pepper. Bring to a boil. Reduce the heat and simmer for 1 hour.

Strain the liquid and cool to room temperature. Refrigerate the liquid, uncovered. Transfer the lamb and vegetables to a bowl, cover, and refrigerate.

On the day you plan to serve the Cassoulet, remove the fat from the top of the reserved cooking stock and bring to a boil. Cook until reduced to 2 cups. Set aside.

Place the soaked beans in a large pot with the carrots, celery, onions, bay leaf, parsley, and peppercorns. Cover with water and simmer for 2 hours or until the beans are tender, adding more water as needed. Discard the bay leaf.

Sprinkle the quartered Cornish game hen with the thyme. Roast in a roasting pan in a preheated 325°F oven for 15 minutes. Remove from the oven and as soon as the hen is cool enough to handle, remove the skin.

To assemble, drain the bean mixture and reserve the cooking liquid. In a deep 3-quart casserole, layer half the beans, then the lamb and game hen. Top with the remaining beans. Add the stock reserved from cooking the lamb to 1 inch from the top, adding the reserved liquid from the beans if necessary.

Combine the bread crumbs and the melted margarine and mix thoroughly. Sprinkle over the top of the casserole. Bake, uncovered, in a preheated 250°F oven for 4 hours. Add more liquid if needed.

Makes 4 servings

EACH SERVING CONTAINS APPROXIMATELY:
620 TOTAL CALORIES / 280 CALORIES IN FAT
90 MG CHOLESTEROL / 460 MG SODIUM
130 MG CALCIUM

BREADS & CEREALS, PANCAKES & SUCH

BREAD IS TRULY the staff of life, and the staff is stronger when the breads are all made from whole grains. More than a third of the world's population gets over half of its daily calories from wheat alone.

We distinguish the different diets of various cultures around the world more by the types of breads and grain products they eat than by any other item in their diets. For example, we have Italian pasta, Mexican tortillas, Indian chapatis, Middle Eastern pita, Chinese pao ping, and a variety of French breads depending upon the region in France.

Even in this country there are regional differences in breads and grains. There are southern corn bread and grits and San Francisco sourdough and Boston brown bread, to name a few.

In ancient times all breads were made from whole grains and were completely unleavened and rather hard in texture. The lighter-textured yeast breads we have today are thought to have been discovered in Egypt when someone, quite by accident, mixed sourdough with new dough and produced a lighter loaf. Hundreds of years elapsed before these same white or refined-grain breads were developed in England. In the nineteenth century the roller mill was invented, and the British were able to produce a pure white flour by removing the germ and the outside bran coating of the wheat kernel, leaving only the endosperm, or soft white center portion of the kernel. Of course by removing the germ or embryo of the berry, they were also taking out all the valuable vitamins and minerals, and by removing the bran, they were getting rid of the fiber. This new white bread was very expensive to produce and was in such limited supply that only royalty and the upper classes could afford it. Thus it was the peasants who were eating the dark, rough whole-grain breads and they were all much healthier than the upper classes who were eating the refined bread. To this day this rough bread is called peasant bread.

An interesting aside is that it took at least fifty years before scientists realized that all the important vitamins, minerals, and fiber were in the bran and the germ they were either discarding or feeding to animals. This discovery took place during World War II, when they stopped refining grains in order to stretch the supply available for bread. The general health of the population improved during this period; however, immediately following the war they went right back to refining as much of the grain as possible and the same health problems recurred primarily due to the lack of enough fiber in the diet.

Dietary fiber is the indigestible part of plant food; it is not absorbed by the body and does not supply calories. It absorbs moisture, adding bulk, and speeds up the transit time of all other foods through the body for proper bowel function. Because of this moisture absorption, it is essential to drink an adequate amount of water along with the necessary amount of fiber. Many people think they are unable to eat high-fiber foods simply because they don't drink enough liquid and therefore experience stomachaches. The solution is to drink water!

Increased dietary fiber is also encouraged for the prevention of heart disease and many types of cancer, as well as constipation.

Wheat, although it is the most popular and often-used grain, is certainly not the whole grain story. Many other grains are readily

Fantasy in Fruit

Breast of Chicken Salad with Goat Cheese and Warm Mushroom Dressing

Minestrone Soup

Light Cinnamon Popovers with Apple Butter

Vegetable Terrine

Polynesian Prawns

Mexican Fiesta Menu

*Bouillabaisse, Salad of young greens with
Jeanne Jones' Light Tarragon Dressing,
and Gingered Fruit Compote*

available that are excellent both for cereals and breads. Oats, in particular, have received a lot of publicity recently due to the fact that scientific studies have shown that oat bran can lower the LDL (low-density lipoprotein) cholesterol in the blood, which is the harmful type of cholesterol that causes hardening of the arteries. This, in turn, raises the ratio of the HDL (high-density lipoprotein) type of cholesterol, which is the beneficial form of blood lipids. Oats have also been shown to be helpful in the diabetic diet.

Rolled oats are certainly one of the most popular hot breakfast cereals; however, some people don't like oatmeal because of its "mushy" texture. For those people I have included an oatmeal-pancake recipe that is truly delicious and very popular on my spa menus. I have never cared much for hot cereals myself because I am partial to crunchy or chewy textures. I have included in this section my favorite hot cereal, which is made with rye berries and is called Danish Rye Cereal (page 220). The rye berries retain their texture in cooking, and therefore you have a hot cereal with lots of texture.

All whole grains and whole-grain flours should be stored in the refrigerator. Since all bugs are born nutrition-oriented, they will always attack the whole grains first.

TORTILLA WEDGES

Because it is impossible to buy fat-free tortilla chips, I always include baking instructions for making your own. Not only are they healthier and less expensive, I think they are tastier, and they certainly contain fewer calories.

10 corn tortillas

Cut the tortillas into eight wedges each. Place them on cookie sheets in a single layer and bake in a preheated 400°F oven for 10 minutes. Turn over and bake for 3 minutes more. Sprinkle with a salt-free seasoning mix of your choice if desired.

Makes 80 wedges

EIGHT WEDGES CONTAIN APPROXIMATELY:
70 TOTAL CALORIES / 10 CALORIES IN FAT
0 MG CHOLESTEROL / 55 MG SODIUM
40 MG CALCIUM

CROUTONS

As with Tortilla Wedges (preceding recipe), I always include baking instructions for croutons because they are healthier, less expensive, and better tasting than anything you can buy. Making your own croutons also allows you to have enormous variety in the type of crouton you use. You can make them with whole-grain bread, as suggested in the recipe, or with sourdough, rye, corn bread, or pumpernickel.

4 slices whole-grain bread

Allow the bread to dry out for several hours, turning occasionally to assist the process.

Cut the bread into ¼-inch squares and place on a cookie sheet in a preheated 300°F oven for 20 minutes or until brown. Turn occasionally so they will brown evenly.

Makes 2 cups

¼ CUP CONTAINS APPROXIMATELY:
30 TOTAL CALORIES / 5 CALORIES IN FAT
0 MG CHOLESTEROL / 60 MG SODIUM
10 MG CALCIUM

LIGHT CINNAMON POPOVERS

Serving these giant popovers will always get you at least one "wow" from an admiring guest impressed with your culinary talents. The really wonderful thing is that you can make them ahead of time and no one will know the difference.

> *Corn-oil margarine*
> *All-purpose flour*
> *4 egg whites, at room temperature*
> *1 cup low-fat milk, at room temperature*
> *1 cup calcium-fortified all-purpose flour*
> *1 teaspoon ground cinnamon*
> *2 tablespoons corn-oil margarine, melted*

Preheat the oven to 450°F. Grease six 3½-inch custard cups with corn-oil margarine, being careful to cover all inner surfaces. Lightly dust with flour.

Combine all the ingredients in a blender container for 15 seconds at medium speed. Do not overmix.

Divide the batter evenly among the custard cups and bake for 20 minutes at 450°. Reduce the oven temperature to 350° and bake for 25 minutes more. Pierce the side of each popover and bake for another 5 minutes.

Serve immediately with Apple Butter (page 61). If you wish to make them ahead, cool to room temperature, wrap tightly with plastic wrap or aluminum foil, and freeze. To serve, unwrap and place on a cookie sheet in a preheated 350° oven for about 15 minutes.

Makes 6 popovers

EACH POPOVER CONTAINS APPROXIMATELY:
130 TOTAL CALORIES / 35 CALORIES IN FAT
1 MG CHOLESTEROL / 55 MG SODIUM
60 MG CALCIUM

PIZZA CRUST

I have purposely made this recipe for two pizza crusts instead of one because it takes practically no more time to make two, and these pizza crusts freeze so successfully that even if you want only one, the next time you're making pizza, you don't have to take the time to make the crust.

> *One 1/4-ounce package active dry yeast (check the date on the package)*
> *1 cup lukewarm water (110° to 115°F)*
> *3 cups whole wheat flour*
> *1 tablespoon olive oil*
> *1/2 teaspoon salt*

Sprinkle the yeast over the water. Stir to dissolve and let stand in a warm place for a few minutes until bubbly.

Add 1½ cups of the flour and mix well. Add the olive oil and salt and stir until well mixed.

Add 1 more cup of flour and mix well. Turn out onto a floured board and knead until smooth and elastic, adding more flour as needed (knead for about 10 to 15 minutes).

Place in an oiled bowl and turn the dough so that the oiled side is up. Cover with wax paper or plastic wrap. Put in a warm place for 1½ to 2 hours or until the dough is doubled in bulk. Punch down. Refrigerate until cold.

Divide the dough into two balls and roll out on a lightly floured board. Place each crust in a 12-inch pizza pan (available in grocery stores). Wrap and freeze if you are not going to use it immediately. Thaw completely before placing sauce, toppings, and cheese on top (see recipe for Pizza, page 126).

Makes two 12-inch crusts

EACH CRUST CONTAINS APPROXIMATELY:
670 TOTAL CALORIES / 95 CALORIES IN FAT
0 MG CHOLESTEROL / 560 MG SODIUM
80 MG CALCIUM

VARIATION:

To make 4- or 6-inch crusts (for Fresh Fruit Pizza, page 229, or for smaller regular pizzas), divide the dough into smaller balls.

SOUTHWESTERN CORN BREAD

This robustly flavored corn bread is particularly good served with soups and salads and is hearty enough to turn them into full meals.

> *2 tablespoons corn oil*
> *1/2 cup finely chopped onions*
> *1/2 cup canned chopped green California chilies*
> *1/4 cup finely chopped red bell pepper (optional)*
> *1 cup yellow cornmeal*
> *1 cup unbleached flour*
> *1 tablespoon baking powder*
> *1/2 teaspoon salt*
> *1/2 teaspoon ground cumin*
> *1/2 teaspoon chili powder*
> *2 ounces sharp Cheddar cheese, shredded (1/2 cup)*
> *1 cup skim milk*
> *1 egg*
> *1 cup cooked corn kernels*
> *Nonstick vegetable coating*

Preheat the oven to 400°F. Heat half the corn oil in a medium skillet. Add the onions, green chilies, and red bell pepper. Sauté until tender, about 5 minutes. DO NOT BROWN.

In a large bowl, combine the cornmeal, flour, baking powder, salt, cumin, and chili powder. Add the cheese and mix again.

In a separate medium bowl, combine the remaining corn oil, the milk, and the egg. Add the onion mixture and the corn. Add this to the dry ingredients and mix just until blended. Do not overmix.

Pour the batter into an 8-by-8-inch pan that has been sprayed with nonstick vegetable coating. Bake for 25 to 30 minutes or until lightly browned and a toothpick inserted in the center comes out clean. Cool for 5 to 10 minutes before cutting.

Makes 16 servings

EACH SERVING CONTAINS APPROXIMATELY:
115 TOTAL CALORIES / 30 CALORIES IN FAT
20 MG CHOLESTEROL / 165 MG SODIUM
100 MG CALCIUM

MAGIC BISCUIT MIX

I created this biscuit mix for a reader who wrote me requesting a recipe for an easy-to-make substitute for commercial mix that was lower in sodium and didn't contain preservatives. I am thrilled with the results and I think you will be too. You can use it in exactly the same way you would use any other biscuit mix—for pancakes, waffles, shortcake, and so on. Throughout the book I have recipes that use this Magic Biscuit Mix, including the following recipes for biscuits. In fact I called it magic because it will work in recipes in ways that literally seem impossible, if not magical. For convenience, you may wish to double this recipe. Most home food processors, however, will hold only a single recipe, so it is usually necessary to make a double recipe in two batches. Store in a tightly covered container either in a cool cupboard or in the refrigerator.

> *3 cups calcium-enriched all-purpose or unbleached flour*
> *1/2 cup nonfat dry milk powder*
> *2 tablespoons baking powder*
> *3/4 teaspoon salt*
> *1/3 cup corn oil*

Mix the dry ingredients in a food processor using a metal blade or with an electric mixer. Slowly pour in the oil as the machine is running. Scrape the sides of the bowl with a rubber spatula. Mix thoroughly again.

Store in a cool place in a tightly covered container.

Makes 5 loosely packed cups of mix

1 CUP CONTAINS APPROXIMATELY:
375 TOTAL CALORIES / 135 CALORIES IN FAT
1 MG CHOLESTEROL / 745 MG SODIUM
380 MG CALCIUM

BISCUITS

Once you have made the Magic Biscuit Mix, these biscuits are so easy to make that they will also seem like magic. Both this biscuit recipe and the Buttermilk Biscuit recipe that follows it can be made in much less time if you prefer to make drop biscuits, because you don't have to knead the dough or roll it out. After you have combined the ingredients, drop the dough by teaspoonful onto an ungreased cookie sheet and bake for 8 to 10 minutes or until golden brown.

1½ cups Magic Biscuit Mix (page 206)
⅓ cup skim milk

Preheat the oven to 450°F. Combine the biscuit mix and milk and beat vigorously by hand. If the dough is sticky, gradually add a little more biscuit mix until the dough is easy to handle.

Turn onto a cloth-covered board that is lightly dusted with biscuit mix. Shape the dough into a ball, then knead about ten times.

Using a rolling pin or your hands, flatten to ½-inch thickness. Press a 2-inch biscuit cutter into biscuit mix and cut out eight biscuits. Place on an ungreased cookie sheet and bake until golden brown, 8 to 10 minutes.

Makes 8 biscuits

EACH BISCUIT CONTAINS APPROXIMATELY:
75 TOTAL CALORIES / 30 CALORIES IN FAT
0 MG CHOLESTEROL / 145 MG SODIUM
85 MG CALCIUM

BUTTERMILK BISCUITS

2 cups Magic Biscuit Mix (page 206)
⅔ cup buttermilk
¼ teaspoon baking soda

Preheat the oven to 450°F. Combine all the ingredients in a large bowl and beat vigorously by hand until a soft dough forms. If the dough is sticky, gradually add a little more biscuit mix until the dough is easy to handle.

Turn onto a cloth-covered board that is lightly dusted with biscuit mix. Shape the dough into a ball, then knead about ten times.

Using a rolling pin or your hands, flatten to ½-inch thickness. Press a 2-inch biscuit cutter into the biscuit mix and cut out twelve biscuits. Place on an ungreased cookie sheet and bake until golden brown, 8 to 10 minutes.

Makes 12 biscuits

EACH BISCUIT CONTAINS APPROXIMATELY:
70 TOTAL CALORIES / 25 CALORIES IN FAT
1 MG CHOLESTEROL / 155 MG SODIUM
80 MG CALCIUM

GINGERBREAD PANCAKES

These sugar-free gingerbread pancakes are one of the most popular breakfast items I have ever created for any menu. When you make the pancake batter for this recipe, if you think it is too thick, add a little water. Each time I make it, I find the consistency is slightly different; also after the batter has been sitting for any length of time it will start to thicken and need to be thinned a little before making the pancakes. Just be careful not to overmix it or the pancakes will not be as light in texture. If you have any pancakes left over, make Gingerbread Pancake Pinwheels for after-school snacks or tea-party finger sandwiches. Spread each pancake with Light Cheese (page 52) and roll the pancake like a jelly roll. To serve, trim off the ends of each pancake roll and then cut it into pinwheels. If you really want to get fancy, using a pastry tube, pipe a little rosette of pastry cream on the top of each pinwheel.

1 cup whole wheat flour
3/4 teaspoon baking soda
1/2 teaspoon ground ginger
1/2 teaspoon ground cinnamon
1/4 teaspoon ground cloves
1/4 teaspoon salt
2 teaspoons instant decaffeinated coffee powder
1/4 cup hot water
1 egg, beaten
One 6-ounce can frozen unsweetened apple juice concentrate
2 tablespoons corn-oil margarine, melted
Nonstick vegetable coating

Combine the flour, baking soda, ginger, cinnamon, cloves, and salt in a large mixing bowl.

In another, smaller bowl, dissolve the instant coffee in the hot water. Add the egg, apple juice concentrate, and melted margarine and mix well.

Add the liquid ingredients to the dry ingredients and mix just enough to moisten the dry ingredients. The mixture will be lumpy.

Pour the batter, 1/4 cup at a time, onto a hot skillet or griddle that has been sprayed lightly with nonstick vegetable coating. Cook until the top of each pancake is covered with tiny bubbles and the bottom is brown. Turn and brown the other side.

Serve with Apple Butter (page 61) and Light Cheese (page 52).

Makes 8 pancakes

EACH PANCAKE CONTAINS APPROXIMATELY:
130 TOTAL CALORIES / 35 CALORIES IN FAT
35 MG CHOLESTEROL / 270 MG SODIUM
20 MG CALCIUM

OATMEAL-RAISIN PANCAKES

For people who don't particularly like cooked oatmeal as a breakfast cereal, this is a wonderful way to get this healthful grain into their breakfast menus. I like to serve them with Apple Butter (page 61). A delicious variation of this recipe is to use banana slices instead of raisins. Spoon the pancake batter on the grill and arrange the banana slices on each pancake before turning it over. I serve Spiced Bananas (page 228) with Oatmeal-Banana Pancakes.

1/4 cup raisins
1 1/2 cups uncooked old-fashioned oatmeal
1/4 teaspoon salt
1/4 teaspoon baking powder
1/4 teaspoon baking soda
1 egg, lightly beaten, or 1/4 cup liquid egg substitute
1 cup plain nonfat yogurt
1 tablespoon corn-oil margarine

Cover the raisins with warm water and allow to soak for 15 minutes. Drain thoroughly.

Put the oatmeal in a blender or food processor with a metal blade and blend for approximately 1 minute or until the consistency of flour is attained. Combine the oat flour, salt, baking powder, and baking soda in a large mixing bowl and mix well.

Combine all the remaining ingredients except for the margarine in another bowl and mix well. Combine the liquid and dry ingredients and mix until just moist. Allow to rest for 5 minutes.

Heat a cast-iron skillet or nonstick pan and melt the margarine. When the pan is hot, wipe out the margarine with a paper towel. Spoon 3 tablespoons of batter into the pan for each pancake. Cook over medium heat until bubbles form on the surface and the underside is lightly browned. Turn over and cook until the other side is lightly browned.

Makes eight 4-inch pancakes

EACH PANCAKE CONTAINS APPROXIMATELY:
105 TOTAL CALORIES / 20 CALORIES IN FAT
35 MG CHOLESTEROL / 135 MG SODIUM
80 MG CALCIUM

CINNAMON-APPLE-PASTA PANCAKES

The first comment I received after putting these pancakes on a spa menu was, "Pasta—for breakfast!" My answer was, "Why not?" Pasta is a grain product, just like breakfast cereals, breads, and muffins. If variety is the spice of life, then why not literally spice up your breakfast menus with pasta?

2 tablespoons chopped walnuts
1 egg plus 1 egg white, lightly beaten
1 tablespoon skim milk
1 tablespoon fructose or 4 teaspoons sugar
1/2 teaspoon ground cinnamon
1 1/2 teaspoons vanilla extract
2 green apples, cored and thinly sliced (1 1/2 cups)
1/4 cup raisins
2 cups cooked spaghetti (about 1/4 pound dry)
1 tablespoon corn-oil margarine

Place the walnuts in a preheated 350°F oven for 8 to 10 minutes. Watch them carefully, as they burn easily.

Combine the eggs, milk, fructose or sugar, cinnamon, vanilla, apples, raisins, and walnuts in a large bowl. Add the spaghetti and mix well.

For each pancake, heat ½ teaspoon of the margarine in a small skillet. Spread ¾ cup of the pasta mixture in the pan, packing it evenly. Cover and cook over medium heat until it is golden brown on the bottom, about 10 minutes. Turn over and brown the other side, about 3 to 5 minutes.

Makes 6 pancakes

EACH PANCAKE CONTAINS APPROXIMATELY:
150 TOTAL CALORIES / 45 CALORIES IN FAT
45 MG CHOLESTEROL / 25 MG SODIUM
20 MG CALCIUM

WHOLE WHEAT CREPES

1 cup skim milk
¾ cup whole wheat flour
¼ teaspoon salt
1 egg, lightly beaten
Corn oil for coating pan

Combine the milk, flour, and salt in a medium bowl and beat with an egg beater until well mixed. Beat in the egg and mix well.

Wipe the inside of a crepe pan with corn oil after the pan is hot. Spoon 2 tablespoons of the crepe batter into the pan and tilt from side to side to spread evenly. When the edges start to curl, turn the crepe with a spatula and brown the other side. Place the crepes in a covered container as you make them in order to keep them pliable.

To freeze the crepes, seperate them with pieces of aluminum foil or wax paper. Wrap tightly and place in the freezer. To use, bring the crepes to room temperature. Put them in a preheated 300°F oven for 20 minutes or until they are soft and pliable. This will preclude their breaking when folded.

Makes 12 crepes

EACH CREPE CONTAINS APPROXIMATELY:
40 TOTAL CALORIES / 10 CALORIES IN FAT
25 MG CHOLESTEROL / 60 MG SODIUM
30 MG CALCIUM

FOUR-GRAIN WAFFLES

These waffles have a wonderful crunchy texture that I love. I like to serve them with Light Cheese (page 52) and Apple Butter (page 61). Or sometimes I make blueberry waffles by adding 1½ cups unthawed frozen blueberries just before folding the egg whites into the batter. If you are making the waffle batter to use later, don't add the frozen blueberries until you're ready to make the waffles. The cooking time in the waffle iron is adequate to thaw the blueberries and plump them up so they look and taste like fresh blueberries. Four-grain cereal is made from wheat, rye, barley, and oats and is available in health food stores.

½ cup uncooked four-grain cereal
2 eggs, separated
4 teaspoons corn oil
2 tablespoons fructose or 3 tablespoons sugar
1⅓ cups skim milk
1¾ cups whole wheat flour
2 teaspoons baking powder
½ teaspoon salt

Soak the cereal in enough water to cover. Set aside.

Combine the egg yolks, oil, fructose or sugar, and milk and mix thoroughly.

Combine the flour, baking powder, and salt and mix well. Drain the cereal and add to the flour mixture. Add the milk mixture to the flour mixture and stir lightly. Add additional milk if necessary to thin sufficiently to ladle.

Beat the egg whites until stiff but not dry and fold into the waffle mixture before baking.

Preheat a waffle iron and pour ½ cup of the mixture at a time onto the hot iron; bake for approximately 6 minutes.

Makes 6 waffles

EACH WAFFLE CONTAINS APPROXIMATELY:
350 TOTAL CALORIES / 55 CALORIES IN FAT
70 MG CHOLESTEROL / 340 MG SODIUM / 180 MG CALCIUM

WAFFLES

These waffles are another in the "magic" series of truly quick-and-easy recipes. If you do not have buttermilk, you can make them with skim milk as well, but reduce the amount of milk to 1 cup and omit the baking soda.

> *Nonstick vegetable coating or 1 teaspoon corn oil*
> *2 cups Magic Biscuit Mix (page 206)*
> *1 egg*
> *1½ cups buttermilk*
> *½ teaspoon baking soda*

Spray a round waffle iron with nonstick vegetable coating or add the corn oil to the waffle batter. Preheat the waffle iron.

Combine the Magic Biscuit Mix, egg, buttermilk, and baking soda (or 1 cup skim milk without the soda). Beat with a rotary beater until smooth.

Pour ½ cup of the mixture into the center of the hot waffle iron. Bake until the steaming stops.

Makes 6 waffles

EACH WAFFLE CONTAINS APPROXIMATELY:
245 TOTAL CALORIES / 90 CALORIES IN FAT
75 MG CHOLESTEROL / 590 MG SODIUM
305 MG CALCIUM

OUR FAMOUS SUGAR-FREE BRAN MUFFINS

Of all of the recipes I have created, this one has become the most popular with all of the spa, hotel, and restaurant guests. We always have trouble making enough of them to meet the demand. Since Apple Butter is an ingredient, it is impossible to make the muffins before making Apple Butter; and since we also serve Apple Butter with these muffins, several chefs have told me they feel like they have gone into the apple butter business. To make Carrot-Bran Muffins, add 1 cup grated carrot to the mixture at the same time the raisins are added.

2 ounces dried unsulfured apples, diced (1 cup)
1 cup unsweetened apple juice
1½ cups uncooked four-grain cereal
¾ cup unprocessed wheat bran
¾ cup raisins
1 cup buttermilk
1 cup Apple Butter (page 61)
1½ cups whole wheat flour
2 teaspoons baking powder
2 teaspoons baking soda
½ teaspoon salt
½ teaspoon ground cinnamon
2 eggs
1 teaspoon vanilla extract
½ cup corn oil
Nonstick vegetable coating

Preheat the oven to 375°F. Combine the diced apples and apple juice in a small bowl. Set aside.

In a large mixing bowl, combine the four-grain cereal, bran, raisins, and buttermilk. Stir in the Apple Butter. Mix the apple mixture and the bran mixture and set aside.

In a third, smaller bowl, combine the flour, baking powder, baking soda, salt, and cinnamon. Set aside.

In a fourth, small bowl, combine the eggs, vanilla, and corn oil and beat lightly. Stir this into the apple/bran mixture. Add the flour mixture and stir until just blended. Do not overmix.

Spray a muffin pan (including the top of the pan) with nonstick vegetable coating. Divide the batter among twelve muffin cups. Heap the batter above the edge of the cups. Bake for 35 minutes or until a toothpick inserted in the center of a muffin comes out clean. Cool for 10 minutes. Remove the muffins from the pan, cutting apart where necessary. Cool on a wire rack.

Makes 12 muffins

EACH MUFFIN CONTAINS APPROXIMATELY:
345 TOTAL CALORIES / 105 CALORIES IN FAT
45 MG CHOLESTEROL / 325 MG SODIUM
90 MG CALCIUM

CRUNCHY WHEAT BERRY BREAD

When making this bread, don't forget to soak the wheat berries for at least 24 hours. You want the bread to have the crunchiness its name implies, but unsoaked wheat berries can be dangerous to your teeth!

Two ¼-ounce packages active dry yeast (check the date on the package)
3 tablespoons fructose or ¼ cup sugar
¼ cup lukewarm water (110° to 115°F)

½ cup low-fat milk
2 tablespoons corn-oil margarine
½ teaspoon salt
1 egg, lightly beaten
¼ cup wheat berries, soaked in water to cover for at least 24
   hours and drained
3 cups whole wheat pastry flour
Corn-oil margarine

Combine the yeast, 1 tablespoon of the fructose or the sugar, and water. Set aside in a warm place and allow to double in bulk. This takes a very short time.

While the yeast is rising, combine milk and margarine in a small saucepan and heat slowly until the margarine melts. Add the remaining fructose or sugar and salt and mix well. Combine the beaten egg with the milk mixture and again mix well.

Combine the milk mixture with the yeast mixture in a large bowl. Add the soaked wheat berries. Add the flour 1 cup at a time, mixing well. The last ½ cup will have to be kneaded in with your hands. Cover and allow to double in bulk in a warm place, about 1½ hours.

Form into a loaf and place in an oiled loaf pan. Cover and again allow to rise until doubled in size, about 30 minutes. Bake in a preheated 325°F oven for 35 to 40 minutes or until the loaf is golden brown and sounds hollow when tapped. Rub the top with a little margarine and put back in the oven for about 3 minutes.

Allow the bread to cool to room temperature on a rack before slicing. To reheat, wrap in foil and place briefly in the oven.

Makes 20 slices

1 SLICE CONTAINS APPROXIMATELY:
90 TOTAL CALORIES / 20 CALORIES IN FAT
15 MG CHOLESTEROL / 65 MG SODIUM
15 MG CALCIUM

HERB BREAD

I love to make this bread because it's so easy and so tasty. Two important tips for the success of this bread include checking the date on the package of yeast to make certain it is still effective and having the egg at room temperature. If the egg is not at room temperature, simply put it in a bowl of lukewarm water long enough to bring it to room temperature before proceeding with the recipe. This bread is especially good served warm.

One ¼-ounce package active dry yeast (check the date on the package)
¼ cup lukewarm water (110° to 115°F)
1 cup low-fat cottage cheese
1 tablespoon fructose or 4 teaspoons sugar
¼ cup finely chopped parsley
¼ cup finely chopped scallion tops
1 egg, lightly beaten
1 teaspoon dried basil, crushed in a mortar and pestle
1 teaspoon dried oregano, crushed in a mortar and pestle
1 teaspoon dried tarragon, crushed in a mortar and pestle
1 teaspoon salt
1 cup whole wheat flour
1 cup unbleached white flour
Vegetable oil for coating pan

Sprinkle the yeast over the water. Stir to dissolve and let stand until bubbly.

Warm the cottage cheese in a small saucepan. Transfer to a large mixing bowl and stir in the yeast. Add the fructose or sugar, the parsley, scallion tops, egg, and seasonings and mix well.

Sift the flours together and add to the cottage cheese/herb mixture, a little at a time, to form a dough. Knead until smooth. Cover with a tea towel and let stand in a warm place for several hours, or until doubled in bulk.

Punch the dough down until it is reduced to its original size. Form into a loaf and place in an oiled loaf pan. Cover with a tea towel and let stand in a warm place until again doubled in bulk.

Preheat the oven to 350°F. Bake for 40 minutes or until the bread has a hollow sound when rapped with the knuckles.

Serve warm or place on a rack to cool. When cool, wrap in foil and store in the refrigerator until ready to use. It slices better when it is cold.

Makes 20 slices

1 SLICE CONTAINS APPROXIMATELY:
60 TOTAL CALORIES / 10 CALORIES IN FAT
15 MG CHOLESTEROL / 160 MG SODIUM
20 MG CALCIUM

CRANBERRY BREAD

I developed this recipe for a holiday menu, but now I use it all during the year because it is so pretty and goes so well with luncheon salads of many types. During the holidays it is fun to make it in tiny loaves and wrap them up for gifts.

Nonstick vegetable coating
2 cups whole wheat flour
1 1/2 teaspoons baking powder
1/2 teaspoon baking soda
1/2 teaspoon salt
1/2 teaspoon ground cinnamon
One 6-ounce can frozen unsweetened apple juice concentrate, thawed
1 egg, lightly beaten
2 tablespoons corn oil
2 teaspoons vanilla extract
1 1/2 cups cranberries, blanched and coarsely chopped (1 cup chopped)

Preheat the oven to 350°F. Spray a standard loaf pan with nonstick vegetable coating.

In a large bowl, combine the flour, baking powder, baking soda, salt, and cinnamon. Mix thoroughly.

In another bowl, combine the apple juice concentrate, egg, corn oil, and vanilla and mix well.

Pour the liquid ingredients into the dry ingredients. Add the cranberries and mix well. Pour into the loaf pan and bake for 45 to 50 minutes.

Makes 24 slices

1 SLICE CONTAINS APPROXIMATELY:
65 TOTAL CALORIES / 15 CALORIES IN FAT
10 MG CHOLESTEROL / 120 MG SODIUM
25 MG CALCIUM

DANISH RYE CEREAL

This is my own favorite cooked hot cereal. I named it Danish Rye Cereal because I think it tastes like a Danish sweet roll, which is also good for you. I cook it in large amounts and store it in the freezer, then reheat it in the microwave for breakfast. I like it best hot, topped with Light Cheese (page 52), but I sometimes use it as a cold ingredient in fruit salads.

1 cup unprocessed rye berries
2 teaspoons ground cinnamon
1 teaspoon caraway seeds
1 tablespoon vanilla extract
3 cups water
¼ cup raisins

Combine all the ingredients except the raisins in a saucepan. Mix well and bring to a boil. Reduce the heat and cook, covered, for 1 hour, stirring occasionally and adding more water if necessary to prevent scorching.

During the last 15 minutes of cooking time, add the raisins and mix well.

Makes 2¹/₂ cups

½ CUP CONTAINS APPROXIMATELY:
125 TOTAL CALORIES / 5 CALORIES IN FAT
0 MG CHOLESTEROL / 1 MG SODIUM
20 MG CALCIUM

DESSERTS

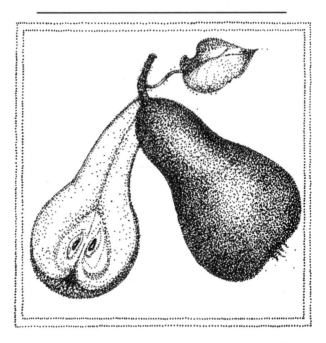

FRUIT IS THE ideal dessert because it is naturally sweet and doesn't contain the fat found in most man-made sweets. It contains no cholesterol, is very low in sodium, and is packed with vitamins and fiber.

Even though everyone's favorite fruits may not be the same, I don't know of anyone who just plain doesn't like fruit. Due to both popular demand and modern refrigerated transportation, there is an incredible variety of fresh fruit available all over the country during most of the year. Vine- and tree-ripened fruits are always both sweeter and more flavorful, but they are not always available.

When you buy fruit that is not quite ripe, allow it to ripen at room temperature before refrigerating it. Refrigerate ripe fruit to prevent spoilage. Don't peel or slice fresh fruits until you are ready to serve them or they will lose some of their vitamin content, dry out, and some, such as apples, will turn brown. To prevent apples from discoloring, brush them with citrus juice immediately after slicing them.

222

Fresh fruit provides the optimum amount of vitamins, and there are many ways to add variety in serving them. You can combine several types of fruit; puree fruits to serve on other fruits as sauces; marinate in fruit juices, wines, or liqueurs; or combine fresh fruits with cooked or canned and dried fruits to create what the French call a composed compote. Fresh fruits also make wonderful accompaniments and sauces for all other types of desserts, such as custards, puddings, cakes, and pies.

Without destroying too many of the vitamins in fruit and still creating very healthy desserts, it is possible to steam, poach, bake, or broil fruit. You can also freeze fruit for sorbets, sherbets, and ice cream.

When poaching peaches, plums, apricots, or cherries, remove the pits before cooking. An interesting aside about these fruits is that the nutlike kernel in the center of the pits is potentially poisonous. I was horrified to learn this because as a child I used to open peach pits and eat the almond flavored "nut" in the center. Fortunately I never had too many of them at one time because supposedly eight to ten of them, if chewed, can release enough hydrogen cyanide to kill you!

When fresh fruits are not available, there is a wide selection of canned fruits packed in water or in natural juices without sugar added. Not only are they better for you, they also taste better than the insipidly sweet fruit packed in heavy syrup.

Dried fruits make wonderful sweet snacks, which can be eaten like cookies or candy. They also make delicious compotes and sauces when cooked. Their high caloric content can be understood easily when you realize that it takes almost 6 pounds of a fresh fruit to yield 1 pound of dried fruit. Raisins or currants have more moisture and flavor if you plump them up first by presoaking them for 15 minutes before adding them to a mixture. When adding them to baked goods, either soak them in water and drain them, or soak them in one of the liquids you are using in the recipe.

I usually don't have very large dessert sections in my books; however, I have received so many letters from my readers requesting revisions of their dessert recipes that I decided to share some of those revised recipes with you. I have also included some of my own favorite spa creations for you to try on your family and friends. When you have a craving for a really rich dessert, eat only half of it. On my menu at the restaurant at Neiman-Marcus in Newport

Beach, California, I offer rich desserts in full portions for "sinners" and half portions for "saints." You would be surprised how few "sinner" portions we serve!

FANTASY IN FRUIT

This dessert has literally become my signature on many menus. It is more colorful if you use two fruit purees as suggested; however, it is easier and also beautiful using just one. When using raspberries, strain the puree to remove the seeds or it will be gritty. This is an incredibly beautiful and very healthy dessert. It is also a practical approach to using up all of the varied types of fresh fruit you may have on hand. I used the Honey Cream variation (see page 250) of the Pastry Cream recipe with Fantasy in Fruit for a Rosh Hashanah dessert in a magazine article and received hundreds of letters from people telling me how much they liked it.

> ½ cup fresh fruit puree (two colors: ¼ cup of each—mango or
> papaya and raspberry are most colorful)
> 1½ cups assorted seasonal fresh fruit, sliced in different shapes
> (melon balls, wedges of citrus, slivers of peach, whole grapes,
> etc.)
> ¼ cup Pastry Cream (page 250)

Place 2 tablespoons of each color puree on each of two large round plates, preferably white. Spread the puree out in an interesting pattern with the back of a spoon.

Arrange ¾ cup of the various fruits in an interesting pattern on the puree, creating a work of art on each plate.

Decorate the fruit with the Pastry Cream. For a truly exciting treat, use a pastry bag and pipe squiggles, swirls, and rosettes onto the fruit.

Makes 2 servings

EACH SERVING CONTAINS APPROXIMATELY (VARIES WITH
FRUIT USED): 140 TOTAL CALORIES / 25 CALORIES IN FAT
10 MG CHOLESTEROL / 45 MG SODIUM
125 MG CALCIUM

VANILLA ICE MILK CREPE WITH PAPAYA - RUM SAUCE

This is both a delicious and an impressive dessert, and it can be made ahead of time. You can make the sauce in the morning and store it in the refrigerator. The crepes may be filled with ice milk and frozen in a single layer in a covered pan or dish. (Be sure to cover it tightly or the ice milk will pick up the flavors of other foods in the freezer.) ·Ten minutes before serving, remove the crepes from the freezer and allow them to soften slightly. I particularly like this dessert after curried dishes.

PAPAYA-RUM SAUCE:

> *1 pound papaya*
> *1 1/2 teaspoons dark rum*
> *1/2 teaspoon vanilla extract*
>
> *1 cup vanilla ice milk*
> *4 Whole Wheat Crepes (page 212)*
> *Ground cinnamon for garnish*
> *Mint sprigs for garnish*

Peel the papaya and remove the seeds. Cube the papaya, place it in a blender container or food processor with a metal blade, and puree. Add the rum and vanilla and blend thoroughly. Refrigerate in a covered container. You should have 1 cup.

When ready to serve, spoon 2 tablespoons of the sauce on each plate, turning the plate to distribute the sauce evenly over the bottom.

Spoon ¼ cup of the ice milk down the center of each crepe. Wrap the crepe around it, placing it in the center of the sauce on the plate, fold side down. Spoon 2 tablespoons Papaya-Rum Sauce over the top. Garnish with a sprinkle of ground cinnamon and a mint sprig.

Makes 4 servings

EACH SERVING CONTAINS APPROXIMATELY:
105 TOTAL CALORIES / 20 CALORIES IN FAT
30 MG CHOLESTEROL / 90 MG SODIUM
85 MG CALCIUM

STRAWBERRIES ROMANOFF

This is the easiest version I have come up with to date of this Russian dessert. It is classically made with whipped cream, but for far less fat and calories this provides a healthier version for a Russian menu—or any other menu!

SAUCE:

> 1 ½ cups skim milk
> 3 tablespoons uncooked Cream of Rice
> 1 tablespoon fructose or 4 teaspoons sugar
> 1 ½ teaspoons vanilla extract
> ¼ teaspoon rum extract
> 2 tablespoons Grand Marnier
> 2 egg whites, at room temperature
>
> 4 cups sliced fresh strawberries
> 8 whole strawberries
> 8 sprigs mint

Bring the milk to a boil in a small saucepan. Add the Cream of Rice and stir for 30 seconds. Remove from the heat and allow to stand for 5 minutes.

Mix well and pour into a blender container. Add the fructose or sugar, the vanilla and rum extracts, and the Grand Marnier and blend until smooth.

Beat the egg whites until stiff but not dry in a small mixing bowl. Pour the milk mixture into another small mixing bowl and fold in the egg whites until smooth.

To serve, spoon ½ cup sliced strawberries into each of eight sherbet glasses. Spoon ¼ cup sauce over the top. Place 1 whole strawberry, with a mint sprig in the center, on top of each serving.

Makes 8 servings

EACH SERVING CONTAINS APPROXIMATELY:
80 TOTAL CALORIES / 5 CALORIES IN FAT
1 MG CHOLESTEROL / 40 MG SODIUM
70 MG CALCIUM

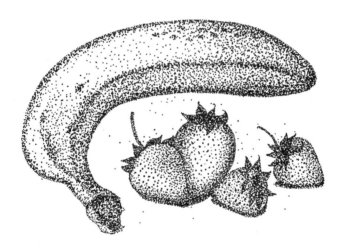

CAROB - YOGURT SUNDAE

This sundae is one of the most popular desserts at the Canyon Ranch Spa in Tucson, Arizona, where it is served appropriately after a "burger and fries." To make a Strawberry-Yogurt Parfait, use the Easy Strawberry Jam (page 60) in place of this Carob Sauce.

CAROB SAUCE:

> *2 tablespoons corn-oil margarine*
> *2 tablespoons unbleached flour*
> *1½ cups boiling water*
> *½ cup roasted carob powder*
> *1½ teaspoons instant coffee powder*
> *¼ cup fructose or ⅓ cup sugar*
> *1 tablespoon vanilla extract*
>
> *1⅓ cups plain nonfat yogurt*
> *Mint sprigs for garnish*

Melt the margarine in a medium saucepan over low heat. Add the flour and cook, stirring constantly, for at least 3 minutes.

Remove from the heat and add the boiling water all at once, stirring with a wire whisk. Add the carob powder, instant coffee, and fructose or sugar and return to heat. Simmer, stirring constantly with a wire whisk, until the sauce is slightly thickened. Remove from the heat, add the vanilla, and mix well. Makes 1¾ cups sauce. Store in the refrigerator.

For each serving, place ⅓ cup yogurt in a champagne glass or compote. Top with 2 tablespoons Carob Sauce. Garnish with a mint sprig.

Makes 4 servings

EACH SERVING CONTAINS APPROXIMATELY:
90 TOTAL CALORIES / 15 CALORIES IN FAT
1 MG CHOLESTEROL / 60 MG SODIUM
150 MG CALCIUM

SPICED BANANAS

Remember when the most famous fruit slogan was "An apple a day keeps the doctor away"? Now researchers tell us that a banana a day is a good idea, too, because of its high potassium content. Spiced Bananas are a quick, easy, and tasty dessert. To turn this recipe into a wonderful topping for other fruit, pancakes, waffles, yogurt, and ice milk, chop the bananas into small pieces rather than quartering them. When adding the ground cloves, be very careful not to add more than a dash. A dash is defined as less than ⅛ teaspoon. A little clove is a wonderful spicy accent; too much can quickly make anything taste like toothpaste!

> *¼ cup frozen unsweetened apple juice concentrate*
> *2 bananas, peeled and quartered lengthwise*
> *¼ teaspoon ground cinnamon*
> *¼ teaspoon ground allspice*
> *⅛ teaspoon ground nutmeg*
> *Dash ground cloves*
> *Mint sprigs for garnish*

Heat the apple juice concentrate in a medium skillet. Add the banana quarters and cook until heated through, about 5 minutes.

Combine the spices and sprinkle over the top of the bananas.

For each serving, place two banana quarters on a plate and spoon 2 teaspoons sauce over the top. Garnish with a mint sprig.

Makes 4 servings

EACH SERVING CONTAINS APPROXIMATELY:
100 TOTAL CALORIES / 5 CALORIES IN FAT
0 MG CHOLESTEROL / 75 MG SODIUM
10 MG CALCIUM

FRESH FRUIT PIZZA

If you want to make Fresh Fruit Pizza in a hurry and you don't have the Pizza Crusts waiting for you in the freezer, you can use either four whole wheat flour tortillas or two pita breads for the crust.

When using pita bread, place it under the broiler just long enough for it to puff up slightly and then separate into two round flat halves. Toast each half lightly before spreading it with the cheese and fruit and proceeding with the recipe. When using tortillas, I also like to toast them lightly before proceeding.

> *1 cup assorted fresh fruit*
> *Apple juice to cover*
> *Four 4-inch Pizza Crusts (see page 204)*
> *½ cup Pastry Cream (page 250)*

Prepare the fruit for poaching. Some fruits are better peeled before poaching, such as peaches, apples, pears, and melons of all types; however, plums, nectarines, and cherries should not be peeled. Slice the fruit and place it in a saucepan with apple juice to cover. Bring to a boil. Reduce the heat and simmer until the fruit can be pierced with a fork. Drain well.

For each serving, spread 2 tablespoons Pastry Cream on a Pizza Crust. Arrange ¼ cup of poached fruit on top. Place under a broiler until hot.

Makes 4 servings

EACH SERVING CONTAINS APPROXIMATELY:
230 TOTAL CALORIES / 45 CALORIES IN FAT
10 MG CHOLESTEROL / 185 MG SODIUM
115 MG CALCIUM

GINGERED FRUIT COMPOTE

This uniquely different dessert keeps well for days in the refrigerator. It is also good served on hot cereal for breakfast. I even like it instead of jam on whole wheat toast.

> *3 tablespoons pine nuts*
> *1 cup water*

½ cup dried apricots, sliced
½ cup dried unsulfured apples, sliced
¼ cup dried currants
¼ cup golden raisins
1½ teaspoons finely chopped peeled ginger
¾ cup Cinnamon-Apple Yogurt Sauce (page 54)
Mint sprigs for garnish
Ground cinnamon for garnish

Place the pine nuts in a preheated 350°F oven for 8 to 10 minutes. Watch carefully, as they burn easily. Set aside.

Combine the water, apricots, and apples in a medium saucepan and bring to a boil. Turn down the heat, cover, and simmer for 20 to 30 minutes or until tender. Remove from the heat and add the currants, raisins, and ginger.

Cool to room temperature, cover, and refrigerate overnight (or at least 12 hours).

To serve, spoon 2 tablespoons of the Cinnamon-Apple Yogurt Sauce into each of six wine goblets. Spoon ¼ cup compote on top of the sauce. Then top with 1½ teaspoons toasted nuts and a sprig of mint. Sprinkle with a light dusting of cinnamon.

Makes six ¼-cup servings

EACH SERVING CONTAINS APPROXIMATELY:
130 TOTAL CALORIES / 15 CALORIES IN FAT
0 MG CHOLESTEROL / 50 MG SODIUM
65 MG CALCIUM

BAKED APPLESAUCE

This applesauce is a good accompaniment to a variety of meats and poultry. It is also a good breakfast as well as a light dessert. For dessert, I like to serve it either with Pastry Cream (page 250) or Cinnamon-Apple Yogurt Sauce (page 54).

1½ pounds cooking apples (4½ cups cubed)
¾ cup water
¾ cup unsweetened apple juice
¼ teaspoon ground nutmeg
¼ teaspoon ground cinnamon
½ teaspoon vanilla extract

Wash, peel, and core the apples. Cut into 1-inch cubes.

Combine the remaining ingredients. Place the diced apples in a glass loaf pan or baking dish (the apples stay more moist in the loaf pan) and pour the juice mixture over the top.

Bake, uncovered, in a preheated 325°F oven for 45 minutes. Remove from the oven and allow to cool to room temperature. Store tightly covered in the refrigerator.

Makes 2 cups

¼ CUP CONTAINS APPROXIMATELY:
90 TOTAL CALORIES / 4 CALORIES IN FAT
0 MG CHOLESTEROL / 110 MG SODIUM
15 MG CALCIUM

SUGAR-FREE APPLE OR PEAR CRISP

As well as being a good dessert after the meal, these fruit crisps make excellent snacks. You can serve them in place of cookies, with coffee or tea or with milk for after-school treats.

1½ pounds apples or pears, peeled, cored, and thinly sliced
3 tablespoons all-purpose flour
¼ cup frozen unsweetened apple juice concentrate
½ teaspoon ground cinnamon
Dash freshly ground nutmeg
3 tablespoons corn-oil margarine, softened
10 graham cracker squares, crushed (¾ cup)

Preheat the oven to 375°F. In an 8-inch-square baking dish, toss the apples or pears with 1 tablespoon of the flour. Add the concentrated apple juice. Coat well.

In a small bowl, combine the remaining 2 tablespoons flour and the spices with the margarine and mix until well blended.

Gradually stir in the graham cracker crumbs until the mixture resembles coarse crumbs. Sprinkle evenly over the fruit.

Bake for 30 minutes or until the topping is lightly browned and the fruit is tender.

Makes sixteen 2-inch-square servings

EACH SERVING CONTAINS APPROXIMATELY:
75 TOTAL CALORIES / 25 CALORIES IN FAT
0 MG CHOLESTEROL / 40 MG SODIUM
10 MG CALCIUM

INDIAN APPLE PUDDING

For a uniquely different sweet after your next Southwestern-style dinner, try this Indian pudding. Because it is sugar-free and full of healthy ingredients, I have even served it for breakfast on spa menus with Light Cheese (page 52) instead of Pastry Cream.

2 cups canned evaporated skimmed milk
1 1/2 teaspoons Minute Tapioca
1 tablespoon yellow cornmeal
1 egg, beaten
1/3 cup frozen unsweetened concentrated apple juice
1/4 teaspoon salt
1/4 teaspoon ground ginger
1/4 teaspoon ground cinnamon
1/2 cup Pastry Cream (page 250)

Preheat the oven to 300°F. Scald the milk in the top of a double boiler over simmering hot water. Stir in the tapioca and cornmeal.

Continue to cook for 10 minutes, stirring occasionally with a wire whisk.

In a medium bowl, beat the egg. Add the apple juice concentrate, salt, ginger, and cinnamon.

Combine the milk mixture and the egg mixture and mix well. Divide the mixture evenly into eight 3-inch ramekins or eight 6-ounce custard cups or pour it into a 1½-quart baking dish. Place small baking dishes on a cookie sheet for easier handling.

Bake the individual puddings for 25 to 30 minutes, the large pudding for 1½ hours. Serve warm with 2 tablespoons Pastry Cream per serving.

Makes four ½-cup servings

EACH SERVING CONTAINS APPROXIMATELY:
220 TOTAL CALORIES / 40 CALORIES IN FAT
85 MG CHOLESTEROL / 440 MG SODIUM
480 MG CALCIUM

APPLE FLUFF

This is a recipe I modified for a reader who wanted a healthier, very easy-to-make recipe for her Cub Scout troop. It is a great recipe for a group of children to make because they can take turns beating the mixture for the 15-minute period it requires.

> *1½ cups frozen unsweetened apple juice concentrate*
> *2 cups water*
> *½ cup uncooked farina or Cream of Wheat*
> *Freshly grated nutmeg for garnish (optional)*

Combine the apple juice concentrate, water, and farina or Cream of Wheat in a large saucepan and bring to a boil over medium heat, stirring constantly.

Reduce the heat to low and cook, stirring occasionally, for about 10 minutes or until thickened.

Pour into a large bowl and beat for 15 minutes with an electric mixer or until the mixture is very light in color and about twice its original volume.

Spoon ½ cup of the mixture into each dessert dish or goblet and refrigerate for up to 2 hours. Garnish with a sprinkle of freshly grated nutmeg.

Makes 10 servings

EACH SERVING CONTAINS APPROXIMATELY:
130 TOTAL CALORIES / N CALORIES IN FAT
0 MG CHOLESTEROL / 180 MG SODIUM
10 MG CALCIUM

RAISIN - RICE PUDDING

This is a nutritious and easy-to-make version of an old favorite. The major difference between this recipe and most of the "old favorites" is that it calls for brown rice and skim milk rather than white rice and cream.

1 cup cooked brown rice
1 cup skim milk
2 eggs
2 tablespoons fructose or 3 tablespoons sugar
1½ teaspoons ground cinnamon
1 teaspoon vanilla extract
½ cup raisins
Freshly ground nutmeg for garnish
Mint sprigs for garnish

Combine all the ingredients except for the garnish and mix well. Pour into a casserole and set the casserole in a larger deep pan. Add boiling water to a depth of ¾ inch.

Bake in a preheated 350°F oven for 1¼ hours.

Spoon ¼ cup of warm pudding into individual dishes and sprinkle lightly with freshly ground nutmeg. Garnish with a sprig of mint.

Makes 2 cups

¼ CUP CONTAINS APPROXIMATELY:
100 TOTAL CALORIES / 15 CALORIES IN FAT
70 MG CHOLESTEROL / 100 MG SODIUM
60 MG CALCIUM

PERNOD SORBET

This is a good dessert after a heavy meal because it is light and not too sweet. It is particularly nice served between courses to clear the palate, as is the custom at most formal wine and food dinners. Many of the sorbets served for this purpose are too sweet and tend to diminish the appetite rather than clearing the palate.

6 ripe pears, peeled, cored, and halved
1 cup water
2 tablespoons Pernod

Combine the pears and water in a large saucepan and bring to a boil. Reduce the heat, cover, and simmer for 20 minutes or until the pears are soft. At this point the liquid should be reduced by half. If not, remove the pears and continue to simmer the liquid until it is reduced by half.

Place the cooked mixture in a blender container and blend until completely smooth. Add the Pernod and mix again. Pour into a sorbet machine and process according to the manufacturer's directions.

Makes 2 cups

2 TABLESPOONS CONTAIN APPROXIMATELY:
40 TOTAL CALORIES / N CALORIES IN FAT
0 MG CHOLESTEROL / 0 MG SODIUM
10 MG CALCIUM

PINEAPPLE PIE

Talk about a tropical treat! If you like piña coladas, you'll love this pie.

1 tablepoon corn-oil margarine, melted
16 graham cracker squares, crushed (1 cup)
¼ cup water
1 envelope unflavored gelatin
2 tablespoons cool water
¼ cup boiling water
¾ cup low-fat cottage cheese
¼ cup skim milk
1 teaspoon vanilla extract
1 teaspoon coconut extract
2 tablespoons fructose or 3 tablespoons sugar
One 20-ounce can crushed pineapple, packed in natural juice, undrained
Ground cinnamon for garnish

Preheat the oven to 350°F. Combine the melted margarine and graham cracker crumbs, mixing thoroughly. Add the ¼ cup water a little at a time until the crumbs are moist enough to hold together (too much water makes the mixture mushy).

Place the crumb mixture in a 9-inch pie pan and press to cover the bottom and sides. Bake for 8 to 10 minutes or until browned. Set aside to cool.

In a small bowl, soften the gelatin in the 2 tablespoons cool water. Add the ¼ cup boiling water and stir until the gelatin is completely dissolved. Combine the gelatin mixture and all the other ingredients except for the pineapple and cinnamon in a blender container and blend until smooth.

Pour the mixture into a large bowl. Add the crushed pineapple and mix well. Pour the mixture into the cooled graham cracker piecrust and sprinkle with cinnamon. Refrigerate until firm before serving.

Makes 12 servings

EACH SERVING CONTAINS APPROXIMATELY:
95 TOTAL CALORIES / 20 CALORIES IN FAT
1 MG CHOLESTEROL / 125 MG SODIUM
25 MG CALCIUM

CHERRY TRIFLE

This recipe is a revision of a very rich dessert a reader wanted to serve for a Valentine's Day party. It was loaded with eggs and cream, and her husband had just been put on a low-cholesterol diet. This is a delicious compromise and contains practically no cholesterol at all. For an Italian Cherry Trifle substitute sweet marsala for the sherry.

2 tablespoons fructose or 3 tablespoons sugar
1 tablespoon cornstarch
¼ cup liquid egg substitute
1 cup skim milk
2 teaspoons vanilla extract
¼ pound angel food cake, torn into bite-size pieces (2 cups)
3 tablespoons sherry
1 cup frozen unsweetened dark sweet cherries, thawed and thoroughly drained

To make the custard, mix the fructose or sugar and the cornstarch in a small saucepan. Add the liquid egg substitute and the milk and mix well. Heat to boiling over medium heat, stirring constantly, until thickened. Remove from the heat; add the vanilla. Cool to room temperature.

Place one-third of the cake pieces in the bottom of a 1-quart glass bowl or soufflé dish. Sprinkle with 1 tablespoon of the sherry. Pour one-third of the custard over the cake. Spoon ⅓ cup of the cherries over the custard. Repeat the process twice. Cover and refrigerate.

Makes 4 servings

EACH SERVING CONTAINS APPROXIMATELY:
190 TOTAL CALORIES / 10 CALORIES IN FAT
1 MG CHOLESTEROL / 140 MG SODIUM
90 MG CALCIUM

CARROT CAKE

In order to keep the calories low enough to serve this carrot cake as a dessert in spas, it does not have the usual cream cheese frosting. If you prefer carrot cake frosted, spread 1 cup of Pastry Cream (page 250) over the top.

½ cup chopped walnuts
2 cups all-purpose flour
2 teaspoons baking soda
2 teaspoons cinnamon
½ teaspoon salt
3 eggs
¾ cup corn oil
¾ cup buttermilk
1½ cups fructose or 2 cups sugar
2 teaspoons vanilla extract
¾ cup canned crushed pineapple, packed in natural juice, drained
4 small carrots, peeled and grated (2 cups)
Nonstick vegetable coating

GLAZE:

> ⅔ *cup fructose or 1 cup sugar*
> ½ *teaspoon baking soda*
> ½ *cup buttermilk*
> ½ *cup corn-oil margarine*
> 1 *tablespoon light corn syrup*
> 1 *teaspoon vanilla extract*

Place the walnuts in a preheated 350°F oven for 8 to 10 minutes. Watch carefully, as they burn easily. Set aside, leaving oven at 350°.

Sift the flour, baking soda, cinnamon, and salt together and set aside. Beat the eggs in a large bowl. Add the oil, buttermilk, fructose or sugar, and vanilla and mix well. Add the flour mixture, pineapple, carrots, and walnuts and stir well. Pour into a 9-by-13-by-2-inch baking pan that has been sprayed with a nonstick vegetable coating and bake for 45 to 50 minutes or until a toothpick inserted in the center comes out clean.

While the cake is baking, make the glaze. Combine all the ingredients except the vanilla in a small saucepan and bring to a boil. Cook for 5 minutes, stirring occasionally. Remove from the heat and stir in the vanilla.

Remove the cake from the oven, poke holes in the top with a fork, and slowly pour the glaze over the hot cake so the glaze will enter the cake through the holes. Cool completely.

Makes 15 pieces (for fewer calories, cut in smaller pieces)

EACH PIECE CONTAINS APPROXIMATELY:
380 TOTAL CALORIES / 185 CALORIES IN FAT
60 MG CHOLESTEROL / 250 MG SODIUM
50 MG CALCIUM

LEMON-CREAM CAKE

Finely grated rind of 2 lemons
3 tablespoons freshly squeezed lemon juice
2 cups sifted all-purpose or unbleached flour

¹/₂ teaspoon baking soda
2¹/₂ teaspoons baking powder
¹/₂ teaspoon salt
1 cup fructose or 1¹/₂ cups sugar
¹/₂ cup corn oil
2 egg yolks
³/₄ cup buttermilk
8 egg whites (1 cup)
¹/₂ teaspoon cream of tartar
2³/₄ cups Lemon Pastry Cream (page 250)

Preheat the oven to 325°F. Mix the lemon rind and lemon juice and set aside.

Sift the flour before measuring. Then sift together the flour, baking soda, baking powder, salt, and fructose or sugar into a large bowl. Add the oil, egg yolks, buttermilk, and lemon juice mixture in that order. Mix with an electric mixer at medium speed until satin smooth.

In another large mixing bowl, combine the egg whites and cream of tartar and beat at high speed with the electric mixer until the whites are very, very stiff (be sure the beaters are free of oil).

Fold the batter very gradually into the beaten egg whites. Fold with a wide spatula in a continuous motion until the batter is completely mixed into the egg whites.

Pour the batter into an ungreased 10-inch tube cake pan. Rotate the pan briskly back and forth to level the batter. Run a knife through the batter to eliminate holes in the cake. Bake for 1 hour and 10 minutes. Turn the cake upside down over a funnel or bottle and cool completely.

Loosen the cake with a spatula. Turn it upside down and hit the pan sharply on the edge of a table. Transfer the cake to a serving plate. Frost the top and sides with the Lemon Pastry Cream.

Makes 16 servings

EACH SERVING CONTAINS APPROXIMATELY:
250 TOTAL CALORIES / 100 CALORIES IN FAT
50 MG CHOLESTEROL / 240 MG SODIUM
190 MG CALCIUM

LEMON FROST

This is an easy, fast, and inexpensive dessert. It is surprisingly good and very refreshing.

> *1 egg white*
> *1/2 cup water*
> *1/2 cup nonfat dry milk powder*
> *1 egg yolk, slightly beaten*
> *1/4 cup fructose or 1/3 cup sugar*
> *1/4 teaspoon grated lemon peel*
> *3 tablespoons freshly squeezed lemon juice*
> *Dash salt*
> *3 graham cracker squares, crushed (3 tablespoons)*

Combine the egg white, water, and milk powder and beat until stiff peaks form.

Combine the egg yolk, fructose or sugar, lemon peel, lemon juice, and salt and mix well. Beat gradually into the whipped egg-white-and-milk mixture.

Sprinkle 2 tablespoons of the graham cracker crumbs in a refrigerator tray and spoon in the lemon mixture. Top with the remaining crumbs. Freeze.

Makes 6 servings

EACH SERVING CONTAINS APPROXIMATELY:
80 TOTAL CALORIES / 10 CALORIES IN FAT
45 MG CHOLESTEROL / 55 MG SODIUM
75 MG CALCIUM

SLIM LEMON PIE

1 tablespoon corn-oil margarine, melted
16 graham cracker squares, crushed (1 cup)
1 envelope unflavored gelatin
¼ cup cold water
½ cup liquid egg substitute
⅔ cup fructose or 1 cup sugar ›
3 tablespoons freshly squeezed lemon juice
Grated rind of 1 lemon
4 egg whites
Lemon wheels for garnish
Mint sprigs for garnish

Preheat oven to 350°F. Combine the melted margarine and graham cracker crumbs, mixing thoroughly. Add the ¼ cup water a little at a time until the crumbs are moist enough to hold together (too much water makes the mixture mushy). Place the crumb mixture in a 9-inch pie pan and press to cover bottom and sides. Bake for 8 to 10 minutes or until lightly browned. Set aside to cool.

Soften the gelatin in the cold water for 5 minutes. In the top of a double boiler, over simmering water, cook the liquid egg substitute, half the fructose or sugar, the lemon juice, and the lemon rind until thick, stirring constantly. Add the softened gelatin and stir until dissolved. Do not boil. Set aside to cool to room temperature.

In a small bowl, beat the egg whites until foamy. Gradually add the remaining fructose or sugar and continue beating until the egg whites are stiff but not dry. Fold into the cooled lemon mixture and pour into the baked shell. Refrigerate for 4 hours or overnight.

To serve, slice into 8 wedges. Garnish each slice with a twisted lemon wheel and a sprig of mint.

Makes 8 servings

EACH SERVING CONTAINS APPROXIMATELY:
155 TOTAL CALORIES / 130 CALORIES IN FAT
0 MG CHOLESTEROL / 150 MG SODIUM
15 MG CALCIUM

PEANUT BUTTER DELIGHT

I love peanut butter so much that I am always trying to figure out a way to make a very little bit of it go a long way by combining it with other ingredients that don't interfere with its basic taste. When blending the ingredients in this recipe, make certain that you blend them long enough to get a really creamy satin-smooth consistency. I serve this in sherbet glasses using an ice-cream scoop to fill them, and garnish with a whole peanut in the shell and a sprig of mint.

1 cup part-skim ricotta cheese
1/4 cup unhomogenized smooth peanut butter
2 tablespoons skim milk
2 1/4 teaspoons vanilla extract
1/2 teaspoon ground cinnamon
4 1/2 teaspoons fructose or 2 tablespoons sugar

Combine all the ingredients in a food processor with a metal blade and blend until satin smooth. Refrigerate in a tightly covered container.

Makes 1 1/4 cups

1/4 CUP CONTAINS APPROXIMATELY:
165 TOTAL CALORIES / 95 CALORIES IN FAT
15 MG CHOLESTEROL / 125 MG SODIUM
150 MG CALCIUM

FLAN

Classic flan is always made with cream. While trying to lower the fat content I found that skim milk makes a flan that is much too watery. I was still able to lighten it enormously over the original version by using a combination of low-fat milk and evaporated skimmed milk. If your flan tends to be a little watery, don't worry about it—just pour off the water and rejoice in the fact that you're not getting all that extra fat in the flan.

2 eggs
1 cup low-fat milk
1 cup canned evaporated skimmed milk
1/8 teaspoon salt
2 tablespoons fructose or 2 1/2 tablespoons sugar
1/2 teaspoon ground coriander
1 teaspoon vanilla extract
1/2 teaspoon maple extract
Ground cinnamon for garnish
Mint sprigs for garnish

Preheat the oven to 225°F. Put all the ingredients except the garnishes in a blender container and blend well.

Pour the mixture into six custard cups and sprinkle the tops generously with cinnamon. Place on a cookie sheet in the center of the oven and bake for 2 hours and 30 minutes or until the flan is set and a knife inserted in the center comes out clean.

Serve warm or cold. Sprinkle each serving with additional cinnamon and garnish with a mint sprig.

Makes 6 servings

EACH SERVING CONTAINS APPROXIMATELY:
120 TOTAL CALORIES / 25 CALORIES IN FAT
140 MG CHOLESTEROL / 180 MG SODIUM
200 MG CALCIUM

PUMPKIN PIE

To make this traditional light pumpkin pie still lower in calories, you can omit the crust.

FILLING:

>3 egg whites
>1 tablespoon corn oil
>1 cup part-skim ricotta
>One 16-ounce can solid-pack pumpkin (2 cups)
>1/3 cup fructose or 1/2 cup sugar
>1/4 teaspoon salt
>1 1/2 teaspoons ground cinnamon
>1/2 teaspoon ground nutmeg
>1/4 teaspoon ground ginger
>1/8 teaspoon ground cloves
>1 teaspoon vanilla extract
>2/3 cup canned evaporated skimmed milk

CRUST:

>1 cup whole wheat pastry flour
>1/4 teaspoon salt
>1/4 cup corn oil
>3 tablespoons ice water
>1 cup Pastry Cream (page 250)

Combine all the ingredients for the filling in a large bowl. Mix thoroughly with an electric mixer or in a food processor with a metal blade. Set aside to rest while you make the crust.

Combine the flour and salt in a 9-inch glass pie dish and mix well. Measure the oil in a large cup. Add the ice water to the oil and mix well, using a fork. Slowly add the liquid to the flour mixture, mixing with the same fork. Continue mixing until all the ingredients are well blended. Press onto the bottom and sides of the dish with your fingertips. Make sure the crust covers the entire inner surface of the dish evenly. Flute the edges if desired.

Mix the filling ingredients again until very smooth. Pour into the prepared pie shell and bake in a preheated 350°F oven for 40 to 45 minutes. Cool and chill.

To serve, cut into eight wedges and top each wedge with 2 tablespoons Pastry Cream.

Makes 8 servings

EACH SERVING CONTAINS APPROXIMATELY:
300 TOTAL CALORIES / 125 CALORIES IN FAT
20 MG CHOLESTEROL / 265 MG SODIUM
265 MG CALCIUM

ROCKY ROAD CAKE

I created this chocolatelike cake for spa menus where I do not use chocolate. It serves as a wonderful placebo for chocoholics who are trying to alter their habits.

¼ cup chopped almonds
1 cup flour
1 teaspoon baking soda
1 teaspoon baking powder
1 cup frozen unsweetened apple juice concentrate, thawed
¼ cup corn-oil margarine
½ cup roasted carob powder
2 tablespoons plain nonfat yogurt
Nonstick vegetable coating
¼ cup Pastry Cream (page 250)
2 tablespoons unsweetened carob chips

Place the chopped almonds in a preheated 350°F oven for 8 to 10 minutes. Watch them carefully, as they burn easily. Set aside.

Raise the oven temperature to 375°.

Sift the flour, baking soda, and baking powder together. In a medium saucepan, mix the apple juice concentrate, margarine, and carob powder. Heat and stir until the margarine is melted and the carob powder is dissolved. Add the flour mixture to the carob mixture and blend.

In a separate small bowl, mix the yogurt with a wire whisk until all the lumps disappear and the yogurt is smooth and creamy. Add to the cake batter and mix gently. Add the almonds and again mix gently.

Pour into an 8-inch round cake pan that has been sprayed with nonstick vegetable coating. Bake at 375° for 20 minutes or until a toothpick inserted in the center comes out clean. Cool completely. Spread the Pastry Cream over the top and sprinkle with the carob chips.

Makes 12 servings

EACH SERVING CONTAINS APPROXIMATELY:
160 TOTAL CALORIES / 55 CALORIES IN FAT
1 MG CHOLESTEROL / 205 MG SODIUM
60 MG CALCIUM

BAKLAVA

Baklava is a classic Middle Eastern dessert that is loaded with butter, honey, and nuts. It is traditionally made in sheets and cut diagonally into diamond-shaped pieces and is almost impossible to portion exactly. I finally figured out a way to lower the calories and control the serving size—by rolling the filo dough like a jelly roll, then slicing it diagonally into the traditionally shaped pieces.

6 tablespoons walnuts
1/2 cup honey
1/4 cup corn-oil margarine
1 teaspoon ground cinnamon

Dash ground cloves
1/2 teaspoon vanilla extract
Vegetable oil
1/2 pound filo dough

Using a food processor with a metal blade, grind the walnuts to the consistency of fine gravel. Set aside.

Combine 1/4 cup of the honey and the margarine in a small saucepan and cook over low heat until the margarine is melted. Add the cinnamon, cloves, and vanilla and mix well.

Oil a 10-by-14-inch cookie sheet.

Place one layer of filo dough on a slightly damp towel. Brush the entire surface lightly with the honey/margarine mixture, using a pastry brush. Add another layer of filo dough and repeat. Sprinkle the top layer with 2 tablespoons of the ground walnuts, leaving a bare edge along one end.

Using the towel to help, roll the filo dough as you would a jelly roll, toward the bare edge and close neatly. Place on the prepared cookie sheet. Brush with another light layer of the honey mixture and slice diagonally into eight even portions, allowing for two half slices at the ends. Make two more rolls in the same manner.

Bake the three rolls in a preheated 250°F oven until brown, about 40 minutes. Watch closely after 30 minutes because the rolls will brown suddenly. Cool. When cool, warm the remaining 1/4 cup honey and paint honey on each roll with a pastry brush.

Makes 24 slices

EACH SLICE CONTAINS APPROXIMATELY:
80 TOTAL CALORIES / 55 CALORIES IN FAT
0 MG CHOLESTEROL / 45 MG SODIUM
5 MG CALCIUM

PASTRY CREAM

This Pastry Cream is really a variation on my Light Cheese (page 52); however, I decided to include it as a separate recipe, with variations for lemon, honey, and maple flavors, in the Dessert section because it is most frequently used here. Pastry Cream can be used to replace a classic French Crème Pâtissière, which would be used to garnish fruits, pies, and cakes but which also adds enormously to their fat and calorie content.

> *1 cup part-skim ricotta cheese*
> *3 tablespoons plain nonfat yogurt*
> *2 tablespoons fructose or 3 tablespoons sugar*
> *1 teaspoon vanilla extract*

Blend all the ingredients in a food processor with a metal blade until satin smooth. Refrigerate in a tightly covered container.

Makes 1 cup

2 TABLESPOONS CONTAIN APPROXIMATELY:
50 TOTAL CALORIES / 20 CALORIES IN FAT
10 MG CHOLESTEROL / 40 MG SODIUM
95 MG CALCIUM

VARIATIONS:

Lemon Pastry Cream: Add 2 tablespoons freshly squeezed lemon juice and 1 teaspoon grated lemon rind, and omit the vanilla extract.

Honey Cream: Substitute 2 tablespoons honey for the fructose or sugar.

Maple Cream: Substitute 2 tablespoons maple syrup for the fructose or sugar.

BEVERAGES

WATER IS BY FAR the healthiest beverage in the world, and it has finally come into its own as a status drink. You can now buy bottled water from almost everyplace in the world, plain or sparkling, flavored or natural, and with price tags ranging from nominal to outrageous. For anyone on a low-sodium diet, there are now many low-sodium soda waters available, as well as bottled distilled water, which is completely sodium-free.

There was a time when your guests would have been rather surprised, if not shocked, to have been offered water at a cocktail party. Now that it is the beverage of choice among many fitness-oriented young urban professionals, it is considered chic in many circles to serve a variety of waters for parties.

Water is also the basic ingredient for the two most popular beverages, coffee and tea. Here we are seeing decaffeinated coffee and caffeine-free herb tea becoming much more popular and available. In fact, even the chemically processed decaffeinated coffees, which some researchers believe contain carcinogens, are being replaced

251

in many places with water-washed (often called the Swiss process) decaffeinated coffees.

Even the makers of many popular cola-type soft drinks that contain caffeine are now changing their formulas and touting the fact that they no longer contain even a trace of caffeine.

Caffeine is a drug that stimulates the adrenal glands to produce more adrenaline, which then acts as a stimulant, giving a false sense of energy.

Healthy alternatives to chocolate milk for children can be either carob milk or milk blended with old-fashioned unhomogenized peanut butter. Carob tastes a lot like chocolate, but it does not contain caffeine or saturated fat as chocolate does. Also it is naturally sweet so it doesn't need a lot of sugar and, being a plant, it contains fiber. It also has about four times the calcium found in chocolate or cocoa and none of the oxalic acid, which binds calcium and prevents its absorption. Carob milk is perfect for teenagers who have allergy problems affecting their complexions because of chocolate.

Also try "fruity" milk. Blend milk and fresh fruit such as peaches, strawberries, and bananas for after-school treats.

With alcohol consumption on the decline, many hotels and restaurants have asked me to create nonalcoholic alternative drinks they can serve for "happy hour." The general decline in the consumption of alcoholic beverages has come about because of the growing interest in fitness and the efforts of dedicated and powerful groups such as MADD (Mothers Against Drunk Driving), who have been instrumental in getting legislation passed for much stricter enforcement of the laws against drunk driving.

In this section I have included a few of these "mocktails," both hot and cold, as well as some of the drinks I have on spa menus.

This section is short because so many recipes in this book can actually be turned into beverages simply by blending the ingredients with enough added liquid to make them easily drinkable. Many of the soups make good hot or cold beverages without any alteration.

It always amazes me when people tell me they are trying to lose weight by going on a liquid diet. *Liquid* certainly cannot be interpreted as low-calorie. There can be just as much nutrition in a liquid diet as in solid food. If you or anyone in your family is ever put on a liquid diet, simply blend up all of your favorite dishes and serve them in mugs!

SUGAR-FREE LEMONADE

This delightfully refreshing summer cooler is delicious just as the recipe is given; however, I often combine it with cold sparkling water and serve it in wineglasses with the meal.

1/2 cup very hot water
Grated zest of 1 lemon
One 6-ounce can frozen unsweetened apple juice concentrate
3/4 cup freshly squeezed lemon juice
3 cups cold water

Combine hot water and the lemon zest and let cool.

Add the apple juice concentrate, mixing well. Add the lemon juice and cold water and mix well again. Refrigerate until ready to serve.

To serve, strain to remove the zest. Pour over ice in tall glasses.

Makes 5 cups

1 CUP CONTAINS APPROXIMATELY:
75 TOTAL CALORIES / N CALORIES IN FAT
0 MG CHOLESTEROL / 180 MG SODIUM
15 MG CALCIUM

STRAWBERRY COOLER

1/2 cup sparkling water
1 cup fresh strawberries
2 teaspoons fructose or 1 tablespoon sugar
1/4 cup ice cubes
1 whole strawberry for garnish

Place all the ingredients in a blender container and blend until frothy.

Serve in a chilled glass and garnish with a whole strawberry on the rim of the glass.

Makes 1 serving

EACH SERVING CONTAINS APPROXIMATELY:
75 TOTAL CALORIES / 5 CALORIES IN FAT
0 MG CHOLESTEROL / 30 MG SODIUM
30 MG CALCIUM

PEACH DAIQUIRI

This recipe is a satisfying and delicious "mocktail" that can easily be turned into a cocktail by substituting a jigger of real rum for the rum extract.

1 large peach, chopped (1 cup)
1 tablespoon freshly squeezed orange juice
1/2 teaspoon freshly squeezed lemon juice
1/2 teaspoon rum extract
1 teaspoon fructose or 1 1/2 teaspoons sugar
1/3 cup crushed ice

Combine all the ingredients in a blender container and blend until smooth and frothy.

Makes 1 cup

1 CUP CONTAINS APPROXIMATELY:
85 TOTAL CALORIES / N CALORIES IN FAT
0 MG CHOLESTEROL / 0 MG SODIUM
10 MG CALCIUM

HOT SPICED CIDER

This hot, soothing beverage is also good served cold.

1 quart apple cider
12 whole cloves
2 cinnamon sticks, broken into pieces
8 whole allspice
4 cinnamon sticks for stirrers (optional)

Combine the first four ingredients in a 2-quart saucepan and bring to a boil. Reduce the heat and simmer for 5 minutes. Pour into 8-ounce mugs, with a cinnamon stick for stirring in each one if desired.

Makes four 8-ounce servings

EACH SERVING CONTAINS APPROXIMATELY:
65 TOTAL CALORIES / 5 CALORIES IN FAT
0 MG CHOLESTEROL / 5 MG SODIUM
25 MG CALCIUM

WASSAIL

I have purposely made this recipe large enough to be served in a punch bowl. It is a festive drink for fall and winter parties and goes well with popcorn, which is a very healthy snack.

2 quarts apple cider
1 quart orange juice
One 6-ounce can frozen unsweetened apple juice concentrate
3 cinnamon sticks, broken
8 whole cloves

Combine all the ingredients in a large pot and bring to a boil. Reduce the heat and simmer, uncovered, for 2 hours. Strain and serve hot.

Makes eighteen ¹/₂-cup servings

EACH SERVING CONTAINS APPROXIMATELY:
100 TOTAL CALORIES / 5 CALORIES IN FAT
0 MG CHOLESTEROL / 55 MG SODIUM
30 MG CALCIUM

SUGAR-FREE WHITE EGGNOG

Traditional holiday drinks don't get any healthier than this. Amazingly enough, it is still delicious!

1 egg
³/₄ cup skim milk
1 tablespoon frozen unsweetened apple juice concentrate
1 teaspoon vanilla extract
¹/₄ teaspoon rum extract
2 ice cubes, crushed
Ground nutmeg or cinnamon for garnish

Dip the whole egg, in its shell, in boiling water for 30 seconds. Break the egg and put the white *only* in a blender container.

Add the milk, apple juice concentrate, vanilla and rum extracts, and ice cubes and blend until smooth and frothy. Pour into a large glass and sprinkle with nutmeg or cinnamon.

Makes 1 serving

EACH SERVING CONTAINS APPROXIMATELY:
125 TOTAL CALORIES / 5 CALORIES IN FAT
3 MG CHOLESTEROL / 220 MG SODIUM
235 MG CALCIUM

BANANA SMOOTHIE

This smoothie is not only a sensational beverage, it is also a satisfying snack drink and my favorite topping for dry breakfast cereals.

1 small banana, sliced and frozen
3/4 cup skim milk
1 slice of banana for garnish
Mint sprig for garnish

Combine the frozen banana and milk in a blender container and blend until frothy. Serve in a chilled glass. Garnish with the slice of banana and mint sprig.

Makes 1 serving

EACH SERVING CONTAINS APPROXIMATELY:
170 TOTAL CALORIES / 10 CALORIES IN FAT
3 MG CHOLESTEROL / 95 MG SODIUM
235 MG CALCIUM

MAKE-BELIEVE MARGARITA

If you want to have a real Mexican fiesta but want to forgo the tequila, this Make-believe Margarita is just what el doctor ordered for your party.

1 egg
1 1/2 cups soda water or Perrier water
2 tablespoons freshly squeezed lime juice
1 tablespoon fructose or 4 teaspoons sugar
1/2 cup crushed ice
1/2 lime
Ice cubes
Lime slices for garnish

Dip the whole egg, in the shell, in boiling water for 30 seconds. Break the egg and put the white *only* in a blender container.

Add the soda water or Perrier water, lime juice, fructose or sugar, and crushed ice. Blend until frothy.

Rub the lime around the rims of four chilled glasses. Fill each glass with ice cubes and pour the Margaritas over them. Garnish with lime slices.

Makes 4 servings

EACH SERVING CONTAINS APPROXIMATELY:
20 TOTAL CALORIES / 0 CALORIES IN FAT
0 MG CHOLESTEROL / 35 MG SODIUM
5 MG CALCIUM

PEANUT BUTTER SHAKE

This shake recipe was published in my column a while ago. I recently received a letter from one of my readers telling me that if I ever ran it again, I should add the warning that it can become habit-forming.

2 cups vanilla ice milk
¹/₄ cup unhomogenized peanut butter
¹/₂ cup skim milk
¹/₂ teaspoon vanilla extract

Combine all the ingredients in a blender container and blend until well mixed.

Makes 2 cups

1 CUP CONTAINS APPROXIMATELY:
220 TOTAL CALORIES / 60 CALORIES IN FAT
20 MG CHOLESTEROL / 145 MG SODIUM
250 MG CALCIUM

GLOSSARY OF TERMS
USED IN LIGHT COOKING

AL DENTE: An Italian term meaning literally "to the tooth." Usually used with reference to pasta, which should be cooked only to the point where it is still resistant to the bite. When used to describe vegetables, it means crisp-tender.

BAKE: To cook in a heated oven.

BARBECUE: To cook over hot coals.

BASTE: To spoon liquid over food while it is cooking, or use a baster for this purpose.

BEAT: To beat with an egg beater or electric mixer in order to add air and increase volume.

BLANCH: To plunge quickly into boiling water. Usually refers to fruits and vegetables. To blanch nuts, cover shelled nuts with cold water and bring to a boil. Remove from the heat and drain, then slip the skins from the nuts.

BLEND: To combine two or more ingredients well, often using a blender or food processor.

BLEND UNTIL FROTHY: To blend until foamy and the volume is almost doubled.

BOIL: To cook food in liquid in which bubbles rise to the surface and break. Water boils at 212°F at sea level.

BONE: To remove all bones. Usually refers to roasts and poultry.

BRAISE: To brown meat well on all sides, then add a small amount of water, stock, juice, or wine. The food is then covered and simmered over low heat or placed in a moderate oven and cooked until tender or as the recipe directs.

BROIL: To cook under the broiler at a designated distance from the heat.

BROWN: To brown in the oven, under a broiler, or in a heavy skillet to the desired color.

BUTTERFLY: To bone and open flat. When using this term with half chicken breasts, it means to cut horizontally and lay open so that they again look like whole breasts.

CHILL: To refrigerate until cold.

CHOP: Using a large chopping knife, to hold the point end down with one hand and use the other hand to chop. Check your hardware or appliance store for other chopping devices.

COARSELY CHOP: To chop in pieces approximately ½ inch square.

COAT: To shake in a paper bag containing coating material (cornmeal, flour, etc.) until coated. You may also use a sifter to sprinkle coating material.

CODDLE: Usually used when referring to eggs. When a raw egg is called for in a recipe, put the egg in boiling water for 30 seconds before using it. Avidin, a component of raw egg whites, is believed to block the absorption of biotin, one of the water-soluble vitamins, but it is extremely sensitive to heat and is inactivated when the egg is coddled.

COOL: To allow to stand at room temperature until no longer warm to the touch.

CORE: To remove the core from fruits such as pears and apples.

COVER TIGHTLY: To seal so that steam cannot escape.

CREAM: With a spoon, to rub against the sides of a bowl until creamy. Food can also be creamed with the use of a pastry blender or food processor.

CRUMBLE: To crush with your hands or a fork into crumblings.

CRUSH: To crush dry herbs with a mortar and pestle before using.

CUBE: To cut into approximately 1-inch cube-shaped pieces or into a specified size.

DEGLAZE: To pour excess fat from the pan in which poultry or meat has been sautéed or roasted and add liquid such as water, stock, wine, or juice, scraping the remaining cooking juices and other accumulated material into the liquid as it simmers in order to obtain a tasty base for poultry or meat sauces.

DICE: To cut into ¼-inch cubes or smaller.

DISSOLVE: To mix dry ingredients with liquid until they are no longer visible in the solution.

DOT: To scatter in small bits over the surface of the food; usually refers to corn-oil margarine.

DREDGE: To sprinkle lightly with flour or coat with flour.

FILLET: To remove all the bones; usually refers to fish.

FINELY CHOP: To chop into pieces smaller than ¼ inch.

FOLD IN: Using a rubber spatula or spoon in a circular motion coming across the bottom, to fold the bottom of a mixture over the top. The motion is slowly repeated until the mixture is folded in as indicated in the recipe.

FORK-TENDER: When food can be pierced easily with a fork.

GRATE: To rub a surface on a grater for desired-size particles. Finely grated and coarsely grated foods require two different size graters.

GREASE: To rub lightly with corn-oil margarine, corn oil, or other oil specified in the recipe.

GRIND: To use a food processor or other food-chopping device or grinder.

JULIENNE-CUT: To cut in strips about ¼ inch by 2 inches.

KNEAD: To place a ball of dough on a floured surface, flatten it down with floured hands, and then fold it toward you, and, with the heels of your hands, press down and flatten again. This motion is continued until the dough is smooth and satiny, or as the recipe directs. Usually refers to bread dough.

MARINATE: To allow a mixture to stand in a marinade for the length of time indicated in the recipe.

MASH: To reduce to a soft pulpy state by beating with a food processor or using pressure with a potato masher. Refers most often to potatoes and other vegetables.

MINCE: To chop as fine as gravel.

PANBROIL: To cook in an ungreased or nonstick skillet, pouring off the fat as it accumulates.

PARBOIL: To boil in water or other liquid until partially cooked. This usually precedes another step in the cooking process.

PARE: To remove the outer covering of foods such as fruits and vegetables with a knife.

PEEL: To remove the outer covering of foods such as oranges, lemons, and bananas.

PIT: To remove the seed or pit from fruits such as peaches and plums.

PLATING: Refers to presentation on plate; "plating a sauce" means putting it on the plate first and placing food on top of it.

POACH: To cook for a short time in simmering liquid.

PREHEAT: To set the oven to a desired temperature and wait until that temperature is reached before putting food in to bake.

PRESS: Usually refers to garlic when using a garlic press.

PUREE: To reduce to a liquid state using a food processor or blender.

REDUCE: To boil a liquid until it has reduced the desired amount in volume.

ROAST: To bake meat or poultry in the oven.

SAUTÉ: To cook in a small amount of water, stock, juice, or wine (and occasionally a little oil) in a skillet.

SCALD: To heat to just under the boiling point, when tiny bubbles begin to form around the sides of a pan. Also called "bring to the boiling point."

SCORE: To make shallow cuts or slits on the surface of a food with a knife.

SCRAPE: To remove the outer skin of foods such as carrots and parsnips with a knife. Also to rub the surface of a food, such as an onion, with a knife in order to produce juice.

SEAR: To brown the surface of a food rapidly over high heat in a hot skillet.

SEED: To remove the small seeds completely from such foods as tomatoes, cucumbers, and bell peppers.

SHRED: To slice thinly or use a food processor, grater, or other shredding device.

SIFT: To put flour, sugar, and so on through a flour sifter or sieve.

SIMMER: To cook just below the boiling point (about 185°F at sea level).

SINGE: To hold over a flame in order to burn off all the feathers or hairs. Usually refers to poultry.

SKEWER: To hold together with metal or wooden skewers or to spear chunks of meat and/or vegetables on wooden skewers as for shish kebab.

SKIN: To remove the skin from such foods as chicken and turkey; sometimes used when referring to onions.

SLICE: To slice through food evenly to a specified thickness with a sharp knife or slicing machine.

SNIP: To cut into small pieces using scissors or kitchen shears.

SPRINKLE: To use your fingers or a spoon to spread garnish over a finished dish or to add ingredients to a recipe as directed.

STEAM: To cook food over boiling water, using either a steamer or a large kettle with a rack placed in the bottom of it to hold the pan or dish of food above the boiling water for the specified time. Collapsible steamer baskets are available in hardware and cookware shops.

STEEP: To allow to stand in hot liquid.

STIFF BUT NOT DRY: This term is often used for egg whites and means they should form soft, well-defined peaks but not be beaten to the point where the peaks look as though they will break.

STIFFLY BEATEN: To beat until the mixture stands in stiff peaks.

STIR: To mix with a spoon in a circular motion until all the ingredients are well blended. If more vigorous stirring is necessary, use a food processor.

SWEAT: To cook, covered, over low heat until the natural moisture of what you are cooking is released; usually used in reference to onions, garlic, or leeks.

THICKEN: To mix a thickening agent such as arrowroot, cornstarch, flour, or cream of rice with a small amount of liquid to be thickened, then add slowly to the hot liquid, stirring constantly. The mixture is then cooked until slightly thickened or until it coats a metal spoon.

THINLY SLICE: To slice vegetables such as cucumbers and onions using the slicing side of a four-sided grater. A food processor or other slicing device may also be used.

TOAST: To brown in a toaster, oven, or under a broiler. Nuts and seeds may be toasted at 350°F until the desired color is attained. They may also be placed in the broiler but must be watched carefully, as they burn easily.

TOSS: To mix from both sides in an under-and-over motion toward the center, using two spoons or a fork and spoon. Usually refers to salads.

WHIP: To beat rapidly with a fork, whisk, egg beater, electric mixer, or food processor and thereby increase the volume of a mixture.

WHISK: To stir, beat, or fold using a wire whisk.

FOOD MEASUREMENTS & EQUIVALENTS

VEGETABLES (FRESH)

Arugula, ½ pound = 2 cups bite-size pieces

Beans, green, 1 pound = 5 cups 1-inch pieces raw

Beets, 1 pound (2½-inch diameter) = 6 cups sliced raw; 2½ cups sliced cooked

Bell pepper, 1 pound (3 medium) = 2 cups finely chopped raw; 4 cups sliced raw

Broccoli, 1 pound (2 stalks) = 6 cups chopped cooked

Cabbage, 2½ pounds (average head) = 10 cups shredded raw; 6¼ cups chopped cooked

Carrots, 1 pound (8 small; 6 medium) = 4 cups grated raw; 3 cups sliced raw

Cauliflower, 1½ pounds (1 average head) = 6 cups chopped cooked

Celery, ½ pound = 1½ cups chopped raw; 1 rib = ½ cup finely chopped raw

Celery root, 1¾ pounds (1 average) = 4 cups grated raw; 2 cups cooked and mashed

Chilies, jalapeño, ½ pound (16 chilies) = 2 cups chopped raw

Corn, 6 ears = 2½ cups cut raw

Cucumber, ½ pound (1 medium) = 1½ cups sliced raw; 1 cup diced raw

Eggplant, 1 pound (1 medium) = twelve ¼-inch slices raw; 6 cups cubed raw

Garlic, 1 clove = 1 teaspoon finely chopped raw

Leeks, white part only, ½ pound (1 pound before trimming) = 2 cups chopped raw; 1 cup chopped cooked

Lettuce, 1½ pounds (1 average head) = 6 cups bite-size pieces

Mushrooms, fresh, ½ pound = 2 cups sliced raw

Onion, ½ pound (1 medium) = 1½ cups finely chopped raw; 2 cups sliced raw

  Boiling onions, 1 pound = 32 (½ ounce each)

  Pearl onions, 10 ounces = 2 cups whole raw

  Scallions, ¼-pound bunch (6 average) = 1 cup chopped raw

Parsley, 1 pound = 8 cups tightly packed raw; 8 cups finely chopped raw

  2 ounces = 1 cup tightly packed raw; 1 cup finely chopped raw

Peppers, see bell peppers

Pimiento, one 4-ounce jar = ½ cup chopped

Potatoes, 1 pound (2 medium all purpose or 6 to 8 new) = 2½ cups diced cooked; 3 cups coarsely chopped or thinly sliced

Pumpkin, 3 pounds (1 average) = 4 cups cooked and mashed

Radicchio, 10 ounces (1 average head) = 2½ cups bite-size pieces

Shallots, ¼ pound = ¼ cup chopped raw

Spinach, 1 pound = 4 cups bite-size pieces raw; 1½ cups cooked

Squash, acorn, 1½ pounds (1 average) = 2 cups cooked mashed

  Banana, 3 pounds (1 average) = 4 cups cooked mashed

  Chayote, 1–1½ pounds (1 average) = ½ cup diced; ¾ cup sliced cooked

  Spaghetti, 5 pounds (1 medium) = 8 cups cooked

  Summer, 1 pound (4 average) = 1 cup chopped cooked

  Zucchini, 1 pound (2 average) = 1¼ cups chopped cooked; 3 cups diced raw; 4 cups thinly sliced raw

Tomatillos, ¼ pound (4 small; 2 large) = 1 cup chopped raw

Tomatoes, 1 pound (3 medium) = 2 cups chopped raw; 1¼ cups chopped cooked
Turnips, 1 pound = 2 cups grated raw; 4 cups bite-size pieces raw; 1¼ cups cooked mashed
Watercress, ¼ pound (1 bunch) = 1 cup loosely packed raw

VEGETABLES (DRIED)

Brown rice, 1 pound = 2½ cups uncooked; 7½ cups cooked
Garbanzo beans (chick-peas), 1 pound = 2 cups dry; 6 cups cooked
Kidney beans, 1 pound = 1½ cups dry; 4 cups cooked
Lentils, ½ pound = 1 cup dry; 2 cups cooked
Lima or navy beans, 1 pound = 2½ cups dry; 6 cups cooked
White rice, 1 pound = 2½ cups uncooked; 5 cups cooked

PASTA

Linguine noodles, 1 pound = 5 cups cooked
Macaroni, 1 pound = 3 cups dry; 12 cups cooked
Oriental noodles, ¾ pound dry = 5 cups cooked
Rotelle pasta, 1 pound = 4 cups dry; 6 cups cooked
Spaghetti, 1 pound = 8 cups cooked

FRUITS (FRESH)

Apples, 1½ pounds (6 small) = 4 cups sliced; 4½ cups chopped
Apricots, 1 pound (6 to 8 average) = 2 cups chopped
Bananas, 1 pound (4 small) = 2 cups mashed
Cantaloupe, 2 pounds (1 average) = 3 cups diced
Cherries, 2 cups = 1 cup pitted
Cranberries, 1 pound = 4½ cups raw
Figs, 1 pound (4 small) = 2 cups chopped
Grapefruit, 1 pound (1 small) = 1 cup sectioned
Grapes, Thompson seedless, ¼ pound = 40 grapes; 1 cup
Lemon, ¼ pound (1 medium) = 3 tablespoons juice; 2 teaspoons grated zest
Limes, ½ pound (5 average) = 4 tablespoons juice; 4 to 5 teaspoons grated zest
Orange, 1 pound (3 average) = 3 cups sectioned
Papaya, 1 pound = 2 cups cubed; 1 cup pureed

Peaches, 1 pound (3 average) = 2 cups chopped
Pears, 1 pound (3 average) = 2 cups chopped
Pineapple, 3 pounds (1 medium) = 2½ cups chopped
Rhubarb, 1 pound (4 stalks) = 2 cups chopped cooked
Tangerines, 1 pound (4 average) = 2 cups sectioned

FRUITS (DRIED)

Apples, 1 pound = 8 cups diced
Apricots, 1 pound = 8 cups diced
Figs, 1 pound (2½ cups) = 4½ cups whole cooked; 2 cups chopped
  raw
Pears, 1 pound (3 cups) = 5½ cups cooked
Prunes, pitted, 1 pound (2½ cups) = 3¾ cups cooked
Raisins, seedless, 1 pound (2¾ cups) = 3¾ cups cooked; 2 cups
  chopped raw

FISH

Crab, ½ pound = 1 cup cooked, canned, fresh, or frozen
Lobster, ½ pound = 1 cup fresh, frozen, or cooked
Oysters, ½ pound = 1 cup raw
Scallops, ½ pound = 1 cup shucked, fresh or frozen
Shrimp, 1 pound = 3 cups shelled cooked
Tuna, 6½- to 7-ounce can = ¾ cup drained

POULTRY

Chicken or turkey, 1 pound = 4 cups chopped cooked

HERBS AND SPICES

Garlic powder, ¼ teaspoon = 2 small garlic cloves
Ginger, ground, ½ teaspoon = 1 teaspoon fresh
Herbs, dried, ½ teaspoon = 1 tablespoon fresh

CHEESE

Cottage cheese, ½ pound = 1 cup
Cheese, ¼ pound = 1 cup grated

EGGS

Eggs, 6 medium = 1 cup whole raw
Egg whites, 8 medium = 1 cup raw

MILK

Dry, instant nonfat powdered, ⅓ cup plus ⅔ cup water = 1 cup
   liquid milk
Dry, noninstant powdered, 3 tablespoons plus 1 cup water = 1 cup
   liquid milk

NUTS

Almonds, 32 chopped = ¼ cup; 8 chopped = 1 tablespoon
Peanuts, 44 chopped = ¼ cup; 11 chopped = 1 tablespoon
Pecans, 20 halves chopped = ¼ cup; 5 halves chopped = 1 table-
   spoon
Walnuts, 12 halves chopped = ¼ cup; 3 halves chopped = 1
   tablespoon

BIBLIOGRAPHY

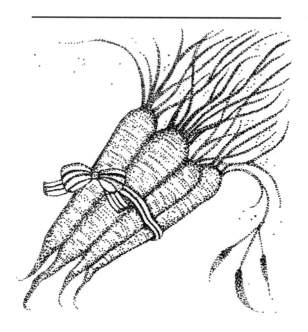

We have used Practorcare, Inc., software for the nutritional analysis throughout this book. Whenever an ingredient was not on this database, we referred to other publications in this bibliography to complete the nutritional information.

Church, Helen Nichols, and Jean A. T. Pennington. *Bowes and Church's Food Values of Portions Commonly Used.* 14th rev. ed. New York: Harper and Row, 1985.

Jones, Jeanne. *The Calculating Cook.* 2d ed. rev. San Francisco: 101 Productions, 1977.

———. *Diet for a Happy Heart.* 2d ed. rev. San Francisco: 101 Productions, 1981.

———. *The Fabulous High-Fiber Diet.* San Francisco: 101 Productions, 1985.

———. *The High-Calcium Diet* (cassette). Chicago: Nightingale-Conant Corporation, 1986.

———. *Jeanne Jones' Food Lover's Diet.* San Francisco: 101 Productions, 1982.

———. *Jet Fuel: The New Food Strategy for the High-Performance Person.* New York: Villard Books, 1984.

———. *More Calculated Cooking.* San Francisco: 101 Productions, 1981.

———. *Secrets of Salt-Free Cooking.* San Francisco: 101 Productions, 1979.

Jones, Jeanne, and Karma Kientzler. *Fitness First: A 14-Day Diet and Exercise Program.* San Francisco: 101 Productions, 1980.

Notelovitz, Morris, M.D., Ph.D., and Marsha Ware. *Stand Tall! Every Woman's Guide to Osteoporosis.* Bantam, 1985.

Practorcare, Inc. *Menu Planner 2000, Practorcare* (software). San Diego: Practorcare, 1986.

U.S. Department of Agriculture. *Nutritive Value of Foods.* USDA Home and Garden Bulletin 72, 1986.

INDEX

273